S

DATE			

THE COMMUNISTS

OTHER BOOKS BY ADAM B. ULAM

The Philosophical Foundations of English Socialism
Titoism and the Cominform
The Russian Political System
The Unfinished Revolution
The New Face of Soviet Totalitarianism
The Bolsheviks
Expansion and Coexistence
The Rivals
The Fall of the American University
Stalin: The Man and His Era
A History of Soviet Russia
In the Name of the People
Ideologies and Illusions
The Unfinished Revolution [rev. ed.]
Russia's Failed Revolutions
Dangerous Relations:
The Soviet Union in World Politics, 1970–1982
Stalin [new edition]
The Kirov Affair (a novel)
Stalin [with new Introduction]

THE
COMMUNISTS

THE STORY OF POWER
AND LOST ILLUSIONS:
1948–1991

Adam B. Ulam

A Robert Stewart Book

CHARLES SCRIBNER'S SONS

NEW YORK

MAXWELL MACMILLAN CANADA
Toronto
MAXWELL MACMILLAN INTERNATIONAL
New York Oxford Singapore Sydney

Charles Scribner's Sons
Macmillan Publishing Company
866 Third Avenue
New York, NY 10022

Maxwell Macmillan Canada, Inc.
1200 Eglinton Avenue East, Suite 200
Don Mills, Ontario M3C 3N1

Macmillan Publishing Company is part of
the Maxwell Communication Group of Companies.

Library of Congress Cataloging-in-Publication Data

Ulam, Adam Bruno.
  The Communists: the story of power and lost illusions:
  1948–1991/ Adam B. Ulam.
    p. cm.
  "A Robert Stewart book."
  Includes bibliographical references and index.
  ISBN 0-684-19236-5
  1. Communism—History. I. Title.
HX36.U415 1992
335.4'09—dc20   91-26981

Macmillan Books are available at special discounts for bulk purchases for sales promotions, premiums, fund-raising, or educational use. For details, contact:

Special Sales Director
Macmillan Publishing Company
866 Third Avenue
New York, NY 10022

10 9 8 7 6 5 4 3 2 1

Printed in the United States of America

CONTENTS

Acknowledgments   *vii*

Introduction   *ix*

1 The First Heretic   *1*

2 The Long Journey   *36*

3 And Then the Great Khan Died   *57*

4 Lifting the Burden of the Past   *108*

5 Reform and Retreat   *129*

6 Toward the Brink   *169*

7 The Great Divide   *203*

8 Death of an Ideology   *240*

9 The Travails of Coexistence   *288*

10 Expansion and Retreat   *318*

11 A Proletarian Revolution   *343*

12 The Ravages of Glasnost   *381*

13 The Unraveling   *424*

Conclusion: The Moment of Truth   *487*

Notes   *495*

Index   *517*

ACKNOWLEDGMENTS

It was Mr. Robert Stewart who suggested that having written about the origin and various phases of the history of Communism, I should now turn to the drama of its decline and disintegration. I have greatly profited from his encouragement and suggestions. I am deeply indebted to Ms. Christine Porto. She not only has helped to turn an untidy manuscript into an orderly one, but has been unsparing and most constructive with her advice on both the substantive and stylistic aspects of my writing.

Work on this book, as on many of my previous ones, took place in the congenial surroundings of the Russian Research Center of Harvard University. The Center has been, in my experience, a unique community of scholars, broadening its members' horizons and imparting both zest and discipline to their endeavors. Among the Center fellows, I am especially in debt for their invariably well-informed advice to David Powell, Mark Kramer, and Lubomyr Hajda. When it came to knotty problems concerning China, I was the beneficiary of having Rod MacFarquhar as my friend and colleague in the Government Department. Thomas Barnett and Alexandra Vacroux were successively my assistants, efficient and patient in providing me not only with research materials, but also with light reading to balance the serious stuff.

INTRODUCTION

"I did not become His Majesty's Prime Minister to preside over the liquidation of the British Empire," declared Winston Churchill at one point in World War II. In the aftermath of the war, colonialism and other forms of arbitrary rule came under increasing attack. And eventually the forces of modernity and rationalism struck at the last bastion of imperialism. When he assumed the duties of the general secretary of the Communist Party of the USSR in March 1985, Mikhail Gorbachev did not propose to dismantle the Soviet empire and dictatorial system. History overruled both statesmen. The British Empire is a thing of the past. At this point not only the "socialist camp" but the entire Soviet power system lies in shambles.

There is, however, a fundamental difference between the two cases. The British Empire receded into history because by the end of World War II the antiquated imperial notions could no longer be reconciled with the democratic spirit of the British institutions. Moscow's rule over other countries collapsed because of the complete bankruptcy of the ideology underlying the Soviet system itself. British democracy, freed of the burden of an empire, remains strong and flourishing. Communism, as a philosophy and a way of life, has been discredited in the Soviet Union and elsewhere.

The simultaneous collapse of an empire and the ideology that engendered it is unprecedented in modern history. Fascism and National Socialism died with the regimes that represented them, but their demise came as a result of a catastrophic military defeat. The Soviet power–Communist complex began unraveling without a war, with the USSR undeniably a superpower and stronger militarily than at any previous time. Nor did the crash follow massive popular uprisings. What no one could have imagined as happening, except in the aftermath of the horrors of a nuclear war or a violent revolution, has come to pass peacefully, and within an amazingly short time.

Why and how it happened is the subject of this book. To anticipate its main argument, much of the story confirms Lord Keynes's dictum that, ultimately, it is ideas that count. Communism and the Soviet state were born out of one world war and experienced their greatest expansion as a consequence of another. In their attempt, which at the time appeared foolhardy, to seize and run a vast country, Lenin and his associates were sustained most of all by the idea of a new international order, where the ultimate victory of their cause would bring the extinction of imperialism and war. That vision, even more than its claim to bring social justice, remained for long the most potent attraction of Communism. Outside of the USSR it persuaded Communists to persist in their slavish obedience to Moscow. At home it was used by the Soviet rulers as justification, also to themselves, for the state of siege they imposed on their society—a necessary, temporary condition in the struggle for a better world, one free from war and exploitation.

Once Stalin was at the helm, the dream of the world revolution gave way to a very prosaic notion of Communism as an instrument of Soviet—his own—power. From an international political movement, Communism was transformed into a partly military, partly religious order. In the USSR its sole function became to assure absolute control of the state and society by the dictator and whoever were his associates of the moment. The expression "ruling party" is thus inexact, for in Stalin's time the mass membership of the Communist Party, whether of the Soviet Union, Poland, or France, was utterly devoid of influence over its policies and actions. Abroad, the function of this peculiar movement was to act as virtual armies of occupation in Communist states or as detachments operating, not always peacefully, to promote the interests of the Soviet Union in non-Communist countries. For all practical purposes, the ideological sustenance of Communism for a quarter of a century reduced itself to two main tenets: worship of the leader and complete submission to Soviet policies of the moment. Ideologically emasculated Communist parties became almost perfect mechanisms for retaining power once it was in their grasp.

It is precisely this last factor that was bound, even before Stalin's death, to mar the otherwise monolithic image of world Communism and to challenge the assumption that there could be no disagreement between any of its components and the Fatherland of Socialism. Programmed for seeking and exercising absolute rule, foreign Communist leaders, upon achieving power in their own countries, would not always readily agree to continue serving as obedient executors of Moscow's commands. And, notably in two cases, those leaders could feel that power came to them as the result of their own and their parties' exertions, rather than as a gift of the Soviet army. Hence the cults of Tito and Mao, which in their own countries were able not only to challenge but to hold at bay that of Stalin.

With the latter's disappearance from the scene, the relationship between the Soviet Union and Communism, both as an ideology and a movement, assumed completely different dimensions. With the exceptions noted above, the cult of *the* leader was the unifying force of Communism both in the USSR and abroad. The oligarchs who succeeded him did not wish, or dare, to try to control their own country as he had. Nor did they expect or wish for equal obedience, not to speak of veneration, from foreign comrades. After March 5, 1953, it became of great importance for the Kremlin to revive Communism as a meaningful creed for its own citizens, as well as an element of cohesion for the entire Communist bloc and movement. Khrushchev's efforts in that direction anticipated those of Gorbachev during the *first* phase of perestroika, 1985–87. Like his successor, Khrushchev tried to portray Marxism-Leninism, once cleansed of its Stalinist accretions, as a constructive and vital force. Had he gone further in his drive for reforms, he may have found, as has Gorbachev, that glasnost—an open society—must spell the doom of Marxism-Leninism.

That the Soviet leaders' and the world's acknowledgment of the bankruptcy of their ideology was delayed for some thirty years must be attributed to the great surge in the Soviet Union's power and international standing, as demonstrated during the 1960s and 1970s. How could you describe as obsolete a system and philosophy that put the first man in outer space, that had surpassed the United States in the production of steel; a government that deployed the most powerful nuclear arsenal in the world? External power shielded from view the inherent weaknesses of the Communist system: the stagnation of the Soviet economy, the increasing discords and crises within the "socialist camp," and the irrelevance of the Marxist-Leninist creed to the conditions of the modern world. In order to survive as the twentieth century drew to its close, the Soviet state and Communism had to continue to expand. "That which stops growing begins to rot," said a Russian minister to a foreign ambassador in Catherine the Great's time when asked why the empire, already the largest in the world, was still seeking fresh conquests. That prescription for survival became even more imperative for the Soviet Union of Khrushchev's and Brezhnev's time. The Soviet Union had to advance, to secure new vassals and clients, to inflict fresh discomfitures on the West. That advance was necessary to shield the Soviet people from the full realization of their deprivations, to convince them that for all of the West's alleged freedoms and riches, it was Communism that was on the march and bound to inherit the world, while capitalism and democracy were in retreat and eventually doomed.

As this book proposes to show, that argument became less and less convincing as modern technology and the increasing difficulty of maintaining rigid repression made it more and more difficult to keep the citizens of the USSR, Poland, or China from becoming aware of what was happening in the democratic world. But more fundamentally, the events of the last three decades argue persuasively that even the Soviet leaders, and before Gorbachev's ascent, had to reach the conclusion that to try to expand Soviet power further was both too dangerous and futile. Too dangerous because such attempts carried increasing risks of a nuclear holocaust. Futile because victories of Communism could no longer be considered assets for the Kremlin. The open hostility of China, the ever-growing difficulty as well as the military and economic burden of propping up the Communist regimes in Eastern Europe and Afghanistan and of the anti-Western governments in the Third World—these all demonstrated the futility of trying to rescue the Soviet system through imperial expansion. And, stripped of its imperial facade, the Communist system in the Soviet Union itself had to begin to crumble.

Also instructive has been the case of China. Once the upholder of militant Marxism and the challenger of Moscow for leadership of the Communist camp, the Beijing regime has also been compelled to give up the antiquated doctrine. A common ideology, instead of providing a bond of friendship, only envenomed the relations between the two Communist powers. To deflect the military danger from the USSR, China was constrained to seek friendship with the United States; to revive its economy, it has resorted to capitalist practices. Formal adherence to Communism remains for the aged rulers of the world's largest nation but a transparent rationalization of their determination to hold on to absolute power.

Yet there has been nothing inevitable or automatic about this process of the unraveling of Communism and Soviet power. Could different policies by the Kremlin or Mao have prevented the Sino-Soviet split, and thus deflected the most damaging blow to the basic premise of Communism? If perestroika and glasnost had been tried much earlier, would they have prolonged the life of the Soviet system? Gorbachev has, and probably correctly, been blamed for not embarking earlier and wholeheartedly on economic reforms, and for his poor sense of timing on the nationalities-federal issue. Would more statesmanlike policies have saved the Soviet Union from its present lamentable condition?

The answers to such questions must be sought not only in terms of political movements, alliances, and economic and military statistics. Paradoxically, for an ideology that sees history determined by impersonal social and economic forces, the fate of Communism has been affected, often decisively, by the personalities of its leaders. It is a remarkable gallery of individuals who have presided over and epitomized first its ascent to being a contender for the world's mastery, then its division into competing regimes and sects. Stalin brought the Soviet Union to the pinnacle of power, but his legacy has been a major reason for its present parlous condition. It was Tito's defiance of Moscow that first suggested that Communism offers no magic formula for dissolving national conflicts, and thus for laying down foundations for a new peaceful world order. Without Mao, China may have remained an ally of the Soviet Union much longer, and thus not dealt a crushing blow to the idea of "proletarian internationalism." Khrushchev, Gomułka and Dubček are, admittedly, lesser figures. Yet each in his way tried to salvage Communism, loosen its authoritarian ways, and make it viable in the modern world. With Gorbachev, we enter upon the final phase of the evolution of Communism toward self-destruction. Perestroika, which began as an attempt to restructure the Soviet system, but still upon the same Communist foundations, has led to the virtual demolition of the entire edifice. With the issue being no longer that of refashioning Communism but of saving the state to which it had given birth, it is a fitting epitaph for the movement that the last successor of Lenin should have sought help from the capitalist West.

THE COMMUNISTS

1

THE FIRST HERETIC

NEVER HAD the threat or promise of Communism loomed larger than it did three years after the conclusion of World War II. A century earlier two young German radicals introduced their fiery challenge to the old order on an exuberant note: "A specter is haunting Europe— the specter of Communism." But in 1848 Marx and Engels spoke for only a tiny sect, and publication of the *Communist Manifesto*, with its message of class war, was a little-noticed incident in the wave of revolutionary convulsions that shook the Old World that year. And that wave, which had been inspired for the most part by nationalist and democratic aspirations rather than calls for a new economic order, soon subsided. Capitalism, instead of being in its death throes as Marx and Engels fondly imagined, was in fact to enter upon a period of vigorous growth and expansion. And for several decades afterward European politics would be dominated not by a supranational creed of class war, but by militant nationalism on the one hand and liberalism on the other.

But what in 1848 had been an expression of youthful bravado became one century later only too true. "Communism is already acknowledged by all European powers to be itself a power," the *Manifesto* had boasted. Now it was more than *a* power; the representative and carrier of the Communist idea, the Soviet Union, was the *dominant* power on the Continent. Eastern Europe lay under Moscow's domination, its vassal regimes rapidly transforming their societies in the Soviet model. No West European state, or all of them together, could match the strength of the Red Army, which, it was generally and probably realistically believed, could, if unleashed by the Kremlin, reach the English Channel in a matter of days. Nor was the threat to Western Europe purely military. The French and Italian Communist parties, as yet obedient tools of the Fatherland of Socialism, enjoyed a wide following in their countries, and it appeared not unreasonable to foresee them conquering power even without the overt assistance of their ideological comrades and masters.

And Communism had long ceased to be a factor only in European politics. In China the Communist forces were now on the offensive, and it was only a question of time before the ramshackle edifice of the Kuomintang would collapse and the world's largest nation would become part of the "camp of socialism," then assumed to be synonymous with the Soviet empire. Elsewhere, in what would become known as the Third World, most notably in Asia and North Africa, the old European empires were rapidly crumbling, and again the Soviet Union, either directly through the local Communist parties or by other means, threatened to acquire dominant influence over the vast areas liberated from European rule.

There was, to be sure, a formidable barrier to what in those days was assumed to be the Soviet drive for world domination. Albeit belatedly, by 1947 the enormous resources of the United States were brought into play to check and contain further Soviet expansion. The Marshall Plan was designed to resuscitate Western Europe's economy from its wartime devastation and to enable it to resist the influence of domestic Communism. The Truman Doctrine pledged U.S. assistance where the threat assumed the form of an insurrection, as in Greece, or Soviet pressure for territorial concessions, as in the case of Turkey. But the main factor, it was widely believed in the West, that kept the USSR from unleashing its vast armies in direct aggression was America's monopoly of the atom bomb. It was only the latter that offset—imperfectly, at that—the Soviet Union's crushing superiority in conventional military forces. The United States, following V-J Day, rapidly demobilized, while the USSR retained millions under arms. Even so, as we now know, and the Soviets at the time surmised, Washington was far from confident about the viability of its nuclear deterrent. For one thing, U.S. stockpiles of those weapons were still quite small, and those were far from possessing the frightful destructive power of the future hydrogen devices. (The closest estimate of the American nuclear stockpile in mid-1948 [the exact figures are still classified] is about fifty.)[1] It was a time before the age of guided missiles, and one had to take a sober view about the likelihood of many American long-range bombers, agonizingly slow by the standards of a few years hence, penetrating the Soviets' antiaircraft defenses. For all the horrors of Hiroshima and Nagasaki, would the possibility of a few Russian cities being similarly stricken restrain the believers in the world mission of Communism from hurtling their armies against the West?

One could not be sure, and no democratic statesman would have the hardiness to put the Soviets to the test. When in May 1948 the USSR in a flagrant violation of its treaty obligations instituted a land blockade of West Berlin, the Western powers did not respond by testing Moscow's resolve by an ultimatum, or by trying to send an armed convoy through the Soviet zone to the besieged city. To do so would have meant risking the unleashing of World War III. There ensued a stalemate, with the United States and Britain supplying West Berlin by air.

We *now* know, and perhaps it should have been realized at the time, that the USSR was neither powerful enough nor ready for a confrontation with the West, as it was then believed. The Soviet armies had been demobilized almost as thoroughly as had those of the United States, for after the frightful losses in the war—more than 20 million lives lost—Soviet man- and woman-power was badly needed in the factories and on the collective farms. Prudent and realistic when it came to foreign policy, Stalin was not going to risk a war with America, the country that quite apart from its possession of the ultimate weapon was currently producing half of the industrial output of the entire world, and which in comparison with the other belligerents had been barely bled in the conflict. The USSR's ominous and defiant posture was in fact designed very largely to mask its vulnerabilities and to discourage Washington and London from trying to interfere with the Kremlin's sovietization of Eastern Europe.

Yet that situation was not understood, or but dimly perceived in the non-Communist world. And even had a realistic assessment of Soviet power and intentions been made by the West's statesmen, it is unlikely that they would have found the picture much more reassuring. What if for the moment the Soviets' threatening policies were not as yet commensurate with their military capabilities? Judging by its performance during the war, the Soviet Union's recuperative powers had to be judged very highly. And with its industrial recovery and growth the Communist state's military power would increase accordingly. America's monopoly of atomic weapons was likely to be short-lived (though in 1948 few scientists thought that it would be broken within a year). Once it was gone, no American quantitative and qualitative superiority in nuclear weapons would be likely to offset the psychological and political effect of even a small stockpile of A-bombs in Moscow's arsenal. A dictatorial regime with the bomb could bluster and bluff in a way that no democracy, and especially the American one, could match.[2]

And so whatever its current but largely hidden weaknesses, the Soviet Union cast an ominous shadow over the world's political scene and the specter of Communism loomed indeed menacingly.

Inherent in that menace was the suspicion in the West that Communism was strong not only because the USSR was now one of the two superpowers. Capitalism and its political philosophy, liberalism, had had their reputation severely damaged by recent events ranging from the Great Depression to the collapse of France in 1940. Communism, as shown by the Soviets' wartime performance, had proved its vitality. Even in democracy's traditional preserve there were many in 1948 who saw in Marxism-Leninism the wave of the future. In the parliamentary elections in France and Italy that year one out of three voters would affirm his preference for the Communist Party. When Winston Churchill had on March 5, 1946, sought in his Iron Curtain speech to shock the West into a sense of urgency about Soviet-Communist expansion, his warning was felt, even in some nonleftist circles, to be unduly provocative and unrealistic. The staid London *Times* gently reproached the former prime minister: instead of squaring off, East and West should seek common ground. Thus Western democracy had much to learn from Communism when it came to "the development of economic and social planning."[3] How strange this would sound some forty years later when leaders of practically all Communist states would unite in praising the market economy and in lamenting their previous practices in that sphere now denounced as the "command administrative" regulation of economic life. But in the 1940s the collectivist economy was eulogized, and not only by the left, as superior to the "anarchy of the free market"!

And so we have the prevalent image of Communism among its opponents: for all of its rapacity and denial of freedom, Communist ideology and the movement were endowed with strength and vitality, and only the utmost effort on the part of the free world could stave off their further advance. Practically no one as yet credited the West with the ability to make the Soviet Union and Communism retreat from the positions they had already occupied. After all, the policy guiding Washington in what was becoming known as the cold war went by the name of *containment*. Its classical formulation in a celebrated article by George Kennan, then a high official of the State Department, envisaged an essentially defensive posture by the West. The United States was not to probe for or try to exploit Soviet weaknesses and vulnerabilities: America's "demands on Russian policy should be put forward in such a manner as to leave the way open for a compliance not too detrimental to Russian prestige."[4] This meant in practice acquiescing to Soviet domination of Eastern Europe. Nor did the doctrine prove effective, at least through the forties, in stemming fresh advances of Communism. Only a few months after its enunciation in February 1948, Czechoslovakia, hitherto preserving features of a parliamentary democracy, though already in the shadow of its powerful neighbor, was brought in line with other states in the area. With an assist from Moscow, the local Communists seized complete power. By this time only one country within the Soviet sphere of interest, Finland, still preserved internal democracy, something most of the contemporary observers believed could be but short-lived.[5]

An even greater and hugely more significant challenge to the containment policy was presented by the situation in China. There 1948 was the year of decision, with the tide of the civil war turning definitely against the Nationalists and with the Communist victory, barring a fortuitous development, being virtually inevitable by its end. In China one encountered yet another dilemma of the strategy of containment: did it extend to the areas where the local Communists were about to seize power on their own, and without direct help or intimidation by the Soviets? And yet another unclarified point of the doctrine: did it put the United States under an obligation to intervene militarily in a situation such as now arose in the Far East? It was fairly clear that short of such an intervention, nothing could really rescue Chiang's regime. Those two questions and their variants would provide ample material for debate and recrimination on the American political scene in the decades to come, but in the meantime China fell under the sway of Communism.

Containment then was proving less than fully satisfactory as a formula for stopping Soviet-Communist expansionism. Did it translate into America's resolve to deter Communist advances anywhere in the world? No—if one judges by Washington's resigned attitude about China once the civil war there resumed. In Europe? Hardly, if one considered the rather supine reaction of the West to what had been in fact a Communist coup in Czechoslovakia. Would the United States react forcefully, at least, to a Soviet challenge to its treaty rights in Central and Western Europe, or as Mr. Kennan's article put it, "confront the Russians with unalterable counterforce" whenever they showed aggressive designs there? Even there the meaning of containment was somewhat ambiguous; the Soviets' blockade of West Berlin was thought (incorrectly) to be designed to force the Western powers out of that outpost. And the airlift through which the United States and Britain were able to sustain the city's life for a whole year could hardly be seen as meeting the Soviets' challenge "with unalterable counterforce." The blockade was lifted by the Soviets in May 1949. But the result was a draw in that battle of the cold war. The Soviets' peremptory challenge failed to make the Western powers abandon their plan to merge their sphere of occupation into what became the Federal Republic of Germany, the prevention of which had been Moscow's real objective in instituting the blockade. But the USSR had not been rebuffed forcefully enough to discourage it from threatening to subject West Berlin to similar ordeals in the future.

Inherent, then, in the current high standing of Communism was both the belief that the USSR was enormously powerful militarily and that its social and economic system held worldwide attraction. Communism seemed awesome in its unity. A democrat could rationalize its acceptance by the Soviet people because of the ruthless system of repression exercised by their own government. Even so, how could one explain that the Russians loyally stuck by their regime during the darkest days of the war? In any case, what explanation was there for the widespread appeal of Communism in China? And certainly the French and Italian Communists' loyalty to Moscow could not be ascribed to their living in fear of its agencies of repression. As of 1948, the most astounding, and to its enemies disturbing, feature of Communism was its apparently monolithic character, the seeming universality of its appeal. In the speech announcing what became known as the Truman Doctrine, the president denounced the Communist way of life as "based upon the will of a minority forcibly imposed upon the majority."[6] Yet at the time, the Communists were thought to be fairly close to becoming majority parties in France and Italy and to ascend to power there through free elections. Communism, Mr. Truman's speech also instructed, was rooted "in the evil soil of poverty and strife." But if so, democracy would have but a doubtful chance of overcoming the rival philosophy's appeal in large areas of the world now becoming emancipated from their European masters. Paradoxical as it must seem in the view of subsequent events, democratic institutions in 1948 appeared completely secure only among the "Anglo-Saxons," as De Gaulle was to dub the two Atlantic powers, the British dominions, and Scandinavia. But even there, would those institutions be able to withstand the stresses of what even under the most optimistic Western assumptions had to be foreseen as a long, long period of neither peace nor war?

Communism, on the other hand, seemed by its very nature to be well adjusted to that condition. The Soviet regime has always rationalized the denial of freedom to its subjects and their economic deprivations as a necessary price for warding off the capitalist enemy and for the building of socialism. The Kremlin did not have to deal with an unruly electorate that might object to suddenly increased military budgets or protest the excessive risk taking in its foreign policy. Citizens of the USSR could not question the policies of their masters. They were habituated even in peacetime to living under the conditions of what could be likened to a state of siege.

And now, that discipline was being imparted to the subjects of other Communist states. In 1947 the Kremlin ordered the creation of the Cominform—to give it its full name, the Communist Information Bureau. Membership in the bureau was comprised of the Communist parties of the Soviet Union, Poland, Yugoslavia, Hungary, Romania, Czechoslovakia, and Bulgaria, as well as those of France and Italy. Superficially, there appeared to be but little rationale for the creation of this intra-Communist body. With or without the Cominform, Moscow's dictates were supposed to be, and usually were, taken as law in Warsaw or Prague, and other headquarters of the participating parties. But the new organization was created precisely to impart international gloss to what in fact still was the Kremlin's autocratic rule over the Communist bloc. Unlike the Comintern, dissolved by Stalin in 1943,[7] the Cominform was to have its seat outside the Soviet Union, in Belgrade. There were other features about the new organization that were designed to endow it with the appearance of equality for the participating members and to anticipate and refute the charge of undue Soviet influence. Andrei Zhdanov, Stalin's chief lieutenant at the time, referred to such "slanders" in his speech at the founding meeting of the Cominform. "The dissolution of the Comintern which conformed to the demands of the labor movement . . . played a positive role. . . . [It] once and for all disposed of the slanderous allegation that Moscow was interfering in the internal affairs of other states, and that the Communist parties in the various states were acting not in the interests of their nation but on orders from outside."[8]

But the Cominform's role was not merely decorative. It was already, if somewhat dimly, perceived by the Kremlin that for all their loyalty to the Fatherland of Socialism and Comrade Stalin, the Communist rulers of Eastern Europe were not free of the ambition to be considered as leaders of their nations and not mere vassals of Moscow. They would not dare to demand to be treated as equals, but it was thought politic for their own sake, as well as for the outside world, to maintain the fiction that, as Zhdanov said on the occasion, "the Soviet Union unswervingly holds the position that political and economic relations between states must be built exclusively on the basis of equality of the parties and mutual respect for their rights." Then if any of the satellite leaders should be unrealistic enough to take the above seriously, and to break ranks, his doom, though decreed by the Kremlin, would be pronounced by and in the name of the international body.

Yet in the months following its establishment, the Cominform had no occasion to act as a disciplinary agency. Nor were its services really required for any meaningful political action. The process of sovietization of Eastern Europe went apace. In the immediate backwash of the war the Communists in most of those countries had observed some restraint, insofar as both their policies and the repression of the anti-Communist forces were restrained. Now such restraint, with Soviet approval if not indeed prodding, was being abandoned. The non-Communist parties in the area, even if at one time partners of the rulers in a variety of popular fronts, had by 1948 become emasculated and impotent. And it was already becoming clear that now that power was fully theirs, the Communist rulers of the satellite states would no longer eschew policies that would transform their society according to the Soviet model: forcible collectivization of agriculture and attack upon organized religions, especially the Catholic Church, being the principal steps in that direction. Such measures were bound to arouse widespread resistance among the people of the unfortunate countries, and it is clear that the leadership of some parties, notably the Polish one, hoped to postpone them for as long as possible. But by 1947–48 Moscow decided that in view of the West's acquiescence in the face of its encroachments in Eastern Europe, there was no longer any reason for Communism there to conceal its true face and to delay measures that would economically and socially, as well as politically, transform the entire area in accordance with the Soviet model. And so the Cominform was to be yet another instrument, as well as a cover-up, for the Soviets' repression of what yet remained in the way of social and political pluralism in the East European countries under its domination.

With one single exception no other post–World War II development was to weigh as heavily on the future fortunes of Communism as the Kremlin's decision to submit its sphere of influence in East Europe to the full rigors of Marxism-Leninism as it was understood at the time. The decision meant that Communist parties in the area, weak as was their popular appeal to begin with,[9] would never be able to free themselves from the opprobrium of being instruments of a foreign power. It is just possible that had they been left to their own devices, allowed to follow domestic policies felt to be suitable to their own societies, rather than having them laid down to the last detail by Moscow, the East European regimes would have relaxed their repressive practices and acquired a degree of legitimacy in the eyes of their own people. As it was, by imposing the Stalinist pattern upon its protégés, the USSR assumed the burden of standing armed guard over some 100 million people, whose aspirations to independence would never be appeased, and whose submission could only be secured by the actuality or threat of Soviet military intervention. And eventually when that threat had faded, the resulting collapse of East European Communism would have fateful reverberations on its fortunes in Russia.

But at the time such perspectives could not as yet be easily perceived. For the outsiders the subordination of the world Communist movement to the policy goals and interests of a superpower appeared both as one of the keys to its success and as its most menacing aspect. And among the faithful, that subordination could be rationalized as the necessary preliminary of a supranational world order that, however repressive its beginning, would eventually usher in an era of peace and social justice.

By the end of the year neither of those beliefs could be held with the same conviction as before. For in the course of 1948 came a challenge to the supremacy of the Soviet Union, a development all the more unexpected and shocking on account of the challenger's being a Communist party considered hitherto most loyal and devoted to the Fatherland of Socialism and to Stalin. Contemporaries viewed with amazement, at times with incredulity, this apparent blow to the

monolithic unity of Communism. And indeed it appeared incredible
that a small Balkan country would dare to stand up to the Soviet
Union, and that its leader, only recently an obscure agent of the
Comintern, could be reckless enough to cross words with and defy
Stalin, then at the height of his power and worldwide prestige.

To be sure, at the time, Yugoslavia's defection did not loom as
significant as it does from today's perspective. Today we see in it a
harbinger of the subsequent dissonances and clashes that would rend
the Communist bloc and eventually bring about its disintegration. At
the time, it was viewed not so much as a gesture of defiance by Tito
but as yet another episode in the Kremlin's assertion of its supreme
authority and chastising of an imperfectly obedient vassal. Few as yet
believed that the Yugoslavs' defiance of the USSR could be long-
lasting or successful. During the initial phase of the dispute the Yugoslav leaders themselves pleaded for a reconciliation and denied any
intention to break ranks or to question the authority of Comrade Stalin.
Hitherto no Communist party had withstood as much as a hint from
Moscow that it should repudiate its leaders and put in their place
those who would meet with Comrade Stalin's approval. Whenever a
much weaker interwar Soviet Union demanded that the foreign Communists change their policies overnight, it was invariably obeyed. And
with the USSR at the height of its powers, it seemed only a question
of time before the Yugoslav Communists would heed Stalin's call and
overthrow Tito and his clique.

Even if against all the odds the Yugoslav Communists would continue to stick by their leaders, it was thought unlikely that Stalin
would for long tolerate something the world had as yet never seen: a
Communist state not submissive to his will. America's enormous
power and A-bomb had not inhibited him from challenging the West
over West Berlin. Compared with the blockade, a Soviet invasion of
the small Balkan country appeared to present no real danger of leading
to a wider military conflict. The United States was not going to risk
a third world war for the sake of preserving Tito's regime, which ever
since its consolidation of power had shown itself to be virulently anti-
Western. And for how long could Yugoslavia withstand the Soviet
military might? At the most it could be a matter of a few weeks.

Yet all such expectations were to be confounded: small, at first
completely isolated politically, Yugoslavia retained its independence
in the face of the Soviet juggernaut. Tito's maverick Communism
would survive, a standing refutation of what had been a cardinal tenet

of Marxism-Leninism: the supranational character of the ideology and movement.

If it did not sound perversely ironic, one might describe the Soviet-Yugoslav dispute as marking the end of the age of innocence of Communism. Here was a startling demonstration of the incompatibility between its universal aspirations and Soviet imperialism, or rather a revelation of how much international Communism had served as the extension of Soviet power. In the beginning Titoism was described as representing national Communism. That explanation has to be qualified. Milovan Djilas, who in 1948 was among Tito's closest associates and who a few years later was to rebel also against his own national party, would write perceptively about the background of the dispute: "Our party remained [after 1945] the most militant, the most doctrinaire, and the most pro-Soviet to the point that, as I mentioned, the Western press called Yugoslavia 'Satellite No. 1.' I resisted such a label. We really did not feel like a satellite. This only confirmed our delusion that the Soviet Union had no control over us and could not reduce us to a vassal. I conclude that the roots of the conflict lay in our feeling, spawned by the revolution, of being an independent power. As we consolidated our authority and became more aware of ourselves as a distinct political entity, we came to know our own possibilities—conflict with the Soviet Union was pre-ordained. . . . Stalin and the Soviet Union were our cornerstone and point of spiritual origin; we even felt ourselves to be a part of their body politic, until we founded our own regime and political differences began to emerge."[10]

"Until we founded our own regime . . . " This is the crucial phrase in Milovan Djilas's analysis of the break between the USSR and what had been until 1948 its most devoted junior partner. Nationalism is thus only a partial explanation of the psychological impulse that sustained the Yugoslav notables in their refusal to grovel before Stalin, and helped them see the Soviet Union through different eyes from those with which they had viewed it as *revolutionaries*. Now they were rulers whose power, and perhaps even lives, were threatened and could be forfeit should they capitulate to the Kremlin. The love of and pride in their own country helped to sustain Tito and his followers in their defiance of Moscow, but strictly speaking those sentiments were not the primary reasons for their embarking upon a struggle against their erstwhile idol and the country they had literally worshiped. Or perhaps, and without any attempt at irony, it might be more correct to say that it was when their power was threatened that the Yugoslav leaders realized that devotion to the country of Lenin and Stalin was second to their patriotism.

Communism in this late phase of Stalinism was indeed far from being a "mystical Messianic movement," as it was still characterized in Mr. Kennan's exposition of the doctrine of containment.[11] For the Kremlin the messianic goal of conquering or converting the world to Marxism-Leninism had long been replaced by a quite prosaic aspiration to expand the power and influence of the USSR and to render it secure from external and internal threats. The only element of the Communist faith that smacked of mysticism was the extravagant worship of Stalin. Whether in Moscow, Paris, or Belgrade, the party member was expected to worship at the altar of the "genius leader of all progressive mankind." In brief, the main if not the only operative part of the ideology was by 1948 an unabashed cult of power, nicely blending with what after 1956 was to become known as the cult of personality.

This absorption with considerations touching on political power, prizing it far above all other aims of Communism, goes far to explain the successes of the movement in the wake of World War II. But as the Yugoslav-Soviet dispute demonstrated, this cult of power was to vitiate the supranational pretensions of Communism. The very same people who as revolutionaries were loyal servitors of Moscow, once masters of their own countries, were bound to resent and combat the Kremlin's demands that they should continue to render unconditional obedience to the Fatherland of Socialism. And this worship at the altar of power was to strip the Communist rulers in Eastern Europe not only of their reverence toward the Soviet Union but of whatever idealism had guided their steps as revolutionaries and fighters against the Nazi oppression. Lenin before the Revolution characterized tsarist Russia as a "prison house of nationalities." In post–World War II Eastern Europe it was Communism that came to deserve that unenviable epithet, with its leaders trying to soften the rigors of Soviet control, while at the same time striving to contain their own people's aspirations for freedom.

The history of the Yugoslav party exemplifies those diverse traits of East European Communism. The German invasion of their country in April 1941 did not at first stir the Yugoslav Communists into armed resistance against the invader. The destruction of the old state and the division of the country into a number of satellite regimes and spheres of occupation provided Tito and his followers—as yet a small clandestine group—with new opportunities to intensify their work and expand their membership. They did not collaborate with the Germans, but did not fight them either. They did try to sabotage, obstruct, and infiltrate the puppet regimes installed by the invader, just as their party had conspired against the old royal Yugoslav government ever since its inception after World War I. In brief, their behavior was of the kind that Moscow expected and demanded from every Communist party after the Nazi-Soviet Pact of 1939. Nor was such behavior surprising. The core of the conspiratorial organization was composed of young zealots for whom their creed was synonymous with the fervent belief in what was then the only socialist state in the world and its legendary chieftain, a belief that as yet held in check the outrage at the rape and sufferings of their own nation. And for their leader, they had a man who in 1937 had been specially selected by the Soviets to turn the party into their obedient tool. The pre-1945 Tito was, and rightly so, completely trusted by the Russians, something that his erstwhile associate asserts "can perhaps be explained by Tito's past, the time he spent in the Soviet Union, his training there, his special links with Soviet intelligence."[12]

It was only after the news of the German invasion of the Soviet Union on June 22, 1941, that the Yugoslav Communists sprang to arms against what was *now* their enemy. Even after the break and their disillusionment, one of the Yugoslav leaders could render testimony of the emotion which at the news propelled his party into struggle: "On June 22, 1941, we did not conclude that 'happy times' had come when the U.S.S.R. would have to liberate our country from German, Hungarian, Italian and Bulgarian occupation. . . . On the contrary, we concluded that the time had come when it was necessary—in the sense of international solidarity against the fascist invaders, in the sense of that truly Marxist-Leninist internationalism which demands of every working man that he give all of himself at the fateful moment for the common cause of working and progressive mankind—to take up arms *en masse* and to sacrifice all. . . ."[13] Patriotic exhilaration now combined with revolutionary enthusiasm to make the Communist-led Partisans the most effective force fighting the invader in Yugoslavia, in fact in the entire Balkan Peninsula. And nowhere else in German-occupied Europe did a Communist resistance movement equal the feat of the Partisans in surging to the forefront in the struggle for national liberation and in proving so intractable for the occupying power. By November 1942 what not long before had been a puny and isolated movement had succeeded in attracting enough non-Communist adherents to create the Antifascist Council of National Liberation. And within one year this front for the Communist Party would proclaim itself the acting government of the liberated territories, with Tito as its prime minister. Unlike what happened in most other East European countries where Communist governments came, so to speak, in the baggage train of the conquering Soviet armies, when at the end of 1944 Soviet troops appeared on Yugoslav soil, Tito's Partisans already controlled most of their country.

To be sure, that achievement could not be credited solely or even mainly to the Partisans' own exertions. German armies had been defeated on all fronts. Tito's standing had been much enhanced when Churchill had decided to shift the Western Allies' aid from the resistance forces, loyal to the royal Yugoslav government-in-exile, to the Partisans, a decision which in fact sealed the former's fate. And of course the *coup de grâce* to the retreating Germans was delivered by the advancing Red Army. Nevertheless the Yugoslav Communists emerged from the war with a sense of achievement that could not help but cause them to differentiate their attitude toward the USSR from that of their East European ideological brethren.

That "truly Marxist-Leninist internationalism," i.e., unbounded faith in and allegiance to Moscow which characterized the Yugoslav Communists' psychology in the beginning of their struggle, was bound to be affected by the wartime experience. For all the nationalist accoutrements that he had donned, Tito never forgot that he was a Communist. For all the desperate situations in which they often found themselves, the Partisans helped the Albanian Communists to organize their own resistance and maintained contacts with the Greek and Bulgarian Communists. All the more striking in that context must have appeared the attitude of Moscow, which, especially during the earlier part of the war, urged Tito to conceal if not indeed to suppress the Communist character of his movement, to concentrate on fighting the Germans, and to not spurn collaboration with the pro–royal government resistance forces. The Soviets' urgings were understandable: until the victory at Stalingrad, Stalin was fighting for survival, and this was no time for ideological scruples or political maneuverings. But in their prevailing state of political innocence his Yugoslav followers must have been uncomprehending and hurt to receive messages chiding them for their ideological fervor.

"Reviewing all your information, one gets the impression that with some justification the followers of England and the Yugoslav government believe that the Partisan movement is assuming a Communist character and that it intends to sovietize Yugoslavia. Why, for instance, was it necessary to organize a special proletarian brigade when the basic and immediate task consists now in the unification of all anti-Hitler elements to crush the occupier and achieve national liberation. . . . We ask you to review seriously your tactics and actions, to check whether you did all you could to create a united and real national front of all enemies of Hitler and Mussolini in order to defeat the occupier and invader, and if not, to take quickly the necessary steps and to inform us about them." This cable, received at the Partisan headquarters on March 5, 1942, is one of several messages from Moscow in the same vein during that year when the military situation on the Eastern Front still posed mortal danger to the Soviet armies.[14] The Partisan leaders were also, and piquantly enough, advised to be cautious and not overly enthusiastic in their pronouncements about the Soviet Union and Stalin.

Such warnings appear to us to be under the circumstances just common sense. But at the same time Tito himself resented such cautions and he anxiously consulted his senior colleagues as to how one should go about persuading Moscow that in their ideological purity the Yugoslav Communists simply could not agree to collaborate with the reactionaries and royalists. And if a fifty-year-old, seasoned veteran privy to the long history of the Comintern's intrigues and infighting could be shocked by such realistic counsel, what would have been the reaction of the rank and file of Yugoslav Communists had they known that Moscow for the moment did not care about their love for Russia and Comrade Stalin? And indeed after the 1948 break those messages were published in Yugoslavia to document what in retrospect was considered as the first signs of the Kremlin's duplicity and indifference to "truly Marxist-Leninist internationalism."

For all such jarring episodes at the war's end, the Yugoslav party remained, in Djilas's words, "the most militant, the most doctrinaire, and the most pro-Soviet." But the achievement of power in their own country had already wrought a subtle psychological change in Tito's people's attitude toward the Soviet Union. It was precisely by remaining so militant and doctrinaire that the Yugoslavs were bound to run into trouble with the Kremlin. What might have been a virtue in a Communist party out of power was in Stalin's eyes a besetting sin in a ruling one, for what he required from the latter was unconditional obedience.

Tito's militancy and doctrinaire approach had been troublesome enough during the war, but now they threatened more than just embarrassment for the Soviet Union. At the war's end Tito's regime, now officially the government of Yugoslavia, far from devoting its full energies to the task of rebuilding its devastated country and healing its ethnic and political conflicts, sought immediate territorial aggrandizement and embarked on a course of violent domestic repression. The Kremlin was far from desiring such demonstrations of ideological zeal on the part of its satraps. Between 1945 and 1947 the Soviets still preferred that the process of sovietization of Eastern Europe be carried out cautiously and gradually, so as not to threaten a premature confrontation with the United States and Britain.

Even more troublesome for Moscow was the new Yugoslavia's foreign policy. Its leader, whose mercurial personality had during the war charmed so many of his Western contacts, now stood revealed not only as a Communist but also as a nationalist zealot. Tito's anti-Western attitude went far beyond at the time what was deemed to be desirable and safe. Two armed American planes that had wandered over Yugoslav airspace were, at Tito's explicit instructions, shot down. The Soviet foreign ministry officials, while in private allegedly praising the Yugoslavs for their harassment of capitalists, warned them sternly that such provocative acts must stop.

Even more exasperating were Tito's territorial vindications vis-à-vis Italy and Austria. In the postwar negotiations Belgrade persistently and rudely pressed to be given a large slice of Austrian Carinthia. But the most insistent and provocative of Yugoslav demands concerned Trieste, which between 1945 and 1948 remained one of the most sensitive spots in Europe. Fantastic as it must seem in retrospect, at times the expansionist zeal of Tito's regime threatened to lead to a military clash. One of the Soviets' subsequent accusations of their erstwhile protégés that rings true was that Tito and his entourage simply could not understand why on the Trieste issue they should not have been supported by the USSR, even at the risk of a military confrontation between it and the Western powers. Communism was on the march. The Soviet Union as witnessed by its own territorial acquisitions could invariably obtain what it wanted from Britain and the United States. The USSR, as the war demonstrated, was also invincible. Why then wouldn't the Soviet comrades press the Yugoslav case with greater firmness? Such an unrealistic view of the situation may seem comical to us, but at the time it was far from being so to the Kremlin. And conversely, the Soviets' refusal to risk a war to satisfy Tito's territorial cupidity was bound to give rise to some dark suspicions on the Yugoslav side: perhaps they were the victims of some clandestine bargain made at their expense during the war. In a 1945 speech Tito irritably proclaimed that his nation refused to become the subject of deals and bargains between the great powers. The main thrust of his speech was directed against the West, but the Soviets, their own suspicions now aroused, protested through their ambassador at what they took to be a slanderous interpretation of their policies.

Yet such differences and mutual suspicions during the years from 1945 to 1947 were known only in the highest circles of both parties. Insofar as everyone else was allowed to know, Soviet-Yugoslav relations during that period flowed smoothly and harmoniously. Nor is it likely that even the leaders had a premonition of how soon and sharply they would clash. That the Soviets were planting their agents in various agencies of the Yugoslav government and military apparatus could not have surprised Tito, an old Comintern hand. And whatever slights to their national *amour propre*, the Belgrade leaders could not be but flattered by being singled out among all the new East European Communists as the most adept pupils of the Fatherland of Socialism. Other East European satellite chiefs were outshadowed by Marshal Tito, both insofar as his prominence at home and his treatment by Stalin were concerned. At the founding meeting of the Cominform the Yugoslav delegates were treated with special honors. It fell to them to criticize the French and Italian Communist parties for not having been more enterprising in trying to gain power in their countries following their liberation,[15] a task the Yugoslavs performed with a great deal of zest. Who could have thought before 1945 that some hitherto virtually unknown Balkan conspirators would be empowered to sit in judgment on world-renowned figures of the two great Western parties?

An equal mark of distinction was the placing of the Cominform's offices and journal in Belgrade. It was only later that the Yugoslavs reflected on the fact that this also enhanced the Soviets' opportunities for spying within their country.

Such was the situation at the beginning of 1948, when from being occasionally strained, Soviet-Yugoslav relations turned into an acri-

monious conflict. The monolithic unity of the world Communist movement was shattered, never really to be restored again. To be sure,
contemporaries could hardly appreciate the historic significance of
the break. For them Yugoslavia's case was an exception that confirmed the rule: there could be no Communism except for that which
the Soviets led and approved. For reasons already adduced, it was
generally believed, certainly in Moscow and other Communist capitals, that it was only a matter of time before Tito and his associates
in defiance must meet their doom.

On the surface the conflict centered around the personalities of the
two contestants. Again, Djilas: "It was around Tito that the conflict
with the Soviet Union first began to crystallize. This was not only
because of Tito's leading and central role but because of the peremptory, authoritarian characteristics of Yugoslav Communism, which
were essentially no different from those of Soviet Communism."[16] Or,
in plain language, it was a contest of wills between Stalin and Tito;
the Soviet despot resented the Balkan dictator's prominence and the
Stalin-like cult of personality with which he surrounded himself in
his own bailiwick. Other reasons advanced by the Soviets in their
letters to the Yugoslav leadership were for the most part contrived or,
coming from whom they did, laughable: the undemocratic character
of the Yugoslav party arrangements, the secrecy in which its decision
making was veiled, the too-radical "leftist-deviationist" character of
the social and economic reforms forced by Belgrade upon its people.
The Kremlin wanted Tito and his associates to recognize humbly their
errors and beg for forgiveness. That was equivalent to asking them
to put their heads into a noose, which at a moment thought appropriate
would be pulled by Stalin. The Yugoslav dictator and his entourage
were not merely to be stripped of power, but were probably to share
the fate of countless previous victims of the "genius leader of all
progressive mankind." Well, in Moscow through 1937, Tito witnessed
the Soviet purges and witch hunts at first hand and at their worst,
and genuine and great as was his devotion to proletarian internationalism, he knew what would be the ultimate price of even a verbal
capitulation.

Internally, the Yugoslav party and state machinery had been, so to
speak, Stalinized, so that by 1948 they proved resistant to the Soviets'
threats, cajoleries, and subversion. The rank and file of the faithful
had to be weaned gradually from their worship of Stalin and Russia,
but the violence, mendacity, and vulgarity of the Kremlin's attacks

upon their leaders were of great help in this respect. The "Cominformists," as Moscow's real or reputed partisans were called, were expeditiously and often very brutally handled by Tito's security service, an apt pupil of the then Soviet predecessor of the KGB.

But even to see the conflict primarily in terms of personalities suggests how greatly the ideological base of Communism had by 1948 been eroded. By now the main obligatory article of faith for every Communist had to be the infallibility of Comrade Stalin. It was mainly by propagating a cult of personality of his own that Tito managed to stave off the danger of an internal revolt. Even a man of exemplary modesty, something certainly not charactcristic of the mercurial Yugoslav leader, would have perceived that a posture of personal humility would be of great disadvantage in his duel with Stalin. And so a man who until his fifties was unknown to the vast majority of his countrymen was built into a legend.

The cult of personality, though so frequently lambasted by the Communist leaders following Stalin's death, was still, though on a much, much lesser scale than in the case of its greatest practitioner, indulged in by virtually all of them. Already in 1948 one had to wonder whether the practice was so ingrained into the psychology of Communism that attempts to eliminate or even restrain it might throw the entire system into disarray. And indeed what has been happening in the Soviet Union since Gorbachev's ascent, and in Yugoslavia since Tito's death in 1980, poses a real question whether a Communist state can dispense with such idolatry and yet preserve its cohesion. Gorbachev wouldn't, Tito's successors couldn't, build a personality cult of their own.

By the same token, the myth of the Communist philosopher-kings was also likely to have disastrous results since it was bound to erode the ideological appeal of Communism. The inanities of Mao's last decade, the frightful legacy Stalin left to his successors, the fate of such minor idol-tyrants as Nicolae Ceauşescu, all attest to the catastrophic consequences of the tendency to deify the leader inherent in Communism. There is no doubt that the timing of the Soviet campaign to oust Tito proceeded from the vanity of one man. Had Stalin's usual political cunning not been warped by his megalomania and suspiciousness, Yugoslavia might have remained a loyal satellite for quite a while longer.

But not even such merely outward harmony could have been preserved indefinitely. Beyond the question of personalities—an old man's vanity, the younger's need to assert himself—there was the basic incompatibility between Soviet Communism as it crystallized after thirty years of its existence, and the internationalist character and aspirations of the movement at large. Quite apart from the personal foibles and whims of the man who by 1948 had ruled it for a generation, its Soviet version has made Communism synonymous with a system of absolute control of the society and the state over which it had acquired power. If Moscow was unwilling—really, because of the nature of the system, unable—to tolerate the slightest degree of autonomy of its subordinates in Kiev or Minsk, how could it, in the long run, continue to view the Communists in Belgrade, Warsaw, or for that matter, Paris or Rome, as allies or partners rather than simply as satraps for whom its every word had to be the law?

From the Kremlin's point of view its attempt first to chastise and then to oust Tito and his associates was perfectly logical. The Yugoslavs were, prior to the outbreak of the dispute, scrupulously loyal and yet were giving themselves airs, as if they were independent. They wanted it to be understood that they had conquered power on their own, and had not, like the Communists elsewhere in Eastern Europe, received it as a gift from the USSR. Imbued by the same expansionist impulse that was so characteristic of the Soviets, Tito and his associates were not satisfied with their absolute rule over their country. The Yugoslavs' aim from 1945 to 1947 was to become the overlords of the Balkans. They had already reduced Albania to the status of what might be called a subsatellite, and they were actively promoting the idea of the merger of Yugoslavia and Bulgaria. At first the union had the support of Moscow, but then in January 1948 the latter peremptorily vetoed the scheme.[17]

It was not then so much what Tito did, but what he might become that required teaching him a lesson and eliminating him—right away if he did not heed it, at a more leisurely pace if he did. It was bad for the morale, i.e., unconditional obedience to Moscow, of the other ruling Communist parties to see the Soviets humoring the Yugoslav dictator. Once their rule was established more firmly in their countries, the Polish, Hungarian, and other Communists might also become emboldened to expect more considerate treatment from their Soviet superiors. And if the leader of a small Balkan country was permitted to carry on in that way, what lesson would it convey for the Chinese Communists when they took over their country? One who at the time was a very active participant in the drama sees some justification in the Soviets' fears of the implications of Yugoslav expansionist ambitions concerning their neighbors. "Our highly idealistic initial aspirations in relation to these countries [e.g., Albania and Bulgaria] may have carried the seeds of hegemony, if only ideologically. Does not politics by definition contain such seeds, though unaware of their presence? Soviet aspirations on the other hand were consciously hegemonic and only superficially cloaked in a codified, ossified ideology."[18]

One remains somewhat unconvinced that Tito's own aspirations vis-à-vis Bulgaria and Albania were highly idealistic, but it is easy to see how the search for even a regional and "idealistic" hegemony by one of the Communist regimes was bound to stir up anxiety and anguish in the Kremlin.

Yet viewed from the broader perspective, the campaign to oust Tito, even if understandable, was bound to be self-defeating. In the past practically every long-lasting imperial system had been built on something more than force. The most successful of them allowed for a considerable degree of local autonomy and for retention of the national and cultural particularities of their component parts. Insofar as the Communist bloc, in 1948 and the years following it, was concerned, the Soviets could not have convinced themselves that, for all the propaganda and indoctrination, Communism had won the allegiance of the majority of the population of the subject nations. As seen in Czechoslovakia, even where it was initially popular, Communist rule became much less so after the people's experience with it. There were then two alternative ways to secure Soviet domination on broader foundations than just that of brute force. One was for Moscow to allow a degree of political pluralism in the domestic politics of its satellites, eschewing any effort to put them into the straitjacket of Soviet-type Communism. The other was to grant to what were in fact Soviet garrisons in those countries—the local Communist parties—a wide latitude of policies, and permit them to think of themselves not as agents of a foreign power but as national leaders in their own right, united with and indebted to Moscow by links of ideology and self-interest.

By approving and helping engineer the Czechoslovak coup of February 1948, the Kremlin gave a signal that the former path was not to its liking. And now later on in the year the break with Yugoslavia served as a vivid illustration that, henceforth, foreign Communists would not be allowed to be masters in their own house or to follow their own paths to socialism.

The repercussions of the Tito affair then led almost inevitably to the fragility of the Soviet-Communist system, a fragility that was to be revealed in 1956, shown again in the sixties in the Sino-Soviet clash, and culminating in the drama of 1988 through 1991. Perhaps force could have remained a dependable element in the cohesion of the empire had China, in the meantime, *not* entered the Communist camp. But the world's largest nation could not have been molded in the image of a Bulgaria or a Hungary.

Stalin's successors, as we shall see, would realize the inadequacy and danger inherent in his concept of empire and would try to devise a more workable and flexible model of a Communist commonwealth. But despite their efforts, intermittent crises and uprisings in the subject states would keep eroding Soviet power. Apart from military intervention, diplomacy would occasionally be brought into play by the Kremlin to preserve the fiction of the stability of the ramshackle East European empire and of the unity of the world Communist movement. But it was the basic structure of Soviet politics at home that kept frustrating all such endeavors. And when belatedly that structure itself became shaky after 1985, the empire would collapse like a house of cards, and that collapse in turn would portend grave consequences for the internal cohesion of the Soviet Union and for the survival of the ideology.

The Yugoslav dispute may well have saved democracy in another small country in the Soviet sphere of influence. And Finland's case reiterates the view that between 1945 and 1948 there had been an alternative to the rapacious methods of Soviet expansionism, methods which though at the time were crowned with success were in the decades ahead to bring such trials and debacles to the USSR. An outside observer at the end of World War II might well have expected Finland to be eventually forced into a mold similar to that of the Communist satellites. As a matter of fact, there were more cogent reasons to expect such a future for the little Baltic country than for Hungary or Romania. Finland had been under Russian rule between 1809 and 1917,[19] a factor of great importance for someone as conscious of history and as imbued with Russian nationalism as Stalin. The Finns, after putting up a gallant fight against the Soviets in the winter war of 1939 and early 1940, joined the Germans in their invasion of the USSR. But to the amazement of observers, at the war's end Finland, while forced to sign a harsh peace treaty and admit Russian military bases on its territory, was for a while not tampered with by the Soviets insofar as its domestic politics was concerned. Yet by the beginning of 1948 there were ominous signs that the Finnish Communists might try to emulate their comrades elsewhere in Eastern Europe, and the Kremlin itself demanded that a Helsinki government delegation come to Moscow, allegedly to negotiate a defense treaty. Before, Stalin's hitherto and uncharacteristic restraint in regard to Finland might well have been conditioned by the memory of the strong emotional reaction in the United States to the Soviet aggression against the little state in 1939–40. But the West's supine reaction to the Communist takeover elsewhere in the area argued by now that such restraint had been unnecessary. Yet providentially there intervened the sharp clash between the USSR and Yugoslavia.[20] In the wake of the coup in Czechoslovakia, with the angry though as yet secret exchanges between Belgrade and Moscow in the face of the approaching Berlin crisis, an attempt to communize Finland might have become the proverbial straw that broke the camel's back, or more concretely, could have shocked the West out of its passivity. And so when the apprehensive Finnish delegates arrived in Moscow, it was the defense treaty which was all that they were required to sign, a treaty that from the Soviet point of view must have been quite superfluous, and hardly seems to have been the real and original reason for the Kremlin's invitation. In any case, shortly afterward the Communist ministers were removed from the Finnish coalition government and their party accepted it quite placidly. Most likely, and perversely, the Communist dictator in Belgrade helped save Finnish democracy!

Here we run into one of recent history's biggest "ifs." What if the Soviets after liberating Europe, instead of then enslaving it to Communism, had been content with the Finnish-type arrangement: having those countries defer to the Kremlin insofar as their foreign and defense policies were concerned, but leaving them free insofar as their domestic policies were concerned? In that case and without Soviet military coercion or its threat, only one country in the area—Yugoslavia, and even there it is debatable—would have been under Communist rule in 1948. And how many troubles and burdens would have been spared for the USSR had it in the wake of the war agreed to the Finlandization of Eastern Europe. It would not have had to stand armed guard for forty years over 100 million sullen people. The threat of a rebirth of German militarism would still have made whoever ruled in Warsaw and Prague and the other capitals look to Moscow for support. Being left to their own devices, the local Communist parties would not have become identified with foreign oppression and might have gained genuine popular support.[21] Communism and the Soviet Union would not have incurred the obloquy that followed the latter's military intervention in Hungary in 1956 and in Czechoslovakia in 1968. It was the Soviet usurpations in Eastern Europe that first stirred up the winds of the cold war. Had the Soviets shown restraint there, East-West coexistence would, in all likelihood, have proved much easier and real détente might have come earlier. And most important, when the time came to restructure the Soviet system itself, the task would not have been rendered so much more complex and difficult by the political earthquake that shook Eastern Europe, the tremors of which have been more than just felt in the USSR.

Well, history cannot be replayed and there is an obvious counter-argument to the above. A diehard defender of the old Soviet order would undoubtedly argue that it was not Stalin but his incompetent successors, especially those after 1985, who are responsible for Communism's present parlous condition. And in a sense even the old despot had erred by not striking at Tito harder and sooner, or once the dispute was out in the open. True proletarian internationalism cannot exist, our hard-liner would assert, without a central authority that wields absolute control over the member parties, and unless those who defy this authority are promptly and harshly punished, the whole movement must lose its appeal and cohesion.

By the summer of 1948 the Kremlin had in fact reached the conclusion that the main trouble with its policies vis-à-vis the satellite states lay in their leniency. Rather disarmingly the Soviets proposed to present the whole dispute for judgment before the Cominform. Let the representatives of the fraternal Communist parties decide who is right. With the Yugoslavs refusing to participate in that charade, the Cominform on June 28 in effect excommunicated their party. The ban would be lifted, it was implied, only after the party purified itself of its heretical leaders, Tito and three others closest to him being specifically listed by name.

Belgrade's answer was to convoke the Yugoslav Communist Party's congress. Such was the hold that the Fatherland of Socialism and the "genius leader of all progessive mankind" still exercised over Communists everywhere that Tito and his associates thought it imprudent to inform the comrades that the split was already irreversible. Instead, they modestly pleaded for an opportunity to prove to their colleagues that their accusations were completely unfounded. And the same motif was evident in the chant the delegates took up at the conclusion of their congress: "Stalin—Tito—Party." The Stalin cult was permitted to linger for a while longer and was terminated only gradually. As late as the 1949 May Day celebrations, pictures of Stalin were still carried in the parades accompanying those of Tito.

It was not until 1950 that the Yugoslav leaders become confident enough of their followers' having been weaned from their psychological dependence on and awe of the Soviet Union to present the dispute as the result of the two parties' irreconcilable views of Communism. The Soviets identified it with the goals and interests of the Soviet state. The Yugoslavs for their part claimed that they represented the true version of Marxism-Leninism, stressing the equality of all the Communist parties and true internationalism. Soviet Communism became corrupted not only by Russian chauvinism and the cult of Stalin but also by the bureaucratic degeneration of the party and state apparatus.

The Yugoslavs now became quite explicit about what they had to put up with during the allegedly harmonious period of their relations with the senior Communist power. In addition to their arrogant and condescending way, the Soviets exploited Yugoslavia economically, just as they did the other satellites. They did this through unequal terms of trade, and by notorious joint companies in which the Russian side supposedly provided management skills and capital, but in fact took control of some of the vital segments of the country's economy.

From the Soviet perspective the clash was soon also transmogrified into an ideological dispute. There could be only one true version of Marxism-Leninism: that represented by Moscow. The Yugoslav party was run in a conspiratorial way rather than by the democratic principles exemplified in the practices of the Communist Party of the USSR. The Tito regime was persecuting those Communists who refused to endorse its anti-Leninist, anti-Soviet policies. Its social and economic measures displayed leftist sectarian characteristics, so as to compensate for and cover up its betrayal of ideology. And what was almost inevitable during the Stalinist phase of Communism, the Kremlin's indictment of the rebels on ideological grounds, was soon supplemented by charges of plain treason: Tito and his clique had sold out to the Western imperialists, they had become (if indeed they had not been all along) agents of Wall Street, and as the vituperative rhetoric of late Stalinism took on an increasingly anti-Semitic coloring, also of the capitalists' ally, the Zionists!

"Titoism" joined "Trotskyism" as a synonym for treason and anti-Soviet malevolence. The latter term had been attached to the multitudes of Communists who perished in Russia in the great terror of the thirties, the great majority never having had the slightest connection with the fallen great of the Bolshevik Revolution. Similarly, the massive purge of the "Titoists" throughout Eastern Europe claimed thousands who in no sense could be described as followers of Tito or as sharing his ideas.

Most of the victims were Communist officials who attracted Moscow's displeasure or suspicion. There were those who in their contacts with the Soviets did not display proper reverence toward the USSR, or hinted about Russian exploitation of their country's economy. There were others who though unfailingly servile toward the Kremlin were still suspect because of their long residence in the West or for having friends and associations outside of the Communist camp.[22] For Moscow's local satraps the open season on Titoists served as a convenient pretext for accusing and destroying their actual and potential rivals. In brief, the mass terror Communists experienced in Eastern Europe was startlingly reminiscent, though on a smaller scale, of what the Soviet Union itself had undergone between 1936 and 1939.

The grim process was highlighted, as had been its antecedents, by the spectacular trials of the once great of East European Communism. They were made to confess to surrealistic tales of treason and subversion. Publicly tried under such circumstances were the once towering figures of their respective Communist regimes: Hungary's László Rajk, Bulgaria's Traicho Kostov, and Czechoslovakia's Rudolf Slansky. They and the lesser lights put in the prisoners' dock with them were pressed to, and usually did, confess[23] to the utterly improbable plots and anti-Soviet conspiracies, this at the bidding of Tito and Western intelligence services, as well as international Zionism. The anti-Semitic motif was most pronounced in the Slansky trial, where the great majority of the accused and condemned were Jewish. As in the great Moscow dramas of 1936, '37 and '38, the usual sentence was that of death. There can be no question from whence came the inspiration for the spectacles, and who instructed the local producers how to stage them.

From one point of view this physical liquidation of hundreds of loyal Communists and the imprisonment and disgrace of many, many others appeared to defy common sense. Rather than coming from political calculation it seemed reminiscent of a savage ritual where an offended deity demanded and obtained propitiation through a mass human sacrifice. But there was also a less exotic reason: as in the Soviet Union in the 1930s, the terror was to be so pervasive as to preclude any potential challenge to the Kremlin and to make unimaginable any self-assertion, no matter how modest, on the part of a Communist leader within the bloc. When it came to the veracity of the charges, the notion of intra-Communist intrigues brewed by Tito and abetted by the CIA and the Zionists was of course on a par with the story of Trotsky and his partisans being servitors of the German General Staff under Hitler. But it was not unreasonable to assume that most East European Communist leaders must have privately sympathized with Tito during the initial phase of his quarrel with Moscow: most of them would have naturally preferred a modicum of autonomy and a lighter Soviet hand. One of them, the Polish leader Władysław Gomułka, was naive enough to declare that Tito should have been conciliated rather than peremptorily condemned.[24] The terror unleashed against the alleged Titoists was in the Kremlin's view an effective way of deterring such aspirations and illusions.

Terror was not the only means through which the Kremlin sought to secure that its vassals should follow the narrow if exceedingly tortuous path of blind obedience to its commands and whims. Already in 1947–48 Moscow had tightened the requirements for the sovietization of its satellites' societies. Before, the satraps in their social and economic policies were allowed to take into account the local circumstances and popular feelings. Until the formation of the Cominform there was some ground for the illusions that had allowed Churchill and Roosevelt to acquiesce in the Soviets' claims at Yalta: the USSR sought a sphere of influence in the old pre-1914 sense of the term, rather than the transformation of the whole area in the Soviet image. Collectivization of agriculture, it was believed, would be introduced, if at all, gradually, not in the brutal manner as had been done in the USSR between 1929 and 1933. There would be no frontal attack on the Catholic Church in countries such as Poland where it had been such an integral part of the society's culture. There would be some room left for the national traditions and customs distinct from those of the imperial powers. Such toleration was already severely constrained before 1948, but the satellite regimes still enjoyed some latitude concerning the pace of the social and economic transformation of their societies. In fact, in their initial outburst against Tito, the Soviets themselves roundly and justifiably criticized the Yugoslav Communists for being doctrinaire and imprudent on those counts.

The heating up of the campaign against the Yugoslavs was accompanied by clear direction to all the People's Democracies, as they were called at the time, to step up their pace of sovietization. As suggested above, the reason for such peremptory orders could hardly be attributed to the Kremlin, still burning with ideological fervor. Considerations of power and of Soviet-Russian nationalism had for some time outweighed the imperatives of Marxism-Leninism insofar as Stalin's and his associates' motivations were concerned. But tightening the screws of social and cultural controls was assumed to be yet another way of immunizing the satellites against Titoism. The notion of "separate roads to socialism," so much touted by the Soviet leaders after the Stalin period, was currently held to be heretical and equivalent to treason.

And so with a heavy heart the satellite leaders embarked upon measures, most of which they knew would meet popular resistance, and some at least, they feared, would prove damaging to their country's economy. Even in 1948 it must have been obvious to any reasonable observer of the Soviet scene that collectivization of agriculture there had become the Achilles' heel of the entire economy. How much more true it would have to be in countries where individual peasant ownership of the land had been of much longer standing than in Russia and where the technical level of cultivation was (certainly in Czechoslovakia and parts of Poland) on a much higher level than in the precollectivization USSR. Yet because of a quarrel between two dictators the East European peasant was now forcibly subjected to regimentation, and his country's economy suffered accordingly.

The initial and sensible drive to diversify the hitherto mainly agrarian economies now assumed a frantic pace reminiscent of the first Soviet Five-Year Plan. In addition to the other obvious flaws of this hurried pace of industrialization, its main burden fell upon what in theory was the ruling class of the Communist state, the workers. Greatly tightened labor discipline and constantly increased work norms had become the grim reality for the Romanian and Polish worker, just as they had been for the Soviet worker since the early thirties. And alongside the workers and peasants, the local intelligentsia had also been made the victim of the Communist regimes' being compelled to cast off the mask of moderation and tolerance, as they were hurried to resemble as much as possible the Soviet model. Scholarly contacts and cultural exchanges with the West had to be terminated. Scientific disciplines then on the index in the USSR, such as genetics, had to be repudiated. Socialist realism became the only permissible mode of expression in literature and the arts. The Catholic Church and other religious denominations were subjected to pressure intended in the first instance to make their hierarchies submit to the government (which in the case of the Catholic churches required breaking their ties with Rome), and then gradually to destroy the influence of religious bodies altogether.

In brief, no social class or group in Eastern Europe was by 1949 spared as the shackles of conformity and repression were being tightened over the whole area. Nor were the rulers themselves exempt from the ordeal. What Milovan Djilas was to dub the new class—the top Communist leaders and bureaucrats, their entourages and families—may already have enjoyed the privileges and material appurtenances of power that were quite incompatible with the egalitarian notions of their ideology. But even more than their subjects, the oligarchs must have suffered from a growing sense of insecurity: a hint from Moscow and not only their high positions and privileges would be forfeit. If a longtime secretary general of the Communist Party of Czechoslovakia could be unmasked overnight as an agent of Western imperialism, then confess in open court and be sent to the gallows, who among the elite of East European Communism could feel safe? And so there was a kernel of rationality in Moscow's machinations. None of its satraps could now hope to emulate Tito's feat: to defy Moscow and yet be sure of carrying his party with him.

And so Yugoslavia was quarantined from the rest of the Communist world. In their initial reaction to the Soviets' accusations, Tito's partisans had hoped that they could convince the Russians that the accusations were unjustified. After their disillusionment on that count they still hoped that now that the Kremlin had dropped its mask, revealing unabashed imperialism, other fraternal parties would provide them at least moral support. Surely Marxism-Leninism was greater than any party, even that of the Fatherland of Socialism. For two years after the break Belgrade was still at pains to demonstrate its allegiance to the faith. It continued its opprobrious oratory about the imperialist West. Though spurned by their Soviet opposite numbers in the U.N., Yugoslavia's delegates continued voting with them and against the United States. When the Korean War broke out, the Yugoslav's pronouncements echoed those of Moscow's: it was the South which with American connivance embarked upon wanton aggression. Yet such repeated demonstrations of Marxist-Leninist probity availed the Yugoslav rebels nothing. The entire Communist world echoed the Soviets' vilification of the upstart Balkan leader and his insolent clique. The Kremlin's absurd charges were repeated not only by the terrorized satellite parties, but also by those that had not undergone the post-1948 rites of purges and repression, most notably the French and Italian ones. The Yugoslavs placed great hopes on the Chinese, whose struggle for power, like their own, had only intermittently been helped by the Russians and who were assumed to have similar grievances against the Kremlin. But here again Belgrade met with disappointment. At this crucial period of China's civil war in 1948–49, Mao's party was not going to risk Stalin's displeasure and perhaps also more than just that by endorsing Tito's cause.

And so the Yugoslav rebels had to undergo another and more fundamental disenchantment: no one in the Communist camp would endorse their position or show an understanding of the predicament in which the party and country found themselves. "Marxist-Leninist" internationalism was demonstrably a fiction. What was strong and enduring about Communism was Soviet power and imperialism.

The subsequent ideological wanderings of Yugoslav Communism were to cast further doubts upon the possibility of the ideological resuscitation of Communism. After their disenchantment with the fraternal parties' behavior in the dispute, the Yugoslavs proposed to demonstrate that there could be another model of Communism than that of the Kremlin; freer and more democratic, attuned to each nation's circumstances and characteristics. And indeed the bitter experiences with Stalin abroad and at home led the regime to become more tolerant and less repressive. There followed a détente with the West; the once most anti-Western of the post-1945 Communist regimes in Eastern Europe was by 1952 soliciting U.S. economic and military help.

But though fully emancipated from the USSR, Tito's Yugoslavia would never free itself from those two basic features of Stalinism: the cult of personality and the one-party system. And herein lay one of the fundamental lessons of the great crises of the Soviet bloc. Stalinism had become so much part and parcel of the ideology and practice of

Communism that it could not be excised from its body without irreparably (though not immediately) injuring the entire organism.

Much and genuinely as the Yugoslavs wanted to be different from their erstwhile comrades and current vilifiers, they could not dispense with these basic appurtenances of the Communist system. Tito's regime would go through all sorts of motions designed to refurbish its image and to provide it with a new democratic-looking facade. Doctrinaire measures adopted during its honeymoon with Moscow, such as the collectivization of agriculture, would be rescinded. The party was renamed the League of the Yugoslav Communists. Democratic gloss was applied to industrial management and local government. All such cosmetic adjustments did not change the realities of personal dictatorship and the police state. Tito's stand against alien domination did undoubtedly gain him a much wider acceptance, even among the non-Communists among his compatriots. But though now genuinely a national leader he would remain to the end very much a dictator, tolerating no interference with his prerogatives.

The hollowness of the apparent democratization of the system was dramatically illustrated by the Djilas affair. The shock of the separation from Moscow transformed one of the dictator's closest associates and friends from a doctrinaire ideologue into a passionate advocate of liberalization and a severe critic of the powers and privileges of the ruling oligarchy. And though Tito, unlike his savage Soviet counterpart, was susceptible to the ties of friendship and comradeship, Djilas was made to pay dearly for his outspokenness. In 1954 he was stripped of his high offices and read out of the party. Much later he would write: "The democratic movement set in motion by our struggle against Stalin was brought to a halt; the party bureaucracy again gained the upper hand."[25] Not exactly a correct reconstruction of the event; unlike the writer, Tito and his other associates had not really been interested in moving toward democracy. They had sought to impart a democratic veneer to their fight for survival and retention of power. For the rest of Tito's long reign his once-close collaborator and friend would be shunned and persecuted by the Yugoslav establishment. Twice Djilas, a former inmate of pre–Communist Yugoslavia's jails, would experience long-term imprisonment under the regime he had helped to bring to power.

Djilas's story is not a mere footnote to the turbulence that shook the Soviet bloc beginning in 1948. It tells us a great deal about post–World War II Communism—that his is the only case of a high Communist notable who forfeited his office and suffered persecution not because he had found himself on the losing side in a struggle for power, but because of genuine ideological scruples and by his own choice.

The Tito affair brought into sharper focus the nature of East European Communist regimes. Imposed upon countries that in most cases lacked democratic traditions or in which they had been of short and uncertain standing, those regimes at first sought to offset their authoritarian ways and gain popular acceptance through progressive social and economic policies. The aspirations of the Communist rulers prior to the trauma of the Soviet-Yugoslav break are perhaps well epitomized by a story related by Djilas. Shortly after they consolidated their power, Yugoslavia's leaders discussed the need for a special jail for political prisoners. "When someone observed that the number of political prisoners might be reduced, the experience of the Soviet Union was cited and naturally Comrade Stalin's doctrine whereby an ever sharpening class struggle must accompany the building of socialism. With the inevitability of ever increasing numbers of political culprits thus being authoritatively established, the assembled dignitaries fell to discussing how to house them. That we had to have a new jail was obvious, and no one argued the point. There were appeals to hygiene and humanity, but if the meeting had one keynote, it was this: on the outside the new prison should resemble anything but a prison; on the inside it should have none of the imperfections or 'conveniences' that Communists had turned to advantage in their illegal prison communications back in the days of the Yugoslav monarchy. . . . By providing for deep, insulated cellars, we would insure that the light of day would not penetrate to the cells, and that no human voices would ever be heard above. We would have windows of insulated glass set in concrete, which would look out on passage ways not on the outside world, but on the inner exercise courts! Finally, we envisioned a clean, wholesome prison, from the water supply and toilets in every room to blankets and food preparation. The need for a new jail would have arisen with any government; our distinction consisted in our planning for complete control over the prisoners, whose isolation had to be certain."[26]

Well, as with most utopias, this blueprint for a new society turned out to be unattainable. The Soviet Union would not allow the Communist masters complete control over their subjects, nor that they should rule over prisoner societies in anything like a "clean, whole-some" way.

The Tito affair, then, enabled the world to see more concretely the nature of Communism in power. But other than that, a superficial observer might well have concluded within a year or two of the split that its broader repercussions did not seem so momentous. Unlike what had been hoped in the West, national Communism did not spread. The Soviet Union's grip on Eastern Europe was stronger than ever before. And now that the USSR broke the U.S. monopoly on nuclear weapons (with its first explosion of an A-bomb in the fall of 1949), its power loomed and was more awesome and menacing. The creation of NATO in 1949 was a tangible proof that the West's alarm over the Soviet threat was in no sense diminished.

And could one say that the threat of Communism, as distinguished from that of Soviet military might, had been reduced as a consequence of the Balkan imbroglio? In the first place, few in 1949 or 1950 would have been inclined to make that distinction. Tito's revolt could still be seen as a fortuitous event rather than as a harbinger of things to come and a symptom of an organic malaise of the world Communist movement. Few as yet gave this maverick Communist regime much chance of surviving.

There was another, much larger stage than Eastern Europe, and there the attractions of Communism and the prestige of the Soviet Union did not appear affected by the appearance of a dissident Communist state. The dissolution of the great Western empires was now taking place at a rapid pace. In some Third World areas, such as what had been French Indochina, Communist movements were in the forefront of the struggle for emancipation and most likely the beneficiaries of its achievement. Elsewhere the non-Communist movements struggling for independence, or the postcolonial regimes already established, as in India, still looked at the Soviet Union with sympathy. Eastern Europe's example notwithstanding, the USSR was assumed, in light of its ideology, to be anti-imperialist and a natural friend of oppressed nations now emerging from or still fighting against Western rule. The Kremlin, needless to say, stressed the anti-imperialist motif in its foreign policies. Few among the emerging nations' leaders and politicians appreciated the true nature of the Soviet state, or the realities of Stalin's treatment of the non-Russian ethnic groups in his own empire. The myth that Communism achieved miracles in modernizing and industrializing once-backward and mainly agrarian economies held powerful attraction for what were beginning to be called the developing nations, no matter what the political complexion of their regimes. The alleged effectiveness of the "Soviet model of development" combined with the indisputable power of the USSR enhanced the image of Communism in the Third World. Few of the emerging states found Western political institutions and customs applicable to their circumstances. Genuine democracy and parliamentarianism seemed hardly attainable in societies with a low level of literacy and general standard of living. All the greater the opportunities for a Kremlin that had displayed no compunction in dealing with dictatorial, or outright despotic, regimes.

To be sure, it would be Stalin's successors rather than the old despot himself who would make a concerted effort to exploit such favorable conditions (from the Kremlin's point of view) for expanding the Soviet Union's power and influence in the Third World; Stalin's attention remained riveted on Europe and on the condition of the Communist camp rather than on the new and seemingly dazzling opportunities that already beckoned in Asia and soon would in Africa.

And whatever the aged dictator's obsessions and peculiarities, his instincts as to what were the important areas and issues in the post–World War II world were correct. The Soviet Union would in the decades ahead score some spectacular successes by exploiting the West's weaknesses and vulnerabilities in the Middle East, Southeast Asia, the Caribbean, and other places where the local dictators and/or liberation movements would naturally gravitate toward the Kremlin. But Europe remained the main battlefield of the cold war, and its resurgence from what had been a steady decline in its vitality and importance ever since 1914 would be the crucial factor in the worldwide contest between the democratic and Communist systems.

Of even greater weight to the Soviet Union would be the preservation and enhancement of the unity and dynamism of the international Communist movement. Paradoxically, the USSR as a superpower would find it both more important and more difficult to maintain that unity than it had as a much weaker and more vulnerable state in the twenties and thirties. Once Stalin's Russia chose to transform its satellites in its own, Communist image, the success or failure of that transformation became supremely important to the political security of the Soviet Union itself. What was the point of the USSR's assuming a variety of risks and burdens incidental to its mission of propagating Communism if shared ideology did not, as in the case of Yugoslavia, secure the loyalty of the "fraternal countries"? And if the central postulate of Marxism-Leninism was a sham, how could one justify what was incurred in its name by the mass of the Soviet people?

In the wake of the Tito affair such questions might well have agitated the minds of Soviet and foreign Communists, even though at the time and for the balance of Stalin's life the former couldn't and the latter wouldn't voice any doubts on those counts. The spell was broken, and the monolithic structure of Communism cracked. For a few more years massive repression within the Communist world and the awe of Soviet military power outside it would obscure the appearance of those fissures. But even before the end of the Stalin era the unity and premises of the movement would be subjected to a much more challenging test. In 1949 Communism would score its greatest victory since the Bolshevik Revolution—the conquest of the world's largest nation. But this victory would present the Soviet Union with its most intractable problem and eventually would bring a signal defeat of Soviet imperialism.

2

THE LONG JOURNEY

THE CHAIRMAN and those accompanying him boarded the train in Beijing on December 6, 1949. It was Mao's first trip abroad, its destination, Moscow, where he was going to meet for the first (and, it turned out, the only) time with Joseph Stalin. The travelers reached the border on the ninth and had to shift to the wider-gauged Soviet railway cars. Those members of the delegation who knew Russian must have been struck, if they were superstitious, by the name of the first Soviet station they stopped at: Otpor (the Russian word for "resistance"). As the train rolled on through the seemingly endless snow-covered expanse of Siberia, a Soviet diplomat assigned to the delegation thought he could sense that Mao's mood was one of growing agitation. At the stops he would but reluctantly emerge from the train to walk in the open air, explaining that he was unaccustomed to the cold and wind of the Siberian winter. He fell ill in Sverdlovsk, almost losing consciousness, and remained unwell—ostensibly with the flu—for the balance of the trip.

As he was approaching Moscow, it would have been natural for Mao to experience mounting anxiety. To be sure, he was not going to the center of world Communism as a humble supplicant. His party and armies had conquered the vast area of mainland China, and with the official proclamation of the People's Republic on October 1, he became the head of the world's most populous nation. The Kuomintang regime which only one and a half years before appeared to have the upper hand in the civil war had fled to Taiwan. He had led his movement to what was the greatest triumph of world Communism since the October Revolution. To an outsider it would have appeared natural that the victorious leader was assured of a rapturous welcome in the Soviet capital. But though he had not met him, he knew enough about his host to suspect that his stay in the USSR might turn out to be an ordeal rather than a series of festivities.

It was Stalin who in the mid-twenties had ordered the Chinese Communists, in the face of their growing apprehensions, to continue collaborating with the Kuomintang. Suddenly, in April 1927, after they had been helping him in the civil war, Chiang Kai-shek turned on his allies and staged the Shanghai massacre of the Communists. The Kremlin then tried to compensate for its nearsightedness by ordering a series of armed uprisings in the country's urban centers. Hastily improvised, they were all crushed by the Nationalists. By the middle of 1928, Communism in China lay utterly shattered.

Or so it appeared in Moscow, where little notice was being taken of the continuing guerrilla struggle in the countryside, led by a former minor official of the party, Mao Zedong. By the end of the decade Chiang Kai-shek, partly by conquest, partly by arrangements with the most influential warlords, succeeded in giving China its first semblance of a real national government since the fall of the Manchu dynasty in 1911. To the Kremlin it seemed foolhardy to imagine that an isolated, peasant-based, movement could resurrect Communism in China, or that it would hold out for long against the superior Kuomintang forces, equipped with modern weapons.

Moscow's skepticism persisted even after Mao and his followers, having "liberated" a sizable area, proclaimed it in 1931 the Chinese Soviet Republic. And soon another consideration came to outweigh the importance of Chinese Communism, insofar as Stalin's foreign policy was concerned. With Japanese militarism on the march—and the consequent threat to the Soviet Far East—and Hitler's coming to power in Germany, Chiang Kai-shek became a valuable potential ally. Hence the Soviet pressure on both warring parties in China to compose their differences and present a united front against the Japanese. Clearly, the Kremlin wanted Tokyo to become bogged down in an endless war in China, so as to lessen the danger to the USSR. Stalin had his wish in 1937 when a truce between Chiang and the Communists spurred a full-scale Japanese invasion.

Nor had Stalin's more recent policies been of a kind to persuade Mao that he was motivated by any other considerations than those pertaining to the Soviet Union's and his own power. The USSR entered the war against Japan only after the latter's fate had been sealed, and mainly so that it could grab Tokyo's real estate, some of it situated in China. On August 14, 1945, the Soviet Union signed the Treaty of Friendship and Alliance with the Kuomintang government. Its provisions had to be painful to Chinese of all political persuasions.[1] China renounced formally any claims of sovereignty over Mongolia, long a Soviet satellite. The Soviets were granted co-ownership of the Manchurian Railway, by now an extensive industrial as well as transportation complex. The USSR would take over from Japan the bridgeheads it had secured on Chinese soil after the Russo-Japanese War of 1904–5: the naval base of Port Arthur and the port facilities of Dairen. Apart from its imperialist greed, the treaty clearly revealed the Kremlin's conviction that the Kuomintang government would indefinitely remain the dominant factor on the Chinese scene, for in return for Chiang's concessions, the Soviets pledged not to deal with or assist any Chinese factions, except that of the official (Kuomintang) government of the republic.

We know also from other sources that Stalin's ideal scenario envisaged the Communists holding on to some territory in the northeast, with the Nationalists in control of most of the mainland, and Russian influence paramount in Manchuria and Sinkiang. Thus, following Japan's collapse, the Red Army, notwithstanding the "pledges" to Chiang (not to deal with any other Chinese movement but his), delivered the stocks of captured arms to Mao's forces, but kept the latter (as well as the Kuomintang's army) from entering Manchuria, which the Soviets looted of some $2 billion worth of industrial equipment. And Stalin, again with scant regard to the August 14 treaty, kept up his secret communications with the Chinese Communist leaders, but only to advise them to try to reach a compromise with the Kuomintang and to refrain from challenging it in a full-scale civil war.

Despite their unwillingness to follow that advice, and despite other transparent signs of Soviet duplicity, the Chinese Communist leaders were at the time in no position to break with the Soviets, or even to voice their disenchantment and grievances. Years later some Western sinologists were to propound the view that at the end of the war Mao may well have been inclined to seek an understanding and cooperation with the United States, and it was only Washington throwing its support behind Chiang that constrained the Chinese Communists to opt for the Soviet camp. But while Mao and his people had, for obvious reasons, been deferential and even cordial in their wartime relations with the American contacts, it is wrong to assume that in 1945, or for many years afterward, they would have been able to sever their

ties to Moscow. Politically and ideologically, such a shift would have
been impossible. It was only Stalin's death that marked the beginning
of their psychological emancipation from what, at least on the surface,
appeared to be slavish dependence and awe of their Russian comrades.

Inwardly, however, and as future events would show, Mao would
register and bitterly resent those rebuffs and slights received from the
"Elder Brother"—the term used for the Soviet Union in Chinese intraparty communications. And at times Mao would come dangerously
close to open criticism of the Elder Brother for not helping his Chinese
sibling more extensively and in the open, and for being unduly apprehensive of how America would react to such help. He tried to nudge
the Soviet comrades into the realization that America was a "paper
tiger," something that could not seem very convincing in 1945 after
Hiroshima and Nagasaki, but which Mao would keep repeating during
the next twenty-five years. Speaking to his followers on August 13,
1945, trying to boost their morale in view of the impending announcement of the Soviet-Kuomintang treaty, Mao affirmed that "relying on the forces we ourselves organize, we can defeat all Chinese
and foreign reactionaries."[2] The implication was clear: they could not
count on effective help from the USSR. But his listeners were urged
not to become depressed because of the fact that the United States
stood behind the Kuomintang: "U.S. imperialism, while outwardly
strong, is inwardly weak." For all their evil machinations, the Americans lacked the necessary endurance in their foreign policies; the
day would come when they would tire of Chiang and abandon him.
This was, to be sure, largely wishful thinking, but it still was a remarkable insight, coming from a man who had never been abroad,
knew no foreign languages, and whose constant preoccupation with
the struggles at home could not have allowed him much time or leisure
to study the outside world.

During his long journey to Moscow, Mao probably reflected on his
prophecy of four years earlier, and how then it had struck the Kremlin
as being wildly overoptimistic. The American imperialists did turn out
to be, as he said on another occasion, "newly upstart and neurotic."[3]
They kept denouncing Communism hysterically, but up until now
had reconciled themselves to its triumph in the world's most populous
country. Yes, he had been proven right. And Stalin, "genius leader of
the world proletariat," had been wrong.

The Soviets' caution about China, and the consequent slights of
their ideological brethren there, continued after the civil war had been

fully resumed in January 1947. The Chinese Communists must have wished for the USSR to recognize them at an early date as at least the de facto government of their country. Such a recognition would have signified Moscow's commitment, and its faith in the eventual Communist victory; it might have discouraged the United States from further helping Chiang and boosted the morale of the People's Liberation Army. But the USSR continued to hedge its bets, maintaining diplomatic relations with the Kuomintang regime. When Nanking was occupied by Mao's forces in April 1949, most of the ambassadors, including the American one, remained in the old capital, but the Soviet diplomat followed the fleeing Nationalist government to Canton, its temporary haven before the final flight to Taiwan.

Even more insulting and disquieting was the Kremlin's probing of the possibility of its establishing a special sphere of influence in the Chinese provinces bordering on Soviet territory. During the last phase of the civil war the Soviets conducted negotiations with the Nationalist governor of Sinkiang. The Communist boss of Manchuria, Gao Gang, went to Moscow in July 1949 and there, as if his province were an independent state, signed a trade agreement with the USSR. It must have cost Mao dearly to acquiesce to such behavior on the part of his subordinate.[4]

The Chinese Communists' loyalty to the Soviet Union was being sorely tried. We now know that on several occasions prior to December 1949, Mao had signaled Moscow of his readiness to come to the USSR and to meet with Stalin or anyone designated by him, so as to clarify the situation and remove any possible misunderstandings between the two parties. In April 1948 the chairman tried virtually to force the Soviets' hand: he and a number of his collaborators repaired to a station on the Sino-Soviet border and from there telegraphed Stalin, asking for an invitation. Instead, they received an incredibly schoolmasterish reply. Its sense was as follows: the revolutionary war in China is going through its decisive period. Chairman Mao, as the commander of the armed forces, ought not to leave his command post. If there are serious problems that ought to be discussed, he—Stalin—would send as his representative a member of the Politburo to discuss the issues with the chairman.[5]

Almost equally incredibly, Mao, the next month, did return to the border to await Stalin's promised emissary, only to be notified there that "because of the unstable military situation" (one would think that, as on the previous occasion, it would have been up to the Chinese to decide that), the mission had to be postponed! Only on January 31,

1949, when the tide of the conflict had definitely turned against the Kuomintang and the People's Liberation Army occupied Beijing, did the emissary, Anastas Mikoyan, arrive at Mao's headquarters. The chairman and his colleagues were eager to hear what the Soviet Union could do for them to speed up the final stages of the war and what economic help they could expect for the devastated country once all of China was theirs. "Mikoyan replied that he had come only to listen, to hear Chairman Mao, and to report to Stalin what had been said."

By May 1949 there could no longer be any doubt that, barring an unlikely massive American intervention, Chiang and his regime would be chased out of the mainland. Under the circumstances, Stalin finally deigned to receive a delegation from the Chinese Communist Party (CCP), though the visit still had to be kept secret.

When the occasion warranted it, Stalin knew how to be hospitable and gracious, even with fellow Communists. The head of the delegation, Liu Shaoqi, the future president of the People's Republic, still later a victim of the Cultural Revolution, was received by the great man five times. During one session Stalin admitted that he had underestimated the Chinese Communists, and had not believed they could prevail in an armed struggle against Chiang. The dictator conducted Liu on a guided tour of one of his *dachas*. Equally tactful was Stalin's invitation to Mao's wife, then undergoing medical treatment in Moscow, to join him and his Chinese guests at a banquet at his residence. And on this occasion he showed himself at his most disarming: the center of the world revolution, he declared, once shifted from [Western] Europe to the USSR, but now it may move to China. He hoped that in time the Younger Brother would surpass the Elder one. Rather judiciously, one would think, Liu felt constrained to protest: for the Chinese Communists the Soviet Union would always be the Elder Brother.

We have not been vouchsafed the information whether those compliments emboldened the Chinese delegates to be frank in discussing thorny issues such as that of Manchuria, Port Arthur, or what the USSR would do if the United States chose at the last moment to intervene militarily on Chiang's side. Presumably, there had been some guarded discussion of those subjects, but their resolution had to await a meeting of the two supreme leaders. There was one substantive question that was resolved to the visitors' satisfaction. While bidding them farewell after the long stay (they arrived in July and departed in August), Stalin expressed surprise at the Chinese comrades' not having yet proclaimed their regime the official government of their country and urged them not to delay the declaration too long. It would not have been tactful to reply that they had waited for so long precisely because the USSR had not been ready to recognize them. A detailed account of what Stalin said was immediately telegraphed to Beijing and "as a result, the Central Committee of [our] party hastened with measures to organize the central national government."

As the above suggests, it was not only a question of the Chinese Communists' respect, admiration, and/or fear of the Soviet Union. Over and above such feelings one senses in their reactions an almost superstitious awe of Stalin. How amazing of the ruling deity of world Communism to admit that he might have made mistakes! How generous of him to grant that in the future the center of revolutionary Marxism might shift to China! Of course, it may have at least passed through Mao's mind when reading the reports of those conversations that such becoming modesty could have been a pose, that Stalin was testing his guests' reactions: how strongly they would object to his self-criticism, how genuine would sound their protestations at his suggestion that one day primacy in the Communist world would pass over to China. But such suspicions would have been inconceivable to a rank-and-file Chinese Communist. Didn't the chairman bring up his party in the worship of Stalin? On the occasion of the latter's sixtieth birthday in 1939, Mao wrote, "Stalin is the leader of world revolution. . . . It is a great event that mankind is blessed with Stalin. . . . Marx is dead and so are Engels and Lenin. Had there been no Stalin, who would be there to give directions?"[6] And so apart from his mystique there were very practical reasons why a foreign Communist leader should shun a clash with the Soviet dictator: a thunderbolt from the Kremlin and his own people might turn against him.

By 1949 there had been, to be sure, one Communist leader who had defied Stalin and so far had gotten away with it. But it was premature to believe that Tito's regime would be able to survive for long in the face of Moscow's condemnation. And the Yugoslav leader had had time to consolidate his party's personal power and had no choice but to stand up to the Russians. Stalin had virtually demanded that he and those close to him commit political suicide. In China, on the other hand, the Communists were still engaged in the mopping-up operations against the Kuomintang's forces on the mainland. Chiang might still strike back from Taiwan. Were Stalin to condemn Mao publicly, the Americans might well renew their assistance to the Nationalists; currently, a violent debate was raging in the United

States over the impending "loss of China," the most weighty argument against American intervention being that it might provoke the USSR and lead to World War III.

And so for all the painful aspects of their relations with the Fatherland of Socialism, the Chinese Communists persevered with public affirmations of their loyalty to it. On April 3, 1949, they issued a declaration denouncing the North Atlantic Treaty and proclaiming their resolve to stand by the side of their "ally, the Soviet Union." On July 1, Mao's emphatic statement came: "We must lean to one side. . . . Not only in China but throughout the world, one must lean either to imperialism or to socialism."[7]

Even after their break with Moscow (or, more properly, since the initiative came from him, after their excommunication by Stalin), the Yugoslav Communists greeted with enthusiasm the progress and victories of the Chinese comrades. But the latter did not reciprocate such compliments. The attitude toward Tito and his alleged heresy was by now considered by Moscow as a litmus test of the loyalty of foreign Communists, and whatever their private feelings on the subject, the Chinese Communists' references to the Balkan leader and his entourage matched those of the Soviets in their scurrility and vehemence. Who would have guessed at the time that in the not too distant future Beijing would violently denounce Moscow for, among other things, its rapprochement with Tito, or that Mao's own break with the Kremlin would in historical significance and the severity of the blow to world Communism dwarf the apostasy of the Yugoslav party?

Nothing on the surface, and insofar as they themselves were concerned, was allowed to mar the image of Mao and his people as faithful disciples and loyal followers of the Soviets and great Stalin. That certainly was the impression of the American policy makers who only a few years before had viewed the Chinese Communists in a different light. Disillusioned by the Kuomintang's corruption and ineptitude, some in Washington had consoled themselves by the thought that Chiang's opponents were in their outlook and policies quite independent of Moscow and fiercely nationalist. At times that appraisal took a grotesque form, such as seeing them mainly as "agrarian reformers," unencumbered by doctrinaire ideologies or other links to international Communism. The Soviets, needless to say, did nothing to dispel those illusions, Molotov on one occasion soothingly assuring President Roosevelt's envoy that the Chinese Communists "were related to Communism in no way at all. It was merely a way of expressing dissatisfaction with their economic conditions and they would forget this inclination when their economic condition improved."[8] Now in the State Department's White Paper on China, Secretary Dean Acheson fulminated against Mao and his party and branded them as "having foresworn their Chinese heritage . . . a party [working] in the interests of a foreign imperialism."[9] While hurtful to their national pride, such accusations suited Mao's and his confederates' interests: why should Stalin now do anything that might disabuse the Americans of their notion that his empire had now acquired several hundred millions of new subjects?

He didn't. The People's Republic of China was proclaimed by Mao in Tienanmen Square on October 1. Zhou Enlai in his capacity as premier and foreign minister informed the local Soviet consul general (the ambassador was away) of the fact the same day. The Soviet press had until then paid scant attention to the historic events in the Far East. This was the year of the seventieth anniversary of the birth of the "genius leader" of world Communism and as the date (December 21) approached, the Soviet public was being deluged with articles, stories, and birthday greetings eulogizing Stalin on a scale unprecedented in history, to be matched again only some twenty years later, when Mao himself was to become the object of a personality cult of similar proportions. What foreign news was being reported touched mainly on Greek Communists, now on the verge of defeat in their civil war, on the villainies of Tito and his clique, and on the trials and executions of alleged Titoist "enemies of the people" in the East European satellites. But on October 3 the Chinese Communists finally made the front page of the Soviet press. The USSR extended diplomatic recognition to their regime, withdrawing it from that of the Nationalists. Other Communist states followed in short order.

And so, in a broader sense, those ten days that Mao spent traversing the distance between Beijing and Moscow were but the last stage of a much, much longer journey.

At noon on December 16, the train carrying the Chinese leader and his entourage pulled into the Yaroslavl railway station. To an outsider it must have appeared inconceivable that his chief host would not be among those greeting the Chinese leader. To be sure, it was not in Stalin's style to welcome in person foreign potentates, no matter how important, upon their arrival in the USSR. During the war he had not seen fit to make an exception for the head of the world's most powerful state and his ally, the president of the United States. When

Franklin Roosevelt's plane touched down in the Crimea on his way to the Yalta conference in February 1945, it was Molotov who had been deputized to greet him on behalf of the Soviet government. For a Communist, this, however, should have been an even more historic, epoch-making event. It signaled a giant step forward by the world revolution, its conquest of a 500-million-strong nation. And yet the Soviet despot did not choose to grace the occasion with his presence.

In fact, the welcome fell short of what the protocol would have required in the case of any head of state. Mao was led quickly past the honor guard, read his address, and was spirited away to his residence. The Chinese interpreter tactfully ascribes this very reserved greeting to the Soviets' concern for Mao's health. "Because of the frigid weather and fear that Chairman Mao could not stand the cold, the welcome ceremony was abbreviated." The head of Communist China was greeted with no greater fanfare than might have been extended to the leader of one of the vassal states of Eastern Europe.

Whatever Mao's feelings, he chose to be courteous and flattering to his host. This opportunity to visit the capital of the world's first socialist state was "one of the most joyful occasions" of his life. He recalled how "after the October Revolution the Soviet government, guided by Lenin and Stalin, annulled immediately the unequal treaties imposed on China by tsarist Russia," an artful implication being that from the very first day of the Revolution Stalin's role was equal to that of Lenin's. Also questionable from the historical point of view was the assertion that "during the past almost thirty years the Soviet people and government have repeatedly helped in the task of the liberation of the Chinese people."[10] Instead of an equally flowery response, Molotov, who headed the Soviet reception committee, advised the guest to get a rest and informed him that Stalin would receive him at six o'clock in his Kremlin office, again a departure from the protocol which demands that the host first pay a courtesy call on the honored guest.

It was not unusual for Stalin to pass from rudeness to cordiality in the treatment of those he aimed to impress: it is a prerogative of a deity to be mysterious and unpredictable in bestowing favors and chastisements. And so on finally receiving Mao (exactly at six o'clock) he was effusive in complimenting him: how young and strong the chairman looked. And introducing him to members of the Politburo, he hailed him as a famous son of the Chinese people who had already made an imperishable contribution to its destiny, why, to that of the whole world. In his reply Mao gave vent to bitterness: he was a man

who for long had suffered setbacks and been ignored, and there was
no one to whom he could turn for help. Was it a spontaneous *cri de
coeur* or premeditated? In any case, Stalin did not let him finish his
complaint: it had all been in the past, Mao was now a victor. Who
would dare to question his stature and achievements?

One might think it excessive to attach so much importance to the
egos and moods of the two men. But as events were to show, Stalin's
personality did affect, and decisively, the future of relations between
the newly born People's Republic and the Soviet Union. After his
death those relations were to undergo, and almost instantaneously, a
basic change in their nature. The memory of the slights and rebuffs
he had experienced at the hands of the Russian comrades was to stay
with Mao, and undoubtedly played a role in his decision in 1959 to
defy openly the erstwhile Elder Brother.

But even before that he proved himself a tenacious negotiator. Right
there at the first meeting Stalin proposed that the two of them sign
a formal agreement on behalf of their countries. Mao refused. Diplomacy was not his strong point, he implied. Let Zhou Enlai, skilled in
such matters, come to Moscow, he proposed, and negotiate a treaty.
Clearly, he did not relish the prospect of negotiating, which would
have also meant hard bargaining, one on one, with Stalin. And the
eventual treaty, he realized, would have to contain concessions hurtful
to Chinese national pride and which would be resented by his followers. Zhou had a brilliant record as a negotiator. During the war,
as his representative at Chiang's headquarters, Zhou had kept the
Communist-Kuomintang agreement from falling to pieces. The ur-
bane prime minister also managed to charm the Americans and almost
persuaded them of the Communists' essentially democratic inclinations. In any case, he, Mao, would not be directly responsible when
some provisions of the agreement seemed to encroach on the People's
Republic's sovereignty.

Mao stayed in the Soviet Union until February 17, 1950. This was
an unusually long period for a head of state and government to stay
abroad, especially under the particular circumstances in China at the
time, with some enclaves of the Kuomintang forces still to be eliminated, and with a multitude of problems facing the new regime and
calling for his personal attention. It was not surprising that stories
appeared in the Western press alleging that Mao was being detained
against his will. Even stranger things had happened in Russia and
world Communism in Stalin's time. To counteract such slanderous

rumors, great publicity was given to Mao's travels around the country and to his appearance with his host at the theater gala in honor of the latter's birthday, where the two of them shared the former imperial box, while the leaders of the Communist states gathered for the occasion were consigned to less prestigious locations.

The birthday celebrations were finally concluded and the other Communist leaders, undoubtedly to their secret relief, were sent home. Mao stayed on. Still no treaty. There was now evident strain permeating the two leaders' encounters, recalls the Russian interpreter, Nikolai Fedorenko. "Stalin seldom looked directly at his interlocutor, but mostly sidelong, once in a while casting a furtive glance at his visitor from afar. . . . Behind his contrived mask there seemed to be something inscrutable, some hypnotic power." Mao, for his part, fended off the attempts to get down to business—the treaty—and regaled his host with stories about "struggles with the Kuomintang; the economic devastation, the agrarian problem, and other almost intractable difficulties faced by his country." In plain language, Mao was resisting Stalin's attempt to make him sign whatever the Soviets would choose to thrust under his nose. Forty years have not dimmed Fedorenko's memory of his inner panic during those sessions: what could be the consequences to him for having been privy to this duel? At times his alarm would interfere with his work as an interpreter. Having trouble with Mao's Hunan dialect, he would at times ask him to write down the sentence. During one such pause, Stalin vented his frustrations on poor Fedorenko: how long did he propose to keep conspiring, asked the despot, with every appearance of seriousness. He hastily explained the difficulty and was immensely relieved to hear, now in a different tone of voice, " 'Well, if you have to go on with your secrets . . . ' I felt almost physically that my head had just been saved from the guillotine." Today the whole episode appears highly comical, but this confession by a man who was subsequently to become a high-ranking Soviet diplomat and an academician is eloquent testimony regarding the atmosphere of those times.

Mao's dilatory tactics eventually met with a qualified success. The Soviet side agreed that the actual conduct of the negotiations should be assumed by Zhou Enlai. On January 21 the Chinese premier and minister of foreign affairs arrived in Moscow. But along with him came special representatives of the Manchurian Communist regime and that of Sinkiang. The public statement about the presence of the delegates from the border areas, the implication that they were negotiating with the Soviets independently of the central government of the People's Republic, and the fact that these representatives were to remain in Moscow for some time after the principal Chinese negotiators had left, must have been at once offensive and deeply disquieting to Mao and his entourage. Sometime before, speaking to the People's Republic's assembly, he pledged, "Our nation will never again be an insulted nation. We have stood up."[11]

The Soviets' attempts to sow dissension within the Chinese leadership bore, at times, almost a childish character. The residence prepared for Zhou was a considerable distance from that of the chairman. Zhou declined the offer and moved in with Mao. The negotiations now went ahead briskly, if not smoothly. When difficulties arose, Stalin still sought to involve Mao in the talks, but the latter would invariably refer him back to his prime minister.

The Kremlin's tactics were transparent to the point of being counterproductive. Mao and his colleagues would have been obtuse not to sense that the completeness of their victory was less than welcome to their hosts. The Russians would have much preferred to have the People's Republic confined to the northeast section of China. Such a Communist state, in constant conflict with the Kuomintang, which would control the rest of the mainland, would have been completely dependent on the USSR, and the latter would not have to deal with it, as now, on an *almost* equal basis.

The Chinese leaders also probably realized that it was not the concern for world revolution that had inhibited Stalin from pressing, rather than just advising, them to arrange a truce with the Nationalists. The crucial phase of their struggle from mid-1948 to spring 1949, when the People's Liberation Army was breaking the spine of the Kuomintang, coincided with a critical period of the cold war—the Soviet blockade of Berlin. It would have then made little sense for Moscow to try to brake the advance of the Communist forces and thus relieve Washington of additional strains on its foreign policy. By the time the blockade had been lifted and tension in Europe had abated, it was much too late for any outside force to try to restrain the triumphant progress of Chinese Communism.

And now in 1950, having lost the opportunity to manipulate the course of the civil war, Stalin was testing the cohesion of the Chinese Communist leadership. There was the ominous example of Eastern Europe, where practically every ruling Communist Party had been pressed by Moscow to carry out purges, with some of their highest officals meeting their doom for alleged Titoism or other heresies appropriate to "the people's enemies." But the Chinese Communists held firm; no one challenged Mao's leadership, and it would be he who, after Stalin's death, would purge his party of those who had been in his view too friendly with the Russians.

For all his realism and ruthlessness, when it came to protecting his own interests as well as those of Communist China, it would be a mistake to see Mao as simply opportunistic or cynical in his politics. Even before the war he had proposed to sinicize Communism, but at least in 1949–50 he was a more genuine believer in proletarian internationalism than "the greatest man of all nations and times," a frequent description of his Soviet counterpart in that year of his seventieth birthday. Perceiving Mao's ambition to be acknowledged as a great theorist as well as practitioner of the revolutionary craft, Stalin, again the flatterer, proposed that a selection of the chairman's speeches and writings be translated and published in the Soviet Union—a signal honor for a foreign Communist. Mao eagerly embraced the idea and rather disarmingly asked Stalin to designate a Soviet scholar learned in Marxism-Leninism to check his writings for ideological correctness. He could be intransigent when negotiating with the Russians, but in some ways, as when it came to the philosophical side of Communism, he felt himself still a disciple, quite different from the Mao of the 1960s, who would blast the Soviet comrades as "capitalist roaders" who had departed from the straight-and-narrow path of true socialism.

With Zhou carrying the main burden of negotiations on the Chinese side and with Molotov, Bulganin, and Malenkov on the Soviet side, the agreement was hammered out by February 14. The Kremlin somewhat indelicately wanted it to be called the Sino-Soviet Treaty of Friendship and Alliance, overlooking the fact that this title was embarrassingly identical with that of the 1945 pact between the USSR and Chiang's government. Zhou insisted on and obtained the addition of "and of Mutual Help." He and Foreign Minister Andrei Vyshinsky were the actual signatories.

The photograph of the signing ceremony appeared in the Soviet press the next day. Stalin and all the members of the Politburo, and Mao and his entourage were present. The Soviet dictator, recalls the Chinese interpreter, stepped forward when the picture was being taken, so as not to appear of lesser height than Mao. Unlike on the occasion of another historical signing, that of the Nazi-Soviet Pact of

1939, Stalin is not smiling; his expression is wistful. Mao, on his left, is staring rigidly into the distance. Equally somber is the expression of the others in attendance, the whole tableau conveying the impression of strain rather than that of a festive occasion. It also must have puzzled the Soviet readers, as it still does us today, why in referring to Mao and the other Chinese delegates the picture's legend, as well as the official communiqué, used "Mister" rather than "Comrade" in front of their names.

As the above suggests, most of the agreements comprising the treaty (if there was, as seems likely, a secret protocol, it has not up to now been made public) must have been reached after some very hard bargaining, neither side getting fully what it wanted. From the Chinese point of view the only completely satisfactory formula was that of the preamble: ". . . the reactionary Kuomintang regime having been overthrown, China became a democratic republic. A new people's government was formed which has united China, entered upon friendship and cooperation with the Soviet Union, and has demonstrated its ability to defend the state independence and territorial integrity of China, as well as the national honor and dignity of the Chinese people."[12]

The alliance part of the treaty did not provide the People's Republic the guarantees it needed for its security. The latter would have required the USSR to come to its help against *any* power that might attack it. But the two parties pledged their assistance only in the case of aggression by Japan and/or "any other state which should unite with Japan directly or indirectly in acts of aggression." Japan was currently totally disarmed. The principal worry of the Chinese Communists had to be the possibility of the Nationalists, with U.S. assistance, launching an invasion of the mainland. In such a contingency nothing in the treaty obligated the USSR to come to the help of the People's Republic.

The Soviets must have initially balked at giving up the property they had acquired on Chinese soil in the wake of World War II. This included co-ownership of the Manchuria Railway, its industrial complex, and the naval base of Port Arthur, and the use of port facilities at Dairen. The Chinese, for their part, could not have acquiesced in such gross derogation of their sovereignty. The compromise spelled out in the treaty provided for the transfer of the railway and the ports to the People's Republic upon the conclusion of a peace treaty with Japan, but in no case later than 1952. In the current world situation there was no earthly chance of the United States and the USSR concurring on a peace treaty with Japan in the foreseeable future. Why then delay the transfer? Mao and his associates must have at least suspected that the Soviets were counting on something happening in the Far East that might enable them to hang on to the enclaves beyond 1952. And so it did.

Both sides acknowledged the independence of Mongolia, i.e., the perpetuation of its status as a Soviet satellite. The Kremlin wanted the February treaty to be accompanied by a trade agreement which would include provisions for setting up joint Sino-Soviet companies for the exploration of oil and mineral resources in Sinkiang, their management and profit to be shared equally between the two sides. For the Chinese this was unpleasantly reminiscent of such arrangements between the Soviets and their East European satellites, a thinly veiled form of economic imperialism at the expense of the "fraternal socialist countries." When the time came for signing the overall treaty, Stalin was told that the commercial part could not be included because "the Chinese text was not ready." When questioned about the reason, Mao calmly replied that yes, it was his side that was responsible for the omission and any other mistakes. The trade agreement with its contentious clause about the joint stock companies was signed separately on March 27.

Having its territory devastated by forty years of almost continuous warfare and its economy in shambles, the People's Republic should have been able to count on generous financial assistance from the Elder Brother. But the latter proved himself so stingy that it is a wonder that the credit agreement, its provisions as embarrassing to the giver as derisory for the recipient, were included in the February 14 declaration. Under the circumstances, the loan was but a pittance: $300 million spread over five years, the money to be spent entirely on purchases from the USSR. In the text of the agreement the Soviets stressed that because of "the ruined condition of China," they were charging but 1 percent interest on the loan, but this hardly offset the gross inadequacy of the sum. True, the Soviet economy was still recovering from the aftereffects of the war, but even Moscow's European satellites had by then received from it larger credits than those extended to the world's largest nation, not to mention the $2 billion the United States had *given* to the Kuomintang regime between 1945 and 1948.

The treaty and what preceded it could not be considered a good augury for the future of Sino-Soviet relations. To be sure, this knowledge was not vouchsafed to those not privy to the tortuous course of the negotiations. To the outside world the most significant fact was that the two Communist giants were now bound in a firm alliance, with a stipulated duration of thirty years—which in itself seemed to give the lie to the rumors of serious disagreements between them. The Soviet Union, whose power already in 1945 loomed so ominous to the West, now had a huge nation on its side. The Chinese Communists, on the brink of military defeat two years before, now obtained a firm grip on the mainland, and it appeared to be only a question of time before they would conquer Taiwan and other islands still held by the Kuomintang. Their victory and now-attested unity with the Soviet Union was a devastating blow to the concept of containment that had been guiding Washington's policies in the cold war. The contest between Communism and what was then called the free world had seemingly taken an ominous turn in favor of the former. America's monopoly of nuclear weapons was now a thing of the past, the Soviets having exploded their first A-bomb almost simultaneously with the proclamation of the People's Republic. It was then widely believed that whatever their shortcomings, the Communists were masters at modernizing their societies in a hurry, especially when it came to anything bearing on military power. How would the West be able to meet the worldwide challenge of Communism when to the already formidable and growing strength of the Soviet Union was added that of an industrialized China?

The mere fact of concluding the treaty thus increased the international standing of both signatory powers. It strengthened, psychologically, the Soviet Union's hand in dealing with the United States, whether on the problem of Germany or any other issue. To the Chinese people it marked the finality of the Kuomintang's defeat and of the Communists' victory. Whatever the fine print of the agreement said, Chiang Kai-shek would not dare to try to reverse the verdict of the civil war, nor would the Americans sponsor such attempts now that the Soviet Union stood shoulder-to-shoulder with the People's Republic. In Eastern Europe the significance of the Sino-Soviet alliance dwarfed that of Yugoslavia's defection, and indeed seemed to portend a speedy end to Titoism: the treaty was a vivid demonstration to the Yugoslav Communists of how isolated they were in defying Moscow and Stalin. They were bound to turn against their heretical leaders. By the same token, the people of East European satellite states received yet another lesson on the irreversibility of Communist domination of their countries, and of the futility of expecting the Americans, sometime, somehow, to rescue them from that predicament.

In Asia the Communist summit and its ostensible results proved a powerful stimulant to what in Communist parlance are wars of national liberation—i.e., the mostly Communist-led movements struggling against either retreating colonialism or native but pro-Western governments. As early as October 1949 at the conference of left-wing Asian and Australian labor organizations, Liu Shaoqi extolled the path taken by the Chinese people in smashing imperialism as a model for other nations in the colonial and semicolonial areas in their fight for independence and socialist democracy. On January 18 the People's Republic took the bold step of recognizing Ho Chi Minh's movement, still far from having conquered even the north of Vietnam—actually, in a position somewhat analogous to that of Chinese Communists in 1945—as the legitimate government of the country. The Soviets had seen no reason to gratuitously offend France, which had been carrying on the main burden of the war against the Vietnamese Communists on behalf of the Bao Dai regime. But now it became awkward not to follow the People's Republic's example, and Moscow on January 30 did extend its recognition to the rebels.

And not only in Indochina, but in Indonesia, Malaya, the Philippines and elsewhere in Asia (Africa was as yet quiescent) the news from Moscow buoyed Communist and other left-wing movements, thus increasing pressures on the Western powers in their retreat from colonialism. The Japanese Communists, echoing the Soviets' denunciations of General MacArthur's occupation policies, entered upon militant and disruptive tactics. As of the beginning of 1950, not only its two leading powers but the entire Communist world received an accession of strength, and a boost in morale.

Yet beneath such appearances there were, as yet barely discernible, strains in the relations between the USSR and the new China. The Kremlin's interest in the success of foreign Communism was strictly limited to those situations where such success would advance the Soviets' own power. By conceding to the People's Republic an *almost* equal status, Moscow to some extent lost its freedom of action. At the time, no other Communist state, not even heretical Yugoslavia, would have dared to precede Moscow in recognizing a foreign regime as China did in the case of Vietnam. It was already possible to predict what would take place some years later: how China, whether directly or indirectly but persistently, would try to push Moscow into a more militant stance vis-à-vis the West, thus exposing it to the danger of a nuclear confrontation with the United States.

Mao's new stature as a world leader was another troublesome consequence of the Moscow parley. There was first of all Stalin's enormous vanity: he did not like sharing the limelight with another man, and at that, one who was fourteen years younger. But there was also a very practical side to his concern: experience had shown that charismatic leaders of foreign Communist parties, and especially when they had risen to power through their own efforts rather than by being Moscow's creatures, could not be depended on to put the interests of the Fatherland of Socialism ahead of those of their own nation. In the case of Yugoslavia, Stalin, as Khrushchev alleges, may well have said in the beginning of the dispute that he had only to shake his little finger and there would be no Tito. And it was the Soviets who had started the unpleasant business by demanding that the Yugoslav leaders confess their sins, i.e., put their heads, and not only figuratively, in a noose, to be jerked by Stalin whenever he wished. But Mao was much more than a chieftain of a small Balkan state. Defection by his party would make nonsense of the whole notion of proletarian internationalism and would irreparably loosen Moscow's hold on foreign Communism. The absolute subordination of world Communism to the dictates of Stalin's Russia could not be then rationalized as the necessary preliminary of the establishment of a supranational socialist world order, which for all its unavoidably harsh initial characteristics would abolish war. That belief, the core of Communism's appeal, would not survive a split between the Soviet Union and China.

The prospect of China's rapid industrialization and of thereby acquiring the sinews of a great military power could be no more pleasing to the Kremlin than it was to the West. Such a China might well put in a claim to the territories which over the centuries tsarist Russia had wrested from the Manchu emperors. In the treaty, Mao and his associates conceded the independence of Mongolia. But the tenacity with which they reclaimed Port Arthur and the Manchurian Railway suggested that after a passage of time a stronger China would present still further territorial claims against its neighbors across the world's longest border. What was now the Soviet Maritime Province with its capital of Vladivostok had been annexed by Russia only as recently as 1860. In 1950 it would have been inconceivable for the Chinese even to hint at the need for the restitution of such areas. But in the long run, as Mao had repeatedly pledged, the new China was committed to reversing the provisions of *all* the unequal treaties the imperialist powers had imposed upon the decadent Manchu emperors. Unlike Chiang's authoritarian yet inefficient regime, the Communist one was bound to make China strong, hence not a reliable partner and not a particularly desirable neighbor.

It would be unreasonable to assume that the Soviets' fears corresponded to Mao's hopes. He was too much of a pragmatic politician, preoccupied with the multitude of problems that his government and people faced, to think that he would live to see Vladivostok under the Chinese flag. He was too much of an ideologue to wish for or contemplate a break with the Elder Brother. But he undoubtedly looked forward to the time when the Kremlin would have to treat Beijing as fully its equal. That, he knew, would not come to pass in Stalin's lifetime, but then he was considerably younger. The Kremlin's rather clumsy attempts to undermine his authority with Zhou and his other colleagues had for the time being backfired; for a Chinese Communist to challenge the chairman would now be unpatriotic, as well as dangerous. The long stay in Moscow had had an opposite effect from what the Kremlin had evidently hoped for: it had enhanced Mao's self-confidence and his determination to protect the interests and prestige of the People's Republic, even if by doing so he had to stand up to Stalin.

To celebrate the signing of the treaty the Chinese delegation proposed to give a reception for some five hundred members of the Soviet elite, and foreign Communist notables currently in Moscow (including Ho Chi Minh, whose presence in the USSR was kept in strict secrecy from the media). When invited in person by Mao, Stalin agreed to attend, already a great favor on his part, since of late he did not frequent large social gatherings, confining his attendance to parties where only a few of the Politburo circle and an especially important foreign guest or two would be present. He added graciously that the Chinese could use for the occasion any suitable location within the precincts of the Kremlin. But his mood changed when he was told that the reception was to be given in a hotel. It was out of the question: he was not in the habit of appearing in public places. Why not the Kremlin? Mao explained that for the Chinese the Kremlin was synonymous with the Soviet government. This was to be *their* reception, and since their embassy, only recently vacated by its Kuomintang tenants, was under repair, it would have to be a hotel. And it was unthinkable that Comrade Stalin would not grace the occasion with his presence. Quite likely it was as difficult for Stalin to break his rule as it had been for him to promise to return Port Arthur to China. But finally, and somewhat irritably, he did agree to come.

And so it was the Metropol, an old run-down Moscow hostelry, that was the scene of the banquet. The invited included not only the party, government, and military bigwigs, but also the cream of the Soviet intellectual and artistic communities. No one except for the hosts and the secret police personnel was in on the secret, and Stalin's arrival created a tremendous sensation. Most of those present, even if fairly high officials, had seen their master only on national holidays, May 1 or November 7, the anniversary of the Revolution, a distant figure on top of the Lenin Mausoleum, reviewing a parade in Red Square. Many years later Ilya Ehrenburg was to record his amazement and awe when he, one of the country's leading journalists and most popular authors, could see Stalin in the flesh for the first and only time. Unused as he was to such mass sociability, the dictator fell in with the festive mood, gaily chatting and clinking glasses with whoever appeared to be around, including a very frightened waiter. Finally, he called for attention and toasted his host. "Dear comrades, we ought to be thankful to history, which has given us this leading Marxist-Leninist and fearless Communist, Mao Zedong. To his health and further successes, bottom up, comrades."

Three days later Mao boarded the train for his return trip. Stalin again was absent and the chairman may have recalled the one occasion on which he had come to the station to bid farewell to a departing foreign dignitary. That was in the terrible spring of 1941 when Europe had been brought under Hitler's heel and the Soviet Union stood in imminent danger of being attacked by Germany from the West and Japan from the east. The last danger was considerably lessened by the USSR's concluding a nonaggression treaty with Japan. Stalin carried his shameless flattering of its foreign minister, Matsuoka Yosuke, to the point of being present at his departure from Moscow to wish him a pleasant journey to Tokyo—a good indication of the inner panic he must have felt at the time. Yet nothing in Mao's farewell speech could have suggested that he was less than gratified with the results of his visit or with the way he had been received. As if to compensate for its absence upon his arrival, he now paid more than a fulsome tribute to Stalin. "We express sincere gratitude to Generalissimus Stalin, the Soviet government and people. . . . Long live the teacher of world revolution, the best friend of the Chinese people, Comrade Stalin."[13]

3

AND THEN THE GREAT KHAN DIED

LITTLE MORE THAN three years were to separate the Sino-Soviet encounter from the death of the "leader and teacher of world revolution." Glasnost, which has provided us with many new details about the Stalin era, has, alas, thrown but little new light on its last, and in some ways most mysterious, period. There was obviously a new purge in the works when the despot died. But what would have been its exact dimensions? Would the new wave of terror, as in 1936–39, strike severely at the highest strata of the party and governmental bureaucracy? How true were the rumors, which have lingered to our own day, about the projected mass expulsion of Jews from the European USSR and other measures of repression that were to engulf them? What were the reasons that prompted the Kremlin to license, if not indeed order, the North Koreans' invasion of the south?

At no other period did Stalin's behavior conform so much to what a Soviet poet was to write about him later. "Though alive, cut off from life by the Kremlin walls he stood over us like a dread spirit."[1] And indeed his dictatorship during those last years seemed almost disembodied: virtually inaccessible to Western visitors and diplomats, seen by his people only infrequently—a distant figure on the top of the Lenin mausoleum at the traditional Soviet celebrations, he appeared detached from routine policy making and political leadership, yet his personality permeated practically every aspect of Soviet life.

As did the Soviet Union's isolation from any but the most formal contacts with the West, so did its dictator's seclusion contribute to the awe of Soviet power felt by the outside world. Few at the time gave any thought to the possibly ruinous consequences that the long-lasting tyranny might have portended for the USSR and Communism.

Both, it was still believed in 1953, were immeasurably more powerful and menacing because of what one man had accomplished. "The transformation of Russia within little more than a quarter century is largely due to the genius, the will power, the energy and ruthlessness of the man born Josif Vissarionovich Djiugashvili," editorialized the *New York Times* on March 8, 1953. And the accompanying summary of Stalin's achievement was also likely to be less than heartening to a believer in democracy.

> The Soviet empire today is an empire far larger, more centralized and *cohesive*, infinitely more powerful than the empire of the tsars. The sixteen Soviet Socialist Republics have an area of 8,173,000 square miles and a polyglot population of 215,409,000. Held tightly within the orbit of this vast Soviet Communist mass are the Eastern European satellites. . . . These add . . . 70,000,000 persons to the Communist sphere. . . . Less firmly held but still *under Russian tutelage* is Communist China with 3,700,000 square miles and 460,000,000 persons, plus embattled North Korea. The area of Communist rule grew by 75 per cent and the population by 440 per cent under Stalin. . . . And behind the Communist armed strength there is the relentless pressure of revolutionary ideology. For all of the Kremlin's lip service to "coexistence" with free democracy, there is no doubt in the West that the Communists see in their destiny the domination of the world. [My italics.]

How strange these praises—which with a bit of rephrasing could have been part of a Communist's tribute to the departed tyrant—must strike us today. But at the time there was sound logic in attributing to Stalin much of the credit for the awe that Communism inspired among its subjects and in the outside world. In a few years the Soviet rulers would themselves proceed to unravel the story of errors and crimes and try to cope with the grave consequences of his legacy. And in time that legacy and the effects of de-Stalinization would combine to shake the very foundations of both the state and the movement over which he had tyrannized for nearly thirty years.

But as of March 5, 1953, the most obvious elements of Stalin's rule were the impression of power and dynamism he had imparted to the Soviet Union and to the Communist movement. From our perspective we can also see that between the end of the war and his death Stalin, or rather his image, blacked out many of the Soviet Union's weaknesses and vulnerabilities. The myth of an indomitable and ruthless leader ready to plunge the world into a third world war rather than to retreat on any major issue that divided it from the West paralyzed the resolve of the democratic leaders and made the United States, then at the height of its power, fearful of challenging the Kremlin on its usurpations in Eastern Europe or, more directly, about the blockade of West Berlin. To digress, the reaction in the West to Stalin's death, of which the *New York Times* columns were typical, again throws ironic light on the current notions of contrasting America's alleged omnipotence in the forties and fifties with its much reduced status in the world today. In statistical terms the United States in those days disposed of resources far outweighing those of Russia's. But psychologically Washington was inhibited from exploiting those resources in taking a more vigorous stand against the Soviet Union. For one thing, the USSR of 1945 to 1953 was believed, mistakenly, to be much stronger than it was in actuality. For another, Stalin was believed, almost equally mistakenly, to be indomitable in his resolve to risk war rather than to surrender any of the Soviet Union's conquests. Containment was purported to be the strategy, and at that rather ambiguous, for preventing the Soviet Union's *further* encroachments. And so perhaps it is no exaggeration to say that it was Joseph Stalin who in a way offset the United States' superiority over the Soviet Union in those crucial years.

One can hardly imagine Khrushchev or Brezhnev matching Stalin's skill and resolution in arranging for the Soviet takeover of Eastern Europe from 1944 to 1947. As mentioned before, the nature of this takeover would prove, and even well before 1991, to have been a Pyrrhic victory for the Soviets. But as of 1953 it must have seemed, even granting the trouble over Yugoslavia, a fantastic achievement. For more than three centuries the tsars had fought and striven, mostly in vain, to obtain a foothold in Central Europe and a sphere of influence over Eastern and Southeastern Europe. And now within a few years and in violation of its wartime pledges to the United States and Britain, the Soviet Union acquired not a sphere of influence in the old, limited sense, but absolute domination over the vast area. For the first time in history all the Slavs were united within one political system, and even the secession of Yugoslavia from the Kremlin's realm could be considered but a quirk not likely to last.

Part of Stalin's success in thus, to use plain language, scaring the

West lay in Western statesmen's suspicion that in dealing with the Kremlin they were facing uncompromising apostles of world revolution, or as Mr. Kennan put it in his celebrated essay, a "mystical Messianic movement." The Western wartime image of a reasonable Stalin who had jettisoned Communist dreams in favor of his country's security had by 1945 been replaced by one of a leader still driven by ambition to conquer the world for Marxism-Leninism. Who but a fanatical ideologue would have scorned participation in the Marshall Plan, thus forfeiting massive American help for his war-devastated country? What else but a blind faith in the historical mission and inevitability of Communism could have made the Soviet leaders provoke the United States with its monopoly of the A-bomb by barring Western access to Berlin? There was but little residue of the "Uncle Joe" legend that beguiled the Americans during the wartime Soviet-U.S. partnership, though as late as 1948 President Truman was incautious enough to opine that it was not Stalin but the people around him who were responsible for the strain in East-West relations. But the vast majority of Truman's countrymen were by then far from sharing his illusions.

Stalin's undoubted skill in handling the West was by the same token an important element contributing to the cult of his personality both at home and abroad. In the Soviet Union the vast apparatus of repression and propaganda worked incessantly to maintain the superhuman image of the dictator. And whatever doubts the Communists outside the Soviet-ruled world may have experienced in the wake of the first shock of the Tito affair, they suppressed them or pretended to in the face of an incomparably greater event: the Communist conquest of mainland China. The new China's leaders' deferential public attitude toward the Russian Elder Brother, their joining in the paeans of praise at the time of Stalin's seventieth birthday, confounded for the time being the gleeful anticipations of the Yugoslavs and the State Department: Mao was far from showing any signs of following in Tito's footsteps. And the signing in February 1950 of the Sino-Soviet alliance delivered a final blow to such hopes.

However unfashionable it may have become to attribute such weight to personalities, it is unquestionable that Stalin not only dominated the Communist world, but between the end of the war and his death stood as a towering figure over the entire international scene. Of the two other statesmen who might have challenged him on that score, Roosevelt was dead, and Churchill, dismissed by the British electorate in 1945, found himself on his return to power in 1951 no longer the leader of an empire but of a country much diminished in status through the inexorable forces of economics and geopolitics. The president of the United States headed the world's most powerful country, but his personal power was limited by the constitutional constraints and the vagaries of democratic politics. Hence it was Stalin who really held in his hands, it was widely and not unjustifiably believed, the fateful choice between peace and war. Even before the onset of the intense phase of the cold war, the world watched anxiously for any sign that might reveal the mysterious potentate's true intentions. In April 1946, when Stalin was still fairly accessible to Western visitors, he received General Walter Bedell Smith, the new American ambassador to the USSR. In the course of the audience Smith, rather undiplomatically one would think, asked, "What does the Soviet Union want and how far is Russia going to go?" Stalin quite likely must have repressed a smile before answering, "We are not going much further."[2]

How far was Stalin going to advance and what risks would he be willing to incur in his passion for expansion were questions that would continue to agitate the Western chanceries throughout the postwar years. In 1948 on the eve of the presidential election Mr. Truman proposed to send Chief Justice Frederick Vinson as a special emissary to the dictator. It would not have been a mere election stunt. As the president explained it disarmingly in his memoirs, he thought that "if we could only get Stalin to unburden himself to someone on our side he could trust, I thought we could get somewhere."[3] Having previously speculated that Stalin might have been led astray by his anti-Western subordinates, Mr. Truman evidently still believed in the despot's omnipotence. And so, perhaps, if a person as prestigious and above the tumult of politics as the chief justice of the United States Supreme Court reassured Stalin about America's peaceful aims and intentions, the cold war might be brought to an end. It was only after Secretary of State George Marshall threatened to resign that the president regretfully abandoned this idea of appealing to Stalin's better instincts.

Churchill, though in a way impressed (and on occasion outwitted) by the Soviet dictator in their wartime encounters, would not have credited him with having such instincts. But for him Stalin also held the key to East-West relations and a word from him might spell the difference between peace and war. Speaking at the celebration of the centenary of the Massachusetts Institute of Technology in Boston in 1949, the former British prime minister evoked for his audience a frightening precedent of the current threat to the West. He recalled how in the thirteenth century Genghis Khan conquered vast areas in Asia and then the Mongols burst upon Eastern Europe, conquering what is now Russia and ravaging Poland and Hungary. The apparently invincible Mongol cavalry was about to invade the heart of the Continent when "the Great Khan died."[4] With their leaders eager to participate in the election of his successor in distant Mongolia, the invading horde turned back and Europe was saved.[5]

This rather indelicate reference to the eventual demise of Stalin (and he was Churchill's junior by five years!) shows well the enormous importance the veteran British statesman attached to his personal role on the world stage. The entire East-West confrontation, which at the time many quite sober observers believed teetered on the brink of actual war, could be decisively affected by this one man.

In light of the above, the fidelity of the world Communist movement to the "genius leader of all progressive mankind" becomes more understandable. With the leaders of foreign Communists it was not merely a question of ideology and the habit of obedience to Moscow that caused them to prostrate themselves before Stalin. People outside the immediate reach of the MGB (later the KGB) lauded him in terms as extravagant as those used by his subordinates in the USSR. Veterans of the Comintern, such as the Italian leader Palmiro Togliatti and the French party's general secretary Maurice Thorez, could have had few illusions about the man they so extolled: unlike the mass of their followers, they knew only too well what happened during the great slaughter of 1936–39 when the Terror engulfed not only Soviet officialdom, but proportionately even more so the foreign Communists who during those dreadful years had had the misfortune of finding themselves in the Soviet Union.[6] The loyalty of the Thorezes, Togliattis, etc., was based neither on naiveté nor the lack of firsthand knowledge about Stalin's Russia. They realized that for the mass of their supporters Communism was synonymous with the awesome Georgian in the Kremlin. Even before the war a man with such world renown as Trotsky utterly failed in his endeavor to create a Communist movement that would be a serious rival to the one bewitched by Stalin. And now after the Soviet Union's ordeal and triumph in the Great Patriotic War, a triumph largely credited to its indomitable leader, how could one challenge his authority, question his infallibility on all issues, whether in politics or, when he chose to write about them in his late years, economics and linguistics? When Stalin ordered that the Communists in the West should actively oppose the Marshall Plan since it would lead to the enslavement of their countries by American imperialists, the Italian and French parties duly obeyed his orders, carrying out their servility to the point of promoting strikes that would hamper the delivery of American goods and similar activities intended to sabotage the great scheme of economic recovery of the West. Their leaders could be under no illusion as to how politically damaging with their electorates such action was, and that it would probably dampen their chances of coming to power. Even more astounding in their utter servility toward the distant divinity of Communism were the declarations in 1949 of the French and Italian parties pledging that if their capitalist governments joined the United States in a war against the USSR they would side with their *ideological* fatherland. Such acts of devotion to the Fatherland of Socialism and its leader bring to mind what a French Socialist said about his Communist fellow countrymen: "They are neither on the left nor on the right. They are in the East!" Such fervent devotion is unlikely to have sprung only from political idealism. It also required a visible human object of worship. The cult of personality was a vital element of the appeal of Communism during the Stalin era.

What happened in the post-Stalin era has enabled us to understand yet another facet of the cult. Paradoxically, this cult obscured the fact that in many ways international Communism was a tool of the Soviet Union's foreign policy. The Stalin legend placed him as apostolic successor to Lenin, thus a leader not merely of a state or nation but of the Revolution. Older foreign Communists (and not many of them survived the purges and the war) knew of course that Stalin was not "the closest and best pupil of Lenin's." But the rank and file in their overwhelming majority had been thoroughly indoctrinated in the Moscow version of the history of the party and the Revolution. Prior to 1953 Mao would occasionally, though most often in a veiled form, criticize the Elder Brother. But even he could not bring himself to utter in public a single word of criticism of the heir of Marx, Engels, and Lenin. And indeed can one find in any document a single instance of such criticism on the part of any foreign Communist prior to the Twentieth Congress of the Communist Party of the USSR? To do so would have meant a definite breach within the movement, stepping over the line separating the true believers from "Trotskyites," "servants of Wall Street and Zionism," and similar categories of betrayal and infamy. Tito and his associates did cross that line. But even they confined their dissent at first to complaints about lesser Soviet officials' behavior, with the implication that Stalin had been misled by his subordinates. It took Belgrade more than two years after the break, and that in the face of Moscow's most scurrilous attacks on Tito, to begin to hint that Stalin was not above criticism and culpable in the dispute.

Personal allegiance to Stalin thus masked somewhat Communism's subservience to Soviet imperialism. And perhaps "masked" is not exactly the right word, for Stalin's policies could not always be identified with the Soviet Union's national interest.[7] How could the purge of the Red Army between 1936 and 1939 and the veritable decimation of its higher officer ranks have contributed to the security of the USSR? Stalin chose to be a Russian nationalist, just as he chose to follow the strictures of Marxism-Leninism—whenever it fit in with his personal power interests. Thus in a perverse sense he was an "internationalist," for whenever it suited his purpose, a sacrifice of millions of lives of his own countrymen could be of no greater moment to him than that of the interests, say, of the Chinese or the French Communists.

With Stalin gone, the worship that had surrounded him could not be transferred to any of his successors. After him the leaders of the Soviet Union had to be cast in an ordinary human mold. In Stalin a worshiping Communist saw one of the men who had made the Revolution, who performed the miracles of industrializing the Soviet Union, led it victoriously through the Great Patriotic War, and frustrated the schemes of the imperialists to stop the spread of Communism. How could one feel anything resembling that emotion about a faceless bureaucrat like Malenkov, the rambunctious and undignified Khrushchev, or that company of elderly bureaucrats who presided over the USSR during the Brezhnev era. In terms of the quantities of nuclear weapons and in production of steel, the Soviet Union was rapidly growing stronger than in Stalin's time, and by Brezhnev's it was incomparably so. But in terms of the awe and veneration, the veritable mystique that surrounded the head of the world Communist movement, the position of Stalin's successors was gradually becoming weaker. And with Brezhnev's demise the last vestiges of that mystique would disappear. The two invalids who then successively and briefly presided over the Communist Party of the USSR could hardly be portrayed as inspirational leaders. And with Gorbachev and perestroika the whole phantasmagoric world of Stalinism, and with it what remained of the leader's reputation, would definitely and irrevocably collapse.

History will have to decide whether Communism had become so permeated with Stalinism that Stalinism's demise had to lead to the opening of fissures within Communism and then its end as a viable world movement. But it is instructive to note that leaders of other Communist states, most notably those that came to assert their independence from the USSR, imitated many features of the despotic style of the Soviet dictator. And it is also noteworthy that after the deaths of Mao and Tito, China's and Yugoslavia's regimes, while still officially hewing to orthodoxy, veered away from the fundamental tenets of Marxism-Leninism. Is it necessary here to describe what has been happening in the Soviet Union following the categorical condemnation of Stalinism by Gorbachev and Company? Is the cult of personality—or in plain English, unbridled dictatorship—an organic part of Marxism-Leninism? As we shall see, Khrushchev's campaign against the cult was carried on under the slogan "Back to Lenin." Stalinism, it was asserted, had been a malignant growth on the ideology and practice of Communism. But as we shall also see, the momentum of perestroika and glasnost has carried the political debate beyond the point where Lenin and his legacy are sacrosanct. Viktor Afanasev, a prominent intellectual and of late increasingly a critic of Gorbachev's policies, was quite explicit on the subject in a public address given in August 1989. "All of us have to screw up our courage and admit not only that socialism is deformed in our country but that in its Marxist-Leninist pure form, it is incapable of development. We have to dismantle a Marxism-Leninism which calls us back to the nineteenth century, while the twentieth century is coming to an end."[8]

Nothing in Stalin's last years suggests any awareness on his part of how disastrous his legacy would prove to his country and to the cause of Communism. On the contrary, he acted and spoke (the latter becoming very infrequent) as if his methods of ruling Russia and the world movement were the only practicable ones. Autocracy suited both of them. In domestic politics any hopes that the regime, having passed the test of war, would become less repressive were soon dissipated. The cold war abroad was paralleled by a politicocultural campaign against alleged contamination from Western ideas at home. Millions of Soviet citizens in uniform had had the chance to see something of the outside world. Though the countries they passed through or occupied had been devastated, they still bore traces of a much higher material and cultural civilization than most Russian men and women had known at home. That and the wartime comradeship at arms with the Atlantic democracy created at least a theoretical possibility of Western ideas and customs becoming better known and more attractive. From an outsider's point of view, the possibility of this vague attraction of the West translating itself into sentiments hostile to the Soviet regime must have appeared very small indeed, yet throughout the immediate postwar years the Soviet government and party organs acted as if the entire Soviet population had been exposed to the danger of wholesale ideological subversion. Hence a vigorous campaign associated with the name of Andrei Zhdanov, Stalin's principal lieutenant at the time, which was aimed at disparaging foreign values and cultural achievements and contrariwise extolling Soviet, and especially Russian, ones.[9] The theater, cinema, plastic arts, literature, etc., were subjected to close scrutiny regarding their adherence to the style and subjects appropriate from the points of view of Soviet patriotism and socialist realism. The struggle against alien influences and the ideological pollution of Soviet society continued after Zhdanov's death in 1948. Chauvinism and obscurantism extended to science. It became unsafe for Soviet scholars to acknowledge the validity of, and to work along the lines of, such scientific achievements as Einstein's theory of relativity, Darwin's theory of evolution, and the entire field of genetics. By the same token, some of the Russian scientists whose achievements were singled out for praise and favor by the regime, sometimes by the leader himself, were in fact just facile popularizers, or as in the notorious case of Trofim Lysenko, sheer charlatans. Lysenko's theories, products of fraudulent experiments, were endorsed by a Central Committee resolution in 1948, and for the balance of Stalin's life the enterprising faker remained a virtual dictator of Soviet biological sciences, his opponents paying with their academic positions—and at least in one case with his life—for their scholarly integrity.

The xenophobic trend in Soviet cultural life was another burden for international Communism in its servitude to the Kremlin. Sympathy for the USSR was in those years quite widespread in the Western intellectual and artistic community, especially among the French and Italian intelligentsia. And here the regime that proclaimed itself to be the vanguard and carrier of "proletarian internationalism" endorsed theories and artistic practices that under different circumstances would have been denounced as phony or laughed out of court by anyone familiar with the given issue in science or the arts. And yet whatever their inner thoughts on such matters, the great majority of intellectuals in foreign Communist parties continued their allegiance.

The alleged worshipers of false foreign values and detractors of the achievements of the great Russian people were being denounced as "cosmopolites," again a strange term of opprobrium to be used by a movement dedicated to the eventual supranational world state. Even stranger on that count must have appeared increasing indications that there was an anti-Semitic undertone to the campaign against "cosmopolites," some of the writers and critics unfortunate enough to be listed as such being further denigrated by the adjective "rootless," usually an indication that the person in question was Jewish.

A diehard admirer of Stalin in today's Russia would reject criticisms on those counts, if not indeed praise his foresight in indulging in such chicaneries. Look what opening the country to Western ideas, what cultural and scientific exchanges with the West have done to the USSR under Gorbachev! Those nostalgic about the old times would also find attenuating circumstances for the anti-Semitism of Stalin's last years. The Soviet Jews, because of their international connections, and especially after the rise of Israel, could never be assumed to have an *undivided loyalty*. The issue of Soviet emigration has been a source of trouble and ideological embarrassment to the USSR from the moment when Brezhnev incautiously agreed to discuss it with the United States: to admit that a sizable part of the population has remained insensitive to the benefits of Soviet life could only be denigrating to the state that claims it has abolished exploitation and ethnic discrimination. And also it was not wrong in those years to extol *Russia* and flatter the national pride of the *Russian* people: "The leading nationality of the Soviet state," as the Georgian-born dictator proclaimed in his speech on V-E Day. For, our unreconstructed Stalinist would claim, it was upon Russia and the Russian's domination of the other nationalities that the Soviet system has been based. To tamper with that domination, as Gorbachev has belatedly discovered, threatens the very existence of the USSR.

As in the Terror of the late thirties, though not as yet on the same scale, the purge struck at the highest levels of the party and government organs. In 1949–50 took place the notorious Leningrad affair, the precise details of which, for all the revelations of glasnost, still remain veiled in mystery. Dismissed from their high offices and eventually executed were a number of high officials, including Nikolai Voznesensky, head of economic planning and a Politburo member,

Alexis Kuznetsov, secretary of the Central Committee, and some others whose careers had begun or who had been associated with the Leningrad party organization under the late Andrei Zhdanov. No evidence has ever been published that would link any of those officials with an act of disloyalty or insubordination toward Stalin. One rumor claimed that their "crime" consisted of urging the dictator to create a separate Russian branch of the party on the model of those of the non-Russian republics rather than having the Russian party subdivision, as it had been since the beginning of the Soviet state, directly within the overall apparatus of the Communist Party of the Soviet Union. Such a proposal would have been quite reasonable and aboveboard; why should little Armenia and Estonia have their national parties while the biggest republic of them all does not? But with Stalin's inordinate suspiciousness it would not have been surprising if he had seen in the proposal an attempt by some of his subordinates to build an independent power base, and in view of his age (he was born in 1879) he could have seen such maneuvers as preliminary moves for the struggle for succession after his death.[10]

In any case, the liquidation of some of the most important party and state leaders was a forceful reminder that victory in the war and all the encomia that accrued to Stalin on its account did not affect his conviction that prophylactic terror was a necessary ingredient of the art of government. Equally astounding to today's reader whether in the USSR or the West must be the fact that all those high-ranking personages were never publicly tried or even denounced. Insofar as the Soviet public was concerned, these people simply vanished from their posts and the news.

Some writers have questioned Stalin's sanity during his last years. "Paranoia" and "morbid suspiciousness" are typical of the characterization of this behavior, the latter almost a standard term applied by the Soviet writers under glasnost to explain this extraordinary man's misdeeds. But Stalin's cruelty and deviousness are not more apparent during those years than in earlier periods of his rule. "Morbid suspiciousness" has to be a professional ailment of tyrants. Without it they would not remain long in power.

As to whether the advancing years affected his judgment, we are again without any clear-cut evidence. If not its initial phase then the consequences of the Yugoslav imbroglio undoubtedly reflected an old man's hurt vanity. A younger and less irascible Stalin would have used diplomacy rather than confrontation and harsh rhetoric in dealing with Tito. But apart from his mistakes on that count, his handling of Soviet foreign policy and of the international Communist movement remained during this last period flexible and skillful. When the occasion demanded it, as during Mao's visit, he could still find the right blend of haughtiness and flattery, of awesomeness and amiability. Soviet diplomacy vis-à-vis the West continued to be artful. Though it was Secretary of State John Foster Dulles who first formulated the concept, it is Stalin who must be credited with initiating the practice of "brinksmanship." The Berlin blockade and the Korean War strained the patience of U.S. policy makers, yet in both cases the USSR had the means to terminate or deflect the crisis if the cold war threatened to turn into a real one: the blockade could be, and eventually was, lifted, and in the case of Korea it was the Chinese Communists who were constrained to pull Stalin's chestnuts out of the fire and to suffer the consequences.

Stalin's successors did not fully share his confidence that the USSR could maintain a high level of tension with the West and yet not run the risk of the latter responding by bellicose measures. But Stalin's evaluation of Western statesmen and of public opinion in their countries proved largely correct: even in the face of such provocation as that over Berlin and Korea, the West was unlikely to react in a manner that might lead to war. The American electorate was not likely to be unduly stirred up by what was happening in and to the countries in East Europe, some of which many a U.S. citizen would have had considerable trouble locating on a map. Winston Churchill might passionately decry the existence of the Iron Curtain, but the premises underlying the foundation of NATO were purely defensive; the United States and its allies did not propose to forcibly pierce the curtain, but only to prevent its being moved farther west. Would the U.S. posture have remained defensive had Washington and American public opinion realized (1) the degree of American military superiority over the USSR and (2) the element of bluff in the Kremlin's seemingly challenging stance toward the West? Stalin evidently thought that unless you press the Americans you run the danger of being pressured by them. Not an unreasonable belief in view of the future course of Soviet-American relations. And indeed, who in Stalin's time would have even dreamed of expostulating with the Kremlin about violations of human rights in Russia?

Cowed though it might have been temporarily, Stalin was far from underestimating America's potential strength and from downgrading its people's resolve once aroused. He had none of Hitler's inane scorn for the fighting qualities of a democracy. His brinksmanship was tempered by great sensitivity to situations and issues that might stir the sluggish transatlantic giant to a more threatening policy, from the Soviet point of view, than that of containment. He did *not* blockade all the routes to West Berlin, and, as noted before, his uncharacteristic indulgence in not attempting to "satellize" Finland might well have been due to his recollections of how the Americans applauded the little country's gallant stand during the winter war of 1939–40. All in all, a pattern of behavior hardly characteristic—certainly not when it came to foreign affairs—of a deranged or senile mind.

Few aging dictators have relished the thought of what might happen to their vast powers after their demise. Mao lent his hand to the liquidation of two of his successive heirs apparent, finally giving his blessing to one who turned out to be a nonentity. Tito had manipulated the party and state machinery of Yugoslavia to make sure that after his death no single individual would be able to step into his shoes. Deng, now well into his ninth decade, has for quite a while been announcing his forthcoming retirement, yet as of 1991, he still retains supreme authority in China.

One would have thought that Stalin, the original and most flagrant practitioner of the cult of personality, should have been especially solicitous in preparing the ground for an orderly succession. He was, after all, not only a national leader but also leader of a world movement. And he must have remembered the disarray into which the party and the Soviet state had been thrown first by Lenin's incapacitating stroke and then his death. How much more important was the need to prevent splits and divisions within the body of Soviet and world Communism should Stalin, now over seventy and in poor health, become incapacitated or die! The cold war was going through its most intense phase and the Korean conflict would soon bring even closer the danger of its turning into a hot one.

Yet in the very nature of things, quite apart from the character of the man, it was impossible for Stalin to assure that the monolithic and absolutist structure of Communism would remain unimpaired after his death. As of 1950, the Communist world was held together not so much by the shared ideology, nor even by awe of the Soviet power, as by the worship of and belief in the infallibility of the leader. A Malenkov or Khrushchev could inherit his offices, but neither, and no one else, could become the object of the idolatry that surrounded the despot. It is insufficient to explain his hold over foreign Communists by the bureaucratic controls exercised by Moscow and the prestige acquired by the USSR in the war. There was also another, almost irrational element, a kind of bewitchment emanating from one man that was instrumental in leading to that submissiveness. The Kremlin's directives were blindly obeyed by the Communists even when they were beyond the grasp of the Soviet security apparatus. We have descriptions of how in Stalin's era the French Communists determined their policies: "Discussion within the Political Bureau and the Secretariat remained secret. When the Russians wanted a specific policy or action it was communicated by Thorez [the then secretary general of the French Communist Party] to the Secretariat. At the key words 'Les camarades nous disent' (The comrades tell us) all further discussion was immediately foreclosed."[11] And the procedure was identical, we can confidently assume, when it came to the Communist parties, say, of Argentina or Norway. Chipped though it had been by the Yugoslav heretics leaving and slamming the door behind them, this monolithic edifice of world Communism still stood, imposing and awesome.

The awareness of the vacuum his death would create did not lead Stalin to search for alternative ways of preserving the unity and cohesion of Communism. In 1950 it was still not too late to steer the movement in the direction of a more genuine "proletarian internationalism" rather than leaving it dependent on the will of one man and completely directed from one center. Yet during the last three years of Stalin's life world Communism was being shaped increasingly in the Soviet image and more and more harnessed to the goals of the foreign policy of the USSR.

Despite what the trumpetings of Soviet propaganda proclaimed, this policy was not premised on the imminent danger of a U.S. attack on the Soviet Union. And indeed no one conversant with what was going on in the West could have seriously believed that Washington and London were preparing or would be able to launch such an attack. For all the intentions of the capitalist ruling elites, they were obviously incapable of pushing their nations into a third world war. Rather, so ran the scenario of Stalin's fears, the imperialists were plotting *indirect* aggression against the Communist bloc through the use of other nations' armies rather than their own, to wrest from the Soviet Union the fruits of its victory in the war.

Here the key issue was that of Germany. In 1949 the three Western powers agreed on their occupation zones being merged into what became the Federal Republic of Germany. Helped by the Marshall Plan, the new state's economy in 1950 was already on its way to what would soon be proclaimed the "German miracle." And there were voices in the West urging that this economically restored (West) Germany be allowed to rearm and join NATO, thus strengthening its potential as a shield against the advance of Communism.

But Stalin did not believe—and his successors would hold on to that disbelief—that a rearmed Germany's role would be that of merely strengthening the defense of the West. The revived German army, the Bundeswehr, would serve as the cat's-paw of American imperialism, the instrument that Washington planned to use to wrest Eastern Europe from Soviet domination and Communism. The Kremlin had no illusions concerning the People's Democracies: their Communist regimes were detested by the people, their hold on power secured by internal repression, backed up by the threat of Soviet military intervention should that repression prove unavailing.

Here then was a potential opening for America's anti-Soviet designs—a way of accomplishing what Secretary Dulles, as if reading the Kremlin's mind and its fears, would in 1953 call the "rollback" of the Soviet sphere of domination and "liberation." A revolt breaks out in East Germany or Czechoslovakia, or still more frighteningly all over the enslaved area. Those anti-Communist uprisings are succored, perhaps even with troops, by West Germany. The Soviet army, of course, could still put out the fire. But what if the United States threatens a nuclear strike against the USSR—should the latter intervene militarily to try to save the satellite regimes? Moscow would then be faced with the alternatives of acquiescing in the loss of Eastern Europe or embarking on all-out war with America at a time when its own stock of A-bombs was still quite small, and when it still lacked a strategic air force capable of retaliating against the American homeland.[12]

With our accumulated hindsight this nightmare of Stalin's appears quite unrealistic. But was it more so than the fears then current in the West—the vision of the Soviet armies sweeping to the English Channel? The fear of a rearmed Germany and what it could portend for the Communist domination of Eastern Europe and, by the same token, for the security of the USSR, explains a great deal about the seeming contradictions in Soviet policies during Stalin's last years. Thus the USSR felt it necessary to respond to the creation of the Federal Republic in 1949 by turning its own zone of occupation into the German Democratic Republic. But at the time and for several years afterward, the new satellite was for the Kremlin a bargaining chip rather than a permanent addition to the Communist camp. Moscow kept tantalizing its erstwhile Western allies by hinting that it might agree to a reunited Germany provided it remained demilitarized. And in 1952 when remilitarization of Germany was being seriously discussed in NATO councils the Soviets were ready to go one step further: they formally proposed to the United States, Britain, and France that "[reunited] Germany will be permitted to have its own armed forces . . . which are necessary for the defense of the country" provided that it would be accompanied by iron-clad guarantees that the new state would remain permanently neutral.[13] German Communists, like any other detachment of the world movement, were in Stalin's eyes expendable whenever his own power interests and the security of the Soviet Union were at stake.

The same motif helps explain the ferocity of the campaign against the alleged Titoists in the People's Democracies. The purges were to solidify Moscow's grip on those countries, fill with awe and terrorize not only the local Communist parties, but their entire population, in the way that the indiscriminate terror in the thirties had been intended to immunize Soviet society against internal subversion. Similar reasons dictated economic and social policies designed to turn East European societies into copies of the Soviet one. And beyond the confines of the Soviet bloc the great Communist parties of the West were constrained to declare publicly that their primary allegiance was to the Soviet Union. It did not matter to Stalin that by trying to sabotage the Marshall Plan and by pledging that they would welcome the Soviet army in the case of war, the French and Italian Communists were in effect scuttling the possibility of their ever coming to power through legal means and alienating the majority of their countrymen. What mattered was to dispel any hopes in Washington that by resurrecting German military might and combining it with nuclear blackmail the West could score a victory over the Soviet Union on the cheap, so to speak, without provoking an all-out war in which the proleft segments of the population in the West would side with the Soviets rather than with their own governments, a war in which the Americans and the British would have to use their own troops rather than German surrogates.

Moscow's posture of seeming unconcern over the prospect of war and the confidence about its outcome should it occur was thus very largely a pose designed to discourage any American attempt to go beyond the policy of containment and to press on the vulnerable segment of Stalin's empire, the East European satellites.

Another Soviet stratagem to deprive what it viewed as the American threat of its nuclear sting was the massive peace campaign launched in 1949 and which reached its crescendo with the Stockholm Appeal in March 1950. A Communist creature, the World Committee of Peace was created in 1949, its main purpose being to support the absolute ban on nuclear weapons as instruments of war. Again Communist parties all over the world had been harnessed to this transparently Soviet-directed campaign. In effect, they were ordered to curtail all their other activities to concentrate on winning public opinion in their countries to the necessity of banishing the specter of atomic war. The Soviets had previously rejected the U.S.-sponsored Baruch Plan, which would have established an international atomic authority under the U.N. with powers to control all aspects of the production and use of fissionable material. The fly in the ointment of the plan from the Soviet point of view was the proviso that a violator of the agreement or of the authority's rules (for example, a state secretly attempting to produce nuclear bombs) would be subject to sanctions imposed by a majority vote of the U.N. Security Council. Thus the right to veto the resolution of the Security Council by one of the five great powers—permanent members of the council—would under the American plan be waived when it came to issues connected with nuclear energy. The USSR stoutly refused to give up its right of veto. This refusal was quite understandable, since the abolition of the veto on any issue vital to the USSR was certain to make it a losing party in any dispute with the West before the U.N. And equally understandable, the United States refused to subject its production and possession of nuclear materials to international control if the veto and with it the Soviet Union's power to block any sanction against the violator of the agreement remained in the U.N. Charter. Discussion of the issue would continue in various agencies of the United Nations, but the gap between the East and the West was and would remain unbridgeable.

The peace campaign was then a massive propaganda effort to outflank the United States on the question of nuclear weapons. For all of its transparent aspects the Soviet gambit was based on sound psychology: the fear of an all-out nuclear confrontation, especially after the Soviet acquisition of the A-bomb, was widespread in the West in the early fifties and probably more acute than at any subsequent period except for the two weeks of the Cuban missile crisis in 1962. The Stockholm peace appeal, with its declaration that world public opinion would consider any government that first uses atomic weapons a war criminal, was signed by millions and had a wide resonance even among those in the West who recognized how the appeal and the entire peace movement was being manipulated by Moscow. Visions of the horror of nuclear war, moral pressures emanating from the peace movement, would thus, as the Korean War soon showed, virtually preclude the possibility of the United States using its nuclear preponderance even as an instrument of diplomacy. It remained for Khrushchev's Soviet Union to explore the possibilities of nuclear diplomacy, and perhaps it is fortunate, judging by his discomfitures on that count, that the United States under Truman and Eisenhower never seriously attempted it.[14]

And so like two boxers moving warily in the ring, apprehensive of testing each other's strength, the two superpowers maneuvered evasively in the cold war, both fearful of an actual confrontation. The United States greatly overestimated the Soviets' strength, and the Kremlin ascribed to the Americans dark designs, a Machiavellian subtlety that was certainly not the style of the Washington policy makers.

The threat of German rearmament and its consequences to the Soviet position in Eastern Europe was one of Stalin's two major concerns in his last years. The other was China.

The Soviet dictator's flattering words to Liu Shaoqi during the latter's visit to Moscow in May in fact mirrored his fears: China in time would replace the USSR as the center of the world revolution, the Younger Brother would surpass the Elder. Now, at the time, the prospects of such a shift in leadership and power relations within the Communist bloc appeared quite distant. But as we have already seen, the whole past history of Sino-Soviet relations, the protracted and contentious course of negotiations that led to the 1950 pact between the two Communist powers, the personality of Mao—all would have appeared as portents of future trouble to anyone on the Soviet side, let alone someone as suspicious and megalomaniacal as Stalin.

To perceive the dimensions of the Chinese problem from the Kremlin's point of view, we must first of all see it against the background of Soviet relations with its European satellites. The term "satellite" itself appears pallid and insufficient in describing the extent of subjugation of those countries to Moscow in the era of late Stalinism. The Soviets did not only control the satellite regimes in the sense of dictating their foreign and domestic policies; they virtually ran, and sometimes directly, the most important segments of their political, economic, and military apparatus. It was well known that the security agencies of those countries were more under the control of the Ministry of State Security in Moscow (the equivalent of today's KGB) than under that of their own political leadership. The Soviet "advisers" supervised the machinery of the terror, stage-managed the most important purge trials, such as those of Rajk in Hungary and Slansky in Czechoslovakia. Soviet generals—for example, Marshal Konstantin Rokossovski in Poland—presided over the satellites' defense establishments. The Russian officers interspersed throughout East European countries' military forces took orders from their counterparts in Moscow, being just nominally subordinated to their own governments. It is thus understandable why the Soviet bloc between 1950 and 1953 could dispense with such contrivances as the Warsaw Treaty Organization. Nor was there any need as yet for something like the future Brezhnev Doctrine. The Soviet armed forces were stationed all over Eastern Europe, and in any case a massive Soviet military intervention was not necessary to affect a People's Democracy's policies, or to change the political leadership of its regime. A telephone call from the Kremlin or a hint from the Soviet ambassador was all that was needed to produce such changes. And as already mentioned, Soviet control of those countries' economic and cultural life was equally extensive and strict.

By contrast, the Chinese Communists, though deferential to the Elder Brother and publicly endorsing the main lines of Soviet domestic and foreign policies, were clearly masters in their own house. Moscow did not have its own man at the head of the People's Republic's military or security forces. It could not dictate the pace of reforms designed to force China's economy into the socialist model. Soviet advisers in China were just that and not like their corresponding numbers in Bulgaria or Romania, agents and executors of policies devised in Moscow.

The Kremlin did claim and for a while obtained special rights in two of China's regions bordering on the USSR. One of the joint Sino-Soviet companies set up under the trade agreement of March 1950 exploited the mineral resources of Sinkiang, which presumably opened the door for a special Soviet position in the province, politically as well as economically. Even more influential, and from Beijing's point of view objectionable, was to be for a while the Soviet role in Manchuria, then industrially the most developed province of the People's

Republic. Under the 1950 treaty the Manchurian Railway was not to revert to Chinese ownerhip before 1952. The Soviet position in Manchuria was buttressed by Moscow's special relationship with the province's regional government headed by Gao Gang. The latter, a member of the Chinese Politburo and evidently at odds with Mao, was, according to Khrushchev's later testimony, very close to the Russians.[15]

Glasnost, which has added a great deal to our knowledge of the Stalin era, has not as yet lifted the veil of secrecy that covers the more delicate aspects of Sino-Soviet relations. We have thus not been vouchsafed more information regarding the Soviet–Gao Gang relationship nor on the Soviet longer-range aims in Manchuria and Sinkiang. On the face of it, the Kremlin's machinations in the two provinces smacked clearly of the old Western imperialist practices, and were undoubtedly viewed as such by Beijing. Following Stalin's death in 1954, Gao Gang was removed from his Manchurian satrapy and shortly afterward stripped of his party offices and put in prison, where he allegedly committed suicide.[16]

How long could such humiliating Soviet privileges (from Beijing's point of view) survive the Communists' consolidation of power and China's inevitable rise to the status of a great power? "Ours will never again be an insulted nation. We have stood up." Those words of Mao's must have forcibly registered in Moscow. As the latter viewed the situation in the beginning of 1950, there were obviously two alternatives for the future relations between the two Communist giants. One was to acquiesce in China's full equality with the USSR and hence in the Communist world's having two centers of power. The other was to work for a situation whereby the People's Republic would be constrained to depend on the Elder Brother and have to defer to his wishes concerning issues such as the Soviets' special position in Manchuria and, more important, to the general lines of foreign policy.

The first alternative would have run against the basic premises of Soviet (Stalin's) statecraft since at least the late twenties. Those premises required that the Communist bloc and world movement have only one center of power, one absolute leader and infallible guide. And this leader saw that anything which even approached what in the late 1950s and 1960s came to be called polycentrism would completely transform the nature of the Soviets' relations even with the European parties. The Kremlin would no longer have a free hand in, say, ordering the Polish Communists around. The latter could seek advice and support in Beijing, hoping to acquire a modicum of independence by playing off the two Communist great powers against each other.[17] It could not escape the Russians' attention that the Yugoslav heretics were gleefully articulating such hopes.

Equally disturbing from Moscow's point of view were other probable implications of admitting the Chinese to anything like equal partnership. Already by *seeming* to accord the People's Republic that status the Kremlin had to some extent lost its freedom of action. Beijing was bent on triggering more wars of "national liberation" in the Third World, thus multiplying the points of conflict between East and West beyond what Moscow might consider prudent. And indeed for almost thirty years following Stalin's death, one would discern in the Soviets' policies continuous anxiety that Beijing was consciously attempting to create a situation, whether in Southeast Asia or in connection with Taiwan, that might precipitate a fatal confrontation between the United States and the USSR. At the same time, such efforts did not preclude the possibility of the People's Republic seeking, as was actually to happen in 1971–72, a rapprochement with the Americans, thus emboldening the latter to take a firmer stance against the USSR.

Polycentrism was equally unacceptable from the doctrinal point of view. The Communist movement had survived such seemingly devastating challenges to orthodoxy as the purge of the Leninist old guard and the Nazi-Soviet Pact because of the general agreement that on all questions of ideology Moscow had the last word. With the cult of Stalin that tenet, already operative in the mid-1920s, acquired the status of dogma. If one were to have two centers of authority in the Communist world, one could already envisage the situation that would arise in the 1960s and 1970s when the Sino-Soviet strife expanded into the ideological sphere, each party denouncing the other for straying from the straight and narrow path of Marxism-Leninism. No, even an outside observer would have to admit that the doctrinal primacy of whoever ruled in Moscow had become as essential to the survival of the cohesion of the Communist movement as was papal infallibility to the preservation of the unity of the Catholic Church. And how could that primacy be maintained if Beijing were raised to an equal status with Moscow?

Could the Soviet system itself survive without Stalin, or whoever succeeded him in the Kremlin, ruling as the undisputed leader and lawgiver to world Communism? In 1950 and until the tyrant's death such a question would have appeared ludicrous. Tito and Mao notwithstanding, a challenge to Stalin's authority was almost unimaginable. But even assuming his disappearance from the scene, the Soviet system loomed impregnable to any threat save that ensuing from an all-out war. The Communist regime, after all, survived the vicissitudes of the interwar years when Russia was weak and isolated in a world dominated by the capitalist powers. It survived the terrible economic crisis of the early 1930s, the trauma of the Great Terror, the catastrophic military defeats of 1941–42. Now the country was one of the two superpowers. Soviet patriotism, the enormous military and industrial resources of the USSR, the habit of obedience instilled in the people by the iron rule over a generation—all these facts appeared bound to assure the perpetuation of the Kremlin's absolute sway, no matter how divided or enfeebled the forces of Marxism-Leninism abroad. So it looked from the outside. But for the rulers, as the intensity of their reaction to the Tito affair demonstrated, anything that struck at the ideological foundation of the edifice that Lenin and Stalin had built was a clear and present danger to their power. And after watching the events of recent years and the reverberations of the collapse of Communism on the domestic politics of the USSR, who can fault their apprehensions?

In other words, there were imperative reasons that the way be found to keep the new Communist colossus in a condition of dependence on the USSR beyond such time as the Chinese Communists consolidated their power and harnessed the nation's huge population to their own great power ambitions.

Looking at the situation realistically, one readily perceives that China's continued deference toward the Elder Brother depended to a large extent on the overall situation in the Far East.

As of the beginning of 1950, a salient element in that situation was the United States' apparent acquiescence, probably not really to the Kremlin's liking, in the Chinese Communists' victory. After its disenchanting experiences with the Kuomintang, the Truman administration was disinclined to take any effective steps to bar Mao's armies from trying to occupy Taiwan and thus eliminate the Nationalists' last major bastion on Chinese soil. Yet anyone cognizant of the American political scene was aware that there were powerful forces which held such acquiescence and the waiting "until the dust settles in Asia" to be a betrayal of America's historical mission of stemming the advance of Communism. Those voices found resonance within official Washington and open support from the U.S. proconsul in Japan, General Douglas MacArthur. The proponents of help to the Kuomintang held

Taiwan essential to the security of what was then known as the free world, and its potential loss as imperiling this country's entire position in the Far East. The pressure to resume massive American aid to the Nationalists was premised on the assumption that it would not only help save Taiwan, but would in due course enable Chiang's forces to threaten the Communists' hold on the mainland. With U.S. official policy precariously tilted in favor of nonintervention in what was still China's civil war, it was at least possible that some untoward event in the Far East might lead Washington to reverse its stand and throw its weight behind the Nationalists.

As has already been noted, the Sino-Soviet alliance, or at least its published text, did not obligate the Soviet Union to assist the People's Republic militarily in the case of a Nationalist attack on the mainland. We do know that, following the signing of the agreement, Soviet military aviation did help the Communist armies in their mopping-up operations and in warding off air raids on the mainland cities by Kuomintang planes. But nothing in the language of the treaty as much as hints at the Soviets' obligation to help the People's Republic in a possible confrontation with the United States, be it through a direct American attack or through the United States helping Chiang Kai-shek in an invasion of continental China. The treaty pledged mutual assistance in the case of aggression by Japan and/or a state allied with it.

As of the moment (the first half of 1950), the Chinese Communist's first and overwhelming priority was the final elimination of the Kuomintang, by the invasion and occupation of Taiwan. They could not have wished for anything happening anywhere in the Far East that might conceivably interfere with that goal. The United States, speaking through President Truman on January 5, reiterated its resolve to stay out of the concluding phases of the Chinese civil war—i.e., it pledged not to help Taiwan militarily. But knowing the pressures under which the Truman administration was finding itself on that issue, one could easily surmise that some dramatic development in the area might well lead the United States to reassess its policy of nonintervention, bar the People's Liberation Army's access to Taiwan, and perhaps carry its collusion with the Nationalists even further.

The invasion of South Korea by the Communist North, which began on June 25, 1950, was then certainly not in Beijing's interest, and it could not, from the Chinese Communists' point of view, have taken place at a worse time. Conversely, and for reasons already adduced, the invasion appears to have fitted Stalin's plans, as at least a partial solution of his Chinese dilemma. "Moscow enjoyed several channels of communication and control in North Korea that rendered [it] a Soviet satellite in the fullest sense of the word."[18] It is little short of ludicrous to maintain, as some still do, that the North Koreans could have planned and executed the invasion on their own, rather than with the Soviets' permission, or even more likely at their explicit orders. The aggressor's forces entered the conflict with up-to-date Soviet motorized equipment, artillery, and aircraft.

Nor could the Korean gambit be considered as yet another attempt to expand the frontiers of the Communist bloc. In itself South Korea was from the Kremlin's point of view a negligible prize, certainly not worth the risk it incurred in authorizing the operation. The invasion and the eventual unification of the peninsula under Communist rule was to serve much broader purposes.

To be sure, Moscow could not have foreseen the exact nature and sequence of America's response to the invasion. President Truman's directives of June 27 and 30 ordering America's first naval and air forces and then ground units to defend South Korea, in all likelihood took Moscow by surprise. How illogical of the Americans, who had reconciled themselves to the loss of a much vaster prize—China—to embark on a full-fledged war to save South Korea! The U.S. reaction was all the more unexpected in view of Secretary of State Acheson's statement in January 1950 that by implication excluded South Korea (as well as Taiwan) from those areas in the Far East where aggression would be met with immediate U.S. armed response.[19]

The rationale of Stalin's sanctioning the Korean gamble must be sought in what was hoped in Moscow would be the larger dividends of a Communist victory in yet another country.

Such a victory would be bound to have a profound psychological impact on Japan. The Communists there had for several months prior to the invasion pursued militant tactics designed to exert additional pressure on the American occupation authorities. This militancy came as a direct result of orders from Moscow, and was at first resisted by the leaders of the Japanese party, several of whom had had close ties with the Chinese Communists before 1945.[20] The USSR clearly tried to stir up as much trouble as possible in Japan, attacking U.S. policies there, renewing the demand that the emperor be tried as a war criminal, in brief trying to create a revolutionary situation in what was at the time an American dependency. It is unlikely that Moscow could have expected such pressures to constrain the Americans to terminate their occupation and agree to a Japanese peace treaty that would be agreeable to the Kremlin. Rather those pressures, plus the invasion, were intended to make Washington reassess its entire Far Eastern policy and strengthen its military presence in the area, steps which would have clearly run against Beijing's wishes and interests.

The invasion was also expected to have direct repercussions on America's stance vis-à-vis the Chinese Communists. The wait-and-see attitude, the chance that after the "dust has settled," i.e., after the Communists conquered Taiwan, the United States would follow Britain's example and accord diplomatic recognition to the People's Republic—these favorable prospects for the Chinese Communists would not survive the eruption of American indignation in the wake of a fresh and brutal case of Communist aggression. To be sure, there was some risk that the sharp edge of the Americans' anger would turn against Moscow. But as the story of the Berlin blockade suggested, the West had been apprehensive of taking any steps that might precipitate a confrontation with the USSR, and its fears were by now very greatly enhanced by the Soviets' acquisition of nuclear weapons.[21] It would be both easier and safer for the Americans to vent their frustration by turning against the Chinese Communists.

For all his super-Machiavellian skills Stalin could not have foreseen that his scheme would lead to what in fact would be, though on a limited scale, war between the United States and China. But what could have been forecast was America's intervention, following the invasion, in the Communist-versus-Nationalist struggle, taking Taiwan under its protection. Mao and his associates, instead of turning their energies to the task of rebuilding their country's shattered society and economy, would have to continue to face the danger of the civil war being reignited on the mainland. They would continue to need Soviet support to save them from even greater dangers. They would not be able to face the consequences of a public disagreement with their Soviet comrades; their foreign and military policies would have to defer to the wishes of the Elder Brother.

It is difficult to resist the conclusion that the Korean imbroglio was instigated by the Russians for the specific purpose of discouraging the Chinese Communists from breaking away from Soviet tutelage. But how did Stalin secure Mao's acquiescence in the venture? It is almost inconceivable that the subject of the forthcoming North Korean attack would not have come up for discussion during Mao's visit to

Moscow. During that visit the Chinese, as we have seen, had proved hard bargainers. Yet they evidently were not able to change the Soviets' decision on a move that ran so clearly against their interests and held so many potential dangers to their freshly and as yet incompletely conquered—or to use their terminology, liberated—country. That the Beijing leadership did know that something would be brewing in Korea and that something might pose a threat to China is strongly suggested by the fact that just prior to the invasion large units of the People's Liberation Army were moved from southern China to the vicinity of the Manchurian-Korean border.[22]

The acquiescence and the subsequent willingness of the Chinese to try to pull Moscow's Korean chestnuts out of the fire can be explained mainly by a phenomenon that for all that has been said still appears incredible from our perspective forty years later: the power and prestige of one man. Stalin could be bargained with when it came to the issues directly affecting their own country, but Mao and his colleagues simply could not question his decisions pertaining to the international dimensions of Comunism. And they were probably also inhibited from protesting by their own long-standing advocacy of wars of "national liberation" and of militant revolutionary tactics all over Asia. How could they, who only four short years before had scorned counsels of prudence and moderation and had challenged the U.S.-backed Kuomintang, now disavow a similar venture by the North Koreans? How greatly Stalin's personality affected Moscow-Beijing relations is attested by what happened after his death. Literally within days of the event the nature of that relationship underwent a dramatic change. China, as Mao had promised, finally "stood up," no longer a deferential Younger Brother but now claiming full equality. And Stalin's successors, much as they resented that prospect, would for the next several years try to placate their no longer submissive Chinese comrades.

The course of events following the invasion went far to justify the Soviets' assumptions in licensing the North Koreans to launch the enterprise. What could not have been foreseen, of course, was America's armed intervention to bolster the South Korean's faltering resistance. But those steps were accompanied by President Truman's ordering the U.S. Seventh Fleet to prevent any military activity in the Taiwan Strait, thus in effect sealing off the Nationalists' redoubt from a Communist invasion. A further proof that the United States was venting its wrath on account of the aggression against the weaker of the Communist powers could be seen in the note the United States addressed to the USSR on June 27. In view of Washington's unexpectedly violent reaction to the invasion, Moscow might well have been fearful of being told something like "Tell your puppets to cease their aggression immediately, or else!" But in fact the Truman administration went to considerable lengths to make its remonstrance as nonthreatening as possible. To emphasize that it was *not* an ultimatum, the paper was designed as an aide-mémoire, a note of record. The Soviet government was asked rather disarmingly to disavow its "responsibility for this unprovoked and unwarranted act," something which Moscow was delighted to do. As to the accompanying American request that the senior Communist power use its influence with the guilty party to get it to cease its depredations, the Soviets in their reply of June 29 solemnly explained that the Democratic People's Republic of Korea was a sovereign state, its policies thus not subject to outside control. And, added the Soviets' note, information at their disposal indicated that it was not the North that was guilty of aggression, but the South.

The Soviet Union did not attempt to block the United Nations' condemnation of the North Koreans and its call to its members to assist the victim of their aggression, thus in effect throwing the authority and support of the world organization behind America's armed intervention. The United States then was able to claim that it was not acting unilaterally, but as the armed instrument of the U.N., part of a force that would also include military contingents drawn from several other of its members. To be sure, the USSR had what might have appeared as a valid excuse for not blocking the U.N. action: ever since the beginning of the year it had chosen to boycott the Security Council's sessions on the grounds that the latter (in line with the U.S. stand on the issue) continued to recognize the Kuomintang regime on Taiwan as the legitimate government of China, thus refusing to seat the People's Republic as one of its permanent members. On the face of it, this was quite a logical and proper affirmation of the friendly bonds uniting the two Communist states. But in view of the subsequent consequences of the Soviet absence, not only the North Koreans but also Beijing would have little cause to appreciate this gesture by their ally and alleged protector.

In the first place, it is exceedingly strange that it was not foreseen in Moscow that whatever else the United States might do following the invasion it was bound to refer the matter to the Security Council and to demand that as a minimum North Korea be branded as the aggressor. The Soviet representative then should have been ready to return to the council at a moment's notice to block any such resolution through the USSR exercising its veto powers. Well, the Soviet absence immediately following the invasion, at the June 25 session, could be rationalized by the need to maintain the fiction that Moscow, like practically everybody else, had been surprised by the affair. But surely it would have been both proper and technically possible for the USSR to suspend the boycott and be represented at the June 27 session. The failure to do so enabled the United States to press for and obtain not only a condemnation of the North Koreans for not terminating their military action but also to get the U.N. and its members to render all possible assistance to the victim of the aggression. Surely it would have been in the interests of North Korea and of the People's Republic that the U.S. military not be backed up by the authority of the United Nations. But the USSR did not terminate its boycott of the Security Council until August, when the Korean War was in full swing and American outrage was already directed almost as much against the Communist Chinese as against the actual perpetrators of the invasion. Was the Soviets' absence from the crucial meetings of the Security Council in June an oversight or was there more to it?

The U.S. interposition of its Seventh Fleet between Taiwan and the mainland bore superficially an impartial character: the Communists were to be barred from invading the island, but by the same token Chiang's forces would not be permitted to launch an attack in the opposite direction. But it was obvious and common knowledge in Beijing as well as in Washington that the latter was at the time completely out of the question: what there remained of the Kuomintang military and naval force was thoroughly demoralized and disorganized by repeated defeats at the hands of the People's Liberation Army, incapable of putting up an effective defense of Taiwan, not to mention staging a major amphibious operation against the mainland. America's "quarantine" of the island was immediately denounced by Mao as revealing the true imperialist character of U.S. policies, a statement echoed by Zhou Enlai's message to the United States branding the action "armed aggression against the territory of China and a gross violation of the United Nations Charter."[23]

Whatever Mao and his associates might have felt about what Stalin had done to them by authorizing the Korean venture, their immediate concern had to be what to do about the war. The North Koreans were rapidly sweeping down the peninsula, but now that the United States had entered the fray, the military situation could soon be dramatically reversed.[24] On July 7 Beijing ordered a massive reinforcement of its forces along the Sino–North Korean border.[25] While scrupulously avoiding any appearance of military help to the North Koreans, Beijing was taking steps to make a future intervention possible.

Such precautionary measures were accompanied by a propaganda campaign against American imperialism, thus preparing the population for the possibility of a military confrontation with the United States. At the same time, Beijing was not bypassing any opportunity to try to avert such an eventuality through diplomatic action. In July the Chinese Communists responded favorably to India's initiative to have the People's Republic seated in the Security Council. The Soviets simultaneously terminated their boycott and the council then explored ways to end the Korean War. Prime Minister Jawaharlal Nehru's proposals to that effect were addressed to Stalin and Secretary of State Dean Acheson, a rather odd coupling of addressees, Stalin being included probably at Beijing's suggestion.[26] Stalin promptly agreed to the proposal, undoubtedly confident that it would be rejected by the State Department, which indeed it was shortly afterward. Beijing could not have hoped for a different outcome, but the maneuver was seen as bringing distinct gains: India (which had officially recognized the Communist regime) would gradually distance itself from the American policies in the Far East, and Stalin had now thrown his personal prestige behind China's postulates. And so perhaps the Americans would think twice about any further hostile acts against the People's Republic.

Such expectations were partly justified. The prevailing view in the Truman administration held that the United States must eschew anything that might enlarge the scope of the war. As it was, until the middle of August the U.N. forces still on the defensive had enough trouble in trying to preserve a foothold on the peninsula. At the same time, for many influential Americans Korea was but an episode in the worldwide struggle between the free world and Communism. The latter was on the march, especially in Asia. One could not fight that advance piecemeal, one had to repel it all along the line, and thus also bolster the Nationalist Chinese redoubt on Taiwan. And it was easy to proceed from that assumption to a further one: the forces of the free world must not always be on the defensive and wait for the Communists to strike the first blow.

In late July, with the situation of the U.N. forces in the Pusan perimeter rather critical, Chiang demonstratively offered thirty thousand Nationalist troops for service in Korea. The offer was refused, and could hardly have been meant seriously. But at the end of the month MacArthur, the U.S. and U.N. commander-in-chief, flew to Taiwan and held conferences with the generalissimo. Three weeks later the outspoken proconsul publicly voiced his conviction that the United States ought to cooperate militarily and otherwise with the Kuomintang's regime and that those wary of provoking Communist China were guilty of defeatism and ignorance of Oriental psychology. Much as the statement was subsequently repudiated as contrary to the official policy of the United States, it could not but increase the already considerable apprehension in Beijing.

The first phase of the Korean War had already taught Mao and his entourage a bitter lesson. Their hopes of developing complete independence in foreign policy and of being the decisive force in determining the course of Communism in all of Asia had been shown as ephemeral. The security of the People's Republic depended ultimately on decisions made in Moscow. Only a few weeks before the conclusion of the civil war, occupation of Taiwan seemed easily within reach; now it was out of sight. Whatever the shifts and vacillations in America's policy, it was virtually certain that it would soon, rather than later, reestablish an alliance with the Kuomintang. At the very least, the Americans would reequip and restrain Chiang's troops and help turn them into an effective fighting force. Prior to June 25 the Communist high command had planned to demobilize a large part of the People's Liberation Army. The tasks at hand—Taiwan, Tibet, and the liquidation of the remaining pockets of Kuomintang resistance on the mainland—did not justify the heavy burden on the economy incurred by maintaining more than 5 million men under arms. By July the situation called for increased rather than reduced military preparedness and expenditures. The task of repairing China's devastated economy and launching it on the path to industrialization and socialism would be delayed and made more difficult, and that in itself dictated continued dependence on Moscow.

Nor could Mao afford at this juncture, and for that matter for the duration of the Korean conflict, to give the slightest indication of diverging from or disagreeing with the policies of the USSR. To do so might well tip the scales in Washington in favor of those who urged further and more vigorous measures against the Chinese Communists. The basic though unstated premise of U.S. policy makers in resisting such pressures was the belief that the threat to the existence of the People's Republic might bring a violent Soviet reaction leading to World War III. After Chinese troops had already entered Korea and dealt heavy blows to the U.N. forces, General Omar Bradley, the chairman of the Joint Chiefs of Staff, was to articulate the administration's rationale for not striking directly at the territory of the People's Republic. An all-out war with China would be, in his famous phrase, a "wrong war, at the wrong place, at the wrong time, and with the wrong enemy." But his statement, even though obliquely, carried the implication that the United States could not and would not wish a war with the "right" enemy, and that such a war indeed might result from, say, an American nuclear strike at Manchuria or other areas of mainland China.

As of August, Moscow, unlike Beijing, could view the situation in the Far East with some equanimity. To be sure, America's armed intervention in Korea and the resulting international crisis was not without its dangers to the Soviet Union. There were grounds to believe that prior to June 27, Moscow may have contemplated drastic steps to get rid of the Tito regime. There had been a growing number of "frontier incidents" along Yugoslavia's borders with Bulgaria and Hungary. The Soviet press's vilification of the heretics grew in intensity. It is quite possible that the Soviets had planned military action in conjunction with their satellites in order to excise this malignant growth from the body of world Communism, but that in view of the United States' unexpectedly violent reaction to one invasion decided that another one would be too risky. It also could not have been to the Kremlin's liking that NATO now intensified its military preparations and placed the rearmament of Germany on its agenda. To underline the seriousness of the situation General Eisenhower was recalled from retirement and placed in command of the forces of the Atlantic Alliance. The atmosphere of crisis constrained the Soviet Union to expand considerably its own military forces at a time when its manpower, badly depleted in the war, was still urgently needed in the factories and collective farms. If Stalin had counted on the Korean venture to lessen the United States' commitment to NATO and concerns over the general situation in Europe, he had miscalculated.

As against such risks and disadvantages, the invasion did bring the expected dividend in strengthing the Soviet position vis-à-vis the People's Republic and rendering impossible any rapprochement between the latter and the West. Whatever the future course of the war, there was every likelihood that China rather than the Soviet Union would continue to be endangered and penalized for the American frustrations over the Korean imbroglio. To be sure, there were some in the United States who specified the Soviet Union as the main villain in the Far Eastern crisis and called for drastic measures against the culprit. The U.S. secretary of the navy went so far as to advocate military action against the USSR should it persist in carrying on aggression through surrogates. And an air-force general was more specific: the United States should strike at "Russia's five A-bomb nests."[27] But such outbursts bespoke exasperation at what seemed an intractable U.S. predicament and ran against the reasoned judgment of the administration and the prevailing sentiment in public opinion. The mere mention of the Soviet A-bomb evoked nightmarish visions of a nuclear war. Secretary Francis Matthews was made to resign, and General Robert Anderson was suspended from his command. The manner in which President Truman hastened to disavow the threats against the USSR must have heartened the Kremlin. Beijing could draw little comfort from the incident: China would not develop its own nuclear weapons for quite a number of years.

Expostulations by Beijing must have been at least partially responsible for Moscow's abandoning its pose of an uninvolved bystander insofar as the Korean crisis was concerned. On August 1 the Soviet representative, Jacob Malik, returned to the Security Council. He followed it by a proposal to solve the crisis through negotiations in which Communist China as well as the two Korean sides would participate. But when the United States demurred—it would not consider any negotiations without the North Koreans withdrawing above the 38th parallel—Malik warned that the continuation of the conflict might lead to a widening of the war, the responsibility for which would lie with the United States. The Soviet Union had thus rather belatedly thrown its *diplomatic* support behind its Communist allies in the Far East. But the threat contained in Malik's statement was still quite vague: nothing in it indicated that the USSR would intervene should the affairs of the North Koreans take an untoward turn, or, more importantly, should the United States step up its measures against the People's Republic.

The affairs of the North Koreans did take an untoward turn in September. With the U.S. forces landing at Inchon on the fifteenth of September the North Korean armies were outflanked, and their withdrawal turned into a rout. Within two weeks U.N. troops recaptured Seoul, and the invader was pushed behind his own borders. And now both the U.N.—really just the United States—and Communist China were faced with difficult choices; for the United States, whether to carry the war to the invader's territory north of the 38th parallel; for China, what it should do in such an eventuality. Washington's temptation to pursue the defeated enemy was well-nigh irresistible. The North Korean army could no longer offer serious resistance. Korea would be reunited under U.N. auspices and the Communist world would finally be taught a badly needed lesson that aggression, whatever its form, does not pay. The main reservations concerning such action centered on possible Soviet reactions. The Truman administration had already been in a quandary as to why Moscow had authorized the invasion. "The United States considered it possible at first that the Korean operation was a feint to lure US forces away from some more vital area where a Soviet attack was planned."[28] Its initial incomprehension was then compounded by the Soviets' inaction at the American threat to North Korea's existence. At first, "the Truman Administration was quite certain that the 'rolling back' of a presumed [*sic!*] Soviet satellite in an area so strategically important to the USSR would inevitably evoke a response."[29] Ironically, despite its rhetorical appeals to the Chinese people not to allow themselves to be used by the Soviets, no one in Washington even considered the hypothesis that there was a built-in tension in the Sino-Soviet alliance and the whole Korean enterprise may have been started by the Kremlin for reasons reflecting that tension.[30]

But as the U.N.-U.S. troops were approaching the border, Washington's inhibition about crossing it were dissolving in view of the absence of any Soviet threats or warning. One might have thought that following the turn in the war the Soviets could have at least had recourse to the formula they would use on several occasions when they wished to intimidate the West without committing themselves to a specific course of action, i.e., solemnly admonish the United States that "the gravest possible consequences would follow should its forces invade or try to subdue a fellow Communist state." But nothing of the kind was heard from Moscow during those crucial weeks. Even before the breakthrough of September 15 the State Department had been surprised—and relieved—that the bombing of targets in North Korea quite close to the Soviet border—even an accidental downing of a Soviet plane by an American one—did not provoke sharp reactions by the USSR. And now in the face of the imminent destruction of its satellite, Moscow displayed complete equanimity. "Such passivity gave encouragement to those within the US Administration who wished a military settlement to the Korean unification problem and to those who wanted to impress on the Communist bloc the resilience and effectiveness of American military power."[31] In pursuance of the National Security Council's decision, General MacArthur was given a free hand to carry the war beyond the 38th parallel. South Korean forces crossed it the next day; U.S. troops followed on October 7.

The Chinese Communists on the other hand were both profuse and emphatic in their warnings that they would not remain passive in the face of the American threat to destroy the Democratic People's Republic of Korea and to place the entire peninsula under the rule of Syngman Rhee's regime. One such warning was issued by Zhou Enlai on September 22. The Beijing leader's statement on the thirtieth was more specific. "The Chinese people will not stand by supinely while their neighbors are being savagely invaded." Simultaneously, high Beijing officials kept repeating to Indian Ambassador Kavalam Panikkar that China was ready to enter the war if the U.S. forces crossed the 38th parallel. But these warnings were being dismissed in Washington as a bluff. It is almost certain that had similar intimations come from Moscow they would have been taken most seriously. And certainly the United States would have been more attentive to the Chinese warnings had they been communicated through the Soviets rather than through India.

We would pay dearly to have full and authenticated information as to what went on between Beijing and Moscow during those hectic days. What we do know suggests that the Soviets, quite in line with their previous conduct, were leaving it up to the Chinese comrades to decide whether they should intervene in the war, or acquiesce in the destruction of a fellow Communist state and thus in effect have the United States (through what they regarded as its puppet [Syngman Rhee's] regime) at their doorstep.

It did not take much knowledge of Mao and his associates to realize that it was most unlikely that they would accept the second alternative. Not that they had any great attachment or regard for their Communist neighbors to the south. Until the outbreak of the war the relations between Beijing and Pyongyang had been quite chilly. The first Chinese ambassador did not arrive in the North Korean capital until August 1950. Though not as cynical about "proletarian internationalism" as Stalin, Mao could not feel very sentimental about North Korea, which had been a Soviet bailiwick and whose precipitate attack on the South placed the interests of the People's Republic in grave jeopardy. But the complete obliteration of the Korean Communist state was another matter. Mao and his associates believed—and who can say with full assurance that they were wrong?—that in their glee over their victory, the Americans would have second thoughts about acquiescing in Communist rule over mainland China. President Truman's repeated assurances that U.S. forces would scrupulously refrain from carrying the hostilities into China or from any activity harmful to the latter had to be taken by Beijing with a grain of salt. Why, then, did the United States stand between Taiwan and the People's Liberation Army? Even if one could believe Truman, there were other influential Americans, including the commander in chief in the Far East, who, elated by the ease with which victory was achieved over one Communist regime, were publicly drawing obvious conclusions in relation to that of China. Wouldn't the United States at the very least help the Nationalists in all sorts of ways and thus reignite the fires of an all-out civil war?

The actual decision to send Chinese forces across the Yalu River into Korea was evidently made at the special Politburo meeting of the CCP on October 1–2.[32] Some of the participants pointed out the risks inherent in a confrontation with the United States. There must have been voices, though we are not told about them, wondering whether and how staunchly the Soviet Union would stand by its ally in case the United States responded by unleashing an all-out war against the People's Republic. But the decisive voice was Mao's. On the second he decided on intervention and informed Stalin accordingly. It was also decided that the troops that engaged in fighting would do so under the guise, to be sure quite transparent, of being volunteers, rather than part of the regular army of the People's Republic. The operation was planned to begin on October 15.

The same Chinese sources claim that the Soviets had previously assured Mao that while they would not join the Chinese "volunteers" in the ground fighting, their air force would actively assist the latter. Great, therefore, was the consternation in Mao's entourage when on October 10 Stalin peremptorily informed Beijing that the USSR would not send its pilots and planes into action in Korea. Orders went out to General Peng Dehuai, designated as the commander of the Chinese People's Volunteers (CPV), that the crossing of the border had to be deferred. Simultaneously, Zhou Enlai was dispatched secretly to Moscow. The Chinese sources would not have Zhou pleading with Stalin to reverse his decision, yet that was obviously what he did. But the "genius leader of the world proletariat" would not change his mind and commit the USSR to an active role in the prospective fighting. All he would promise was that the Soviet air force would help to protect *Manchuria* against American raids. The USSR would also be ready to train the People's Republic pilots. If the Chinese went back on their decision, the Soviet dictator added, it was their business, and he hoped that at least they would allow the Korean Communists to set up an exile government on the People's Republic's territory. The Chinese sources refrain from a straightforward characterization of the Soviets' behavior. They simply inform us that it took Mao several sleepless nights before he decided to stick by his initial decision. On October 19, 1950, "volunteer" troops entered Korea.[33]

What happened during the first phase of the Chinese intervention in the Korean conflict confused Washington policy makers and has not ceased to puzzle Western historians and analysts of the war. On October 25 the "volunteers" made their presence felt by routing some South Korean units. On November 1 they engaged and pushed back some U.S. divisions; then having delivered these blows, the Chinese broke off the action on November 7. For the next three weeks their military forces disappeared from sight insofar as the U.N.-U.S. command was concerned. The mystery was compounded by a Chinese gesture quite out of keeping with their future conduct in the war. On November 21 they released and directed back to the U.N. lines a number of wounded Americans the "volunteers" had captured during their initial thrust. The standard Chinese explanation of these bizarre tactics has portrayed them as a brilliant ruse designed to lure the imperialists to advance further without taking the necessary precautions and thus make all the easier the next and devastating blow by the CPV. Western observers and future analysts have sought answers in Mao's theory of "protracted war" or some other esoteric peculiarity of the Chinese Communists' thinking on military affairs. Why the reluctance to come up with the obvious answer? Well, for the Chinese interpreters and memoir writers, that unwillingness springs from national pride; while for the Western writers the then and subsequent vehemence of Beijing's anti-American propaganda, both for domestic and external use, warrants ruling out the possibility that the break in fighting was meant as a propitiatory gesture. Yet how can we avoid the conclusion that the Chinese hoped that, having been taught a lesson, the United States would pull its forces back to the 38th parallel, or at least keep them at some distance from the Yalu and the border? Beijing then would be spared the cruel dilemma of risking what might turn out to be an all-out war with the world's most powerful nation, a war in which, considering its recent experience, it could hardly count on massive help from its ally.

Well, the lesson turned out to have had the opposite effect. Some in the American government indeed argued that "MacArthur . . . instead of pushing to and then holding the line at the Yalu River . . . should . . . hold the high ground to the south of it."[34] But the American commander-in-chief considered the Chinese maneuver as yet another bluff and insisted on pushing all the way to the Yalu. The president and his advisers were for their part victims of a not uncommon fallacy: since *they* knew that the United States did *not* plan to extend the war to China, there was no reason for the Communists to feel threatened. MacArthur was authorized to resume the advance, which he did on November 24, amazingly enough taking no precautions against a possible Chinese counteroffensive. When the latter materialized, this time on a massive scale on the twenty-sixth and twenty-seventh, the two prongs of the advancing U.S. forces found themselves in the imminent danger of entrapment. It was only with great difficulty and at the cost of heavy casualties that the army and marine units under attack managed to disengage themselves, but only to be forced to retreat as rapidly as they had advanced. December 1950 became the most calamitous month in American military history. The enemy recaptured the North Korean capital on December 4. At the end of the year, far from having erased the Communist role in North Korea, the U.N. forces were trying to establish a defensive line drawn roughly along the 38th parallel. With the New Year, a renewed Chinese offensive pushed the U.N. forces further south. Once more the Communists occupied Seoul. As of the beginning of 1951, both the Joint Chiefs of Staff in Washington and General MacArthur's headquarters in Tokyo had to give serious thought to the grim possibility of evacuating the United Nations forces from Korea.

Chinese victories and U.S. distress over them combined to portend great dangers for the People's Republic. Mao and his colleagues must have realized that they might have to pay a terrible price for inflicting defeat and humiliation upon America. They must have anticipated such U.S. reactions as that of General Bradley, who on December 3, "contemplating evacuation of Korea . . . asked how much the United States could afford to lose without further action against the PRC [People's Republic of China] and suggested what sort of reaction would occur in Congress and among the armed forces if military action against China did not follow a US withdrawal from Korea."[35] General MacArthur in his communication with Washington suggested immediate retaliatory steps, including bombing of targets in Manchuria, authorizing the Kuomintang regime to launch raids upon the mainland, and employment of its troops in action in Korea. Beyond such measures there arose a real possibility that, baffled and outraged by the drastic reversal in the course of the war, the United States would have recourse to the use of nuclear weapons. The prospect of nuclear devastation being visited on the troop concentrations and communication links in Manchuria and even upon the great urban centers of Communist China appeared so close during those hectic days of December that British Prime Minister Clement Attlee flew to Washington to implore Truman not to authorize the use of the fearsome weapons. The British and America's other allies also made it clear that they were resolutely opposed to an extension of the war against China, both on the grounds that such an extension would weaken the position of NATO in Europe, and above all, that it might well lead to Soviet intervention and escalation to World War III. For the moment, the expostulations strengthened the hand of those Washington policy makers who opposed hasty and drastic measures. But how long could counsels of moderation prevail in the face of the rising clamor that American lives were being needlessly sacrificed because the United States was fighting with one hand tied behind its back?

Despite such fearful odds against them, the Chinese (the North Koreans now clearly subordinate to them insofar as political and military decisions were concerned) continued efforts to drive the U.S.-U.N. forces out of the entire peninsula. There was a mixture of fatalism and sober calculation in Beijing's defiance of the world's most powerful nation. Ever since the events of November the Communists saw a military clash with the United States as inevitable. Better to strike the first blow and to impress the United States with Beijing's resolve in fighting capabilities so that the enemy would think twice about expanding the scope of the war. It was public knowledge that America's allies were alarmed at that prospect, and they refused to countenance full-scale hostilities against China and/or bringing the Kuomintang into the picture. And the Soviets, with their special sources of information about what was going on in Washington's inner councils,[36] had probably convinced Mao that President Truman and Secretary of State Acheson were resisting their military advisers' pleas for unilateral U.S. action against the Chinese mainland.

As in every postwar East-West crisis, the frightful possibility of the use of nuclear weapons had to weigh heavily on the judgment and actions of all actors in the drama. Though there is no evidence to back up this statement, one can hazard a guess that the entire Korean venture would not have been authorized by the Kremlin had the USSR not exploded its first A-bomb a few months prior to the invasion. And as suggested above, the psychological impact of the Soviet achievement on both the governments and public opinion in the West went far beyond what in the immediate context was its military significance: in 1950–51 the Soviets could have had but a few of the dreaded weapons, and they had not as yet produced a long-range bomber capable of reaching U.S. shores. But whatever the experts might say, after October 1949 the Americans, not to mention the British and the French, became much more apprehensive about the possibility of a confrontation with the USSR than they had been before. Thus it is understandable that when in the wake of the massive Chinese intervention the U.S. military leaders were drawing contingency plans for the use of nuclear weapons against the People's Republic, the president and his political advisers balked at such plans, fearful of what the *USSR* might do. At the height of the panic over U.S. reverses in Korea, President Truman at a press conference did indeed mention the possibility of the A-bomb being used, but immediately qualified his statement. In answer to a question whether the U.S. options to stop the Chinese onslaught included the use of the bomb, he replied, "That includes every weapon we have," but then added, "I don't want to see it used. It is a terrible weapon, and it should not be used on innocent men, women and children."[37] One does not have to question the genuineness of the president's moral objections to the use of the bomb to suggest that there was another reason why in 1950 he would not authorize what he had in 1945.

On the surface the Chinese leaders exuded what could only be described as nonchalance concerning the threat of a nuclear strike by the United States. Even before the Korean drama unfolded, Mao had characterized the A-bomb as a "paper tiger." While discussing the subject with an Indian diplomat (undoubtedly for the benefit of Washington and London), Zhou Enlai also pooh-poohed the harm the bomb might do to the People's Republic. It certainly could not be used on the battlefield, for then it would work its devastation on U.S. troops as well as those of the CPV.[38] As to its use against the territory of China, the country was vast and mostly agrarian, and could not be brought to its knees by the bombing of a few cities.

Both men were too intelligent to believe what they were saying. To be sure, even later in the hydrogen-bomb era Mao would intermittently horrify the Soviets by proclaiming that a true Communist had no reason to be afraid of a nuclear war.[39] The memories of Hiroshima and Nagasaki were still very vivid. While the superbomb and guided missiles were still to come, the U.S. arsenal at the time included some four hundred warheads, the explosive power of each weapon being five to ten times greater than that of the 1945 model.[40] There was no reason for the Chinese leadership to ignore the fact that a country with the United States' industrial potential must have accumulated by now a large stock of nuclear weapons, each more destructive than the Hiroshima prototype.

Beijing's bravado about the bomb was feigned. Behind it, however, was a realistic assumption that it was the fear of what the USSR might do in retaliation that would keep America from using the bomb against China. Indeed, this was probably the main part of Stalin's explanation to the Chinese leadership why the Soviet Union should not get directly involved in Korea: if it came to an all-out war, American nuclear bombs would rain on both the USSR and the People's Republic. It was by standing aside from actual fighting that the Soviets were most effectively protecting the Chinese comrades. And indeed, anyone studying what went on in the inner councils of the U.S. government at the time must reach the conclusion that what ultimately tipped the scales against a direct U.S. strike at Communist China, whether with A-bombs or through other means, was the apprehensive uncertainty about Soviet reactions.

Well, glasnost has not as yet helped us to determine whether such apprehensions were justified or whether, as a few in the Truman administration suspected, Stalin was ready to fight the Korean War to the last Chinese "volunteer" and would not have become unduly perturbed if a few A-bombs were dropped on China. The latter hypothesis is rather farfetched: obliteration of the People's Republic would have been a severe blow to the Soviet Union's interests and prestige.

On the other hand, nothing indicates that once the danger of America's escalation of the war against the People's Republic had become more remote, the Soviets would have been pleased by a speedy termination of the conflict. Fortunes of the war would seesaw for the next two and a half years. By the middle of 1951 it became fairly clear that barring some untoward development, neither side would be able to score a complete victory: the Chinese because they could not prevail militarily, the Americans because, as signaled by General MacArthur's dismissal in April, they would continue to observe self-imposed constraints against carrying the war beyond Korea. And it was with an eye to preventing such an untoward development that a Soviet delegate to the Security Council proposed on June 23, 1951, armistice talks between the two sides—the Chinese "volunteers" and North Koreans on the one hand, and the U.N. (U.S.) on the other. The talks began on July 10. There seemed to be every reason to expect that the negotiations should speedily lead to a cease-fire. The Chinese "volunteers" could no longer hope to push the Americans out of Korea, and the U.S., whose forces were now back around the 38th parallel, was quite ready to agree to the restoration of the pre–June 25, 1950, division of Korea. But the talks would drag on for two years, as would the intermittent fighting. Why? There were of course a number of contentious points to be settled, but none to warrant that long a delay. But if the two main parties, the U.S. and China, had every reason to wish for a speedy truce, the Soviet Union, not present at the negotiations but whose influence was very much felt, did not.

A protracted stalemate in the Far East was obviously believed by the Kremlin to be in its interests. There were several benefits accruing to Moscow: Korea distracted the United States from Europe and caused dissonance within NATO. The war led to a cooling off in American relations with the nonaligned nations, such as India. But the main gain lay in the war's demonstrating to the Chinese Communists how greatly the security of the People's Republic depended on the Soviet Union, and how desperate their situation might become were they to lose Moscow's support. Beyond the reasons already mentioned, the People's Liberation Army was dependent on the USSR for equipment and munitions. The alleged volunteers entered the war with obsolete and primitive weapons. It was very largely modern Soviet arms that enabled the CPV to dull the edge of the U.S. counteroffensive. Russia also sent up-to-date jet fighters to reduce the margin of American supremacy in the air, and to strengthen the U.S. inhibition against bombing targets in Manchuria. "To Korea went Soviet [military] advisers, including outstanding army generals."[41] In brief, China would not have been able to stay in the war and to avoid a catastrophic defeat without Soviet help.

For all of that, the costs to the USSR were minimal as compared with the huge burdens and sacrifices, not to mention risks, incurred by the People's Republic. The only Soviet personnel engaged in actual fighting consisted of a small number of pilots sent to defend the Yalu River bridges and the CPV's communication routes between Manchuria and the front. They wore Chinese uniforms and in the event of capture were to identify themselves as citizens of the PRC.[42] China, on the other hand, sent to Korea in the course of the war 2,300,000 troops, or two-thirds of its field army, including its entire armored force and most of its aviation units. The "volunteers" suffered almost 400,000 casualties.[43] Among those killed was one of Mao's sons. In view of such sacrifices it is almost unbelievable that Soviet military equipment sent to the Chinese did not come free. They had to pay their Russian allies for the arms they used in fighting what was essentially Russia's war.

In some of the recent Chinese accounts of the war, criticism of the Soviets, though muted, still comes through. A member of the delegation that was sent to Moscow in 1951 to procure modern weapons said: "It is easy for the Soviets to be cocky and chauvinistic. . . . Their representatives, after we stated our needs, declared sarcastically . . . that to meet our demands they would have to build another trans-Siberian railway. . . . Their great power chauvinism did not form overnight. . . . They were afraid of offending the United States and bringing trouble upon themselves." And much of the equipment finally purchased from the Russians turned out to be defective, adds our author.[44]

The military exertions in Korea also had to have serious consequences for the economy of a country that had barely begun its recovery from a civil war. Politically, the Mao regime felt it necessary to respond to the emergency abroad by stepping up repression at home. In the course of 1951 the struggle against the alleged counterrevolutionaries led to the imprisonment and execution of more than 2 million people.[45] Both its foreign and domestic policies made it unlikely that the PRC would, in the foreseeable future, be able to establish any meaningful links with the West, something that appeared quite close before June 25, 1950.

Mao and his colleagues must have felt acutely the unfairness of the predicament into which they had been thrust by their Soviet comrades. For reasons we have already discussed, they had to contain their bitterness during the next few years. Even after Stalin's death, and in view of the completely changed nature of Sino-Soviet relations, it would not have been in Beijing's interest to dispel the fiction of the "unbreakable friendship" between the two major Communist powers. But then after the dramatic break with the Soviets in 1960, one would have expected the Chinese sources to abandon their inhibitions and speak frankly about the Korean War and how they were duped by the Soviets. Yet, while indulging prior to 1982 in the most violent invective against Khrushchev and his successors, the Chinese Communists chose to show remarkable restraint in criticizing the Soviets' behavior during the Stalin era. It was national pride that has not allowed them to state unambiguously that they had been awed and manipulated by the Soviet tyrant. Mao and other leaders obviously felt that it would be humiliating for themselves and deeply disillusioning to their people to admit that in intervening in Korea, Communist China was not responding to the call of "proletarian internationalism" but was acting under compulsion. And as so often happens in such cases, some of the propagators of the legend may have convinced themselves that it was selfless idealism that had led to the sending of the "volunteers" to fight the Yankee imperialists, and not the web of intrigue woven around the People's Republic by the Kremlin.

At the same time, the trauma of the war, not of their own making, but which they had to fight, left an indelible mark on the Chinese Communists' attitude toward the Elder Brother. Never again would Beijing trust the Soviets or believe that the Kremlin could or would put the interests of the world revolution above those of the USSR.

The experience of the Soviets' duplicity in 1950 accounts for what otherwise would be inexplicable: Mao's regime's violent and vituperative response to Moscow when the latter, after the first American bombing of North Vietnam in 1965, proposed joint steps to help the fellow Communist state. On their face the Soviets' proposals were reasonable and straightforward: the People's Republic was to allow Soviet military supplies for embattled Hanoi to be transported across its territory. Beijing's refusal was couched in such abusive terms that it was almost incoherent. Mao must have felt that here was but the first move in yet another Kremlin game to entrap China into a confrontation with the United States.

The Korean War thus laid the psychological groundwork for the Sino-Soviet dispute of the 1960s and 1970s, and that split in turn was to be a major cause of the erosion of the ideological pretensions of

Communism and eventually of the catastrophe that has overcome the movement in recent years.

The course of the war after 1951 need detain us only insofar as the deadlock bears on the relationship between the two Communist powers. Beijing could register several other occasions demonstrating how one-sided that relationship was in terms of who profited from it. One such example was the conference held in San Francisco in September 1951 summoned by the United States to rush through a peace treaty with Japan. Communist China was not invited, and it could not have been pleased by the USSR's attendance at the conference. To be sure, Deputy Foreign Minister Andrei Gromyko, after having failed to block the treaty, refused to sign the final draft. Even so, the Americans showed themselves rather deferential to Soviet susceptibilities. In the treaty Japan was made to renounce formally southern Sakhalin and the Kurile Islands, its pre-1945 territories now under Soviet occupation, an act of courtesy toward the Soviet Union that might have at least been postponed until such time as it deigned to sign the peace treaty.

Another example of the Chinese Communists' unequal status vis-à-vis the USSR came during Zhou Enlai's visit to Moscow in August 1952, this time not a secret. Again the negotiations were rather protracted, the visit lasting one month. In the end, the Chinese plenipotentiaries succeeded in wresting from their covetous hosts the Manchurian Railway complex which was to be returned to the People's Republic by the end of the year. But another piece of Soviet property on Chinese soil which Moscow had promised to relinquish in the Friendship Treaty of 1950, the naval base of Port Arthur, would remain in its hands "until such time as peace treaties between the Chinese People's Republic and Japan and the Soviet Union are concluded." At the time, prospects for such treaties being concluded in the foreseeable future were extremely dim and the provision would imply that the Soviets might retain Port Arthur indefinitely. This emendation of the 1950 treaty was allegedly made at the express request of China and rationalized on the grounds that the presence of the Soviet garrison and naval units on the territory of the PRC gave it additional protection from "the recurrence of Japanese aggression." Equally unconvincing for those who knew the real story of relations between the two powers was another statement of Zhou's that the inviolable friendship between China and the USSR would extend "not only from day to day, but from generation to generation."[46]

How long was Stalin ready to let the People's Republic continue its unequal struggle against the United States? We don't and probably never will know a precise answer to that question. Complete destruction of the Communist regime in China would have emboldened the West to the point where the Soviet empire in Europe might have found itself imperiled. But one who bore the responsibility for millions of deaths of his own countrymen was unlikely to have flinched at even the most grievous devastation visited upon a "fraternal" country if that could help the Soviet Union to preserve its domination of the Communist world.

In the long run, such a ruthless and perfidious policy was bound to backfire. The experience of having withstood alone the challenge of war with the world's most powerful nation enhanced the morale and nationalism of the Chinese Communists and allowed China within a few years to really "stand up" and defy its alleged protector and ally.

While official declarations bespoke friendship, the Soviet media hardly concealed the Kremlin's ambivalent attitude toward the Chinese comrades. The press, for the most part, attributed the setbacks suffered by the United States equally to the North Korean and Chinese armies in that order. The feats of the Chinese People's Volunteers were ungraciously, if realistically, qualified by reminders that they were made possible because of the self-imposed restraint of the United States and that that restraint sprang in turn from the Americans' fear of the USSR. This motif would be echoed by the Soviet historians down to our own day. For example: "In the failure of the American plans to expand aggression the decisive role was played by the Soviet-Chinese alliance. This was more than once admitted by American public figures who lamented especially the fact that the alliance was the main restraint upon 'free use' of American naval and air force."[47] The more recent Russian analysts of Sino-Soviet relations must find the Korean War period embarrassing, for they virtually ignore it. One such work of 635 pages devotes but two brief paragraphs to the subject.[48]

Prolongation of the conflict was not without certain risks for the USSR. As exemplified by their unexpected reaction to the June 1950 invasion, the Americans' moods and moves in foreign policy were not easily predictable. By 1952 public opinion was increasingly restless and exasperated by the stalemated war and the restraints that the Truman administration observed in its conduct. How long would Washington be able to resist pressures epitomized by the hero's welcome accorded to the dismissed commander in chief in the Far East and the general acclaim with which MacArthur's motto, "In War There Is No Substitute for Victory," was received by the nation? And it was not out of the question that not only China but also the senior Communist power might suffer from the consequences of the Americans' wrath and impatience.

The Kremlin sought to minimize such dangers by a variety of conciliatory gestures to the West. The most important among them was the March 10, 1952, Moscow initiative on Germany. The Soviet Union proposed negotiations between the four occupying powers that would lead to a peace treaty with, and unification of, Germany. The USSR was willing to contemplate its complete withdrawal of the occupation troops, and—this went quite beyond its previous position on the subject—would not object if unified Germany rearmed. There was a catch from the West's point of view. The new Germany would be pledged to neutrality. Still, the proposal went quite a way to meet the West's postulates. On the face of it, the Kremlin was willing to sacrifice the German Democratic Republic, for no one could have any illusions even then as to how the German Communists would fare in free elections. By now the experiences of Yalta and Potsdam had taught the United States to be wary of any, even the most conciliatory, Soviet invitations to the negotiating table, so Washington quite peremptorily refused even to discuss the proposal. If the Soviets really meant it, then the West missed an opportunity that would not recur for another thirty-seven years, to erase the GDR and secure a united democratic German state.

Despite its rejection of the proposal, Washington must have felt reassured by its conciliatory tone. It helped dissipate the lingering suspicions that Moscow had started the Korean adventure so as to distract U.S. attention from Europe, where the Soviets would thus be able to victimize yet another country. But what was Beijing to make of the Soviets' initiative on Germany? If the USSR did not want to intervene directly in Korea, then it could at least succor its sorely tried ally by increasing its pressure on the West elsewhere. Instead, the Soviets were evidently trying to appease the imperialists and offering to sacrifice Communist Germany!

Time was growing short for the man who had been devising and in most cases getting away with such intricate deceptions. Stalin's last public speech was delivered at the Nineteenth Congress of the Communist Party of the Soviet Union held in October 1952. Though it was addressed to problems of world Communism, there was no special mention of Mao's party. It was lumped together with other People's Democracies. The only foreign Communist leaders named in the speech were Thorez and Togliatti, who were singled out for praise because of their declarations that the French and Italian people would not fight against the Soviet Union. The artificer of the Korean War did not neglect to add that "as for the Soviet Union, its interests are altogether indivisible from the cause of world peace."[49]

In January 1953 came ominous signs that the tyrant was preparing yet another mass purge of the party and state apparatus. But on March 6 the Soviet people were informed that as of 9:50 P.M. the preceding day, "the heart of Lenin's comrade in arms, the inspired continuator of Lenin's cause, the wise leader and teacher of the Communist Party and the Soviet people—Josif Vissarionovich Stalin—has stopped beating." And in this very same statement Stalin's heirs felt constrained to emphasize what he himself refused to acknowlege only a few months before: the special role of China in the Communist world and China's importance to the USSR: "The people of the Soviet Union are, under the banner of proletarian internationalism, strengthening and developing in all ways fraternal friendship with the great Chinese people."[50]

The changes in Soviet foreign policy that occurred after Stalin's death can be traced to his successors' acute feeling of insecurity. The sorcerer who cast a spell on the West that made it greatly overestimate Russia's strength, who maneuvered the Chinese into a Sisyphus-like labor of contesting Korea with the Americans, was gone, and his disciples were too unsure of themselves to continue such dangerous games. Their greatest fear centered on the domestic situation: Stalin's henchmen were afraid of the Soviet people and of each other. They realized they had to initiate a thaw, i.e., to discard the most oppressive features of Stalinism. Their state of mind was to be graphically portrayed by Khrushchev: "We were scared—really scared. We were afraid the thaw might unleash a flood, which we wouldn't be able to control and which could drown us. How could it drown us? It could have overflowed the banks of the Soviet riverbed and formed a tidal wave which would have washed all the barriers and retaining walls of our society."[51] Not a bad description of what actually began to happen—some thirty-five years later.

One could no more run world Communism in Stalin's manner than one could rule Russia in the old way. The struggle for the succession between the despot's satraps, their all too visible sense of vulnerability both of the USSR vis-à-vis the West and of the Soviet system domestically, made it impossible for the Kremlin even to try to control the "fraternal parties" as it had done prior to March 5, 1953. Conversely, the affairs of the latter assumed special importance for the new bosses of the Kremlin. It would have been preposterous to suggest that Stalin's control of the levers of power was in any sense threatened or weakened by Tito's apostasy. But under the new order of things whoever ruled the Soviet Union was no longer immune from some of the pressures and vulnerabilities that attend political leaders of democracies. In the United States the Democrats' resounding defeat in the 1952 elections was due in some measure to the legend that the Truman administration "lost China" as well as to its getting involved in an unwinnable war. None of Stalin's successors would be in a position where he could be sure that a major setback in foreign policy, especially another defection from the Communist camp, might not sweep him from power. Conversely, the strength and viability of other Communist regimes, their continued deference to Moscow—now to be secured not only by intimidation but up to a degree through diplomacy—would rebound to the credit of the man at the top of the Soviet establishment. And of course in this connection Sino-Soviet relations assumed new and special importance.

How dramatic a change in those relations was vividly illustrated within days of the great event. On March 10 the Soviet press carried Mao's fulsome tribute to Stalin. The prose was what could be expected: ". . . the greatest genius of the era, great teacher of the world Communist movement . . ." But the picture accompanying the panegyric had some unusual features. It purported to be a photograph of Mao with Stalin and the current (but not for long) number-one man in the Soviet hierarchy, Georgi Malenkov, taken allegedly at the time of the chairman's visit to Moscow. The message was clear: here you had a proof that the new prime minister of the USSR stood, so to speak, in apostolic succession to Stalin, and had the blessing of the most prestigious leader of foreign Communism. It did not take much power of observation for the reader to note something unnatural in the way the three gentlemen had posed for the picture. In fact, it was a fake, a crude composograph made from the picture taken at the ceremony of the signing of the Sino-Soviet alliance on February 14, 1950. Malenkov was there, but as one of about twenty other dignitaries surrounding the two bosses. Only a regime in considerable disarray could have perpetrated such a transparent propaganda trick; how many of the readers would not recall the genuine photograph which all the

Soviet newspapers carried just three years before? Only a leadership very unsure of itself would try to bolster its prestige by invoking the moral support of a foreign Communist leader.

Beijing thus became the immediate and chief beneficiary of Stalin's death. A Chinese economic mission had been in Moscow cooling its heels for several months. On March 26 the Soviets signed new agreements providing extensive economic assistance to the People's Republic, including large loans, provisions for sending technical experts, and technology transfers.

Zhou Enlai, who represented China at the obsequies (with the obvious exception of Yugoslavia, the People's Republic's regime was the only Communist one not represented by its top leader, Mao choosing to be absent), was given the honor of being one of the four principal pallbearers, the others being the ruling trio of Malenkov, Molotov, and Lavrenti Beria. Also during those March days, V. V. Kuznetsov, then close to the summit of Soviet officialdom, replaced a professional diplomat as the Soviet envoy to Beijing. All such steps testified to a rather frantic attempt to gain the Chinese Communists' goodwill and make up for past indignities. The capitalists, the communiqué on Stalin's death asserted, calculated that "the heavy loss we have borne will lead to disorder and confusion in our ranks." Sino-Soviet unity was the best way to confound such expectations.

But Mao's regime needed more than such honors and the recognition of its new status in the Kremlin's eyes. Its first priority had to be an end to the burdens and dangers of the Korean War. With a Republican administration in office in Washington, the dangers escalated. The new president announced on February 2 that the Seventh Fleet would no longer bar Chiang's forces on Taiwan from attacking the mainland. This was largely symbolic because in fact the American navy had not interfered with the Nationalists' occasional raids on coastal points, and Taiwan's armed forces were hardly in a position to launch a full-scale invasion. Still, the "unleashing of Chiang Kai-shek" was a portent of worse things to come. General Eisenhower was to write in his memoirs that he conveyed a warning to Beijing through Indian intermediaries that unless a cease-fire was expeditiously arranged, the United States would rethink its inhibition about the use of nuclear weapons. Even if such threats had actually been made, the cease-fire negotiations continued to be stymied, with the main stumbling block being the Communists' insistence that the prisoners of war in U.N. hands be repatriated rather than being given a free choice as to where to go after being released (which would enable Chinese "volunteers" to opt for Taiwan and North Koreans for the South).

"Then on March 30 Zhou Enlai, returning from Stalin's funeral in Moscow, announced a major Chinese concession. On the largest single point of disagreement, he reversed the previous Communist insistence that all Chinese and North Korean prisoners must be repatriated by force, if necessary."[52] Even if circumstantial, the evidence that it was Stalin's death that removed obstacles to a cease-fire is well nigh overwhelming. Just to quote one source, McGeorge Bundy, a former National Security adviser, wrote: "A Chinese friend of high professional standing told me in 1983 that he had heard from three separate individuals that they had been told by Zhou Enlai himself that Stalin's death was what made the armistice possible."[53] The armistice long sought by both Washington and Beijing finally materialized on July 27.

For the Americans the lesson of the conflict remained ambiguous. As against some public figures and analysts who would insist that "we cannot afford new Koreas," there were those arguing that, on the contrary, in the nuclear age the United States could not afford any other kind of war. In the early 1960s this ambiguity colored American policy makers' perceptions of the situation in Southeast Asia and was to weigh heavily on Washington's policies during the ordeal of Vietnam.

For the Chinese the lesson of Korea was quite unambiguous: they had been used by the Russians. The fiction of the "unbreakable friendship" of the two regimes would be maintained by Beijing only as long as it would suit its purposes, which turned out to be not quite seven years.

By amassing so much power over world Communism, Stalin made it almost inevitable that once he was gone the unity of the movement would start unraveling. And eventually, like the edifice of Soviet power at home, proletarian internationalism would collapse under the debris of Stalinism.

4

LIFTING THE BURDEN
OF THE PAST

"THERE WERE DEMONSTRATIONS IN EAST BERLIN.... The demonstrators . . . carried signs and shouted slogans demanding freedom. . . . Ministers who tried to address the crowds were shouted down. On the next day the demonstrations developed into riots, in the course of which government buildings were set on fire [and] Russian flags were torn down."[1]

No, the date of these reports is not the fall of 1989 or the winter of 1990. These disturbances took place in East Germany in the spring of 1953.

The sense of weakness and vulnerability the Soviet rulers experienced following the event of March 5, 1953, communicated itself to their subject peoples. In East Germany the popular unrest was triggered—as it would be in 1989—by the satellite regime attempting, hurriedly and awkwardly, to put on a liberal image. In late May the East German government acknowledged publicly its errors in connection with the hasty collectivization and nationalization of small industry and retail trade, and promised to undo those measures. The party and government recognized that sovietization of East German society was responsible for "numerous persons having left the Republic."[2] Contrite German Communists promised, rather unconvincingly, to stop political harassment of students and intellectuals. And, again sounding like their unfortunate successors in the moment of truth in 1989, the German satraps of the Kremlin sought to beguile their subjects with promises to strive for greater intercourse and eventual unification with West Germany. "In its resolution the Politburo has been guided by the great aim of German unification which demands from both sides concrete measures that facilitate drawing together. . . . The Politburo decided . . . to facilitate traffic between the German Democratic Republic and West Germany. . . . Scientists and artists in particular are to be enabled to attend conferences in West Germany."[3]

Such liberalization was currently being promised, and to a degree practiced, by other satellite regimes. But the case of East Germany is especially intriguing. There had been recurrent rumors that the then ruling Kremlin trio of Malenkov, Beria, and Molotov had become seriously alarmed about the dangers inherent in the international position of the USSR vis-à-vis the West. With their master gone, with the new administration in Washington threatening to replace containment by policies leading to the liberation of captive nations and the "rollback" of the Communist sphere, the triumvirs reputedly were willing to go quite far in appeasing the West on the German question. The same rumors, which were to be confirmed in 1991, identified Beria as one who was ready virtually to concede East Germany to the West. It may well be that this is what Khrushchev had in mind when he wrote in his memoirs: "More than once I'd confided to Malenkov and Bulganin that I regarded Beria as an adventurist in foreign policy. . . . The enemies of socialism and of the international Communist movement saw what Beria was up to, and would have made good use of it for their own purposes if Beria had not been unmasked and removed."[4]

We are still waiting for glasnost to shed light on the complex intrigues and maneuvers that followed Stalin's death, both within and without the Soviet Union. And here one of the main mysteries touches on East Germany. The Kremlin had clearly inspired the East Germans' liberal gestures. At the same time, Moscow made some conciliatory moves on its own. The Soviet military commander in East Germany was divested of political authority, which was transferred to a civilian high commissioner. And the latter was formally charged with the duty "to maintain relations with the representatives of the occupation authorities of the U.S.A., Britain and France in all questions of an all-German character arising out of the agreed decisions of the Four Powers on Germany."[5] Such language had not been used by the Soviet government since before the Berlin blockade of 1948!

All the more puzzling were the measures the German Communist government took in the middle of June, when it raised the standard work norms, thus in effect cutting wages. Against the background of the previous concessions and greatly raised popular expectations, this was clearly a provocation and led to the demonstrations and riots of which we spoke. But who was behind this provocation? Was it the Berlin Communist regime, fearful of being orphaned by Moscow and hoping that a revolt would bring a Soviet military intervention? Or did the Kremlin decide it could not afford even the appearance of being ready to sacrifice East Germany, and thus sought an occasion to display its mailed fist? In any case, this preview of Budapest in 1956 and of the Prague Spring of 1968 ended, as they would, with Soviet tanks and soldiers crushing the uprising.

The East-West dialogue over Germany reverted to its post–Berlin blockade pattern. But the suppression of the revolt was not followed by a reversion to Stalinist practices. The satellite regime revoked the increased work norms, and announced other social and economic concessions to the population. Several officials were discharged, and some imprisoned. As Khrushchev would try to explain it much later, "We knew we would have to find other ways of establishing East Germany on a solid Marxist-Leninist footing. . . . We would have to strip the thin coating of Stalinism from our policies and reactivate the ideas of Lenin."[6] Alas, that coating was quite thick, and it would take more than thirty years to rub off.

The East German drama was soon followed by one in the Kremlin: the arrest on June 26, 1953, of Lavrenti Beria. Of all the ironies attending Soviet history this was surely one of the greatest: the most opprobrious of Stalin's henchmen was purged (he was to be executed in December) because in his bid for supreme power he advocated liberal nationality policies within the USSR and a rapprochement with the West!

The events in East Germany during that tempestuous spring of 1953 are instructive on many counts. Stalin's successors clearly lacked his aplomb and confidence that they could always gauge correctly the mood and potential reactions of the Western capitals, maintain a high level of tension in East-West relations, and yet avoid war. Just as they had sought to humor Mao's susceptibilities, the new leaders looked for ways to reduce the risk of a confrontation with the United States. How great that risk was estimated to be in that year of Stalin's death and the Eisenhower-Dulles team taking over in Washington is vividly illustrated by the increase in Soviet military effectives: from the pre–Korean War figure of 2.8 million men under arms, they would expand by 1955 to 5.8 million.[7]

The desire to assuage the West's fears was evident in a speech on

Soviet foreign policy delivered on August 8, 1953, by Malenkov, then ensconced (though already quite shakily) as top man in the Kremlin. The speech marked the passage from the most tense period of the cold war to what would be dubbed "peaceful coexistence." The prime minister disavowed Stalin's territorial claims on Turkey, one of the main factors that had led to the Truman Doctrine. Bound also to find a favorable reception in the West was the announcement of the restoration of diplomatic relations with Israel,[8] and that the USSR, as a token of its desire to improve relations with Yugoslavia and Greece, was returning its ambassadors to their capitals.

What undoubtedly led to the greatest relief in the West was Malenkov's avowal that the new weapons (hydrogen-bomb devices had by now been tested both by the United States and the USSR) made a new world war too horrible to contemplate. Such a war would have catastrophic consequences for *all* belligerents. This was a new tack for Soviet propaganda, which hitherto had proclaimed that a nuclear confrontation, destructive as it was bound to be all around, would finish off only capitalism, with Communism surviving and continuing its advance. Though clearly sheer bluster, this contrived equanimity at the prospect of a nuclear war had to frighten the West. And now this admission of the obvious by the top Soviet leader augured the possibility of realistic East-West negotiations on the contentious issues.

Alas, on second thought the Kremlin must have decided that it would be counterproductive to have the West's fears *completely* dispelled. Malenkov's admission was soon retracted, and the theme of Communism being able to survive a nuclear holocaust would not be abandoned by the Soviets until 1977. It was then in a speech delivered in Tula that Brezhnev admitted that there could be no victor in a nuclear war. But it was only with Gorbachev that the motif of the unwinnability of such wars would be fully developed and emphasized by the Soviet leadership.

The tentative character of Soviet moves on East Germany and the nuclear question was a good indication of the volatile character of Soviet politics during the transition period. But that volatility was due not merely to the struggle for succession. At stake and discussed in the inner Kremlin councils was not only what changes were needed in Soviet domestic and foreign policies, but also a new approach to the problems of world Communism. The workers' uprising in the GDR signaled the need for rethinking the status of East European countries. The lesson was obvious. One must no longer rely primarily on terror and police methods to keep the "fraternal countries" in line. Nor could their economic and social policies continue to be ordained by Moscow down to the last detail, with the Soviets also directly controlling the personnel of the army and the secret police. Persisting in such practices and in economic exploitation of those countries ran the risk of further popular uprisings. And the local Communist parties, weakened by the purges, would not be able to handle the growing unrest.

As the Kremlin's blueprint for East Europe was to unfold during the next three years, it became clear that its dominant faction was far from wishing that the Soviet empire be transformed into a commonwealth, where each member would be free to arrange its internal affairs and have the right to endorse or to stand apart from the others' policies. Moscow, while relaxing its grip, insisted on having the final say on foreign policy and defense matters. Nor would Poland or Bulgaria be allowed to abandon or significantly vary the one-party, Communist structure of its politics and society.

Yet it would be incorrect to see the Kremlin's effort to resuscitate "proletarian internationalism" as insincere or motivated only by prudential reasons. Some who presided over the destinies of Soviet Communism in the post-1953 period, certainly Nikita Khrushchev, were genuinely committed to recapturing what they believed had been the dynamic and humanitarian features of early Communism. Freed from the excrescences of Stalinism, they believed Communism would once again become the catalyst of social and economic progress. Shared ideology would become a more important bond between countries of the socialist camp. And Marxism-Leninism, no longer prostituted as a rationale for despotism and once again truly internationalist in its spirit, would greatly enhance its appeal not only to its traditional constituency—the workers and intellectuals of the industrialized countries—but also to the new nations emerging in the wake of the dissolution of the old colonial empires.

Unlike their successors in the eighties, the would-be architects of the first perestroika were ideologues, their outlook confined within the categories of Marxism-Leninism, their formative years coinciding with the drama and romance of the Revolution, the Civil War, and the first years of the construction of socialism and the heady visions of Communism inheriting the world. Nikita Khrushchev, who was born in 1894 and joined the party in 1918, epitomized the generation of party activists for whom Communism was not just the official cult and the stilted phrases learned in the party school, but a living faith that enabled a small detachment of its followers to conquer a vast country, hold it against overwhelming odds in a civil war, and then in the face of the hostility of the entire capitalist world, to raise Russia—the Soviet Union—to the status of a superpower. It would have been inconceivable for such people to see all those developments, as well as the prodigious spread of Communism all over the world, as just accidents of history. The world mission of Communism, the capitalists' malevolent designs against the Fatherland of Socialism, the identity of interests among states belonging to the socialist camp, were for Stalin's successors self-evident truths.

To be sure, this fidelity to the ideology had been tempered by more than thirty years' experience of wielding power and managing the international Communist movement. The traditional goals and slogans were no longer believed in or pursued with the same intensity: the world revolution had long been a distant goal rather than, as to Lenin and his Bolsheviks, something very tangible and a guide to action. The hostile attitude of the capitalist powers did not preclude, indeed in the nuclear age urged, the necessity of peaceful coexistence. Soon after the October Revolution, Lenin would have been willing to sacrifice his hold on Russia if by doing so he could have precipitated the triumph of Communism in Germany or another highly industrialized country. But by 1953 no Soviet leader, no matter how ideologically or internationally minded, would have been ready to give up his party's or his country's vital interests for the sake of even the most spectacular success of Communism on the world stage.

This mixture of Soviet nationalism and ideological fervor was well exemplified in the man who presided over the preview of perestroika in the 1950s. Nikita Khrushchev surged to the front in the summer of 1953 when he took over the top post in the party, which Malenkov had to give up when he became chairman of the Council of Ministers. By the middle of 1954 it was the first secretary ("general" in the title having been jettisoned as being too reminiscent of Stalin) who was clearly the number-one man in the Soviet hierarchy, though this fact was not formally acknowledged until Malenkov's resignation as prime minister in February 1955. Most of the domestic measures of de-Stalinization, such as the repudiation of mass terror and the curbs on the secret police powers, probably represented a consensus in the Politburo, where there were still diehard Stalinists such as Molotov and Lazar Kaganovich. It is also quite likely that there were no dissenters among the elite when it came to the adoption of a friendlier attitude toward the West. But as events were to show, it was mainly Nikita Khrushchev who insisted on and carried out a more basic restructuring of domestic and intra-Communist-state policies in a more liberal direction. As a former Yugoslav ambassador to Moscow, not particularly friendly to the first secretary, was to write, "Khrushchev opposed the official ideologists and theoreticians in the Soviet Communist party and state, [those] who could still only repeat the old Stalinist slogans about socialism and Communism."[9]

Viewed from the perspective of the late eighties, the changes that Soviet society and world Communism underwent during what might be called the Khrushchev era[10] appear unsubstantial compared with those undertaken by Gorbachev. But the latter's virtual dismantling of the structure that Lenin had built would not have been possible without his predecessor's tortuous, and in some sense psycholocially more difficult, repudiation of Stalin. True, Khrushchev did not preside over anything that might be described as a basic reform of the system, nor did he intend to. The system's essential characteristics—the police state, one party's monopoly of power, and the individual's strict subordination to the state—emerged virtually unaffected by the post–March 5, 1953, changes. But following that date it was as if the whole Soviet society of the vast country gradually recovered from a spell that prior to March 1953 produced intermittent moods of frantic fear and hysterical exaltation. In more prosaic terms, the Soviet Union cast off a terror culture and took the first difficult steps toward becoming a civil society.

What it was before the tyrant's death is best conveyed by Osip Mandelstam's poem which, denounced to the secret police by at least one of the six people to whom it was read, cost the poet first his freedom and then his life. There under the rule of the "murderer and the killer of the peasants" the people's sense of reality became attenuated to the point where "we live as if there were no ground under our feet—ten paces away and our voices cannot be heard."

With Khrushchev that landscape of fear began to recede. Unfree as the Soviet people still were, they could begin to feel solid ground under their feet. And then society began to hear voices of protest and dissent. To be sure, most who thus spoke would soon be chastised or silenced. But now their courage and sacrifice were not in vain. And occasionally even the regime would listen. Khrushchev authorized the publication of a novella by a hitherto entirely unknown writer. With the appearance of Solzhenitsyn's *One Day in the Life of Ivan Denisovich*, the spell of fearful silence would be definitely broken; the voice of protest against what had been and at the time had not entirely ceased to be the inhuman Soviet system would be heard not only by Soviet society but also by the entire world.

By thus allowing a larger, if by Western standards still inadequate, scope for free expression, Khrushchev hoped to revivify Marxism-Leninism and once more have ideology rather than fear serve as the foundation and source of the legitimacy of Communism at home and abroad. But as the future was to show, he had unwittingly opened a Pandora's box from which would emerge criticisms of the by now stale ideological formulas and scathing depictions of the realities of Soviet life. Dissent would become a crucial stage on the road to perestroika.

The same philosophy and hope that were behind the domestic changes dictated the Khrushchev regime's policies in its East European empire. The Kremlin not only permitted but urged measures of liberalization in its satellites. But if the wager on ideology was to prove countereffective in the Soviet Union, it became much more so in the other Communist-ruled countries. What enabled Soviet society to withstand the shock of de-Stalinization was the fact that the regime could count on and identify itself with the emotional appeal of what was officially described as Soviet patriotism, a euphemism for Russian nationalism with a thin ideological coating. Even so, many of the non-Russian citizens of the USSR shared in the patriotic elation at the victory in the war, and at their country's rise to the status of a superpower. It was Soviet patriotism more than ideology that now provided the main element of social cohesion and gave the regime legitimacy in the eyes of its subjects. By contrast, Leninism, though still meaningful and a path to the promised land for the Communists of Nikita Khrushchev's generation, was no longer a living faith for most of the party members, not to mention the population at large. Much as the first secretary would try to restore the original revolutionary faith as the main prop of the system, he too would be constrained to emphasize the Soviet Union's growing strength and influence throughout the world as the chief vindication of the Communist Party's rule.

But Polish, Hungarian, and other nationalisms could not serve as allies and sources of popular support for the local regimes. On the contrary, whatever popular support accrued to these regimes in the years immediately after the war was due to their carrying out very badly needed economic and social reforms in countries which with some exceptions had, prior to 1939, been governed undemocratically. But even during that initial, largely constructive phrase, Communism was resented by the Poles, Hungarians, and other captive populations because it was felt to be synonymous with foreign rule. That feeling was greatly enhanced when following Tito's apostasy in 1948 the East European regimes were ordered by Moscow to become both more repressive and doctrinaire in their policies. Terror, forced collectivization, persecution of religious bodies (especially the Catholic Church), all those measures to recast East European societies in the Stalinist mold, made Communism synonymous with a repressive and exploitative alien rule. And conversely, even in a country like Czechoslovakia, where the arrival of the Red Army during World War II had been greeted as liberation rather than an exchange of one foreign master for another, the Soviet Union now stood compromised as the overlord of its tyrannous regime.

Characteristically, only one Communist government enhanced its popularity between 1948 and 1953. As we have already seen, prior to 1948 Tito's regime had been the most doctrinaire and repressive among those of the satellites. Yet after that year the Yugoslav Communists' courageous stand against Moscow won them the respect and grudging support of most of its opponents. The lesson was clear: Communism in power could gain genuine popular support only if it was not seen as the servant of a foreign state, and if it did not run against national pride and interests.

And so it was against formidable odds that the Kremlin would wage its campaign to change the image of Marxism-Leninism in its East European empire. The first steps in the campaign were intended to induce the satellites to follow the example of the Fatherland of Socialism and to purge their politics of Stalinism. In the USSR the cult of the infallible and omnipotent leader was replaced by the notion of collective leadership of the party and the state. And so in Eastern Europe, Moscow's principal satraps hastened to demote the local bosses and reduce them to the status parallel to Malenkov's in the Soviet Union: first among equals within the ruling oligarchy, rather than as they had appeared before March 1953—little Stalins.

A more substantive and welcome dividend of the tyrant's death to millions of East Europeans was the dismantling of the mass terror that ever since 1948 had been spreading like a plague over the area and which except for Stalin's fortunate demise would in all likelihood have reached the horrifying dimensions of the Soviet purges of 1936 through 1939. In every satellite except one the terror had been highlighted by show trials of erstwhile Communist leaders, who like members of Lenin's old guard in similar dramas in Moscow between 1936 and 1938 were made to plead guilty to opprobrious charges, centered on their alleged Titoism and spying for the West. The main figures in those productions were László Rajk in Hungary, Traicho Kostov in Bulgaria, and most recently (November 1952) the former general secretary of the Communist Party of Czechoslovakia, Rudolf Slansky. They and most of their fellow accused, also high party officials, had been sent to their doom. The absurdity of the charges—all of those sentenced were subsequently fully exonerated by their regimes—reinforces the impression that in the Kremlin's view those phantasmagoric theatricalities had nothing to do with their actors' real or alleged transgressions. Periodic winnowing of the satellite parties' elites was simply a prophylactic measure designed to inoculate the local parties against the virus of Titoism or any other form of disloyalty to the Kremlin. But again, as in Russia during the terrible thirties, terror claimed victims not only at the top of the political pyramid. It was spreading to all strata of society.

And now with the maker of this surrealistic world gone, the pall of fear would be gradually lifted between 1953 and 1956. The satellites reverted to their pre-1948 status of being "normal" police states.

Of all the Communist regimes, the Polish one had been most refractory in bowing to the Kremlin's injunction to apply systematic terror. The inherent unpopularity of Communism in this predominantly Catholic country with strong traditions of anti-Russian sentiments mitigated against Moscow's Polish satraps applying too hastily a Soviet prescription and probably accounted for Moscow's atypical patience on that count. To be sure, when it came to mass arrests of its real and alleged opponents, and to their tortures at the hands of the secret police, the Polish government was not far behind the others in the satellite herd. But Warsaw had refused to make what after 1948 was considered an obligatory sacrificial offering to the vengeful deity in the Kremlin: to stage a show trial and send disgraced Communist notables to their doom.

The Kremlin's patience, however, had its limits. And so there is little doubt that had Stalin survived a few more months Władysław Gomułka and a number of other fallen Polish Communist greats would have shared the fate of Kostov and Slansky.

In fact, unlike in the case of the others, chosen, it would seem at random, to be stamped as accomplices of "Tito, Zionists, and Wall Street," there were cogent reasons for Gomułka's being on Moscow's purge list. Not that this uncomplicated and, as the events later on would suggest, rather simple-minded man was anything but a loyal Communist, or in any sense disloyal to the Soviet Union. But there is no doubt that his Communism was tempered by a measure of nationalism. In 1947 he had reservations about the creation of the Cominform, believing realistically that it would only institutionalize and increase Soviet interference in the affairs of the People's Democracies. Later he was reported to have been in favor of conciliating rather than dealing summarily with Tito. A homegrown Communist rather than one who had spent long years in Russia, Gomułka, while still in the underground during the Nazi occupation, was selected by his comrades rather than appointed by Moscow. Altogether a formidable array of sins by the pre-1953 Kremlin's criteria. And he was Polish to boot![11]

In 1948 after his colleagues on the Central Committee chorused their indignation about his nationalism and his deviation, Gomułka was made to resign as the general secretary. As usual in such cases, there followed for him a succession of government jobs of diminishing importance, then dismissal and expulsion from the party, and in 1951, arrest. Normally, the subsequent tale should have been summarized quite cryptically: trial, confession, execution. But Gomułka's story was to take an unusual turn. He was released from imprisonment in 1954 and in two years would be acclaimed not only by the party but by the bulk of his countrymen as the national leader. Because of a strange conjunction of events, this quite ordinary man, not overly endowed intellectually, would bring the Communist regime a fleeting moment of popular acceptance, then see it once more excoriated by society, and finally, as an emeritus, would witness the utter collapse of Polish Communism. Gomułka's second career epitomizes how the Communist movement sought to recoup its ideological meaning and mission. His personal tragedy goes far to explain why it failed.

As of 1954, the winds of change were coursing increasingly through the Communist world. Just as in the Soviet Union the power of the secret police was considerably curtailed and the institution itself subjected to stricter party controls, so was similar reorganization taking place throughout Eastern Europe. The People's Democracies were now free to regulate the pace of their transition to socialism, to modify or even stop the collectivization of agriculture. The drastic labor discipline under which the workers could be imprisoned for economic "crimes" such as absenteeism, being late to work, and unsatifactory productivity was now discarded as it had been in the Soviet Union already in the last days of March 1953. It was in an imitation of the USSR, if not at its explicit instructions, that East European Communism was shedding some of its Stalinist trappings. Had the men in the Kremlin been conversant with European history, they might have recalled the words of a nineteenth-century Italian patriot from Venice, then part of the Habsburg empire: "We don't want Austria to be more liberal towards us. We want it to go away and leave us to be free." Welcome as the new, more humane policies were to the long-suffering subject nations, they did not add up to what some years later would be called socialism with a human face.

If in their satellites the Soviets sought to revivify "proletarian internationalism" by reforms, then China, a problem of much vaster magnitude, had to be cajoled through diplomacy. No more patronizing gestures toward the Beijing regime, which, freed from the burden of the Korean War, basked in the aura of a great power. The People's Republic had scored a major success at the 1954 Geneva Conference, which put a (temporary) stop to the Indochinese War and led to the creation of a Communist state in North Vietnam. It was China that more than any other party at the conference had to be pleased with its results. As long as the French continued their futile efforts to deny all of Vietnam to Ho Chi Minh and his people, there was always the danger of the United States intervening and of China, on the analogy of Korea, becoming involved in the war. The USSR on the other hand had to view the Geneva settlement with mixed feelings. True, it marked another victory for Communism, but Hanoi *at the time* was much closer to Beijing than to Moscow. As long as the war continued, the USSR had a convenient way of pressuring France by holding before it the prospect of being an intermediary between it and the Vietnamese comrades in exchange for Paris not agreeing to West Germany's becoming rearmed and joining NATO. Now that lever of pressure was lost.

Communist China's debut in the international councils was also satisfying to its masters from the symbolic point of view. Though the

Americans, who sullenly refused to acknowledge the partition of Vietnam, snubbed the Chinese delegation, the representatives of other powers showed marked deference toward Zhou Enlai, none more so than Molotov.

Thus gone were the days when the People's Republic's highest dignitaries would travel to Moscow as supplicants, with no Soviet official of the Politburo deigning to return their visits.[12] On the occasion of the fiftieth anniversary of the proclamation of the People's Republic, the Soviet delegation to Beijing was headed by Khrushchev, in fact if not yet in name the number-one man in the Kremlin, and included three other Politburo members.

The ebullient first secretary was bringing fresh Soviet concessions for his hosts. Finally, after all the delays Port Arthur, which under the 1950 treaty should have been evacuated by the Russians in 1952, was now to be returned to the People's Republic within six months. The USSR also agreed to turn over to the Chinese, with only partial compensation, its share in the several joint Sino-Soviet mining and commercial companies, which like similar enterprises in Eastern Europe had been Moscow's devices for exploiting the host country's resources. And in addition to those offerings the erstwhile Elder Brother (the term would now disappear from use) pledged to expand greatly its economic and technological assistance to its ally.

On their face the Soviets' concessions did not appear extraordinary. The USSR would soon evacuate its naval base in Finland and pull its troops out of Austria. Colonial-type economic exploitation through the device of joint companies would be brought to an end, also in other Communist states. But Khrushchev's visit even more than the 1950 treaty marked an end to Russian expansion in East Asia, which, beginning in the seventeenth century, saw the Russians wresting vast areas from what had then been the Manchu empire. The latest acquisition was Mongolia, a Soviet puppet state since the early twenties, which was formally released from Chinese sovereignty only in 1945 in pursuance of Moscow's treaty with the Kuomintang government of China. And now in their heady mood of national pride and exultation at the growing international prestige of the People's Republic, its leaders were not above hinting to their Soviet guests that Russian expansion should be reversed. Years later Mao would reveal that it was on this occasion that he proposed to Khrushchev Mongolia's being returned to Chinese sovereignty.[13] The chairman could not have seriously expected his Soviet guest to agree or even to discuss the issue.

But the incident is characteristic of the changed atmosphere in Sino-Soviet relations, and how the outward appearance of unity and cordiality between the two Communist giants concealed growing tensions and mutual suspicions.

Mao's treading on his Soviet visitor's toes may appear strange in view of his country's still precarious position in relation to the United States. The Americans at about the same time concluded a mutual defense treaty with Chiang's regime in Taiwan, which formally sanctioned the presence of American naval and military forces on and around the island, and pledged to come to the aid of the nationalists if attacked. Quite apart from denying Taiwan to the Communists, Beijing now had to face the possibility that a Nationalist raid on the mainland might lead to an ambiguous situation in which the United States would feel impelled to intervene. The danger was enhanced by the Republican administration's rhetoric about "massive [nuclear] retaliation" in any future Korea-like conflict. And it was generally known that prior to the French debacle at Dien Bien Phu consideration was given in Washington to the possible use of nuclear weapons against the Vietnamese Communists. China's security still rested ultimately on its alliance with the USSR, and it would seem injudicious for Mao to have risked arousing the Soviets' susceptibilities.

But like Stalin before him, the chairman believed that he could distinguish between what was rhetoric and what sounded like a real threat in the Americans' declarations and policies. It is also quite likely that already at this point the Chinese suspected the Kremlin, or at least its Khrushchev faction, of trying to arrive at an accommodation with the West, and of being quite ready to sacrifice for its sake the interests of the People's Republic. If so, an attitude of docility on the part of Beijing would only encourage the Russians to take their ally for granted, and not to be inhibited in their circuitous maneuvers to reach détente with the capitalists. Contrariwise, a self-assertive stand toward Moscow, making it understand that the alliance was not a one-sided affair, would keep the Kremlin on the right path in dealing with the West—that is, the path of confrontation.

From the Soviet point of view, preserving the appearances of "unbreakable friendship between the Soviet Union and the Great People's Republic" had a twofold importance. An open split might, as it would from 1960 on, make it virtually impossible to make ideology once more a binding link between the Communist regimes and parties. It would mark the beginning of an end of "proletarian internationalism." In the second place, having the most populous nation in the world as an ally was a tremendous asset for Soviet diplomacy when dealing with the West, and in enhancing the Soviet image in the Third World. The mere size and alleged unity of the "Sino-Soviet bloc," as the State Department usually referred to the alliance in those days, goes far to explain why Secretary Dulles's "rollback of the Soviet sphere" and "liberalization" remained empty rhetoric.

There was another, personal angle to the Kremlin's efforts to propitiate the Chinese comrades. The situation at the top of the Soviet political pyramid was quite unstable. Khrushchev, while the dominant figure, was not invulnerable insofar as his control of the party was concerned. Popular among the rank and file, he did not have firm support within the Politburo, its conservative faction headed by Molotov objecting to the pace of de-Stalinization and of the relaxation of Soviet controls over East Europe. As of the middle 1950s, he could not have afforded an open break with China, which in all likelihood would have led to the end of his political career.

As it was, his star was still rising, as demonstrated by the removal of Malenkov as prime minister in 1955. Though the first secretary's leadership was still not undisputed—it was Bulganin who stepped in as premier and Malenkov remained in the Politburo—the Soviet Union's policies carry increasingly the first secretary's personal imprint.

Khrushchev was clearly a believer in bold improvisation and the importance of personal contacts. For the next ten years the world would be treated to the spectacle of Khrushchev traveling all over the globe, dropping in on Communist, capitalist, and nonaligned countries, dispensing alluring entreaties and chilling threats, his uninhibited and often raucous ways providing a glaring contrast with those of a sinister predecessor who, as far as the Soviet bloc knew, seldom stirred from behind the Kremlin walls.

The most startling visit of all in 1955 was one to Yugoslavia. Soviet relations with that country had been steadily improving during the past two years, but it still required considerable effrontery on Khrushchev's part to invite himself to meet the man whom not long ago he and other Soviet big shots had been vilifying as an "agent of Wall Street and the Zionists." The strain told in what was even for Khrushchev unusually rambunctious behavior: at one point he stopped a tour of the countryside to engage in a wrestling match with Mikoyan.

Later, overcome by drink at an official reception, the first secretary passed out and had to be carried to his quarters.

But such comic incidents ought not to obscure the seriousness and importance of the occasion. Here were the leaders of a superpower appearing as supplicants before those of a small Balkan country, pleading with the men they once sought to destroy not only for a reconciliation, but that Yugoslavia should resume its rightful place in the Communist camp. Were the latter to take place, not only would the Soviet Union recover an ally, but it would also be a vindication and reassertion of the international message and mission of Marxism-Leninism.

To underline the Soviets' repentance, Khrushchev did not bring with him Molotov, who as foreign minister of the USSR should have logically been included in the delegation, but who in Tito's eyes had been, after Stalin, most responsible for the opprobrious charges against him. The first secretary displayed less sublety in his statement upon arrival when he blamed the past troubles on "Beria . . . and other exposed enemies of the people . . . the contemptible agents of imperialism who had fraudulently wormed their way into the ranks of our party."[14] This rather ridiculous obfuscation of what really happened in 1948 was received rather coldly by Marshal Tito, who may have reflected that the language used by his guests about Beria and other deposed Soviet leaders was quite similar to the epithets applied by the Soviets not so long ago to himself and other Yugoslav notables.

At the moment, the Yugoslavs were ready to place intrastate relations with the USSR on a friendly basis, but resisted the proposals for closer links between the two Communist parties and for their country's full reentry into the Communist family of nations. What stood in the way of a closer rapprochement was first of all the Russians' failure up until then to explicitly denounce Stalin and Stalinism, something which for the imperious Marshal Tito was a question not only of *amour propre* but of practical politics: how could Eastern Europe, in fact Communism everywhere, be secured from Soviet domination and oppression unless the old pattern of the Kremlin's tyranny were unambiguously renounced? Also, since 1950 the Yugoslavs had developed close and profitable ties with the West. They were beneficiaries of American military and economic assistance. Tito's independent stance had gained him a great deal of prestige among the uncommitted nations and in left-wing non-Communist circles throughout the world. Little Yugoslavia had achieved a position on the international scene quite out of proportion to its size and power. To be completely reintegrated into the Soviet bloc would have meant the loss of those benefits, until and unless that bloc were completely transformed on the basis of full equality of its members, something which in 1955 was far from being the case.

There were on the other hand good reasons for Tito to leave the door open to a further rapprochement. Once liberated from the spell of doctrinaire Communism, Yugoslavia's leaders had adopted a number of reforms designed to distinguish their brand of ideology and society from the Stalinist model. But measures such as the cessation of forced collectivization and giving the workers a formal share in management did not affect the basic facts of one party's domination of national life, and one man's dictatorship. With the waning of ideological zeal, there grew the Communist notables' taste for the privileges and emoluments of power. Those who like Milovan Djilas argued that the logical follow-up of the break with Stalinism should be progress toward genuine freedom were shunted aside, he himself to suffer persecution and imprisonment for suggesting an end to the one-party system. The original nationalist elation among the rank and file of the League of Yugoslav Communists (renaming the party was one of the cosmetic changes adopted by the regime) had given way to restlessness and a feeling of ideological vacuum. Perhaps a renewed link with the "socialist camp" might revive that sense of mission without which any authoritarian party turns inevitably into a mass of mere officeholders and office-seekers.

The Belgrade visit concluded with both sides subscribing to a declaration reiterating the usual pieties about the need for peaceful coexistence between nations irrespective of their different ideologies and social systems. More meaningful from the Yugoslav point of view was the Soviets' willingness to sign the statement affirming that "questions of the internal structure, differences of social systems, and differences of concrete forms in developing socialism are matters to be decided exclusively by the people of the given country."[15] But even before, the Kremlin had in fact conceded the right of the individual Communist states to pursue their own paths to socialism, so that the most the Yugoslavs could claim was that they made the Soviet comrades state that explicitly.

The assiduous wooing of Tito by the Russians continued throughout 1955–56. From the Western perspective it may appear exceedingly strange that the hard-bitten, pragmatic men of the Kremlin should have invested so much effort in trying to bring what was, after all, a minor power back into the fold. But it was not only friendship with Yugoslavia that was at stake in this frantic courtship of the erstwhile heretic. If there was one constant theme of Soviet domestic and foreign policies during the Khrushchev era, it was the attempt to reaffirm the validity of Marxism-Leninism as a guide to action at home and abroad. For the first secretary and his associates the importance of ideology transcended the usual meaning of the word: it was a magic that if correctly applied would advance the Soviet Union's most important goals—it would enable the USSR to catch up with and overcome America in economic development, and also, despite all the growing below-the-surface tensions, the ideological bond would save and solidify the Sino-Soviet alliance. It was by following the path prescribed by Marxism-Leninism that the Soviet Union could go on expanding its power and prestige in the world and yet avoid a nuclear confrontation with the West. But if the ideology was to help achieve all such near miracles, it had first to prove its effectiveness in bringing about a reunion between two Communist regimes that would never have become estranged except for the vanity and obstinacy of an old tyrant.

The Yugoslav angle led to one of the few allusions to foreign policy in Khrushchev's indictment of Stalin. In his celebrated speech at the Twentieth Congress of the Communist Party of the Soviet Union in February 1956, he said: "The July [1955] Plenum of the [Soviet] Central Committee studied in detail the reasons for the development of the conflict with Yugoslavia. It was a shameful role which Stalin played here. The Yugoslav 'affair' contained no problem which could not have been solved through party discussions among comrades."[16] The first secretary then enlivened the subject by relating how Stalin on the occasion of the break allegedly told him, "I will shake my little finger and there will be no more Tito." Well, the late dictator, as some in the audience must have known from their own experience, was never so direct in expressing his prejudices and giving vent to his vanity. The story, like another one in the speech about Stalin plotting World War II campaigns on a globe, could not have contributed to the speaker's reputation for veracity.

The speech sought to destroy both the personal and the political side of the Stalin legend. The benevolent father of his people was now exposed as a supreme egotist and sadist, capable of sacrificing everything and anybody for the sake of his own power and glory. The once infallible and indomitable leader was revealed as having ignored all the warnings about the impending German attack, and then having cringed after the early Soviet defeats. And those initial defeats were largely due to Stalin having had decimated the Soviets' military cadres in the 1937–39 purges. On several occasions the tyrant's decisions as commander-in-chief during the war resulted in military disasters. "The Germans surrounded our Army concentrations and consequently we lost hundreds of thousands of our soldiers. This is Stalin's military 'genius'; this is what it cost us."[17]

How could a man like that have achieved leadership of a party and world movement that have claimed to embody and carry forth the principles of human liberation from oppression and want? Here is the most unconvincing part of Khrushchev's speech. The pre-1934 Stalin was portrayed as a positive character and a resourceful leader who fought to preserve Lenin's legacy. "At that time Stalin gained great popularity, sympathy and support."[18] No participant in the Twentieth Party Congress could have ignored the fact that during that allegedly benevolent period of Stalin's rule he had carried out forced collectivization of the peasant holdings, a measure whose consequences claimed more victims than all of the post-1934 purges, and a policy which quite apart from its human cost has in the long run proved to be the most disastrous failure of Soviet social engineering. But to criticize the policies adopted between Lenin's death and 1934 would have meant condemnation of the greater part of the political and socioeconomic features of the Soviet system, something that would be attempted only with perestroika and which, possibly because it came belatedly, would place Communism and the Soviet state in grave jeopardy.

The "secret speech" was an act of considerable political courage on the part of Khrushchev. One must not, however, exaggerate the risks he took. His personal assistant at the time was to write in his recollections: "How could Khrushchev give that speech about Stalin, knowing that the overwhelming majority of delegates would oppose the revelations? . . . That was one of those very rare occasions in history when a political leader has risked his personal power and even his life for the sake of highest social principles."[19] Well, that is a bit melodramatic. While many in the audience must have suffered a traumatic shock hearing the first secretary confirm what they long must have suspected, or knew from personal experience, it is unlikely that many of those present would have sprung to the defense of Stalin's good name. And as events were to show, an overwhelming majority of the party's rank and file and middle echelons would support the gist and the conclusions of the "secret speech." Where it did encounter hostility was among Stalin's principal accomplices still on the Presidium. They had consented to what might be described as silent de-Stalinization as practiced since 1953. But people like Molotov and Malenkov could have no illusions what telling the party even the partial truth about the sinister and sordid past might portend for their own future.

In talking to his assistant Khrushchev was later to rationalize his candor as a concern for ideology: "How many years did we believe in that man, praised and worshiped him. . . . Once I became the party's head, I felt obliged to tell the truth about the past, come what may. Lenin had taught us that a party that tells the truth would never go down. We are drawing lessons from the past and would like the fraternal parties to do likewise. Then our joint victory will be assured."[20]

Perhaps the shock therapy applied by the first secretary would have been more effective in recharging Communism with ideological dynamism had he chosen or been in a position to be more forthright. In the first place, it was a serious psychological error to attempt to keep the contents of the speech secret from the general public. It was characteristic of a certain naiveté in his makeup that he could have said in all seriousness: "We cannot let this matter get out of the Party, especially not into the press. It is for this reason that we are considering it here at a closed Congress session. We ought to know the limits; we should not give ammunition to the enemy; we should not wash our dirty linen before their eyes."[21] How could a speech delivered before more than two thousand delegates, including foreign Communists, fail to become quickly and widely known both at home and abroad? And why were the broad masses of the Soviet people to be denied the knowledge of Stalin's crimes? Were they also, like the foreign capitalists, "the enemy" who should not be told the truth about Stalin? And so, Khrushchev being at once naive and devious, the "secret speech" lost much of its intended therapeutic effect.

Also, judging by subsequent events, Khrushchev told either too much or not enough. Too much if the regime did not plan to embark on a comprehensive reform of the system that had been shaped by the man denounced by the first secretary; too little if the world was to be convinced that Communism was now genuinely committed to seeking new directions. As a one-time Khrushchev intimate would write under perestroika, " 'Khrushchevism' as a recipe for the resurgence of Communism failed to work. To use a turn of phrase employed by one of Khrushchev's chief enemies, Mao Zedong, the first secretary walked on two legs: with one he would boldly step forward, the other dragged, getting stuck in the slime of the past."[22] An incongruous criticism coming from Mao, himself hardly an apostle of liberalism. For Alexander Solzhenitsyn the tragedy of Khrushchev consisted in his being unable to carry out anything he started to its logical conclusion, "least of all the fight for freedom."

At that time, could any Soviet statesman have carried that fight to its logical conclusion? After all, even that very incomplete indictment of Stalin, full of evasions and half-truths, created a veritable trauma for many in the Soviet party, shocked and divided the world Communist movement, and triggered a crisis and rebellion in the USSR and abroad. And isn't what is happening currently a sufficient proof that real glasnost can hardly coexist with Communism? After 1985 it was the much fuller openness about the past as much as any other factor that has led to a not very orderly retreat from the tenets and practices of Marxism-Leninism in the Soviet Union, and utterly shattered Communism in East Europe. And so one could argue in February 1956 that what Khrushchev did and did not say has to be seen in terms of the political realities of the moment.

Yet it is arguable that on many counts Communism was in a better condition to absorb the shock of glasnost in the late fifties than it would be thirty years later. But because it was half-hearted, the attempt to exorcise Stalinism from the Soviet past still left a considerable residue of it in the Soviet and other Communist systems.

5

REFORM AND RETREAT

THE ANGUISH AND SHOCK felt by the Communist world in the wake
of the Twentieth Congress's revelations was thus deepened, rather
than lessened, by their being veiled in circumlocutions. For the rank
and file of the faithful, their allegiance to the creed could not but be
shaken by this stark account of crimes and abuses that surpassed the
worst things the capitalists had been saying about Communism and
its practice in the Fatherland of Socialism. There followed the inevitable question: Had all those horrors been caused by just one man?
To the more sophisticated among the foreign leaders, the shock consisted not in what Khrushchev said—they knew or suspected much
more than he had chosen to reveal—but in the enormous embarrassment of having been revealed as dupes or accomplices of the
tyrant. There was an additional problem. What did the Kremlin intend
to signal by those startling confessions?

One of the wiliest of the foreign leaders, the Italian Palmiro Togliatti,
found it quite harrowing to deal with that question when confronted
by it in a newspaper interview.[1] Did the condemnation of Stalin mean
that Soviet Communism and the entire movement were to undergo
basic reforms? his interviewers probed. Well, not quite. "I may be
mistaken, but in my opinion, any institutional changes in the Soviet
Union are not foreseen today, nor do the criticisms formulated openly
at the Twentieth Congress imply the necessity for such changes. . . .
To think of a multiparty system in the Soviet Union seems impossible
to us,"[2] but then the veteran Communist and one-time Stalin's confidant could not refrain from voicing his anger at the superficiality of
the official Soviet explanation of what had transpired. "First, all that
was good was attributed to the superhuman positive qualities of one

man. Now all that is evil is attributed to his equally exceptional and even astonishing faults. . . . The real problems are evaded, which are why and how Soviet society could reach, and did reach, certain forms alien to the democratic way and to the legality it had set for itself, even to the point of degeneration."³

But what were the real problems that the Kremlin had been evading? Well, Togliatti and for that matter the Soviet Communist bigwigs who felt constrained to comment upon the "revelations" proved themselves to be extremely agile in evading *that* question. As far as the international Communist movement was concerned, the answer should have been obvious. The root cause of the trouble had lain in the foreign parties blindly following Moscow's—i.e., until March 1953 Stalin's—directives. But such admissions would have been even more damaging to the Italian, French, and other parties than the litany of Stalin's crimes recited by Khrushchev. And so the erstwhile longtime official of the Comintern allowed that Stalin's errors contributed "to making the relations between the Soviet Communists and the Communists of other countries somewhat outward and formal," surely a masterpiece of understatement. But even that feeble admission was immediately qualified by Togliatti's assertion, as untrue as it was a non sequitur, that those "outward relations" could not lessen the foreign Communists' trust in the Soviet Union "because we did not have and could not have any idea of the facts that now have been revealed."⁴ And the Italian party's leader expressed great indignation at those propagating "the foolish myth that the Communist parties receive step-by-step instructions, directives and orders from Moscow."⁵

What emerges from Togliatti's verbal calisthenics is not only his discomfiture at the Soviet comrades' confessions and contrition, but also anxiety as to what they could mean to the future of international Communism. How could the latter be run without absolute and constant control by that infallible center—the Kremlin? Did the secret speech herald any institutional changes in the Soviet Union that would constrain the foreign Communist parties to alter their own authoritarian structures? Those concerns were at the time typical of the attitude of Communist notables all over the world. Much as some of them may have secretly resented their servile situation vis-à-vis the Kremlin, they had become dependent on it not only politically but psychologically. That dependence, in many ways not resulting from rational consideration but rather reminiscent of a drug addict, had practically eroded the foreign Communists' capacity to formulate their own policies and make independent decisions. As we have seen, this was especially true of Communists not in power, as in the case of the two great parties in the West—the French and Italian. But for the movement, more than thirty years of Moscow's absolute domination had come close to vitiating any genuine ideological impulses.

It was only under special circumstances, as in China and after 1948 in Yugoslavia, that the Communist parties were able or felt compelled to chart an independent course. And in both cases this was made possible by an exceptionally strong and charismatic leadership. As for the other Communist parties, Moscow's psychological hold on them had already been shaken by Stalin's death. But it was Khrushchev's harsh accounting of the tyrant's misdeeds that appeared to presage the political demise of Stalinism, and with it Moscow's sway over the world movement. Hence reactions such as Togliatti's.

Tito and Mao had to view de-Stalinization in a different light. For the Yugoslav ex-heretic, now assiduously courted by Moscow, Khrushchev's admission represented a very satisfying vindication of his personal and his party's stand in 1948. He and his small country had prevailed in a political struggle with a superpower. They had been proven right while the most prestigious leaders in world Communism were exposed as dupes or fainthearted conscripts, unwilling or unable to raise their voice in defense of their countries' national interest and against the Soviets' usurpations. And now the marshal, never renowned for modesty, would repeatedly and in a somewhat schoolmasterish way, dispense his advice to the Russians and other Communist regimes as to how they ought to go about liquidating the remnants of Stalinism. Throughout 1956, and especially after the events in Poland and Hungary, Tito kept expatiating on the theme.

He also, but more insistently than Togliatti and his like, refused to accept the Soviet version of what lay behind the past abuses and errors. The Russians tried to put all the blame on one man: "because Stalin had grown old, he had become a little mad and started to commit various mistakes." As against it, "we have been saying that here it was not a question of the cult of personality alone, but of a system which had made possible the creation of that cult." The roots of the cult, he went on, lay "in the bureaucratic apparatus, in the method of leadership and the so-called one-man rule and in ignoring the role and aspirations of the working masses."[6] And the marshal proceeded to excoriate various Communists still in power who, according to him, clung to Stalinist ways and who, not surprisingly, had been the very same people who vilified Yugoslavia when that was the fashion in the socialist camp.

In expanding his critique beyond the cult of personality and blaming "the system" as well as one man, Tito was quite explicit as to what had been wrong with the system as far as intra-Communist relations were concerned: the Soviets' interference in the affairs of other Communist regimes and parties. Even under Khrushchev, he implied, the Soviet Union had refused to treat other socialist countries on the basis of complete equality, under the pretense that it must protect them from the machinations of the West, which sought to restore capitalism there. "In other words, this means that they [the Russians] lack sufficient confidence in the internal revolutionary forces of these countries. In my opinion this is wrong, and the root of all later mistakes lies in insufficient confidence in the socialist forces of these peoples."[7]

But when it came to criticizing the domestic aspects of "the system," Tito's argument did not represent an advance on that of Togliatti's: the same ritualistic condemnation of the evils of the bureaucratic apparatus and of Stalinism's ignoring the needs and aspirations of the working masses. But of course neither he nor any other Communist at the time could or would plead for social, not to mention political, pluralism. To condemn explicitly the authoritarian features of the Stalinist system would have meant condemning his own rule over Yugoslavia and his own methods of dealing with opposition either within the Communist Party, as illustrated by Djilas's case, or outside of it. And, as a matter of fact, Tito had been developing quite a personality cult of his own.

Mao and other leaders of Chinese Communism had no reason to feel nostalgic about Stalin. And even more than the Yugoslavs they had been the beneficiaries of the tyrant's death and of their Russian comrades' awkward attempts to deal with its political consequences. The Soviet Union would never again be able to lord it over them as it had before March 5, 1953, or virtually compel them to save the situation for them as it had in the Korean War. But like other Communist leaders, Mao could not be pleased by what the secret speech did to the reputation of Marxism-Leninism and its worldwide movement. In the wake of the Twentieth Congress the Chinese media hastened to place their approval on the Soviet comrades' exposure of the evils of the cult of personality. But later on in a closed party meeting Mao in his rambling way kept criticizing Khrushchev's indiscretions.

"The criticism of Stalin has a two-sided nature. One side has real benefit; one side is not good. To expose the cult of Stalin, to tear off the lid, to liberate people, this is a liberation movement; but his [Khrushchev's] method of exposing Stalin is incorrect. He has not made a good analysis, [but tried to] club him to death with a single blow."[8]

On another occasion Mao good-naturedly observed that Stalin was quite right in killing counterrevolutionaries—after all, the Chinese Communists themselves killed a lot of the breed, some seven hundred thousand during the first three years they were in power. But Stalin also indulged in "incorrect killing" of genuine revolutionaries, who for one or another reasons displeased him.[9] As behooved a follower of scientific socialism, Mao would also try to express the problems in quantitative terms: "Wasn't Stalin thirty percent wrong and seventy percent right?"[10] But then the Chairman also had a poetic side to his nature. In his famous speech of February 27, 1957, which among numerous other themes contained the famous slogan about letting a hundred flowers bloom, Mao resorted to an appropriate simile. "Stalin in the past was 100 percent a fragrant flower; Khrushchev in one stroke turned him into a poisonous weed. Now Stalin is again fragrant."[11]

Such seeming trifling with a deadly serious subject was in all likelihood intentional. Mao did not want his followers to reflect deeply on the potential danger inherent in the worship of *the* leader or on what it was about Communism that enabled one man to achieve so much power and to do so much harm. By the time Sino-Soviet relations worsened—toward the end of the 1950s—the Chinese Communists would demonstratively revert to the theme of Stalin having been unjustly slandered by Khrushchev and other Soviet "revisionists." They would point to the Hungarian revolt as demonstrating the damage done to the cause of international Communism by such intemperate criticisms.

In delivering his severe judgment on Stalin, Khrushchev may well have thought that it would be gladly endorsed by foreign Communists who had for so long suffered under the despot's arbitrary and cruel domination. Surely their leaders would welcome an opportunity to fashion their policies in accordance with their nations' and parties' interests rather than those of the Soviet Union and would eagerly embrace the opportunity to be Moscow's, to be sure junior, partner, rather than vassals. Thus liberated, the foreign parties would be able to enhance their popular appeal and recoup the ideological dynamism that allegedly characterized the movement before the full onset of the cult of personality.

But as we have seen, such calculations ignored the important differences between the political conditions in the USSR and those relevant to the situation in foreign Communist parties. In the former the Communist regime had lasted for forty years. Whatever its past transgressions and current chicaneries few people could conceive of an alternative to the party's rule. Ironically, the influence of Stalinism had been so strong and all-pervading that for the time being de-Stalinization could not seriously affect the party's hold on power. To be sure, the Twentieth Congress was both a symptom and a cause of a deep crisis within the Soviet Communist establishment. But for the moment the issue was how far the party would go in moderating its authoritarian ways and not whether it should rule or not, with the Khrushchev faction pushing for considerable liberalization and some candor about the past, and the Molotov-Malenkov group in the Politburo holding out for severe limits on reforms and against the continued exposure of Stalin's crimes.

With other ruling parties the question was one of being able to survive the repercussions of the secret speech. It had severely undermined the morale of both leaders and the rank and file. And with what might be called the Communist garrisons in the Soviet bloc countries severely demoralized and thrown into confusion, would those regimes be able to withstand mass revolts like those in East Germany in the spring of 1953, but now quite likely to occur on a much larger scale, and not in just one country? True, the Soviet army's presence or shadow weighed heavily over East Europe, thus discouraging any prospects of its being liberated from foreign domination and foreign-imposed ideology. But as of the early fall of 1956, one could still hope that the Soviets would not interfere militarily if a puppet regime were threatened; after all, fear of wider complications and of a possible escalation of the conflict to the point of bringing about an East-West confrontation kept Stalin from invading Yugoslavia. To be sure, ever since 1949 there had been contingency plans for a Soviet armed strike against Tito, with the Hungarian, Romanian, and Albanian forces joining the Red Army in invading the country to crush the heretical regime.[12] What became known later as the Brezhnev Doctrine—the socialist camp's *duty* to intervene militarily if one of its members departed from the straight and narrow path of Marxism-

Leninism—was still in the future. With their Communist rulers thrown into confusion and unsure of themselves, the people of the Kremlin's fiefdoms in East Europe might become emboldened enough to try to throw off the yoke.

Less dangerous, but if anything even more embarrassing, was the situation of the great Communist parties of the West, principally those of France and Italy. Their rank-and-file members, not having had a firsthand experience with terror, had every reason to be more astounded and shocked by the revelations than their Soviet or Hungarian comrades (on the other hand, even though they hadn't lived under a Communist regime, they could still nourish few illusions about what it would mean in practice). The two parties had had great hopes of coming to power through legal, parliamentary means with the assistance of other left-wing radical groups. But now the latter, like Pietro Nenni's socialists in Italy, would prove increasingly reluctant to be seen as allies of a party whose Soviet comrades and guides had now owned up to such sordid doings in the past.

In the Soviet Union what might be called the crisis of faith caused by the condemnation of Stalin found its reflection in the birth of dissent—acts of defiance of the regime and the ruling ideology by individuals, most of them conscious of the fact that the regime could not be overthrown but could and must be made to acknowledge more fully its past crimes and still-present oppression. But abroad the same crisis threatened, and in one case would actually lead to, rebellion. With the realization that he miscalculated the effects that his (partial) candor would have on Eastern Europe, the first secretary sought desperately to appease and reassure the leaders of the Communist parties of the area. The USSR, he made clear, did not intend to withdraw its support of them, nor would it leave them unprotected from their foreign and domestic enemies. The fraternal parties would have to reexamine their policies and procedures and eliminate from them the remnants of the bad habits from the period of the "cult of personality." By doing so the fraternal parties would not only gain greater trust of their people, but would also solidify their links with the Fatherland of Socialism and advance the cause of Communism throughout the world.

The Kremlin's attention was focused not on what in Communist parlance are the masses but on the Communist elites. The latter were to be reshaped, cleansed of the residue of Stalinism. They would now know how to rule without terror and would be seen by their peoples as being solicitous of their national interests while still preserving their loyalty to Moscow. And that loyalty would now spring not so much from fear, as in the bad old days, but out of a genuine feeling of ideological solidarity and common political and economic interests.

Rather incautiously, but in line with his impetuous way of doing things, Khrushchev decided that it was Marshal Tito and the Yugoslav party that could serve as an example of the kind of virtues that the East European Communists might well seek to emulate. The Kremlin's frantic wooing of the Balkan dictator finally prevailed over his previous reservations about agreeing to closer relations with the USSR, as well as about the two fraternal parties resuming a direct liaison. And indeed it is difficult to think of a small country being courted so assiduously by a great power as was Yugoslavia by the USSR in 1956. Quite apart from a flattering reference to Tito and his associates in the secret speech, the Kremlin took two other measures in the spring that were likely to make the imperious marshal feel more warmly about the Soviet comrades. On April 18 an announcement was made of the dissolution of the Cominform. The only notable event in the nine-year-old history of the moribund organization was the ejection from its midst of Yugoslavia, and the subsequent anathema placed upon it by the ill-fated successor of the Comintern. Equally pleasing to the *amour propre* of the Yugoslav leadership must have been the dismissal of Molotov from his post as foreign minister. For the Yugoslavs as well as for many others, this one-time deputy of Stalin's was also seen as the main opponent of the course of liberalization at home and abroad.

Both measures would have been taken anyway before too long, but their timing was influenced by Marshal Tito's setting out in June to visit Moscow. He had been invited there in 1948, just as the crisis between the two regimes was going to burst upon the world, but prudently chose not to go. Now he spent three weeks in the USSR and was feted and glorified there more than any other visitor, Communist or capitalist, had been since 1945. Not even Mao had had a reception as cordial and attended by so much fuss. An official statement signed for the Soviets by Nikolai Bulganin registered the two governments' agreement on a number of important international issues, something that could not be too pleasing to the United States, which for the past six years had helped the maverick Communist regime economically and with military supplies. The declaration was accompanied by something Khrushchev had sought but had been denied on his visit to Belgrade the preceding year: a statement of common aims and solidarity by the two Communist parties, this time with the first secretary as a cosignatory. All of which came out at the end of a triumphal tour throughout the Soviet Union by the one-time prodigal son of Communism, now a highly valued friend and ally. Tito's advice was sought on the best ways of allaying the unrest in the socialist camp. To use a historical simile, this was a Canossa in reverse, the highest authority in the world movement professing its repentance, the former heretic applauded and presented as an example to all the faithful.

Alas, as in so many cases with Khrushchev's improvisations, his hopes of drawing solid benefits from this veritable love feast were to be largely disappointed. In the first place, Tito, much as he sought and in some ways needed this rapprochement, had no intention of being drawn back into the Soviet bloc, even if it was to be run along much more liberal lines than before. It simply made no sense for Yugoslavia to revert to the status of a junior partner, even if the most favored one, of the USSR. Tito would continue to keep profitable ties with the West and in fact would maneuver with considerable skill between the United States and the USSR.

Another dividend the Russians hoped to draw from the reconciliation was the strengthening of the Communist regimes in East Europe. Their subjects would, it was hoped, realize now that the Soviet Union no longer required abject submission to its dictates on the part of its allies, that under Moscow's benign guidance nationalism could be reconciled with membership in the socialist camp. But many would draw a different lesson from Titoism: if it was possible to stand up to the Kremlin and not be crushed, why then be content with partial rather than full independence? Besides, to the bulk of the population in the satellites, Yugoslavia was hardly an enticing model as far as its domestic politics was concerned: it was still under an oppressive authoritarian regime. And to the people at large it was not only alien domination but their own domestic Communism, no matter how nationalist its trappings might become, that was distasteful. In brief, Khrushchev's Tito gambit made the USSR and Communism less feared but hardly more popular among the subjects of Moscow's European empire.

Yet it would be inaccurate and unfair to brand the Soviet Union's new policy a total failure. If it contributed to the convulsions that shook Eastern Europe in the fall of 1956, it also probably prevented them from turning into a cataclysm. Had the Kremlin clung to the old methods in running its empire, they would in the longer run have triggered revolutions far surpassing the Hungarian one in their scope and intensity. De-Stalinization bared many of the ailments afflicting Communism and enabled the patient to carry on for quite a while longer. But it failed to effect a lasting cure.

The crucial test of the success or failure of the new image of Communism was bound to come in Poland. In no other country was Communism resisted and resented as strongly. No other nation had as long-lasting and persistent a tradition of struggle against Russian imperialism, whether in its tsarist form before 1914, or in the Soviet form since the concluding phases of World War II. The heavy burden of history had affected also the Soviets' attitude on almost every issue connected with their western neighbor. No other foreign Communists resident in the Soviet Union during the Great Terror of 1936–39 had been purged as ruthlessly and thoroughly as the Polish ones. In 1938 the Comintern dissolved the Communist Party of Poland for allegedly having been infiltrated and permeated by Trotskyites and agents of the Warsaw government. So extensive had been the purge of those Polish Communists, on whom the Soviet security organs could lay their hands before 1939, that when it came to installing the Communist regime in the country in 1944–45, some of even its highest officials had to be recruited from among those Polish Communists who between 1937 and the beginning of the war had been inmates of the gulag. That the new regime imposed by the Red Army did not encounter more widespread popular resistance (and the last anti-Communist partisans were not eliminated until 1947) was made possible only by the debilitating effect on the nation of the terrible years of German occupation. As in the other satellites, political repression became more severe in the wake of the Tito affair. The ranks of Polish Communists were purged of alleged Titoists and nationalists, notably of the former general secretary of the Polish Workers' Party[13] and his associates. And as we already noted, it was the Kremlin's recognition of the vulnerability of its vassal regime in Poland that had saved Gomułka and other erstwhile party notables from being produced in a show trial as was done elsewhere, notably in Hungary, Bulgaria, and Czechoslovakia, where the former Communist greats were doomed at Moscow's orders.

And so it was in Poland that one could expect the most serious repercussions of Soviet Communism loosening its hold over its empire.

Indeed, after March 1953 the regime relaxed its repressive policies, though for a while it continued unabated the campaign against the Catholic Church, which after nine years of Communist power remained a bastion of resistance to the alien rule and ideology.[14] As elsewhere in the Communist world before Khrushchev's bombshell at the Twentieth Congress, past departures from socialist legality—a pallid euphemism for terror—were conveniently ascribed to the secret police and its Soviet overlord, Beria. Equally in line with the prevailing fashion in the Communist states, the authority of the security service was curtailed. Several of its high officials were dismissed, some of them subsequently expelled from the party and imprisoned. Few among the Communist rank and file, not to mention the general public, could be taken in by such transparent attempts to deflect the blame for the past misdeeds and the continuing oppression from those really responsible—the party bosses and their Soviet masters. Even more than in other satellites, with the possible exception of Hungary in 1953 through 1956, Poland experienced a period of mounting popular anger and anxiety. For its part, the regime, as a consequence of lacking clear-cut directives from Moscow, was becoming less and less self-assured in dealing with society. Society in turn was both expectant and fearful, sensing the government's lack of self-assurance, yet apprehensive lest the liberal interlude be followed by a Soviet-ordered crackdown.

The effect of the "secret speech" on the fragile morale of the Polish Communists was epitomized by what happened to their leader, Bolesław Bierut. First secretary of the party and president of the country, he became ill while attending the Twentieth Congress in Moscow and died shortly after his return to Warsaw on March 12. The Central Committee's session devoted to the election of his successor was attended by Khrushchev, another sign of the stress and uncertainty characterizing intra-Communist relations at the time. Under Stalin it was not necessary for a Soviet dignitary to be present at such deliberations to secure the election of a candidate favored by Moscow; a telephone call was sufficient. This time the highest Soviet official had to intervene personally to veto the candidacy of Roman Zambrowski, unacceptable to the Kremlin mostly because of his Jewish origin. The man selected as Bierut's successor was Edward Ochab, who had an irreproachable pro-Soviet and Aryan background, and who had distinguished himself by the violence of his denunciations of Gomułka once the former leader's political doom had been decreed by the Soviets. No one at the time could have predicted what would be one of the most astounding events in that topsy-turvy Communist world of 1956: Ochab, one of the chief engineers of Gomułka's fall, would within a few months be instrumental not only in rehabilitating the former general secretary of the Polish Party, but also in reinstating him in power.

The new leader found it necessary to trim his sails to the prevailing wind. His first public pronouncements duly denounced the cult of personality and its reverberations in Poland, expressed contrition for past mistakes, and promised, without going into specifics, the democratization of political life and greater openness in the party and the government. But the growing social malaise could not be dissipated by oratory nor by other propitiatory gestures by the government such as the release of political prisoners and further and more severe measures against the former secret-service officials. For a while the regime would persist in the belief—common to dictatorial regimes whether of the left or the right—that it was the intellectuals who were the propagators of discontent while the masses were and would remain inert. Such illusions were sharply dispelled by the June 1956 events in Poznań, one of the major cities and industrial centers of Poland.

The Poznań strikes and riots initiated the cycle of Polish workers' revolts that would periodically shake and eventually would contribute to the collapse of the Communist edifice in the country. The years 1956, 1970, 1976, 1980, and 1989 are milestones in the history of a society trying to free itself from the oppressive and inefficient rule of an autocratic bureaucracy. The first date is all the more memorable because it was a classical case of a spontaneous workers' outburst against insufferable living and working conditions such as, according to the canons of Marxism, are bound to take place in capitalist societies but should be by definition impossible under socialism. Yet here was a strike and a demonstration that originated within the factories and which no subsequent government investigator was able to trace back to any political agitators or the baneful influences of some intellectual circle.

In its passion for rapid industrialization—second only to that for power for the Communists—the Polish regime, like most of the fraternal countries, placed heavy burdens on the working class: the constant raising of work norms, thus making industrial labor more intensive and strenuous; a pay scale that, while favoring the specially productive workers and innovators, did not protect the rank and file against a decline in their real wages; scant consideration for industrial safety and hygiene whenever their claims might get in the way of increased production. The worker in what was supposed to be the workers' and peasants' state lacked a spokesman for his professional interests, the labor unions being strictly controlled by the party.

The winds of change coursing through the Communist world were thus bound to turn what had been the working masses' sullen resentment into active protest. News about what was going on in the USSR was communicated by the official media in a bowdlerized form, but even so it tended to have an electrifying effect on the public. A Communist author, referring to a labor-union journal of the period in Poznań, anachronistically and piquantly named *On Stalin's Watch*, notes its transformation beginning in March 1956. "Until then the journal had been following the line laid down by the regime and sounded like a government publication. But subsequently it gradually became filled with criticisms [of the regime] and aired the workers' postulates. . . . The impulse for that bolder attitude came from reading and talking about the Twentieth Congress of the Communist Party of the Soviet Union. . . . During the discussions the workers raised not only economic but also political issues as they touched both on the local and national situation."[15] Similar meetings, and one assumes tempestuous discussions, were taking place throughout the country. The party spokesmen confronting the often unruly audiences sought to reassure them that what had happened under Stalin would never be repeated. But they should remember not only the crimes of the past. There had also been real achievements: the elimination of unemployment and much wider access to higher education. And now the party was determined to carry out basic reforms and to raise the standard of living. Socialism was still the only path for Poland. The Communist regime was all the stronger for being able, unlike the capitalists, to admit openly past transgressions and thus make certain that they could not recur.

Poznań workers were not reassured. By the end of June the situation in the city, the fourth-largest in the country, grew tense. The official labor unions were bypassed at mass meetings. In factories elected representatives confronted the management with the alternatives of satisfying their demands or facing a strike. The workers' demands touched on such basic grievances as not being paid for overtime, constant increases in the work norms, thus effectively lowering the real wages, and the lamentable working conditions.[16] Poznań economic bureaucrats referred the workers to the ministries in Warsaw, thus increasing the population's impatience with the local bosses. In the capital the delegates received verbal assurances that the workers' needs would be attended to, but in the meantime tension within the working population of Poznań was building up, threatening an explosion. Officials from the capital hastened to the city to forestall a strike by making fresh offers, but it was too late. It was not only the recent grievances and scant faith in the government's promises but also the delayed reaction to more than a decade of Communist misrule and mismanagement that was fueling the turbulence and triggered off the strikes and the riots. "The workers were outraged by [the officials'] dilatoriness in taking up their complaints and the manner by which their delegates have been treated."[17]

The strike, the first major one in the annals of Communist Poland, erupted on June 28, 1956, and spread instantly to Poznań's fifty thousand workers. After the work stoppage came mass demonstrations, which turned into riots and then escalated into a veritable revolt. What precipitated the latter was an attempt by the security forces to disperse the crowd, which until then, though unruly, had not turned to violence. The demonstrators responded by seizing the loudspeaker from a party official who had been trying to calm them and roughing him up. The speeches now took on an increasingly political character. "They spoke about raising wages and lowering prices, the need for more housing, but also about freedom in general and the restoration of religious lessons to the schools' curriculum. . . . One of the speakers proposed the overthrow of the government."[18]

And now in the classical style of an urban revolt there followed the storming of the party and security services' headquarters, seizure of the jail, and the freeing of the inmates. Some of the assailants helped themselves to the arms seized from unresisting jail guards and policemen. Fire was first exchanged during the storming of the secret-police headquarters. In the course of the day practically all public buildings, including those of the court and procuracy, were ravaged and partly destroyed.

Confronted by the revolt, the government ordered regular army units into the city. As the then First Secretary Edward Ochab was to reminisce several years later: "We sent too many soldiers, far too many. One company would have been enough. One should have settled the whole business more quietly and quickly."[19] As it was, two divisions and three hundred tanks moved into the city and restored a semblance of order by the evening of the twenty-ninth. As is usual in such cases, there is no reliable accounting of the number of victims, but the most reasonable estimates point to about one hundred killed and three hundred wounded.

The government's first version of the Poznań affair placed the responsiblity for it on outside agitators and criminal elements who, playing upon the workers' genuine grievances, pushed them into what developed into a counterrevolutionary riot and rebellion. Following that argument, it was easy to see the whole affair as resulting from a plot by the Western imperialists, who through their agents masterminded the entire operation. A Soviet source hastened with a helpful hint that the plot was financed by "American monopoly capitalism" which had special funds for the subversion of law and order in the socialist camp. The Polish prime minister, Józef Cyrankiewicz, in his radio address on the twenty-ninth, chimed in with bloodcurdling threats: "Let any madcap provocateur who would dare to raise his hand against the people know that this hand will be severed by the people with the full approval of the working class."[20]

Yet such grotesque posturing no longer intimidated society but only increased its indignation. Even within the party there was a widespread feeling that the prime minister's Stalinist-sounding oratory was anachronistic and counterproductive. Talk about the imperialist agents quickly died down. The Soviets, as if oblivious to the lessons of the Twentieth Congress, pressed the Poles to continue to stick to the capitalist-plot version of the cause of the disturbances, but as Ochab would recall, "I rejected those suggestions, as did the majority of the Politburo. We had a spirited discussion with the Soviet comrades, who insisted. . . . There are no proofs, I said."[21] In a way this was proof of the first secretary's growing emancipation from subservience to the Kremlin: no predecessor of his would have rejected the Soviets' demand that he blame the capitalists for some disaster simply because there were no proofs!

But it would be his successor who would spell out the true lesson of Poznań: "The reasons for the Poznań tragedy and for the discontent of the entire working class lie in us, in the leadership of the party and of the government. For years we had been on the verge of an explosion."[22] The possibility of such an explosion was very much on the Polish leaders' minds during the spring and summer of 1956. It was clear that the regime could not indefinitely rely on the armed forces, and another Poznań might possibly be the beginning of a country-wide uprising.

The dilemma facing the Communists was twofold. They were discredited in the eyes of their own society not only on account of their social and economic policies, but also and primarily because they were still seen as puppets of Moscow. To be accepted by society, i.e., to be able to carry on without constant fear of another and much greater upheaval, the regime would have to demonstrate that it could and would, when national interests were involved, stand up to the Soviet Union. On the other hand, the support of the latter was vital to the preservation of the current Communist elite's powers. Should the regime's policies seriously displease the Kremlin, it might react in one of two ways, each fatal to the interests of the ruling group. The Soviets might intervene militarily to install a regime composed of people who would be content to remain subservient to them. Or, a much less likely alternative but one that could not be precluded after the Twentieth Congress, they could disinterest themselves completely in what was happening to Polish Communism, in which case no Communist government, no matter how liberal its policies, would be allowed by the Polish people to remain in power for any appreciable length of time.

The problem before Ochab and his comrades was therefore to map a course that would make them appear to be legitimate guardians of the national interest in the eyes of their own people, while at the same time being seen by the Kremlin as dependable and deferential partners. This admittedly difficult problem preoccupied the attention of the Polish Politburo throughout the spring and summer of that memorable year.

The Soviets were suspicious about what the Polish comrades might be planning, and they continued to watch their policy-making deliberations. Premier Bulganin and Marshal Georgi Zhukov, currently minister of defense, happened to descend on Warsaw in July, their visit coinciding with a session of the Central Committee. Zhukov's presence was a poignant reminder, though one hardly was needed, that the Kremlin, if necessary, could always back up its advice to a fraternal party with some persuasive action. The occasion passed without any overt clashes, even though Bulganin in a public speech continued to maintain the capitalist-plot version of the Poznań events.

In fact, Ochab and some of his colleagues were contemplating a gambit that, as they knew, might well provoke the Russians to armed intervention. In their desperate search for something that might gain the regime a solid lease on life and even genuine support among the people, they turned to the one Communist who enjoyed widespread popularity and could soothe the nation's dangerous mood: Władysław Gomułka. The former general secretary and later "Titoist" had recently been cleared of all charges, readmitted to the party, and of late was much courted by his very repentant ex-colleagues. His ordeal gained Gomułka universal respect and sympathy, especially since it was widely believed that the main reason for his disgrace and imprisonment had been his refusal to kowtow to the Russians. By the same token, for all of their recent friendship with Tito, the Soviets were wary of those East European politicians who had been purged for real or alleged "national Communism." The risk inherent in restoring Gomułka to an important position was all the greater because as Ochab knew, there was a strong faction within the Soviet Politburo that had opposed Khrushchev's fawning on Tito and the general line of his policy on Eastern Europe. The elevation of a reputed "national Communist" to be one of the leaders of traditionally anti-Russian Poland might tip the scales in the Kremlin in favor of the Molotov-Malenkov faction and then bring a harsh rebuff to Poland as a lesson to others who would put national concerns over "proletarian internationalism."

For all such possible complications and danger Ochab and his like-minded colleagues stuck to their scheme. For them the man whom they once had vilified and humiliated had become, and especially after Poznań, a precious resource, a possessor of magic that could turn their peoples' disdain and exasperation with Communist rule into a positive and cooperative attitude. Many of them were undoubtedly motivated by the desire to cling to their jobs and privileges, but it would be unfair to deny that some saw Gomułka's reinstatement as correcting a past injustice and benefiting the country as well as the party. His return to power would be hailed as a signal for less doctrinaire and more rational policies. He was known to have opposed forcible collectivization of Polish agriculture and could be expected to call a halt to the persecution of the Church.

Coupling the reinstatement of Gomułka with more liberal policies was opposed by the party conservatives who, from the suburb of Warsaw where they held their semiconspiratorial meetings, became known as the Natolin group. The Natolin crowd was against any steps

that might displease the Soviet comrades. If Gomułka was to be rein-
stated, then he should be placed in a position where he would have
no real influence on policies. Polish Communism could remain in
power only by keeping strict controls over society, and liberalization
was bound to be interpreted as weakness and lead to further pressures
on the government. If public opinion was to be mollified, some of the
conservatives argued, this could be best done by appealing to anti-
Semitic sentiments. Previous excesses and errors could be blamed on
Jews in the party and the security apparatus.

But whatever might have been the effect of such demagoguery, the
conservatives' position could prevail only if fully backed by Moscow.
And possibly because of its own divided councils, the Soviet leadership
refrained from sending a clear signal to Poland. Khrushchev himself
had not stood in the way of Gomułka's full rehabilitation. But during
their inspection trip to Warsaw, Bulganin and Zhukov gave their Polish hosts to understand that the Soviets would not look favorably upon
Gomułka's being entrusted with the leadership. The Ochab faction
then conducted long and tortuous negotiations with this now clearly
indispensable man: wouldn't he agree to become once again a member
of the Central Committee, or even the Politburo and/or deputy prime
minister? But Gomułka would have had to be very obtuse not to realize
the strength of his position. Like any sensible man under the circumstances, he would settle for nothing short of his old job.

With Moscow unwilling or unable to send clear signals, with the
Polish Communists deeply divided, the situation was growing more
and more tense throughout the spring and summer of 1956. As a
prominent Communist leader was to assess the crisis thirty years later:
"Already in May it became clear to everybody that Ochab would not
be able to carry out far-reaching reforms or meet the needs of the
hour. A moment might come when he would not be able to continue
as first secretary because what he represented clashed with the expectations of society."[23] What was most unusual for a Communist was
Ochab's own recognition that he was incapable of coping with the
situation and his willingness to step down. Now that the forty-odd-
year period of Communist rule in East Europe has passed into history,
one cannot cite another case where the top figure of a regime had
surrendered his post voluntarily. Usually no matter how old or ailing,
the Communist bosses would desperately cling to power, with only
death, an order from the Kremlin, or extreme pressure by their colleagues terminating their rule.

And so there was no easy way out of the predicament that faced Polish Communism. To continue as before threatened a popular revolt, to break decisively with the past risked Soviet military intervention. Ochab was to recollect: "I was well aware that if it came to a serious conflict in Poland, the Soviet Union, no matter what potential complications . . . would hardly hesitate [to intervene]. That is why I wanted to prevent the crisis from escalating and at the same time keep the Polish Communist Party from becoming isolated within our socialist camp. I felt it especially important to keep open channels of communication with the Chinese party . . . and to continue assuring them about our firm resolution to follow socialist principles in our domestic and foreign policies."[24]

At the end of September the first secretary and some other notables attended the Eighth Congress of the Chinese Communist Party as guests. There Ochab acquainted Beijing's leaders with the dilemmas facing Polish Communism and assured them that despite anything they might have heard from the Soviet Union, their Polish comrades would keep the faith. The Poles found it rather difficult to have confidential discussions with their Chinese counterparts since at all the social events during the congress the Soviet ambassador kept chaperoning conversations with their hosts. Finally, the Chinese helped Ochab and his entourage to shake off the inquisitive diplomat and to have a heart-to-heart talk with some of the highest-ranking officials of the People's Republic, who expressed understanding of their Polish guests' problems and their desire to be allowed "to settle among ourselves matters that concern Poland."

Ochab's account throws an interesting light on intra-Communist relations in the year of the "secret speech." The Poles frankly pleaded for more than their hosts' sympathy in case they would find themselves in a sharp conflict with the USSR. The Chinese for their own part were only too willing to encourage them to stand up to the Kremlin. After being reassured about Gomułka's orthodoxy and his fidelity to "proletarian internationalism," Zhou Enlai and other Beijing bigwigs expressed no objection to his being recalled to a responsible position, even leadership, in the party. Ochab also relates that in 1957 Zhou told him that at the height of the October crisis when the Soviets were on the verge of armed intervention in Poland, he, Zhou, contacted Moscow and strongly urged that "even if the Poles are wrong or making a mistake, they must be allowed to resolve their difficulties themselves."[25]

What is less credible, for reasons that will be seen here, is Ochab's conclusion that it was Beijing's plea that proved to be decisive in dissuading the Kremlin from resorting to armed force during the crisis. But the entire story is highly instructive in showing that already in 1956 the Chinese Communists were more than ready to advise the fraternal parties to act independently of Moscow and were thus making life more difficult for their Soviet comrades.

What transpired in China evidently emboldened those Polish Communists who wanted Gomułka back at the helm. By the time negotiations between him and the Politburo were concluded in the middle of October, the once and future leader prevailed on all the contentious points. He would take over the post of first secretary vacated by Ochab; the party would be guided by his views on agriculture and other crucial economic and social issues; people unacceptable to him, in most cases on account of being too close to Moscow, would be removed from the party's leadership. Notable among those to be purged from the Politburo was Marshal Konstantin Rokossovski, a longtime and prestigious Soviet military commander of Polish origin who in 1949 was assigned by the Kremlin to head Poland's armed forces. Now this gift of Stalin's was to be sent back to the Soviet Union, as were several other former Russian officers holding commands in the Polish army. All these measures were to be formally implemented, it was announced, at the meeting of the Central Committee scheduled for October 19.

The results of the negotiations represented a resounding defeat for the Natolin forces. In their panic some of the members appealed to the Soviets. It is a measure of the confusion prevailing at the time within the Soviet leadership, probably on account of the continuing struggle between the Khrushchev and the Molotov factions, that the Russians, usually so alert and well informed about what was going on in the Communist camp, did not have a prepared game plan for Poland and reacted belatedly to the developments there. It was only the night before the scheduled Central Committee session that the Soviet ambassador called Ochab and requested its postponement. The request was rejected by the Polish Politburo, a startling demonstration of how much things had changed in the last few months.

The nineteenth was a day of high historical drama. The Central Committeee met amid rumors, later authenticated, that some units of the army still commanded by Rokossovski were moving on Warsaw. Similar reports were circulated concerning the Soviet troops in Poland.

Unlike the army, the Polish security forces were controlled by the proponents of the changes, and they were put on alert. In preparation for an eventual clash, Gomułka's partisans also mobilized workers in Warsaw's principal factories. Everything seemed to presage the kind of tragic scenario that in a few weeks would unfold in Hungary.

Opening the session of the Central Committee in the morning, Ochab moved to immediately co-opt into its ranks Gomułka and three of his closest followers. He then shook his audience by announcing the arrival in Warsaw of Khrushchev, accompanied by Molotov, Mikoyan, and Kaganovich. Consequently, the first secretary asked that the session be adjourned until the evening to allow him and his colleagues in the Politburo to confer with the Soviet comrades, adding that Gomułka would also participate in the discussion.

What Ochab did not disclose was what happened at the airport upon the arrival of the Soviet guests. It was only later that he described their rather unfraternal behavior. Hardly out of the plane, Khrushchev shook his fist at the Polish notables. Demonstratively, he first exchanged greetings with a number of Soviet military and embassy officials, and only then, still with threatening gestures, turned to his hosts. Ochab credits himself with giving his irascible and uncouth guest a lesson in manners and then instructing him about his own and his colleagues' determination to be masters in their own house. "It is we who are responsible for running our country, and we act as we see fit. Those are our internal affairs. [But] we would not do anything that might threaten the interests of our allies, epecially those of the USSR."[26]

Even without the knowledge of the airport scene the committee members reacted indignantly to the announcement. "Why adjourn the meeting?" shouted one member; let Khrushchev and Company wait. Another argued they should elect the new leadership first and only then hold consultations with the Soviets. Only a few months before—more precisely, prior to the Twentieth Congress—the committee members' attitude toward the Kremlin's envoys, even with much less prestigious names than these, would have been one of reverence; now their coming uninvited was seen as a blatant effort, almost grotesque in its lack of subtlety, to harass and intimidate fellow Communists and in a way that, if successful, would discredit them even further in the eyes of the Polish people. But their initial outrage was soon tempered by the realization of what was at stake. The committee agreed to the adjournment, but in a mood that did not augur well for the Soviets' hopes to pressure the Poles into making important concessions. Not since 1948 was the Kremlin's authority over world Communism so clearly and openly challenged. But then in the case of Yugoslavia that defiance was made possible by Tito's almost Stalin-like grip on all the levers of power. Here the Polish Communists were far from effectively controlling their country. Their defiance came from a desperate need to gain their countrymen's trust and, certainly in some cases, self-respect.

The negotiations stretched late into the night. One version has it that on seeing Gomułka among the Polish delegates, Khrushchev exclaimed, "What is this agent of Wall Street and Zionists doing here?" A more reliable account has the Soviets complaining that they were the last ones to be informed about the impending changes in the leadership. They spoke bitterly about anti-Soviet propaganda, allegedly tolerated by the Polish authorities. When Khrushchev, still in a threatening mood, shouted that they could tell who the enemies of the Soviet Union were, Gomułka coldly retorted: "Ochab is an enemy. I am an enemy. You are beginning to carry on as you used to in the bad old times."[27] Did the Soviet comrades consult with the Poles when they planned to change their leadership, inquired Ochab, a remark that appealed to Khrushchev's sense of humor and made him moderate his bullying way.

The official version of the encounter presented to the Central Committee on October 20 admitted that the discussions had been tempestuous, but that the Polish side refused to give ground. "We tried to calm the Soviet comrades . . . about our intentions and the future course of action. . . . We tried to explain the process of democratization we are carrying on, its essence, general meaning, and its irreversibility."[28]

The report was rather awkwardly inconsistent when it asserted that the changes in the Polish leadership "were from the beginning to the end of the discussion treated as concerning exclusively our party and our Central Committee." In the end the Poles' resolution prevailed over Khrushchev's bluff and bluster, and what one must assume were more fundamental objections from the Molotov-Kaganovich corner. The only alternative the Soviets had was the use of armed force. But as Rokossovski must have informed them, Polish soldiers could not be relied upon in such a case and a Soviet military occupation of the country loomed as a very difficult and expensive operation. The people, as the Natolin faction acknowledged, were overwhelmingly behind the proposed changes, with Gomułka at the moment a national hero. And so the Soviet potentates put a good face upon their discomfiture: they had every confidence that Comrade Gomułka would steer Polish Communism along the correct line. But why, oh why, didn't Comrade Ochab and others tell them what they were preparing?

The Central Committee resumed its deliberations on October 20 in an atmosphere of general relief. The proreform forces were exultant but still wary. The uninvited guests had flown back to Moscow, but, knowing the Soviet comrades, one could not exclude the possibility, alas, of their going back on their word. (As indeed would soon occur in Hungary.) "Comrade" Marshal Rokossovski was closely questioned about the reports of Polish and Soviet troop movements. Were they true? Who ordered them? The victor of Stalingrad explained lamely that the troops under his command were simply going through their usual fall exercises. As for the Soviet units, yes indeed they had been moving toward the major Polish urban centers. But then, as instructed by the Politburo, he contacted their commander, his wartime comrade-in-arms Marshal Ivan Konev, and asked that the troops be returned to their usual location. He concluded, not very convincingly: "We must not—one does not—have the right to suspect the Polish army of ever being used against the government and the party. . . . It is only at their order that the army will act."[29] The committee, with some nudging by the leaders, decided to pass over the troublesome issue. But even the most obtuse member must have realized that it was only by a narrow margin that they had avoided the Soviet military coup and quite likely a civil war.

"When I spoke several years ago at the Plenum of the Central Committee, I was convinced that I was speaking to it for the last time." It was thus that Gomułka began his victor's address. "The intervening seven years have done much harm. The legacy of that period, what it has done to the party, the working class, to the nation, has in many ways been more than alarming."[30] He criticized severely the economic policies of the past. As might have been expected, his sharpest condemnation was reserved for the cult of personality. "The essence of that cult consisted in a veritable ladder of cults . . . at the summit of the ladder stood Stalin. . . . [Below him] were the first secretaries of the central committees of the various countries. They also were credited with attributes of infallibility and wisdom. But their cult prevailed only over the territory of their countries. . . . The system permeated the minds, formed the thinking of the party members. . . . The system violated the principles of democracy and justice. . . . Slander, falsehood, provocation were employed as the means of holding on to power. We are finished with that state of affairs, or rather we are in the process of putting an end to it once and for all. We greatly appreciate what has been done at the Twentieth Congress of the Communist Party of the Soviet Union, which has helped us so much in our own task."[31]

Those who heard Gomułka on both occasions must have marveled at the apparent transformation of the man. His 1949 speech, while not exactly conforming to the model of confession and self-accusation of Stalinist times, was still one of a broken man. Now, although he was technically not yet the first secretary, his address had the ring of authority: they had before them not merely the party's, but the nation's leader. And he spoke against a background of tremendous popular excitement and agitation, with mass meetings held throughout the country, the crowds demonstrating in his support, demanding an end to the persecution of the Church, and though as a rule disciplined and refraining from violence, breaking out occasionally with anti-Soviet slogans. Gomułka's address, in addition to an indictment of the past, promised a freer future: the general democratization of political life, a halt to forced collectivization, and strict observance of the law. While the speaker promised loyalty and cooperation with the Soviet Union, there was no mistaking his determination that Poland, certainly in its domestic affairs, should pursue a completely independent course, "the Polish path to socialism."

For the committee there was now no alternative to formal acceptance of the authority of the man who a few years back had with the complicity or at least acquiescence of many of those present been chased out of the party, imprisoned, and set on the road to the gallows. Now almost equally meekly the assembled notables approved of Gomułka's choices for the new Politburo. The list did not include Marshal Rokossovski. In a last-minute effort to save something from defeat, a number of Natolin diehards still pushed his candidacy, pleading that the marshal's exclusion would incense the Russians. But in a secret balloting Stalin's gift to Poland failed reelection by a wide margin. After a decent interval the renowned commander, obviously miscast in his role in Poland, would be released as minister of defense and would return to the country in whose service he earned his real laurels. In what was almost an anticlimax, the committee by an open and unanimous vote ratified the choice of Gomułka as first secretary.

The new leader's first and harrowing concern was to contain and becalm the popular enthusiasm and agitation that helped carry him to power. His choice by the party came very largely as a result of cold calculations by his colleagues, who saw him as the only man who could rehabilitate Communism in Poland and prevent a mass uprising. But to the crowds of workers and students who had been demonstrating, his was a victory *over* Communism and a resounding defeat for the Soviet Union and its Polish puppets. Now the people's expectations and excitement threatened to overflow safe bounds and to lead to demands to sever all ties with the Soviet Union, and in the first instance to have Soviet troops removed from the territory of the republic.

On October 24, Gomułka for the first time in eight years addressed a mass meeting in Warsaw. He had to stress again and again that Polish-Soviet relations would from now on be based on complete equality. "All concrete matters affecting our internal affairs will be solved in accordance with the attitude of our party and the government. It depends entirely on us whether and how long the Soviet experts will be retained in our army. We received assurances from Comrade Khrushchev that the Soviet troops in Polish territory will return within two days to their bases."[32]

The crowd of half a million cheered those assurances but remained silent when the first secretary tried to explain the reason why some Soviet army units must remain on Polish soil and warned against anti-Soviet agitation. By this time the events in Hungary were approaching their climax and some signs carried by the crowd extolled the Hungarian struggle for freedom. An eyewitness at the time, a high party official, was to reminisce that Gomułka for all his outward composure was greatly agitated and fearful that the meeting might be followed by anti-Soviet riots, an assault on the embassy of the USSR or even attacks on the local party and the security-service headquarters.[33] Nothing could illustrate better how for the crowd, at least to a substantial portion of it, Gomułka's popularity and prestige came from his having been a victim of Communism, rather than from being currently its highest official. By the same token, both he and his fellow leaders realized only too well that they were still not out of danger as far as the Kremlin's options were concerned, but that its acquiescence in the Polish coup had been grudging and was not irrevocable.

Gradually, the tumultuous and dangerous mood of the masses subsided. The new leadership moved quickly to remove the most notorious

Natolin partisans from responsible party and government positions. There began an exodus of the Soviet experts who under Rokossowski had infiltrated the Polish armed forces.

The most important step in calming public opinion, however, was the regime's new opening toward the Church. Only one week after Gomułka's elevation the authorities hastened to release Cardinal Stefan Wyszyński, incarcerated since 1953. There followed the freeing of several other imprisoned prelates and clergymen. But it was not only the question of a cessation of persecution; the party needed the active assistance of the Church to help reconcile the people to the fact that Poland, while considerably freer, was still under a Communist regime and still closely tied to the Soviet Union. And so the government entered into negotiations with the Church hierarchy in which it speedily agreed to most of its postulates: the reintroduction of religious instruction in schools, non-interference with the Church's pastoral and charitable activities, and permission for building more churches. In return, Cardinal Wyszyński threw his great moral authority behind the regime's efforts to assuage the aroused passions and expectations and to restore public order. An official statement by the episcopate proclaimed that "as a result of transformations in public life aimed at the consolidation of legality, justice, peaceful coexistence, the raising of social morality and the righting of wrongs the government and the State authorities would find in the Church hierarchy and clergy full understanding."[34] The survival of the Communist regime in Poland would for the remainder of its existence—thirty-three years—depend on two powers. First on the Soviet Union, for after the October hopes and expectations had been dissipated, it was mainly the fear of Soviet armed intervention that enabled the Communists to hold on to power, even if this fear did not stop the semi-revolution of 1970 and the upheaval of 1980–81. Equally important in that survival was the role of the Church: for all of its basic disagreement with Marxian ideology, the Church maintained steadily that whatever the grievances of the faithful and the people at large, they must not be allowed to lead to violence.

For two years the regime would continue to draw dividends from the capital which accrued to it in the October coup. And during that period Gomułka, uniquely for a Communist figure, would enjoy genuine popularity and the trust of the nation. In the immediate wake of October and in view of the tragic events in Hungary both the Poles and the Soviets could congratulate themselves for avoiding what could have been an even more painful and tragic conflict had the Kremlin not acquiesced in the Warsaw coup.

The October 19 agreement between the two sides was subsequently confirmed and expanded when a Polish delegation headed by Gomułka came to Moscow on November 18. The USSR and Poland agreed on "the similarity of goals" in their foreign policies. The thorny question of the Soviet troops was settled by both sides agreeing that the Soviet army units would continue to be stationed in Poland under the Warsaw Pact provisions, but their movements and use outside their bases would have to be sanctioned by the Polish government. As a means of reparation for its previous and extensive economic exploitation of Poland (which often took the form of the Soviets receiving Polish raw materials at below the world market prices), the USSR canceled $500 million of the Polish debt, and granted new credits to Warsaw. Thousands of Polish citizens still retained in the USSR, some of them since the Soviet occupation of 1939–41 of the eastern part of the republic, were to be returned to their country.

The agreement was to serve as a pattern for similar arrangements with other People's Democracies. They too were provided compensation through long-term loans and sometimes outright cancellation of previous indebtedness incurred during the Stalinist exploitation of the satellites' resources. Soviet troops were withdrawn from some of them, and where they remained, their stationing was linked to the Warsaw Treaty, thus, at least on the face of it, removing the stigma of military occupation and suggesting an arrangement similiar to that of NATO's. Soviet interference in the affairs of its allies became as a rule less intrusive and direct, carried out through hints and advice rather than command. The substance of Soviet imperial power was retained, while the manner of its exercise became more restrained and hence more acceptable to the ruling parties and to their subjects. Had the Hungarian drama not taken place one might have well believed at the end of 1956 that the new spirit in the Kremlin was amenable to the eventual development of a genuine Communist commonwealth of nations, and that "proletarian internationalism," so grotesquely distorted by Stalin, might indeed come into its own.

But quite apart from the jarring effect of the invasion of Hungary, such hopes were to prove excessive. Again one is reminded of Solzhenitsyn's observation about Khrushchev's inability to carry through to the end any of the major reforms he had started, an observation that has often been heard in reference to Gorbachev. To be sure, neither at the time, nor even after his rout of the Molotov group in June 1957, was the first secretary in a position to make decisions on such issues entirely on his own. Yet even by his own lights, Khrushchev could not reconcile himself to the idea of complete freedom, as against autonomy, for other Communist states and parties. He did not want to terrorize or coerce other leaders, but he became bitter and threatening when their policies and actions diverged to any significant degree from those of the Kremlin. Just as the collapse of expectations based on the "secret speech" led within the Soviet Union to the birth of dissent, so elsewhere in the Communist bloc similar disenchantment would produce attempts to expand what in the Kremlin's view were the permissible limits of national autonomy. Even Khrushchev's reconciliation with Tito was predicated upon the assumption that Yugoslavia could, this time through friendliness and flattery rather than threats, be brought back into the Communist camp and once again follow Moscow's lead.

The year 1956 then did not really put an end to the vicious circle that had been a feature of East European politics since World War II. Communism was loathed or at least resented largely because it came, so to speak, in the baggage train of the Red Army. And the Soviet Union was feared and disliked, even in the countries where previously there had been little or no anti-Russian feeling—for example, Czechoslovakia or Bulgaria—mainly because it had imposed Communist regimes upon those hapless nations and apparently stood ready to back them up with military might.

The Polish scenario seemed to offer the hope of breaking the vicious circle and resolving the main dilemma of Communism in East Europe. The Soviets had tried to stop what they considered untoward developments in Poland and, having failed, acquiesced in the new look of the Polish regime rather than sending in troops and tanks. And the Polish Communists, having withstood Soviet pressure, gained a measure of popularity among their own people. Here, then, was a lesson that might apply to other regimes in the area: if the USSR were consistently to pursue the policy of noninterference in their internal affairs, the other regimes would be constrained to follow the path of reform and, like the Polish one, gain respect in the eyes of their own people. This, incidentally, would relieve the USSR of the burden of standing armed guard over some 100 million people. At the same time, Moscow's security interests would not suffer because with the memories of the war still fresh, no country in the bloc would willingly forsake the Soviet shield against a revival of Germany's militarism and its likely sequel, territorial vindications. One suspects that no amount of liberalization on their part could have in the long run preserved the Communist parties' monopoly of power. But then the evolution toward political pluralism would have been gradual and peaceful, and its eventual consummation would not have posed any danger to the USSR.

The Polish drama, however, was almost immediately followed by the Hungarian tragedy, which rudely shook, if not entirely shattered, most of the hopes and speculations aroused by the Warsaw events.

The latter had in a way helped precipitate the Hungarian uprising. What had been in Poland a coup within the Communist Party, even though carried on a wave of popular unrest, was instrumental in triggering the Hungarian revolt *against* Communism. There were significant differences in the background of the two crises. The campaign against the alleged Titoists had been much more brutal and claimed more victims in Hungary than in its neighbor to the north. The Warsaw leadership, despite the Soviets' pressure, managed first to delay and, once Stalin died, to avoid the frightful spectacle of a show trial of Communist notables. In Budapest already in 1949 there was staged such a trial featuring the former interior minister, László Rajk, who having duly confessed to a variety of grotesquely improbable crimes was along with most of the others accused (most of them also former Communists) dispatched to the gallows. The man who bore direct responsibility for the judicial murders was the party's first secretary, Mátyás Rákosi. He was allowed to remain in that post until 1956, even in the face of the growing revulsion against him in the party, not to speak of the people at large.

After March 5, 1953, the Soviets, as we have seen, insisted on the local Stalins being brought down a notch and on at least the appearance of collective leadership. And so Rákosi had to lay down his other job of prime minister, which was taken over by Imre Nagy. Though known as a moderate and reform-minded man, Nagy rather surprisingly had not suffered imprisonment during his long pre-1945 stay in the USSR and was equally fortunate during the open season on "Titoists" and other "people's enemies" between 1948 and 1953. By the same token, this well-meaning but politically not very skillful man lacked that aura of martyrdom that had been such an asset of Poland's Gomułka and had helped him to recoup power. Nagy's rather brief stay as prime minister (July 1953 to January 1955) was marked by an amnesty for political prisoners and attempts to introduce more liberal and less dogmatic social and economic policies. But the latter was sabotaged by the party apparatus headed by Rákosi, who finally managed to remove his rival from all his government party posts and in December of 1955 had him expelled from the party. The abrupt halt to reform further stirred the political atmosphere, provoking especially strong protests among the intellectuals and students. It could only have been the political divisions and struggles within the Soviet elite that made Moscow not heed, until it was too late, the danger signals from Hungary.

The reverberations of the Twentieth Congress constrained Rákosi to fall in line with de-Stalinization policies. One of the crucial measures had to be the rehabilitation of the Hungarian victims of Stalinism, including Rajk. By now such admissions served only to incense public opinion, and the Kremlin was finally compelled to intervene. Its expert on handling the more delicate aspects of intra-Communist affairs, Anastas Mikoyan, was dispatched to Budapest in July 1956. The very next day Rákosi resigned as first secretary, pleading ill health but also acknowledging his mistake in "the field of the cult of personality and socialist legality." As a Yugoslav observer saw it: "The Russians were ready . . . to back Rákosi and through him carry out the 'de-Stalinization' of Hungary! When even the Russians realized that such an operation was not possible in Hungary, they chose Rákosi's closest collaborator, instead of picking some less compromised person."[35]

The person in question was Ernö Gerö, and as one might have suspected from the above, he was not much of an improvement on his predecessor, nor was he able to stabilize the situation and prevent the eventual explosion.

Gerö tried to appease public opinion by gestures such as staging a ceremonial reburial of Rajk's remains. But this attempt by the regime to gain sympathy by striking a contrite pose backfired. The gruesome ceremony brought vast crowds into the streets of Budapest, their attitude toward the regime unmistakably hostile.

For all of the undemocratic character of its internal politics, Yugoslavia, because of its government's courageous stand in 1948, still enjoyed great prestige throughout Eastern Europe. And so hoping that some of that popularity would rub off on them, Gerö and his associates invited themselves in the fateful month of October to Belgrade. Marshal Tito, then at the very apogee of his international standing—assiduously courted by both East and West—deigned to receive the Hungarian delegation and to express, though not overenthusiastically, his approval of the new Budapest leadership.

But the week of October 15–23, which the hapless leaders spent in Yugoslavia, saw the situation at home evolve very quickly. Hungarians seeking a path to a freer life now shifted their attention from Yugoslavia to Poland. The news of what on the face of it was a successful defiance of the Soviet Union by the reform-minded faction of the Polish United Workers' Party (the successor of the Polish Workers' Party) and the assumption of its leadership by a man trusted by the nation provoked demonstrations in Budapest that were met at first with weak and confused reactions by the authorities. "The university students announced plans for a silent sympathy demonstration in front of the Polish embassy. . . . At 12:53 was broadcast a decision of the Ministry of the Interior prohibiting the demonstration. At 2:23 P.M. the decision of the Ministry was rescinded."[36]

From gestures of sympathy with the apparently victorious Poles, the Hungarian demonstrators turned to their own concerns. There had been meetings before that heard demands for the return of Imre Nagy to the government and urging the pullout of Soviet troops from the country's soil. Demonstrations soon turned into riots. The popular mood was inflamed by Gerö's radio address in which he denounced those attacking the government for, among other sins, slandering the Soviet Union. "They assert that we are trading with the Soviet Union on an unequal footing, that our relations with the Soviet Union allegedly are not based on equality and that our independence must . . . be defended not against the imperialists but against the Soviet Union."[37] Along with that succinct summary of what was in fact the nature of Soviet-Hungarian relations, the apparently humorless party boss made another unfortunate statement. "We, of course, want a socialist democracy and not a bourgeois one."[38]

Within twenty-four hours that "socialist democracy" was shattered. The government lost control of the situation. Sometime during the night of October 23–24 the Central Committee of what no longer could be called the ruling party, trying to retrieve something from the situation, voted to invite Nagy to assume the post of prime minister. But by the time Nagy, whose appointment a few days before would have prevented the outbreak of the uprising, could take up his duties on the morning of the twenty-fourth, Soviet tanks were rolling through the streets of Budapest. The formal request for Soviet intervention was made by a member of the Hungarian Politburo, the Hungarian leadership's role being thus in startling contrast to that of the Polish Party, which a few days before threatened armed resistance should Soviet troops attempt to move on Warsaw.

Also, unlike Poland, the party high command virtually disintegrated within hours of the beginning of the rebellion. Street fighting was not stopped by the announcement that Gerö had been replaced as first secretary by János Kádár, whose reputation as a reformer and anti-Stalinist was based on a prison term he had suffered during the post-1948 hunt for the Titoists. But neither Nagy nor Kádár were able to get a handle on the situation, with the crowds assaulting government and party buildings and attacking Soviet tanks with Molotov cocktails. What contributed to the eventual tragedy of the Hungarian revolution was the fact that during those last days of October all the relevant political forces were rendered impotent. "The Communist Party no longer existed. The opposition had disintegrated. The state apparatus ceased to exist."[39] And for the moment the Soviet leaders had still not recovered from the Polish shock, some of them being far from reconciled to the new order in Warsaw. What many in the USSR had feared, ever since Khrushchev delivered his indictment of Stalinism, was taking place in Hungary: what had begun as a movement to reform the Communist regime had turned into a revolution against Communism.

Taking note of this, the roster of the new government announced by Nagy on the twenty-seventh included prominent non-Communists. He then proclaimed an end to the one-party system and promised to dissolve the secret police. By the twenty-ninth there could be some hope that things were sorting themselves out. The government had ordered a cease-fire. The Soviet troops began to pull out. Soviet emissaries Mikhail Suslov and Anastas Mikoyan, who were commuting almost daily between Moscow and Budapest, now brought a reassuring message: the Soviets would not use force to upset the new order. On the thirtieth a formal statement by the Kremlin on the principles that would henceforth regulate "friendship and cooperation between the Soviet Union and the socialist states" promised that they would be based on respect for the individual countries' independence, and noninterference in their internal affairs. At the time—but how briefly—the statement was meant seriously. Moscow would not reject a variant of the Polish solution for Hungary. With divided counsels in the Kremlin, and with the Suez Crisis offering new opportunities but also presenting new potential dangers for the Soviet Union in the Middle East, Khrushchev must have hoped for the Hungarian crisis to subside to preclude the need for a further and this time massive Soviet military intervention. At the same time, it is obvious that the Soviet troops had as early as October 23 been put on alert should such an intervention prove necessary.

What did tip the scales in favor of military intervention? As of the twenty-ninth, both Foreign Minister Dmitri Shepilov and Defense Minister Marshal Zhukov had issued statements implying support of the Nagy government and confidence in its ability to master the situation. But the October 30 declaration, of which we spoke, specified that a member state could withdraw from the Warsaw Treaty Organization only on the basis of an agreement by all the signatories to the pact—i.e., with Soviet approval. At the same time, his government in danger of being swept away by the momentum of the revolution, Imre Nagy sought to appease the anti-Communist forces by announcing, as if in defiance of the declaration, that Hungary was withdrawing from the Warsaw Pact and was appealing to the United Nations to protect its neutrality.

With the Hungarian situation coming to a boil, the Kremlin was thrown into agitated confusion. Khrushchev's and some other Soviet leaders' wanderings between the first and third of November speak for themselves. On the former date the first secretary, accompanied by Molotov and Malenkov, had traveled to Brest Litovsk to confer with Gomułka and Ochab. He and Malenkov then flew to Bucharest to take counsel with the Romanian and Czechoslovak Communist leaders, afterward to Sofia for a talk with the Bulgarians. Nor were the Chinese omitted during that frantic round of consultations, the number-two man in Beijing, Liu Shaoqi, being currently in Moscow.

On the evening of November 2 the harassed Kremlin chief and Malenkov, obviously holding the brief for the other Politburo (Presidium) faction, descended on Marshal Tito's luxurious retreat on the island of Brioni off the Adriatic coast. Khrushchev, though no longer a youngster, must still have possessed considerable stamina. He could not have had much sleep in the preceding hours, and now the talks with Tito and his main lieutenants went uninterruptedly from 7 P.M. to 5 A.M.[40]

For a few months prior to the Polish and Hungarian crises, Tito had been Khrushchev's confidential adviser on East European affairs. But now the Soviet boss was coming mainly to seek the marshal's approval for a course of action already decided on, rather than to ask him whether or not to intervene militarily in Hungary.

The first secretary was emphatic that the USSR had to intervene and in a manner that would speedily crush all resistance. "What is there left for us to do. . . . If we let things take their course the West would say we are either stupid or weak. . . . We cannot possibly permit it either as Communists and internationalists or as the Soviet state." He was quite frank about the domestic reasons for the projected intervention. "There were people in the Soviet Union who would say that as long as Stalin was in command everybody obeyed, but that now that they had come to power, Russia had suffered defeat and the loss of Hungary." And Khrushchev intimated that "this might be said primarily by the Soviet army, which was one of the reasons why they were intervening in Hungary."[41] Nagy, he also asserted, was either a tool of imperialism or had for long been its agent, and to let him carry on would lead to the restoration of capitalism in the country.

The speech was vintage Khrushchev. He could not have thought for a moment that his Yugoslav hosts would believe the nonsense about Nagy. Only a bit more credible was his allegation that it was the military that had been pressuring him for intervention. (In less than a year he would fire Marshal Zhukov without encountering any trouble on that count from other marshals and generals.) Nor could the argument about Hungary's quitting the Warsaw Pact be fully convincing: Yugoslavia was not a member of the organization and yet it was *as of then* a "fraternal Communist state" in good standing.

Yet against all that bluster there was one motif that had to appeal to Tito: this was a domino situation. If Communism in Hungary could be overthrown by a popular uprising, what East European regime could feel safe? And so the marshal, after lecturing his visitors to his usual refrain of "if you had only listened to me when," reluctantly agreed that the Soviets had no other choice in the matter. As a participant in the meeting, the Yugoslav ambassador to the USSR recorded, "We were also concerned at the swing of events to the right, toward counterrrevolution, when we saw the Nagy government allowing Communists to be murdered and hanged."[42]

To be sure, passions unleashed by the uprising did lead to violence, including a number of lynchings of officals of the secret police and others suspected of having been minions of the Rákosi-Gerö team. The list of alleged victims of "counterrevolutionary terror" published by the Kádár regime after the suppression of the revolution contains

215 names, of whom around twenty are described as having been summarily executed, with the rest evidently casualties of the fighting.[43] As of October 31, order by and large had been restored and excesses brought to an end. But the vision of a popular uprising against Communism, of mobs invading party and secret-police headquarters, had to be deeply disturbing to Tito, as it was to other Communist chieftains of Eastern Europe. And so with a heavy heart, and probably not without a thought at the back of his mind that this might set a precedent for some future Soviet intervention in Yugoslavia, he fell in with the Moscow plan to invade Hungary and crush the uprising.

His approval was accompanied by several suggestions concerning the political side of the intervention. The latter should be preceded by the formation of a new Hungarian government, which while condemning Nagy and his supporters should make and publicize its sharp break from the policies and personalities of the Rákosi-Gerö era. Who could head such a government? Two prominent Hungarian Communists had just fled from Budapest to Moscow, Ferenc Münnich and Kádár. Khrushchev leaned toward Münnich. Too old and too much compromised by his past association with the old regime, objected Tito. Better take Kádár, purified, so to speak, by his having been put in jail by Rákosi. Khrushchev let himself be convinced, or quite possibly he had wanted Kádár all along but thought it politic to show his host how much he valued his advice.

The Yugoslav official's account of the Brioni meeting expresses obvious embarrassment: here were Tito and his associates, whose defiance of Stalin had inspired hope throughout captive Eastern Europe, now advising the Russians on the most efficacious ways of suppressing another nation's desperate striving for freedom.

And if the Yugoslav leaders thought their invidious game would prevent or at least minimize further bloodshed, such hopes were soon exposed as chimerical. On November 4, Soviet military units opened a full-scale assault on Budapest and other cities. They were met with spirited resistance, but poorly armed workers' militia and a few military units could be no match for Soviet tanks and heavy artillery. Nagy, and several of his fellow ministers, with whom the Soviets until the very moment of the assault had kept up deceptive negotiations, sought refuge in the Yugoslav embassy. The Russian verdict on the situation as expressed in *Pravda* on the same day was peremptory: "Imre Nagy turned out to be, objectively, an accomplice of the reactionary forces. . . . The task of barring the way to reaction in Hungary was to be carried out without the slightest delay—such is the course dictated by events." On the seventh, Kádár and his hastily improvised cabinet returned to the Soviet-controlled capital. Like his Soviet sponsors, Kádár would try to appease the popular resistance and strikes that had broken out all over the country by mendacious promises, hinting at the possibility of eventual free elections and a multiparty system. But the pattern of deception was fully unraveled on November 22, when on leaving the Yugoslav embassy, Nagy and his associates, previously given a pledge of safe conduct, were seized by the Soviet military. Hungary's ordeal continued through the bleak winter of 1956-57. The balance sheet of the uprising was grim. Even by Kádár's government's own admission some 2,000 people had been killed in Budapest alone during November. The official figures listed 105 executions for "crimes against the people." The actual number was probably ten times as great.[44] Close to 200,000 people, 2 percent of the country's total population, escaped to the West across the Austrian frontier. It would be a sort of poetic justice that more than thirty years later the same frontier would be crossed by thousands of East German refugees, their flight precipitating the fall of the Berlin Communist regime, the central feature of the utter collapse of Communist power all over Eastern Europe, including Hungary.

For the moment, however, and a long time to come, the incipient "new thinking" in Soviet policy, insofar as it touched on the Kremlin's relations with other Communist states, had been shattered. The Stalinist pattern would not return, but neither would the hopes that those countries or even their regimes would be allowed to enjoy anything like genuine freedom of action. The Hungarian revolt had been defeated, but so, in a much deeper sense, had been the idea of "proletarian internationalism," the notion that ideological links could be an effective bond of unity within the Communist camp. It was clearer than ever before that this camp was kept together by the Soviet Union's military power. The Warsaw Treaty Organization (often called the Warsaw Pact), called into being in 1955 supposedly because of the need to offset NATO now that Germany, in the process of remilitarization, had joined its ranks, would in fact become a synonym for, and an instrument of, the Soviet Union's protectorate over Eastern Europe. The expectations raised by the Polish October had rudely been dispelled by the Hungarian November. In Poland itself Gomułka's approval, even though qualified, of what happened south of its borders dealt a blow to his prestige among the people, thus beginning the rapid process of the erosion of his popularity.

Another consequence of the Budapest imbroglio was a drastic change in the Soviet's attitude toward Yugoslavia. On further reflection, and probably goaded by the Molotov-Malenkov faction, Khrushchev no longer saw in Tito a trusted guide in the politics of Eastern Europe, but one whose unfortunate example had been responsible for much of the trouble the USSR had been experiencing there lately. Already a few days after Brioni, Khrushchev floored the Yugoslav ambassador by telling him that "nobody in the Soviet Union could interpret the failure to hand over Nagy, and the other organizers of the counterrevolution, as anything but evidence that they had long been acting on instructions from Yugoslavia and that Yugoslavia was responsible for what they had done."[45] This incredible bullying and prevarication was stoutly resisted by the ambassador, but it casts a rather strange light on the Yugoslavs' subsequent protestations that they were surprised and shocked when Nagy and his companions, in flight from their embassy under a safe conduct from the Kádár government, were seized by the Russians.

The Soviets' fresh unhappiness with Tito was not diminished by the schoolmasterish tone he now adopted over Moscow's actions in Hungary. In his November 11 Tula speech the Yugoslav leader was at his haughtiest: "And of course, if it meant saving socialism in Hungary, then, comrades, we can say that although we are against interference [in a country's internal affairs], Soviet intervention was necessary. But had the [Soviets] done everything that should have been done earlier, there would not have been any need for military intervention. This error was, unfortunately, a result of their idea that military power can solve everything.[46] Even if the statement was condescending, the last sentence was so right on target that it evoked indignant protestations in the Soviet media. The Yugoslavs were now officially blamed as carriers of the virulent virus of national Communism. Early in 1957 the USSR canceled several commercial agreements with Yugoslavia. The nonsense about Tito being largely responsible for the anti-Soviet character of the October 1956 Budapest uprising was repeated on the occasion of Kádár's visit to Moscow in March 1957, with both the visitor and his official host, Marshal Bulganin, indulging in derogatory remarks about Yugoslavia. USSR-Yugoslav relations did improve following Khrushchev's triumph over the "antiparty" Molotov group in June 1957, but a full reconciliation had to await the eruption of a much more serious, Moscow-Beijing, dispute.

And speaking of China, the reverberations of the Hungarian drama affected areas and issues transcending Eastern Europe. Many Western Communists were outraged, quite a number of them tearing up their party cards, and so were some left-wing sympathizers. Such reactions were neither unanticipated nor particularly disturbing to Moscow, which knew from past experience that after the wave of moral indignation had subsided most of the left-wing intellectuals in the West would revert to the more congenial task of criticizing their own societies and the United States. Still, they marked a further step in that disenchantment with the USSR that began with the revelations at the Twentieth Party Congress.

Much more serious were the consequences within the Soviet Union itself. The Molotov-Malenkov faction could and did resume its refrain that Khrushchev's ill-considered liberalism brought the entire Communist bloc to the edge of disaster. The embattled first secretary now adopted an unfortunate, and as it turned out, counterproductive course of a partial withdrawal of his repudiation of Stalinism. At the New Year's reception in the Kremlin, the Soviet elite and the diplomatic corps were treated to a harangue by Khrushchev in which he attacked those "who divide Soviet leaders into Stalinists and anti-Stalinists, hoping in this way to cause a split in the Soviet and other Communist parties." He himself received his political education under Stalin and was proud of it![47] He expatiated on the theme later at a gala evening at the Chinese embassy, telling his audience that Stalin had taught Communists how to deal with their enemies. Whether sincere or not, such avowals could only weaken his own position and embolden his opponents within the ruling elite. He had compromised his image as a reformer without gaining any solid political advantage.

Even more serious was the effect of Khrushchev's turnabout on the future of Sino-Soviet relations. As already noted, the brutal repression of Hungary revealed not only his personal political weakness, but that of the Soviet Union's. Would the USSR always have to stand armed guard over some 100 million people in Eastern Europe? What if Hungarian-type troubles erupted simultaneously in several countries of the area? And would the Western powers, which at the time were fortunately tied in knots over the Suez crisis, remain passive during the next crisis?

To forestall such alarming possibilities the Kremlin leadership invoked the help of China. Beijing's approval had already been sought before the invasion of Hungary. And now Khrushchev and his colleagues felt constrained to ask for China's overt and explicit support of its policies in Eastern Europe. It was at Moscow's request that Zhou Enlai interrupted his tour of Asia to pay a visit to Moscow, Warsaw, and Budapest in January of 1957. In all those capitals he stressed China's solidarity with the Soviet Union, describing it repeatedly as the leader of the socialist bloc and expressing approval of its intrabloc policies. Consummate diplomat that he was, Zhou varied his approach and oratory according to the place and occasion. In Warsaw, while expressing his support for the Kádár government, he did not refer to the Soviet armed intervention. In Budapest he attacked the "Nagy clique." In Moscow he dealt at length on the help the Soviet Union had rendered China, and praised the Soviet role in protecting the Hungarian people from the designs of the imperialists.

Chinese help, the Kremlin must have realized, could not come free. That the Soviets needed it was already a somewhat humiliating confession of their political vulnerability and an acknowledgment of China's growing importance. On both counts it was bound to increase Beijing's demands for full partnership in directing the world Communist movement, i.e., for giving Mao and his people direct influence on Soviet foreign policy. As a Yugoslav observer astutely noted: "It seems as though the Russians are now in favor of recognizing the Chinese as equal partners of the Soviet Union in the leadership of the socialist camp, even if it is at the moment to the Soviet disadvantage. More important now is Chinese support for Soviet policy; the question of prestige can be taken care of later."[48]

The year 1956 began as one of hope within the Communist movement. The Soviet Union appeared on the verge of what would be called many years later "perestroika." In Eastern Europe the Communist regimes promised to undergo a similar transformation, and from being the USSR's satellites seemed about to advance to the status of its partners. But the Twentieth Congress and Khrushchev's speech did not fully exorcise the ghost of Stalin: the man was denounced but the institutional bulwarks of Stalinism—the party's absolute control over society and control of that party by a small inner group—remained untouched. The satellites' evolution toward what in the future would be called "socialism with a human face," the evolution that appeared to have had such a promising beginning in Poland, was soon checked and partly reversed by the suppression of Hungary. Communism once again failed to pass the test as a plausible foundation of a stable world order. The Yugoslav-Soviet estrangement occurred not merely because of the personalities involved and an unfortunate turn of events. It was a telling demonstration that because of the very nature of its system the USSR could not maintain relations with another Communist state on the basis of equality rather than that of domination. It was the recognition by both sides of that ineluctable fact that brought new strains in the relations between Moscow and Belgrade.

For the West, 1956 signaled the end of an era: the Suez venture forcibly demonstrated the incongruity and futility of imperialist ventures in the age of mass communications and of nuclear weapons. Superficially, what happened in Hungary put that lesson in question: an imperial power suppressed a national rising. But the resort to arms marked in the longer run a political defeat: as against quite recent hopes, ideological links proved too weak to secure the unity of the socialist camp and to keep a Communist regime in power. And the realities of the nuclear age would make military power by itself an inadequte safeguard of the cohesion and security of the Communist bloc. Thus Hungary was a harbinger of the future defeats and of the eventual collapse of "proletarian internationalism" and of its steady companion, Soviet imperialism.

6

TOWARD THE BRINK

WHY DIDN'T perestroika, of which the Twentieth Congress appears to have been a harbinger, begin in the late 1950s, rather than belatedly and lamely in the 1980s? From the perspective of 1991, it can be seen that Khrushchev, even if in a hopelessly roundabout and awkward way, did seek an amelioration of relations with the West. Why, then, did détente appear but ephemerally in 1972, and then more concretely only in 1985?

Allowing for some oversimplification, the answer to both questions must be Communist China. It was the People's Republic's presence on the world scene and the conscious policy of Beijing's leaders that proved to be a very serious obstacle to basic reforms within the Communist world, and even more so when it came to reaching any enduring accommodation between the Soviet Union and the West. We have already noted that China's joining the socialist camp increased the Soviet Union's weight enormously in international relations, appeared to make nonsense of the American doctrine of containment, and enhanced the aura of Communism as the wave of the future. But as we have also seen, from the Kremlin's point of view the stupendous success of the Chinese comrades was far from welcome. Even before the "unbreakable friendship between the Soviet Union and the great Chinese people" was exposed as hollow rhetoric, the relationship between the two Communist powers was in fact a very strained one.

On the Soviet side there had to be mounting irritation at the realization of how much the alliance limited Moscow's freedom of action. For one thing, whatever advantages the USSR derived from China's support, that support did not come free. It is understandable that the Kremlin could not be enthusiastic at the prospect of China's becoming a nuclear power; and as we shall see, by 1959 the vision of a China armed with nuclear weapons would become as frightening to the Soviets as it had long been to the United States. And so the Russians dragged their feet in helping the People's Republic's research-and-development efforts on the dreaded weapon. "In contrast to its at least halfhearted backing of the Chinese missile efforts, the Soviet Union . . . confined its support of the nuclear program to industrial applications."[1] But then came a moment when the Kremlin was constrained to be more forthcoming: "Just as the Chinese were putting in place the start-up organizational system to oversee the strategic weapons program, the anti-Communist (and anti-Soviet) eruptions in Poland and Hungary increased China's bargaining power. . . . The Soviet Union, in an attempt to consolidate its deteriorating position in the socialist community . . . needed the support of the Chinese and was forced to make concessions to them in their demands for strategic weapons aid."[2] Thus in October 1957 came the Sino-Soviet New Defense Technical Agreement, according to which the Soviet Union promised to deliver to China the prototype A-bomb, as well as missiles and other relevant materials and technical data. The Soviets' reluctance, and Beijing's unabashed pressure, to exploit their allies' discomfiture throw vivid light on that allegedly "unshakable friendship." It was an uncomfortable alliance. Mao's and his associates' attitude was clearly based on the assumption that an eventual break was inevitable and that they must squeeze the last possible ounce of help out of the USSR before it came.

Another and fundamental cause of tension between the two Communist giants lay in their different perspectives on the international situation. The USSR was seen by the Chinese, and essentially, if not completely, correctly, as a status quo power. While many in the West still thought of Moscow's ultimate aims in terms of conquering the world for Communism, the Chinese knew better: the Russians needed and wanted peace. The world Communist movement was viewed by Stalin's successors, as it had been by him, as a useful appendage of Soviet foreign policy, an instrument for exerting pressure on the capitalists and keeping them off-balance.

The USSR also could not afford to cast off its image as the vanguard of world revolution and be seen as completely peaceful and accommodating toward the West, for the latter would then increase immeasurably its own pressures on the Soviets, demand reunification of Germany, question the legitimacy of the Communist regimes in

Eastern Europe, and God knows what else. Here then was Khru-shchev's dilemma: On the one hand, he sought through summitry and various, usually oversubtle, schemes to establish a modus vivendi with the United States, one that would considerably lower the level of international tension and yet preserve for the USSR its post–World War II empire. But in order to avoid the impression that such advances came as a result of Soviet fears and weaknesses, the temperamental first secretary would also, sometimes simultaneously, engage in missile-rattling boasts that the USSR was not afraid of a nuclear war and voice confidence that Communism would eventually prevail over the entire planet.

It was Beijing's enduring concern that the Kremlin might break out of this vicious circle and reach genuine détente with the West. Khrushchev's real goals were not new foreign conquests, but economic and political reform at home that would advance the welfare of the Soviet consumer and rid society of the remnants of Stalinism. To be sure, Nikita Sergeievich could not have envisaged, let alone approved of, what would happen in Soviet politics within thirty years: for him the Communist Party was, and had to remain, the sole repository of political power. But he was striving, even if inconsistently, to democratize procedures *within* the party, to curb the influence of the bureaucracy, and to chase out of its ranks the remaining devotees of Stalinism. On the economic front he was eager for the USSR to catch up with the West not only in heavy industry but also in providing consumer goods.

He was a believer, but with none of that fervor and urgency that inspired Lenin and his followers right after the Revolution and that made them, even if briefly, place the interests of the world movement over those of the Soviet state. For Khrushchev the latter definitely came first, and a Communist world was a distant goal, best advanced by the Soviet Union growing, in peace, ever stronger and more prosperous.

It was difficult for the West to perceive a reformer and advocate of peaceful coexistence in a man so given to threatening bombast and devious stratagems, which on several occasions brought the United States and the USSR to the brink of a confrontation. But for Mao and his colleagues, Khrushchev, ever since the beginning of his ascendance in Soviet politics, was an open book: and as such he represented everything they feared and loathed in post-Stalin Russia.

There was first of all an ideological chasm between the two leaderships, or if one wants to be precise, sharp political and personal divergencies and animosities rationalized in ideological terms. For the Chinese, Khrushchev had departed, both in his domestic and foreign policies, from the straight-and-narrow path of Marxism-Leninism. Mao believed, like the Molotov-Malenkov faction, that an explicit condemnation of Stalinism was unnecessary and its consequences greatly damaging to Communism everywhere. Such betrayal and self-inflicted humiliation indulged in by the leaders of the Soviet party, Beijing's logic continued, could not be accidental. But as the Chinese Communists would repeatedly trumpet after the break became open, it must have reflected an ideological heresy—revisionism—which had been allowed to permeate Soviet Communism. As for Khrushchev himself, he was to become, in the colorful idiom of the Chinese, a "capitalist roader" willing, if he could get away with it, to lead his country away from socialism and to have Soviet society penetrated and molded by Western ideas.

Ideological strictures were intermingled with political and economic grievances. Any sign of a U.S.-Soviet rapprochement, even the holding of a summit, had to be construed in Beijing as a threat and a Soviet attempt (even if the Western statesmen were too obtuse to perceive it as such) to sell out the People's Republic in exchange for some American concessions. It was the Soviet Union's duty to press the capitalist world unrelentingly and to force upon it fresh retreats and capitulations. Any obvious slackening in the Soviet Union's exertions on behalf of world Communism was in itself bound to be seen in Washington as a sign that Moscow would not be unduly perturbed if the United States were to attack China. Contrariwise, it was the Soviets' bounden duty to pressure the United States to abandon its protection of Chiang's regime and thus allow the People's Republic to take over Taiwan and to secure its rightful place in the United Nations.

But how did China, by far the weaker of the two powers, manage to influence the Soviet Union's policy so as to inhibit a reconciliation with the West and continue to do so, as we shall see, even after the Moscow-Beijing break in 1960? Prior to the break, the USSR's weight on the international arena and its bargaining power vis-à-vis the West benefited enormously from the fiction of Sino-Soviet unity. Despite the rumors of dissonance between the two Communist giants, the West could not but be awed by the fact that the Communist bloc comprised one-third of mankind. After the split, Beijing's ability to influence Soviet policies derived in the main from the condition of world Communism. The Kremlin felt that it could not afford policies that would seem to confirm Beijing's charges that the Russians were betraying the interests of Communism as well as those of national liberation movements throughout the world. Here then is a poignant irony of history: the Soviets, who for so long and so uninhibitedly exploited those movements for their own goals, were to find themselves increasingly constrained in their actions and pushed to risk their vital interests because of what was happening in Southeast Asia or in the Middle East. From being its absolute master, the Soviet Union would by the 1960s find itself in some ways a captive of international Communism. Moscow's expansionist thrust would continue in the face of an even more startling paradox: those fresh conquests of Communism, whether in Ethiopia or Afghanistan, were not bringing the USSR anything beyond vast expense and new dangers. And as of this day, the fatuity of Soviet, as of any other, imperialism in the era of mass communication and nuclear weapons has been illustrated by the shattering impact that the collapse of the Soviet external empire has had on the unity and cohesion of the USSR itself.

Such developments could be but dimly foreseen in the wake of the Hungarian revolution. The year 1957 was one of trials and tribulations for Khrushchev. What had been brewing ever since the Twentieth Congress came to a head on June 19, when by seven votes to four the Presidium voted to remove Khrushchev from the position of first secretary. To the consternation of his colleagues, he refused to abide by the vote, appealing the decision to the full Central Committee, a flaunting of precedent that left the Molotov-Malenkov faction confused and aghast. The Central Committee, whose members had been hastily collected by army planes, provided courtesy of Khrushchev's supporter Marshal Zhukov, turned the tables on the conspiring party elders. Branded the "antiparty" group, three of them—Molotov, Malenkov, and Kaganovich—were immediately dismissed from the Presidium and other high posts. The other anti-Khrushchev plotters, notably Bulganin and Marshal Klimenti Voroshilov, were publicly identified and disgraced as such only later, to obscure the fact that it was the majority in the highest party organ that had voted against the first secretary. It was only in March 1958 that Khrushchev, replacing Bulganin, added premiership to his other offices.[3]

The disgraced oligarchs were blamed not only for their factionalism and opposition to the liberalization in domestic politics. They also— and especially Molotov, proclaimed the Central Committee resolution reading them out of its ranks—tried to obstruct desirable changes in the foreign policy of the USSR, decried the rapprochement with Yugoslavia, and refused to admit that the Soviet model for a transition to socialism was not obligatory for other Communist countries. On the face of it, Khrushchev scored a resounding victory and had the party reaffirm his policies that had been put in question by Hungary. Having prevailed over his domestic opponents, the first secretary received in effect a vote of confidence for his democratic reforms and for new initiatives in foreign relations. After June 1957 the first secretary would no longer have to appease his intraparty critics by speaking favorably of Stalin. The difficulties and constraints on his plans would now come mainly from another quarter.

Though the image of the new Communism was tarnished by Hungary, never since the onset of the cold war has the Soviet Union's prestige stood so high as it did in the fall of 1957. It was partly a consequence of the West's still suffering from the post-Suez disarray, with Great Britain hastening to liquidate its remaining imperial commitments and France weakened domestically and externally by the Algerian War. But it was mainly its own technological feats that enhanced the Soviet Union's standing in the international arena. In October the Soviets launched the first artificial earth satellite. It is difficult now after the passage of more than thirty years to appreciate the sensation and awe aroused throughout the world by Sputnik. The USSR suddenly appeared to have a solid lead over the United States in the race to conquer extraterrestrial space. The Americans, so confident and boastful about their technological superiority, now had tangible proof that socialism could catch up and surpass capitalism when it came to industrial and scientific achievements—a theme that would now be repeatedly trumpeted by Khrushchev. Sputnik and the subsequent Soviet space achievements would be advertised by Moscow, and largely accepted as such by the world, as a vindication of Communism and a convincing refutation of the notion that it is only under Western-style democracy that science and technology can fully flourish. This motif would then be strengthened by the Soviets being first to launch manned space flights. It is not too much to say that for the next twelve years, until the U.S. astronauts landed on the moon in 1969, the Russian cosmonauts' achievements would serve as an important psychological prop of the otherwise faltering reputation of Marxism-Leninism, and by the same token would obscure the economic and social weaknesses of the Soviet system.

But the significance of Sputnik was not limited to the effect it had on the national *amour propre* in the USSR and America. Its launching and successful flight was a sign of the Soviet breakthrough in missile technology, and an ominous warning that America's advantage over the USSR when it came to the quantity and quality of long-range bombers no longer assured it of superiority in the delivery of nuclear weapons. Though the experts may have known better, to the public the "nuclear umbrella" that had been assumed to be the main U.S. element protecting the security of the West all of a sudden appeared to have been blown away. The myth of the "missile gap," which had allegedly developed in favor of Moscow, would be an important inhibiting factor on U.S. policies for several years, and of course it would be relentlessly exploited by the Soviets.

Great as the political and ideological benefits of the Soviets' scientific triumph were, they could not at the time divert the Kremlin's attention from the real and widening gap that was developing between its position on international issues and that of Communist China. The launching of Sputnik ushered in celebrations of the fortieth anniversary of the Russian Revolution. Its central feature was the gathering of the representatives of sixty-four Communist parties in Moscow. The solemn occasion called for a declaration defining the political and ideological stance of the socialist camp in the current world situation. What was also needed, some of the participants had argued before the conference, was a sort of coordinating organ, if not a formal organization like the late, unlamented Cominform, then a journal, which would provide ideological guidance to the movement.

The task of preparing what was hoped to be the momentous declaration—the Communist profession of faith—fell naturally to the thirteen ruling parties. All but one were represented by their top leader, the exception being the Yugoslav delegation: Marshal Tito, quite likely smelling trouble, excused himself on grounds of bad health.

Mao's mood and stay in Moscow presented a marked contrast to his previous visit there. This time he traveled by air and on his arrival was greeted by the top Soviet hierarchs, headed by Khrushchev. In a way, it was Mao who was the central figure at the conference, his imperious bearing an object of awe among the non-Russian delegations, and a source of hardly concealed irritation on the part of his hosts.

The Sino-Soviet dissonances went far beyond the question of personalities (though the incipient hostility between Mao and Khrushchev, reflecting intellectual arrogance in the former and choleric temperament in the latter, was not an insignificant part of the picture). The Chinese wanted to make the declaration as militant-sounding as possible, committing the bloc to an unrelenting struggle against U.S. imperialism and stressing that the path to socialism may involve revolutionary violence and hence condemning any ambivalence by the Communists vis-à-vis the West. "Revisionism," as such sinful ambivalence was classified, though not explicitly stated, was understood by everybody to refer to the behavior of the Yugoslav party. The Russians, in fact if not in their rhetoric quite close to what Beijing decried as revisionism, were of course anxious to soften the tone of the manifest. Ironically, it was also Mao who insisted that the declaration spell out clearly and unmistakably the Soviet Union's leadership of the socialist camp. This, as the Kremlin must have well and bitterly understood, was far from being a plea for Moscow to actually dictate the policies of the camp as a whole, still less for Soviet domination of the internal policies of the individual Communist-ruled countries. The Soviet Union was supposed to lead in the sense of assuming the primary responsibility for the advance of the Communist bloc, i.e., leading in the way an officer leads his men into battle, being the first to expose himself to enemy fire.

But just as they had recently appeased the Chinese when it came to military hardware and nuclear technology, the Soviet leaders, probably smoldering internally, also felt compelled to appease them ideologically and to accept Beijing's phrasing for the joint declaration. As Khrushchev told the Yugoslav ambassador, "Mao Zedong was so insistent over these proposals that he had said they must be included in the declaration even if it were signed only by the Chinese and the Russians."[4]

Not surprisingly, the Yugoslav delegation refused to subcribe to the statement, which by implication condemned them as heretics. For some time now the Chinese media had been assailing Tito and the Yugoslav party. In Beijing's eyes the former wanted, and quite often succeeded in having, the best of both the Communist and the Western worlds. By Mao's lights, Khrushchev and his colleagues held, even if covertly, similar views. And so the only way of keeping the Soviet comrades from straying off the straight line and falling into the pit of revisionism and ignoble coexistence with the imperialists was to harry them incessantly, not to allow them to steer Communism away from militancy. In the present situation, with Khrushchev worried about West German rearmament and the possibility of the Americans allowing Bonn to acquire nuclear weapons, what signal would be sent to the West if the Chinese walked out of the conference? Militant rhetoric might not prevent Moscow from eventually holding hands with the Americans, but for the moment it kept the latter confused and unable to divine what Khrushchev was really after.

Nor could the tone of the declaration be pleasing to the Poles, with Gomułka still suspicious of any formula threatening his party's freedom of action. But after strenuous lobbying by the Chinese, the Polish delegates agreed that the declaration condemn "revisionism," this being balanced by its censure of "dogmatism" and "sectarianism" (i.e., excessive ideological rigidity). Reluctantly, Gomułka was also persuaded to go along with the formula about the Soviet Union's leadership of the "socialist camp." One success scored by the opponents of centralization of the movement was their blocking of any new international structure similar to the Cominform. (A journal for ideological guidance of the movement was agreed upon. It began to be published in Prague in the fall of 1958, but soon sank into complete insignificance.)

Why such great perplexities about formal declarations that, as the past had amply demonstrated, could not be really binding on any of the signatories? To a large extent, those concerns reflected the realization that the Communist world was becoming polycentric and was in danger of losing even an appearance of cohesion. Hence the need for ideological incantations that somehow would arrest the process. And so with the Yugoslavs abstaining, the other twelve ruling Communist parties subcribed to the declaration.

The Soviets still hoped to avoid a break with Beijing. As for the Chinese, it is rather unlikely that at that time, November 1957, they were consciously set on a collision course with the USSR. Mao's own feelings about the Soviet comrades were highly ambivalent. To be sure, they were for him primarily "Russians," i.e., heirs of an imperialist tradition in Asia going back centuries before the 1917 Revolution. And quite in line with that tradition they would not, unless pressed, view China as an equal partner. At the same time, Mao admired the Soviets' achievements and power. In fact, he had quite an unrealistic view as to how powerful the USSR was in relation to the West. And so as long as possible that power should be utilized to advance the goals of world Communism, and incidentally those of

China, rather than serving just the selfish interests of the Kremlin. China then would stick to her alliance with Moscow, as long as it could serve as a block to any accommodation between the Soviet Union and the United States.

Mao's performance at the conference followed two themes, seemingly somewhat contradictory, but both designed to convince his audience that the Communist world neither needed nor really would be able to appease the capitalist one.

Such appeasement, or rapprochement, between the two, Mao argued, was unnecessary because the Soviet Union had now reached such a position of strength in relation to the United States that the Communist bloc could safely pursue more militant policies without the West's being able or daring to counter them with any effectiveness. In his speech to the conference on November 18, the chairman listed first the defeats suffered by the imperialists since World War II: the triumphs of the socialist camp in China, in Vietnam and Korea, the collapse of the European powers' colonial empires. But then he got to the heart of the matter: the decisive breakthrough achieved by the Soviet Union in military technology as demonstrated by Sputnik and the development of the land-based intercontinental missile. How could the imperialists dare to start a third world war in view of those weapons in the hands of the socialist camp? "It is my opinion that the international situation has now reached a new turning point. . . . There is a Chinese saying, 'Either the East wind prevails over the West wind or the West wind prevails over the East Wind.' It is characteristic of the situation today, I believe, that the East wind is prevailing over the West wind. That is to say, the forces of socialism are overwhelmingly superior to the forces of imperialism."[5]

The other tack pursued by Mao was, one suspects, not uninfluenced by Khrushchev's own tactics. In his intermittent attempts to bully the West, the latter would occasionally hint that the Kremlin was not overly frightened over the prospect of a nuclear confrontation. The USSR would not only survive but would emerge victorious from the conflict. Such seeming equanimity over the horrendous possibility could not but impress Western statesmen: of course, the first secretary must have known better and was just bluffing, but could one be sure?

And now before the leaders of world Communism, Mao was even more explicit in his seeming insouciance concerning the possibility of a nuclear holocaust. What if it destroyed half of mankind? The other half would still survive, as would socialism, and it would be imperialism and capitalism that would be forever destroyed. "We Chinese have not yet completed our construction, and we desire peace. However, if imperialism insists on fighting a war, we will have no alternative but to make up our minds and fight to the finish."[6]

Like Khrushchev, Mao *did* know better. What then was the purpose of uttering such inanities? Most likely to tantalize his audience, to demonstrate the uncompromising zeal of his party, which would not shrink from making any sacrifices to remain true to the goals of Marxism-Leninism. But he was also warning his Soviet hosts, saying in effect, "You may cast us off and make a deal behind our back with the U.S. imperialists. But then you must know it would still be within our power to ignite a world conflict that inevitably would draw in the Soviet Union. So you better defer to our needs and wishes." Like those hapless Western diplomats viewing Khrushchev, so the Soviets must have hoped that Mao was bluffing. No intelligent man could *really* be so nonchalant about the possibility of half of mankind perishing within a few hours. But could they be sure? It was an impossible dilemma: How could one go on and continue to cooperate and be allies of those impossible people? How could one afford the scandal and the blow of an open break?

Some in the audience could not believe their ears. A delegate from one of the smaller Communist countries tried to expostulate with the Chinese leader: his whole nation might be wiped out by a few H-bombs. Mao was unperturbed. Yes, some entire nations might have to be sacrificed to assure the victory of socialism, and that was the important thing and not what happens to the 14 million Czechs and Slovaks. Judging from their statements about Mao following the break, the Russians must have wondered whether their Chinese guest was not developing maniacal traits not dissimilar to those of the late Josif Vissarionovich.

Such impressions may have been strengthened by other circumstances pertaining to his speech. Though apparently in fine physical shape, Mao, unlike other speakers on the occasion, did not deign to stand up while delivering his address but remained seated. He was quite indelicate in reminding his audience about Khrushchev's clash with the antiparty group the preceding June, and in terms suggesting that both parties were at fault. At those words Mikoyan rose from his chair, demonstratively stared at the table at which the Chinese delegation were seated, and for a few moments turned his back on the speaker. After that, "statements about the 'monolithic unity' of the

Soviet Union and China, which we hear at every step, do not sound particularly convincing."[7]

At a reception following that emotion-laden meeting in the Kremlin's great St. George's Hall, Mao was polite even toward the Yugoslav "renegades and capitalist roaders," as they soon would be dubbed in the Chinese media. He was playing, one suspects, the role of the proverbial inscrutable and unfathomable Oriental. When told by the Yugoslav ambassador that his government hoped to raise the performance of its agriculture in two or three years, the Chinese leader expressed his skepticism: it might take twenty, thirty, or more years! One day he would tell an interviewer that it would take one thousand years to improve Sino-Soviet relations!

Instead of reaffirming the unity, the conference offered yet another confirmation of the deep fissures in the international Communist movement. It was an oversimplification to view the problem, as most Western commentators did then and for many years afterward, in left-right terms: the Yugoslavs being moderate and urging a conciliatory approach toward the West, as well as following less radical economic and social policies at home; the Chinese at the other end of the spectrum on both counts, with the Communist Party of the USSR somewhere in the middle. The situation was much more complex and reflected primarily the power relationships between the two main Communist states rather than genuine ideological differences. What would become explicit in the late 1970s was already inherent in the situation at the end of the 1950s: what held the movement together was the power and prestige of the Soviet Union, and not ideology. It was this power that made possible the survival of the Communist regimes in Eastern Europe. If the Chinese as yet did not break off from the bloc, it was because they still hoped to draw concrete advantages from being officially allied to Moscow. In Western Europe the French and Italian Communist parties kept their ties with the Soviets, strained though they had become after the revelations of the Twentieth Congress and Hungary, partly because of habit, but also because of the prestige of the country which had put Sputnik in space and was believed, falsely, to have surpassed the United States in military might. The ideological motif was stronger in the Third World, but even there links with the Soviet Union developed not so much because of the appeal of Marxism-Leninism (even though the Soviet model of economic development then exerted its deceptive fascination on the politicians in the former colonial and semicolonial areas and was seen by them as a miraculous shortcut to industrialization and modernization) but because the regime in the new nations and the "national liberation movements" struggling for power hoped for and in many cases received the Soviet Union's material and political support. It was really the belief in the Soviet Union's power that maintained the appearance of Marxism-Leninism as a doctrine on the march in the world. Once the Soviet Union's power or rather its readiness and ability to use it came to be questioned, that image would almost immediately turn into a mirage.

The growing, if from the Western eyes still concealed, estrangement between the two Communist giants (only a few perceptive observers—General Charles de Gaulle, for one—foresaw prior to 1959 the forthcoming clash) was bound to find its reverberations in the ideological sphere. Many would argue the other way around: Mao's people were the true faithful. The Soviets had grown weary of the strictures of Marxism-Leninism. Hence the dissonances and the final break. But as we have seen on many occasions, it is concrete political disputes, whether in domestic politics or between the Communist states, that usually lead the contending parties to accuse each other of deviations and heresies. It was after the Soviets had tried to overthrow Tito that he discovered Stalinism to be contrary to the principles of Marxism-Leninism and the Yugoslavs embarked on a number of political and economic innovations designed to demonstrate that theirs, in distinction to the Soviets, was the correct version of Leninism. And so with the Chinese Communists: for all the growing difficulties with the Russian comrades, they had until the end of 1957 not only admired but emulated the main lines of Soviet policies. Mao believed that Khrushchev's *public* denunciation of Stalin went much too far, yet within weeks of the Twentieth Congress his party chimed in, though in a more restrained way, with a condemnation of the cult of personality. And the Soviet campaign of de-Stalinization and internal liberalization was echoed by Beijing's own version of glasnost, enunciated by Mao on May 2, 1956, with his celebrated formula "Let a hundred flowers bloom, let a hundred schools contend." Mao may have intended his licensing of what, translated into prose, may be called a modicum of intellectual freedom, to serve as a check on the bureaucracy and thus an enhancement of his personal power, something he would try later on a much vaster scale and with catastrophic results during the Cultural Revolution. But it did not take him long to realize that the resulting outburst of free speech might threaten the very basis of authoritarianism. As he was to say, holding on to the same tiresome metaphors, on February 16, 1957, "The Soviet way is to have only fragrant flowers and no poisonous weeds. In reality many poisonous weeds live in disguise under the name of fragrant flowers."[8]

Well, the Soviets' political soil appeared of late quite favorable to the growth of such noxious weeds: excessive liberalization at home, insufficient vigilance in regard to revisionism, lack of militancy in marshaling the socialist camp against the imperialists. And so there had to be some organic, i.e., ideological, reasons for this unfortunate condition of Soviet society, and it was up to China to demonstrate what Marxism-Leninism meant in practice when it came to both domestic and international policies.

The loss of faith in the Soviet Union as the ideological guide led the People's Republic to jettison the Soviet model of economic and social development and to seek a shortcut to modernization and socialism. But there was another, and probably more important, reason for Mao to launch a complex of policies that became known as the Great Leap Forward. For all the concessions recently wrested from the Soviets, the chairman and his colleagues must have realized by the beginning of 1958 that time might be running out on the "unshakable unity of the Soviet and Chinese peoples," and that they had no assurance that the USSR would continue indefinitely its economic and technological assistance to the People's Republic. Hence the need to industrialize and to build up the defensive potential of the country in a hurry. With their now complete psychological emancipation from the awe of the Elder Brother, Chinese Communists believed that they could attain some of the basic prerequisites of socialist society much faster than had their Soviet comrades. In 1958 Communists all over the world, whatever they thought of Stalin on other counts, still considered his collectivization of Soviet agriculture as a grand feat of social engineering: in a few years he had succeeded in converting some 20 million individual peasant holdings into about 250,000 collective and state farms. China had followed that example, and by 1957–58 its agriculture had been collectivized. But, in Marxist-Leninist parlance, the standard collective farm still retained a few noncollectivist features: individual family dwellings, the peasant's small private plot, as well as material incentives for work done on the collective's land. The Great Leap was to merge several collective farms into people's communes, which in Marxist semantics was a "higher" form of production unit because there the principle of private property is entirely erased and its members live, as well as work, in common. If collectivization was already distasteful from the point of view of the individual peasant, so attached to his land, and of agricultural productivity, then this turning of collective farms into huge communes comprising 2,000 to 4,000 households—i.e., up to 20,000 people— would be a veritable cataclysm and cripple the countryside, contributing to the great famines of the early 1960s.

It was intellectual fervor, and the impulse to do the Russians one better (they, for some decades now, had been stuck with the old type of collective farm!), that prompted this Leap into catastrophe. A passage from Mao's speech on the communes is perhaps characteristic of the incoherent enthusiasm with which the leadership embarked on the ill-fated experiment. "They are called people's communes first [because] they are public. Lots of people, a vast area of land, a large scale of production; all their undertakings are done in a big way. [They] integrate government [administration] with commune to establish public mess halls, and private plots are eliminated. . . . The Soviet Union practices the use of high rewards and heavy punishments, emphasizing [only] material incentives. We now practice socialism, and have the sprouts of communism. Schools, factories and neighborhoods can all establish people's communes. In a few years big communes will be organized to include everyone."[9]

Here, then, is an invidious note: In the USSR they have to rely on material incentives and sanctions. We Chinese can rely on the public spirit and zeal of our people, so that we can achieve a higher stage of socialism than they have in the USSR. As a matter of fact, Mao intimated that the Leap would in some ways carry Chinese society into the realm of Communism where, according to Marx and Engels, there is such an abundance of goods that one can begin to dispense with the money economy and reward workers according to their needs, rather than according to the usual yardsticks. Never mind that according to the canons of Marxism this stage could come only after a long period of socialism, i.e., only in a highly industrialized society. Even though more than 80 percent of China's population was occupied in agrarian pursuits, and even though, according to Marxist canons, the country had not yet entered the stage of socialism, let alone a state appropriate for the Communist stage, the wonderful spirit of the Chinese people would enable them to improve upon the doctrine and to leap into the most advanced phase of historical development. In contrast, Mao implied (and soon the Chinese would become explicit on the point), socialism in the USSR had become stymied, due to the inordinate growth of such evil weeds as bureaucratism and Russian nationalism. Soviet society had become thoroughly petty bourgeois in its tone, hence its dependence on material rewards and punishments.

Statements such as the one above were not just idle musings, or even made just for propaganda purposes. Unfortunately for China, its rulers decided that not only must they be one up on the Russians, but also that theirs was a truer and purer brand of Communism than that practiced in the Fatherland of Socialism. In 1957 Khrushchev had prophesied that in fifteen years the USSR would overtake the United States not only in the production of such basic sinews of industrialization as steel and cement (he was right on that count), but also in the production of most consumer goods. Well, the Chinese began by modestly predicting that their industrial output would surpass that of Great Britain, also in fifteen years. But then utter fantasy took over. The Great Leap Forward, in addition to prescribing an egalitarian paradise, laid down a scheme for making the countryside a mighty industrial base. Why limit the production of steel to the urban factories? No other feature of the Great Leap Forward was as fantastic as the villages blossoming forth with small foundries. Peasants would bring broken pots and pans and other metal junk and feed them to the furnace. Here then was another postulate of Marx that was being triumphantly achieved in China: the abolition of contradictions between the city and the countryside. Such was the degree of self-intoxication of the leaders that Mao soon abandoned comparisons with Great Britain. The latter was no longer a major power, and China, on the strength of its ideological elan and innovations, was going to catch up in steel production with the Soviet Union and the United States. The actual production figure for steel in 1957 was about 5 million tons. But then China's heavy industry, helped by thousands of those innovative rural furnaces, would take off and catch up with the USSR by 1960 and the United States two years later. By the mid-1970s, while those two powers' steel production would hover around a beggarly 120 million or so tons, the People's Republic would be producing 700 million tons of steel.[10]

The One Hundred Flowers campaign expired by the end of 1957, and with it died the regime's tolerance of diversity in intellectual styles and views. The discarding of what might be called this very modest version of glasnost marked the end of the period when Beijing tried consciously to adjust its internal policies to those of the Soviet Union.

Henceforth it would make a virtue of being as different as possible, presenting its policies as being truer, if not to the letter then to the spirit of Marxism-Leninism, than those practiced in the "bourgeoisified" Soviet Union. The simmering conflict with Moscow stimulated the Chinese Communists' self-image as being at once innovative and fundamentalist when it came to ideology. And conversely this ideological stance intensified their anti-Russian feelings. The Soviets were not only neo-imperialists (the term would not be used until the mid-1960s, but it is implicit in Chinese criticisms of the USSR from 1958 on), but also ideological renegades.

The Soviets, for their part, had to view the vast delusion of the Great Leap Forward with more than just concern about what it would do to the economy of a fraternal country (and what it might mean in terms of future Chinese demands that the Soviets bail them out). The pre-1958 Soviet evaluation of Mao and his companions was based on assumptions that, difficult as they were, they were still open to reason and that they were sound Communists, i.e., practical people and not wild zealots. Mao's nonchalance about the possibility of a nuclear war must have already shaken these assumptions, and now there was this business of village "steel mills" and other inane features of the Leap. And here the Soviet Union stood pledged to defend the People's Republic if attacked (even though, as we have seen, that pledge was not unambiguous), and had promised to help it develop nuclear weapons and other appurtenances of up-to-date military technology.

With his defeat of the "antiparty group" in June 1957, Khrushchev's position at home became much stronger. But as has been noted, Soviet attempts to appease China continued through the rest of the year, reaching their climax with the military-technology agreement of October and the twelve parties' declaration in November. Had he followed his personal inclinations, Khrushchev, as his later behavior suggests, might well have chosen to be more assertive toward Beijing a year or two before the actual break. But there were two major considerations that kept him hoping against hope that a break might yet be avoided.

In the first place, he still clung to the idea of rebuilding the world Communist movement upon new principles that would allow the individual parties and countries considerable latitude in their polices and yet demonstrate the viability of Marxism-Leninism as an ideology and an alternative to the international capitalist system.

The other reason was more practical. The first secretary was about to enter upon his complex game of trying to persuade or force the

West to agree to a resolution of the German problem that would be in line with what the Kremlin believed were the Soviet Union's vital interests in the question. Those interests required firm, ironclad guarantees that the German Federal Republic would never be allowed to possess, manufacture, or control (be it even partially) nuclear weapons. The Soviets had learned to live with a nuclear-armed America, and despite Moscow's intermittent rhetoric on the subject, they were confident that unless blatantly provoked, Washington would never unleash a nuclear holocaust. But the possession of even a small quantity of the dreaded weapons in the hands of the "Bonn revanchists," as the West German regime of Chancellor Konrad Adenauer would often be described by the Soviets, might lead precisely to such a provocation.[11]

The second objective concerning the German issue was the recogniton by the West of the German Democratic Republic. The position of the Communist bloc in Eastern Europe was endangered as long as the legitimacy of the Communist German state was questioned and while that state was hemorrhaging through the massive flight of its citizens (mainly through West Berlin) to the Federal Republic. The vulnerability and "illegitimacy" of the Communist regime in East Germany reflected on the situation of the Polish, Czech, and other states in the socialist camp.

The West, primarily the United States, was not going to recognize East Germany unless literally pushed to the wall. And as for nuclear weapons and Bonn, the Americans did not understand why Khrushchev should be worried about it—at the moment West Germany did not possess any such weapons, the ones on its territory being under the control of the American supreme commander of the NATO forces. And if the Americans understood how much the Kremlin was apprehensive about the possibility of Bonn's "finger on the atomic trigger," they might well use that fear as a bargaining chip: either allow free elections in East Germany or we give the bomb to Bonn! And so, rather than articulating his fears, Khrushchev hoped to achieve his objectives by forcing the West to agree to a German peace treaty that would embody them.

But the Soviet Union's bargaining position vis-à-vis the United States and its allies would be considerably weakened if it became obvious that the Kremlin no longer had 600 million or so Chinese on its side. And so the Soviet leader persisted in trying to preserve the facade of friendship and unity with China.

One sacrifice on the altar of that fast-fading friendship was the Soviet Union's recent rapprochement with Yugoslavia. True, after Hungary, Khrushchev himself became disenchanted with the notion of Tito as a guide and exemplar to other Communist regimes in Eastern Europe. Still, he would have preferred to avoid a major clash with Belgrade. Such a clash would bring back unhappy memories of 1948 and in conjunction with the recent Hungarian drama would lead to many in both West and East concluding that the Soviets were reverting to the bad old Stalinist ways.

So to keep their relations with Belgrade in balance, the Soviets announced in March 1958 that of course they would be sending a delegation to the forthcoming congress of the League of Yugoslav Communists, the head of that delegation to be one of the lesser lights of the Soviet elite. One month later Khrushchev announced that not only would there be no delegation, but that the Soviet party would refrain from sending its greetings to the congress. And as might be expected, other Communist parties felt constrained to follow the Soviet lead and to decline the invitation.

The alleged cause of Moscow's demonstrative snub was the draft of the theses for the congress. They contained nothing new, spelling out simply those ideological and political premises of Yugoslavia's domestic and foreign course that had not changed in the last few years and which the Russians knew and applauded in 1956 when relations between the two countries and parties were at their warmest. The congress's program thus reasserted the country's need to maintain good relations with both East and West, to follow its own road to socialism, and contained other thoroughly unsensational stuff. As Khrushchev indirectly confessed to the Yugoslav ambassador, it was pressure from Beijing that led to this new campaign against Tito. As a matter of fact, the Yugoslavs had moderated their program in a pro-Soviet direction, largely at the urging of the Hungarians and Poles, for whom continued Soviet-Yugoslav friendship was for obvious reasons of great importance. But Moscow did not alter its stand, even though its actual criticism of the unfortunate "theses" was quite moderate in comparison with that coming from China. A Beijing daily repeated uninhibitedly the old slander of 1948 that in propagating revisionism, the Yugoslavs were following the instructions of the American imperialists.

This campaign of vilification was to continue for some time, but on the Soviet side it was halfhearted and rather contrived. (The Yugoslav

ambassador recalls that at a diplomatic reception he was taxed by
Mikoyan with Yugoslavia's acceptance of aid from the United States.
"I reminded him that we invariably heard that Soviet reproach whenever there was a worsening of relations between us. I recalled a meeting in the Kremlin in June 1956 . . . when Khrushchev stated that
they had nothing against Yugoslavia taking American credits and
accepting American aid, and that the Soviet Union was also ready to
take American credits on the same terms.")[12] Soviet offers of credits
were withdrawn, and previously projected state visits were demonstratively canceled. But there was no new break in relations between
Moscow and Belgrade. Conversely, Sino-Yugoslav relations were practically severed. The Yugoslavs easily diagnosed the trouble as spring-
ing from China's rejection and fear of the whole principle of peaceful
coexistence between Communism and the West, of which Yugoslavia
was a visible symbol and a beneficiary. Little Albania was the only
other Communist country to share fully Beijing's intense enmity to
Tito. Its rulers recalled how prior to 1948 the Yugoslav Communists
tried to lord it over them, and hence were fearful of their neighbor.
Hostility to Yugoslavia and revisionism became thus the basis of Albania's links to Beijing and of that long-lasting alliance between the
smallest and the most populous of Communist states. And as relations
between the Soviet Union and the People's Republic worsened over
the course of the next two years, so a new thaw would come into
those between Moscow and Belgrade.

The magic formula that would enable the Communist movement
to recoup its unity and at the same time avoid the uniformity and
rigidity that characterized Stalin's times kept eluding Khrushchev. As
of the middle of 1958, he was still hoping to appease China, and in
yet another attempt to avoid a break, he authorized a measure that,
apart from its inhumanity, he must have known would still further
antagonize many within and without the Communist bloc, especially
those Western radicals sympathetic to the USSR but critical of its role
in Hungary. Nagy and his closest associates, who had been lured out
of the Yugoslav embassy in November 1956, were then arrested by
the Soviet military and imprisoned in Romania. Nothing further was
heard of them until the announcement (made simultaneously in Moscow and Budapest) on June 16, 1958, that Nagy and three others had
been tried, condemned to death, and executed. To paraphrase Talleyrand, this judicial murder was worse than a crime, it was a major

political blunder. It would haunt the Kádár regime despite all its subsequent efforts at reform and liberalization, and would contribute to
the eventual crash of Communism in Hungary. The executions must
have been approved in Moscow. Why after a year and a half remind
the world of the whole grisly business in Hungary? The Kremlin
obviously wanted to impress upon those who in its opinion needed
impressing that it was serious in its struggle against "revisionism."
In fact, this barbarous and unnecessary epilogue to the martyrdom
of Hungary weakened still further the capacity of the East European
Communist regimes to find support among their peoples. As for the
intended lesson as to what might be expected by those leaders who
defy the USSR and lead their parties astray, that lesson would soon
be undermined by China's openly questioning the ideological and
political orthodoxy of the Soviet leadership itself. Relying on Chinese
support (though in no sense could it assure its leaders of military
security), Albania later would go much further and with impunity in
defying Moscow than had Nagy and his associates.

The cumulative evidence of what transpired in 1958 suggests
strongly that, try as they might, the Soviets could not appease the
Chinese enough to preserve even an appearance of the "unshakable
friendship." The only way to have satisfied Mao and his friends fully
would have been to turn over to them virtual control of Soviet foreign
policy, and that of course was inconceivable.

A vivid example of how Mao proposed to pressure Moscow even on
issues not directly affecting the People's Republic came during one
of the perennial Middle Eastern crises. This one opened on July 13,
1958, with the overthrow of the pro-Western regime in Iraq and its
replacement by one that chose to position itself quite close to the
Soviet Union. There was alarm in the West that a similar fate might
be in store for two other pro-Western regimes in the area—Lebanon's
and Jordan's—and that the Soviet Union, already close to Nasser's
Egypt, would now establish a virtual protectorate over the eastern rim
of the Mediterranean. Following the Suez imbroglio, the United States
sought to provide for such a contingency by a congressional resolution
embodying what became known as the Eisenhower Doctrine. It envisaged U.S. aid for the countries in the Middle East "to secure and
protect the territorial integrity and political independence of such
nations requesting such aid against overt armed aggression from any
nation controlled by International Communism."[13] This classical lan-

guage of the cold war was now invoked to bolster the faltering regimes in Lebanon and Jordan. The Americans landed Marines in Lebanon; the British sent parachute units to Jordan.

The crisis, welcome though the toppling of a pro-Western regime was to the USSR, confronted it with a difficult dilemma. In its freshly assumed role as a protector of the Arabs and a Middle Eastern power, the Soviet Union could not afford to do nothing in the face of what in Communist semantics was a blatant display of imperialism by the West. At the same time, Khrushchev's main interest was to reach an accommodation with the West concerning Germany. The Middle Eastern affair thus tended to divert the Kremlin from its chief concern and presented a threat. Were the USSR to challenge the West's intervention, the situation might soon escalate to a danger point.

As one might have expected, Khrushchev reacted to the crisis with a typical mixture of bluff and bluster on the one hand and cajolery on the other. President Eisenhower and Prime Minister Macmillan were reminded in an official Soviet communication that the USSR had an ample armory of modern weapons, including hydrogen bombs and intercontinental ballistic missiles. And, added the incorrigible bluffer, "the powers which have started the aggression are playing with fire. It is always easier to kindle the fire than to put it out."[14] But then came the first secretary's favorite gambit: a plea for summitry. The Soviets proposed that the governments of the Big Four (Great Britain, the USSR, the United States, France) plus *India* confer on the situation, if need be within the context of the U.N. Security Council, Khrushchev being quite willing to come to the United States to attend its meeting.

One can well imagine the emotions the Soviet proposal must have aroused in Beijing. There was first and foremost a feeling of bitter resentment at Khrushchev's willingness to attend a meeting at the Security Council, where he, as head of the Soviet government, would meet the ambassador representing the fraudulent regime of Taiwan, and from which representatives of the legitimate government of China would be absent. The People's Republic's relations with India had lately become strained. And here was Khrushchev proposing to bring India in on the negotiations, thus compounding the slight to Beijing! Finally, it could not have escaped Mao's attention that Khrushchev was in fact inviting himself to the United States and that it would be the first visit by the head of the Soviet government to the heartland of capitalism and neoimperialism. Surely, he would want to discuss other issues with the imperialists than just the Middle Eastern crisis, which, as the Chinese must have known, had been blown by him out of all proportion.

The reaction from China must have been prompt and drastic. With his usual bombast Khrushchev had been pretending that the world was imminently in danger of a conflagration: "Time is precious as the guns are already beginning to fire. . . . There is not a minute to be lost." Then, on July 31, unmindful that if the danger was so great he should be in Moscow, he flew to Beijing for what turned out to be a four-day visit.

There was still some willingness on the Chinese side to keep up appearances. The communiqué issued at the conclusion of the talks contained China's endorsement of Khrushchev's proposals. But the visit certainly cooled off his enthusiasm for a summit meeting. On August 5, after his return to Moscow, the first secretary (and now also prime minister) claimed that the Anglo-American position made such a meeting impossible. And of course the USSR would not negotiate within the Security Council, "where most of its members are states which belong to the aggressive blocs and where the great Chinese People's Republic is not represented."[15]

Khrushchev's own confused account of what transpired at the meeting is probably designed to conceal rather than reveal the gist of his conversations with Mao.[16] It is probable that the Chinese price for formally endorsing the Soviets' stand, rather than denouncing it, was more Soviet military and technological help, and that is why the first secretary brought with him the Soviet minister of defense, Marshal Rodion Malinovsky. But there was evidently some talk about the USSR having naval bases on Chinese territory, something that, according to that not overly reliably acount, Mao categorically refused.

The Middle Eastern crisis, which had aroused considerable anxiety in the West, soon subsided without any of the horrendous consequences threatened by Khrushchev. After the passage of more than thirty years, it is easy to view the whole episode in a humorous light. But at the time Western statesmen could not take the Soviet leader's bluster lightheartedly. He, for his own part, was denied, due to Chinese pressure, the opportunity to inveigle the West into negotiations, in which, after brushing aside the contrived Middle Eastern crisis, he would in all likelihood have raised the problem of Germany. How long would the Soviet Union keep sacrificing its vital interests out of deference to Mao, a man, Khrushchev notes (and on this he is quite credible), who had for some time impressed him as acting and talking in a manner quite reminiscent of the late J. V. Stalin? And even in his personal relations with Soviet dignitaries, Mao could intermittently be haughty and intentionally crude. Talking during his Moscow visit with Voroshilov, who though a member of the "antiparty group" was allowed to linger for a while as head of state, Mao observed jokingly that "everyone over seventy should be buried to the strains of rousing music, not funeral music, because he had (finally) relieved the earth of his presence."[17] At the time, Marshal Voroshilov was seventy-six years old.

On August 23, 1958, the Chinese began massive shelling from the mainland of the islands of Quemoy and Matsu. Did Mao warn Khrushchev during his visit that Beijing proposed to stir up things in the Taiwan Strait, and what assurances could he have gotten of Soviet support? As yet there are no clear-cut answers to these questions. But all the evidence at our disposal points strongly to the conclusion that this heavy shelling of the Chinese Nationalists' foreposts was designed not as a prelude to an attempt to land there and seize the islands, but mainly as a means of testing Washington's and Moscow's reactions.

It was no secret that the U.S. authorities viewed with irritation Chiang's holding on to the islands, which were within a few miles of the Communist-held mainland and had no relevance, except perhaps psychologically, to the defense of Taiwan itself. Yet the generalissimo had placed there about 100,000 Nationalist troops, one-fourth of his entire force, and in 1955 obtained a qualified American pledge to defend them, though formally they were not covered by the U.S.–Republic of China Mutual Defense Treaty of 1954. Clearly, Chiang's interest lay in maintaining the tension between Washington and Beijing at a high level, and even the slightest sign of possible détente between the two, such as the contacts begun in 1955 through their ambassadors in Warsaw, had to be seen by him as a grave danger. Holding on to Quemoy and Matsu, to the Communists an infuriating reminder of the U.S. imperialists' interference in their domestic affairs, was a good way for the Nationalists to keep up that tension, and perhaps of goading the Communists to an outright attack, which just might bring American nuclear retaliation against the People's Republic.

But though breathing fire in their rhetoric, in their actions the Chinese Communists knew how to be prudent, at least when it came to anything that might bring an actual confrontation with the United

States. And so the new installment of the Quemoy-Matsu crisis in August and September 1958 was only partly due to Beijing's hope that it might frighten Chiang, and indirectly the Americans, enough to make them evacuate the islands, so tantalizingly close that in fact only the shadow of a hydrogen bomb stood between them and the People's Liberation Army. The other, and quite likely the main, reason for the bombardment, and the frantic propaganda campaign directed at the Nationalist garrisons that accompanied it, was to put Moscow on the spot. If the Americans threatened the People's Republic, would the Soviet comrades stand loyally by their allies and in turn threaten the United States with nuclear retaliation? In that case, and since Beijing actually had no intention of invading the islands (unless they were abandoned by Chiang without fighting), by putting all those threats to the test the People's Republic would still reap the dividend of worsened United States-USSR relations, and thus block Khrushchev's schemes for an accommodation with the West. Or, if the Soviets, as one might anticipate, just hemmed and hawed, then the Chinese Communists would get a true measure of the Kremlin's attitude toward them and know what to expect in the future.

Well, the USSR did not exactly flunk the test, but it hardly passed it with flying colors. There is no doubt that the Kremlin saw the whole Quemoy-Matsu business as an unsubtle attempt to inveigle the USSR into a confrontation with the United States. Later, Soviet sources were to characterize it as a provocation. "At the end of August the People's Republic conducted bombardment of the islands . . . declaring that it was being done as a punitive measure in answer to the provocations by the partisans of Chiang Kai-shek. . . . Beijing intended by this action to worsen Soviet-American relations and through invoking the mechanism of the Sino-Soviet alliance to widen the conflict so as to bring about an armed confrontation in the Far East."[18]

Washington, not being privy to such an insight into the Chinese Communists' motivation, saw the bombardment as a preliminary to an invasion of the islands by the People's Liberation Army. On September 4, Secretary Dulles warned in a public statement that such an invasion "would forecast a widespread use of force in the Far East which would endanger vital free world positions and the security of the United States. Acquiescence therein would threaten peace everywhere."[19] And so if the Chinese Communists invaded, the United States would not remain a spectator.

Up until the time of Dulles's speech, the Soviet Union had not taken an official position on the crisis, and that probably led Beijing to signal that it did not wish an armed confrontation with the United States. On the sixth Zhou Enlai declared his government's willingness to resume the Warsaw ambassadorial talks with the United States that had been suspended some time before.

Now that the immediate danger had receded, the Kremlin rallied to its ally's side. On the seventh Khrushchev addressed a long, verbose letter to Eisenhower built around the theme "An attack on the Chinese People's Republic . . . is an attack on the Soviet Union," [20] but still not specifying what the USSR might do should the United States send its forces to repel an attack on the islands.

A correspondence ensued between President Eisenhower (who had previously expressed the wish that the damned islands might sink) and the first secretary. On September 19, when it was already fairly clear that there would be no rash move on either side, Khrushchev became bolder and more specific in his warnings, informing the president in yet another sententious letter that "those who harbor plans for an atomic attack on the Chinese People's Republic should not forget that the other side, too, has atomic and hydrogen weapons—and the appropriate means to deliver them—and if the Chinese People's Republic falls victim to such an attack, the aggressor will at once suffer a rebuff by the same means."[21]

The conflict that many, certainly in the West, believed posed a serious danger of a nuclear war petered out almost on a comic note. On October 6, Beijing's minister of defense ordered the shelling suspended for one week and announced that his forces would not prevent supplies from reaching the islands, provided that the ships bringing them were not escorted by U.S. warships. The Americans speedily discontinued the escort service. Another bizarre announcement from the Chinese Communists came on the twenty-fifth: they would shell the islands on alternate dates!

But to the instigators of the affair its outcome could not have appeared funny. The People's Republic had been humiliated; it was not the United States that had turned out to be a "paper tiger." Nor could Moscow find anything amusing in the whole sequence of events. The Chinese comrades had not even consulted them before precipitating a situation that could have involved the Soviet Union in the calamity of all-out war. As Soviet historians were to write about the Taiwan Strait crisis many years later, "All those actions were undertaken by the People's Republic without any [prior] consultation with the USSR, even though such consultations were clearly stipulated by the Sino-Soviet Pact of Friendship and Mutual Aid."[22]

But if the Chinese did not warn Moscow specifically about their forthcoming cannonade and attempted blockade of Quemoy, it is reasonable to assume that they did warn them (probably during Khrushchev's visit) about the likelihood of future clashes with the Nationalists, and asked the Soviets for diplomatic and, if need be, military assistance should the United States threaten to intervene. The Soviets' retort must have been that they could not assume direct military obligations unless they were put in control of any prospective joint Sino-Soviet defense measures and operations. Khrushchev in his recollections of the meeting with Mao mentions only his request for submarine bases on China's coast. But as the Chinese government's statement in 1963 was to suggest, the Russians had gone much further in their demands. "In 1958 the leadership of the CPSU [Communist Party of the Soviet Union] put forward unreasonable demands designed to put China under Soviet military control. These unreasonable demands were rightly and firmly rejected by the Chinese government."[23] The Soviet position was on its face quite sensible: If Beijing wanted the USSR to backstop its military moves and thus incur the risk of a clash with the United States, then the Soviet Union should be in control of the operation both diplomatically and militarily. No Soviet, or for that matter any other national, leader would leave a decision on a potentially life-and-death matter entirely to a foreign government. But the Chinese also had a case. Where was the Soviets' support, even diplomatic, when they most needed it? In 1963 at the height of its most indiscreet and indecorous (but by the same token to a student of Sino-Soviet relations, most valuable) public correspondence with Beijing, the Soviets credited themselves with selfless protection of numerous nations from the imperialists. "The Soviet Union without hesitation has thrown in all its international weight, all its military might, to stay the hand raised by the aggressor over countries large or small, geographically distant or near to us. . . . This was the case when tension flared up in the Taiwan Strait—and the Chinese people and leaders certainly remember this."[24] The Chinese, one hardly needs to say, would not endorse this Soviet version of the crisis. "In August and September 1958 the situation in the Taiwan Strait was indeed tense as a result of the aggression and provocation by the US imperialists; the Soviet leaders expressed their support for China on September 7 and 19 [when] although the situation in the Taiwan Strait was tense, there was no possibility that a nuclear war would break out and no need for the Soviet Union to support China with nuclear weapons. It was only when they were convinced that this was the situation that the Soviet leaders expressed their support for China."25

From one point of view the Taiwan Strait episode was a typical cold-war crisis with both sides playing the game of bluff and brinksmanship. (Would the United States really have attacked the mainland with nuclear weapons the minute the People's Liberation Army landed [it virtually could have swum there] on Quemoy?) But for both Communist powers the turmoil over these islands, insignificant in themselves, marked a definite turn from an alliance, frayed as it had become since 1950, toward first a controversy and then open hostility. The Chinese Communists would never again try a dangerous gamble like their indirect challenge to the United States in the Taiwan Strait, since now they knew (whereas before, they suspected) that the Soviet Union would not back them up. The Soviet Union's leaders were now convinced that the Chinese wanted to make impossible the prospect of peaceful coexistence with the West, and also suspected that Beijing was not averse to inveigling them into a military confrontation with the United States. Subsequently, Soviet analysts would refer to an alleged statement by Mao of how satisfying it is to sit atop a mountain and watch two tigers devour each other.

The possibility of a mutually suicidal struggle between the United States and the Soviet Union was very much on the mind of Nikita Khrushchev. To an outsider the Russian leader appeared to be a man committed to the expansion of Communism and of Soviet influence, especially in the Third World, at the same time that he sought, rather incomprehensibly, summit meetings with the leaders of the West. But Khrushchev's priority was an agreement with the United States and its allies. As already mentioned, the key provision of such an agreement would have been a resolution of the nuclear arms problem. This problem appeared to Khrushchev in a different light than it would to both Soviet and American statesmen after 1970, who would put as their first priority placing quantitative and qualitative limits on their respective stockpiles of weapons and vehicles of delivery. Nikita Sergeievich felt, and quite rightly, that the greatest danger to the world lay in the potential spread of nuclear arms to other powers beyond those already having them at the time (1958)—the United States, the USSR, and Great Britain. For reasons already stated, the Soviets feared most West Germany's acquisition of the dreaded weapons. And by now there was another power that the Kremlin wished would remain without these bombs, warheads, and missiles as long as possible— the People's Republic of China. In line with Khrushchev's strategy, which was to maneuver the Americans into agreeing on a nuclear ban on West Germany without realizing how important it was for the Soviets, the Kremlin had already tried several tacks. There had been, for example the Rapacki Plan, formally proposed by the Poles, but undoubtedly authored in Moscow, which would have West Germany as part of a "denuclearized zone of Central Europe." But none of the stratagems worked. The Americans would not buy them.

And so Khrushchev would try again, in his roundabout and devious way, to reach his objectives, leading first through a Central European capital, then an island in the Caribbean, failing in both cases, but not before the Russian's oversubtle schemes had brought the world as close to a nuclear holocaust as it ever had been.

On November 27, 1958, the Soviet government addressed a note to the three Western powers. Its main argument was simple. It was high time, thirteen years after the war, to have a German peace treaty. The treaty had to recognize the facts of life: the existence of the two Germanys. Were the Western powers to persist in their refusal to negotiate a treaty and to recognize the German Democratic Republic, the USSR would make a separate treaty with the latter, divesting itself of any responsibility as an occupying power. It would then be up to East Germany to regulate American, British, and French access to West Berlin through its territory. And if East Germany banned such access and the West should think of using force, then the Western chanceries ought to keep in mind that the Soviet Union and other Warsaw Pact countries would be bound to come to their ally's aid.

To translate: you sign a peace treaty on our terms or you'll have another blockade of West Berlin, and this time we may not allow you to supply the city by air.

The note did not mention nuclear weapons, but it dwelt at length on West Berlin's being used by the West for the purposes of subverting the socialist regimes of East Europe, and as a center of espionage, etc. The Soviet Union was quite willing to have West Berlin declared a demilitarized, free city, but of course this had to be done through a peace treaty. The USSR also declared that it would not, for the next six months, cause any alteration in Western access to the city. But after that . . . !

Thus began what was and still is known as the second Berlin "crisis," which would tantalize the world for nearly four years.

It is difficult to see why at the time so many in the West really did believe that Khrushchev wanted to grab the city. Without being a mind reader, and by simply reading the note carefully and knowing the background, one could easily conclude that West Berlin was for him, as it had been for Stalin in 1948, an instrument to pry concessions out of the Western allies; in this case a Germany treaty. To repeat, this treaty would first of all constrain the Americans to give up their unyielding opposition to recognizing East Germany. But then, and probably to the Soviets more important, there would have been another provision, one containing ironclad guarantees against the Federal Republic's deployment of nuclear weapons. There had been some talk within NATO about West Germany being allowed to possess such weapons, but at the time it was very unlikely that such permission would be granted. Had the Soviet leader been less obvious on that issue, it is quite likely he could have been reassured. But there still would have remained the stumbling block of Washington's and Bonn's categorical refusal to recognize the German Democratic Republic. The Americans, it seemed, would rather fight than agree to have access to West Berlin formally controlled by the latter, i.e., to have an East German, and not a Soviet, official, stamp a traveler's papers.

Where did China fit into the picture? On December 21 the People's Republic endorsed the Soviet note. "China fully supports the proposal of the Soviet government and firmly maintains that the occupation regime in West Berlin must be abolished. . . . The cancerous tumor of West Berlin, which poisons the European and world situation, must be removed."[26]

This was the next to the last time that the Chinese Communists endorsed a major Soviet diplomatic initiative. To be sure, it strengthened Moscow's hand vis-à-vis the West to have such a reaffirmation of the "unshakable friendship" and of the People's Republic's support, even on a purely European issue. But Khrushchev could not have been overly pleased by the tone of the Chinese note, which made it appear that the Soviet demands concerned almost exclusively the withdrawal of foreign troops from Berlin and termination of the state of occupation of West Berlin, thus reinforcing the impression in the West that all that the Soviets wanted was to grab the city. And of course it suited Beijing's purpose to have such an impression widespread.

As for Khrushchev's real purpose, his subsequent tactics in the crisis did not serve it well. He kept up his threats over Berlin, but when the crisis would reach a really dangerous point, he would back down and give the West another opportunity and more time to settle this vexatious Berlin business.

In the meantime, he was laying down yet another scheme, this one designed to keep China from obtaining the bomb. If Berlin was the West's exposed nerve, pressing of which would eventually make the United States forswear nuclear weapons for West Germany, then China's nuclear abstinence could be secured only by persuasion. But how could Mao and Company, especially in their present mood, be persuaded to give up their efforts to produce a weapon, the possession of which they believed would free them from American nuclear black-mail, and thus eventually would enable them to reclaim Taiwan? There is a great deal of evidence, admittedly circumstantial, that Khrushchev hoped to urge Beijing to give up or at least to postpone its nuclear ambitions by dangling before the Chinese Communists the possibility of recouping Taiwan peacefully. Eternal optimist that he was, the Soviet statesman believed that the Americans might give up protecting the Nationalists on the island in exchange precisely for China's not seeking to enter the atomic club. On both counts he was vastly overoptimistic. The Chinese would not give up their right to nuclear weapons, now considered by them to be essential for their security. The United States, frightened as American public opinion was by the prospect of China's acquiring the bomb, would not be, for quite a number of years, willing to lessen its support of Chiang. But Nikita Sergeievich would keep trying until one day in October 1962.

His scheme was unfolded at the Twenty-first Congress of the CPSU in January 1959. There, in his review of international affairs, the first secretary included a pregnant sentence: "One can and must construct in the Far East and the whole Pacific Ocean area a zone of peace, and first of all a zone free of atomic weapons."[27]

The message was clear. The United States should remove nuclear weapons from its bases in Japan, from Taiwan, and from its Seventh Fleet. China would have to agree to forsake the right to manufacture nuclear weapons, becoming part of the atomic-free zone. But it cer-tainly might be worthwhile to Beijing if in return the United States would remove its weapons and thus its shield over Taiwan, leaving Chiang to his fate.

As yet, Khrushchev was not ready to spell out his proposals. So the passage about the Pacific nuclear free zone could be taken for a propaganda slogan and not much more than that. It brought no reaction. What was registered was what the first secretary had to say about Berlin, confirming his suspended ultimatum and indulging in jibes about West Germans.

He was still eager to hold on to the fading alliance. Thus, to please the Chinese, he berated Tito and his party. What were those non-sensical things the Yugoslavs were saying about a conflict developing between Moscow and Beijing? They would never see a quarrel between the two fraternal countries any more than they would be able to see their own ears!

And indeed the Twenty-first Congress was a swan song of Sino-Soviet friendship. Khrushchev's speech was cordially endorsed by Zhou Enlai, who headed the Chinese delegation, and a message from Mao himself stressed once more the "unshakable unity of the socialist camp." For the Soviets, that unity was becoming very expensive. On February 9 it was announced that the USSR had granted China its most extensive parcel of economic and technological aid to date: 5 billion rubles' worth of economic and technological services and goods, to be produced during the next seven years. Alas, this second honeymoon would last but a few weeks.

It is not reported whether at the end of 1959 Marshal Tito and his collaborators could see their own ears. But though the Sino-Soviet quarrel became known to the world in 1960, insofar as the leaders on both sides were concerned, it was in fact brought to a boil during the preceding year. The decisive factor was Beijing's by now firm conviction that Khrushchev and the Soviet leadership were bent upon destroying the cause of Marxism-Leninism, or in more realistic language, were seeking to make a deal, possibly at China's expense, with the United States. And a bit later came another conviction: they, the Chinese, could not keep the Soviet Union from a sinful rapprochement with the capitalists by quarreling with the Russians in private. It could only be by publicly branding Khrushchev and his ilk as revisionists, unmasking their schemes, that Beijing could hope not so much to shame them out of a betrayal but to complicate their relations with other Communist parties and "national liberation movements" to the point where they would have to pretend at least to behave as good Marxists-Leninists.

Furious as they had been for a long time at the Chinese comrades, the Soviet leaders, on the contrary, did not wish for a public break. As the Chinese calculated, but not only for those reasons, such a break would weaken Khrushchev's hand in dealing with the Americans. He would no longer be able to speak for the Communist bloc as a whole, with the Americans seeing not only the Soviet power but those countless millions of Chinese behind him. And so when the break did come, the first U.S. reaction was one of incredulity (similar to the initial belief in 1948 that the Stalin-Tito business was contrived to fool the free world), followed by the feeling that because he was quarreling with Mao, Khrushchev was now less dangerous.

One cannot, however, analyze the dispute in purely rational terms. Once the policy differences became insurmountable, other, often emotional factors came to play a role in further aggravating relations. The Chinese remembered the territories that prerevolutionary Russia had snatched from the Manchu empire. Even before 1959–60, maps were printed in the People's Republic showing large areas of the Asian USSR as belonging by right to China. Mutual criticism would occasionally assume chauvinist, and even racist, undertones. To the Russians it appeared preposterous that representatives of a backward country should presume to give lessons in Marxism to the leader of the Fatherland of Socialism. Beijing, for its part, would hint that the Soviets were insensitive to the aspirations of the Third World so long oppressed by the white imperialists. From the time they first met, it was obvious that Khrushchev could not stand Mao, while the latter, apart from holding the first secretary to be a renegade Marxist, also viewed him the way a nineteenth-century mandarin might have looked at a European "barbarian."

The Chinese Communists' behavior, or more precisely, Mao's behavior, grew increasingly erratic. The inanities of the Great Leap Forward were catching up with the country's economy. Already in the spring of 1959 there were signs pointing to a bad harvest and a general downturn in agriculture. The problem was aggravated by a large part of a peasant working force wasting its time on frantic and futile labor on the backyard furnaces. Confronted by harbingers of an economic disaster and rising criticisms within the party, Mao would intermittently call for pressing the peasant harder on the one hand and on the other would moderate his push for communes and for fantastic figures in steel and grain production.

Economic troubles were paralleled by political ones. A rebellion in Tibet led Beijing to suppress that country's autonomy. That in turn triggered a conflict with India. Ever since the Bandung Conference, when, thanks largely to Zhou Enlai's skill and charm, China gained the sympathy and support of other Asian countries, friendly relations with New Delhi was the cornerstone of the People's Republic's bid for leadership in the Third World. Now the two largest nations in Asia (and the world) found themselves at odds.

Internally, the catastrophic Leap and the latent crisis in Sino-Soviet relations brought a challenge to Mao's leadership. He sought to deflect criticism by yielding his post as head of state to Liu Shaoqi, but remaining chairman of the party. Still, opposition to Mao erupted at the July-August meeting of the Central Committee in Lushan. Marshal Peng Dehuai pointed out the folly of forcing the communes and the grotesque steel drive on the country's millions of peasants. In 1930, Stalin, when confronted with the catastrophic effects of forced collectivization on Russian agriculture, proclaimed brazenly that he had been misunderstood; this had been the fault of his overzealous subordinates. Now the chairman followed the example of the man he had both hated and admired. With his customary earthiness he turned the tables on his critics: "Comrades, you should analyze your own responsibility and your stomachs will feel much more comfortable if you move your bowels and break wind."[28] Beyond dispensing such homely prescriptions, Mao felt it advisable to have Peng, until then minister of defense, and some other high offcials, dismissed. In 1966–67, amid the Cultural Revolution, a massive folly surpassing even that of the Great Leap, Peng, who had led the Chinese volunteers in Korea, would find himself accused of having tried, at the Russians' instigation, to overthrow Mao. At the time, the Soviet connection was already hinted at by Mao himself, alongside the charge that the hero of the Korean War had never been a true Marxist.[29]

Soviet reaction to what was transpiring in China is succinctly described by Khrushchev (though reminiscing about them ten years later, he was somewhat confused about the sequence of events): "When Mao started pushing the idea that China could catch up with America in five years, he took the offensive against us, and he did so out in the open. It was about this same time that he started to organize communes and build his samovar blast furnaces. . . . Mao Zedong also declared that peaceful coexistence was a bourgeois pacifist notion."[30]

7

THE GREAT DIVIDE

TENSION BETWEEN the two allies had built up to an almost un-
bearable degree. Yet, hoping against hope, Khrushchev was reluctant
to give up either of his two major goals: the preservation of at least
the appearance of unity in the Communist bloc, and détente with the
United States. As usually happens in such cases, he would lose on
both counts. On the Chinese side one notes through 1959 an almost
masochistic longing for further and more concrete proofs of the Soviets' betrayal. A major one came in June 1959: "The promised prototype atomic bomb removed from a Soviet train at the last moment
never reached China, nor did the Chinese realize their early hope of
drawing on the most advanced Soviet knowledge and technologies."[1]

The Chinese correctly saw this action as a clear violation by the
Soviets of the technological and defense agreement of 1957. Their
bitter reaction to the Kremlin's going back on its word was revealed
to the world only in 1963 in an official statement. "In the eyes of the
Soviet leaders, the whole world and the destiny of all mankind revolve
around nuclear weapons. Therefore they hold on tightly to their nuclear weapons, afraid that someone might take them away or come
to possess them, and so break up their monopoly. They are very nervous."[2] This was an unwitting tribute to Khrushchev: he was quite
right to be nervous—the destiny of mankind, alas, *does* revolve around
nuclear weapons. But if Beijing was so indignant, why didn't the
Chinese drop the other shoe then and there?

Well, for all of his emotionalism about the Russians, there was a
cold and calculating side to Mao, especially when it came to foreign
policy. There was still some help to be squeezed out of Moscow. Then
he had been under pressure from his colleagues not only about the

Great Leap, but also about his antagonism to the Soviets, which was jeopardizing not only the military-technological development but the general economic one as well.

At the moment, neither of the Communist powers wished to publicize their disagreements. Khrushchev had been invited to visit the United States by President Eisenhower, in return for which he announced that his six months' time limit on the resolution of the "Berlin problem" was no longer binding. Beijing could not be overjoyed at the announcement of the visit, but it is quite likely that the Soviets had tried to soften the blow by promising to take up with the Americans the question of Taiwan. To trumpet the break with the USSR now would have meant forfeiting the chance, small as it was, of the Americans' giving up or moderating their sponsorship of the Nationalists. By the same token, an open clash with Khrushchev might well drive him to plot with Washington against the People's Republic.

Flattering as it was to Khrushchev's ego, the trip, the first time a ruler of Russia had stepped on American soil, proved barren of political results. No opportunity arose for the Soviet statesman either to plot against or to intercede on behalf of the People's Republic. Khrushchev *did* ask the president whether he wanted to talk about China. To quote Eisenhower: "I answered that I thought there was little use to do so for the simple reason that Red China had put herself beyond the pale insofar as the United States was concerned."[3] But what if the president had been more alert and asked his guest to go on? Would Khrushchev have intimated that if the United States removed the Seventh Fleet from the Taiwan Strait, he would be able to persuade the Chinese to stop working on the A-bomb? Or would he have confessed the trouble he was having with those impossible people? In any case, and probably with an inward groan, the first secretary assured the president "that allegations of differences between the Soviets and Red China . . . were ridiculous by their very nature. He and Mao Tse-tung were good friends. . . . The two nations would always stand together in any international dispute."

Nor was there any progress on another issue close to Khrushchev's heart. The Americans still thought he was after Berlin and would not budge on the issue. There is much evidence that the Soviet leader had hoped not merely for another exercise in summitry but for a real rapprochement with the West, somewhat on the order of what was to transpire in the late 1980s. To cement human as well as diplomatic ties with America, he brought with him not only his wife but also prominent figures from the Soviet scientific and cultural establishment. The Americans did not catch on, and as the tour progressed, Khrushchev's mood grew irritable. Still an optimist, he invited the president to pay a return visit in 1960. With Eisenhower in Russia, perhaps they could get down to business.

But the visit was seen quite differently by Beijing. Khrushchev evidently established close personal relations with the archimperialist Eisenhower (this was the famous but, alas, evanescent "spirit of Camp David"). He had put the Berlin issue on hold, rather than pressing the West with further ultimatums. (The first secretary had always denied that there was an element of threat in his stance on Germany— he had simply said that the matter had to be settled by such and such a date or else!) Who, knowing the Russian trickster, would really believe that what actually transpired in the talks was truthfully represented by the bland U.S.-Soviet official communiqué? The mounting Chinese irritation was compounded by what happened a few days before Khrushchev flew to America. There had been a border clash between Indian and Chinese soldiers that brought to light a boundary dispute between the two Asian powers. An official Tass communiqué on the affair was neutral in its tone, professing Soviet friendship with both. This fed another Chinese suspicion: the USSR was getting too intimate with India—were the Soviets thinking of setting up the latter as a countervailing force in Asia to the People's Republic? How could they profess neutrality in a dispute that arose out of India's attempt to grab territory that of right belonged to a member of the socialist camp? The Soviets for their part were also suspicious: what was the sense of Beijing suddenly making an issue over some uninhabited, worthless territory? Were the Chinese trying to sabotage Khrushchev's trip and wreck prospects for peaceful coexistence?

On his return to Moscow the Soviet leader gave himself a triumphant reception during which he again spoke warmly of Eisenhower. But almost immediately afterward he had to fly to Beijing.

This was to be the last visit by Moscow's number-one man to China until the also unfortunate (but in quite a different sense) 1989 Gorbachev visit to a very disorderly Beijing. And in a way this coupling is symbolic: it was very largely because the chasm between the two Communist powers was not bridged in 1959—and would grow even greater during the quarter of a century following it—that thirty years later both regimes would be in considerable trouble and the star of Communism would have set.

Four years later this is what the Central Committee of the Communist Party of China had to say about Khrushchev's visit. "Back from the Camp David talks [he] went so far as to try to sell China the U.S. plot of 'two Chinas' and at the state banquet celebrating the Tenth Anniversary of the founding of the People's Republic of China, he read China a lecture against 'testing by force the stability of the capitalist system.'"[4]

Actually, what the Soviet leader tried to sell to the Chinese was the need for patience on the issue of Taiwan. His logic was irrefutable: the People's Republic was in no position to seize Taiwan unless the United States lifted its protective shield over it. So why make bellicose statements that only increased Washington's fears and hostility? The Soviet state in its beginnings acquiesced in having large territories remain temporarily outside its borders. Was Lenin then fainthearted or betraying socialism? Chinese leaders reacted frostily to such pleadings, and they were not enraptured when their visitor eulogized Eisenhower as a man of peace.

Mao, acccording to one Khrushchev version, did not choose to quarrel openly with him,[5] but instead unleashed his foreign minister Marshal Chen Yi to attack the head of the Soviet delegation. Chen Yi became quite unpleasant on the subject of the Kremlin's neutrality in the Sino-Soviet border dispute. " 'How could you make such a statement?' he blurted out. 'Don't you know Nehru must be destroyed if the progressive forces in India are to prevail?' "[6] For a second-rank Chinese official to use such language to the head of the Soviet party and government would indeed have been quite shocking, and it is possible that Khrushchev in his recollections confuses what was said in 1959 with the tone of Chinese utterances about the Soviets after 1960, when indeed no epithets would be strong enough to characterize the Russians and their perfidious leader.

Whatever the actual tone of the Beijing discussions, it remains a fact that again the two powers chose not to reveal their disagreements to the world but to reassert in public that famous "unshakable unity." The Chinese goverment placed on record its support of the Soviet Union's disarmament proposals.

Did Khrushchev on that occasion return to his plan for "the Pacific atomic-free zone." that is, for China to give up its nuclear pursuits in return for the United States stopping its protection of Taiwan from the Communists? Though both Soviet and Chinese sources are silent on this subject, this is quite likely in view of subsequent developments.

He certainly would have tried to justify his invitation to Eisenhower by presenting it as a way to get the Americans to agree to a German peace treaty that would ban nuclear weapons for or in the Federal Republic. And it would have been entirely in line with Khrushchev's approach to such problems to argue while in Beijing that China would not have to give up *entirely* its ambitions to have nuclear weapons. The People's Republic was still quite far from developing and testing its first A-bomb. It could then *promise* not to do so, and once the United States withdrew the Seventh Fleet from the Taiwan Strait, Beijing could resume its nuclear endeavors.

Sometime earlier Mao declared that as long as his country did not have nuclear weapons it would be bullied, something of a contradiction of his frequent assertion that the A-bomb was a "paper tiger." And evidently Beijing now felt that it was being bullied by the USSR, and asked to sacrifice its vital interests at the altar of peaceful coexistence between the Soviet Union and the capitalists.

Was it entirely out of the question that Khrushchev in his guilty passion for coexistence would presume to speak on behalf of the People's Republic and declare on its behalf that it would not produce nuclear weapons? Evidently not, in Beijing's view. At the meeting of the Warsaw Pact states in Moscow on Feburary 4, 1960, the Chinese delegate (the People's Republic's representatives attended the meeting as observers) made a statement clearly addressed to such a possiblity. "The Chinese Government has to declare to the world that any international disarmament agreement and all other international agreements which are arrived at without the formal participation of the Chinese People's Republic and the signature of its delegate cannot of course have any binding force on China."[7]

The Warsaw Treaty Organization's meeting at which China's representative delivered this rebuff to Khrushchev's schemes took place under somewhat mysterious circumstances. The foreign ministers of the member states (and observers from the Communist states in Asia) had been meeting since February 1, but it was only on the third that the announcement was issued about the meeting being held. One must assume that Moscow did not know what to expect: would Beijing's delegate endorse the strongly procoexistence statement by the member states, or would he create a scandal by denouncing the Soviet Union then and there? As it was, the Chinese representative's performance, while falling far short of the Kremlin's hopes, still was not an explicit attack. The declaration by the member states fitted in

completely, needless to say, with the Soviet position, hailing the Soviets, especially Khrushchev's endeavors on behalf of peace and conciliation with the West. The visit to America was credited with having
broken "the ice of the cold war . . . in the relations between the two
strongest powers in the world—the USSR and the United States."[8]
Much hope was expressed about the forthcoming May summit of the
Big Four in Paris, even more about the scheduled summer visit by
President Eisenhower to Russia. The language in the document
should have made it plain to the West that what the Soviets were after
was not Berlin but a German peace treaty: "The conclusion of a peace
treaty, the renunciation of all ideas of revenge, or revision of frontiers,
the renunciation of the policy of Germany's remilitarization and *atomic
arming,* such is the best road to words ensuring the security of all
European nations."[9] (My italics.) The Chinese delegate, on the contrary, poured cold water on all such hopes. "The actions of the United
States prove that its imperialist nature will not change."[10] The Communist bloc, he implied, did not have to be so cautious in combating
the imperialists, since it was really stronger: ". . . in the most important fields of science and technology the Soviet Union has left the
United States far behind."[11] The United States was also becoming
politically isolated and militarily weak, and its economic situation was
growing quite vulnerable.

It is unlikely that given the general context of the speech, Khrushchev could have been comforted by such compliments, nor could
he have much confidence in the speaker's pledge that "the Chinese
Communist Party and the Chinese people have always taken the safe-
guarding of the unity of the socialist camp headed by the Soviet Union
as their sacred international duty."[12]

The overt phase of the Sino-Soviet dispute is usually dated from
April 6, 1960, when the *Red Flag,* a Chinese organ, published an
article entitled "Long Live Leninism." A heavy, didactic piece replete
with numerous references to the canons of Marxism, it did not attack
Soviet policies explicitly, but its violent language about Tito and other
unnamed "revisionists" made its intent unmistakable: the other shoe
had been dropped. The article was attributed by the Soviets to Mao,
but its scholarly—indeed, scholastic—paraphernalia must have been
composed by professionals in such matters, with Mao probably au-
thoring or suggesting the polemical part of the philippic. It was certainly his personal touch to inject the "life can be beautiful after an
atomic war" motif: "We consistently oppose the launching of criminal

wars by imperialism. . . . But should the imperialists impose such sacrifices on the peoples of various countries, we believe that just as the
experience of the Russian revolution and Chinese revolution shows,
those sacrifices would be repaid. On the debris of a dead imperialism,
the victorious people would create very swiftly a civilization thousands
of times higher than the capitalist system and a truly beautiful system
for themselves."[13]

One can easily imagine the Kremlin's reaction to Mao's propounding
such absurdities—hitherto he had chosen to express his insouciance
about the bomb only within intra-Communist gatherings. What
chance was there now for Khrushchev and his schemes to lay to rest
the specter of a nuclear war?

It is unlikely that Khrushchev ever read T. S. Eliot. But he would
have appreciated the poet's notion that "April is the cruelest month,"
and indeed the month brought him rebuffs from the West as well as
the East. Mao's insolence was paralleled by the Americans' obtuseness. The two highest officials of the State Department, Secretary
Christian Herter and Under Secretary Douglas Dillon, made statements that indicated to the Soviet leader that the German part of his
master plan was not faring any better than the Chinese one. Both
gentlemen displayed symptoms of tunnel vision: all they saw as the
issue in international affairs was Berlin, and that was what Khrushchev was after. "He desires West Berlin to be free from protection,
free from security, free from its commercial and cultural ties with
West Germany—and cut off from freedom itself."[14] U.S. officials simply could not see that when the Soviets talked about making Berlin
a free city, it was simply a gimmick to make the Western powers
amenable to serious talk about a peace treaty for Germany. As usual,
when they felt they were being bullied, the Americans became rigid
and unyielding. There was little point negotiating with the Russians
unless they first agreed to remove their troops from East European
countries and granted self-determination to East Germany and North
Korea, said Dillon. The Soviet leader could only complain that such
speeches were quite inconsistent with the spirit of Camp David, and
he came closer, but not close enough, to saying that it was not West
Berlin that he coveted, but progress on peace and disarmament. But
if Khrushchev, as the Chinese were to say, was obsessed with nuclear
weapons, then his Western protagonists were equally so with West
Berlin and the need to protect it from being snatched away by the
Communists. So the incorrigible bluffer felt compelled once again to

raise the stakes: were the Western powers to refuse to sign a German peace treaty, then the USSR would have no recourse but to sign such a treaty unilaterally with East Germany. It is with the latter that the West would then have to negotiate about access to Berlin.

Under the circumstances, the approaching Big Four summit in May threatened to become an embarrassment to Soviet diplomacy. The U.S. stand there had already been delineated by Dillon's speech: there was no hope of any constructive approach to the German problem. As "the cruelest month" drew to a close, the Kremlin stood badly in need of something that might distract the world's attention from the predictable fiasco of the forthcoming summit and the inability of Khrushchev to fulfill his threats.

That something dropped literally from the skies on May 1 in the form of pilot Gary Powers and his U-2 plane, brought down by Soviet missiles. Those high-altitude overflights of the Soviet Union by specially constructed American planes with photographic equipment had been going on since 1956, providing Washington with valuable information about the Soviets' military installations and preparedness. The Soviets, while not overjoyed about this crass espionage, had not been able to shoot down any of the planes prior to the unfortunate Powers's. They consequently chose not to protest the overflights, a story that would have taken a lot of wind out of their claims of superiority in military technology. Now that their rockets did bring down the plane and they held the pilot, Khrushchev had an excellent pretext to scuttle the summit meeting and to disinvite Eisenhower. There is no question but that he would have moderated his reaction to the incident had he thought that there was still a chance to advance his plans. As it was, and in view of the Americans' incredibly clumsy efforts at explanation—first denying any spying intention, then admitting it and acknowledging the president's ultimate responsibility for the flights—Khrushchev could be excused for exploding. He had been praising Eisenhower as a man of peace and a wise statesman. Now this praise backfired: not only was Eisenhower unable to free himself from the baneful influence of Chancellor Adenauer and his own State Department and strike a bargain over Germany, but by allowing his name to be associated with aerial spying, he made the Soviet leader appear ridiculous. And indeed, as he had heaped praise on Eisenhower, he now grew bitter and vindictive about the president. The world now held its breath, half expecting Khrushchev to make good on his threat to have the USSR sign a peace treaty with East

Germany. But in Berlin, where he flew after aborting the Paris summit, the choleric leader, after indulging in new threats and taunts, merely appealed for another summit once the United State had a new president. How dangerous even verbal explosions had become in this age was shown by the fact that the United States secretary of defense had ordered a worldwide alert of American forces.

That vivid demonstration of the perils of inflammatory rhetoric was probably partly responsible for the fact that the clash with the West did not bring an improvement in Sino-Soviet relations. On the contrary, the conflict now intensified and both sides, abandoning euphemisms, began to belabor each other in public.

The first such confrontation took place at the Congress of the Romanian Communist Party in late June. The representatives of forty-odd other parties witnessed for the first time an uninhibited exchange between Khrushchev and Peng Zhen, head of the Chinese delegation. By appearing in person and being able to count on support from the great majority of other parties, Khrushchev may have thought that he would be able to intimidate the Chinese, especially since they were not represented by their most prestigious leaders. A few years later Beijing had the following to say about Khrushchev's behavior in Bucharest: "Khrushchev took the lead in organizing a great converging onslaught on the Chinese Communist Party. . . . He vilified [its members] . . . as 'madmen' wanting to unleash war, pure nationalists, 'dogmatic, left wing adventurists.' "[15]

This was no longer a question of divergence on specific political or even ideological issues. Such reasons were brought in since it is difficult for Communists to engage in a quarrel without accusing each other of ideological sins. In the Kremlin's idiom, Mao's people became "left-wing sectarians and dogmatists"; for Beijing, almost needless to say, the Soviet leadership had for some time followed the "revisionist" heresy. The real essence of the quarrel lay in the clash of state and national interests, as seen by the elites of the two contending parties. It is that clash that led to and aggravated the ideological conflict and not vice versa.

The outside world did not see it this way. Viewed from Washington or London, the Communist bloc was on the offensive, with differences between Moscow and Beijing being those merely of emphasis or tactics. The Communist bloc, or as it was still anachronistically called by many, the "Sino-Soviet" bloc, was trying to seize Berlin. With the European powers' empires crumbling, the Communists were out to ensnare the new nations. The Kremlin was contributing to the turmoil in the Congo, which was breaking out from under Belgian rule. It was attacking, as yet only politically, the West's positions in other parts of black Africa and the Middle East. Whatever the dissonances between the two Communist powers, they appeared of lesser significance than the explosion in the Third World and the fact that Communism was establishing footholds there, either directly or through its sponsorship of "national liberation" movements. The American doctrine of containment now seemed ridiculously out of date, for Soviet influence was extending to areas where there was not a single Soviet soldier, and where the Communist Party was nonexistent or insignificant; thus Egypt, Ghana, and most startlingly, Castro's Cuba.

Yet against such apparent successes of Communism the most important development of 1960 was the breakup of the Communist bloc, and this time with convincing evidence that proletarian internationalism did not work. In July and August the Soviet Union abruptly terminated its entire technological and economic assistance to China. In 1964 the Chinese party's Central Committee was to refer scathingly to that decision: "You were going completely against Communist ethics when you took advantage of China's natural disasters to adopt these grave measures . . . [you] unscrupulously withdrew the 1390 Soviet experts working in China, tore up 343 contracts . . . and scrapped 257 projects of scientific and technological cooperation."[16] Indeed, at the time, famine had struck large parts of China. Millions were literally starving, and the government was unable to provide food even to the personnel of the most important projects. In one factory that produced fissionable materials "dropsy afflicted two-thirds of the staff and workers. . . . The belt tightening at Lanzhou disproportionately fell on the women and children and on Party members, for the ordinary staff and workers got supplementary food allowances. Even then the wives and children . . . reduced their grain ration and saved food for their husbands so that they could engage in hard work."[17] Of what importance, against the timing of the Soviet blow, could be those esoteric and pedantic quarrels about "dogmatism" and "revisionism"? The Chinese would neither forgive nor forget.

Had the Soviets' help been phased out or withdrawn under different circumstances, their official explanation for the step would have been fairly convincing. The Russians were being spied upon, and their technical advice was often disregarded. Imbued by the spirit of the Great Leap, the Chinese put inordinate and unreasonable demands on the experts. But under the circumstances the effect of the Soviets' pullout in several critical industries was comparable to a surgeon withdrawing in the middle of an operation. In some places the experts, prior to leaving, engaged in virtual sabotage. The Chinese crew in Lanzhou "faced a jumbled pile of pipes and machinery that the departing Soviet specialists had ordered dumped in their wake."[18] Blueprints and crucial parts of the equipment would disappear along with departing guests.

Politically, the blow was clearly calculated by the Kremlin to teach the Chinese a lesson and to destroy Mao politically. He had already found himself in serious trouble: blamed within the party for the catastrophic Leap, and by his generals for endangering technological assistance from the USSR. The communes and the fatuous backyard "steel mills" were being liquidated, but not before they, along with the drought, had contributed to the disastrous famine. It is quite possible that for the moment actual power was in the hands of Liu Shaoqi and Deng Xiaoping, with Mao's even nominal leadership being in jeopardy.

But Khrushchev made a cardinal psychological mistake if he thought that the Soviet blow would help to dispose of Mao. As on other occasions, Chinese national pride reasserted itself in the face of foreign pressure: after an interval Mao recouped supreme power and the Chinese now poured such vast effort and resources into their nuclear endeavors that they would have the A-bomb much sooner than the Kremlin had expected.

For the moment the catastrophic internal conditions in the People's Republic argued against a definitive and open break with Moscow. With millions starving, never was a moment so propitious for the Nationalists to invade and reignite civil war on the mainland. And wouldn't the Americans be tempted to license such an adventure on Chiang's part if they were sure that there would be no reaction from the USSR?

Elementary prudence dictated continuation of some sort of a dialogue with the Soviet Union. And on the other side the hope of bringing China into line, and the mirage of reasserting the unity of the bloc, still deluded the Kremlin. In September a Chinese delegation traveled to Moscow. Then again in October. Finally, in November a prestigious group headed by Liu Shaoqi and Deng Xiaoping joined there in the conference of eighty-one Communist parties.

Mao's absence was all the more noticeable since most other delegations were headed by their parties' number-one person. If China's leadership was in some disarray, that of the Soviet party was also showing the effects of the pressure of events. Khrushchev had just returned from a session of the United Nations General Assembly in New York. He had gone there, one suspects, as much out of sheer spite to vent his recent frustrations on Eisenhower and the Americans as to court the newly independent states of Asia and Africa, and to welcome a new ally, Fidel Castro. The strain under which the first secretary had found himself told in his boorish behavior, shouting to people from the balcony of his New York residence and banging his shoe during a session of the General Assembly. On the surface Soviet policies had reverted to their standard cold war, anti-U.S. pattern. No longer the genial would-be-host of the president, Khrushchev had recently warned Eisenhower that before he undertook anything against Castro's Cuba, he should remember that the USSR now had long-range rockets, and nuclear weapons to mount on them.

The West was duly apprehensive. Concern over Berlin and the by now proverbial fear—"What will the Russians do?"—was an important factor in the 1960 U.S. presidential election. The collapse of the Paris summit and the heightened level of international tension very likely made the difference in John F. Kennedy's narrow win over the Republican candidate.

But the Chinese knew better: for all his irritation and exhibitionism Khrushchev still chased after détente with the West and was scandalously oblivious of Soviet obligations to international Communism and national liberation movements. The tone of the Soviet government's pronouncements on the Congo crisis was strident, and the Kremlin was again escalating its pressure on Berlin. Yet all those moves were intended, Beijing had good reason to believe, to soften the West and persuade it to have serious negotiations on two issues the Soviets cared most about: the German peace treaty and nuclear arms control and nonproliferation. The Soviet Union's withdrawal of technological assistance to the Chinese nuclear project was a closely held secret, but the USSR was publicly pursuing another approach that might be used to interdict nuclear weapons for Beijing. For some time now the Soviet Union, Great Britain, and the United States had been observing a moratorium on above-ground nuclear testing. The Kremlin might well try (it would do so in 1963) to make such a ban universal, which would then preclude countries like China from testing their first A-bomb.

But such practical and urgent problems did not get a hearing at the conference of eighty-one parties. Instead, the meeting alternated between the discussion of scholastic-sounding ideological formulas and spirited clashes between the Chinese representatives and the Soviets, assisted on this count by most of the European parties' representatives. On China's side there were only a few of the Asian parties and Albania.

Why did Enver Hoxha, the ruler of the diminutive Balkan state, come out so strongly on China's side, and why would Albania proudly advertise its pro-Chinese stand until the Sino-American détente in the 1970s? The answer shows how far the attrition of internationalism within the Communist movement had progressed by this point. Despite its claims to the contrary, Albania's turn to China and against the USSR had little to do with ideology. Seen from Tirana, a Soviet détente with the West was bound to again warm up relations between the USSR and Yugoslavia. And the latter, the Albanian leaders well remembered, had in the past shown the inclination to dominate, if not indeed to swallow, its little neighbor. And so it was logical for Hoxha and his acolytes to seek support of the Communist power that favored militant tactics vis-à-vis the West and that was bitterly hostile to Tito's revisionism. Within the Communist bloc, ideology had become to a large extent only a veneer for power politics. Emboldened by the encouragement of the government of the largest nation in the world, Albania had evicted Soviet naval units from a base they had established on its Adriatic coast, and at the conference its leader's references to the Soviet Union were scurrilous. Preoccupation with power had permeated the movement. His job security at stake, the leader of a minor Communist state became abusive and sarcastic about the Fatherland of Socialism. How different was the spirit of the Communist movement after October 1917 when Lenin would have willingly sacrificed his own and the Bolsheviks' power over Russia if by doing so they could have speeded up a revolution in Germany and then have it engulf all of the West.

Proletarian internationalism had become a facade behind which now raged the struggle of power interests of the various parties and regimes. As the Chinese were to characterize the atmosphere of the meeting: "It is true that, both before and during the meeting, the leadership of the CPSU engineered converging assaults on the Chinese Communist Party by a number of representatives of fraternal parties, and relying on a so-called majority attempted to bring the delegations of the Chinese and other Marxist-Leninist parties to their knees and to compel them to accept its revisionist line and views. However, the attempts to impose things on others met with failure."[19] The parties lined up, predictably, according to what the two contestants would do for, or to, them. The major Asian parties, except for India's, went along with China, or tried to maneuver between the two Communist giants, as did the North Koreans. The Indonesians and North Vietnamese had an obvious stake in the movement's reasserting its militant stance toward the West: a U.S.-Soviet détente would obviously impede them from achieving their goals—Indonesians from seizing power in their country, the North Vietnamese from conquering the South. By the same token, the East European ruling parties and the French and the Italians strongly supported the Soviets. The European comrades recoiled from the Chinese attacks on peaceful coexistence, which they saw, as did the Kremlin, as increasing chances for a nuclear war. Also for the Poles and Hungarians the reaffirmation of peaceful coexistence meant a greater latitude in their relations with the Soviets, for the Italians and French a better chance to appeal more strongly to the electorates in their countries. The Yugoslav party, currently consigned to the limbo (in Beijing's view, hell) of "revisionism," was conspicious by its absence.

"Ah, Nikita Sergeievich, he never carried anything to its conclusion." This lament of Solzhenitsyn's could also be an epitaph for the conference of eighty-one parties. Here was an opportunity for Khrushchev to line up an overwhelming majority of the Communist parties solidly behind his policy of coexistence and détente with the West, let the Chinese do their damnedest. A version of perestroika, healing of the Soviet system, real rapprochement with the United States, and negotiations about nuclear arms reduction and control might have begun then and there. The Chinese would have walked out, but it was fairly obvious they soon would break away in any case. But the first secretary was still chasing the phantom of Communist unity, still believed in the power of ritualistic incantations to bridge the chasm between Moscow and Beijing. Hence for all the fireworks at the conference, it concluded with a tortuously phrased declaration subscribed to by all the eighty-one participants. The document reflected mostly Soviet postulates on issues such as coexistence with capitalism, the possibility of peaceful transition to socialism, etc. But in almost each case the departure from the militant line was qualified by reservations insisted upon by the Chinese, so that as a whole the declaration sounded more like a challenge and a threat to the West than an acknowledgment of the realities of international life.

But what mattered more than the stilted propaganda idiom of the statement was the effect of the clash on Soviet policies. Though they carried the great majority of the conferees with them, though the Chinese did not get their way with the declaration, they had put the Soviets on the defensive. It was a novel experience for representatives of the Communist movement from all over the world to hear the leadership of the Soviet party scathingly criticized, with Deng Xiaoping aiming his attack directly at Khrushchev. The latter gave as well as he took. But he could not bring himself to break clearly and openly with the Chinese. And so he was placed in the paradoxical situation of simultaneously bad-mouthing China and still trying to appease it, of searching for a way to détente with the United States while maintaining some appearance of unity of the Communist world.

Yet could the two be reconciled? A true and lasting détente depended ultimately on the West's becoming persuaded that the USSR was a "normal" state and, as such, concerned about its security and the promotion of the welfare of its citizens, no longer pursuing the dream of world revolution. Had the Kremlin's actions and rhetoric adhered convincingly to that image, no major problem in contention between the East and the West—that of Germany, of nuclear arms control, the Middle East—could have been impervious to a peaceful solution. To preserve the unity of the Communist world, i.e., to have China pay at least lip service to it, the Soviet Union would have to strive after a different image: a power still bent on expansion and the worldwide victory of Marxism-Leninism. Here then was the dilemma facing Khrushchev and ultimately his personal tragedy: being unwilling to give up either of the goals, he would succeed in neither.

For the moment and through October 1962 the indefatigable improviser would still cling to the hope of finding a way out of the dilemma. If the Soviet Union must not seek to induce the West into détente by being reasonable and laying its cards on the table, then it could scare the United States into a rapprochement. And for its own part China would be induced to admit the necessity and benefits of peaceful coexistence once the Soviet Union achieved an understanding with the capitalists not by making concessions but by *forcing* an agreement upon them.

How was such a seemingly impossible feat to be accomplished? One factor that could encourage Khrushchev was the current Western perception of the power of the Communist bloc. Extravagant as it sounds today, this self-appraisal in the declaration of the eighty-one parties did not sound greatly exaggerated to a contemporary observer of the international scene in the early sixties: "The near future will bring the forces of peace and socialism new successes. The USSR will become the leading industrial power of the world. China will become a mighty industrial state. The socialist system will be turning out more than half the world industrial product. . . . The working class movement in the capitalist countries and the national liberation movements in the colonies and dependencies will achieve new victories. . . . The superiority of the forces of socialism and peace will be absolute."[20] Never had the fear of a nuclear war resulting from a clash between the United States and the USSR been so acute as during that period. Apart from an exaggerated image of Soviet power, nuclear as well as conventional, there was a widespread belief that the USSR was way ahead of America in many important branches of military technology. The Soviet Union was the first to put a man into orbit, another seeming proof of the missile gap, of the Soviets' superiority when it came to the means of delivery of the dreaded weapon.

One would have thought that the U-2 flights, which had gone on for several years before the fiasco in May, would have enabled the U.S. government to correct this exaggerated impression of Soviet military capabilities and establish that if there was a missile gap it was in our favor. But Khrushchev's missile-rattling had to lead to the deepest apprehension even among the best-informed circles in Washington, not to mention the other Western capitals.

In addition to the awe of Soviet military might, the Kremlin leader had another card when it came to pressuring the United States and its allies. Incongruously enough, it was China. By now (1960–61) there was some awareness abroad of the troubles between the Kremlin and Beijing, but hardly of how deep and bitter their disagreements already were. The Soviet Union was still thought in the West to be capable of exercising a moderating influence on the policies of the People's Republic, something considered to be of crucial importance since hard as the Soviet leaders were, their Chinese counterparts were believed to be fanatical ideologues, unrelenting in their hostility toward the United States. Fearful as Western governments and public opinion were of the Soviet Union's power and intentions, the prospect of China's acquiring nuclear bombs and missiles was in some ways even more alarming to them. Wouldn't the West be tractable on Ger-

many, Berlin, and some other contentious questions, if in return
Khrushchev could guarantee that China would abandon, or at least
postpone, the development of its own A-bomb?

There was one obvious catch: as we have already seen, the Chinese
had already and categorically rejected Soviet intimations that they
give up their ambition to join the nuclear club. But as the subsequent
course of events would show, Khrushchev had not given up on the
idea. What if the issue were raised again under circumstances that
would make China's pledge of nuclear abstinence appear not as a
concession to the imperialists but part of a spectacular coup that would
bring solid advantages to the Communist bloc in general, and to China
in particular?

At the beginning of 1961 the polemic between the two Communist
powers was somewhat muted. This reflected not a real détente but
the fact that both had cogent reasons not to advertise their quarrel.
The People's Republic suffered from a severe economic crisis, falling
industrial production, and famine conditions in large parts of the country. In the Kremlin there may have already been gestating the 1962
Caribbean stratagem that would require Chinese cooperation.

Though not advertised—they would only be revealed in 1963—
troubles between the two "fraternal countries" continued on several
fronts. There were serious border clashes. Thousands of the Turkic
inhabitants of Sinkiang were fleeing across the border into the USSR,
escaping the central government's repression. In order to change the
province's national character, the Beijing authorities were importing
large numbers of ethnic Chinese there, and so the natives were fleeing
en masse to their kindred in the Central Asian republics of the Soviet
Union. China was later to accuse Moscow of sponsoring subversion
on its territory and "enticing and coercing tens of thousands of
Chinese citizens into flight and refusing to return them to the People's
Republic, an astounding event, unheard of in the relations between
socialist countries."[21] Border clashes were to remain a persistent side
show of the Sino-Soviet dispute for a number of years, at times threatening to turn into localized warfare.

Another bone of contention was Albania. The Balkan country had
lined up behind Beijing, its leaders, especially Enver Hoxha, indulging
in the kind of invective about the Soviet Union that the Chinese as
yet thought prudent to eschew. There was no doubt, however, that
the Albanians were being encouraged by the Chinese. When the Soviets withdrew their economic aid to the little country, China moved

in to help. With millions starving in the People's Republic, its regime did not hesitate to divert some of the foodstuffs purchased abroad to Albania.

Whatever the divergencies within the Communist or, as it was still and anachronistically called in the West, the Sino-Soviet bloc, they seemed to be secondary to the main drama on the world stage: the escalating tension between East and West. The new American administration came into office determined to arrest what it viewed as a dangerous drift toward a confrontation over Berlin. To do so it sought first of all to impress Moscow with its firmness in meeting the Communist challenge on other fronts. But its initial efforts in that direction led to resounding failure. Ill conceived and badly planned, the invasion of Cuba ended in April in the disaster of the Bay of Pigs. In Laos, a CIA sponsored coup, which had pushed out the neutralist government, led to a Communist counteroffensive, bolstered by supplies flown in from the Soviet Union.

Cuba's accession to the Communist camp had at first occasioned some doubts and hesitations in the Kremlin. On the one hand, it was a signal triumph for Marxism-Leninism, a vivid demonstration of the potency of its appeal in the Third World. It came as a result of a completely voluntary decision by Castro and his acolytes, with not a single Soviet soldier on the island. Here was a startling confirmation of the Chinese notion of the East wind prevailing over the West one, of the configuration of world forces favoring militant tactics by the Communist bloc.

At the same time, Khrushchev greeted warily the new recruit to the socialist camp. Would Washington really tolerate a Communist regime in the Western Hemisphere, ninety miles from the U.S. shore? And most important, wouldn't the Americans, incensed over what they viewed as a breach in the Monroe Doctrine, become all the more inflexible on Germany and other issues more important to the USSR than who ruled the island in the Caribbean? The extent of Soviet reservations was indicated by the fact that with Castro already set on an anti-American course and soliciting his admittance to the bloc, the Soviets kept delaying the resumption of formal diplomatic relations with Cuba (they had been broken under Batista), undoubtedly out of apprehension over possible American reactions. They were resumed only in May after the U-2 episode, when Khrushchev had already decided that he could not expect anything tangible from the forthcoming summit and Eisenhower's visit to Russia.

Once the die was cast, there was every reason for the Kremlin to back Castro vigorously. Hence Khrushchev's peroration about Cuba being protected by Soviet intercontinental missiles, and his threatening and insulting message to Kennedy *after* it became clear that the invasion had fizzled out and the United States would not back it up with its own forces. As over Suez and in the Quemoy-Matsu affair, the Soviet leader was quite ready to threaten that the USSR would intervene once it was clear that he would not have to come through on his threats.

But even within the harsh and abusive message one could spot a plea and a bait for a rapprochement with the United States: "We wish to build up our relations with the United States in such a manner that the Soviet Union and the United States, as the two most powerful states in the world, would stop saber-rattling and bringing forward their military and economic advantage."[22]

The failure of U.S. policy in Cuba and Laos did not bring the Soviets over to the Chinese position that the capitalist world could be pressed with impunity and without seeking an accommodation with it. The Soviet Union would press harder and would take greater risks, now that the United States had stumbled, but the goal would remain an accommodation with the West, an accommodation that would serve the Soviets' interests rather than the interests of international Communism.

President Kennedy's motto that one must not negotiate from fear was put to a hard test throughout the balance of 1961. Khrushchev's favorite technique was precisely to try to frighten his protagonists into negotiations, to mix threats with enticements. Those tactics worked in Laos. The Soviets' militant pose was probably instrumental in dissuading the United States from intervening there directly, the affairs of the little kingdom being eventually referrred to the Geneva powers conference (i.e., including China).[23] It would take the Soviet Union's spectacular retreat in the second Cuban crisis to embolden Washington to comtemplate a major military involvement in Indochina.

Under the circumstances, the major diplomatic event of the year, the Kennedy-Khrushchev summit in Vienna, could not lead to any concrete agreements. In the wake of a painful setback for his administration, the president could not afford to yield on the issues of Berlin and Germany. The Soviet leader, for his part, was not as yet ready to unfold his plans, some of the props for the subsequent Russian move not being as yet in place; or, to put it differently, the Chinese stood in the way of the Soviet Union openly seeking an accommodation with the United States. Rather, one suspects, Khrushchev agreed to the U.S. solicitation for a summit largely to size up the young president. The latter was at a serious psychological disadvantage in confronting the Russian, since the meeting came only weeks after the Bay of Pigs. It was also awkward for Kennedy to face the man who had recently sent him what was probably the most insulting message ever received by a president of the United States from a foreign government. Khrushchev pressed his advantage, issuing yet another ultimatum about West Berlin, proving intransigent on the conditions for a nuclear test ban and the reorganization of the U.N., and in general trying to bully rather than negotiate. As would all his successors, the president went to the summit hopeful that once in a congenial setting the Soviet leaders would discard their propaganda bombast and ideological idiom and would address themselves seriously to removing the danger to peace. But personal contacts, the president's efforts at amiability and establishing a real dialogue were not reciprocated by Khrushchev and his entourage. The first secretary persisted in ideological diatribes and scornfully rebuffed Kennedy's explanation that the new Democratic administration looked favorably upon social and political reforms, decolonization, and other winds of change coursing through the world. It was difficult for the Americans to perceive that behind all that Soviet bravado there was real concern and anxiety about the condition of the Communist world. As with Eisenhower, Khrushchev again was telling fibs: the USSR and China continued to be close friends and allies. Had he (Khrushchev) been in Mao's place, he would have long ago attacked and seized Taiwan. Even more brazen, since this lie would be literally exploded within a few weeks, was his assurance that the Soviet Union would not be the first to resume nuclear tests.

There was to be no "spirit of Vienna"; the president grimly predicted a long, hard winter. And so would be the summer and the fall. Encouraged by what they perceived as the Americans' lack of self-assurance, the Soviets escalated the war of nerves. In August they licensed the East German authorities to erect the Berlin Wall and construct barriers all along their frontier. One aspect of the Berlin problem had thus been resolved through an act of force: the flight from East Germany, which had cost it 3 million citizens, most of them at the most productive age and endowed with professional skills, would be reduced to a trickle.

At the end of the month, equally suddenly, the West was astounded and shocked by the Soviet Union's resumption of atmospheric nuclear tests. They continued for two months and concluded with the mightiest bang yet: a fifty-six-megaton bomb. Those who in the late 1980s were to complain that America's standing in the world had greatly declined from what it had been in the sixties and seventies would do well to recall the feeling of alarm and almost helplessness that swept Washington in the wake of those Soviet pyrotechnics. Some classes of American reservists were recalled to active duty and defense estimates went up. The administration's alarm and puzzlement as to how to respond to the Soviet challenge was reflected by its effort to encourage the construction of fallout shelters. There was now vivid apprehension that the Soviets were irrevocably committed to ousting the West from Berlin and a corresponding conviction, at least in Washington and Bonn, that that enclave of the free world must be defended, even at the risk of nuclear confrontation.

Though responsible for the crisis, Moscow must have viewed the situation with an almost equal sense of exasperation. The Americans were frightened but not, so to speak, in a constructive way: they persisted in thinking that the game was about Berlin. The effects of Soviet militancy were also disappointing insofar as the Chinese were concerned; they applauded the escalating conflict between the Soviet Union and America, but were showing no sign of drawing closer to the former. On the contrary, by their demonstrative support of Albania, with which Moscow had now broken both party and state relations, Beijing was intentionally widening the rift within the world Communist movement. It was strange that the Western chanceries and analysts could come close to believing that Khrushchev was ready to risk a nuclear confrontation, while he was impotent to prevent the Hoxha regime from ejecting Soviet naval units from Albanian ports and from executing pro-Moscow officials of his party. Those high-risk policies (or, as after his ouster, Khrushchev's colleagues would characterize them, "harebrained schemes") were not bringing the Soviet Union closer to their real goals, détente with the United States and China. They were having, in fact, the opposite effect.

These contradictions were plainly visible, if still unperceived in the West, during the deliberations of the Twenty-second Congress of the CPSU, which assembled on October 17.

There was first of all a demonstration of the breach, this time unmistakable and public, between the two Communist powers. Khrushchev erupted with a violent attack on the Albanian leaders. The Chinese now decided to dispense with euphemisms in their dispute with the Kremlin. Zhou Enlai, in his capacity as the head of the Chinese delegation, the last one to attend the Soviet party's congress, replied in kind. "Open and one-sided attack upon any fraternal party does not contribute to solidarity, does not resolve the problem. To expose openly a dispute between fraternal parties and fraternal countries for enemies to see cannot be considered a serious Marxist-Leninist approach."[24] After this salvo the Chinese walked out of the congress. Zhou followed it with another symbolic gesture. The congress had witnessed the most comprehensive and concerted denunciation of Stalin to date, far surpassing Khrushchev's performance on that count in his 1956 secret speech. The Chinese representative thought if fitting before his departure from Moscow to deposit a wreath on the tyrant's tomb, inscribed "To the memory of a great Marxist-Leninist." On his return to Beijing, Zhou was demonstratively greeted at the airport by the entire Chinese leadership, headed by Mao.

This signaled a definite parting of the ways between the two parties, the two branches of the movement. Like all crusading faiths, Communism had drawn its strength and appeal from its unity and its claim to infallibility. That unity had broken down. By the time the two parties would attempt to patch up their differences, the faith would have eroded.

For the moment, neither side realized that by aiming blows at each other, and in full view of the world, they were striking also at the ideological basis of their own regimes. Both viewed what had happened as a separation rather than an irremediable split. The Chinese hoped that what they considered the revolutionary climate of international relations would render futile the Kremlin's strivings for détente with the capitalists. The Russians had still not lost hope that they could inveigle China into their scheme for such a détente.

To contemporary Western analysts, the significance of the Twenty-second Congress lay mainly in what was taken as the Soviets' renewed and escalated demands and threats about the need to resolve the "Berlin crisis" by the end of the year. Even the effect of the Chinese walkout took second place to the anxiety over the bellicose-sounding rhetoric of Khrushchev and his defense minister, Malinovsky.

Yet from our perpective the congress must be seen as centered on two quite different goals. One, a renovation of the Soviet system, was in some ways not dissimilar to what in twenty-odd years would be dubbed perestroika. The other, and consequent upon the former motif, was the bid for détente, if not indeed partnership, with the United States. Unlike Gorbachev's, Khrushchev's perestroika was planned within the context of the party's monopoly of power. But the party was to be refurbished and cleaned of the residues of Stalinism. Its repudiation was signaled by the removal of the tyrant's mummy from the mausoleum where it had reposed next to Lenin's. The dictator's crimes were now spelled out much more extensively than at the Twentieth Congress and for the whole world to hear and read. There was to be erected a monument with the names of those martyred in the thirties and forties inscribed upon it—surely an impractical idea in view of the number of victims, but one taken up again by Gorbachev in 1988.

More workable was the provision in the party's new program that limited its hierarchy to three terms in office—a maximum of fifteen years; this provision, if subsequently observed, which it was not, would have prevented, or at least curtailed, the rise of the gerontocratic oligarchy that would have such baneful influence under Brezhnev. The program promised a new deal for the Soviet consumer: within two decades production of basic foodstuffs would surpass that of the United States. By 1980 Soviet society would be entering the era of Communism, the state bureaucracy to be reduced in numbers and functions.

Hardly a convincing blueprint for the future. But its formulation was a vivid proof that the leaders recognized the danger of the growing atrophy of the ideological base of the system.

Casual reading of the proceedings of the congress would hardly lead to the conclusion that one of its main motifs was a plea for détente with America. On the contrary, the stress seemed to be on a militant and threatening stance toward the West. Apart from the usual bluff and bluster from Khrushchev on Berlin, the delegates were treated to a bloodcurdling speech by his minister of defense, Marshall Malinovsky. The marshal cited some horrifying statistics: eight Soviet multimegaton bombs could dispose of all West Germany; a single nuclear strike against the United States would leave at least 50 million dead. The USSR had rockets capable of reaching any point on the globe, as well as nuclear warheads with the power of up to a hundred megatons. The speaker seemingly echoed Mao's contention that a nuclear war, should the imperialists provoke one, was bound to end with the socialist camp victorious and capitalism gone forever.

Nothing was spared to impress and frighten the West, and one may wonder whether the delegates themselves could have been reassured rather than frightened by the grim statistics.

The foreign minister's speech was a counterpoint to the rhetoric of intimidation. To be sure, it would have been difficult for Washington to take Gromyko's honeyed words seriously after those fireworks produced by Khrushchev and his defense minister. Gromyko portrayed the Vienna meeting as one of the most momentous and positive events of modern times. Kennedy's encounter with Khrushchev was presented as having taken place in a cordial atmosphere. Having just heard Zhou Enlai describe the U.S. government as "the worst enemy of peace" and its current administration as "the wiliest and most adventurist yet," the foreign minister was still uninhibited in his words of praise for certain aspects of American policies, referring to a recent statement by Secretary of State Dean Rusk as "wise and sober," and called on both countries "to harvest the fruits of the victory" in World War II.

Such diplomatic insincerities might be dismissed as insignificant except for a statement by the foreign minister that must have impressed and shocked the Chinese delegates more than anything else that had been said at the congress: "Our country places special importance on the character of the relations between the two giants— the Soviet Union and the United States. If those two countries united their efforts in the cause of peace, who would dare and who would be in a position to threaten peace? Nobody, there is no such power in the world."[25] This statement was a startling contradiction to the spirit and language of the declarations of the Communist conclaves of 1957 and 1960, with their boasts about the invincible power of the socialist camp and their denigration of the United States. This could not have been a casual flourish on the part of Gromyko. As all such pronouncements on such a solemn occasion, it had undoubtedly been carefully discussed, crafted, and authorized by the Politburo. In a way, that passage in the foreign minister's speech had to be taken more seriously as indicative of the Kremlin's frame of mind than if it had come from Khrushchev, given to occasional improvisations that might or might not be approved by his colleagues. And so it had to be read as a warning to Beijing as well as a come-on to Washington.

Afterward, in the midst of the acrimonious exchange between the two "fraternal" parties in 1963, the Chinese presented their estimate of the Twenty-second Congress. "It marked a new low in the CPSU's leadership's efforts to oppose Marxism-Leninism and split . . . the international Communist movement."[26] Beijing restated its indignation at Khrushchev's attack on the Albanians—and its rejection of the negative assessment of Stalin. As to the Soviet party's program, even a cursory perusal showed "that it is an out-and-out revisionist program which totally violates the fundamental theories of Marxism-Leninism and the revolutionary principle. . . . It substitutes humanism for the Marxist-Leninist theory of class struggle and substitutes the bourgeois slogans of 'freedom,' 'equality,' and 'fraternity' for the ideals of Communim."[27] The diatribe went on to allege that when Zhou told Khrushchev about his party's objections, the latter brusquely informed him that indeed the Soviets had listened to the Chinese comrades after Stalin's death as they were then badly in need of their support, but now that their system had emerged from the post-Stalin trauma, they did not propose to have their policy dictated by anyone.

The last allegation sounds more like a Chinese reconstruction of the rationale of the Soviets' behavior rather than a description of what actually happened. Temperamental as he was, Khrushchev still would hardly have been so unceremonious and offensively frank. He still needed Chinese support for what would turn out to be the biggest and most dangerous gamble of his political life.

If one of the purposes of foreign-policy statements at the Twenty-second Congress had been to frighten and/or cajole the West into a new posture on the German question, then nothing during the subsequent months indicated that the Soviets were succeeding. At the congress Khrushchev came close to saying outright that it was not West Berlin that he was after. "The main thing is to decide the issues, to liquidate the remnants of the war, to sign a peace treaty with Germany. That is the most important and essential problem."[28] But again, how could the West take this postulate at its face value, surrounded as it was in the speech by a profusion of threats and boasts.

The incongruities in Soviet relations with China and the United States continued through the first half of 1962. There was a sharp conflict with both countries. Yet for all of its polemic with Beijing, the USSR still signed a trade agreement with the People's Republic. The latter's protégé, Albania, was thrown out of the Warsaw Pact and its economic equivalent, Comecon.

There was no slackening of Soviet pressure on Berlin, with Soviet military planes occasionally buzzing passenger planes as they made their approaches to the Western enclave, continuous chicanery on the land routes, and threats of an actual confrontation between Soviet and Western garrisons. At the same time, the diplomatic dialogue continued, as did the negotiations about a nuclear test ban. At times the Soviets appeared close to an agreement banning atmospheric nuclear tests, but then they would raise fresh objections or reservations. Why continue negotiations on nuclear arms control while the fundamental problem of East-West relations—that of "Berlin" and Germany—still remained unresolved and might lead, judging by the Kremlin's rhetoric, to a violent clash?

The concurrent negotiations became explicable if we assume that the Kremlin was already considering a plan that it hoped would resolve both the nuclear control and the German issues. And there is overwhelming, if as yet circumstantial, evidence that the plan was closely connected with what would become known as the Cuban missile crisis of October 1962.

The crisis was preceded by a most eventful summer. There was a series of ominous developments during those most nerve-racking months: almost daily incidents about the Berlin Wall, Khrushchev's repeated hints that America lacked the guts to fight for Berlin, incongruously interspersed with claims that the West was preparing for war and that the Bonn government was planning to acquire its own nuclear weapons. And there were signs that the West's solidarity was under great strain: the British government was almost ready to trade the recognition of East Germany for a guarantee of safe access to Berlin; the White House was searching for some formula that would relieve the tension without leading to the West's capitulation, while De Gaulle's France and Adenauer's Federal Republic firmly held out against any deal.

In July there began a new series of Soviet nuclear tests and special and highly publicized maneuvers of the Soviet naval forces, including nuclear-armed submarines. The Geneva conference reconvened about the same time; but insofar as the nuclear test ban was concerned, no progress was registered and the talks recessed on September 7.

In view of the above facts, could one seriously believe that sometime during the summer the Soviet and American governments concluded a far-reaching secret agreement on nuclear arms control? Certainly, nothing of the kind has ever been intimated by the American side, at the time or since then. And Washington would have been more than eager to greet such an agreement and *not* to keep it secret, both because it would have marked a hopeful turn in the dangerously tense

East-West relations, and could be of considerable help in the coming congressional elections, where President Kennedy's party would be greatly aided by such a development. So how is one to interpret the following statement made publicly by the government of the People's Republic on August 15, 1963: "On August 25, 1962, two days before the United States and Britain put forward their draft treaty on the partial halting of nuclear tests, the Soviet Government notified China that U.S. Secretary of State Rusk proposed an agreement stipulating that, firstly, the nuclear powers should undertake to refrain from transferring nuclear weapons and technical information concerning their manufacture to nonnuclear countries, and, secondly, that the countries not in possession of nuclear weapons should undertake to refrain from manufacturing them, from seeking them from the nuclear powers, or from accepting technical information concerning their manufacture. The Soviet government gave an affirmative reply to this proposal of Rusk's."[29]

This allegation by Beijing was never denied by the Soviet authorities. In fact, Soviet statements during the bitter argument raging at the time between the two regimes confirm that such an approach indeed was made.

If the story of a U.S. Soviet agreement is patently untrue, then the Chinese statement that was quoted obviously left a great deal unsaid. It went on to refer to those memoranda sent by Beijing to the Soviet government dated September 3, 1962, October 20, 1962, and June 2, 1963, in which the Chinese side said that it was up to Moscow to dispose of its own weapons and technical knowledge but "that the Chinese goverment hoped *the Soviet Government would not infringe on China's sovereign rights* and act for China in assuming an obligation to refrain from manufacturing nuclear weapons." And so the Kremlin must have repeatedly asked the Chinese to be empowered "to act for China" and repeatedly been told, as the statement says, "that we would not tolerate the conclusion of any sort of treaty between the Soviet Government and the United States which aimed at depriving the Chinese people of their right to take steps to resist the nuclear threats of US imperialism."

But what could have given the Kremlin the grounds to hope that the Chinese, who had rebuffed them on that issue before and categorically, would now agree to give up their ambition to become a nuclear power? As early as April 1956, Mao had written: "If we are not to be bullied in the present-day world, we cannot do without the

bomb."[30] After 1959, with the Soviet experts and technical help no
longer at their disposal, the Chinese increased the scope and pace of
their effort to build the bomb. It must have greatly increased the strain
on the country's economy, suffering from the aftershock of the Great
Leap and of the famine that in two years is reported to have claimed
30 million lives. After such sacrifices, what could make Mao and his
colleagues change their mind?

Here the dates are important. It is logical to assume that it was
some special communication or entreaties that had provoked the
Chinese memoranda of September 3 and October 20. What else was
the USSR doing at the time in addition to escalating its threatening
rhetoric on Berlin? Why, secretly and hurriedly constructing the missile launching pads in Cuba! Could this have been a mere coinci-
dence? Most unlikely. The Berlin problem, the Soviets' exhortation
to the Chinese to give up their nuclear ambitions, Soviet missiles in
Cuba—it all fits together.

As American intelligence sources were to establish during and after
the crisis, work on the missile installations began in early July. After
they had been completed, in early November, the launching pads
would have accommodated twenty-four medium range (500–1,000
miles) and sixteen intermediate-range (1,000–2,000 miles) missiles.
The large Soviet shipments of men and supplies that summer did not
escape notice. But Washington was being repeatedly assured that no
offensive weapons were or would be placed in Cuba—all that the
USSR was sending consisted of other supplies, like antiaircraft defensive rockets, planes, radar, etc., accompanied by Soviet techni-
cians. In answer to increased agitation in the United States over the
volume of the shipments, an official Tass agency release stressed that
in view of its possession of intercontinental missiles, there was no
need for the USSR to place nuclear weapons on the island. "The
Soviet Union has the capability from its own territory to render assistance to any peace-loving state, and not only Cuba."[31] It was only
on October 14 that an American spy plane's overflight established the
existence of the launching sites and their purpose. As late as October
18, Foreign Minister Gromyko at his meeting with President Kennedy
in Washington denied categorically the rumor that the Soviet Union
had or would place any offensive weapons in Cuba. The president did
not tip his hand, and it was only on the twenty-second in his address
to the nation that he revealed the grave news and the U.S. counter-

measures: a naval blockade, "quarantine" of Cuba, and the decision to respond to any nuclear missile fired from there by full retaliation against Cuba *and* the USSR.[32]

There followed six days of unprecedented tension, of what was then felt to be and by many is still considered, the closest the world got to a nuclear holocaust. The Kremlin was caught in a cruel dilemma: to give in to the American demands and to face humiliation (and for Khrushchev a debilitating defeat), or to face the unimaginable danger. That such danger was believed by Moscow to be real is suggested by the measures taken in the wake of Kennedy's speech. The Ministry of Defense proclaimed an alert for the rocket, air, and submarine branches of the armed forces and canceled all leaves. An alert was also issued for Warsaw Pact forces. There must have been a temptation to respond to the blockade of Cuba by similar measures in relation to West Berlin. But it would have meant another step toward the abyss. On October 25 came the decision, though not yet an announcement, to pull back from the confrontation.

By the twenty-eighth the danger had passed. The USSR would dismantle the installations and pull out the missiles it already had there from the island in return for a face-saving pledge by the United States not to invade Cuba. Khrushchev's great gamble had failed.

Twenty-nine years later, and in the era of glasnost, the official Soviet version of why the USSR sought to place missiles in the Caribbean remains the same as Khrushchev's after his scheme had exploded: they were to defend the island from an American invasion. Yet this explanation is nonsensical on several counts. In the first place, at the time there was no likelihood of the Americans invading. And the installations were being constructed in such a hurry that the sites could not be adequately camouflaged or protected with ground-to-air missiles, which might well have prevented their detection. More basically, if the motivation was to protect Cuba, this could be, and as a matter of fact was, though not very convincingly, done by the Soviets threatening retaliation for an invasion with the home-based intercontinental missiles. To place missiles right there, on the island, could *not* serve as a deterrent, since they would have to be used (i.e., sent against U.S. targets) the moment the first American wave of invasion hit the island.

The last point brings us to the crowning absurdity of the "they were there to protect Cuba" hypothesis: the Soviet Union being ready, for the sake of saving Castro and his regime, to plunge into a nuclear war, an immediate effect of which would have been the annihilation of the island's population.

An alternative explanation proposed by some American political analysts is hardly more convincing. It attributes the Kremlin's action to its aspiration to erase the real "missile gap," which at the time and despite the previous and widespread belief to the contrary, worked in America's favor. And so to compensate for their inferiority in intercontinental ballistic missiles, the Soviets tried to smuggle forty missiles of lesser range into a location next door to the United States.

The implausibility of this variant is immediately apparent. Who with any knowledge of America could assume that its people would stand for these weapons being there indefinitely? And if the Soviets were so misinformed as to believe that, why did they proceed in such secrecy?

No, the only explanation that makes sense is to assume that the missiles were being placed there not to defend Castro nor to reverse the missile gap, but to be used for bargaining.

The area of the installations was controlled entirely by Soviet troops. It is rather doubtful whether Castro himself was aware of all the angles of the enterprise. It is also unclear whether the missiles were to be armed with warheads. Probably not, since the latter were not needed for the desired effect and the Soviets were wary of placing nuclear weapons outside the USSR, even if, as in this case, they were fully controlled by their own people.

Having despaired of forcing the United States to agree to a German treaty by pressing on the West's exposed nerve—Berlin—the Kremlin hoped to achieve this goal by a Cuban gambit. Agitation over what in the West was believed to be Berlin was rising to a boiling point during those October days prior to Kennedy's bombshell on October 22. Khrushchev had let the president know through several channels that he would not start anything prior to the American congressional elections. But along with this condescending assurance came a stern warning: after that the German problem must be solved. Khrushchev would be coming to New York in late November to address the United Nations. Prior to his departure for Moscow on October 19, Gromyko had also been pressing on Berlin—if the United States continued dithering, the USSR, this time definitely, would sign a peace treaty with East Germany. He had been contemptuous of the American effort to impress Moscow by calling up reservists: this was not 1812, and an additional 150,000 people under arms could make no difference.

But forty nuclear missiles might and would. The likely scenario has Khrushchev in his speech before the U.N. General Assembly, first, to shock the world by revealing the existence of the missiles and then to amaze it by Soviet reasonability: the Soviet Union was ready to withdraw its weapons from Cuba if the United States and the West agreed to meet their quite reasonable proposals to resolve the most pressing international problems.

One such proposal must have been a German peace treaty that would recognize the sovereignty of the German Democratic Republic and contain, even more importantly, ironclad guarantees against West Germany's ever receiving or manufacturing nuclear bombs.

The other part of the undelivered part-ultimatum/part-enticement must have concerned China. The Kremlin had sought repeatedly Beijing's authorization to speak for it on matters concerning nuclear arms control. Its arguments had a certain unintended humor: even if the People's Republic succeeded after great effort and expense in producing an A-bomb, it would not increase its security substantially. Its stock of nuclear arms would for long be dwarfed by that of the United States. So why not let the USSR protect China with its nuclear force, thus leaving it free to apply its resources to the improvement of its economy, rather than to the development of expensive and really ueless atomic baubles?

Disarming as such arguments seem, they were not found so by Mao and his associates. But what if by a dramatic coup the Soviet Union extracted from the United States the promise to abandon its protection of Taiwan and to remove nuclear weapons from its Pacific bases? The Chinese in return would be asked to give up or at least postpone their development of the A-bomb and they would be able to do so without a loss of face.

On paper the Kremlin game plan may have looked promising. The Americans, to be sure, were not going to like to be more or less roped into a German peace settlement, but then it would be just an acknowledgment of the realities and relieve them of anxiety about Berlin. And they could be only grateful for being relieved of an even greater worry: the vision of Mao having a nuclear arsenal at his dispoal.

But psychologically the plan was flawed. Had Khrushchev achieved his element of surprise in November, America's reaction might still have been as determined and fatalistic in facing the possibility of a nuclear war rather than submitting to blackmail as it was in October.

More assuredly, nothing and nobody could have persuaded the Chinese leadership to give up the effort to develop nuclear weapons, possession of which they equated with achieving the status of a great power, and hence with the elimination of the last traces of China's dependence on the Soviet Union.

Khrushchev's chances of persuading Beijing to go along with his oversubtle schemes could not have been improved by the eruption on October 20 of yet another crisis: border war between China and India. China's attack along two sectors of the disputed frontier in the Himalayas was the culmination of a long-standing border dispute, but it also may have been due to the irritation in Beijing over the increasingly close relations between the USSR and India, manifested by actions such as the former contracting to provide India with the latest-model jet engines and other advanced military technology. The campaign lasted a month and concluded with a decisive military setback for India. The USSR, caught in an embarrassing diplomatic situation, could only advise both sides to settle their differences and eventually urged New Delhi to accept China's rather humiliating conditions for a cease-fire. All of which failed to propitiate China, which denounced Moscow for assuming neutrality in a dispute involving a Communist state.

The failure of Khrushchev's daring plan to solve the outstanding international problems by one master stroke was to have important and long-lasting reverberations. Even though it was not understood what the Soviets were really after, the world viewed the conclusion of the affair as a resounding Soviet defeat. The height of the crisis was barely over when one by one the leaders of the East European Communist states descended on Moscow seeking explanations and reassurances. Khrushchev's capitulation infuriated Fidel Castro, supposedly because he was not consulted about the decision to pull out the missiles, but probably also and primarily because belatedly he came to understand the real purpose behind them. The Soviets' master troubleshooter, Anastas Mikoyan, had to spend three weeks in Cuba trying to calm the outraged Castro.[33]

By contrast, in another Communist country the resolution of the crisis was received with unconcealed glee. As long as the confrontation between the United States and the USSR persisted and threatened war, the Chinese supported the Russians with flamboyant declarations, but once the Soviets yielded, they were both indignant and pleased at the discomfiture of Khrushchev and his fellow "revision-

ists." Their Russian comrades' explanations of why it had been necessary to start the whole business were treated with contempt. As
Beijing's official statement was to spell out later on, "During the Caribbean crisis the Soviet leaders committed both the error of adven-
turism and the error of capitulationism . . . before the Soviet Union
sent rockets into Cuba, there did not exist a crisis of the United States
using nuclear weapons in the Caribbean Sea, and of a nuclear war
breaking out. If it should be said that such a crisis did arise, it was a
result of the rash action of the Soviet leaders."[34]

It is obvious from the above that the Kremlin had not warned any
of the fraternal parties of its forthcoming coup in Cuba, nor had it
informed them of what it sought to accomplish there. It would be
fascinating to know exactly what Khrushchev was planning to say in
his address to the U.N. General Assembly. But of course he never
went there; after the collapse of his scheme there was no point. The
Berlin crisis? It simply vanished as those missile installations were
being dismantled—no more ultimatums, threats, and harassments of
communications with West Berlin. The magician had run out of tricks.

His postmortem on the missile crisis was delivered on December
12 to the Supreme Soviet. There Khrushchev stuck lamely to his
version: it was all done to protect Cuba. Once Kennedy promised that
it would not be attacked, there was no reason to keep the missiles
there. As to the taunts by the Albanians "and those who support them"
about the USSR's "capitulationism," he replied in kind: did anyone
consider the Chinese cowardly because they tolerated foreign occupation of Hong Kong and Macao? Almost equally outrageous to Beijing
must have been the speaker's warm references to Yugoslavia and to
the arch-"revisionist," Marshal Tito, once again an honored guest of
the Soviet Union.

The Cuban crisis looms almost as important in the history of Communism as does Stalin's death. The latter loosened the Soviet Union's
hold on the movement; the crisis, though in an indirect way, demonstrated the incompatibility between the national interest of the
USSR and the professed goals of international Communism. Marxism-
Leninism assumes, by definition, a constant state of tension, if not
actual conflict, between the socialist camp and the capitalist world.
Yet common sense urged that the maintenance of such tension was,
in this nuclear age, fraught with incalculable danger, and that it was
imperative for the security of the USSR to seek an arrangement with
the United States that would remove, or at least greatly reduce, that

danger. By putting missiles in Cuba the Soviet Union sought to achieve at once both détente with and a victory over the West. The attempt failed. It was a most salutary failure: Khrushchev had blundered into what might have been a cataclysm but what fortunately turned out to be a vivid demonstration of how modern weaponry has rendered anachronistic so many of the ideological dogmas of Communism. As Gorbachev would say in 1986, "The character of comtemporary weapons does not allow any country the grounds to hope that it can protect itself only by military technological means, by a defense system, no matter how strong. . . . To achieve security one has to seek it through political means. Security cannot indefinitely be based upon the fear of retaliation . . . not to mention the absurdity and immorality of a situation when the whole world becomes hostage to nuclear war."[35]

But to enunciate that obvious fact clearly and fully in 1962 would have meant to give up any hope of restoring the unity of world Communism, hence a death blow to the ideological premises of the doctrine. And that in turn, as Gorbachev would find out, would have endangered the survival of the Communist regime in the Soviet Union itself. And so attempts at a détente with the West were still constrained in 1963 by the Soviet Union's simultaneously pursuing the mirage of a reconciliation with China. Goals sought in the two sets of negotiations were much more modest than those that had inspired the Cuban gambit. From China all that the Kremlin could realistically hope for was its abstaining from a public polemic, not objecting too vehemently to the prospective nuclear test ban agreement between the USSR, the United States, and Britain. Did the Soviets try to inveigle Beijing into subcribing to this agreement, which in effect would have inhibited their acquiring a nuclear arsenal (an untested weapon is not operational)? This seems suggested by the Chinese statement of September 1, 1963, already quoted, saying that as late as June 6 the People's Republic once again warned the Soviet government "not to infringe on China's sovereign rights" by presuming to speak for China on matters affecting nuclear arms control. But it is more than doubtful whether at this late date the Soviets could have had any illusions on that score—the Chinese were simply overly suspicious.

From the West, Khrushchev sought what would probably have been included in his Cuban crisis package had he not been caught in flagrante: a modest but significant step toward nuclear arms control. Negotiations on the test ban were confined to the three current members of the nuclear club, but the agreement was to be open to other countries, who by signing would in effect forsake the development of their own nuclear weapons.

After much pushing and backing the Chinese finally sent a delegation to Moscow. That not much was expected from the direct talks was indicated already by the fact that the delegation was headed by the acerbic and acknowledgedly anti-Russian Deng Xiaoping rather than the suave and diplomatic Zhou. To begin to appease Beijing the Kremlin would have had to break off negotiations with the United States and Britain and, fresh from a nuclear war scare, adopt once more a militant stand toward the West, as well as break with Tito. Deng's demands were phrased in a Marxist-Leninist idiom, but their essence was simply that the Soviet Union should resume its collision course with the United States. As the Soviets were to expostulate later, the Chinese leadership viewed with equanimity the prospect of a nuclear war. "Apparently the people who refer to the thermonuclear weapon as a 'paper tiger' are not fully aware of the destructive force of this weapon."[36] The negotiations, mired in an endless dispute, finally recessed on July 20.

Five days later the test-ban accord was signed. Through it the three nuclear powers (the United States, Great Britain, and the USSR) agreed to abstain from all except underground tests. Modest as this first tentative step toward nuclear arms control was, it was received furiously in Beijing: "big fraud to fool the people of the world. . . . It is unthinkable for the Chinese people to be a party to this dirty fraud. . . . The policy pursued by the Soviet government is one of allying with the forces of war to oppose forces of peace—allying with the United States to oppose China."[37] This was but an opening salvo in an exchange of "open letters" between the two regimes, their tone an incongruous blend of fishwives exchanging petty insults with that of medieval clerics hurling pronouncements of excommunication against each other. Yet distinct from both is the motif of a plot pervading both sides of the correspondence. The Chinese evidently persuaded themselves, or at least made a convincing appearance of believing, that the innocuous-sounding (and in fact so) test ban was part of a diabolical plot by the United States and the USSR to blackmail the People's Republic and to render it impotent. On the Soviet side there was an equal insistence that the Chinese were plotting to provoke a nuclear war between the two superpowers. Beijing's argument, or, more properly, indictment, is more comprehensive: it lists a whole series of Soviet transgressions, beginning with the Twentieth Congress, where Khrushchev slandered Stalin, to the Kremlin's collusion with the "renegade Tito." "Ever since the Twentieth Congress of the CPSU we watched with concern as the leadership of the CPSU took the road of revisionism. . . . We believed its errors were not just accidental . . . but rather a whole series of errors of principle which endanger the interests of the entire socialist camp and the international Communist movement."[38] There was, of course, an ideological potion mixed into the brew: the Soviet leadership's sins and errors proceeded from its abandonment of the cause of revolution, its espousal of revisionist notions such as "parliamentary cretinism" (i.e., repudiation of violence as a path to socialism), its narrow nationalist selfishness.

The Soviets, never at a loss when it comes to vituperation, were still rather on the defensive in this exchange of propaganda fire: no, they were not lukewarm in promoting the cause of world revolution, they were stalwart in defending the interests of the Communist movement. It was the men in Beijing who had departed from the straight-and-narrow path of Marxism-Leninism; their views, in fact, were quite reminiscent of the heresy of the late, unlamented Trotsky.

The polemic inevitably slid into personalities. The Chinese, who must have invested a lot of time and effort into researching the material for their insults, came up with a collage of Khrushchev's quotes about Stalin when the dictator was alive—quite different from what he had to say about that great Marxist at the Twentieth and Twenty-second congresses! Why did the Chinese dogmatists defend so strenuously the dead tyrant, the Russians rhetorically asked, and found an answer in "the idolization of Mao Zedong in which Chinese propaganda is intensively engaged. . . . We are witnessing a campaign against the very foundations of Marxism-Leninism that is unparalleled since the time of Trotskyism."[39]

It was the bomb which was at the center of the dispute. As the Chinese complained petulantly and pathetically about their Soviet protagonists, ". . . in their eyes the countries and people that do not have nuclear weapons are not worth a single glance, and the struggle waged in the interests of the people of the world is unrealistic. All they see is nuclear weapons, and in their opinion the only thing that is realistic is to divide spheres of influence with the imperialists who possess nuclear weapons."[40] This was a grossly oversimplified and tendentious, but not wholly incorrect, presentation of the Kremlin's motivation.

From the Soviet side came equally insistent charges that Beijing was indifferent to the danger of a thermonuclear conflict, and insinuations that China indeed would be pleased if such a conflict erupted between the two superpowers. This also seems too strong. If not Mao himself, then the other Chinese notables were aware of what a nuclear war would mean, and not only for the actual belligerents. But there is no question that all the leaders perceived any Washington-Moscow rapprochement as a clear danger for the People's Republic, and, conversely, had a vested interest in maintaining a high level of tension between the West and the USSR.

The issue of nuclear weapons illuminated the inability of Communism to serve as a viable ideological link for an international community. Both sides in the great dispute revealed by 1963 that they were more frightened of and basically antagonistic toward each other than toward the capitalist world. The power of the USSR was no longer viewed as a protective shield by China but as a direct threat, surpassing that posed by the United States. In a few years, and not unreasonably, the Chinese rulers would believe that if assured of U.S. approval, the Soviet Union would not hesitate to destroy Chinese nuclear installations.

From the Kremlin's viewpoint it was the prospect of China's future power—nuclear weapons added to the country's vast population—that was alarming. The only relationship the Soviet Union could have with another state in the socialist camp was one of domination or of sharp conflict. Common ideological antecedents would only make the clash of Soviet and Chinese nationalism all the sharper, thus demonstrating the inability of Marxism-Leninism to create a new world order. And that failure would be a prelude to the historic defeat of Communism.

8

DEATH OF AN IDEOLOGY

ERUPTING INTO THE OPEN and violently in 1963, the Sino-Soviet conflict shook the edifice of world Communism. At the time, it did not bring it down. But from our perspective, one can see that the consequences of the clash were in a way similar to those wrought by a distant earthquake, which undermines the foundations of a city's buildings, rendering them vulnerable to aftershocks. Eventually, unless the damage is repaired, even a slight tremor will bring a collapse.

And so with international Communism. Successive shocks followed the bitter polemic that revealed the depth of the crisis. The year 1964 brought the fall of Nikita Khrushchev and with it an end to the effort to mend the Soviet political system and to reform its still-Stalinist structure. China's Cultural Revolution, begun in 1966, was allegedly intended by its maker to recoup for Communism its populistic meaning and revolutionary fervor. Instead, it plunged the country into anarchy; and its end saw the reemergence of authoritarian rule by the party bureaucracy. In Czechoslovakia in 1968, the world witnessed yet another attempt to repair Communist ideology by infusing it with elements of democracy. It is unlikely that the experiment would have succeeded even if it had been allowed to work itself out. Similar efforts in Yugoslavia in the early fifties and in Poland in the mid-to-late fifties had failed, since they ran into the impossibility of reconciling the party's monopoly of power with any meaningful definition of democracy. In any case, Soviet military intervention cut short the "Prague Spring."

Perhaps even more important than the failure of those attempts at internal reforms was the inability of Communism to regain its worldwide unity and undo the Sino-Soviet split. From the beginning of the dispute, neither the Soviets nor the Chinese would admit that its source lay in the clash of national interests, and that ideology was unable to bridge their differences, or was in fact mostly irrelevant to the conflict. Both sides professed to be confident that, in time, the other party (presumably under new leaders) would recognize the error of its ways, revert to the true path of Marxism-Leninism, and all would be well again with world Communism. Thus for Mao and his associates the main ideological sin of the Soviet leaders consisted in their seeking a rapprochement with the West rather than working unceasingly for world revolution. The Soviets, equally strenuously though in less extravagant language, affirmed their fidelity to the cause and maintained that it was Beijing that was guilty of ideological betrayal. By dividing the socialist camp for their own selfish reasons, the Chinese were in fact helping the capitalists. By 1972 both sides had been proved right, and the ideological part of their dispute was exposed as hollow. By then the People's Republic and the USSR, each in its own way, had sought and achieved détente with the United States, and, ironically, in view of what had been said and done in the past, it was China that drew much closer to the United States, its relations with the latter soon assuming the character of an unofficial alliance.

The relative unimportance of the ideological factor insofar as the genesis of the dispute was concerned was not at first appreciated in the West. Many there, and not merely among the intellectuals, embraced the stereotype of the Chinese Communists as being imbued with the revolutionary zeal of neophytes, while, by contrast, the Kremlin leaders were paying only lip service to Marxism-Leninism, being mainly interested in advancing Soviet imperial interests. Similar contrasts were drawn between the two Communist societies: one having undergone "embourgeoisement" and far-reaching bureaucratization, while China adhered much more closely to the populistic and egalitarian precepts of the doctrine.

Such stereotypes were not entirely without foundation. But as the two powers' attitude toward the Vietnam situation was soon to demonstrate, Soviet foreign policy, while not ideologically motivated, still had to abide by certain ideological constraints, while Beijing, on the other hand, was capable of quite far-reaching realism, bordering on cynicism, when it came to assuming risks for the sake of a fellow and embattled Communist country. During the initial period of their rule, Mao and Company were indeed imbued with the conviction that

Marxist-Leninist faith could move mountains—witness the absurdities of the Great Leap. That they hurried after Mao's death into economic policies they had hitherto denounced as ultrarevisionist is good proof that in domestic as well as in foreign policies they were not so much different from the Russian comrades.

Each side saw clearly through the other's pretensions and protestations. The Kremlin's chief ideological spokesman, Mikhail Suslov, analyzed Chinese motivations for their foreign policy in words that should have been heeded in the West: "With a stubbornness worthy of a better cause, the Chinese leaders attempt to prevent the improvement of Soviet-American relations, representing this as 'plotting with the imperialists.'" At the same time, the Chinese government makes "feverish attempts to improve relations with Britain, France, Japan, West Germany, and Italy. It is quite clear that they would not refuse to improve relations with the United States, but as yet do not see favorable circumstances for such an endeavor."[1] Who in America would have believed at the time that Suslov was right, and that in eight years the president of the United States would be stepping on Chinese soil to hold friendly negotations with Mao and Zhou?

Also not far off the mark was the by now standard Chinese characterization of Russian foreign policies as being mainly imperialist in character. In August of the same year (1964) Mao, in an interview with a group of Japanese journalists, indulged in an attack on the USSR which was so far-reaching that it left the Soviets, who by now should have been accustomed to expect such things from Beijing, at first unable to react. It was weeks later that a summary of the interview was published in the Soviet press and only after vain attempts to make Beijing repudiate its text, already circulated in Japan. Mao was in his best Russia-baiting form: the USSR was a robber imperialist state, stealing territories from its friends as well as its enemies. In Europe it appropriated part of Romania, gave eastern Germany to Poland after taking eastern Poland for itself, chasing out the local inhabitants. Then much of the Asiatic USSR should belong by rights to the People's Republic, having been wrested by force from the Manchu empire in the nineteenth century. How about Mongolia? Mao reclaimed it for China in 1954 when Khrushchev had visited Beijing, but the Soviets refused even to talk about it. "The Russians took everything they could!" Someday, Mao implied, China would demand the restitution of those territories taken from it by the USSR. He added an interesting tidbit: the Soviets had asked Beijing to stop the polemic, which had scandalized the Communist world, for at least three months; the Chinese were not going to stop it for as much as three days!

It was with an almost masochistic glee that *Pravda* expatiated on Mao's interview, its commentary occupying one-fourth of its September 2, 1964 issue. Mao's outburst was cited as proof that the Chinese Communists' complaints about the Soviet Union had nothing to do with ideology. "Behind the cover of a theoretical dispute, one can see ever more clearly the malevolent political intentions of the leadership of the Chinese Communist Party. . . . As can be seen from what Mao had said, China's leaders now don't even try to cover up their expansionist goals. As we can learn from the Japanese press, Mao did not even mention any ideological question . . . not a word about Marxism-Leninism, socialism, the unity of the working class in the struggle for the interests of the world's workers and national liberation movements." And, the article gloomily concluded, "we can now see in full light the designs of the Chinese leaders, those designs having nothing to do with the struggle for the victory of peace and socialism. They are clearly inspired by great power chauvinism and hegemonism."

The last two terms were routinely used by the Chinese in characterizing their Soviet adversaries' motivations. As seen from the above, both sides were careful to attribute malevolent intentions to the leaders of the "fraternal" (and temporarily hostile) party, thus indulging in the polite fiction that its rank and file were innocent of anti-Soviet or anti-Chinese sentiments. The Kremlin's feelings about Mao, hitherto unknown to outsiders, were now openly and venomously expressed, as in the speech by Suslov to which we have already referred. "The leadership of the Chinese Communist Party is trying to propagate the cult of personality of Mao . . . so that he, like Stalin in his time, would tower God-like over all the Marxist-Leninist parties and would decide all questions of their policy and activity according to his whim."[2] On the same occasion other speakers picked up the anti-Mao cue, one of them mocking the chairman's literary strivings. His labored poems, he declared amid general laughter, were now being presented as important contributions to China's culture! Thus spoke the Soviets about the man who until a few years before was hailed in their press as an outstanding Marxist-Leninist.

The Chinese, needless to say, returned the compliment. In the colorful English of Beijing's publication for foreigners, Khrushchev became "the number-one capitalist roader," the embodiment of Soviet perfidy and betrayal of Marxism. Nikita Sergeievich's successors, though evidently not thought to be worthy of individual distinction, were branded collectively as "Khrushchev's heirs," and were viewed as equally, if not more, treacherous.

There was a significant difference in the way the two parties defended their leaders. Chinese propaganda scorned the task of answering the Soviet gibes about Mao. The Great Helmsman was above criticism. The Soviets, on the other hand, and probably because Khrushchev's position since the Cuban fiasco had become quite shaky, tended to be suspiciously touchy in their defense of the first secretary. Suslov, soon the central figure in the plot to oust him, was almost lyrical in his praise at the February 1964 meeting of the Central Committee: "Our nation knows well and has boundless confidence in Nikita Sergeievich Khrushchev, a passionate revolutionary, outstanding follower of Lenin's tradition, indefatigable fighter for peace and Communism. . . . We Soviet people credit our successes to the untiring efforts of Nikita Sergeievich for the benefit of our nation, for the welfare of all toilers in the world. . . . He expresses the deepest thoughts and dreams of the Soviet people. . . . The Chinese, and not only they, should get it through their thick heads that our Central Committee, headed by this faithful Leninist, Nikita Sergeievich Khrushchev, is more than ever united and monolithic."[3]

Almost exactly eight months later this "indefatigable fighter for peace and Communism" was overthrown by a Kremlin coup. Unlike in 1957 when the Central Committee at his urging reversed the Presidium's dismissal of the first secretary, this time the plot was carefully prepared and encountered no resistance, its victim himself, according to reports, strangely passive and hardly defending himself.

As of now, it is difficult to determine what role considerations of foreign policy played in Khrushchev's fall. The failure of his intricate Cuban missile gambit must have been one reason for his former colleagues' uncharitable reference (in justifying their action) to the fallen leader's "harebrained schemes."

The main reasons for the ouster were, however, to be sought among domestic considerations. The oligarchs grew increasingly concerned about their leader's continuing garrulity about the crimes and disasters of the Stalin era. A full accounting for the past, they felt, and rightly so—look what happened in the late 1980s—would almost certainly bring a wave of revulsion against the party that had authorized or permitted such monstrous doings. And during his last two years in power, Nikita Sergeievich had embarked on a number of measures—

mostly symbolic, to be sure—that looked suspiciously like an attempt
to curtail the prerogatives of the Presidium earlier and later the Politburo. He would bring outsiders to the meetings of the party's highest
policy making organs. There was, toward the end of his reign, an
attempt to refashion the structure of the party at the lower levels. And
of late, Khrushchev had started to define his goal as having the Soviet
Union become "the state of all the people," a vague phrase, but one
that probably sent shivers down the spines of his fellow oligarchs.

Khrushchev was the last true believer, and his evident goal was to
re-create in the party and society what he took to be the spirit of
Lenin's times. As has been postulated here and as Gorbachev would
discover in 1989, no reforms that left the party's authority intact could
have been reconciled with a genuine "state of all the people." Still, if
allowed to work itself out, Khrushchev's reforming zeal might well
have enabled the Soviet system to be better prepared for the eventual
transition to social pluralism than it was to be in the 1980s when a
belated effort in that direction brought it to the verge of complete
collapse.

Unlike Khrushchev, who joined the party in 1918 and retained to
the last some of the revolutionary era's turbulent and venturesome
spirit, his successors—Brezhnev, as head of the party, and Kosygin,
as head of the government—had their political physiognomy shaped
by their service in the Stalinist bureaucracy. Their formative years
having been spent in the difficult task of trying to avoid the fate of
so many of their fellow bureaucrats during the Great Terror, they were
amply endowed with the survivors' inherent caution and conservatism.

Domestically, the changing of the guard meant the Soviet system
settling firmly into ogligarcho-bureaucratic form. There would be no
recurrence of terror, but equally there would be no toleration, as there
occasionally was before 1965, of noncomformity. Khrushchev had
licensed the publication of Solzhenitsyn's *One Day in the Life of Ivan
Denisovich*. The Brezhnev regime would track down and punish any
manifestation of dissidence in literature and the arts, not to mention
politics. The campaign against Stalinism had served between 1956
and 1964 as a kind of surrogate for intellectual, and in a way political,
freedom. Now that outlet had been firmly shut off. The official image
of Stalin was no longer that of a tyrant (with some redeeming features)
but of an "outstanding Marxist-Leninist and party leader." Stalin's
birthdays would be regularly commemorated; the highest party offi-

cial's title became again "general" rather than "first" secretary. By contrast, it was the more recent leader's name that would be carefully excised from official histories and scrupulously avoided by the media. Khrushchev's populistic style of leadership was followed by the rather distant manner of his successors. Brezhnev's usually stern expression and Kosygin's bilious one, both reminiscent in their behavior of masters in a reform school, seemed to convey a message to their subjects: "Now then, there will be no more nonsense."

Operations of the Soviet government were traditionally run in a conspiratorial way, the people seldom being privy to where and how decisions affecting their lives and welfare were being made. This pattern was somewhat relaxed, as we have seen, between 1956 and 1964, with outsiders being admitted to the meetings of decision making organs and Central Committee sessions being often fully reported. Under Brezhnev such practices were discontinued and what little there had been of glasnost was eliminated.

In one respect the new rulers were to show themselves more indulgent than their predecessor: they were much more solicitous of the interests of the upper ranks of the party and government bureaucrats, or the *nomenklatura*, as they were collectively known. Terrorized under Stalin, and kept on a short leash by his irascible successor, those people could now relax: short of a spectacular dereliction or insubordination, they would no longer have to meet strict standards of performance or be subject to a peremptory dismissal. It was as if the oligarchs of the Politburo (the Presidium was formally so renamed in 1966) had entered upon an unwritten compact with the lower-ranking members of the official elite (the latter not to interfere with the oligarchs' power) in exchange for being granted virtual job security. While creating a kind of bureaucrats' paradise, the arrangement was hardly conducive to efficiency and high morale in the party and state apparatus. Cronyism and government corruption, not unknown before, became widespread. With rare exceptions, only death or extreme debility was allowed to deplete the ranks of the highest policy making organs, the vacancies usually being filled by men close in age to the departed. Thus by the end of the Brezhnev era the Soviet Union was ruled by a veritable gerontocracy. Fearful of innovations, whether in politics or the economy, the aged rulers were to persist in sweeping under the rug the most perplexing problems of Soviet society and world Communism. It is not to be wondered that after twenty years of *immobilisme*, a belated effort at reform was to lead to chaos and the crumbling of the authoritarian structure.

As far as its international situation was concerned, the Soviet Union under Brezhnev presented a picture of power and stability. The country's still-impressive economic growth during the first Brezhnev decade (about 5 percent annual increase in GNP, 1965–70; 4 percent annually, 1970–75) enabled the USSR to catch up and in some cases surpass the United States in several basic categories of industrial production such as steel. Even more impressive, or alarming, depending on one's point of view, was the growth of the Soviet nuclear arsenal: by 1970 the number and megatonnage of their land-based intercontinental ballistic missiles had far surpassed that of America's.

For all of its domestic weaknesses, the Soviet Union's credentials as one of the world's two most powerful states were unquestionable. And, indeed, and this is especially true of the Brezhnev-Kosygin time, the regime's overall policies seemed almost consciously designed to inculcate in its people the lesson that for all of its internal shortcomings and unfulfilled promises, it was under Communism that the Soviet Union had steadily advanced in power and worldwide influence. On the other hand, foreign successes were to suggest that the capitalist democracies, for all their reputed freedoms and riches, had been in retreat. Sedate and conservative at home, the Soviet leadership during those two decades pursued quite adventurous policies abroad. Though they were not accompanied by as much bluff and bluster as had been the case under Khrushchev, the Kremlin's moves on the international scene were not without occasional and considerable risks. That the leaders, as prudent as those who guided the Soviet state after 1964, were not averse to taking such risks could only mean that they were firmly convinced that the regime's internal security was largely dependent on the advance of its external power, and hence required a dynamic and expansionist foreign policy.

But ironically and almost inevitably, such policies were to contribute to the eventual destabilization of the Soviet system. The superpower paraphernalia, and keeping up with the United States in this respect, was bound to be increasingly costly. There was the enormous cost of the Soviet military establishment, estimated in the 1970s to be absorbing 18 to 20 percent of the country's GNP. Competition with the United States for influence in the Third World meant that the USSR had to shoulder a by now sizable burden of economic and technological assistance to the new nations. And, like its capitalist rival, it was discovering that giving them even substantial aid did not necessarily turn its recipients into reliable friends, while cutting it off was bound to alienate them. Heading the "socialist camp" was also proving increasingly costly. Keeping its East European partners docile required not only giving up the previous exploitative Soviet practices, but occasionally, as after the invasion of Czechoslovakia, massive aid to shore up their economies. The same was even truer of the Kremlin's non-European protégés. Stalin's Russia unabashedly charged China for the military matériel it provided in the Korean War. The changed appearance of the Communist world meant that such an unsentimental approach was no longer possible when it came to helping North Vietnam and the Vietcong in their struggle against the United States. Cuba's economy was kept going only with continuous and heavy Soviet subsidies. As some European powers previously discovered, imperialism in the post–World War II era did not pay off, certainly not in economic terms.

Superficially, nonetheless, Soviet foreign policy in the period following Khrushchev's fall did not seem to warrant such a negative appraisal. On the contrary, as viewed from abroad the Brezhnev-Kosygin team was steering the Soviet ship of state quite successfully through the rocks and shoals of the international scene. Moscow's prestige was being enhanced, and the gains abroad helped obscure the Soviet Union's domestic problems and, to a lesser extent, those of world Communism.

This development had to be all the more gratifying because as of the end of 1964 the USSR's overall international posture appeared quite shaky. The longtime goal of America's policy makers of containing Russia's political and ideological expansion was close to realization, though not on account of any masterstrokes of Washington's diplomacy or strategy.

The Sino-Soviet split, whose full significance and gravity were not recognized in the West, put in question the whole rationale of ideological expansion. As yet nobody (except the Russians) could envisage China moderating its violent anti-American attitude, still less becoming a semi-ally of the United States. Still, with the two Communist powers squaring off against each other, both were suffering a loss of influence in the Third World. The USSR was vulnerable to Beijing's charge of trying to reach an accommodation with the United States and the former colonial powers. China, even though more in tune with the militant Third World regimes' "national liberation movements," was hardly in a position to provide them with economic help and military hardware on a scale similar to Russia's. The erstwhile external allies were busy trying to undercut each other's influence in the Third World and the international Communist movement.

In the mid-1960s the problems posed by the Chinese challenge were compounded by the apparent failure of the Soviets' policies toward Western Europe. The aims of the Kremlin's diplomacy in that area—international recognition of the East German state and of Poland's western borders, and stopping or at least putting a brake on the Federal Republic's rearmament—were no closer to realization in 1964 than they had been at the end of World War II. Before his ouster Khrushchev had planned a state visit to West Germany, a clear recognition that the technique of bluff and bluster had not worked and that the Russians realized they had to resort to diplomacy to alleviate what the Kremlin still viewed (though not as strongly as its propaganda tried to make one believe) as the German danger.

But even more troublesome from the Soviet point of view was the momentum toward the economic unity of Western Europe. The success of the Common Market, the historically unprecedented outburst of economic prosperity in areas ravaged by World War II, the erosion of such ancient enmities as that between France and Germany—all these developments presaged a Europe united politically as well as economically, and thus capable of becoming a third superpower. As such, it would restore the politicomilitary balance on the Continent and stop the erosion of Western influence elsewhere. More than that, this new political organism, by its combination of freedom and prosperity, would exert an irresistible influence on the Communist countries of Eastern Europe. What at one time sounded like the extravagant rhetoric of American diplomacy—the "rollback and liberation" of the Soviet sphere of domination—could in a few years, if the trend continued, become a very real danger to the Soviet empire.

Nobody as yet could foresee the rapidity with which, once Moscow's controls slackened, the Communist regimes in the East would be toppled. But it was possible to envisage that if such a cataclysmic event took place, it would pose an immediate danger to the multinational structure of the Soviet Union itself.

What was actually to happen in the late 1980s was probably not dissimilar to the Kremlin's fears that we have just described. That the USSR was able to stave off that nightmare for more than twenty years was due mainly to the good luck of the Brezhnev regime: shortly after its coming to power, its two rivals embarked upon policies which, because of the crippling effects they had on their international standing, enabled the Soviet Union to escape containment and, for a period, to revive the image of its brand of Communism as a viable and dynamic force.

America's massive involvement in the war in Southeast Asia and the consequences of that involvement helped the Soviet Union, both directly and indirectly, in several ways. It distracted attention from, and minimized the impact of, the Sino-Soviet split. The fact that a small Asian country and a guerrilla movement were withstanding the power of the U.S. military seemed to reaffirm the vitality of Communism. That that feat was made possible through the Soviet Union's help tended to reaffirm Moscow's ideological credentials and to reassure those Communists who had been inclined to believe Chinese insinuations that the USSR had become a status quo power.

Equally important were the Vietnam War's repercussions on America's friends. America's discomfiture weakened its ties with the European allies and undercut its power to prod them to synchronize their policies toward the Soviet Union. They would instead try to negotiate with the USSR separately, General de Gaulle's ephemeral vision of "Europe from the Channel to the Urals" and Chancellor Willy Brandt's Ostpolitik offering Moscow new diplomatic opportunities and gains. The United States itself would seek Moscow's help in trying to get out of the Vietnam imbroglio, while the Soviets, for their part, would be able to put détente on hold, postponing it until such time as it would best suit their interests.

America's foreign setbacks were paralleled by China's domestic ones, the latter also working to Soviet advantage. The Cultural Revolution plunged the People's Republic into virtual anarchy. The spectacle of the Beijing regime literally tearing itself apart severely undercut China's appeal even to the most radical and militant elements in other Communist parties and national liberation movements. The danger to the Soviets' dominant position in the socialist camp had passed.

America's travail's in Vietnam and the Chinese Communists' domestic aberrations helped the Soviet Union recoup much of what it had lost as a result of the Cuban missile crisis and the Sino-Soviet split. In contrast to its rivals' predicaments and entanglements, Moscow's foreign image appeared one of prudence and steadfastness. Yet from our perspective it might be questioned whether this fortuitous turn of events proved, in the long run, beneficial to the interests of Soviet Communism. Relief from what only shortly before appeared as almost insuperable dilemmas reinforced the new leadership's inherent conservatism and made it appear unnecessary to tackle the basic problems at home or to rethink the country's role in world affairs and in the international Communist movement. Domestic and foreign policies reverted to the traditional ways: strictly authoritarian at home, cautiously expansionist abroad. Dissent, that offspring of imperfect de-Stalinization, was being firmly repressed, and on the whole Soviet society presented a placid appearance. The drama of Vietnam and the tragicomedy of the Cultural Revolution tended to obscure and minimize the effects of such foreign policy blunders as spurring Egypt and other Arab states to their disastrous 1967 confrontation with Israel. The defeat of the Soviet Union's protégés in the Six-Day War should have sent a warning about overcommitting the country's resources and prestige in an area not of primary importance to Soviet security. The Kremlin's recourse to military intervention a year later in Czechoslovakia illustrated another aspect of the imperialist strivings: the USSR had to stand armed guard over 110 million people in Communist East Europe. Neither event shook the Soviet leaders out of their complacency nor led them to rethink their international role.

America's overcommitment in Vietman could not have been thought at first to provide reasons for such complacency. On the contrary, the U.S. bombing of North Vietnam, which began in February 1965, and the subsequent massive infusion of American troops into the South, put the Brezhnev-Kosygin team on the spot only a few months after it assumed power. How far would the USSR go in helping a relatively small Communist country that lacked up-to-date military technology to cope with America's crushing superiority in the air? What would Moscow do to assist a Communist-led guerrilla movement to fight the Saigon regime, which in the Communist world, and with some justification, was called a U.S. puppet?

Vietnam's division (ordained by the Geneva Conference of 1954) into two states, one Communist, the other an American protégé, became, as was true in regard to similar arrangements in Germany and Korea, a festering sore of international life. Prior to 1964, Moscow had been wary to step directly into the caldron of Indochinese politics: its attention was centered on other areas and issues. Still, it felt that it had to keep some control over the local Communist movements lest they fall exclusively under China's influence. When the CIA engineered a coup in Laos, the USSR rushed supplies to the Communist forces in the little kingdom. But then it sought negotiations that concluded with both Moscow and Washington agreeing on a neutralist regime, with pro-Communists allowed to remain in control of a part of Laos. This arrangement thus enabled North Vietnam to continue to use Laos as well as Cambodia as conduits for sending men and supplies to the guerrilla forces in the South. In themselves the former French possessions in Indochina were, from Moscow's point of view, unimportant; as far as Soviet-American relations were concerned, the activities of Communist movements there were a nuisance. But here was the rub: were Beijing able to stir Vietnam and the Communist forces in Laos and Cambodia into an all-out offensive, Moscow would not be able to avoid entanglement and would be faced with some very difficult choices. Moscow therefore much preferred the local Communists to "cool" it. On the other hand, Beijing urged its friends in the area to be more militant. Thus North Vietnam found itself in a position to play upon those differences between the two Communist powers and, when the right moment came, to exploit their conflict to advance its cherished aim: the "liberation" of the South.

In 1960 Hanoi evidently concluded that the moment had come. In December, in a secret location in the South, the National Liberation Front of South Vietnam (NLF) was organized. Henceforth guerrilla activities increased to the point that in 1964 the Saigon regime, despite all the American help it received in military supplies and the growing number of military "advisers," found itself close to collapse. Its internal structure riven by corruption and constant changes and squabbles within the leadership, and with the NLF actually controlling large areas of the countryside, South Vietnam appeared unable to survive without the direct and massive military assistance of the United States.

Such help was to materalize in 1965. That it came was largely the result of Washington's oversimplified reading of the Sino-Soviet split. The American policy makers came to believe, and rightly so, that the Soviet Union was no longer the propagator of world revolution, and that certainly as far as the Vietnam situation was concerned, its preference would have been for a diplomatic solution. On the other hand, the Chinese leaders were perceived by the Americans to be driven by fanatical zeal and the conviction that, certainly in the Third World, the West was unable to arrest the triumphant march of militant

Marxism-Leninism. It was therefore incumbent upon the United States to demonstrate to Beijing that "wars of liberation" do not pay, and that America was no "paper tiger" when it came to protecting its friends. And so the Communist aggression and subversion in South Vietnam had to be met head-on. The Russians would understand and approve.

This analysis overlooked the very important fact that as far as intra-Communist bloc policies were concerned, the Soviet Union no longer disposed of the absolute freedom of action it had had under Stalin. Moscow had good reasons to be irritated by the North Vietnamese Communists for heeding Beijing's views and publicly dissociating itself from the Soviet stand on international issues. Thus Hanoi had refused to sign the nuclear test ban agreement, not because it had the remotest chance or intention of developing atomic weapons of its own, but because China had condemned the agreement as a Soviet-American plot. In August 1964, in a preview of the American air attacks to come, President Lyndon Johnson ordered the bombing of North Vietnam's naval units in retaliation for an alleged attack by its torpedo boats on an American destroyer. It was soon reported that Khrushchev, then in the waning weeks of his power, called what became known as the Tonkin Gulf incident a "Chinese provocation."[4]

For for all their discomfiture concerning North Vietnam, the Russians could not afford a peremptory refusal when asked to assist a Communist country that found itself pitted against American power. To do so, and especially in 1965 when China's position within the socialist camp had not yet been shaken by the inanities of the Cultural Revolution, would have lent credibility to the Maoist charge that the Kremlin was betraying the cause of national liberation.

For all their obviousness, the Chinese tactics seemed to work: the USSR had been forced to become an active, if indirect, partner in the North Vietnamese's struggle to conquer the South. And thus by openly helping to destroy an American-sponsored regime, the USSR would be jeopardizing or at least greatly complicating any Soviet-American accommodation. Mao and his colleagues may well have congratulated themselves that they were repaying the Russians for their Korean gambit. In 1950 China had been obligated to try to bail the Soviets out and thereby incurred the bitter hostility of the United States. Now the situation was to be reversed.

To be sure, the analogy was not exact: as yet no Soviet volunteers had been sent to battle the Americans on Vietnamese soil. Moscow proposed to limit its help to providing war matériel and technical advisers to its Communist ally. A nuclear power, the USSR would not incur risks commensurate to those borne during the Korean War by the People's Republic. And to allay American hostility, Moscow, while helping North Vietnam and the Vietcong, would try to play the role of an honest broker, acting as an intermediary between Washington and Hanoi, urging a peaceful solution of the Indochinese conflict.

Yet in the beginning the Kremlin had to be apprehensive about whether its two-sided game could work, and whether it would be able to avoid a deeper and more perilous involvement in Vietnam. There was a possibility, indeed a probability, that massive military intervention by the United States would turn the scales in favor of the Saigon government. The Kremlin would then be discredited as the champion of the Communist cause, having at the same time forfeited whatever gains it had made in its relations with the United States since the signing of the Nuclear Test Ban Treaty.

The crucial test of the Soviets' dual role in Indochina—helper and abettor of North Vietnamese aggression on the one hand, and would-be peacemaker on the other—came between February 1965 and March 1966. Early in the former month a Soviet delegation headed by Kosygin visited Hanoi. It brought North Vietnam promises of economic help as well as military supplies and advice. The gist of the latter was evidently to persuade the North Vietnamese leaders that the best route to an eventual takeover of the South was via the conference table, rather than by escalating the Vietcong's attacks on the Saigon regime. A negotiated agreement similar to that reached on Laos would provide for a coalition government which, after a short interval, would lead to a full Communist takeover, since the United States, having saved face, would no longer resist such a solution too strenuously. The Soviets may well have learned through their intelligence channels that the preceding summer the Johnson administration had decided once the American presidential elections were over to step up its activities in Vietnam and, if necessary, to put pressure on the North in order to bar a resolution of the conflict by force.

While Kosygin was conferring in Hanoi, the Americans dropped the other shoe. Their first air attack on North Vietnam was supposedly in retaliation for a Vietcong raid on an American base in the South. In fact, it was the beginning of the systematic bombing of the North as the means of forcing Hanoi to discontinue its support and direction of the guerrilla movement in the South.

The bombings thus meant that the United States had abandoned the constraints it observed in the Korean case, when the Chinese intervention in the war was *not* followed (despite the American commander's protests) by attacks on China's mainland. This time it was not quite the "massive retaliation" threatened by Secretary Dulles in 1953 in case America had to cope with another Communist aggression. The targets were, at least in theory, to be limited to military and communications centers, and nuclear weapons were not to be used. Still, it was a clear breach of what hitherto had been "the rules" of the cold war.

On Washington's side, the decision to bomb was clearly influenced by what we have already seen was not an entirely correct perception of the intra-Communist-bloc situation: the Soviet Union, with its vast nuclear power, was not committed to North Vietnam and its struggle in the South nearly as strongly as it had been to China in 1950, while the latter, no longer under the Soviet nuclear umbrella, would not be likely to risk another confrontation with the United States, the Johnson administration having made it clear that this time no holds would be barred.

In fact, Washington was to be proved wrong in its assumptions about the Soviet reaction to its Vietnam moves. Had the USSR refused to react to the bombings by committing itself more strongly to Hanoi, its role as the leader of the "socialist camp" would have been questioned by even the most moderate elements in the Communist world. But also disappointed were Beijing's expectations that Vietnam would constrain Moscow to enter upon a sharp collision course with the United States and to break up any attempts at a détente. Admittedly, the bombings were pushing the Kremlin in that direction. But its initial response was a course of action designed to frustrate both China's and America's hopes. Tough talk about "the gravest consequence" that would follow if the United States persisted in attacking the North, hints of the possibility of Soviet "volunteers" being sent to Vietnam, were combined with continued urgings that all the contentious issues be brought to the negotiating table. At the same time, and quite successfully, Moscow was trying to turn the tables on Beijing by proposing joint action with it to ward off the American threat to Hanoi.

Following the American raids, the USSR formally requested the People's Republic to expedite the transfer of Soviet war matériel and military specialists to North Vietnam. Moscow also asked to be allowed to set up bases in southern China from which its air force could assist in protecting North Vietnamese airspace. Those requests to cooperate in helping a fellow Communist state, on their surface quite sensible from the point of view of proletarian internationalism, were categorically rejected by Beijing.

The reasons for this rejection throw an interesting light on the Chinese leaders' alleged solicitude for their Vietnamese comrades, whom they had repeatedly urged to cast off all restraint in their struggle to liberate the South. Obviously, in Mao's scheme of things the most desirable Soviet response to the imperialist threat would have been a sharp challenge to the United States, say over Berlin, rather than just helping to defend North Vietnam. And did the Russians really want to help, or were there ulterior motives behind their proposals? Take their demand for air bases in southern China: if the Soviet pilots flew missions against U.S. planes and warships from Chinese soil, wouldn't the Americans retaliate against the People's Republic? The proposal for a massive shipment of supplies to the beleaguered Communist nation was yet another potential trap. North Vietnam would become so dependent on Soviet supplies that by threatening to cut them off Moscow could dictate its policies. It was quite in the Kremlin's style to strike a deal with the Americans: you meet our modest demands on the German issue and we will make the North Vietnamese see reason. The Communists fighting wars of national liberation should rely on their own resources rather than on the promises of the perfidious "Kremlin tsars."

Paradoxically, then, the threat to a fellow Communist state, instead of bringing the Soviet Union and the People's Republic closer together, served to further worsen their mutual relations, thus bringing out in full relief the essentially nationalistic and self-serving motivations of the leaders. On both sides there had been some semblance of a rapprochment following Khrushchev's ouster. Zhou Enlai visited Moscow (where he demonstratively deposited a wreath on Stalin's tomb near the Kremlin wall); there had been a brief cessation of the bitter polemics. But once the Vietnam situation heated up, the Chinese Communists resumed their campaign of vilification of the Soviet comrades, presenting Moscow as being more concerned about its relations with the United States than about North Vietnam's struggle. As an official Chinese source, undoubtedly truthfully, reported, "When Kosygin passed through Beijing on his visit to Vietnam in February 1965 and exchanged views with the Chinese leaders, he stressed the need to help the United States 'find a way out of Vietnam.' This was firmly rebuffed by the Chinese leaders."[5]

This statement tells us more than Beijing might have wished: even the prospect of Hanoi's securing most of what it wanted (i.e., an arrangement which, after an interval, would enable it to take over the South) was unacceptable to the Chinese leaders, if the road to it had to lead through negotiations. It was much more preferable to have the United States mired in an indecisive war in Indochina, thus exposing. U.S.-Soviet relations to constant strain.

It took considerable skill—and luck—for the Hanoi leadership to be able to remain in the eye of the hurricane rather than to be swept into the storm raging between Beijing and Moscow. The North Vietnamese could not afford to alienate either of the senior Communist powers. China was their neighbor, and the Chinese Communists' epic struggle for power had been an inspiration and a model for their own. In the past they also appreciated Beijing's strivings to turn the entire international Communist movement to a more militant path and thus to keep the USSR from placing undue constraints on their campaign to conquer the South. But Ho Chi Minh and his people would have been very obtuse if they had not seen through China's game by the time the United States began its massive intervention in the war. Beijing was good at cheering them on, but real help in war matériel to carry on the guerrilla campaign, to keep North Vietnam's economy going, and to stave off American air raids had to come from the Russians. It was mainly on account of what Moscow might do that the Americans felt restrained from carrying out more intense and indiscriminate bombing, or even, as some in Washington had been suggesting, from invading the North. To be sure, Soviet help was not a consequence of sheer ideological solicitude on the part of the Kremlin, but tied to broader considerations. Still, China's attitude must by now have been revealed as being much more unsentimental, to the point of near callousness. The North Vietnamese could not fail to perceive that their Chinese comrades' primary interest in the war touched on what it was doing to U.S.-Soviet relations, with but little consideration for what the struggle was costing in human lives and suffering, or

even the possibility that if it heeded Beijing's injunction not to negotiate under any conditions, North Vietnam might eventually lose
the war.

Hanoi's urgent remonstrations were needed for the People's Republic to agree to have Soviet matériel shipped through its territory,
but it was still interfered with by the Chinese, alleging that the weapons the USSR was sending were obsolete and in insufficient quantity.
Nor was there any inhibition on China's part in revealing the reasons
for its obstruction of aid to fellow Communists. "If we are to take
united action on the question of Vietnam with the new leaders of the
CPSU who are pursuing Khrushchev's revisionist line, wouldn't we
help them to deceive the people of the world? Wouldn't we be helping
them to bring the question of Vietnam within the orbit of U.S.-Soviet
collaboration?"[6]

Once victory was theirs, the North Vietnamese would demonstrate
that they had neither forgotten nor forgiven China's cold-blooded attitude at the time of their greatest peril. It would be one of the main
factors in the sharp clashes between the two Communist states that
eventually would lead to open warfare.

At the time, fear of offending China was still strong enough to make
Hanoi absent itself from the conference of the major Communist
parties summoned to Moscow in March 1965. The Soviets' hope was
evidently to secure a condemnation of Beijing's policies or perhaps
China's formal excommunication and ejection from the socialist camp.
Of the twenty-six invited parties, only eighteen sent delegates. Predictably, in view of the abstentions and the Vietnamese situation, the
meeting did not lead to any concrete decisions. Even the most pro-
Soviet parties felt that this was not the moment to aggravate the
Communist world's disunity. Still, Beijing was infuriated by the mere
fact that the meeting took place.

Simultaneously, there was an even more vivid illustration of how
tempestuous the relations between the People's Republic and the
USSR had become. On March 4, 1965, the Soviet authorities organized a "spontaneous" people's protest against the latest imperialist
iniquities in Vietnam—in front of the American embassy. As usual
for such contrived spectacles, the crowd, after shouting anti-American
slogans and being seemingly restrained by the police, was supposed
to disperse. But on this occasion the demonstration did in fact become
genuine when the Chinese students in its forefront broke through
the police protective cordon and hurled stones at the building and

manhandled Soviet militiamen. Citizens of Moscow were treated to the unusual sight of representatives of the authorities being beaten up by foreigners. This was the last straw in the Kremlin's eyes and brought the instantaneous termination of the cultural exchanges between the two still formally allied states. The students were expelled, to receive heroes' welcomes on their return to their homeland.

One year later the Hanoi leadership felt it could no longer afford to keep a distance between itself and Moscow. It sent a delegation to the Twenty-third Congress of the CPSU, which was boycotted by the Chinese and a few other partisans of Beijing, notably the Albanian and Japanese Communists.

The intervening year had been an eventful one in the Communist world. The pace and scope of the struggle in Southeast Asia intensified, the United States continuing to bomb the North and greatly increasing its land and air forces in South Vietnam. Soviet support in war matériel and in warding off America's still more drastic escalation of its attacks upon the North had become essential to the latter's capacity to continue the struggle. China's help, on the other hand, had been marginal.

Beijing's international standing had been further shaken by the disaster that overcame its strongest partisan in Asia, the Indonesian Communist Party. Indonesia itself, once a favorite of the USSR in the Third World, had of late been drawing away from Moscow and closer to the People's Republic. Its mercurial leader, Sukarno, had expansionist ambitions that thrust his country into a confrontation with Malaysia. Indonesia's harassment and intermittent guerrilla infiltration of the neighboring state required the latter to seek help from Britain and threatened at one time to lead to a second major war in Southeast Asia. In January 1965, abetted by China and against Soviet advice, Indonesia withdrew from the United Nations. In his bid for dictatorial power Sukarno himself had come to rely increasingly upon the Communists. In September, with the assistance of some elements in the Communist Party, Sukarno attempted a coup that would remove the last obstacle to his full rule—the cohesive leadership of the armed forces. The coup failed. The generals took over, and though for a while retaining Sukarno as a figurehead, embarked on a ruthless purge of his allies. More than 100,000 Communists are estimated to have been killed, the strongest and most influential party of any Asian non-Communist state virtually erased. Moscow's reaction was one of barely concealed relief; had the coup succeeded, this land of 100 million people, of much greater economic and political importance than Vietnam, the most populous Moslem state in the world, would have become China's satellite. The USSR did not even go through the motions of suspending its diplomatic relations with Indonesia, and it was only after the generals' regime had been firmly entrenched that Brezhnev saw fit to condemn the anti-Communist terror.

China's prestige was further hurt by the failure to help its only non-Communist friend in Asia, Pakistan, in its hour of need. This friendship, another example of Beijing's freedom from ideological compunctions when it suited its interest, had resulted from both countries' antagonism toward India. The USSR's now extensive economic and military help to the world's second-most-populous country was seen, and justifiably so, as an effort to build it into a countervailing power in Asia to China. "The new leaders of the CPSU . . . have carried further their alliance against China with the Indian reactionaries who are controlled by the American imperialists. . . . They granted India aid to the tune of 900 million dollars in one year, which is more than all the loans Khrushchev extended to India in nine years. They have speeded up their plans for military aid to India."[7]

When the ever-festering conflict between the two states sharing the subcontinent burst into actual fighting in August 1965, China brought troops to the Indian border and addressed ominous threats to New Delhi. The USSR lined up behind its friend, a Tass communiqué conveying an oblique warning to China. Such diplomatic sparring between Moscow and Beijing would become quite frequent during the next twenty years, with both powers acting like boxers warily circling each other and voicing threats but never actually coming to blows (except for some very minor border fighting in the late 1960s). But this time the Indian-Pakistani affair ended in a Soviet diplomatic victory. Both sides accepted Soviet mediation, and at the subsequent conference held in Tashkent their leaders heeded Premier Kosygin's counsel to renounce the use of force and to return their troops to where they had been stationed before the fighting. For China the outcome of the whole affair meant a considerable loss of face and a derogation of its status as the leading Asian power.

It had been a bad year for Beijing, and in view of that as well as more pressing considerations, it is easy to understand why North Vietnam felt constrained to lean more on the Soviet Union. Still, in his speech at the Twenty-third Party Congress the leader of North Vietnam's delegation expressed profuse thanks to China as well as to his hosts for the assistance they had rendered in their struggle against American imperialism and its puppet regime in the South. Hanoi could afford an occasional disagreement with China but not yet its open enmity. Both its representative and that of the NLF (to keep up the appearance of its independent status) pleaded in their speeches for the restoration of unity in the Communist bloc and hinted, ever so obliquely, that fears of U.S. reaction should not inhibit the USSR from taking more vigorous steps in furthering their cause.

Some other foreign guests at the Congress were in a position to be more explicit in criticizing the insufficiency of the Soviet response to the by now routine American raids on the North. For the more militant parties the raids represented a dangerous precedent and to tolerate them would embolden the imperialists to try similar tactics elsewhere. "Imperialism must be slapped hard in Vietnam," pleaded the spokesman for the Cuban Communist Party. "For the victory over imperialism in Vietnam it is necessary to arrest, using all available means and taking the necessary risks, that criminal aggression which is the bombing of the Democratic Republic of Vietnam."[8] It was natural that Castro, intent on exporting his model of revolution to other Latin American countries, should have been especially sensitive on this issue. Soviet toleration of this new American strategy of containment threatened the advance of Communism everywhere. Therefore, "It is necessary, should the circumstances demand it, to be ready for a [decisive] battle in Vietnam in order to defend the territorial integrity and the very existence of this fraternal country. The struggle in Vietnam poses a basic question of principles for the entire Communist movement, and especially for the Communist states."[9]

The thinly disguised appeal that the USSR meet the United States head-on in Vietnam even at the risk of a nuclear confrontation drew scattered boos from the normally disciplined audience. Certainly, an overwhelming majority of delegates as well as many foreign guests must have felt outraged that the representative of a regime which owed its survival to the USSR had the presumption to urge upon it fresh commitments involving incalculable risks.

This call (echoed by a handful of representatives of other foreign parties) for the Soviet Union to be ready to sacrifice all on the altar of "proletarian internationalism" met with an unmistakable rebuff in Brezhnev's concluding speech to the Congress: "We have had the opportunity to hear the speeches of our comrades-in-arms, our foreign friends. . . . Listening to them, we were reassured that our class brothers around the world realize that the main help to their revolutionary struggle and our main contribution to it lies in the successful construction of Communism in our country."[10] Those sobering words were received by the delegates, the record notes, with "tumultuous applause."

The intensity of the applause was a good indication of the growing weariness and impatience of the party elite—those feelings undoubtedly stronger among the rank and file—with the dangers and burdens that "proletarian internationalism" imposed upon their country. No vital interest of the Soviet state was at stake in the struggle in Southeast Asia; the struggle had been pushed to its present and critical phase very largely because of China's maneuvers and intrigues. Some in the audience may well have felt that if the Chinese were so keen on advancing the cause of Marxism-Leninism throughout the world, the Soviet Union should let them assume the obligations and risks attendant on shielding North Vietnam from an all-out assault by the United States.

But for the Soviet Union to have adopted such a policy would have meant an abdication of its role as the leader of the world movement, a confession of ideological bankruptcy. And that in turn would have undermined the very foundation of the Soviet system. Some years later Solzhenitsyn would write, "It is not authoritarianism itself which is intolerable, but the ideological lies that are daily foisted upon us," and he suggested, perhaps tongue-in-cheek, that the proprietorship of the antiquated creed be turned over, so to speak, to Beijing. But the Kremlin, and probably the writer himself, knew better: authoritarianism could not long survive a repudiation of ideology.

The Soviet leaders then could not afford, whatever their private feelings, to leave North Vietnam to its own devices or to be indifferent to the course of the struggle for the South. In the eyes of the world, Vietnam was seen as a testing ground of the appeal and strength of Communism, at least insofar as the Third World was concerned. The Vietcong were battling and holding their own against the rapidly growing number of American combat troops as well as those of the Saigon regime. The U.S. air strikes of increasing severity did not seem to break Hanoi's determination to see the war through. Were Moscow to opt out of the picture, it would bring vociferous protests and condemnations from even the most pro-Soviet and anti-Chinese elements in the movement.

While the jettisoning of foreign commitments incurred on behalf of proletarian internationalism might have been popular at home, it would in the long run lead to the questioning of the rationale of the Communist regime. Brezhnev would have been hard put to define in concrete terms what "successful Communist construction" meant. A more egalitarian society? A much higher standard of living? But why did these goals require authoritarian controls and vast spending on defense? On the other hand, the twin themes relating to the foreign dimension of Communism—the obligation to advance the cause of socialism and national liberation and the need to counter the threat posed by the capitalist camp—had retained a measure of credibility, if not among the population at large then among the party faithful. The Kremlin simply *had* to sustain the Soviet commitment to the Vietnamese comrades.

And whatever the initial hesitations, after 1966 this commitment could be seen as not only unavoidable but also justified in terms of the political benefits it was bringing to the Soviet Union. The United States, for all of its greatly enhanced military presence, was proving incapable of dealing a decisive blow to the Vietcong or of forcing Hanoi either to give up its support of the insurrection or to negotiate. America could not lose militarily, but short of desperate measures such as invading the North or resorting to nuclear weapons, it would not win. And in view of the growing revulsion against the war at home and the surge of anti-American feelings abroad, Washington was unlikely to resort to such measures. Under the circumstances, the Soviet Union did not have to undertake steps that would place it on a collision course with the United States. Moscow would follow the path of what in Pentagon parlance could be described as "measured response," helping its friends at each instance of U.S. military escalation, but not beyond the point where it became too dangerous.

Those voices within the Communist camp that had protested the insufficiency of Soviet aid had by 1967–68 been largely stilled. Moscow's policies, it was now conceded, preserved the right balance: they enabled the NLF and the North Vietnamese to resist the imperialists' encroachments and yet avoided the kind of challenge to the United States that might result in a worldwide conflagration.

Soviet influence in Hanoi now topped that of China's. It was not only that the North Vietnamese (along with most of the other parties) blamed Beijing for the rift in the Communist world and the failure of the two Communist powers to synchronize their policies in Southeastern Asia, a failure that at one time threatened the cause of liberation of the South with disaster. As already mentioned, China's aid in the struggle could not match Moscow's, especially when it came to sophisticated military equipment designed to combat American air raids on the North and to minimize the American land forces' technological superiority over the Vietcong in the South. Beijing's contribution came mostly in the form of construction battalions sent to North Vietnam to repair its communications, now constantly under U.S. air attack. Other than that and the not very significant financial infusions, China's help consisted in bracing slogans and advice: Rely on your own forces—imperialism cannot prevail over an aroused people; be wary of Greeks bearing gifts, i.e., of the Russians, who may sell you out so as to make a deal with the United States.

Initially, and until the American resolve to make Vietnam an object lesson that "wars of national liberation don't pay" began to crumble, such suspicions were very rife in Beijing. They accounted, as we have already seen, for China's refusal to have Soviet bases on its soil to expedite shipments to North Vietnam. But even after Washington had realized that it was Moscow's help that was a crucial factor in North Vietnam's and the NLF's being able to carry on, China's nightmare of a collusion between the United States and the USSR persisted: on May 28, Foreign Minister Chen Yi spoke openly about the possibility of the Soviets and Americans not only making a deal, but joining hands to attack China.

That massive eruption of irrationality—the Cultural Revolution—was just around the corner, but in its *foreign* policy Mao's regime could display flexibility and prudence. In May 1966 Zhou Enlai stated in an interview that "China will not take an initiative to provoke a war with the United States."[11] And much as this reassurance might have appeared lost amid the chorus of threats and imprecations hurled against the United States in connection with its role in Indochina, Beijing would continue to maintain open channels of communication with Washington at the periodic Warsaw ambassadorial-level talks between the two countries.

What the Kremlin might have expected or perhaps even hoped for following America's massive military intervention—a replay of the Korean situation with the American army fighting Chinese volunteers—became by the end of 1967 quite unlikely. Beijing was too wary, and the Johnson administration was quite persuaded that the war it already had on its hands was enough: the American people would not approve its extension.

By 1968 the Soviet leaders could congratulate themselves: against considerable odds they stumbled into success in Vietnam. They were helping a fraternal country and a liberation movement but incurring no casualties on that account. The war was costing the United States something on the order of $30 billion annually; the corresponding figure for the USSR was below $1 billion. The world's attention was focused on Southeast Asia and the reverberations of the war in the United States and elsewhere rather than on the internal problems of the USSR.

The success was all the more important because it came in the wake of a series of setbacks for Communism: the revelations about the Stalin era, the suppression of Hungary, the Cuban fiasco, and the Sino-Soviet split. In 1968 there occurred in the capitalist West what might be called a cultural minirevolution: the rise of the New Left, the student upheavals in France and West Germany, and the great escalation of the antiwar protests in the United States. By contrast, the Soviet Union presented a picture of stability at home and of steadfastness in its foreign policy. To be sure, that image was soon to be damaged by the invasion of Czechoslovakia. Even so, the Vietnamese Communists' feat in standing up to the greatest power in the world appeared to portend the resumption of Communism's victorious march and the Soviet Union's becoming once more the uncontested leader of the world movement.

Nor did this seeming resumption by Moscow of its ideological mission threaten its long-term goal of reaching détente with the United States. The Johnson administration, exasperated by its predicament, clung more than ever to the notion that the USSR should be an intermediary between it and Hanoi to help bring about peace with honor. As far as American public opinion was concerned, the hope of a military solution in Vietnam had been severely shaken. On January 3 the Vietcong launched attacks on all the major urban centers, thus confounding the notion that its strength was confined solely to the countryside. Militarily, this offensive turned out to be a disaster for the rebels; their attacks were beaten off and they suffered huge casualties. But before the war-weary American public there opened now the prospect of an unending conflict in Southeast Asia with more and more of America's manpower required just to contain the Vietcong.

Responding to the popular mood, President Johnson on March 31, 1968, announced far-reaching changes in the conduct of the war: the U.S. land forces would not be substantially increased; most of North

Vietnam's territory would be exempt from air raids. Combined with the president's statement that he would not seek reelection, this amounted to a virtual avowal that the past U.S. strategy had failed and that Washington now sought a solution through negotiations.

The cessation of the bombing was Hanoi's condition for holding peace talks. Johnson's declaration led then to the first tentative contacts between Washington and Hanoi, though the latter kept insisting that peace negotiations in the formal sense could not start until there was a complete and unconditional halt to the U.S. air raids on the North. On October 31 the president did comply, ordering an end to the aerial campaign though not precluding its resumption if needed in the future.

The subsequent course of fighting in and negotiation over Vietnam cannot be pursued here in detail. What is of interest to us is the significance of the Vietnam story to the fortunes of international Communism, and in particular to the relations between China and the USSR. On this account President Johnson's announcement of October 31, 1968, takes on special importance. To be sure, the American air raids on the North would be resumed on several occasions during the subsequent four years. Yet by being constrained to desist from them in principle, the United States enabled Moscow to score a brilliant diplomatic and ideological success. It had been the USSR that had some years before been put on the spot and upbraided for being incapable or unwilling to coerce the Americans to stop this form of aggression against a fraternal socialist nation. Had this American experiment with "massive retaliation" succeeded in its objective—to force North Vietnam to give up its struggle for the South—it could have had ominous consequences for future wars of "national liberation." Washington would be tempted to try the same medicine in other cases of what it considered Communist subversion of pro-Western regimes. Between 1965 and 1968 Soviet aid, technological and military, was a crucial factor in enabling Hanoi to withstand this "air piracy," as it was branded in Communist parlance, and to make the United States pay a considerable price in planes and pilots. But it was the U.S. recognition that even its enormous air power could not sway the course of a national liberation struggle that fully vindicated Moscow's tactics and refuted decisively China's slander about the Kremlin's faintheartedness.

North Vietnam's willingness to negotiate with its opponents was another point on which, in the eyes of the Communist world, the

Soviets scored heavily over the Chinese. Hanoi, probably on the Soviets' insistence, began talks with the United States even before the
complete halt of the American air attacks: with the precedent of Korea
in mind, no one on either side could have had any illusion of the talks'
bringing a speedy conclusion to the war, or even moderating the
character and intensity of the fighting. But the mere fact of holding
the talks was a rebuff to the Chinese, whose position was that a
revolutionary movement must not negotiate with the imperialists but
go on fighting them until the victorious end. Such peremptory and
petulant advice ignored the fact that the Chinese Communists themselves had not scorned negotiations with the Kuomintang following
World War II and that those negotiations, by providing a breathing
spell for their armed forces, contributed to their success once the civil
war was reignited. China in the past had also welcomed truce talks
in the Korean War and had participated in the Geneva Conference of
1954, which had agreed on the division of Vietnam. In both those
cases Beijing had been eager for a peaceful compromise solution. The
classical Maoist model of revolutionary warfare did not preclude negotiations as a potentially useful tool in the struggle. You may distract
the enemy, test his staying power, and impress him with your resolution. Like many of the allegedly ideological postulates of the Beijing
government, this one reflected its self-interest and its opposition to
any initiative on Vietnam that was supported by Moscow.

To what extent did the latter influence North Vietnam's policies
and strategies? The Soviets, needless to say, were not very explicit on
the subject. American requests (occasionally assuming the form of
supplications) that the USSR employ its good offices with the North
Vietnamese and make them see reason, a peace that would enable a
non-Communist South Vietnam to survive, were usually met in Moscow by stern reminders that the Democratic Republic of Vietnam was
a sovereign state that took no orders from anybody. But intermittently
the Russians would hint coyly that, yes, if the United States were
really interested in a peaceful solution in Indochina, Moscow might
try to persuade its friends there to give serious consideration to American proposals.

In fact, the Soviets did exercise considerable influence over Hanoi,
especially between 1966 and 1969 when the Cultural Revolution
drastically reduced China's role as an actor on the international scene.
But, conversely, public support of Hanoi, now a symbol as well as a
tangible example of Communism on the march, was of great value

to the Soviet Union. North Vietnam's absence from the conference
of Communist parties summoned to Moscow in June 1969 was largely
responsible for the failure of the gathering. The Kremlin's obvious
hope had been to secure from the seventy-five parties attending a
condemnation of the Chinese leadership. Indeed, Brezhnev let loose
with a diatribe against the Chinese leaders, singling out "Mao Zedong
and his partisans who already ten years ago began their assault on
the principles of scientific Communism."[12] Even though the great
majority of the parties represented were appalled by the spectacle
furnished by the Cultural Revolution, they balked at aggravating divisions within the movement, the final declaration falling far short of
an unqualified censure of Maoism. Even so, a number of parties,
including the Italian one, subscribed only to that part of the proclamation that urged unity of all progressive forces in the struggle against
imperialism. Where the participants did reach unanimity was in a
statement calling for "independence, freedom and peace" for Vietnam
and in hailing the provisional government of the Republic of South
Vietnam, recently proclaimed by the National Liberation Front.

The absence of North Vietnam and of its creature, the National
Liberation Front, from the seventy-five-party conclave was thus instrumental in blocking the Soviet Union's presumed goal in sum-
moning it, i.e., to read China out of the socialist camp. Even the Italian
Communists, already professing uneasiness over the authoritarian
features of Communism not only in China but in the Soviet Union
itself, felt that to formalize the split in the movement at a time when
Marxism-Leninism was being put to the test in Vietnam would make
nonsense of the whole notion of proletarian internationalism. Even to
the most staid and nonmilitant Communists, the struggle in Southeast
Asia offered the hope that their movement and ideology were the wave
of the future. Capitalist Western Europe had risen from the ashes and
was experiencing a period of unprecedented prosperity. The reputation of Communism had been damaged by the revelations about Stalinism and by the now open and increasingly acrimonious conflict
between the USSR and the People's Republic. But in 1969, and for
several years afterward, this unraveling of the Communist movement,
and erosion of the doctrine, were seemingly being refuted by a Communist movement in a Third World country being able to withstand
the most powerful capitalist power. This then was not the moment
for the Soviet Union and China to advertise and aggravate their mutual
enmity.

Viewed from our perspective, the struggle in Vietnam was not so much a proving ground of the validity and appeal of Marxism, in a non-Western setting, as a contest of wills between a militant and tightly disciplined movement (whose adherents were motivated by nationalism rather than ideological stimuli) and a democracy whose citizens increasingly questioned the need for its soldiers to fight and die in a civil war in a distant land. Whatever the appeal of the Vietcong to the population in the South, it was based largely on its success in appropriating the theme of anticolonialism, as well as in its superior morale and discipline, as contrasted with the forces of the Saigon regime.

It was a belated recognition of this fact that shortly after the inauguration of Richard Nixon as president led American policy makers to initiate what became known as "Vietnamization." The United States would gradually withdraw its ground troops while building up Saigon's army and fully maintaining its own air and naval presence in the area. By now all that Washington could hope for was a military stalemate in the South which, along with the threat of renewed bombing, would force North Vietnam to negotiate seriously and possibly accept a compromise solution in the undeclared war. By 1969 it had already lasted longer than any previous foreign conflict in this country's history.

While the new approach by Washington did succeed in building up the strength and effectiveness of the Saigon regime's forces, it could not reverse the trend toward an eventual Communist victory. Saigon's had been, going back even before 1960, an *inefficient* authoritarian regime, suffering from frequent changes in its leadership, divided counsels, and opposition not only from left-wing elements, but also from a number of other political and religious groups. The phased withdrawal of American troops was bound to lower still further the morale of the anti-Communist forces, since despite all of Washington's assurances to the contrary, it had to be taken as an indication of America's resignation to a solution which, while preserving appearances, would in the long run almost inevitably lead to the absorption of the South (and quite likely also of the neighboring states of Laos and Cambodia) by the Communists.

As viewed from Washington, the only hope of averting such an outcome lay in exploiting the Sino-Soviet conflict, creating a situation in which it would be in the interest of both Moscow and Beijing to pressure their North Vietnamese comrades to settle for less than a complete victory. This was the objective of the complex diplomatic game carried out by the Nixon-Kissinger team during the next three years; the game, which while it did not save American protégés in the South, contributed to making the division of the Communist world deeper and irremediable.

We discussed before how the USSR faced with seemingly intractable problems in its foreign and domestic policies was able to overcome them and recover its diplomatic balance very largely because of the crippling effects on its rival of the Cultural Revolution. Relief, however, was temporary. The appalling spectacle which unfolded in China between 1966 and 1969—its reverberations lasting long beyond the latter date—reflected on Communism as a whole, and thus in the long run could not but prove detrimental also to the USSR. The Cultural Revolution revealed the irrationality lurking beneath Communist ideology and practice, and not only in the country that underwent the Revolution.

"Grotesque" is the first term which comes to mind in dealing with that period in China's history. Historians and political scientists would attribute the collapse of Communism in the 1980s to a variety of causes: its anachronistic economics, the erosion of its ideological foundations, its denial of individual freedom. But quite apart from those weighty reasons, the crash was precipitated by what might be called a revolution of common sense. The people rebelled against the yoke of an ideology that described itself as "scientific socialism," but the practice of which had been reduced to a quasi-religious worship of "the party" as the repository of all wisdom, supplemented by the cult of "the leader," a semidivine figure, infallible in all his policies and pronouncements. And no other period in the history of the movement, except for those years of the height of terror under Stalin, demonstrates this irrational tendency of Communism as vividly as does the Cultural Revolution.

Mao's cult came to resemble that of the late Soviet dictator but in some ways took on an even more ludicrous form. For all the heroics attributed to him, Stalin was never credited with superior athletic skills. But as the Chinese media reported on July 16, 1966, Mao bested several world swimming records in the course of his nine-mile swim in the Yangtze. Foreign partisans of the Chinese Communists tried to rationalize this embarrassing incident: the chairman and those close to him were obviously trying to reassure the people of China that, although seventy-three, their leader was in perfect physical as well as mental condition, and thus fully fit to preside over the political drama of national regeneration that was about to unfold. Unfortunately for such "deeper" interpretations, we have the evidence that Mao simply fancied himself as a swimmer and felt that he should be admired as such, as well as on other counts. In 1959 in a speech before the Military Affairs Committee of the People's Congress, Mao, apropos of nothing in particular, turned to the subject of swimming: "I really learned to swim well only in 1954 . . . [at] an indoor swimming pool. I went there every evening with my bag, changed my clothes and for three months without interruption I studied the nature of the water. Water doesn't drown people. Water is afraid of people. . . . The Yangtze at Wuhan is water, so it is possible to swim in the Yangtze at Wuhan."[13] Such garrulity and the chairman's eagerness to let others in on autobiographical data might be thought of as of little consequence or even disarming. But it inevitably makes one wonder whether some of the more bizarre policies of that very bizarre period of Chinese history might have had their source in Mao's personal whim, rather than requiring a sophisticated ideological and political explanation.

There were, of course, tangible political reasons for one aspect of the Cultural Revolution: the smashing of the party and government apparatus as it had existed between 1949 and 1966 and making the cult of Mao virtually the only foundation of the legitimacy of the regime. Much as he had been extolled and had stood immune from public criticism (a modicum of the cult of personality was an almost inevitable feature of every Communist regime prior to perestroika), the Great Helmsman's power prior to 1966 had not been unlimited: on most issues he had to defer to the opinions of fellow members of the Standing Committee of the Politburo. As had Stalin in the 1920s, so Mao, beginning with the late 1950s, chafed under constraints placed upon him by the party oligarchy and the party apparatus. Failure of the Great Leap Forward brought the hitherto covert anti-Mao feelings to the surface. At the time, he managed to defeat the opposition, and its spokesman, Marshal Peng Dehuai, was dismissed and disgraced. The subsequent intraparty machinations, combined with the growing economic distress and famine conditions, constrained Mao to lay down his functions as head of state. Much older than Stalin when he was scheming for absolute power, Mao evidently felt a growing sense of isolation and the threat of being turned into a figurehead.

Stalin relied mainly on the political (usually misnamed "secret") police to suppress his actual and potential opponents and *then* to unleash mass terror to benumb the entire nation. Mao had recourse to the youth who had been brought up to idolize him and who now responded to the appeal to protect the beloved leader from his personal enemies and the "capitalist roaders" who had perfidiously infiltrated the organs of power. In March 1966 came the signal: [Mao] "said his intention was to support fully the left wing radically and that he would establish armies to bring about a 'Cultural Revolution' in China."[14]

The armies soon materialized in the form of bands of fanatical youths, the Red Guards. Carefully manipulated by the chairman's partisans, among whom an important role was played by his wife, Jiang Qing, they attacked both the party and the government bureaucracy. A wave of unrest swept China's universities and other schools. It does not take much to stir up the young against those in authority and against traditional ways. In this case the titillation of rebellion was enhanced by the knowledge that the idolized chairman was with the young rebels, and that it was at his behest that they were stamping out the reactionary elements that still somehow survived in the people's China.

There followed a contrived wave of turbulence that then turned into what seemed like an elemental revolution against what had been the Communist establishment. Encouraged by esoteric slogans such as "Bombard the Headquarters," crowds of frenzied young people were let loose on the ministries, invaded the party office, and beat and humiliated officials of all ranks, often with consummate sadism. Early in the game those oligarchs whom Mao had suspected of having tried to supplant him were repeatedly assaulted and publicly disgraced even before their dismissal and imprisonment. Once the number-two man in the regime and head of state, Liu Shaoqi was publicly denounced as "China's Khrushchev" and the "number-one capitalist roader," and he and his wife were brutally paraded at public meetings with the frenzied crowds yelling insults.

The penchant for colorful jargon and vivid vocabulary always characteristic of Chinese Communism reached new heights in the Cultural Revolution. The Red Guards were out to combat "four type members": "landlords, wealthy farmers, antirevolutionaries, and bad elements." The Guards' struggle was allegedly on behalf of the "Red five elements," consisting of "workers, poor Chinese farmers, zealous youth, revolutionary activists, and poor city residents."[15] By 1967 the entire structure of the party and the central government lay in shambles. Not only Liu, but a number of other once-prestigious oligarchs, such as Deng Xiaoping, long general secretary of the party, and Peng Zhen, Beijing's boss, were stripped of their posts and vilified. Mao's wrath was visited even on those no longer in a position of power. Marshal Peng Dehuai, in disgrace since 1959, was imprisoned and physically abused. Suffering from cancer, the old warrior was eventually allowed to be hospitalized but was denied treatment for his condition. On his deathbed, Liu Shaoqi was informed of a resolution of the Central Committee that characterized the veteran revolutionary as "a sinful running dog of imperialism, modern revisionism and the Kuomintang. . . . The exposure of the true antirevolutionary . . . is a great victory for Mao's thought and the Proletarian Revolution."[16]

While his alleged and potential rivals and enemies were being destroyed politically and often physically, Mao's cult assumed the proportions of a nationwide hysteria. Pictures taken at the time would suggest that no one would venture out of his home without carrying the Little Red Book of Comrade Mao's writings. The Great Helmsman was being extolled in terms that anywhere else would have been taken as subversively satirical; he was interminably cheered at his public appearances, his most commonplace utterances throwing the crowds into a St. Vitus–like fit of rapture.

And yet he still was not at the pinnacle all by himself. The army having become the only island of relative stability amid the sea of anarchy, its head, Marshal Lin Biao, was elevated to the number-two position in the party-government hierarchy and in 1969 was proclaimed officially to be Mao's heir designate. The past record of such arrangements, especially under totalitarian regimes, did not warrant much confidence that this one would lead to an orderly succession. To make things worse, the sixty-five-year-old heir apparent was ailing and understandably impatient.

In August 1971, Mao, then on a tour of the provinces, recalled that he and his would-be successor did not see eye to eye on some intellectual problems. "I told Comrade Lin Biao that some of the things he said were not accurate. For example, he said that a genius appears in the world only infrequently. . . . This does not fit the facts. Marx and Engels were contemporaries, and not one century had elapsed before we had Lenin and Stalin, so how could you say that a genius appears only once in a few centuries?"[17] Few of his listeners on that occasion could have been left in doubt as to what was likely to happen to a man who entertained such shallow views on history.

The actual circumstances of Marshal Lin's death have remained mysterious to this day. The official version to which the Chinese government has stuck accused the marshal of having plotted on several occasions to have Mao assassinated. His treachery unmasked, the villain, accompanied by his wife, son, and some other plotters, attempted to flee to the Soviet Union, but his plane crashed in Mongolia on September 12, 1971. There are several questionable aspects of the story, but whatever the truth, the whole affair was a blow to Maoism. Within five years the chairman had matched Stalin's feat of destroying in the 1930s the cadres of the ruling party; his methods, while not as sanguinary as those of the Soviet despot, were still of the utmost ruthlessness. Of those who along with Mao had guided Chinese Communism through all of its vicissitudes to victory, only Zhou Enlai managed to hold on to power during the Cultural Revolution, and only a few others, notably Deng, were hardy enough to survive persecution and to reemerge on the political scene during Mao's final phase and after his death.

Ten years after Mao's death the Beijing regime allowed and even encouraged realistic appraisals of the revolution of unreason that with his blessing had gripped the unfortunate society. One of its most lamentable features was the wanton orgy of destruction and violence. The Red Guards were uninhibited about their cultural nihilism: "We are critics of all that belongs to the Old World. We will criticize and smash to pieces all that belongs to the Old World . . . old ways of thinking, the old culture, the old traditions. . . ."[18] And indeed this destructive zeal translated itself into a wave of vandalism that led the Red Guards to lay their hands on and destroy historical monuments and works of art, many of them among the most precious relics of Chinese civilization. The same impulse led to a widespread persecution of intellectuals, the closing of the universities (those students not enrolled in the Red Guards being sent to do physical labor in the countryside), and to the harnessing of the entire educational apparatus to the study of the "thought of Mao Zedong."

Had it not involved a vast incidence of personal tragedy,[19] several aspects of the Cultural Revolution would strike us as irresistibly funny. It could not have been easy for today's Communist China, in which Mao is still revered, to place on record the more preposterous features of his personality cult, but to its credit the Deng regime did authorize the publication of the most compromising and hilarious details. "The loyalty dance was simply moving your body in rhythm with the chanting of Mao's sayings, and one would wave one's hands and move one's feet in gestures of loyalty. . . . Once at the railroad station in Pan Yang people were not allowed to board trains unless they first performed the loyalty dance."[20]

Equally incredible but also authenticated is the story of the Red Guards' insistence that the message of red and green traffic lights be reversed—it was unbecoming that red should stand for "stop," rather than signal vigorous forward motion! It took the authority and persuasiveness of Zhou Enlai himself to block the inane scheme. But our impulse to laugh is stifled when we read another item from a chronicle of that period: after the party boss of Yunnan was denounced as failing in his zeal for Mao, there was a wholesale witch hunt throughout the province that cost fourteen thousand people their lives. Depressing in a different way are the stories of the Red Guards sacking libraries and bookstores for books "inimical to the ideas of Mao Zedong."

Insofar as he tried to provide a rationale for unleashing the epidemic of unreason, Mao urged the need for purifying his society of bureaucratic and elitist elements. To an old friend, Edgar Snow, who interviewed him in 1970, he explained that "the party has fallen into the revisionist [Soviet] road to capitalism—creating a new class, an elite of bureaucratic power wielders, a mandarinate of cadres divorced from labor and the people."[21] The American journalist interpreted his goal: "In a word, Mao demanded that the proletarian successors to power reenact the revolutionary life experience of his own generation . . ."

Whatever one thinks of Mao's sincerity, the fact remains that while destroying the previous bureaucratic apparatus and much else the Cultural Revolution led to a proliferation of new bureaucracies and factions. True, fourteen out of the seventeen pre-1966 Politburo members were suppressed, but their place was taken not by rank-and-file workers but by other party notables from the "group for the affairs of Cultural Revolution," the high command of the Red Guards. Nor was the new elite more united ideologically and more zealous than its predecessor. There ensued brisk infighting, often leading to actual armed clashes between the various factions of the Red Guards. After 1971 the regime would blame Lin Biao for trying to exploit the turmoil and to manipulate the Red Guards so as to prepare the way for his coup. In some provinces the local military commanders turned their troops on the young fanatics to preserve an appearance of order. Mao's wife acted throughout the period as the patron of the radical wing of the movement, obviously hoping to use it in her own bid for supreme power.

As to the chairman himself, he remained, as behooved a divinity, enigmatic, his statements intermittently praising and scolding the turbulent mass of his fanatical followers. As time went on, however, Mao grew increasingly critical of the Red Guards, at times accusing them of spreading anarchy, betraying his expectations and disappointing the hopes of China's workers and peasants. By the end of 1967 control over the local organs of government and the task of taming the Guards was delegated to the army. With other branches of the government in a skeletonlike condition, the military commanders assumed for the time being the role of the ruling oligarchy, presided over by Mao and Lin. China seemed to have relapsed into a kind of warlordism. The Politburo elected at the Ninth Congress of the Chinese Communist Party included fifteen military figures among its twenty-one members.

As the Cultural Revolution was winding down in 1968–69 its main instrument, the Red Guards, became themselves the target of repression. Some 7 million of their most active members were sent to work on the land in distant provinces. Speaking of the youth who had worked so strenuously to promote his cult, Mao was quite unsentimental: "It is very necessary to send educated young people to the countryside so that poor peasants might give them real education."[22]

Yet, as of 1969–70, it still appeared problematical whether having opened the floodgates to anarchy the Great Helmsman, then seventy-six, would be able to recover control of the Communist ship of state and save it from being wrecked. Apart from the threat of the irretrievable disintegration of the central government or its complete takeover by the military, the Cultural Revolution magnified the foreign danger. This was a period of turbulence on the world scene. Had the United States not been mired in the Vietnam imbroglio, it is not inconceivable that Washington would have licensed the Nationalists to try their luck and invade the mainland, American fears of China having been enhanced by its possession and development of nuclear weapons. As it was, the U.S. involvement in Southeast Asia and the resultant domestic political travails (Vietnam had triggered what might be described as America's own version of the rebellion of the youth and the disarray of society) made the incoming Nixon administration ready to try a new approach to China, if and when the current madness there had subsided. In December 1969 the United States and the People's Republic resumed those rather bizarre meetings held between the two countres' representatives in Warsaw.

But if the threat from the "imperialist camp" was lessened (and it could never be entirely discounted), that posed by a "fraternal socialist" country had greatly increased.

The Cultural Revolution was viewed by Moscow first with amusement and then with growing concern. In the beginning the Soviets were content to comment sardonically on the lighter features of the upheaval, such as the preposterous lengths to which the cult of Mao was carried. More practically the Kremlin could feel, and justifiably so, that in view of what was going on there, China no longer threatened Soviet domination of the world Communist movement. But the initial amusement was soon followed by increased apprehension. The apparent irrationality of Beijing's actions combined with their as yet modest but expanding and technologically improving nuclear weaponry was no laughing matter. It would have been sheer madness for the Chinese to attack the USSR in view of the latter's crushing superiority in conventional, not to mention nuclear, arms, but then, wasn't the entire Cultural Revolution an exercise in madness? China's progress in nuclear weapons was one of the few developments not visibly affected by the irrationality of the political scene; in 1967 came the first test of the H-bomb, and it was obviously not long before the People's Republic would dispose of missiles capable of reaching the heart of the European USSR.

Violent xenophobia was inherent in the Cultural Revolution, and the Soviet Union, both on nationalistic as well as ideological grounds, was one of its main targets. An invariable part of the accusations made against disgraced notables such as Liu Shaoqi was their alleged pro-Russian orientation. At the high point of the Red Guards' outrages, their detachments subjected the Soviet embassy in Beijing to a veritable siege. Soviet diplomats (just as was the case with other foreign diplomatic personnel) were molested and beaten. On occasion, bands of hooligans would break into the embassy compound and ravage the premises. On August 7, 1969, armed Chinese border guards seized a Soviet ship and placed its officers under arrest. It took a personal protest by Premier Kosygin to Zhou Enlai to have the ship and its crew released. As Soviet sources glumly report, throughout 1976 alone, Chinese authorities instigated "more than 200 major provocatory acts" toward Soviet personnel in the country, evoking "more than 90" diplomatic protests from Moscow, most of them, needless to say, unanswered and/or ineffective.[23]

Under the circumstances, it would have been surprising had the Sino-Soviet border, the longest in the world, remained unaffected. There had been sporadic trouble there from the beginning of the decade. That and the clashing territorial claims led in March 1969 to serious fighting along the Ussuri River, with quite a few casualties on both sides. The initial attack was perpetrated by the Chinese. The Soviets struck back, inflicting more than a thousand casualties on the Chinese border troops.

Moscow's reaction to the Chinese provocations was one of public indignation accompanied by ominous-sounding warnings. Yet on the whole, except for the March 1969 episodes, the Kremlin eschewed a violent response, its posture that of an innocent party trying patiently to persuade the offender of the irrationality of his ways. And in fact the Soviets' attitude was probably premised on the assumption that they were dealing with irresponsible, currently quite irrational people who had to be humored. Prime Minister Kosygin hoped to intercept Zhou Enlai during the funeral ceremonies for Ho Chi Minh in Hanoi in September 1969. His Chinese counterpart hastened his departure from North Vietnam's capital so as to avoid a meeting. Kosygin was halfway home, in Tashkent, when Zhou Enlai condescended to let him know that he would meet him in Beijing. Zhou's hospitality did not extend to asking his Soviet guest to stay overnight; their meeting took place at the Beijing airport.

Moscow's attempts to lower the level of tension between the two Communist giants could not be equated with appeasement. Beginning at least in 1967, the possibility of a full-scale war with China had to be on the minds of the Soviet leaders, even before they began to strengthen their military forces in the Far East. By 1972 they would have about one-quarter of their ground troops and air units there. And officials of the Nixon administration would be directly queried as to the American reaction should the USSR find itself compelled to launch a surgical strike against China's nuclear facilities.[24]

With their inherent suspiciousness and the by now firmly ingrained habit of believing the worst about the Soviet comrades, Mao and Company could not have been left in doubt about the danger threatening them from the north. And even if belatedly, they must have sensed that that danger was greatly enhanced by the parlous condition into which they had plunged China.

Even though the catastrophic consequences of the Cultural Revolution were plainly visible by the end of the 1960s, it was difficult to arrest its momentum and restore any sense of normalcy. What little in the way of rationality and continuity China's domestic and especially foreign policies retained throughout the period had largely been due to one man, Zhou Enlai. It was he who tried, not always successfully, to soften the savage treatment of those party and government notables who had fallen afoul of Mao, who sought to persuade the Red Guards to abandon their attacks upon foreign legations and personnel, and who throughout appeared to be the only force for sanity and moderation amid the general chaos. It was Zhou who almost single-handedly managed to preserve for China a semblance of foreign policy and who tried to assuage the anti-Soviet passions of his chief.

Yet at the height of the Cultural Revolution even Zhou's position became shaky. According to Chinese sources, both Lin Biao and Jiang Qing saw the veteran statesman as an obstacle to their schemes, and with Mao's apparent acquiescence kept inciting the Red Guards against him. On one occasion mobs of young fanatics were allowed to break into the premier's residence and for eighteen hours harangued the man who virtually alone was carrying the burden of day-to-day direction of China's government.[25] And Zhou had to adhere to the rites of the Revolution, attend mass meetings devoted to the worship of Mao and the denunciation of the "people's enemies," and, the Little Red Book in his hands, join in the chanting of the inane slogans of the Great Proletarian Cultural Revolution.

A modicum of rationality returned to Chinese politics in 1969. The year marks both the culmination and the ebb of the Cultural Revolution. It was largely the sobering perception of the Soviet threat that broke the spell. Diplomacy regained its place in Beijing's scheme of things. On the one hand, there was an endeavor to reduce the immediate threat by responding to the Soviet's conciliatory gestures— for example, the Kosygin-Zhou meeting, and as one of its results, the initiation of the Sino-Soviet negotiations on the contentious border issues (negotiations that would drag on indecisively until the era of perestroika). On the other hand, as we have also seen, Chinese diplomacy, while still fulminating against American imperialism and its misdeeds in Southeast Asia, began to probe the possibility of a rapprochement with the United States.

Simultaneously, the regime (and by this point the term can again be used meaningfully after a hiatus of three years) did not preclude the possibility of war breaking out suddenly. It was from this time that the People's Republic launched a comprehensive program of civil defense. Huge underground shelters were dug in major Chinese cities. Superficially, the effort might still have seemed irrational, a tremendous investment of money and manpower for shelters that could not provide real protection against nuclear weapons.[26] But the construction of veritable subterranean cities was also, and perhaps primarily, intended to divert the nation's attention and energies from that compulsive and destructive milling around to which the Cultural Revolution had been reduced. The same dual purpose was evident by 1969 in the complete assumption of authority by the local military commanders over the revolutionary committees.

As masses of city dwellers (the figures range from 20 million upward) were under compulsion wending their way to the countryside, and largely to the outlying provinces, China in other respects was resuming the appearance of Communist normalcy. Party committees smashed during the "bombarding of the headquarters" were being reconstituted. The People's Republic's heads of foreign missions who had been recalled during the frantic days—the Cultural Revolution scorned formal ties with the capitalists' and the revisionists' governments—were returning to their posts. Some features of the Cultural Revolution would persist past Mao's death in 1976 and through the subsequent purge of his widow and her partners in the "Gang of Four," notably the sudden shifts in the leadership. But the egalitarian and anarchic impulses loosed upon society between 1966 and 1969 would be severely repressed. Chinese domestic policies would soon remind one of what Beijing would, even into the late 1970s, castigate as revisionism. But the reverberations of that era of chaos and spurious enthusiasm are still being felt.

As often happens with revolutions, this one aggravated the evils it had proposed to eliminate. It is unclear to what extent the party high command really sought to limit Mao's powers before 1966. But from the Revolution there emerged real plots, one evidently going beyond a scheme to turn him into a figurehead and envisaging murder. For those conversant with Soviet history the fate of Lin Biao must have been a vivid reminder of how close Maoism had come to Stalinism at its worst. Extolled as the chairman's closest comrade-in-arms and a devoted pupil, Lin was in the fall of 1969 proclaimed in the new constitution of the People's Republic as Mao's deputy and heir. One and a half years later the crash: according to the official version, an elaborate plot frustrated largely through Zhou's vigilance and then Lin's and other conspirators' (including his wife and son) flight and death. Understatement has never been a characteristic of the Chinese Communists and at the Tenth Party Congress in 1973, Zhou Enlai left his audience in no doubt as to what the late marshal really was like under his mask of a devoted disciple of Mao: "A bourgeois careerist, plotter, hypocrite, renegade, traitor to the country, adventurer." It was something of an anticlimax for official propaganda to brand the wretch as having also been a follower of Confucius, the regime currently carrying on a spirited campaign against the philosophy of the ancient sage.[27] Was Lin, as also charged, conspiring with the Russians? This seems quite unlikely, but the real circumstances of the affair must await the Chinese version of glasnost, something which at the moment appears rather distant.

What might be called anti-Sovietism became by 1969 a regular and major part of the Chinese Communists' ideological fare. There would be an occasional break in the clouds. In 1970 the respective ambassadors returned to the capitals to which they were accredited, ending four years of virtual severance of diplomatic relations. From time to time Beijing would address a perfunctory message to Moscow, as on the anniversary of the October Revolution. The Kremlin would intermittently profess amicable sentiments toward the erring but still "fraternal socialist" state. But such gestures could not affect the by now enduring hostility between the two regimes, ironically still bound by the Treaty of Friendship and Mutual Assistance that would not expire until 1980 but which for two-thirds of its duration must certainly have been the most bizarre and unusual "alliance" in modern history.

Though the Communist camp was still its main battleground, the conflict was seen increasingly, even by the parties concerned, as a clash of national interests. The target of Beijing's verbal attack was identified as "the new Kremlin tsars" as often as the "revisionists and renegades." For the Soviets their protagonists had become the Chinese "chauvinists and hegemonists," as well as "the left-wing and sectarian dogmatists." The ideological veneer of the dispute was wearing thin, *but so were the importance and premises of the ideology itself.* The initial impact of the Cultural Revolution had, as we have seen, greatly benefited the international standing of the USSR. Beijing could no longer be seen as a viable competitor for the leadership of the world Communist movement. But by the same token, by damaging the reputation and unity of the movement, the extravagances of the Cultural Revolution helped render Moscow's leadership both less meaningful and more precarious. As shown by the 1969 conference of the seventy-five Communist parties, the Kremlin could no longer wave a magic wand that would make the fraternal parties toe the line, even in the sense of making them subscribe to a very general declaration of principles. Some of the most revisionist (in the sense that the term was used by the Chinese) parties, such as the Italian, saw the situation as affording them an opportunity not only to dissociate themselves from the Chinese stand but also to proclaim their emancipation from Moscow. In the West the image of Communism was being damaged not only by what was going on in China, but also by the reverberations of the Soviet invasion of Czechoslovakia. Within the bloc, Ceauşescu's Romania, while practicing crass revisionism, had retained and strengthened its friendly ties with Beijing and had virtually emancipated itself from Moscow's influence as far as its foreign policy was concerned. Vietnam obscured but could not arrest what from today's perspective can be seen as the terminal crisis of "proletarian internationalism."

The two Communist powers maneuvered wearily around each other. China was finding it difficult to break out of the self-imposed isolation of 1966 to 1969. Within the Communist bloc, North Vietnam, North Korea, and Romania remained friendly; the first two in a negative sense, i.e., not wishing to alienate their giant neighbor, while Romania found it convenient to play off the People's Republic against the USSR so as to emancipate itself from the latter. In a special category, there was faithful Albania, and rather significantly Beijing now sought better relations with Yugoslavia, its independent stand toward Moscow now found to offset Tito's revisionist sins.

It is a measure of Mao's regime's eagerness to resume an international role that China, a poor country, its economy still further strained by the side effects of the Cultural Revolution,[28] spent $1.2 billion in foreign aid during 1970–71, the lion's share going to Third World countries.

How greatly the internal disarray had affected Beijing's international standing was vividly illustrated by what happened in 1971 to China's only non-Communist friend in Asia, Pakistan. Six years before, the threat of Chinese intervention was a major factor in persuading India to accept Soviet advice to terminate hostilities against Pakistan. But in 1971 the USSR no longer urged moderation and restraint upon New Delhi. Emboldened by the treaty of friendship and cooperation, a virtual alliance with the Soviet Union, India took the occasion of a popular revolt in East Bengal to invade its neighbor and to amputate its eastern part, which became the independent republic of Bangladesh. This time China's threats (as well as U.S. warnings) were disregarded. China proved incapable of protecting the state that had relied on its support, and Beijing's passive if verbally furious reaction is explained only by the leaders' fear of an armed clash with the Soviet Union.

Vietnam, the Cultural Revolution, the escalation of the Sino-Soviet conflict—all these developments culminated in the great turnabout in world Communism in 1971–72. Both Moscow and Beijing turned away, now definitely and explicitly, from Marxism-Leninism as a guide to their foreign policies. Both were seeking an accommodation with the chief capitalist state, and their policies under the thin veneer of ideological rhetoric would from now on bear a strictly pragmatic realpolitik character.

This shift was all the more remarkable because the first few years of the decade were not good years for what in Communist parlance would for another decade remain "the imperialist camp." The United States had to acknowledge virtual defeat in Vietnam and was soon plunged into a constitutional crisis that debilitated its foreign policy for the rest of the decade. The Middle Eastern crisis of 1973 and its reverberations would demonstrate the precariousness of that prosperity in which the Western world had hitherto basked. The flourishing state of the capitalist economies and their prodigious and uninterrupted growth during the past two decades had stood as a vivid refutation of Marxism-Leninism. But first the oil embargo by the Arab states and then the exactions by OPEC (Organization of Petroleum Exporting Countries) as a whole wreaked havoc with the entire economic and social mechanism of the non-Communist world. For all their vast industrial, not to mention military, power, the Western democracies, after 1973, proved incapable of any concerted action that would remove the sword of Damocles OPEC held over their economies. For those still clinging to Communist ideology, there could now reappear the enticing vision of the collapse of capitalism, to be sure not for the reasons Marx and Lenin prophesied but because of factors arising out of international politics.

The post-Vietnam-and-Watergate debility of American foreign policy and the crippling effects of the energy crisis on the entire West did in fact embolden the Kremlin. It enabled the USSR to have its

cake and eat it too; to pursue the path of détente and at the same
time engage in expansionist ventures throughout the 1970s. This
expansionism, though, had but the merest ideological gloss. The real
motivation behind it was the need to compensate by forceful foreign
policy for the stagnation at home and to counter the ever-growing
evidence of the failure of Communism as a guide, whether to domestic
or foreign policies.

Such an erosion of ideological impulses was something that could
be expected in the case of the Soviets, with their now quite long record
of "revisionist" practices. What was surprising, and in its consequences shattering for the worldwide prospects of Communism, was
the simultaneous hauling down of the flag of militant Marxism-
Leninism by Mao's China.

The death throes of "proletarian internationalism" can be dated from
1972, when both Communist powers reached détente with the United
States. In the case of the Soviet Union, this rapprochement with the
main capitalist power was the culmination of conscious efforts of
Soviet diplomacy going back at least to Khrushchev's revival of summitry in the mid-1950s. Though the Soviet leaders before Gorbachev
were never to state it explicitly, they had long understood that the
advent of nuclear weapons rendered ideologies of little importance
compared to the imperative need of developing a mechanism of international relations which could assure peaceful coexistence. During
the entire period the vast shadow cast over international relations by
China had been at the same time, perversely, one of the main incentives for the Kremlin to seek a rapprochement with the United States
and the chief obstacle to achieving it. An incentive because Moscow
had to watch with apprehension the People's Republic's ambition to
become, and in a hurry, a great industrial and military power. They
also had to fear that consciously or unconsciously Mao might push
the entire Communist bloc into a war with the West. And China for
a long time effectively blocked an understanding between the two
superpowers both by trying to aggravate East-West tension in areas
such as Vietnam and Indonesia and by threatening to split irrevocably
the world movement.

By 1970–71 Mao and his partisans, far from being in a position to
block Soviet-American détente, were seeking to anticipate and offset
it by reaching their own accommodation with America. The Cultural
Revolution had led to a catastrophic lowering of China's standing not
only within the Communist world but in the international community

at large. Beijing now had to take seriously the danger of a Soviet military strike. In much of the literature on the subject, this change in China's evaluation of the Soviet threat has been attributed to the impression created through the invasion of Czechoslovakia by the Warsaw Pact forces and its alleged rationale—the Brezhnev Doctrine.[29] But at the time, much as they condemned the USSR for the invasion (as well as the reforms of the Dubček regime, which in their eyes represented inadmissible ultrarevisionism), the Chinese leaders evidenced little alarm on that count—China was not little Czechoslovakia. It was only two years later, and after some real evidence that what Beijing had noisily alleged for years a U.S. Soviet understanding, and not merely on Vietnam—was really in the cards, that China decided to beat Moscow to the punch.

America's willingness to seek a compromise solution to the Vietnam War could also be seen as one of the reasons the Chinese Communists decided to move toward détente with the United States. Much as they had denounced Washington's previous peace proposals as shams and imperialist trickery, they came to see them as genuine attempts at a settlement. The United States was now seen as neither a "paper tiger," nor, as they had long depicted it, a Communist version of the Evil Empire. While in foreign policy Mao and his colleagues, notably Zhou Enlai, had always shown greater realism than in their domestic course, the bitter experience of three years of turmoil was conducive to the return of greater rationality in both spheres. The ideological blinders dropped off. As China emerged from what might be likened to a nationwide nervous breakdown, the regime would embark on a completely new course, first abroad and then belatedly at home. To be sure, one element of foreign policy would remain unchanged—Beijing's staunch and consistent hostility toward the USSR.

The diplomatic maneuvers of 1970 to 1972 involved very intricate moves on the part of the three concerned powers, concluding with the most far-reaching rapprochement to date between the United States and the Communist powers, a preview of what in fifteen years would be a complete and—one has good reason to hope—enduring accommodation between all three—the United States, the Soviet Union, and the People's Republic. But as of 1973 none of the concerned parties succeeded in realizing its main objectives. The Soviet Union sought détente with the United States in order to enlist the latter as an ally against China or at least to block a Sino-American rapprochement. Well, Moscow did reach a number of important agreements with the United States. After Nixon's visit to the USSR in 1972, the Brezhnev regime could boast of having achieved through patient diplomacy (as well as on account of America's predicament over Vietnam) much that Khrushchev had sought and failed to obtain with his pyrotechnics: what in 1973 appeared to be a lasting solution of the German problem; a nuclear arms control agreement on terms favorable to the USSR, as well as expanded economic and technological intercourse with the West. But the Soviets' suggestions about a joint front against China were rebuffed, as seen in Henry Kissinger's description of his interview in 1973 with Brezhnev: "He [Brezhnev] had found the Chinese treacherous, arrogant, beyond the human pale. . . . China's growing military might was a menace to everybody. Any military assistance to it by the United States would lead to war. . . . I warned that history proved America would not be indifferent to an attack on China."[30]

The United States for its part had sought a general understanding with the Soviet Union. Its first priority, however, was to induce Moscow to pressure Hanoi to agree to a settlement of the Vietnam War on terms that would allow Washington to claim it had secured peace with honor. The Kremlin's intercession was undoubtedly instrumental in making North Vietnam agree to a truce whose provisions fell quite short of what the United States had hoped to gain. The United States under the Paris agreements of January 1973 obtained the return of its prisoners, plus a face-saving but extremely fragile arrangement in the South. Enclaves of Vietcong rule and of North Vietnamese troops would remain on the latter's territory after American withdrawal. Predictably, the ramshackle arrangement—and with it the South Vietnamese government—would collapse within two years.

China, as signaled by President Nixon's visit in February 1972, achieved its aim of breaking out of political isolation. The Chinese leaders could now set at rest their fears of the Americans and the "social imperialists" (the Soviets, in Beijing's current parlance) ganging up on them. Though full diplomatic ties between the United States and the People's Republic would not be established until 1979, the two countries entered upon a relationship that would soon develop into an informal alliance. But whatever security this arrangement gave the People's Republic against a Soviet attack, it was purchased at the price of Beijing's ideological credibility.

And indeed, though this would not become obvious for some time, the fact that both the USSR and China had sought and achieved a rapprochement with the United States provided the most definitive proof and vivid demonstration to date of the obsolescence of the ideological premises of Communism. What happened to the cardinal tenet of Communist philosophy that only the advance of socialism and the elimination of capitalism could free the world from the scourge of war and lead to a durable peace? Here was the palpable evidence that shared ideology, if anything, helped precipitate the two Communist powers to the brink of war, and that in order to deflect that danger each of them was constrained to seek a rapprochement with the main capitalist power. The Soviet Union's status as a superpower would for quite a while continue to obscure its internal weaknesses and vulnerabilities. It would still be able to score points in the international arena, with U.S. foreign policy still reeling following Vietnam, the constitutional crisis, and the oil shock. But such gains would not be able to obscure the much more fundamental crisis of world Communism. With neither Moscow nor Beijing being able to reunite and revivify the movement, now torn by dissension and having lost a sense of mission, both regimes would have to stand or fall by their domestic records.

9

THE TRAVAILS OF
COEXISTENCE

IN AND BY ITSELF the Soviet-American détente, inaugurated officially by Nixon's visit to Moscow in 1972, proved to be of less than momentous significance. To be sure, apart from the agreements on concrete issues, Nixon and Brezhnev affixed their signatures to a document that promised to change drastically the nature of relations between the two superpowers. *Basic Principles of Mutual Relations Between the United States and the Union of Soviet Socialist Republics* stated that "in the nuclear age there is no alternative to conducting mutual relations on the basis of peaceful coexistence."[1] That incontrovertible truth was followed by a pledge that even states bound by the closest friendship would have found difficult to abide by: ". . . efforts to obtain unilateral advantages at the expense of the other, directly or indirectly, would be shunned by the United States and the Soviet Union as inconsistent with their new relationship."

Political analysts and practical politicians soon had reasons to question whether détente marked a sharp break with the past: the Middle Eastern crisis of 1973 ranged the USSR and the United States on the side of their respective clients, and though the moment of danger soon passed and both superpowers pushed their respective allies toward an accommodation, the whole affair demonstrated the fragility of the new relationship. Indeed, the next few years would witness the unraveling of détente. The Soviet Union would not deny itself the opportunity to seek "unilateral advantages" at the expense of the United States, profiting by the latter's domestic and foreign troubles in the wake of Watergate and Vietnam. The Soviets would continue collecting client states in the Third World: Angola, Ethiopia, Afghanistan, though at the same time Egypt's emancipation from Soviet influence and reconciliation with the United States would increasingly put in question the point of the entire game. In any case, to judge by concrete developments and policies, the international situation at the end of the decade would appear just as tense as it was before Nixon's visit to Moscow in 1972, before SALT I and the whole array of other bilateral treaties.

The main significance of Soviet-American détente did not lie, however, in its effect on the relationship of the two powers. That relationship would depend, no matter what any declaration of "basic principles of mutual relations" might proclaim, on the correlation of forces on the international scene, and each regime's perception of the other's internal cohesion. The importance of the 1972 Soviet and Chinese rapprochements with the United States lay to a great extent in the fact that they went far in making explicit what had long been implied in the Soviets', if not so much in China's, policies: the repudiation of militant Marxism. To be sure, that repudiation may well have been intended as a tactical maneuver rather than a permanent stance. But reasons that prompted the new posture of the Communist powers—the ineluctable facts of the nuclear age, and of the irreparable split in the Communist world—would with the passage of time, become only more self-evident and pressing.

Could Communism remain in power after jettisoning a crucial part of its ideological baggage? To most students of the movement, Communist or not, that question, prior to perestroika, would have appeared preposterous. Communist regimes, certainly not those of the Soviet Union and China, did not depend on ideological incantations to maintain themselves in power. Their strength lay in their unique understanding of the anatomy of politics, in their ability to manipulate the various levers of power: on the psychological side, propaganda; on the operative one, the secret police and the armed forces.

What happened under perestroika provides a vivid proof that those instruments of power at the disposal of a Communist regime by themselves were unable to save it from internal erosion. Those ideological incantations scorned by pragmatic politicians would be thus shown to have been vital in preserving the system as long as the rulers who recited them did so with some conviction. The time came when a critic of Communism could write, "I see present-day Soviet society as being marked . . . by ideological indifference and the cynical use of ideology as a convenient facade."[2] And very soon after that Andrei Sakharov wrote that the facade itself had collapsed. In one case the

regime felt constrained to admit the bankruptcy of Communist ideology; in another, China, the rulers, while granting the anachronism
of Marxism-Leninism as a guide to concrete policies, are still using
it as a rationale for their attempts to cling to power.

There are two ways of viewing this ideological retreat, which turned
into a rout. One is to record the fact that Communism was unable to
survive the surgical operation performed upon the movement to excise
Stalinism from its body—a procedure begun by Khrushchev and continued, after a long interval, under Gorbachev. Another explanation,
and one not inconsistent with the former, sees Communism as incapable of enduring *peaceful* competition with what it has traditionally
referred to as capitalism. In trying to describe what would be the likely
effects of Soviet-American détente in the early 1970s, a leading Soviet
publicist stressed that the rapprochement did not mean the end of
rivalry between the two systems. "There can be no question as to
whether the struggle between the two systems will or will not continue. That struggle is historically unavoidable." But détente was to
strip this rivalry of its elements of danger—". . . military confrontation,
an armaments race—and dangerous clashes"—and confine it to an
"ideological rivalry and competition in many spheres."[3] If that competition was to be *entirely* peaceful—and by the mid-eighties the
Kremlin would be persuaded that it had to be such—the alternative
was too dangerous—then it was a competition that Communism could
not win.

Why it was so was most dramatically illustrated by Eastern Europe
between 1968 and 1980. Ironically, this was the period when, outside
of Europe, Communism scored those successes to which we have just
referred. But in almost all such cases the successes of the Soviet Union
in gaining new clients were predicated on the use of armed force,
whether by the local revolutionaries with Moscow providing material
and political support, as in Vietnam, or through the Soviet bloc rushing
in an auxiliary armed force, as with the Cubans in Angola, or, finally,
through a massive military intervention by the USSR itself, as in
Afghanistan (which of course in the long run could hardly have been
qualified as a success). Eastern Europe, on the contrary, tested the
Soviet Union's ability to preserve through peaceful means the cohesion of the socialist camp, and beyond it the capacity of Communism
to endure peaceful coexistence. On both counts the Soviet Union
failed.

The year 1968 was a milestone in many ways. The Soviet invasion of Czechoslovakia, or, if one wants to be pedantic, intervention by the armed forces of the Warsaw Treaty Organization, had widespread reverberations, some of which became evident as late as twenty years later and which contributed to that elemental revulsion against Communism that in turn led to what still seems like the miraculous and almost instantaneous liberation of Eastern Europe in 1989–90. Superficially, Czechoslovakia in 1968 was but a repetition of the Hungarian drama of 1956. But in fact there were very significant differences. The Kremlin chose to intervene not in a situation where the Communist regime was in imminent danger of being overthrown, but where it *seemed* to be firmly in control and where, unlike on the previous occasion, there was not a veritable revolution, acts of violence against the local Communists and other symptoms of disarray, allegedly threatening to plunge Hungary into anarchy. In 1956 de-Stalinization was still in its initial stage following the Twentieth Party Congress. Moscow's move could be interpreted, if not excused, as being motivated by something approaching panic at the prospect of similar uprisings sweeping over all of Eastern Europe. Advice from Beijing strongly urged Soviet intervention. In 1968 the post-Stalin and post-Hungary pattern of intrabloc relations *appeared* to be firmly set. By invading Czechoslovakia, the Soviet Union was moving against reform and not, as the Kremlin believed, a revolution against Communism.

The Hungarian revolution and the manner in which it was repressed created a considerable shock in the West. The Czechoslovak drama led, on the other hand, to greater perturbances within the Communist world, and that for self-evident reasons: Moscow was cracking down on a "fraternal" regime that on several occasions had reiterated its loyalty to the Soviet Union. Alexander Dubček's regime, unlike Nagy's, did not propose to take the country out of the Warsaw Treaty Organization, nor was it on the point of giving up the Communist Party's monopoly of power.

What attracted relatively little attention in the West were the reverberations of the Prague Spring within the USSR. It was noted that there had been a minidemonstration in Red Square, the handful of participants protesting the invasion. There were other, not numerous, voices of protest. But as all the dissenters came from a small segment of the intelligentsia, they were assumed to be of little consequence. The majority of those Soviet people who gave it a thought, it was believed in the West and correctly so, held with their leaders that their armies' sacrifices in liberating Czechoslovakia imposed special obligations on the latter. But overt protest was but a tip of the iceberg. Some of the most orthodox members of the CPSU were later to reveal that the invasion of a fellow socialist country had troubled them greatly and contributed to their mounting revulsion against the ethos of the Brezhnev era. Stalin had been dead for fifteen years, and Stalin-like measures and the corresponding rhetoric emanating from the Kremlin could not fail to create unease among the new generation of Communists.

Quite apart from the Soviet intervention there was another, broader question illuminated by the Czechoslovak events. The invasion demonstrated that Soviet Communism in its Brezhnev version would not tolerate diversity. But even in theory, could Communism coexist with a pluralist society? The very expression "socialism with a human face," applied to what had been happening in Czechoslovakia during the first months of 1968, had ironic implications: there was something inhuman about Communism as hitherto practiced. But if, as went another ritualistic maxim of post-Stalin Soviet rhetoric, it was legitimate to pursue different paths to socialism, would the one followed by Dubček and his associates keep them within safe parameters, i.e., preserving the monopoly of power of the Communist Party? Once more we are back to Khrushchev's avowal as to his and his colleagues' state of mind when they decided that reforms were necessary in the wake of Stalin's death: "We were scared, really scared. We were afraid the thaw might unleash a flood . . . which could drown us . . . a tidal wave which would have washed away all the barriers and retaining walls of our society."

Well, Dubček and his associates were trying—and being partly pushed to it by events—to reform the most Stalinist of the East European regimes. An exemplary party member in the pre- and post-Stalin times, Alexander Dubček certainly did not conceive his mission to be that of presiding over the liquidation of Communism in Czechoslovakia. But as in the case with Gorbachev twenty years later, this loyal, even if reform-minded, follower of Marxism-Leninism would be pushed by the logic of the evolving situation to the point where the very essence of Communism was being threatened. When in 1988 Gorbachev was paying a visit to a still-Communist Czechoslovakia, a member of his entourage was asked what difference there was between perestroika and what had been happening during the Prague Spring. The Soviet spokesman's answer, if not exactly to the point, still contained an ironic insight: "Twenty years." Would Dubček, except for the Soviet intervention, have landed where Gorbachev would land almost a generation later: with the Communist Party and its power virtually disintegrating under his stewardship? Well, the Kremlin did not wait for the answer, and we today can give only a tentative one: Communism could not have retained the monopoly of power, but the chances of the Communist Party retaining a significant role in the life of society would have been immeasurably greater in 1968 than turned out to be possible in 1990. By postponing a radical cure, the Soviet regime made almost inevitable the current agony of Communism in the USSR and its death all over Eastern Europe.

The dilemma of Communism (and not only in Czechoslovakia) in trying to reform itself was excellently described by the man who upon its sudden but not unexpected death became his country's president. Writing in April 1968, with the Communist Party already under the new and liberal-minded leadership, Václav Havel stated very well the inherent limitations of reforms under one-party rule: ". . . democracy is a matter not of faith, but of *guarantees*. Even if we admit that the public 'competition of views' is the first condition, the most important means to and the natural result of democracy, its very essence—and the true source of our guarantees—is something else, namely public and legal *competition for power*."[4] Like Khrushchev in 1956, Dubček and his liberal-minded colleagues in 1968 were as yet light-years away from any notion of a multiparty system. In both cases progress and reform were equated with imparting a new spirit into the ruling party, transforming it from an oligarcho-bureaucratic institution into a forum for discussion, making it truly responsible to public opinion. Havel had some cogent notions on that count too: "I also consider as illusory the assumption that internal democratization of the leading party (willingness to tolerate something like internal party opposition) offers a sufficient guarantee of democracy. I hold this position not only because, in principle, the only democracy is one which applies equally to everybody, but also because it has been the bitter experience of every revolution that if the political group which takes over does not restore *control from outside* in time, it must sooner or later also lose its *own internal control* and begin, slowly but surely, to degenerate."[5]

Havel's tract, written in April 1968, is a testimony to the irrepressible pressure of events upon Communism. In 1965 no one throughout Eastern Europe would have dared or thought it useful to theorize about transition from the standard-model Communist society to a politically pluralist one. What was then the most that the countries within the Soviet Union's sphere in Eastern Europe could expect was the current status of Poland under Gomułka: the party retaining its monopoly of power; closely tied to but not closely supervised in its internal politics by the USSR; some latitude in controls over intellectual and artistic life. The case of Hungary in 1956 was an eloquent warning of how dangerous it was to aspire to go further. Then the fall of Khrushchev in 1964 was another signal that the era of reforms was over, insofar as the Soviet Union was concerned. And here Havel's plea, issued within a few months of the change of leadership of the Communist Party of Czechoslovakia, was a call for far-reaching reforms, not merely for democratization within the party, but for democracy, period.

The Brezhnev regime, while it put an end to de-Stalinization at home, placed no barriers to further liberalization elsewhere in the socialist camp, provided it was done cautiously and without impinging on the holy of holies: the special role and power of the Communist Party. Moderate reform was viewed by the Kremlin to be a safety valve rather than a prelude to further trouble. Sticking to the old ways of Stalinism was, by contrast, believed to be not only anachronistic, but fraught with danger. Prior to 1968, the Czechoslovak regime had shown itself retrograde. A gigantic statue of Stalin continued to impart something of the pre-1953 atmosphere to Prague long after similar monuments had been discreetly dismantled in other East European capitals. A diehard Stalinist, Antonin Novotný had stayed as both the first secretary and president, his regime laggard on such issues as rehabilitating the victims of the 1949–52 purges of the fictitious Titoists and "agents of American imperialists and Zionists." Pressures were building up, and after Brezhnev's visit to Prague in December 1967, the Soviets decided it was not in their interest to preserve the rule of the discredited satrap. In January 1968, Novotný was replaced as the head of the party by Alexander Dubček, and in March he was pushed out of the presidency.

The new leader's background bespoke his loyalty to the Soviet Union. A second-generation Communist, he had spent his childhood and early adolescence in the Soviet Union, his faith evidently unaffected by the grim reality of Stalin's Russia. After the war he moved steadily up the party ladder, becoming in 1963 the first secretary of its Slovak component. Still youthful (forty-six) at the time of his ascension to the leadership, he must have seemed both to his colleagues as well as to the Kremlin the right man to guide Czechoslovakia along the path of moderate reform.

The subsequent course of events showed Dubček and his associates not so much initiating reforms or having a clear conception of how, precisely, "socialism with a human face" could be institutionalized, but as driven by events. Once unleashed, the pent-up grievances and hitherto frustrated aspirations, especially those of the intelligentsia, pushed the leadership to dismantle the police-state features of the regime. The latter responded with vague formulas and promises that only whetted the intelligentsia's appetite for further and concrete democratization. The Action Program of the Communist Party, voted by its Central Committee in April, was more meaningful as an indictment of the regime's past practices than as a clear blueprint for the future. The document promised democratization, but immediately qualified this promise: "The Party realizes that ideological antagonists of socialism may try to abuse the process of democratization . . . bourgeois ideology can be challenged only in open ideological struggle before all of the people. . . . We trust that in such a struggle all sections of our society will contribute actively towards the victory of truth, which is on the side of socialism."[6] And so after twenty years of Communism the party still deemed it necessary to combat bourgeois ideology! And if during the twenty preceding years it had failed to prevail in that struggle, though employing methods going far beyond those of ideological persuasion, how could the good citizens of Czechoslovakia be confident that the truth was on the side of socialism?

Nor was the manifesto much more convincing when, even if infrequently, it promised concrete measures of liberation. "Legal norms must provide a more precise guarantee *of the freedom of speech*, minority opinions and interests (again within the framework of socialist laws and in harmony with the principle that decisions are taken in accordance with the will of the majority) . . . the constitutional freedom of movement, particularly that of travel abroad for our citizens, must be precisely guaranteed by the law."[7] Here again one might wonder how under the mechanics of the Communist state one could determine which was the majority opinion and which the minority. As for the promises of various freedoms, they were already amply guaranteed in writing in the Czechoslovak constitution, just as in those of other Communist states. The trick was how to make them a living reality within the context of a one-party state and with the Kremlin casting a wary eye at what had become a revolution of rising expectations.

And so for a few months of 1968 the little country became the testing ground of two propositions that held the key to the future of Communism not only in Czechoslovakia but everywhere. Could Communism reform itself, gain popular acceptance, and yet retain some distinctive characteristics of a world philosophy, demonstrating the viability of at least some tenets of Marxism-Leninism? And would the Kremlin allow the experiment to run its course, or would it, by intervening, reject the possibility of any middle ground between neo-Stalinism, as currently in force in the USSR, and a genuinely pluralist society?

The tragedy of Dubček and his like-minded associates lay in the fact that they firmly believed that such middle ground did in fact exist, and that the Soviet comrades would not interfere with their efforts to reach it. For Tito in 1948 the crucial problem had been that of power: was he or the Soviets going to run Yugoslavia? And to prevent Stalin from subverting his party, he had to resort to some of Stalin's methods. And the problem of power was also crucial in Gomułka's defiance of the Kremlin in 1956, not from the personal point of view as in Tito's case, but from a national one: it was Polish Communists who were to run their own country, not Russian Communists or their puppets. In both cases, as the intervening years have shown, the basic Communist structure of the state and society was not put in question: the Yugoslav and Polish regimes had become more tolerant, but their people remained unfree.

Unlike the other two leaders, Dubček and his colleagues placed reform, even though they may not have had a clear conception of what it would involve, ahead of the question of power. This was their great merit, but at the same time it proved to be a debilitating weakness. They launched upon reforms without first making secure their domination of the party and the state. They allowed diehard Stalinists and opportunists, ready to move whenever signaled by Moscow, to retain important positions within the leadership. And when the showdown approached, they did not, like the Yugoslavs and Poles on the previous occasions, impress the Kremlin with their determination to fight rather than yield.

The Czechoslovak drama was a predecessor of perestroika in yet some other respects. To be sure, the national problem as it appeared in 1968 was but a pale preview of the gravity and complexity of the one that confronts the USSR today. But the task of reform was still further hindered and complicated by the growing volume of Slovak aspirations to greater political autonomy, demands that were exploited by the enemies of reform and those who were behind them. The surfacing of this problem was thus an added challenge both to the system and to those who would reform it.

Even more central to the task of healing society, and again a harbinger of what would become *the* problem of Communism in its terminal phase in the 1990s and in every country under its tottering rule, was the problem of the economy. Czechoslovakia's record on this count was better than that of any other European Communist state with the possible exception of East Germany. Its economy was well balanced between industry and agriculture. Its standard of living was considerably higher than that of the Fatherland of Socialism. But in its program of action the new leadership acknowledged how Communism had failed to deliver on that count as well: "We still lag some thirty-forty percent behind advanced Western countries . . . despite the successes we can exhibit, the state of our economy does not correspond to the situation of an industrially advanced country more than twenty years after the war. There is still a shortage of some types of goods, both retail and those for the supply of enterprises. . . . The volume of unfinished projects is growing, and the environment in which the working people are living, laboring, doing their purchasing, commuting to work, is getting worse or is improving only slowly."[8]

The authors, good Communists that they were, could not bring themselves to blame the growing difficulties of their economy on the inherent flaws of the economic theory derived from Marxism-Leninism. Thus we have the two contradictory statements separated by a single paragraph: "The problem lies above all in the unsuitable structure of our economy. . . . We have failed to take advantage of the superiority of socialist development."[9]

By the 1980s, economic stagnation and the resulting low standard of living, as compared with the West, were to become acknowledged by virtually all Communist regimes. Even before, China was to abandon what might be called Marxist-Leninist fundamentalism in favor of encouraging private enterprise and the profit motive—a startling reversal for the regime that until Mao's death kept denouncing the Soviet economy for its allegedly capitalist characteristics. But until perestroika the masters of the Kremlin kept congratulating themselves on the advantages of their planning and centralization of economic life as against capitalism, chronically plagued by inflation and unemployment. It is all the more instructive and striking how already in 1968 the Czechoslovak reformers focused on the cardinal deficiencies of the Soviet-type economy: its built-in inability to keep up with the technological progress of the second Industrial Revolution, the overemphasis on the quantitative aspect of industrial production, and the overcentralized and bureaucratized structure that leaves little room for individual initiative and innovations. The economic guide on Dubček's team, Ota Šik, stated those conclusions in language virtually identical to that employed by Gorbachev's economic advisers when they belatedly launched their program of economic renewal, and retreat from the obsolete verities of "scientific socialism": ". . . development based on industrial expansion and mobilizing fresh manpower carries with it the built-in risk of stagnation. . . . That is why a large part of our working force finds itself operating in an increasingly bad environment, using obsolescent techniques . . . even the newly constructed plants fall short of the highest technological standards."[10]

In 1968 it took some foresight to see the harm that would be done by the traditional Communist approach to economic management, what the unanimous chorus of Soviet economists in the late 1980s would denounce as the "command administrative" system of economy. At that time Soviet industry and that of the other members of the socialist camp could still boast of high rates of growth; the USSR's production of steel and of some other basic industrial products would soon overcome that of the United States. But the Czechoslovak party's blueprint for reforms already called for changing the emphasis from central controls to individual initiative and the free market. The inefficiency of the Soviet-type organization of agriculture, i.e., of the reliance on cooperative and state farms, had long been acknowledged in the Communist world, though ideological considerations would, except in the case of China, keep the system limping along for some time to come. But on other sectors of the economy, the Czech reformers were uninhibited in their criticism: "Neither the standard form of productive forces, nor the character of work in services . . . warrants the present high degree of centralization in their management and organization, which involves quite unnecessary administration and burdens the services with inexpedient costs."[11] And a plea for what must be the key measure in revivifying and modernizing the stagnant economies: letting market forces rather than an administrative fiat fix prices. "The present system of retail prices is markedly divorced from the costs of production, gives an incorrect orientation to the structure of personal consumption of the population—including the consumption of food—and reduces the possible level of satisfying their requirements. . . . Rational price relations cannot be fixed and proclaimed by State authority: it is necessary to enable market forces to influence their creation."[12]

In Moscow the Action Program promulgated by the Czechoslovak Central Committee must have aroused mixed feelings. On its face there was little in it that should have aroused the undue apprehensions of the Kremlin. The Czech Communists were belatedly moving in the direction of liberalizing their system without abandoning their deference toward the Soviet Union and the unique role of their party. The part of the program touching on international relations was carefully phrased so as not to offend the sensitivites of the Soviet comrades. Czechoslovak foreign policy would remain based on "alliance and cooperation with the Soviet Union and the other socialist states. . . . We shall strive . . . to continue on the basis of mutual respect, to intensify sovereignty, and equality and international solidarity."[13] The Prague reformers proposed to depart from what had been the Soviet model of economic organization and planning. But Hungary had already considerably modified that pattern without arousing any special Soviet apprehensions or protests. The program spoke about expanding economic relations with the capitalist countries and in general about improving relations with them in the spirit of peaceful coexistence. But here again Romania had gone quite far in that direction, not to mention its flirtation with China, and the USSR, while not happy about it, had refrained from any steps against, or even a polemic with, Bucharest. What was it then that bothered Moscow about Czechoslovakia, and why already by April and May was the Soviet Union issuing ominous, if as yet veiled, warnings to Dubček and his associates?

What clearly concerned Moscow was the climate of the Prague Spring: the atmosphere of euphoria and expectation that permeated large sections of the Czech and Slovak populations, and the currents of public opinion that were pushing the regime to go beyond the cautious blueprint of political reform sketched in the Action Program. After its bitter experience with what the new team in the Kremlin dubbed as Khrushchev's "harebrained schemes," the Soviet oligarchs were deeply distrustful of anything that smacked of spontaneity and populism. Part of the reason they tolerated Romania's insubordinate behavior in foreign policy was the fact that for all his departures from what Moscow considered as the straight and narrow path of proletarian internationalism, Ceaușescu was firmly in control of his party and country. There was no question of a challenge to Communism in Romania. The Czechoslovak situation, on the other hand, threatened to get out of hand.

Moscow's political hypochondria was enhanced by the overall situation in the Soviet bloc. Albania persisted in its sullen anti-Soviet attitude. (The Hoxha regime, allied with China, would become sorely disillusioned by its protector's rapprochement with the United States, and by the end of the 1970s would denounce both Communist powers for their betrayal of Marxism-Leninism and for hobnobbing with the American imperialists.) Romania was another ex-satellite which, benefiting by the Sino-Soviet dispute, had thrown off Moscow's control of its foreign policy. It continued its membership in the Warsaw Treaty Organization, but otherwise its regime's position on international issues was not much different from that of Tito's Yugoslavia.

Ever since 1956, i.e., since its repudiation of Stalinism, the Kremlin had kept reiterating that it was permissible for other Communist countries to follow different paths to socialism than that taken by the Soviet Union. In practical language this translated into "We don't care how you resolve your economic and other problems as long as you don't let power slip out of the hands of the party and as long as you remain loyal to the USSR." But despite the Dubček regime's careful observation of such strictures—and indeed at no time in 1968–69 was there any sign of the new leader or his closest advisers having the slightest intention of defying the USSR or seeking a multiparty democracy—the Kremlin intermittently feared that the path it had taken would lead it eventually into a morass of a political crisis that would threaten not only Czechoslovak Communism but the cohesion of other East European regimes.

Superficially, it might have seemed that the Kremlin ought to have rejoiced in the popularity of the new leadership of a fraternal Communist party, a popularity such as had not been enjoyed by it for twenty years.[14] But by now Moscow could have had few illusions left about the possibility of any of its vassal regimes succeeding in gaining, and especially retaining, popular support.

Poland was a point in question. Gomułka's return to the leadership in 1956 had been even more welcomed and acclaimed than the ascent of Dubček and other liberals to the top posts in Czechoslovakia. And indeed for about two years Gomułka had justified Soviet hopes and the Poles' expectations: Eastern Europe witnessed a hitherto unusual situation—a Communist government not only at peace, but genuinely popular with its own people and yet irreproachably loyal to the USSR. But beginning in 1958 this idyllic picture began to change rapidly for the worse. Gomulka's credit with his own people was being exhausted, the one-time national hero revealing himself more and more as a narrow-minded and irascible bureaucrat and ideologue. Once in power, the fervent advocate of the "Polish way to socialism" (which, except for freedom from compulsory collectivization, had never been defined), became a conservative in the Moscow mold. The Polish economy continued to be run according to the Soviet model and thus remained minimally responsive to the needs of the consumer. Neither Khrushchev (who retrospectively considered his acquiescence in Gomułka's return to power as one of his outstanding achievements) nor Brezhnev could complain about Poland's foreign policy; it followed faithfully the Soviets' guidance—for example, when it broke off relations with Israel following the Six-Day War in 1967. By the mid-1960s, Gomułka had forfeited the support he had once enjoyed among the intelligentsia, with controls over intellectual life becoming almost as rigorous as before the Polish October of 1956.

Characteristic of the regime's growing intolerance and of its now voluntary subservience to Moscow was its closing of the production of *Dziady* ("Forefathers' Eve"), a nineteenth-century classic of Polish literature. The play, with its bitter indictment of tsarist Russia's oppression of Poland, was believed by the authorities, and not without reason, likely to make its audiences reflect on more recent facets of Soviet-Polish relations. But as often happens in such cases, this clumsy measure of intellectual repression had an effect opposite to that intended: a wave of protests and manifestations swept the country, many of them going beyond the issue of censorship and aimed against the regime's overall policies.

The Polish case was demonstrating the inherent difficulty, at least in Eastern Europe, of a lasting reconciliation between Communist reality and popular aspirations. Or to put it more vividly, the government and the people had lost patience with each other. For the former it appeared both puzzling and impermissible that the bulk of its people should not acquiesce in its rule, remain grateful that they no longer had to live under Stalinism and put up with the Soviet Union's direct interference in the affairs of their country. By the same token, for the majority of the people, especially the intelligentsia and the young, the government had forfeited their respect. They had greeted the Polish October enthusiastically because they believed the new leaders would steer the nation along the path of democracy. Instead, all that appeared to have changed was that the old Communist repressive practices bore the label "Made in Poland" in place of the former "Made in Moscow."

Confronted with this impasse and perhaps encouraged by some circles in the USSR, some party activists had recourse to demagoguery. Apart from any moral considerations, the preaching of anti-Semitism seemed to be preposterously incongruous for a country that as a consequence of the Holocaust and postwar emigration had only some 30,000 Jews in a population of 31 million. But as people of Jewish origin had occupied important posts in the pre-1956 government and party and now many were among the leading dissidents and critics on the political scene, anti-Semitism appeared, to the unscrupulous within the leadership, to be an effective way to deflect popular discontent from the ruling party. The Jews were being blamed for both the repression under Stalinism and for the current, allegedly unrealistic and dangerous (because they might bring Soviet intervention) demands for democratization and intellectual freedom. Such incongruities did not perturb the advocates of intolerance, who saw these tactics as the means of the party regaining a foothold among the masses. Several Communist notables objected to this transparent demagoguery, so inconsistent with the stated principles of Marxism. Others tried, as was currently the fashion in the Soviet Union, to obscure the racist character of the campaign by protesting that their criticism was directed against the Zionists and others allegedly estranged from the national values, rather than the generality of people of Jewish extraction. In any event, there was a purge not only of the remaining Jewish officials, but also of many of those failing the racial test in the professions and academic life. Some of the oligarchs, notably the minister of the interior, Mieczysław Moczar, and the party boss of Silesia, Edward Gierek, sought to link the assault on "Zionism" with an attempt to unseat Gomułka, who though constrained finally to join in the campaign did so in a halfhearted and obviously embarrassed manner.

The anti-Jewish gambit proved of no help to the regime. Having previously lost popularity, it now gambled away the residue of respect it had gained because of Gomułka's and his associates' (some of whom, repelled by such tactics, now left public life) courageous stand in 1956. Student demonstrations and protests among the intellectuals continued throughout the spring of 1968. Symptomatic of society's rejection of the system and, in startling contrast to the popular attitudes of 1956, also of the faith in the possibility of its regeneration, was the high incidence of dissidence among the children of the Polish *nomenklatura*, the most privileged segment of university youth. This in turn led to the dismissals from office and other acts directed against their parents. The Polish path to socialism had been tried and found wanting, and Gomułka, its would-be standard bearer was now greatly discredited in the eyes of both the party activists and the public. But he would retain nominal leadership of Polish Communism for another two and a half years, mainly because of Soviet support. Enfeebled like its leader, the regime survived the crisis, largely for a similar reason— the implicit threat of Soviet intervention.

The Polish turmoil was of considerable importance to the fortunes of "proletarian internationalism." It had an important bearing on Soviet apprehensions about what was going on at the same time in Czechoslovakia. More fundamentally, it posed once more the question that had been repeatedly asked ever since Tito had defied Stalin in 1948: was Communism capable of reforming itself? Since then all such efforts—Tito's, Khrushchev's, Nagy's, and now Gomułka's—had failed, and the would-be reformers, after a Sisyphus-like uphill struggle, were constrained or forced to let their societies slip back into a neo-Stalinist mold.

The underlying dilemma was stated tersely by a proponent of the Prague Spring: "Is the Communist Party still able to resolve questions concerning the state and the nation in accordance with the ground rules of European politics that have been valid since the French Revolution? That is to say, is it still able, first, to ascertain the will of the people and to respect the sovereignty of the people as the source of all power in the state, standing above personalities and institutions, the Communist Party itself not excluded?"[15]

Well, Communism had always paid lip service to democracy and popular sovereignty. But by the second half of the twentieth century, what had been slogans had become concrete conditions of a properly functioning society. The Communist state had been an efficient machine of repression, enabling its self-perpetuating oligarchy to hold on to power. By 1968 political freedom could be seen as more than just a slogan or an ideal: it was becoming an imperative condition of a country's social and economic progress. Modern technology and communications were making it increasingly difficult for a repressive political system to elicit its people's creative energies and to satisfy their material, not to mention spiritual and political, wants and aspirations. What was the insight of some of the Czech and Slovak reformers in 1968 would become by the 1980s a commonplace and a basic premise of the makers of Soviet perestroika: the argument for democratization does not have to rely solely on solemn invocations of human rights and dignity; it has to do also with the quality of the environment, with the quality and adequate supply of consumer goods, with widespread use of computers and similarly prosaic but crucial problems.

Could Communist power be reconciled with the logic of modernization? Ivan Sviták, the writer we've quoted, kept probing that question: "The Communist Party is faced with a critical dilemma: to win over millions of people to its perspective of democratic socialism, or to retain 100,000 persons in their official posts? Will the Communists regard the Party as a political party of the people? . . . Or will they regard it as a power apparatus designed to use any means at its disposal in order to uphold naked power over the masses that have no rights? . . . Is the Communist Party able in the final analysis to change from a military bureaucratic organization into a civilian party that respects fundamental human rights . . . ?"[16]

The author, who had been expelled from the Communist Party and now considered himself an independent Marxist, concluded that the task of renovation and modernization could not be accomplished by democratization only *within* the Communist Party. The party, if seriously committed to reform, had to take its chances on genuinely free elections to the legislature, i.e., elections open to other movements. "The road toward power and toward the leading role in this nation of ours travelled by the Czechoslovak Communist Party's Central Committee can be travelled only via a properly elected parliament; today everything else is compromised as a fraud."[17]

Sviták's views were hardly representative of even the most radically inclined members of the Dubček circle. Neither the first secretary nor his reform-minded associates conceived their role as that of presiding over the liquidation of Communist rule in Czechoslovakia. But the Soviet observers of the events there, as well as nervous officials in other "fraternal" countries, could be excused for seeing the aberrant

Communist's demands as portents of what was likely to happen—unless the dangerous course of reforms was stopped before it could affect the character and the dominant role of the Communist Party.

Those foreign Communist notables had to take even more seriously another reform manifesto. Authored by a novelist, Ludwík Vaculík, whose unorthodoxy in 1967 had earned him expulsion from the party, it had been cosigned by a number of prominent intellectuals, people in public life as well as ordinary workers. The article, titled "2,000 Words to Workers, Farmers, Scientists, Artists, and Everyone," contained a scathing indictment of the Communist Party's past. "The Communist Party, which after the war possessed the great trust of the people, gradually exchanged this trust for offices until it had all the offices and nothing else. . . . The main guilt and the greatest deception perpetrated by these rulers was that they presented their arbitrary rule as the will of the workers."[18] Without attacking the current party leadership, the manifesto urged continuous pressure on the party so that it would have to cleanse its ranks of remaining doctrinaires and conservatives. Hence the need to organize action committees at every level and in every community to watch over actions of the officials—a call for an alternative structure of political power.

What must have aroused special interest in Moscow was the reference in "2,000 Words" to the possibility of armed Soviet intervention. At the time the broadside appeared (the end of June), the Warsaw Treaty Organization had concluded military maneuvers in Czechoslovakia, and Soviet army units left the country. But "2,000 Words" was explicit on the subject that hitherto had not been publicly broached: ". . . the recent great apprehension results from the possibility that foreign forces may interfere with our internal development. Faced with all those superior forces, the only thing we can do is to hold our own and not start anything. We can assure our government that we will back it—with weapons if necessary, as long as it does what we give it the mandate to do."[19]

Sviták's articles and Vaculík's broadside were signs that the pervasive movement for democratization was assuming a momentum of its own. This was noted in the USSR, where an authoritative spokesman chose to treat "2,000 Words" as a call for the overthrow of the Communist regime. "[The authors of '2,000 Words'] speak on behalf of the reactionary antisocialist forces . . . which are attacking the CCP [the Czechoslovak Communist Party] and the working class."[20] And the writer was fairly explicit as to what might happen should antisocialist activities and writings continue unchecked: "Such tactics are not new. They were resorted to by the counterrevolutionary elements in Hungary which in 1956 sought to undermine the socialist institutions of the Hungarian people. Now, twelve years later, the tactics of those who would like to undermine the foundations of socialism in Czechoslovakia are even more subtle and insidious."

The leadership, though it repudiated what it dubbed the extremists' demands, found it could neither dissipate the Soviets' suspicion nor reassure its own people that the pace of reforms would not slacken. Could Dubček have maneuvered successfully between his people's anticipations and the Soviets' threats? Perhaps; had he been more decisive, he might have impressed the Soviets as one who would not let the democratization movement get out of hand, while at the same time convincing his people that he would not compromise the essence of the reforms for fear of the Russians. But strangely enough for a man of his experience, Dubček proved rather naive in gauging the Kremlin's reactions and somewhat passive when it came to asserting his leadership. "Sitting at the head of the large table, Alexander Dubček more or less attentively followed the ever-thickening goulash of opinion that such debates [between the top officials of the party] always created. He let things democratically take their course until even he felt the comrades had completely unburdened themselves, and then he would recite his credo: what we must do above all is concentrate our forces on the positive tasks."[21] Alas, the situation called for some "negative" measures: if Dubček wanted to reassure public opinion, he should have purged the leadership of its still considerable component of enemies of reform; if he meant to allay the suspicions of the Kremlin and to impress it, he ought to have shown himself to be more in control of the situation. The only East European leaders who had challenged the Kremlin and gotten away with it were men of the dictatorial mien: most notably, Tito, Ceauşescu, and Albania's Enver Hoxha. Gomułka did exhibit similar characteristics in 1956, but within a few years lapsed into subservience to the USSR.

Reference to "positive tasks" brings into view another rather troublesome aspect of the various attempts to reform Communism. For the most part, the term "reforms" was applied to the *removal* of some noxious and/or impractical features of Communism as hitherto practiced. Tito put an end to the Soviet Union's protectorate over Yugoslavia; Khrushchev discontinued the most repressive features of Stalinism. Gomułka for a while stopped the Soviets' interference in

Poland's internal affairs. In each case the emphasis was on removing the objectionable features of the status quo rather than on fresh initiatives that would open new vistas of social and economic progress. The reformers' case had always been that, freed from its unnatural, mostly Stalinist excrescences, Communism would reveal what its fathers and countless followers for over a century had intended it to be: a scientific approach to coping with modern society and, at the spiritual and political level, a liberating philosophy of life. Yet the evidence of what might be called constructive attempts to remold Communist societies had not been impressive: terror and the most doctrinaire policies were gone, but the essential characteristics of the police state and of the ubiquitous bureaucratic rule remained. Hence the conviction, shared at both ends of the political spectrum, by both the proponents of democracy and the diehard conservatives, that the liberal model of Communism—"socialism with a human face"—was a mirage. Real democratization of the Communist regime would almost inevitably lead to its eventual dissolution. Those Communists who urged far-reaching reforms were the gravediggers of Marxism-Leninism.

In 1968 such a verdict would still have been premature. The Czech-Slovak reformers were confident that, given time and Soviet understanding, they could work out a new form of populistic Communism free from the evil practices of the past but preserving a vital and leading role for the party. With our own hindsight in 1991, it is arguable that it would have been in the Soviet interest to allow the experiment to proceed. It had a better chance of succeeding in Czechoslovakia than elsewhere. And even if eventually the sacrosanct principle of the Communist Party's monopoly of power would have had to yield to political pluralism, what did the Soviet Union have to lose? The old formula of proletarian internationalism had broken down. In China all power was being wielded by the Communists (even if the party apparatus itself was currently in a shambles). Yet, short of an actual war, Moscow's relations with Beijing could not have been worse. Czechoslovakia, allowed to work out its own destiny, would assuredly have remained a loyal ally of the Soviet Union and a member of the Warsaw Treaty Organization, as would other members of the Soviet bloc in Eastern Europe, should a similar evolution take place elsewhere.

We can assume that there were voices within the Kremlin urging patience and moderation in dealing with the reformers and stressing the possible damage to the international image of both Communism and the Soviet Union should the latter move in with armed force. Except for the trouble with China, the USSR was in a very favorable situation both objectively and vis-à-vis the capitalist world. Its economy was growing at a pace surpassing that of the West. It had about put an end to U.S. nuclear superiority. The United States was hopelessly embroiled in Southeast Asia; the entire Atlantic alliance was experiencing considerable strains. As a matter of fact, for the West, 1968 was the year of its own version of the Cultural Revolution; not only in the United States, but also in France and West Germany the young appeared to have risen in a massive revolt against the establishment. At the time, this revolt was taken much more seriously than its consequences have justified: it was the traditional codes of morals rather than the capitalist system that cracked under the strain of what the Marxists would call "the inherent contradictions of bourgeois society." The crisis of the West, most notably the consequences of the Vietnam imbroglio in the United States, tended to obscure the memory of the Soviets' foreign-policy discomfitures, such as the brutal repression of Hungary in 1956 and the quite recent embarrassment in the wake of the Middle Eastern war. The USSR was then in a favorable position: its indulgence toward Czechoslovakia, toward its Warsaw Pact partners in general, would not have been interpreted as resulting from weakness, but rather as denoting statesmanship and self-confidence.

Against such considerations, there had been counterarguments, going back practically to Dubček's assumption of power, pleading that unless promptly arrested, the sequence of events in Czechoslovakia would lead to ominous reverberations throughout the entire Socialist bloc and perhaps even in the Soviet Union. Much of that pressure came from the bosses of the "fraternal countries," notably from East Germany's Walter Ulbricht and Poland's Gomułka (who, at the time, as we have seen, had special reasons to be concerned about untoward events anywhere in the bloc). They expostulated with their Kremlin colleagues that the reform euphoria in Czechoslovakia was having a demoralizing effect on their own people, especially on the young. If not stopped in time, the entire affair would lead to a counterrevolution all over Eastern Europe. Criticisms and warnings about the course taken by the Dubček leadership were already voiced at the March 23 meeting of the representatives of the Soviet and five Eastern European parties. That the meeting was called expressly to censor the Czechoslovaks was evident from the absence of the Romanian Communists, who refused throughout to join in any attempt to discipline the aberrant party, holding it as impermissible interference in the internal affairs of a sovereign country. Hungary's delegates, though attending the conference, were more nuanced in their stance than the now rabidly antireform Ulbricht and Gomułka: Kádár's regime was following its own path to socialism insofar as its economic policy was concerned, and its political course was also more relaxed than in the other "fraternal states."

Within four months, warnings and criticism gave way to threats. Another conclave, this time of the leaders of the Soviet Union and of its closest partners in the socialist camp (Bulgaria, Hungary, the GDR, and Poland), held in Warsaw, addressed on July 18 an open letter to the Central Committee of the Czech and Slovak comrades. The key sentence in the letter did not need an elaboration: "Never will we consent to allow imperialism, *whether by peaceful* or non-peaceful means, *from within* or without, to make a breach in the socialist system and change the balance of power in Europe in its favor."[22] (My italics.) But what was it that the signatories, headed by Brezhnev, found so menacing in what the Czechoslovak authorities were doing, or, more precisely, not doing? Here again the letter is quite explicit. The Communist world, the document states, had supported Prague's drive to reform the system. "We do not appear before you as representatives of yesterday who would want to hinder your correction of errors and shortcomings, including the violation of socialist legality that had taken place."[23] But all that was on the assumption that "your party, keeping a firm hold on the levers of power, would direct the whole process in the interests of socialism without allowing anti-Communist reactionaries to exploit it for their own purposes."[24]

When it comes to concrete charges and grievances, the defenders of Marxist-Leninist orthodoxy are much less explicit. It is only halfheartedly that the document insinuates that the "German revanchists" from the Federal Republic may be in cahoots with some elements in Czechoslovakia. Equally unsubstantiated are allegations that the various clubs and organizations that had sprung up in the wake of the change in leadership had become "headquarters for the forces of reaction."

What emerges from the verbose content of the threatening harangue is that the Czechoslovak Communists had sinned mainly by dismantling censorship and licensing freedom of speech, and to a great extent also that of the press. This was then the central issue in the whole anti-Prague campaign. The party, which in word and action was loyal to the USSR in its foreign policy, unlike that of Romania's, following faithfully in the footsteps of the Soviet Union, was being put on trial because it had failed to curb the free flow of information and opinion. By the summer the little country had become the focal point of hectic diplomatic and propaganda activity. Foreign rulers journeyed to what could already be described as an embattled state: some, like Marshal Tito, to encourage the Prague regime in its stance; others, like Ulbricht, to implore it to change its ways. The most appropriate hint and advice came from Hungary's Kádár, who allegedly told Dubček: "Don't you know with what kind of people you're dealing?" The leading Communist parties in the West, notably the Italian and the French, warned Moscow against repeating its 1956 Hungarian gambit. So did a number of prestigious and long-standing Soviet sympathizers in the West.

By the middle of July the Kremlin must have felt that the case for intervention was very strong. Moscow could tolerate, though with considerable distaste and bad humor, Romania's independent behavior in foreign policy, for in his domestic policy Ceauşescu ran a tidy totalitarian state. Finland could be permitted to retain democracy because it had not been a Communist state. But the breakdown of the system in Czechoslovakia might start an epidemic. In Eastern Europe the domino theory was a very reasonable conjecture.

Still, there must have been considerable hesitation and divided counsels in Moscow, obviously having to do with the timing and mechanics of intervention. Some in the Politburo very likely argued that the invasion be deferred until such time as the Dubček regime, pushed to the wall by escalating popular demands, would itself ask for Soviet help. And then how would Czechoslovakia have to be run if and when . . .? Would it require a straightforward Soviet military occupation or could one find a Czechoslovak Kádár? There was no lack of candidates for the latter role. Dubček had not been able to get rid of all the enemies of reform within the upper levels of the party and government apparatus, and some of them were notorious for their special ties to Moscow. But by the same token, would such a person be acceptable to, or rather be tolerated, by the party and the country? It is important to note how with the passage of time the Soviet leadership had become less self-assured and more hesitant to assert its rule of the Communist bloc by an act of force. In 1968 the Soviet

Union was much stronger, militarily and industrially, than in 1956, but it was now weighing the pros and cons of military intervention much more carefully than it had before its invasion of Hungary.

It was in order to gauge the chances of the little country offering armed resistance and to test the cohesion of the Czechoslovak leadership that the Kremlin, following the Warsaw letter, sought a meeting between the Politburos of the two parties. After some sparring as to the location of the meeting, whether it should take place on Soviet or Czechoslovak soil, it was agreed to meet in the Slovak border town of Čierna on the Tisza.

What actually transpired at the meeting can be characterized as the exact opposite of the official communiqué's description of its atmosphere of "complete frankness, sincerity and mutual understanding." To be sure, there was some frankness on the Soviet notables' part: they criticized various aspects of the Prague Spring, and there were opprobrious personal attacks on some of the leading reformers (thus a Soviet Politburo member referred caustically to the fact that one of them present at the meeting, Francis Kriegel, was of Jewish origin). But eventually the Moscow delegation professed to be satisfied by their hosts' professions of good faith. Another Communist summit meeting a few days later in Bratislava (this time with the leaders of four other parties, signatories of the Warsaw letter) put another seal of apparent approval on the Czechoslovak reforms. On their return to Prague, Dubček and his colleagues shared their illusions with the public: the Soviet colleagues had been reassured, reforms would continue, all was well at the Communist Olympus.

In fact, Brezhnev and his lieutenants had good reasons to be satisfied by the Čierna and Bratislava meetings but for reasons quite different from those imagined by Dubček. The Soviets confirmed their impression that the recalcitrant party's leadership was split and that there were high Czech and Slovak officials who would lend themselves to their purposes. And if the leadership was not firmly united behind Dubček's policies, it was very likely that there would be no armed resistance when the Soviets invaded. As one of those in the forefront of reforms was to recollect: "Let me impress on you one important factor which ten years after the Prague Spring tends to be more and more forgotten. The Dubček leadership was *never* united. It always contained a strong group of conservatives who would simply not hear it mentioned that our reforms might lead to a conflict with Moscow. Dubček himself was absolutely convinced that none of the proposed changes could be brought to fruition unless we carried the Russians with us. . . . The last thing we wanted to do was to challenge the Soviet leadership."[25]

If not the Čierna, then certainly the Bratislava meeting was a smoke screen: by August 3 the Warsaw Pact forces were in a position to strike while the assembled leaders of the five "fraternal" parties were beguiling the Dubček team with their assurances of friendship and understanding. In the short interval before the actual strike, Romania's Ceauşescu and Hungary's Kádár visited the unfortunate country and tried to convey to Dubček the gravity of the situation. But despite all the portents, hints, and warnings, the first secretary remained incredulous: he had lived among the Russians and he simply could not believe that they would perpetrate an act at once so brutal and senseless.

On the night of August 20–21, the forces of the Warsaw Pact countries (with the exception of Romania) or, more precisely, a Soviet army of some 400,000 with token detachments from Poland, the GDR, Bulgaria, and Hungary launched an invasion of the little country of 14 million people. From the military point of view the occupation proceeded smoothly; there was no organized armed resistance and few actual clashes between the Russian soldiers and the population. It was mostly the young who demonstrated against, and in a very few cases fought, the invaders. The total number of those killed in such actions was below one hundred. On the other hand, there was a large-scale passive resistance, the attitude of the population toward the intruders at once scornful and defiant. The invasion followed, according to the official Soviet statement, an appeal for help from the fraternal countries by unnamed Czechoslovak party and government leaders. And, indeed, a number of high officials had known in advance about the invasion and stood ready to collaborate with the Soviets. But such was the general revulsion at the coup that the collaborators did not dare to identify themselves before their people. Dubček and several of his progressive colleagues on the Czechoslovak Presidium-Politburo were seized literally at gunpoint. But the Soviet authorities' attempt to launch a new "revolutionary," i.e., puppet, government à la Kádár's in 1956 broke down both because of the prospective leaders' fears and because of President Ludwík Svoboda's courageous refusal to heed the invaders' demands.

The scene now shifted to Moscow, where Dubček and the other kidnapped leaders, provisionally released from captivity, engaged in negotiations with the Soviet Politburo as to the exact form of capitulation by their regime. Bullied by the Soviets and pressured by their conservative colleagues who joined them for the negotiations,[26] they finally agreed to a partial surrender: they would be allowed to resume their posts, but had to promise to crack down on the "antisocialist forces." The Soviet army would stay in Czechoslovakia until the situation was "normalized." As the official communiqué on "Soviet-Czechoslovak talks held in Moscow from August 23 to 26" humorlessly stated, "The allied countries' troops that temporarily entered Czechoslovak territory will not interfere in the internal affairs of the Czechoslovak Socialist Republic."[27]

The negotiations, if they can be described as such, threw some interesting light on the Soviet leaders' current attitudes on international affairs, and toward "fraternal" parties. A liberal Czech leader who participated in that weird exercise recalls the scene. "Brezhnev was personally and sincerely angered that Dubček had betrayed his trust by not having every step he took approved beforehand in the Kremlin."[28] The Soviet general secretary also asserted, according to the same source, that the USSR would defend the integrity of the Communist bloc in Europe even at the risk of a general war. At the same time, he pooh-poohed any possibility of outside support for a maverick Communist regime. President Johnson, said Brezhnev mendaciously, had assured him prior to the invasion that the United States would not become involved. "You are counting on the Communist movement in Western Europe, but that won't amount to anything for fifty years,"[29] added the Soviet leader.

And so the defeated exponents of "socialism with a human face" were allowed to return to their country and their party and government posts, acutely aware that they were now on probation and not only in regard to their official positions. One of them, in a broadcast to the nation, tried to communicate the sense of the recent events: "Our country was suddenly submerged by a gigantic storm that it was impossible and hopeless for us to face with the means at our disposal. . . . It is the tragedy of a small nation whose country is located in a particularly sensitive region of our continent. . . . It is also the tragedy of an effort toward social renewal."[30]

The speaker then summarized what would be the practical consequences of the rape. "We shall have to take special measures in the field of radio, television and the press to prevent writings against foreign policy requirements and the interests of the republic. In the domain of liberty of associations the required measures will lead to the dissolution of political clubs and to a ban on the formation of new political parties. For this the government will avail itself of certain special powers."[31]

The incongruous situation of the authors of the Prague Spring now presiding over its liquidation could not be sustained for long. It was thought unwise to make martyrs of the leading reformers, so after being dismissed as first secretary in April 1969, Dubček was for a short while given jobs of purely nominal importance before being finally consigned to private life. Similar tactics were followed in regard to most of his lieutenants. The Soviets showed themselves equally cautious when it came to replacing them: the ultraconservative among the Czech and Slovak Communists, known to have schemed with Moscow before August 20, were not licensed to occupy the top positions. Leadership of Czechoslovak Communism was entrusted to Gustáv Husák. Imprisoned under Stalinism, the new first secretary had also been a follower of the liberal line prior to the invasion, but thereafter adjusted rapidly to the requirements of the moment and of the Kremlin, remaining its faithful servitor until the very moment of the great crash of Communism all over Eastern Europe. And as it was being discarded on the proverbial rubbish heap of history, the Czech and Slovak people remembered the one who against great odds had tried to humanize the system: though history had now bypassed him and what he had stood for, Alexander Dubček was in 1990 brought out of obscurity to be chairman of the Czechoslovak national assembly.

The attempt to reconcile Communism with political pluralism and with the national pride of the Czechs and Slovaks had failed. But for "proletarian internationalism," as well as for the Kremlin, it was but a Pyrrhic victory. The very caution with which the Soviets maneuvered both before and after the invasion, the relative mildness of the reprisals against those who had offended the Kremlin (certainly in comparison to those visited on the participants in the Hungarian revolution of 1956) testified that for all the brutal character of the descent upon the little country, the Soviet oligarchs were losing their self-assurance. That the invasion was a testimony to the failure of Marxism-Leninism rather than its reassertion was sensed by Castro, who delivered a very ambivalent assessment of the Soviets' actions. Yes, he approved of it, but "what are the causes, the factors and the circumstances that made it possible—after twenty years of Communism in Czechoslovakia—

that a group of persons whose names do not even appear anywhere would have to request other countries of the socialist camp, asking them to send their armies to prevent the triumph of the counter-revolution?" And, continued the Cuban dictator (who sounded suspiciously as if he had doubts about the wisdom of his having cast his lot with the Soviets), why does the USSR chastise Czechoslovak Communists while cultivating good relations with Tito's Yugoslavia, which had strayed much farther off the true path than Czechoslovakia? In fact, why does Moscow seek détente with the United States and sponsor the nuclear nonproliferation treaty jointly with the latter if, as ran the justification of the invasion, the American imperialists have been trying to subvert the Communist countries of Eastern Europe? And an even more direct question: "Will Warsaw Pact divisions be sent to Cuba if the Yankee imperialists attack our country, or simply if, in the face of the threat of an attack by the Yankee imperialists, our country requests it?"[32] And so where is the consistency in Moscow's actions, asked Castro, at the time bitterly disappointed that the Russians were not assisting his efforts to become the Lenin of Latin American.

Castro's insight that the invasion reflected an underlying weakness of the international structure of Communism, and hence of Marxism-Leninism, was not, however, widely shared. What the world did see was that the Soviet Union had violated, and with impunity, the sovereignty of yet another small country. Within the Communist bloc, reactions varied from rather embarrassed approval to scathing condemnation of the wanton act. That of Beijing was predictable: damnable as the behavior of the Czechoslovak revisionists had been, the Kremlin's reaction to it was yet another illustration that what it really wants is "to found a colonial empire with the Soviet revisionists clique as the overlord, and redivide the world in collaboration with US imperialism."[33] Romania's Ceaușescu told his people to prepare to fight if the Soviet Union should try to extend its solicitude for Communist orthodoxy to their country. In the West the Italian party was emphatic in its condemnation; the French party, as usual when it came to criticizing the Soviet Union, was much less so.

Reverberations to the invasion within the Soviet Union were also somewhat deceptive. The ubiquitous propaganda machine swung into action with factory meetings called upon to vote to approve their government's action to save a fraternal country from the wiles of NATO imperialists and to save socialism. Insofar as he gave any thought to the matter at all, the proverbial Soviet man or woman in the street was unlikely to be shocked by what had transpired, his approval or indifference based not on any ideological premise but on the fact stressed again and again by official propaganda: thousands of Soviet lives had been expended in liberating Eastern Europe from the Nazis. But within the wide circles of the intelligentsia, the "we liberated you" argument was less persuasive. One cannot gauge the full depth of disapproval and revulsion at what the government had done by its external manifestations: a few intellectuals refusing to sign declarations pledging solidarity with "the fraternal countries fulfilling their highest internationalist duties by defending socialism in Czechoslovakia." The protestors clearly risked the loss of their jobs, if not more. The one public manifestation may have also seemed quixotic: *seven* dissidents sitting down in Red Square and unfurling Czechoslovak flags. Yet the overt protest was but a tip of the iceberg: many more, and not exclusively among the intelligentsia, felt that the armed intervention was a convincing proof that the Brezhnev regime was now definitely committed to the repressive status quo at home as well as within the entire bloc. One whose commitment to dissent became firmer because of the invasion was Academician Sakharov. Dissent in the Soviet Union received an infusion of strength, if not in the number of its adherents, then in the depth of their moral commitment.

The uneasiness over its wanton act led the Kremlin to seek a theoretical formula to explain the use of force against a fraternal country. Again this shows the Kremlin's lessened self-confidence. Under Stalin or even Khrushchev the Soviet regime considered a recourse to force whenever it saw it as warranted in Eastern Europe as something that hardly needed an explanation or apology. The theoretical case for what misleadingly came to be known as the Brezhnev Doctrine was presented in a September 26, 1968, article in *Pravda* under the signature of one S. Kovalev. The operative sentences in the article read: "Every Communist Party is responsible not only to its own people, but also to all the socialist countries and the entire Communist movement," and "the class approach to the matter cannot be discarded in the name of legalistic considerations."

Whatever the logic of the argument from the point of view of Marxism-Leninism, no alert reader could have failed to note the jarring inconsistencies in the application of the supposed doctrine of limited sovereignty of the Communist states and the responsibility of the movement as a whole—in practical terms, the USSR—to act as the watchdog of orthodoxy. Why hasn't the alleged doctrine been applied to China, a country which according to repeated Soviet declarations has long sinned viciously against proletarian internationalism? And to repeat after Castro: How about Yugoslavia? Or Albania and Romania? Here then was a formula that, instead of providing a rationale or a method of securing unity among the Communist states, served only to illuminate the failures and inconsistencies of Communism in its international dimension.

And failures in that dimension were bound to affect the internal cohesion of Communist societies, that of the USSR not excepted; in fact, they already had. One of the partisans of the Prague Spring wrote most presciently: "The occupation of Czechoslovakia initiated a period of general crisis for monopolistic socialism in Eastern Europe. There is no exit from this situation because the road to reform was rejected by Moscow. Willy-nilly, the power elite . . . will become trapped in the fundamental contradictions of the system, the growing demand for consumer goods and the stagnation in production. The militaristic and imperialistic direction of production will increasingly limit the existing consumption level. The devastating contradictions of monopolistic socialism must lead to a repressive policy against the working class and the majority of the population because . . . the power elite must manipulate manpower as it manipulates any other production resource. Through police repression it must ensure the docility of the labor force."[34]

10

EXPANSION AND RETREAT

WE CONCLUDED WITH A Czech philosopher's scorching characterization of "monopolistic socialism." This neatly turned the tables on
the Communist sages for whom the entire economic and political
nature of the Western world, and of the United States in particular,
was summarized as "monopolistic capitalism." It was the latter which
according to the canons of Marxism-Leninism is condemned to
socioeconomic crises of ever more intense character, culminating in
its utter collapse. And like many of the predictions of Marxism, this
oracular formula turned out to be truer of Communism than of the
capitalist system.

The inherent contradictions of Communism were never more vividly displayed than during the decade of the 1970s. The outer facade
of the movement—the military power of the Soviet Union and its
ability to score repeated political and diplomatic successes in the global
competition with the West—had never been more impressive. Yet at
the same time the foundations of the movement—its unity, its ability
to adjust to the demands of the age and to inspire the loyalty of its
followers—were being steadily eroded. And so a belated attempt to
restructure the edifice would leave it in shambles.

Until the end of the decade, no one could have foreseen such an
outcome. What one did see was the tremendous and growing military
strength of the USSR. With SALT I, the Soviet Union was in fact
acknowledged as having become the equal of the United States in
nuclear weapons, indeed superior in some categories, such as land-
based intercontinental missiles. This latter factor, Western critics of
the agreement argued, went far to destroy the credibility of the American "nuclear umbrella" over Western Europe. Were the Soviets to

invade Western Europe, would a U.S. president be prepared to order a nuclear strike against the USSR when cognizant of the fact that after it Moscow would still be able to visit utter devastation on this country? Or, a still more alarming scenario: an invasion of the West, accompanied by a Soviet preemptive strike that would leave this country with but a feeble force to retaliate.

Barring collective insanity of the collective leadership in the Kremlin, such scenarios were utterly unrealistic. But the mere fact that those concerns had to be felt by statesmen and the public alike detracted attention from the perennial crisis of Soviet agriculture, the drastic slowing down of growth of the Soviet GNP, and the rumblings signaling the approach of yet another explosion in Eastern Europe.

Equally important in obscuring the weaknesses of the Soviet system were the political successes scored by the Soviet Union, in most cases at the expense of the prestige and influence of its main capitalist rival. Today the agreements of the early 1970s, through which the West in fact recognized East Germany, and the Federal Republic acknowledged Poland's "new" (i.e., since 1945) western borders, appear as but a commonsense recognition of the realities of European politics of the period. But at the time, those agreements, as well as Ostpolitik itself, were clear consequences of America's lowered prestige and of the Soviet's enhanced power. The West had agreed to Germany's remaining divided, as it then looked, forever. Could Communist power be in decline if it had forced the United States and its allies to back down on an issue that for a generation they had maintained to be nonnegotiable and involving a moral principle, in defense of which the democracies would fight rather than yield?

Détente as a whole was another element reinforcing the impression of the durability and stability of the Soviet Union and, for all the rumblings of discontent there, of the entire East European Communist bloc. Benefits of détente appeared to accrue mainly to the USSR and its vassal states: increased trade with and credits from the West, and access to its technology. And in political terms détente perceptibly loosened the ties between Western Europe and the United States. What the West had hoped to obtain in return, namely, the discontinuance by the USSR of its "efforts to obtain unilateral advantages" at the expense of America and its allies, had not materialized. Whatever had been Soviet intentions in that respect, when Brezhnev and Nixon signed their agreements (1972), the subsequent train of events convinced the Kremlin that such pledges did not have to be taken too seriously. America's resolve and foreign policy were crippled in the wake of Watergate and Vietnam; the economy of the West was shaken by the repercussions of the OPEC exactions. Between 1972 and 1976 the configuration of forces on the international scene appeared to have shifted in the Soviet Union's favor. As an Asian Communist phrased it with disarming candor in 1976, "The confrontation of socialism and imperialism in Indochina had demonstrated that *with the help of the Soviet Union* one can achieve national liberation without threatening either world peace or détente."[1] (My italics.)

What Brezhnev said on the same occasion (the Twenty-fifth Party Congress) also indicated the Soviet leaders' growing self-confidence and conviction that the four years that elasped from the Moscow summit meeting had brought changes that presented the USSR with new and tantalizing opportunities: no objective person could deny that the influence of the socialist countries on the development of international affairs grew ever stronger, ever further-reaching.[2]

The general secretary could not resist the temptation to paint the West's troubles in the darkest hues: "During the last five years the capitalist world has experienced an economic crisis, the seriousness and extent of which . . . can only be compared with that of the beginning of the thirties." This rather ominous evocation of the Great Depression was accompanied by references to "the ideological and political crisis of bourgeois society." This crisis, the speaker noted, with an unmistakable reference to his erstwhile partner in détente, Richard Nixon, "has afflicted all the institutions . . . undermined the most basic moral standards, with corruption reaching the highest level of the state apparatus." And the complacent conclusion: "The events of the last years have once again, and convincingly, demonstrated that the capitalist system has no future."[3]

The Soviet Union's power and the vitality of world communism thus appeared impressive when seen against the background of the economic and other troubles experienced by the great democracies. Throughout much of the 1970s it was easy to overlook the fact that the ailments affecting America's body politic resulted from an unfortunate conjunction of mistaken policies and chance events, while those afflicting the Soviet Union and Communism were organic: the incompatibility of the ideology with the modern world and the growing decrepitude of the Soviet system insofar as its economic and social condition was concerned. Ten years after the general secretary's boastful assessment of the world situation, a successor of Brezhnev's would,

though as yet in a cautious form, admit how that system, based allegedly on scientific socialism, had failed to meet the test of the time:
"For a number of years now, and not only because of objective factors,
but also and principally because of subjective ones, the activity of the
Party and state organs has failed to meet the needs of the
hour. . . . Inertia, the paralysis of the form and methods governing our
system, the decreasing dynamism of our work force, growth of
bureaucracy—all that has done a great deal of harm to our mission."[4]
But what was readily perceptible in the mid-1970s were the apparently
"objective factors" that had paralyzed U.S. foreign policy and made
Washington unable to continue the advance of Soviet influence in
the Third World. A North Vietnamese general summarized candidly
and succinctly the reasons that emboldened his government to disregard the Paris agreements of 1973 and to embark two years later
upon the absorption of the South: "The internal contradictions within
the U.S. administration and among U.S. political parties had intensified. The Watergate scandal had seriously affected the entire United
States. . . . [It] faced economic recession, mounting inflation, serious
unemployment and an oil crisis."[5]

With the credibility of American commitment to containment undermined, the Kremlin saw little risk in intensifying its expansionist
policies. Moscow's drive to secure new clients and dependents in the
Third World was now relentless and ubiquitous. Were members of
the Soviet ruling elite not stolid, unimaginative, elderly men, one
would have thought that their frantic rush to score fresh gains at the
expense of the West had its source in their doubts about the viability
of their own system and in the need to compensate for the ever more
perceptible disintegration of international Communism and the erosion of its ideology. The armed clashes on the Sino-Soviet border, the
inability to "catch up with and surpass the West" in economic and
technological development, the inability of the Soviet Union to secure
the loyalty of its East European partners except by standing armed
guard over them—all this was somehow to be offset by the accession
to the socialist camp of Angola, Ethiopia, and Afghanistan.

The new acquisitions—and how ephemeral they would prove to
be—owed more to the temporary disarray of the United States' foreign
policy and the Soviets' greater freedom of operation on the international scene than to the inherent attraction of Marxism-Leninism.
True, the notion of the "Soviet model of development" still held some
attraction as allegedly the most efficacious path from underdevelop-

ment to modernization, even though the examples of Taiwan and South Korea, to name two countries, have already made this notion quite questionable. Marxism-Leninism was still in vogue among the intelligentsia of the new nations freshly emancipated from or with recollections of European colonialism, though by now it was often China, rather than the Soviet Union, that benefited from this ideological propinquity.

But Moscow's gains in the Third World came mainly as the result of a projection of Soviet power. The classical case in point was that of Angola. The dissolution of the decrepit Portuguese empire in Africa had been anticipated ever since the early 1960s, and both the USSR and the United States had by then established ties with the guerrilla factions fighting Lisbon's ever more precarious hold on Angola. The CIA's entry in the race (Washington could not openly sponsor the insurgents because of the U.S.-NATO links with Portugal) was a movement called the National Front for the Liberation of Angola (FNLA); the Soviets fairly openly threw their support behind the Popular Liberation Movement of Angola (MPLA). With the collapse of Portugal's authoritarian regime in 1974, the little country gave up its anachronistic attempt to hold on to its colonial possessions. After a brief interval when the various Angolan factions strove to agree on a coalition government, there erupted a full-fledged civil war. The FNLA and another group, the National Union for the Total Independence of Angola (UNITA), which enjoyed sympathy but little tangible support from China, combined their forces against the pro-Moscow MPLA, and at first appeared on the way to victory. But the situation was soon drastically changed when the Soviets provided their protégés with massive military help, including MIG jets, ground-to-air missiles, and other sophisticated, up-to-date equipment. What proved to be the decisive element in the struggle was the infusion of Cuban troops to help the MPLA. And so in 1976 Angola became the first African country with a clearly Communist regime. The anti-MPLA factions, assisted not so covertly anymore by the United States, had continued their struggle, but the self-proclaimed Marxism-Leninist government was recognized by the Organization of African Unity as the legitimate one as of February 11, 1976.

The use of surrogate troops as the means of projecting its power was an innovative technique of Moscow's imperial drive. Military and secret police personnel from other Communist countries, most frequently East Germany, had been employed before to assist Soviet clients and allies. But this time it was, given the circumstances, a sizable army, combat units, and not merely instructors. There were halfhearted attempts to present the intervention as being an entirely Cuban operation both in its conception and execution. But even on its face such an interpretation was absurd; the USSR had obviously equipped and provided transport for some fifteen thousand Cuban soldiers sent to Angola in 1975–76. Frustrated in his ambition to become Latin America's Lenin, Castro obviously relished the prospect of Cuba's becoming the vanguard of the advance of Marxism-Leninism in Africa. But the design and the logistics of the venture were clearly Moscow's. For the West the whole affair had to appear as not only a definite setback, insofar as Communism now had a foothold in the turbulent area of southern Africa, but also an ominous precedent. With the volatile conditions of politics south of the Sahara, many of its precariously situated governments could be easily destabilized or even overthrown by the injection of a few thousand soldiers equipped with modern weapons and provided with Soviet advisers. It now appeared only too understandable and menacing why during the past twenty years the USSR had expanded considerable effort and resources on developing a powerful navy. Moscow's insouciance at Washington's expostulations that the Angolan enterprise was inconsistent with the spirit of détente must have been almost equally alarming. When on one of his visits to Moscow, Secretary of State Kissinger proposed to discuss the issue, Foreign Minister Gromyko publicly announced that the American could indeed talk about it with his advisers; the USSR did not propose to interfere in what was strictly the business of two sovereign states, Angola and Cuba.

Having established, and with impunity, the precedent of using a third country's troops to secure and maintain its influence over a Third World nation, the Kremlin would now make it a regular practice. The next case was that of Ethiopia. Here it was the native authoritarian regime, rather than that of a colonial power, that had collapsed amid revolutionary stirrings. What finally emerged following the overthrow of the monarchy in 1974 was the dictatorship of Colonel Mengistu Haile Mariam, presiding over a military junta, the Provisional Military Administrative Council, also known as the Derg. Secessionist movements within Ethiopia as well as war with neighboring Somalia drove the Derg into the Soviets' arms. After Mengistu's visit to Moscow in 1977 the Soviet Union hastened to provide him with a steady flow of war matériel and military instructors. And then came Cuban soldiers.

By the middle of 1978 some eleven thousand of them were fighting on Ethiopia's side in its war with Somalia. By adopting the Ethiopian regime, Moscow forfeited its hitherto close ties with Somalia. The latter expelled its Russian advisers and terminated the Soviet Union's use of the port of Berbera. To put it in direct terms, the Soviet Union traded an alliance with a small African country for a protectorate over a much larger one. True, Moscow would have liked to swallow Ethiopia and to have Somalia too, but the awkward attempts of Soviet diplomacy to persuade the two regimes that instead of fighting over disputed territories they should form a federation did not find much response.

The Cuban troops were also used to strengthen the Soviets' hold over another Horn of Africa area, South Yemen, whose political leadership, thought to be shaky in its allegiance to Moscow, was overthrown in July 1978 and replaced by a more trustworthy one.

Even at the time it was difficult to see of what benefit to the USSR were such conquests. There was not an iota of ideological justification for trying to extend any economic or social features of Marxism-Leninism to two undeveloped nations. Insofar as it would be tried, it would only compound their difficulties in achieving even a rudimentary level of modernization. The pro-Soviet regimes in both Angola and, especially, Ethiopia would continue to be involved in civil war, their survival thus placing a considerable burden on the USSR both financially and diplomatically. On the latter count the threat of the Cuban-Ethiopian forces invading Somalia's territory brought a strong reaction from Washington as well as from the Arab League, of which Somalia was a member. There was similarly no reason pertinent to the security of the Soviet Union that could justify those operations in Africa. The only rationale for those expensive ventures could be found in the expansionist itch of the Kremlin, which in turn was a sort of public relations campaign designed to persuade the Soviet people and world public opinion that for all of the setbacks on the domestic and international Communist fronts, the USSR was advancing in the worldwide competition with the main capitalist power, while the United States and the West in general were in retreat.

Moscow's role on the international scene in the 1970s could in a way be likened to that of a scavenger picking up dictators and regimes whose shaky domestic and international situation made it imperative that they lean for support on a foreign power. In that game the USSR enjoyed obvious advantages over the United States: the Kremlin was

not restrained by an inquisitive congress and squeamish public opinion that would require repeated proofs of democratic virtue from the
governments this country protected and helped. For Moscow, on the
other hand, it appeared of no consequence that Colonel Mengistu's
regime engaged in bloody repression and that its fatuous attempts to
practice "scientific socialism" in a society that was barely emerging
from feudalism would year after year cause famines over large areas.
The Soviet consumer neither knew nor would have been able to protest
the extent of the burden placed on his country's economy by those
incongruous newcomers to the "socialist camp."

Years before, in condemning Mao's statement asserting China's
historical claims on huge areas of Asiatic USSR, the Soviet press
editorialized sanctimoniously: "History teaches us that no country
ever achieved grandeur on the path of military gambles and aggression. The true greatness of a nation is reached through the path of
social progress, friendship and cooperation."[6] By the late 1970s the
Chinese Communists were unequivocal in passing judgment on their
erstwhile Soviet comrades' expansionist strivings: "Of the two imperialist powers, it is the Soviet Union which is more ferocious, reckless and treacherous, and the most dangerous source of world
war. . . . The Soviet Union has decided to employ an offensive strategy
to encroach on the sovereignty of all other countries and weaken and
supplant US influence in all parts of the world."[7]

Contrary to what Beijing was saying (but hardly believed), the Soviet Union was far from seeking a new world war. Its interest was
centered rather on maintaining a degree of instability and tension in
areas where the West was most vulnerable. An observer of the Middle
East scene could not agree that the Soviet Union's goal was a *resolution* of the basic crisis of the area, i.e., a solution that would make
Arab states accept the existence of Israel and at the same time satisfy
the Palestinians' aspirations. Rather, Soviet policies appeared designed to keep the pot boiling and thus perpetuate the Arabs' estrangement from the United States. In 1967 Moscow had egged Egypt
into a confrontation with the Jewish state, but when the latter inflicted
a military defeat on the Arabs, the USSR backed out of a dangerous
situation. In subsequent years the Soviet Union supported the main
Arab power, Egypt, up to a point, that point being an outright confrontation with the United States. To be sure, that point was *almost*
reached in the course of the 1973 war. But it had to have been transparent to the Arab leaders that their ally and alleged protector had

other than their own interests at heart, that in a sense they were being used in a much larger game that the Soviet Union was playing against the United States. It was then not greatly surprising when the Arab regime that had borne the main burden of the growing confrontation with Israel chose to reverse the pattern—use the Soviets' support up to the point where a timely shift to the other side would benefit its situation. Egypt's Sadat, having squeezed as much as was possible out of its inconstant ally—saving Egypt from a military disaster in 1973 and billions in credits and arms—moved nimbly to line up with the United States. In 1976 Sadat abrogated the Soviet-Egyptian friendship treaty. Two years later, with President Carter acting as the honest broker, Egypt and Israel reached an agreement that terminated the state of war that had officially existed since the Jewish state's creation, established diplomatic relations, and returned the Sinai Peninsula to Egypt.

Egypt's case should have gone far in convincing the Soviet rulers of the futility of their brand of neo-imperialism. The USSR had poured billions of dollars into trying to bolster this linchpin of the Soviet position in the Middle East. The liaison—a more appropriate term in this case than alliance—brought Moscow considerable embarrassment and a blow to its prestige in 1967, as well as what briefly appeared to be the danger of a military clash with the United States in 1973. And all that had been wasted. The Middle East remained one of the most turbulent danger areas in the world, the Arab-Israeli conflict one of the most intractable and explosive issues in international relations. But what were the advantages that Moscow derived from that situation? It was obviously the source of considerable satisfaction to the Kremlin that the festering crisis handicapped America's position in the area, most of the Arab states blaming the United States' moral and material support of Israel for the latter's intransigence on the issue of the Palestinian state. Against this had to be weighed the risk of some fresh incident leading to another possibility of a clash between the two superpowers, and the continuing drain on the Soviets' resources. There was no question of trying to advance the cause of Communism in the Middle East nor did the Kremlin ever pretend there was; dictatorial regimes such as Syria's and Iraq's remained close to the Soviet Union for purely opportunistic reasons. Any attempt by Moscow to dictate the domestic politics of those countries would have led, as it had in the case of Egypt, to the termination of the close relationship. All that the Soviet Union required of its clients in the

Arab world was that they maintain a consistently anti-American stance.

The incongruity and ideological fatuity in measuring Soviet successes in terms of American setbacks was even more fully demonstrated in the Soviet reactions to the Iranian revolution. The fall of the shah's regime in February 1979 and its replacement by a quasi-theocracy headed by the Ayatollah Khomeini was greeted by Moscow with unconcealed glee. Even at the outset there were scant reasons for such an attitude. The shah had hardly been an exemplary ally of the United States. In 1973–74, Iran had been a prime mover in OPEC's quadrupling of oil prices and fully exploiting its monopoly position. The shah's attitude toward the USSR had all along been conciliatory, and as long as he seemed to be firmly in power, Mohammad Reza Pahlavi was treated with deference by the Soviets, officially invited and feted in Moscow and other Communist captials.

The fundamentalist Moslem character of the revolution ought to have been of immediate concern to the USSR, with its large Moslem population and with a certain native restiveness in the Central Asian republics noticeable already in the 1970s. Yet what seemed to count above all was that another ally of the United States had been toppled and that the revolution was assuming an increasingly anti-Western character. There were awkward attempts to apply a progressive gloss to what by Marxist-Leninist standards was a reactionary and obscurantist outburst of religious fanaticism: "There is nothing unusual in the fact that the struggle against the imperial regime has been led by religious activists. The peculiarity of the Iranian situation consists in the fact that the majority of the population there is under the influence of the Shiite branch of Islam, whose slogans under the given circumstances had a progressive character. . . . [The slogans] call for the people's struggle against the monarchy and foreign oppression and for heeding the social needs of the masses."[8] With the chances of American military intervention following the shah's flight from the country utterly nil, the Soviets gravely warned Washington that an old Soviet-Persian treaty authorized the entry of Russian troops into Iran in case a third power tried to interfere militarily in the country's affairs. With the revolution several months old and clearly revealed to be directed against all foreign, and not merely Western, influences and ties, the Soviets still hoped to replace America as Iran's ally. Brezhnev addressed flattering messages to Khomeini in which the aged ayatollah, with scant consideration for diplomatic protocol, was

styled as "the leader of the Iranian people." The press painted se-
ductive pictures of the benefits of future Moscow-Tehran collaboration: "The USSR sided resolutely with the Iranian revolution and has
made a great contribution to preventing foreign interference in the
country's domestic affairs. As for itself, the Soviet Union, in view of
its peace-loving policy, never has engaged nor, needless to say, would
engage in such interference. And now with the revolution having
triumphed, the USSR is ready to do its utmost to strengthen still
further and expand Soviet-Iranian relations."[9]

Alas, the hopes of, so to speak, coopting Khomeini and enlisting
the oil-rich country among the Soviet Union's clients were not realized. Next to the "Great Satan" itself—the United States—it was the
USSR that became the object of enmity and vilification by the Iranian
fanatics. The Tudeh (i.e., Communist) Party was suppressed, its members picturesquely described by the official press as "sons of Satan,
atheists, the evil of the earth." What proved of much greater significance and struck directly at the Soviet Union's interests was the help
the new Iran extended to the Afghan rebels battling their pro-Moscow
government. Khomeini publicly expressed his hope that just as the
people of Iran had overthrown the puppets of one infidel imperialist
power—the United States—so those of Afghanistan would do the
same to the puppets of the USSR. As an Afghan refugee broadcast
from Tehran proclaimed, " . . . our nation is struggling against an
aggressive army of the criminal Soviet Union and will not rest until
final victory and establishment of the Islamic Republic of Afghanistan." And some of Moslem fundamentalism did spill over the Iranian-
Soviet border. In 1989 and 1990 crowds demonstrating against
Moscow's policies in Soviet Azerbaijan would carry Islamic flags and
portraits of the ayatollah. But it would only be under perestroika that
the Soviet leaders would acknowledge publicly that what affected
America unfavorably did not redound automatically to their own country's benefit, and that in fact international instability was a threat to
both superpowers, as well as to the world community as a whole. It
was a much-belated insight.

A future historian analyzing the checkered course of the Communist movement and of its vanguard, the Soviet Union, would have
to acknowledge the unique ability of the men who had guided its
destinies to have their cake and eat it too. Unlike National Socialism
and other fascist philosophies that stormed throughout the twentieth
century, Communism did not subsist on a philosophy that advanced

claims of racial or national superiority and extolled force as the catalyst for progress. Marxism, in its Leninist version, proclaimed itself to be the heir and fulfillment of the humanitarian aspirations and values of the modern age: world peace, social justice, and democracy. Once in power, the practices of Communism began to diverge more and more from its declared ideology. Yet even in its most horrifying phase under Stalinism, Soviet Communism could and did claim that its repressive measures and its harnessing of the international movement to the dictates of Moscow and the dictator were regrettable but necessary steps toward the achievement of those universal values.

One way of looking at the years from Stalin's death to perestroika is to see them as a sharpening confrontation between the ideology of Communism and what it had in fact become. The 1950s and 1960s went far in dispelling the most ambitious promise of the ideology: that of the establishment of a supranational order, which however cruel and destructive its beginning would, through an eventual worldwide commonwealth of socialist states, eliminate war. Common ideology proved the catalyst of hostility rather than unity between Communist China and the Communist USSR. It was not proletarian internationalism but armed force that kept Hungary in the socialist camp, and as the case of Czechoslovakia once again confirmed, this camp had become a euphemism for the Soviet empire.

With the 1970s the Soviet regime's endeavor to find an ideological rationale entered a new phase. It would be incorrect to accuse the Brezhnev-Kosygin team of entirely overlooking the danger signals on the domestic and intra-Communist-affairs fronts. It sensed the latent danger in what would prove to be both the litmus test of perestroika and Gorbachev's undoing—the nationalities question. Intermittently, the leaders would, though not very convincingly, plead their readiness to meet Beijing halfway and turn a new leaf in their relations with other Communist parties. The Kremlin would persevere in its efforts not to let its expansionist strivings get in the way of détente.

Yet with their conservative cast of mind the rulers would not think of innovative solutions to the perennial problems if such solutions involved risks of diminishing the role of the party or of undermining the image of the USSR as advancing on the world stage. Problems and difficulties as they surfaced were met in the traditional way: soothing rhetoric, and when the regime saw a threat to its power, by repression. Since the government neither could nor would deal with political nonconformity in the pre-1953 manner, political protests and clandestine publications (samizdat) had become a constant feature of Soviet life. Under the circumstances the achievement of the relative handful of dissidents had been considerable: they put an oppressive political system on the defensive. Just as the end of mass terror made civil courage relevant to Soviet society, so the Kremlin's search for détente and international respectability permitted dissent to survive as an enduring force and harbinger of what in the following decade would become glasnost. Though less liberal than its predecessor, the Brezhnev regime felt constrained to deal more cautiously and selectively with its critics and malcontents. The majority of them, to be sure, were being incarcerated in prisons, camps, or special psychiatric institutions. But some, in whose cases more brutal methods would have been counterproductive in terms of public opinion at home and abroad, had been expelled or allowed to emigrate. And a few (though closely watched and officially ostracized) were left at large—ostensibly a proof of the regime's broad-mindedness.

Dissent covered a wide variety of issues, and much as it occasionally embarrassed the regime, it certainly did not pose any clear and present danger to the regime's *power,* although it undermined its claim to moral legitimacy in the eyes of a not inconsiderable segment of the population. What in retrospect is most notable about the voices of dissent in the 1970s is that for the most part they were quite moderate: none urged a violent overthrow of the system; few thought possible the replacement of the existing system by democracy in the near future. Rather the bulk of criticism was addressed to various aspects of unfreedom in the Soviet Union: the regime's intolerance of non-conformity, whether in the politics, the arts and literature, or other fields; the absence of an independent judiciary; the Soviet government's persecution of religious cults; repression of self-assertion by the non-Russian nationalities of the USSR; and myriad other grievances.

Apart from the basic issue of authoritarianism-versus-pluralism (not necessarily of a democratic variety), it was the national question that figured most prominently on the agenda of dissent, just as it had been the key problem of this multinational society both before and after the Revolution. What agitated the proponents of autonomy of the individual republics was not only the obvious fact that beneath the facade of constitutional federalism, the USSR was under the rule of the Communist Party, a unitary state, but also the predominantly *Russian* character of that rule. How greatly official Soviet political culture was permeated by Russian nationalism is well reflected by the tributes leaders of the non-Russian republics felt constrained to pay the great Russian nation, and how they recalled with rapture the moment when their country entered (i.e., had been subjugated by) what was then the Russian Empire. Thus, at the Twenty-sixth Congress of the CPSU, Eduard Shevardnadze, then first secretary of the Georgian party, said, "In two years we shall solemnly celebrate the two hundredth anniversary of the union with Russia. . . . [The Georgian people's] dream was realized. Russia broke through the darkness and became the torchbearer. Together with Russia and led by the great Russian people, other brotherly nations broke away from the darkness."[10] So said Shevardnadze, who in a few years would become one of the most fervent proponents of perestroika. His Armenian counterpart was no less effusive: "The hundred-fiftieth anniversary of East Armenia's union with Russia was for us a major and glorious occasion. . . . History has fully confirmed the insight of Engels's words that Russia has played a progressive role insofar as the countries of the Orient are concerned. . . . The great and beneficent deeds, the profound internationalism of the Russian people, have been an inspiration to us, to all the Soviet peoples. Brotherly friendship with the great Russian people . . . is for us a priceless moral, political, and social treasure."[11]

Well, as a matter of fact, the Russian Empire was for Engels, as for Marx, a bulwark of despotism and reaction. Servile tributes to the Russian's civilizing mission also would not have pleased Lenin, who called tsarist Russia a "prison house of nationalities," and who, on his deathbed, expressed fears about Russian chauvinism overlaying the Soviet system.

That such statements were expected from non-Russian Communist notables was in itself evidence of the sensitivity of the national problem. With the non-Russian population of the country close to 50 percent of the population by the beginning 1980s, and other ethnic groups, notably in the Central Asian republics, multiplying at a much faster rate than the Slavic components, the problem assumed additional gravity.

A perspicacious authoritarian ruler, unless capable of benumbing society with terror, as was Stalin, would not rely entirely on repression but would try also to anticipate and assuage popular grievances. Yet where the crucial questions were concerned, this insight was lacking in the Kremlin councils. Just as the Brezhnev regime cracked down on the Czechoslovak reformers, so in domestic policies its response to the burgeoning national grievances of the non-Russians was one of suppression and intensified attempts at Russification. An anonymous Byelorussian depicted in a samizdat pamphlet the plight of his nation. "We are now witnessing in Byelorussia a process of wide-scale assimilation. Those responsible for this process of national, spiritual castration are acting under the banners of 'internationalism' and 'inevitable fusion of nations.'" And he goes on to protest the "repeated attempts of the Byelorussians' powerful neighbors," i.e., the Russians, acting under the aegis of Soviet authorities, to subvert his people's national identity, thus creating "in this corner of civilized Europe something of a 'cultural' parallel of colonial Africa."[12]

Similar complaints about the disparagement of the local cultures, about staffing the top local party and government posts with nonnatives, most often Russians, came from other Union republics. Even for the highest-placed non-Russian dignitaries, repeated homages to the Russian people and denigration of their own nation's status became, as we have already seen, the condition of their holding on to their jobs. Peter Shelest, the party boss of the Ukraine, was removed from his satrapy in 1972 and before too long was fired from the Politburo for displaying what in Moscow was viewed as excessive interest and pride in his nation's past. (Ironically, in 1968 he had been a strong proponent of a crackdown on the Czechoslovak reformers, whose activities, Shelest argued, were inciting Ukrainian nationalism.) His successor, Vladimir Shcherbitsky, learned the lesson, as shown in his speech before a Ukrainian audience. "To be an internationalist, means to express feelings of friendship and brotherhood towards all peoples of our country, and first of all, toward the great Russian people, their culture, their language—the language of Lenin. . . . To be an internationalist, means to lead an uncompromising struggle against nationalism, and in particular against the worst enemy of the Ukrainian people, Ukrainian bourgeois nationalism, and also against international Zionism; it means to be intolerant of any manifestations of national narrow-mindedness and national conceit."[13]

Russian nationalism had been erected into a major prop of the Soviet system by Stalin. Another, and incongruous, legacy from the tyrant's days was the federal structure of the USSR, with its member republics being accorded under the "Stalin" constitution of 1936 the right to secede from the Union. The passage of time had made what had been fantastically unrealistic under Stalin, if not as yet a source of real danger to the unity of the Soviet state, then a somewhat ambiguous and potentially embarrassing formula. In 1977, Brezhnev felt that the time had come for his own constitution, so a new one, in almost all respects a faithful copy of the 1936 document, was proclaimed with a great deal of fanfare. But what is of interest, in view of what would happen within a few years, is that some within the top leadership thought that the occasion should be used to abolish federalism and have the country divided according to some other than national—possibly economic—criteria. Much as such symbolic shoving of the nationality problem under the rug would have pleased the ruling circles, it was finally decided that even a symbolic blow at the rights of the nationalities could have explosive consequences. The federal structure was somewhat modified, but preserved. And so what was mockery under Stalin and an inconvenient fiction under Brezhnev would with Gorbachev become an all too real threat to the entire Soviet body politic.

Soviet totalitarianism and imperialism had always been obscured, if not effectively concealed, by a veneer of democratic and internationalist phraseology and formulas. But as the Kremlin's ability to intimidate its people and foreign vassals decreased, the rhetoric once thought harmless became for the men of the Kremlin first an embarrassment, then a source of danger. A word from Moscow used to be sufficient to make the most intransigent foreign Communists toe the line. Now, even putting aside Yugoslavia's emancipation and China's apostasy, the Kremlin's word was no longer the law for the major Communist parties outside the socialist camp, and criticisms of Soviet foreign and even domestic policies were no longer taboo. That principle of the equality of all Communists—for generations followed in the breach—now came close to being an alarming possibility.

Who in Stalin's time would have dreamed of invoking those admittedly liberal and democratic provisions of the Soviet constitution against the tyranny of the regime? Even after the despot's death the constitution remained a sort of never-never land, with neither friend nor foe of Communism being able to see the rights and freedoms "guaranteed" under it as having the slightest relevance to real life. The function of the constitution in some ways was reminiscent of the Lenin Mausoleum: it was a sanctuary of the past, of the ideals and beliefs of the progenitors of Communism and, like the mummy of the maker of the Revolution, dead and of only symbolic significance to the present. With the Brezhnev reign this seeming corpse began to stir. The constitutional rights had hardly become the living law of the land, but some of them had advanced from the status of political mythology to that of political issues. Thus the issue of nationalities. And for the first time since the early 1920s, society witnessed political trials. The great Moscow judicial proceedings staged during the Great Terror could hardly be classified as such; they were theater, where each of the accused, reciting his part as instructed by the secret police and the prosecution, was only an actor. Now purveryors of samizdat, nonconformist satirical writers, and political demonstrators were tried for real rather than fictitious acts of political protest, some of the accused refusing to confess and recant and taking their stand on the basis of the law. The courts remained an instrument of party rule, passing sentences as instructed from above, but the judges now had the unfamiliar experience of the defendants invoking the constitution, such as its Article 50: "Citizens of the USSR are guaranteed freedom of speech, of the press, and of assembly, meetings, street processions, and demonstrations." Equally striking was the appearance of a handful of lawyers who really defended their clients, rather than, as of old, acting as auxiliaries of the prosecution.

It was not only the ruling oligarchy that was aging, the average age of the members of the Politburo being by the end of the decade over seventy. The Soviet system itself was displaying an unmistakable symptom of senility: the inability of the authoritarian organism to repel the virus of liberal and democratic ideas as effectively as in years gone by.

That sclerotic condition of the Soviet state was enhanced by, and in its turn contributed to, the plight of international Communism. The Western Communist parties sought in the 1970s to distance themselves somewhat from their Soviet comrades. Once their idol and master, the Soviet Union now appeared to their leaders in a different light: no longer a venerable and exacting parent, but a somewhat disreputable elder relative, still rich and influential, to be sure, and hence to be cultivated, but one no longer to be closely associated with and invariably obeyed.

This new posture adopted by the Western parties became known as Euro-Communism. The French party formally abrogated the harsher-sounding parts of its program, including the commitment to proletarian dictatorship (i.e., one-party rule). Italian Communists became quite outspoken in their criticism of various aspects of the Kremlin's policies, denouncing the invasion of Czechoslovakia, assailing the persecution of dissenters, and accepting, though not unambiguously, their country's membership in the European Economic Community and NATO. Criticism of the once-worshiped Fatherland of Socialism now became quite fashionable in Western Communist and left-wing circles. The Spanish leader Santiago Carrillo was so outspoken in his attacks on Moscow's policies that his speeches had to be ignored or heavily censored in the Soviet press.

To some extent such attitudes followed from political opportunism: the success of the European Common Market and the need to heed the changed mood of the democratic electorates made subservience to Moscow more costly than ever for Western Communism. But the new posture also reflected a degree of disenchantment: militarily more powerful than ever before, expanding in the Third World, the Soviet Union had somehow become less awe-inspiring. The transgressions of Stalinism, as revealed since 1956, the repression of Hungary and Czechoslovakia, dissent—all sapped the moral authority that Moscow once exercised over the movement. The split with China undermined faith in the old formulas and methods: could one really believe that Communism was going to inherit the earth if its two largest powers were at swords' points?

Pessimism about the avowed goals of their movement was perceptible even among the aging oligarchs in the Kremlin. Brezhnev's remark to his involuntary Czechoslovak guests in 1968 that something may come out of Western Communism in *fifty years* was probably typical of the attitudes of those men, solicitous mainly of their own power. Their predecessors, beginning with Stalin, may have been equally skeptical about the possibility of a world revolution in their lifetime, but if so, they were better at concealing their doubts. The pursuit of détente and rapprochement with the West was in itself proof—as the Chinese had argued even when moving in the same direction—that the Soviets' missionary zeal had given way to sheer opportunism. Along with security for their political system the rulers also sought what might be called international respectability. It was the search for the latter that impelled them to take a step that they must have almost immediately and deeply regretted and which continued to haunt them for the balance of the Brezhnev period. In 1975 the Soviet Union subscribed to the Helsinki Final Act, the product of the Conference on Security and Cooperation in Europe. The act was not only an agreement pertaining to security in the strict sense of the term. Its signatories, thirty-three European states plus Canada, pledged themselves to a charter of European peace and comity that obligated them to observe certain standards not only in their foreign policies but also in the domestic ones touching on human rights.

It was the latter part of the agreement that was to prove to be a burden to Soviet policy makers. The original Moscow motivation in pressing for a European security conference was understandable: the need to have an international sanction of Europe's territorial status quo as prescribed at the Potsdam Conference in 1945 but never formally ratified in a peace treaty. The various agreements concluded between 1969 and 1972 under détente and Ostpolitik appeared to have removed the need for a general European conference to affirm the principle of inviolability of the 1945 settlement. But the aging Soviet policy makers were no longer as nimble in their diplomatic maneuvers as before, and so they still pressed for and obtained their conference, whose Final Act reasserted not only the permanence of the European territorial arrangement (mainly of Poland's western borders, and of the existence of the German Democratic Republic), but also much else that would greatly embarrass the Soviet Union.

It was not merely détente but the changed conditions of the world community that rendered Soviet society more open to foreign scrutiny and influences. In placing his signature on a declaration affirming very basic human and political rights, Brezhnev (who was present on the occasion, along with other leaders of the signatory states) quite likely believed that he was subscribing to harmless rhetoric. How could the Soviet reality of 1975 be reconciled with the opening declaration? It stated, among other things, that "the participating states will respect human rights and fundamental freedoms, including freedom of thought, conscience, religion. . . . They will promote and encourage the effective exercise of civil, political, social . . . rights [which] derive from the inherent dignity of the human person."[14] Had the noble principles enunciated in the Final Act been applied in earnest to Soviet domestic and foreign policies, perestroika and glasnost would have had their start right then and there, with the former having a much better chance of succeeding then than after yet another decade of stagnation.

It would, however, have been unimaginable for the Brezhnev-Kosygin team to come up with such initiatives. By the same token, the Politburo oligarchs no longer had the self-confidence that enabled them to entirely ignore their international obligations. Now those pledges, just as the hitherto dormant provisions of the constitution, rubbed off, however slightly, on Soviet reality. The dissidents would invoke the Helsinki Final Act as the legal and moral basis of their stand. The act put the signatories under an obligation to facilitate regulations governing emigration of its citizens. This placed an added emphasis on an already complex and painful area of Soviet domestic policy (also closely connected with foreign policy): a widespread and often frustrated desire of groups such as the Jews and ethnic Germans to be allowed to leave the USSR. Jewish emigration had already been a bone of contention between the United States and the USSR. In the honeymoon period of détente, 1972 and 1973, some sixty-five thousand Jews had been allowed to leave. But subsequently Moscow, offended by the U.S. Congress's attempt to tie the issue of free emigration to the Soviet-American trade treaty, put added obstacles in the way of Jewish emigration. The number of exit visas was greatly reduced, and even those eventually allowed to leave were subjected to interminable delays and chicaneries. And here was the Final Act, a standing reprimand to the authorities and an encouragement to those who insolently declared their intention to shake the dust of the Fatherland of Socialism off their feet. Some within the ruling oligarchy would undoubtedly have been inclined to say good riddance to the departure of people who found Soviet life uncongenial, especially in view of the surfacing anti-Semitic and xenophobic feelings. But to authorize mass migration, and especially at the importunities of the capitalists, would have further damaged that gloss of internationalism still felt to be of importance for the preservation of the system.

And so foreign expansion could not really compensate for, nor effectively obscure, the internal malaise of the Soviet state: the growing meaninglessness of ideology for the mass of its citizens and the loss of economic and social dynamism. Capable neither of countenancing reform nor of effectively eradicating the spreading, if still mostly passive, discontent, the ruling oligarchs marked time.

Mao Zedong's death in 1976 briefly revived Moscow's hopes that the Sino-Soviet split, the chief reason for the waning of ideology, could now be mended and world Communism might regain its former vitality. Another variant of the Soviets' hopes after the demise of the Great Helmsman (which had been preceded by that of Zhou Enlai) was that China now would enter a period of sharp intraparty struggle for succession. One gets the impression that the Kremlin would not have been unduly displeased to see the vast country lapse into a condition of prolonged civil war. But all such hopes remained unfulfilled. The Beijing regime went through a brief period of confusion and intraparty clashes, but those clashes did not last long enough to make any faction seek Moscow's help. The "Gang of Four," headed by Mao's widow, was quickly suppressed and after a while it was Deng Xiaoping who emerged on top, though eschewing any title that would indicate he was the real boss of the party and government. Deng was known for his strong anti-Russian feelings, but it is doubtful that, at the time, any Chinese leader or faction that could have emerged on top would have listened to Moscow's blandishments. Distrust of the Soviets had by now been built into the Chinese Communists' code of beliefs. Nationally, and within the party, the attacks on the Kremlin's "new tsars" solidified support for Deng.

Where Deng's elevation did make a difference was in making Beijing's policies more pragmatic. The masterful oldster had always seemed freer of doctrinaire zeal than any other Chinese notable, except for Zhou, and unlike the latter, he seldom concealed his skepticism about Mao's more extravagant improvisations. By 1978, Deng replaced Mao's designated successor, Hua Guofeng, as China's principal policy maker. Gone was what might be called Marxist-Leninist fundamentalism, that unreasonable straining after ideological purity and extreme egalitarianism that had been one of the most distinct and catastrophic characteristics of the Cultural Revolution. The new leader, in trying to epitomize the fresh approach, resorted to one of those cryptic sayings that have traditionally, and to an outsider somewhat comically, been employed to signal a major policy change: It doesn't matter whether the cat was black or white, as long as it did its duty by mice! And so quasi-capitalist measures were all right as long as they advanced the economy and welfare of the Communist state. The most significant change involved the abandonment of the collective farm system and the eventual return to family farming. As one might have expected, this injection of common sense into the picture resulted in an impressive rise in the volume of agricultural production. From its ruthless pursuit and extermination of the "capitalist roaders," Chinese Communists now turned to active encouragement of small- and medium-scale commercial and industrial enterprises that could now be individually owned. This also had highly beneficial effects on the country's economy.

So here was another "Great Leap Forward," and this time it was real. Those seeming doctrinaire zealots who only a few years ago denounced violently what they saw as the revisionist policies of the USSR and Yugoslavia, now leapt beyond "revisionism," landing, insofar as their economic system was concerned, in a modified form of capitalism. Here was another example of the pressure of modern life upon the tenets and practices of Marxism-Leninism. If the leaders of Soviet Communism still balked at following their erstwhile Chinese friends' example and embarking upon economic pragmatism, this was not only because of their general inertia when it came to social and economic matters. They were obviously apprehensive that economic reforms might lead to massive pressure for political ones (and the events of 1989 in Beijing were to prove them not completely wrong). Perhaps "erosion" is not an adequate description of what was happening in the 1970s to the entire edifice of "scientific socialism." Many of its tenets had become lifeless formulas, adherents of the creed observing them not out of a genuine belief but because of a superstitious fear that to abandon them would endanger the one precept of Communism to which they were still desperately clinging: one-party rule.

It was not, however, the ideological travails of the two major Communist regimes but the signs of their escalating discord that attracted the attention of the world as the decade was nearing its end. The immediate confrontation—through surrogates—of the two Communist powers took place in Indochina. Vietnam by this time had placed itself wholeheartedly in the Soviet camp. China had for a while the consolation of having a protégé in the Khmer Rouge regime in Cambodia, much as the latter had gained the unenviable distinction of dealing more cruelly with its own people than any other dictatorship in modern history, whether of the left or the right. In December 1978 the Vietnamese invaded Cambodia and quickly succeeded in imposing a Vietnamese-sponsored Cambodian government over most of the country. This in turn led to the Chinese attack upon its former Communist ally, Beijing's forces on February 17, 1979, crossing into Vietnam all along the border. What happened during the melee did not enhance either Moscow's or Beijing's prestige. The much better equipped and trained Vietnamese troops inflicted heavy losses on the People's Army, which withdrew on March 5; the Chinese government announced rather lamely that its troops had fulfilled their assigned task, having taught Hanoi a lesson. On the other side there was the undeniable fact that with its ally being attacked, the USSR confined its assistance to it mainly to ominous warnings and the dispatch of some supplies. One had to wonder what, if anything, the USSR would have done had China's troops reached the outskirts of Hanoi.

In April 1978 a leftist coup in Afghanistan brought to power a pro-Communist government. Though the former regime had been quite friendly to Moscow, the Soviet Union hastened to recognize and throw its protective mantle over the new one. But the latter embarked upon radical social reforms uncongenial to the traditionalist mores of the country and offensive to the religious feelings of the people. The difficulties were compounded by the bitter rivalry between two factions of the Communist movement. Within one year the situation both within the regime and in the country at large grew critical: the rulers were murderously set against each other; there was a nationwide uprising against what in the eyes of the majority of the fiercely nationalistic population was a puppet government run from Moscow.

What prompted the Soviets' intervention? The stories published under glasnost were to affirm that the decision to intervene had been reached by Brezhnev with the assistance of just three other Politburo members (no, not Gorbachev, then a candidate member), all of them conveniently deceased when the stories were given out in 1989. The Soviet invasion in December 1979 bore a brutal character. Among those killed was the head of the Communist regime, to whom only three months earlier Brezhnev and Kosygin dispatched a message congratulating him on his "election" (which followed the murder of his predecessor). Now he was disposed of not because, as the Soviet press alleged, he had been the tool of Washington and Beijing,[15] but simply because he could not cope with the situation and would not step aside.

The Kremlin must have thought that to allow a Communist regime, especially in a country neighboring on the USSR, to collapse would have been a dangerous precedent. But to American public opinion this *was* a dangerous precedent of a different kind. The Americans, though sternly disapproving, had gotten used to Soviet military interventions in their East European neighbors' affairs. But in Asia! The aggression brought to an end Soviet-American détente. SALT II, already in difficulty in the U.S. Senate, was definitely set aside and a major grain sale to the USSR canceled.

Substantial as were the immediate costs of the aggression in terms of its foreign reverberations, its eventual price was much greater. Like the proverbial straw that broke the camel's back, Afghanistan exposed both the burden and the futility of Soviet expansionism. Previously, it had been largely expansion through intimidation. Now the Soviet soldier had to fight the ruthless, fiercely nationalistic enemy in an area ideally suited for partisan warfare. If the entire drive for expansion was to serve the Soviet rulers as a public relations campaign for the faltering system and the nearly bankrupt ideology, Afghanistan proved a particularly unfortunate and countereffective investment—a Vietnam in reverse. At first there were great fears abroad that the invasion was part of a scheme to despoil Pakistan and deal the West a crippling blow in the entire Persian Gulf area. But as the picture unfolded and the Soviet and puppet troops could barely hold their own against the Mujahedin, those fears gave way to the recognition of Soviet vulnerabilities. Pakistan allowed itself to become a conduit for American supplies to the guerrillas and, along with Iran, helped the partisans' operations.

If the Soviet Union's performance in Afghanistan relieved its neighbors of excessive fears, it also failed to impress its citizens. In some nine years of fighting, the Soviets' casualties were roughly one-fourth of those suffered by the United States in Vietnam. Nevertheless, the war could not but contribute to society's growing unease about its government quite beyond the question of what the Soviet soldiers were doing in Afghanistan. In the first place, the Kremlin was performing poorly in the one area in which hitherto it had been assumed to be quite efficient. Nothing injures the reputation of an authoritarian government more than when, having resorted to repression or aggression, it shows itself halfhearted and inefficient (we shall see it demonstrated in the case of Poland). And here was the famous Soviet army, incapable of subduing a backward country, suffering reverses at the hands of primitively armed partisans. Hoping to minimize the domestic reverberations of the ill-conceived venture, Moscow kept its military contingent relatively small (below 150,000) and composed mostly of aviation and mechanized troops. Even so, the resentment at Soviet youth having to discharge what was officially described as their debt to "proletarian internationalism" was, as would be revealed under glasnost, quite widespread. The Kremlin had long justified its expansionism by representing it as support for "wars of national liberation." It was a fitting irony that it was a real struggle for freedom from alien oppression that dealt a telling blow to Soviet imperialism.

So many pressures accumulating on world Communism and its vanguard, the Soviet state! And the new decade opened with the death of a man whose career, more than that of any other Communist leader, epitomized the drama of the movement that had set out to conquer the world, and provided a kaleidoscopic vision of its triumphs and failures.

Josip Broz Tito died in May 1980, having survived (amazingly, in view of what a life it had been) and ruled his country until almost ninety. Here was a man who, as behooved a Communist hero, came from the lowest social strata. He was born a peasant and then became an industrial worker in his youth. But his lifestyle when he was in power came to resemble that of old-fashioned royalty. He, in old Yugoslavia, had been a courageous fighter for his ideals, but that did not deter him from being brutally oppressive when master of his country. Once a loyal and worshipful follower of Stalin, Tito did not hesitate, when his country's independence and his personal power were at stake, to embark on what then seemed a suicidal attempt to challenge the tyrant and the enormous might of the USSR. His defiance opened a new era in the history of Communism, but contrary to the early expectations, his own brand of Communism was toward the end not much different from that of Brezhnev's in the USSR. And it is not surprising in a man whose life witnessed so many shifts and paradoxes that he bequeathed a most burdensome legacy to his successors: the political arrangements he had devised made it virtually impossible for the country to be ruled dictatorially or, conversely, to be guided along an orderly path to democracy.

Yugoslavia had not fulfilled its earlier promise to combine national emancipation with a new, freer version of Communism. In Czechoslovakia attempts in that direction were brutally terminated. It fell to another East European country to demonstrate a fresh and revolutionary approach to the problem.

11

A PROLETARIAN
REVOLUTION

IT WAS THE INVASION OF POLAND that triggered World War II. Later it was the dispute over Poland's borders and its future government that divided the Grand Alliance of Britain, the United States, and the USSR. And the dispute, only equivocally settled at Yalta and Potsdam, in turn set the stage for that East-West conflict that endured until our own day.[1] Poland's fate—a Communist regime and Soviet domination—became that of all of Eastern Europe.

And it was thus fitting that it would be in this victimized country that one observed most clearly the growing vulnerabilities and ailments of "proletarian internationalism," leading eventually to its disintegration. The final crash of Communism in Eastern Europe was precipitated by its crisis within the USSR. But what made that crash inevitable once Moscow relaxed its iron grip was well illustrated by what took place in Poland in 1970 and 1980, and in a different sense by what did *not* happen after December 13, 1981.

December 1970, and in a much more massive way August 1980, witnessed revolutions in the classical Marxist sense: spontaneous uprisings of the industrial workers against the exploiters. Compared to them, the events of 1917 in Russia hardly deserve the name of a *proletarian* revolution. The February Revolution was sparked by mutinous soldiers and the Great October one was in reality a coup d'état carried out by the Bolshevik Party. While adhering to the Marxist scenario, the Polish revolt did not follow its Leninist variant; Polish workers did not rise against the capitalist class. What they saw as the exploiter was the state, run by a Communist oligarchy. The only comparable action in recent times, and on a much smaller scale, had been the uprising of the East German workers in June 1953.

December 13, 1981, signaled a major setback for the Polish workers, but hardly a victory for their Communist rulers. The latter proclaimed martial law, dissolved Solidarity—the association of free labor and professional unions—and imprisoned its leaders. The formal structure of Communist power was preserved. But without romanticizing the 1980–81 episode, one can still see it as concluding not in a defeat for the Polish revolution but something closer to a standstill between the nation and the rulers. The Communist Party retained power, but not authority. The best proof of this lies in the fact that the government did not dare to follow the proclamation of martial law by effective steps to eradicate revolutionary sentiments and antiregime agitation within society. The government did not feel strong enough to apply drastic measures, mete out death sentences, and indulge in severe repression as had been done in Hungary after the revolt of 1956. In Poland during the next few years the leading dissenters were being intermittently arrested and released. Strong-arm measures were being applied to the rank and file. In general, the regime's repressive policies were of a kind to enhance the irritation of society but not to cow it. It is not a figure of speech to say that Solidarity remained very much alive.

That it should have been so reflected largely some specifically Polish conditions. There was, for one, the power of the Catholic Church and the regime's reluctance to risk a confrontation with it should the state resort to terror. This power was significantly enhanced by the election in 1978 of the cardinal-archbishop of Cracow to the papacy. There was also the factor of sheer size. It would have been much more complicated and difficult to use the Kremlin's ultimate means of keeping the Eastern Europe countries in line—Soviet troops and tanks— in Poland than it had been when dealing with the Hungarian rebels and the Czech and Slovak reformers. It was the Soviets who advised moderation and the avoidance of terroristic measures to their Polish protégés, and reinforced their own scruples and fears when it came to dealing with Solidarity.

But the schizophrenic appearance of Polish society after 1981—a veneer of Communist power along with popular rejection of, and scorn for, Communism—was also due to something that was happening not only in Poland, but elsewhere in the bloc, and also, though it could not be seen as clearly, in the Soviet Union: the growing irrelevance of ideology. The almost explicit rationale the Communist rulers employed for their coup of December 13, 1981, speaks for itself. They did not do it, they practically told the nation, in the name of Marxism-

Leninism. It had to be done to save Poland from a military intervention by the USSR. In the eyes of the nation, this was only partially the truth; the *nomenklatura* did it also because its members wanted to hang on to their jobs. Even during the most oppressive period of its rule, Communism in Eastern Europe had had some genuine believers among the workers, the young, and the intellectuals. For many of them, Khrushchev's revelations and Hungary did not erase the belief in socialism: purified of its Stalinist excrescences, abstracted from Soviet imperialism, Communism was still a viable ideology. It offered social justice, and promises of material and moral progress. Czechoslovakia dampened those expectations but did not entirely extinguish them.

But by 1980 such hopes and illusions were almost entirely gone. And what is important and helps us understand the developments of the 1980s in the Soviet Union was the fact that, as shown by the Polish regime's behavior after it repressed (but did not destroy) Solidarity, the rulers themselves came to share, not openly of course, the disenchantment. They were finding the doctrine and its practical precepts incapable of coping with the complexities of modern economic and social life. Even the most cynical Soviet oligarch had to be shaken at the spectacle of millions of Polish workers rising unanimously against Communism. One could not delude oneself, as had been possible in the case of Hungary in 1956 and Czechoslovakia in 1968, that the whole trouble was provoked by those perpetually disgruntled intellectuals.

For the masses living under it, the very term "Communism" had become associated with an overgrown, inefficient, and arrogant bureaucracy, with economic and technological backwardness, and with industrial pollution and devastation of the environment. In the not so distant past, one could still hope for a different kind of Communism, with names like Tito, Gomułka, Ceauşescu standing as beacons of such hopes. But now they were seen as not really diverging from the traditional model of Communist leaders, except when it came to their relations with Moscow. Tito could still be admired for his skill in maneuvering between the Eastern and Western blocs. But Communism as practiced in Yugoslavia bore the same depressing countenance as elsewhere. Gomułka, once a national hero, stood revealed as a doctrinaire, narrow-minded party boss. Ceauşescu's courageous defiance of the Soviets in 1968 could by the 1980s no longer obscure the repression in Romania or his quite advanced cult of personality.

Those once highly advertised separate roads to socialism were all seen as ending in a blind alley.

The Polish rulers' predicament was thus but the most dramatic manifestation of what characterized all the ruling Communist elites as the decade of the 1980s opened: their almost sole preoccupation now was how to retain power.

The Gomułka regime's nationalist credentials had been fatally damaged in 1968 when it lent its hand to the invasion of Czechoslovakia. Poland had been in a strong position to refuse military participation and follow the example of Romania, which got away with this act of insubordination toward Moscow. But in fact Gomułka, along with Ulbricht, had been the strongest proponent of curbing the Prague regime's experiment in reform. Participation, even if symbolic, of the Polish units in the invasion was a humiliating commentary on the traditional device of Polish nationalism that called upon the people to struggle "for your own and everyone else's freedom." The regime's standing with its own nation had suffered even more as a result of its repression of the students and Gomułka's toleration of the anti-Semitic propaganda in which some of his associates had indulged. So there was plenty of combustible material around as the 1960s drew to their end.

Even in 1970 it was already discernible that one of the basic flaws of the economy of the countries of the socialist bloc was the unrealistic price system, especially when it came to articles of common consumption. As if to compensate its subjects for their political deprivations and generally low wages, the Communist regimes tried to keep the price of basic commodities artificially low. This in turn tended then, just as of this writing it does now in the USSR, to keep the economy out of balance. By 1970 the Polish economy was clearly stagnating. The government proposed then to embark on an ambitious program of reforms to impart dynamism and introduce fresh incentives to industrial production. One aspect of the plan envisaged raising prices on a wide variety of articles of consumption.

Raising prices in a Communist country has to be, as in any centrally managed economy, a delicate and politically somewhat risky operation. No Communist boss could be unmindful of the fact that even in the USSR such rises, especially on foodstuffs, had led on occasion to disorders, some of them, notably the riots in the south of Russia in 1961, requiring the use of army troops to quell them. One would have thought then that the government would observe some elementary precautions: stagger the rises rather than announcing them all at once; prepare society for the measure; couple the announcement with the promise of providing additional material protection for the lowest paid group of wage earners.

In the event, the government did exactly the opposite of what prudence would have required. There was no psychological preparation for the blow that would affect the entire population but would strike most directly at the poorer working strata. No "safety net" was provided for the lowest-paid. And to compound its imprudence, the government announced the rise on December 12: quite a Christmas present for the Polish masses! Had the whole tragedy of errors taken place in Stalin's time, those guilty of the idiocy might well have been brought to trial and forced to confess that theirs had been a vicious plot to discredit socialism and that they undertook it at the bidding of agents of the capitalist powers.

In fact, the initiative came from a group of economists who obviously had been living in a Communist version of an ivory tower, and the plan was then recommended to the Politburo by First Secretary Gomułka and received its unanimous approval. Price increases affected a wide range of foodstuffs—for example, some 17 percent for meat and meat products, 31 percent for cereals, about 12 percent for fish. There were also sizable increases on a variety of building materials. Coal, widely used for heating in this petroleum-less country, went up 10 percent. Prices were lowered on a number of commodities, but those items, such as refrigerators and washing machines, were, in the Poland of 1970, luxury items, accessible only to the more affluent.

Danger signs appeared already at the meetings of the party organizations in factories throughout the country held on the eve of the announcement of the increases to the general public. At the Lenin Shipyard in Gdańsk (Danzig), from now on one of the focal points of the revolution, the news was greeted with expressions of outrage by the workers. The party notable who had been explaining the Politburo's decision was ruffled enough to break into threats against the workers and, finally losing control of himself, shouted: "I did not come here to plead for your approval. You must do as you're told. I, myself, don't need your help."[2] In twenty years' time those words might well serve as part of the epitaph of Polish Communism.

Similar scenes occurred throughout the country, the audiences, composed entirely of party members, breaking into angry imprecations against the government.

Undaunted by the warning signals, Gomułka in a radio and TV speech announced the increases to the general public. The next day, fittingly the thirteenth, saw the explosion: strikes erupted in all the industrial enterprises along the Baltic seaboard. From the beginning one heard demands for the resignation of the highest party and government officials, including Gomułka. There followed mass meetings and demonstrations. The crowds were chanting: "We want bread"; "Back to the old prices"; "We demand higher wages." Such manifestations broke out simultaneously in several locations along the coast. It is important to bear in mind that even the official investigations were unable to establish any links between what was happening in Gdańsk and in other cities. There was no central staff, no leaders masterminding the eruptions. "Spontaneous" is, in this case, not an empty or rhetorical term.

The initial phase of the movement centered around the protest against the measures threatening the workers' livelihood. But already during the first days the motif of injured human dignity and national pride was surfacing along with the material grievances. The very first day a crowd, thousands strong, gathered before the Gdańsk party headquarters. As behooved a revolutionary manifestation, there was singing. And the songs sung provide good evidence as to what was on the minds of the angry people. There was still, though already sounding anachronistic, the anthem of the world proletariat, the "Internationale." But along with it the crowd joined in singing the national anthem and a hymn blessing patriotic and religious motifs, with its refrain, "Render us, O Lord, freedom for our Fatherland."

There was another and significant facet of the striking workers' behavior. A crowd penetrated the premises of the Gdańsk Polytechnic Institute. Here the speakers appealed to the students to join their movement and apologized for the workers' behavior in 1968 when they watched passively the authorities' repression of the students and intellectuals.

In the following days the street manifestations assumed massive proportions and began to spread to other parts of the country. There had been clashes with the police and isolated incidents of hooliganism and looting of the stores. It was still not too late for the government to calm the aroused passions and avoid bloodshed. The situation called for the top leader, the man who, for all his dereliction, had still not entirely lost his moral authority with the masses, to confront the workers in person to explain and plead for a social truce. But instead of repairing to Gdańsk or Szczecin (Stettin), Gomułka summoned the party and government hierarchs to his office in Warsaw. Here on December 15, 1970, it was decided to proclaim a state of emergency in Gdańsk and in the neighboring communities, and to empower army troops to use live ammunition to protect state and party buildings and to quell the disturbances. A member of the Politburo dispatched to the area of the disorders instructed the local authorities: "We are faced with a counterrevolution that must be put down by force. Even if some three hundred workers are killed, such measures would be necessary to suppress the uprising."[3]

Shooting did take place the next day in Gdańsk, with army troops opening fire on the workers who were allegedly attacking them with stones. There was abundant irony in the Lenin Shipyard becoming the central area of the struggle. The exasperated authorities at one point threatened to destroy this bastion of counterrevolution.

The government representatives with incomprehensible obtuseness persisted in throwing oil on the fire. One dignitary in a televised speech upbraided the strikers for their "demagogic" demands and felt the moment opportune to tell the nation that the shipyard employees, even before, had worked poorly and loafed on their jobs. Clashes between the army and the crowds of workers, the former now equipped with tanks and machine guns, the latter with stones and Molotov cocktails, continued for several days. The Lenin Shipyard was finally cleared of the sit-down strikers after they had been threatened with an artillery bombardment that would raze the entire works. An equally perverse symbolism could be read in some other coincidences of names and events: the Paris Commune Shipyard was stormed by government forces; Karl Marx Street witnessed a confrontation between a defiant mob and army tanks! It was only after the announcement of changes in the highest posts of the regime on December 20 that the fighting died down. Strikes and disorders, both along the coast and in the interior, continued for several weeks. The official and unreliable reports spoke of 44 persons dead, 190 wounded, and 2,300 arrests. In fact, the number of those killed in the entire affair ran well over one hundred.

The workers' revolt subsided. It proved to have been a rehearsal for the revolution of 1980, rather than a real revolution in itself. There were several reasons why the events took that turn. One was that the 1970 revolt was not merely spontaneous but also chaotic. It dissipated its efforts in street manifestations and clashes with the army, rather than sticking, as its 1980 successor did, to what is the workers' strongest weapon: the sit-down strike. The undisciplined and often rowdy behavior of the 1970 strikers was also in striking contrast with what would happen under Solidarity in 1980. As it was, the burning of party buildings, the occasional beatings of officials and militiamen, and the looting of stores did not enhance the image of the uprising.

Well, as Lenin had said, one does not enter the realm of revolution as if walking on a polished floor. The spark thrown in Gdańsk might still have ignited a conflagration throughout the entire country, no matter how rude and reprehensible some aspects of the revolt. But just in time the party notables realized that continued reliance on brute force could only have fatal results. They were helped in reaching that conclusion by a communication from the Soviet comrades. On December 18 the Polish Politburo received a message from its Moscow counterpart strongly urging a political solution to the crisis. This was a definite death knell for the Gomułka leadership. Covered with reproaches and accusations by his colleagues (who until the troubles escalated had gone along with his decisions), the discredited leader tried to hold on to his job. Then, felled by a heart attack, he finally succumbed to the pressure and offered his resignation.

The man elected to succeed him, Edward Gierek, until then party boss of Silesia, had aspired to the top job for some time and had tried to trip Gomułka. Not a doctrinaire like his predecessor, and a man with wider horizons (before World War II he had been a miner in France and Belgium and joined their Communist parties), Gierek by the same token fit quite well the more recent model of the opportunistic party boss. Removed along with Gomułka were the longtime prime minister, Józef Cyrankiewicz, and several other party notables considered to be Gomułka's men. But their successors, just as Gierek himself, were in no sense newcomers to the ruling team. They were party bureaucrats who had shared with the fallen first secretary the responsibility for all the flawed policies of the past few years.

In his first public speech Gierek struck the pose of one who despite his high office (which, as he assured his listeners, he had not sought) remained at heart a simple worker who could empathize with what the workers on the coast and elsewhere had been feeling and demanding. Very soon, and predictably, he placed the blame for all the past troubles on Gomułka and on his insensitive, and by now discharged, subordinates.

The new leader hastened to repair to Moscow as well as to some other capitals of the socialist camp. These visits were designed not only to inform and reassure the comrades about the recent and unfortunate happenings in his country, but also to seek help to tide the Polish economy over its current and rocky period.

"Recent events have, and painfully, made us realize the basic truth, that the party must always maintain close contact with the working class and the nation and that it must not speak in a different language from that of the workers," said Edward Gierek in a nationwide broadcast.[4] Unwittingly, the very statement epitomized how the reality of politics in what was supposed to be the workers' state departed from the ideal of Marxism-Leninism. According to the latter, the party was supposed to be the emanation of the working class and not something separate from it. Even when trying to mollify the workers, the party boss had to acknowledge the gap that separated the rulers from the ruled, and how only a near catastrophe would impel the former to try to appease and cajole the latter.

For the moment the gap was to be filled with rhetoric and material concessions. One cannot resist the impression that for the deposed oligarchs the rebellious workers had assumed the guise of counter-revolutionaries or louts and hooligans. Then their successors viewed the strikers in a hardly more flattering light: unruly children to be distracted with flattery and promises of some baubles. It did not take a very sophisticated analyst to recognize that for the first secretary, as for his predecessors, the art of governance consisted in the party, or rather its elite, successfully manipulating the nation rather than representing its wishes and aspirations.

For the time being, both contestants were ready for a truce. To be sure, toward the end of January 1971 a sit-down strike flared up again in Szczecin. Now, for once, the party leadership displayed courage and imagination. A prestigious party-government delegation, headed by Gierek, set out for Szczecin. It included the man who ten years later would find himself in the center of the storm, Wojciech Jaruzelski, then minister of defense. In the troubled city Gierek, by himself and without security guards, confronted a group of strikers guarding the entrance to the struck shipyard: "I am Gierek, first secretary of the party; will you let me in?"[5] And then followed a long dialogue between the party boss and the workers. The first secretary's performance could not but impress the workers, who had seldom been granted the sight of any party notables and then only to be scolded or threatened. In reminiscing about the encounter several years and several bitter experiences later, some participants confessed that they had in fact been taken in by the first secretary's apparent sincerity and promises of reforms. In fact, the political and professional outlook of the strike leaders of this particular shipyard was still quite narrow, and it was difficult for these simple people not to be impressed and a bit intimidated by the great person who suddenly appeared among them. They did, rather awkwardly, express their demands, such as for genuinely elected workers' councils. Gierek, a seasoned debater and persuader, had little difficulty in fobbing them off with vague promises: of course, all those arrested for promoting the strike would be freed (but not if found guilty of other derelictions); yes, there would be free elections to professional councils (but they must remember that it is up to the party to appraise what has happened and to draw appropriate conclusions). A participant in the meeting, who recalled the occasion in 1981, concluded that "it was a great mistake on our part not to be more unyielding and to make concrete demands . . . [but] we believed him. . . . There were tears in his eyes . . . .We ought not to have yielded unless guaranteed of real changes in the relationship of the authorities to society, between the worker and the employer [i.e., the state]."[6] The strike was called off.

The first secretary then visited the storm center. Here he found the going harder, since the Gdańsk workers displayed, to use Marxist terminology, more highly developed class consciousness and hence less willingness to trust vague promises. Unlike in Szczecin, the strikers' grievances reached beyond the professional and local issues and their language was harsher: "Why does the [official] press lie . . . ? Why did they shoot at the workers?" The demands were more forthright: not only for free labor unions, but also that those who had ordered the shootings should be fittingly punished. The press and other media must be free to tell the truth. And there was the as yet random *cri de coeur* that in time would preempt other grievances and demands: "The government ought to be elected by all of us and not just by the party."[7]

This was a point of great danger to the regime: if the workers remained incensed, strikes might flare up again all over the country. But Gierek rose to the occasion: as in Szczecin, but now more convincingly, he addressed the audience not as the bureaucrat-in-chief, but as one of them, speaking to fellow workers: "We shall never allow those tragic events to be repeated. . . . I need your trust and support. . . . With your help we shall reach our common goals. Will you help?" And the crowd chanted back, "We will, we will."[8] Shouting along with the rest of the crowd was the still-unknown Lech Wałęsa.

As in 1956, changes in the leadership helped save the Communist regime in Poland. But unlike on the previous date, that change was not accompanied by a nationwide euphoria and the feeling that the country was on the way to regaining its independence. There was a patriotic undertone to the revolt on the coast, but its edge was directed at the system: for the striking workers, the Communist system, and never mind whether it was run from Moscow or Warsaw, had failed to provide a satisfactory life. And so it was not with any renewed faith in Marxism-Leninism that they were returning to their factories— that faith had eroded among a great majority of them before 1970— but simply with the hope that the new leaders could do a better job. In 1956 the word "socialism" still had a strong emotional connotation for many workers, and perhaps even more for the young intelligentsia and the students. They were ready to believe in it, especially if it could be dissociated from subservience to the Soviet Union. The year 1968 marked the definite demise of the young intelligentsia's romance with Marxism. What was characteristic of the events in 1970 was that neither side resorted to the idioms of Marxism-Leninism. The authorities appealed to the strikers to return to work and preserve order not in the name of socialism, but simply for their own and their country's sake. And the workers' class consciousness, as noted, took the form of sharp antagonism to what they considered to be their real exploiters, the local and central bureaucracy of the Polish People's Republic.

Whatever confidence or toleration Polish society, and especially the working class, was ready to extend to the regime depended now on the very prosaic question of whether Gierek at the helm could pull the country out of the economic stagnation that characterized the last years of Gomułka's reign. In February the government canceled the price increases of December 1970. There was no genuine effort on the part of the regime to fulfill other promises to the workers. The two dignitaries most directly responsible for the brutal repression of the strikers were punished by being made ambassadors! The labor unions continued to be run by the party bureaucrats. And once passions cooled, the regime proceeded to apply punitive measures to those it identified as the main activists in the strike movement. The revolt had ended, but it was not succeeded by social peace, still less by a genuine reconciliation between the rulers and society. The sense of alienation that now prevailed among the people was exemplified by what one of the veterans of the strike was to write some years later. "From December 1970 to August 1980 I felt stripped of my national identity. Quite simply, Poland became for me a geographic expression. Even though I had been brought up in a strong patriotic tradition, it was all the same to me whether I would live in Canada or Bangladesh, rather than Poland . . . . I lost completely the sense of being Polish."[9]

That this sense of alienation did not lead to a new wave of strikes and worse was due to the Gierek regime's ability to sustain for some years the impression of economic progress. In the wake of the workers' revolt the USSR and some other countries of the socialist bloc hastened forth with assistance. Then came East-West détente and with it an opportunity to tap the Western money market. The Soviet Union had in the past frowned on its protégés establishing extensive trade and financial ties with the capitalists—this was in the Kremlin's eyes one of the besetting sins of Romania, as well as a suspicious item in the Czechoslovak reformers' plans. But now, and sensibly enough, since the Czech and Polish crises proved to be expensive for the USSR, Moscow withdrew its objections. The Polish government sought and obtained large credits from the West. They were used largely to build up heavy industry and secure foreign earnings, which were applied to import technology and consumer goods from abroad. This expanded trade with the West provided a shaky basis for rapid economic growth and a rising standard of living. For a few years the formula worked like magic. Poland's GNP rose almost 60 percent between 1971 and 1976; real wages increased at an annual rate of 8 percent. Poland, along with Hungary, where a similar economic strategy was being followed (but more moderately and prudently), became a leading exponent of socialist consumerism.

"Living on borrowed time" was a very exact characterization of the Polish economy in the 1970s. Yet it should have been clear from the outset that Gierek's strategy was unsound. Agriculture was neglected in favor of heavy industry. And the latter, financed by foreign loans, was largely geared to producing for the Western market, already shrinking after 1973 because of the recession triggered by the rise in oil prices. It is difficult to decide who was more thoughtless, the foreign bankers who poured money into the unbalanced economy, or the government for not using credits to modernize and rebuild the country's infrastructure. The government kept constructing new industrial complexes which, due to their obsolete technology, produced shoddy and noncompetitive goods. At the same time, Poland, once a major food exporter, paid heavily for agricultural imports. In 1975–76 the bubble began to burst. Much of the now reduced hard currency earnings had to be devoted to servicing foreign debts. Inflation had cut into the recent gains in living standards.

The ineluctable facts of economics finally caught up with the regime. By 1976 peasants were refusing to sell grain and produce to the state procurement agencies, demanding higher prices. The government, which according to Western economists had been subsidizing food prices to the tune of some $5 billion a year, felt it could not afford to pay more and that the burden had to be shared by the consumer. In June the regime bit the bullet: retail food prices went up by 60 percent. The workers' reaction might have been expected: instantaneous strikes. In one place a crowd tore up railway tracks; in another, strikers manhandled officials and burned the party headquarters. That was enough; within twenty-four hours the price increases were canceled.

The government capitulated to the enraged consumers. As was noted in the West, presciently though prematurely, "the events in Poland . . . exposed more openly than any earlier happenings in recent years how tenuous is the surface tranquility of Eastern Europe. This vivid demonstration by the Polish workers of their veto power over Warsaw government decisions must inevitably have given ideas to the people of the Soviet Union and of other Soviet satellites."[10]

As had been the case with many faltering authoritarian regimes, Gierek's tried to compensate for its moment of weakness by a display of brutality. Those accused of participation in the riots were not only arrested, but often severely beaten. Many were tried and almost invariably sentenced to imprisonment. But as also happens in such situations, this blend of weakness and brutality proved counterproductive: in 1976 an institution was born that proved crucial in the series of events that led to the mortal wounding of the Communist regime in 1980 and then, after a comalike existence, its expiration nine years later.

The institution was the Committee to Defend Workers (the Polish initials are KOR), which was founded by a group of intellectuals at first to assist the arrested workers who had been turned over to the courts. Among its members were some of the leading cultural and intellectual figures in the country. KOR's stated purpose was to help with the legal defense of the arrested and to render financial assistance to the discharged workers' families. But almost immediately this supposedly apolitical group of intellectuals, containing several former partisans of the regime, became in fact the general staff of Polish dissent. It is from its midst that the future consultants to Solidarity were to come. The prestige of the individuals associated with KOR made it awkward for the authorities to deal with them by the usual police methods: a well-known writer or a veteran of the socialist movement could not be beaten or peremptorily thrown into jail without creating a further wave of popular reprobation. Younger and less prestigious members would intermittently be arrested, and held for a short time, then released. As in the contemporary Soviet Union, dissent became a way of life for many, especially the young intellectuals. But while in the USSR in the 1970s this was confined to a seemingly isolated group, in Poland it emanated from all classes and institutions in society: the workers, the Church, the intelligentsia. Sullenly tolerated by the working class, by and large repudiated by the intelligentsia, the Communist regime had really no sizable constituency in the nation. With KOR in the vanguard, open, semiopen, and clandestine dissent spread widely. The volume of underground literature, discussion groups, and press dwarfed quantitatively the current Soviet samizdat. In the four years that remained to the Gierek leadership, there grew up in Poland, a Western observer noted, a veritable counterculture of dissent.[11] But perhaps "counter" is inappropriate, for the writings and activities of the dissidents were certainly more representative of the nation's mood than the voice of those who ruled it.

That the party more or less tolerated the cacophony of dissent was clearly due to its diffidence. Domestically, it could not be sure that a systematic and thorough crackdown would not lead to a major explosion. As far as its relations with the West were concerned, Warsaw wanted to preserve the image of an enlightened Communist regime that did not resort to crude repression. Such an image was necessary if the Western governments were to continue to allow, indeed to encourage, their banks to pour money into a bankrupt economy. And the regime's restraint did in fact impress many in the West. Statesmen as astute as France's Valéry Giscard d'Estaing and Germany's Helmut Schmidt cultivated Gierek, whom they believed to be very influential with the Kremlin and, for a Communist, quite pro-Western. One recalls the gaffe committed by President Gerald Ford who in his debate with Jimmy Carter during the presidential campaign of 1976 asserted that Poland was quite independent of the USSR. And though such naiveté might well have contributed to Ford's defeat, his victorious rival paid a visit to Warsaw the next year and was quite complimentary in his remarks on Poland's record on human rights. Inevitably, one sees an analogy to Gorbachev, who by 1990 was less popular at home than in the West. But the Soviet statesman did preside, even though shakily, over a real liberalization of the system. Gierek and his associates were just posturing.

As to the real physiognomy of the regime, one gets an insight into it from the rules governing censorship of the media. An official of the office of censorship who had defected abroad transmitted to KOR the secret instructions according to which his office was expected to regulate what could and could not be published and broadcast by the media. The latter were not supposed to inform the public about the import of technology from the West because "too much of such information might lead the average reader to believe that the modernization of our economy is based on the equipment we receive from the developed capitalist countries."[12] Conversely and logically, the media were forbidden to mention any defects or poor quality of the industrial machinery purchased in the USSR. What is more serious is the prohibition of any mention of diseases and ailments incurred by workers because of unsanitary working conditions and of the incidents of food poisoning in factory canteens. "From the materials about the protection of or threats to the environment, one must eliminate any items about the danger to human life and health caused by industrial pollution and use of chemical products in agriculture. This prohibition applies also to the concrete cases of dangerous pollution of the atmosphere, water, soil, and food products."[13] If the public was to be kept ignorant about the defilement of the environment by its own government, the same delicacy need not be observed in regard to a "fraternal country." The media were to be allowed to transmit the information about the pollution of Polish rivers flowing from Czechoslovakia, provided that it was attributed to industrial activities in that country. Commentaries are superfluous.

Equanimity about the ruinous effects their economic policies had on the environment was not peculiar to Polish Communist leaders. One thinks of Chernobyl and what glasnost revealed about similar derelictions in the USSR: the pollution of rivers and lakes, the salinity of the soil in once-fertile regions, the lack of elementary precautions in constructing nuclear plants. What is most striking about this attitude of the rulers is not so much its cynicism, but its shortsightedness: this disregard of environmental common sense had to be counterproductive as far as their industrial and general economic goals were concerned. And not only the masses but they themselves and their families had to be affected by the polluted air and water.

One is also struck by the inherent absurdity of many of the guidelines for the Polish censors. A good example is the directive on prices. "Without approval by the proper authorities, it is not permitted to release information about the prices for consumer and other goods being raised or lowered. . . . One must eliminate all criticisms of the prices of new items appearing on the market."[14] So, unless he read about it in the paper or heard it on the radio, the Polish consumer would not realize that he had to pay more for a loaf of bread, nor was he smart enough to understand that by classifying a standard article as new, or of higher quality, the government is in fact raising prices. The handbook is filled with such inanities. There are absurdly detailed instructions on how to avoid anything that might be construed, God forbid, as criticizing things Soviet. There are exhaustive lists of people whose names are taboo for being less than enthusiastic about People's Poland—artists and writers whose names are well known to the public and whose works are widely circulated. At times the regime appears to be wrestling with itself: here is a film or a book which, because of some slip on the part of the authorities, has been allowed to be shown or published, but must not be mentioned in the media. The government has concluded a kind of truce with the Catholic Church, but your censor must be careful about any material presenting the Church in a positive light—for instance, one must not allow anything suggesting that "the Church has rendered great services to the nation."[15] It is a strange sense of political paranoia and unreality that pervades the document. If one could apply such terms to political entities, one would be tempted to diagnose the condition of Polish Communism as approaching a nervous breakdown.

To be fair, the government did make some efforts to avoid being stultified by its own propaganda and to seek objective evaluations of the condition of the country. In 1977 the Council of Experts was instituted, a body including academics, journalists, and other professional people, many of them not members of the party. Its confidential reports were destined mainly for the top boss—Gierek. In a way, the institution epitomized the regime's Hamlet-like posture: its diffidence about what it was telling the nation, and yet unwillingness to tolerate glasnost; its earnest endeavor to find out how things really were,

provided the information was kept secret, accessible only to those at
the apex of the party pyramid. But again there was a faintly preposterous air about the whole enterprise. What those professors and other
experts communicated in great secrecy should, for the most part, have
been obvious to any thinking person. And of course they could not
be *entirely* candid—for example, to say what many of them must have
felt: "It is not so much you [the government], it is the system."

Even so, our experts' observations are of interest. Here it is suggested, tactfully but unmistakably, that the government's standing
with society is going down. "As the result of the June [price riots of
1976] the ties between the authorities and society were weakened
still further."[16] And the reasons for this widening chasm are, even if
somewhat euphemistically, spelled out: society is being told incessantly about the successes of the government's policies while in fact
the country is facing growing hardships. One of the main reasons for
the regime's—well, the authors cannot quite bring themselves to call
it unpopularity—"failure to deepen its ties with society" lies in the
average citizen's attitudes. "He feels himself utterly without any influence over what is happening in his place of work, his city, in the
party and social organizations."[17] The authors are seldom explicit in
distributing blame for the travails of the nation, but still one cannot
miss the point of their cautiously phrased litany of grievances. "There
has grown a sense of the prevalence of injustice when it comes to the
treatment of the individual and the defense of human rights. . . . The
institutions of socialist democracy have become a facade. . . . There
has grown up a belief about the existence of widespread corruption."

When it comes to concrete suggestions of how the situation might
be improved (i.e., what the regime ought to do), the writers again are
cautious and indirect: it would be highly desirable if the actual role
of the legislative institutions corresponded more to what their function
is supposed to be according to the constitution, if the workers' councils
in the factories were genuinely elected, if what the people are told in
the mass media were closer to what was actually happening.

But what cannot be glossed over and comes out more clearly from
the reports than from their timid suggestions are the grim data about
the nation's condition. The year that had passed since the 1976 riots
had seen a significant growth of absenteeism in the factories. Productivity and the quality of labor of the industrial workers had declined. Society as a whole had grown indifferent to the loosening of
social discipline, to hooliganism. The data on alcoholism were shat-

tering: Poland now had the unenviable distinction of being first in the world as far as the consumption of spirits per head was concerned. Twelve years before, the number of alcoholics was estimated at 1.4 million. By 1977 it had reached 5 million (i.e., well over 10 percent of the total population). Every day it could be assumed that 3.3 million persons were in a state of intoxication.

While many of the 250 or so people drawn into the work of the Council of Experts were not party members, it is unlikely that the government would have called for advice from individuals thought unfriendly to the system. And yet for all the circumlocution in the writing, it is a grim picture of Polish society that emerges from the report, and for all the rapporteurs' discretion, there is no doubt as to who bears most of the responsibility for that condition. Furthermore, the most that the writers can suggest in the way of improving the situation are palliatives: the government should be more attentive to public opinion (but how can that opinion be really gauged in a police state?); it might endow the legislative bodies with some authority (but in the absence of political pluralism, how can they be really representative?); it ought to curb the bureaucracy (but how can it be done without undercutting the party's monopoly of power?).

Following the events of 1980–81, a writer was to note that the "greatest challenge to Communist rule in East Europe has come from Poland."[18] In the late 1970s such a statement would have appeared rather extravagant. True, the regime was in sore straits, but by the same token society appeared drained of the spirit of rebelliousness. The events of 1970 and 1976, though not lacking in patriotic undertones, were centered around the economic postulates of the workers. It was not as yet readily perceived how the existence of KOR and the general burst of dissidence was endowing the working masses with wider horizons. But what accounted most for the apparent passivity of the nation, visibly restive under unpopular rule, was the same factor that had protected the regime since its inception: the widespread conviction that any major challenge to it would bring Soviet military intervention. The Gierek team, for its part, kept reminding society that it had an influential friend. In 1975 the government had proposed to place in the constitution a statement affirming the country's eternal friendship with the Fatherland of Socialism. At the time this formal recognition of vassaldom had to be abandoned because of widespread protest. But for all such reactions, few in Poland could believe that an attempt to overthrow the regime, or to make a fundamental change in the nature of that regime—say, something in the nature of what the Czech reformers had attempted in 1968—would be tolerated by Moscow.

At the same time, the Kremlin was strangely unconcerned about the course of events in Poland, displaying none of that watchfulness with which through the winter and spring of 1968 it had followed the developments in Czechoslovakia. The Soviet oligarchs disregarded warnings coming from several sources, including their ambassador in Warsaw, that Gierek's economic policies, as well as his excessive toleration of dissent, threatened disaster. But just as Gierek managed to charm some Western statesmen, so he managed to convince Brezhnev and Company of his reliability and his ability to handle the situation. It was little realized in Moscow that the Polish boss's skill in manipulating the party and state machinery and in getting rid of potential rivals was not matched by an ability to contain indefinitely his countrymen's grievances and aspirations. And then the elderly men of the Kremlin were set in their ways, partial to the people they had come to know, and disliked seeing new faces in positions of responsibility, whether at home or abroad. (To be sure, they slipped in 1978 by promoting and bringing into their midst a relative youngster—the forty-seven-year-old Mikhail S. Gorbachev.) Gierek continued to be one of the select group of East European Communist leaders whom Brezhnev would invite to share his summer vacations in the Crimea.

An important though ambiguous element in the Polish situation was the role of the Catholic Church. Ever since 1956 when the regime concluded it could not afford open warfare against the Church, the relationship between the two parties had been somewhat reminiscent of that between the United States and the USSR: occasional sharp conflicts, periodic rapprochements and détentes, both sides recognizing that an all-out war was out of the question. The Church openly proclaimed its grievances: difficulties in procuring permits to build new churches, antireligious motifs in the education of the youth, and other difficulties of coexistence with the regime. The latter watched enviously the Church's growing moral authority and its political implications. But whenever in trouble, as in 1970 and 1976, the regime—just as its Soviet sponsor—would seek to allay the tensions by summitry: the first secretary would seek a meeting—one might almost call it an audience—with the primate of Poland, and as between the two superpowers, the mere fact of such a meeting having taken place would have a soothing effect on the public.

As seen from the above, the Church's role was that of a severe critic of the regime, but not its enemy in the sense of pressing for its overthrow. It could never compromise with the materialistic and atheistic philosophy professed by the rulers, but true to its traditional mission, it would not approve of the kind of defiance of the authorities that might lead to violence and bloodshed. On the whole, as grudgingly conceded by the regime, the Church's influence was important in preserving social peace. Some officials interpreted the Church's policies rather cynically: the government, by trying to bar (even if not very effectively) Western ideas and trends from entering the country, was thereby also protecting Polish Catholicism from the ailments and disputes that ever since Vatican II had assailed the faithful in the democracies. They should be thankful for living under Communism, a minister instructed a group of clergy: unlike what was happening in the West, they did not have to cope with liberation theology and rebellious priests and nuns.

For all of the Church's hierarchical structure and discipline, the attitude of the clergy was of course not uniform. Some bishops would have gone quite far in conciliating the authorities; others, and many of the rank-and-file priests, lent their support to dissent. But it was the masterly primate Cardinal Stefan Wyszyński who had the last word in laying down the general policy, and his stance was one of neither collaboration nor defiance of the Communist state.

Still, and inevitably, whatever strengthened the authority of the Church weakened that of the party. And so it must have caused considerable uneasiness among the rulers when in 1978 a countryman of theirs, until then the cardinal-archbishop of Cracow, was elevated to the papacy. The euphoric reception by the nation of John Paul II on his visit to Poland the following year reaffirmed not only the strength of religious sentiment among the masses, but also by implication the irrelevance of Marxism-Leninism to the Polish scene.

For all the superficial placidity of society, it should have been clear by the late 1970s that the next economic crisis might trigger more than just riots and strikes. If the Kremlin and the Warsaw regime were heedless of the danger, then the same could not be said about the forces of dissent. The May 1979 issue of the *Information Bulletin of KOR*, distributed almost openly, carried an article entitled "The

Country's Situation and the Tasks of the Opposition." The author wrote, "Our basic premise must be the fear that we are threatened by our society exploding with anger on a scale much vaster than on all the previous occasions [those of June 1956, December 1970, and June 1976] taken together."[19] Why should the possibility of such an explosion have been viewed with apprehension by an opponent of the regime? Well, the Polish reader would have readily understood, though it was not even hinted at in the article, that an all-out assault on the regime would almost inevitably bring a Soviet invasion. How then, according to the writer, was the danger to be deflected? By society pressuring the regime to make significant concessions, both political and economic. Such concessions then would be the starting point of the peaceful political evolution of the country, which, though the author does not say so explicitly, would lead to the end of one-party rule and to democracy.

Another dissident publication, *The Path*, the organ of a group calling itself the Movement for the Protection of Human Rights, also signaled the approach of a potential disaster: "The authorities of the Polish People's Republic have lost the ability to direct the nation. . . . After thirty-five years the entire system lies in fact in ruin, and goes on functioning only due to inertia. . . . Society's resistance [to the government], weak and unorganized during the first postwar decade, has grown from the 1950s on into a continuous and spontaneous pressure. . . . Superimposed upon the Polish situation is the crisis of the entire Soviet system. . . . More and more, one hears opinions that Poland is on the brink of a sudden huge explosion [that] might destroy the existing structure of power."[20]

The new crisis ripened in the late spring of 1980. In view of the approaching storm, there was an air of unreality about the government's posturing and trying to advertise its role as a bridge between East and West. In May, Gierek hosted Brezhnev and the president of France, Valéry Giscard d'Estaing, in Warsaw. A few days later he held conversations with David Rockefeller, head of the Chase Manhattan Bank. On June 21 the first secretary delivered himself of an exceedingly bad prediction: "Knowing our nation, confident of its creative forces, we look with confidence to the future."[21] Those creative forces were indeed to manifest themselves, but in a manner unanticipated by the hapless party boss.

Higher prices for meat and some other products were introduced on July 1. Strikes were already breaking out in central Poland when

Gierek repaired to Strasbourg to receive the medal of the International Institute for Human Rights. By the middle of the month some 80,000 workers in 1,977 factories had laid down their tools. And then, to use a quip most appropriate to this situation, it was "déjà vu all over again." The Lenin Shipyard in Gdańsk became the scene of unrest. But there was a dramatic addition to the old script. Unlike in the 1970 and 1976 strikes, which lacked real direction, this time a leader did emerge. Lech Wałęsa was his name and he was an electrician by profession, who four years before had been discharged by the management and had been active since then in the attempts to organize free labor unions. He now addressed the milling workers, gained their confidence, and became their spokesman in the negotiations with the authorities of the shipyard. At first his fellow-worker negotiators were ready to settle for a pay raise, but buoyed by the news of the eruption of new strikes all along the Baltic seaboard, Wałęsa's eloquence carried the day: the strike would not only continue, but it turned into a movement with demands far transcending the questions of pay and working conditions.

With leadership came not only a sense of purpose, but also organization and discipline. The experiences of 1970 and 1976 taught them, wrote one of the strikers, that they must not leave their factories and indulge in demonstrations that would inevitably turn into riots. And so it was strictly a sit-down strike, and its growing dimension left the government with but two alternatives: to storm the factories, with all that implied, or to negotiate, no longer with workers in individual factories but with the Interfactory Strike Committee, which would soon speak not only for the strikers on the Baltic but for the entire working class, and in a sense for the nation. Gierek, his vacations on the Black Sea with Brezhnev and other Communist notables rudely interrupted, still failed to grasp the magnitude of the upheaval. His television address of August 17 followed the old script: pledges of immediate material concessions to the workers, combined with vague promises of eventual political and social reforms. And there were threats. A bowdlerized version presented to the Soviet leaders gave them the first inkling that something out of the ordinary was going on in Poland. "Referring to the situation in some enterprises on the Baltic, E. Gierek noted that certain irresponsible elements have tried to explore the isolated [*sic!*] work stoppages for hostile political purposes. . . . 'We shall not tolerate any action directed at the political and social order in Poland. . . . In that respect, nobody should expect concessions, compromises or even hesitations.' "[22] As those words appeared in print, the government was dispatching an emissary to Gdańsk empowered to promise almost anything if it could only arrest the avalanche. And in a nervous reflex the Central Committee of the party began to sack some of the highest party and state officials believed to be particularly objectionable to society.

When the government representative confronted Wałęsa and his associates, their demands had by now escalated. They were grouped under twenty-one headings. There was a historical irony in the number. When the Communist International was organized in 1920 by Lenin, its statute listed twenty-one conditions that had to be met by the participating parties. And now this same figure marked the prelude to what would become the final act of the drama of international Communism.

How alien the *Weltanschauung* of Communism had become to the Polish workers was demonstrated by yet another symbolic event. There in the courtyard of the industrial complex named after the father of Communism was celebrated on September 17 the Catholic Mass, with the strikers then lining up to receive Communion. This then became a daily event. And in addition to divine help, Wałęsa sought counsel from the intelligentsia and dissidents. To the regime's added discomfiture, several members of KOR were enlisted as consultants to the strike committee. Among them was Tadeusz Mazowiecki, who nine years later would be the first prime minister after the collapse of the Communist regime, and then, what in 1980 would have seemed equally fantastic, Wałęsa's rival for the presidency.

On August 31 the government's plenipotentiaries signed an agreement that on the face of it spelled an almost complete victory for the workers. The government commission pledged that the state would guarantee and ensure complete respect and autonomy for the new labor unions in all aspects of their activity. Other concessions also echoed the workers' demands: generous pay raises, a shortened work week, additional social benefits, and the right to strike. In the mood of the moment few gave much thought to the possible effects of those concessions on the faltering economy.

The nation's attention was riveted to the regime's pledge to abide by the constitution, to allow freedom of expression, and to release political prisoners. And the ideological bankruptcy of the regime was underlined by the Communist authorities' agreeing "to ensure that the radio will transmit the Sunday [Catholic] mass under a special accord with the episcopate."[23] Equally unheard of (if put into practice) for a Communist country was the promise that henceforth "radio, television, the press and publications should be used to transmit a variety of ideas, views and opinions."

These concessions went far beyond what Dubček and his fellow reformers had aspired to in 1968.

The shadow of the Soviet Union hung heavily over the negotiations. Hence the workers' pledge that their future unions "do not intend to play the role of a political party." They agreed further that under the circumstances (this sounded almost ironic) the Communist Party should continue to play "the leading role in the state." And unmistakably with an eye toward the east, the victorious workers declared that they did not desire to tamper with "Poland's existing system of alliances." For the moment and the foreseeable future, few would question the necessity of Poland's remaining within the Soviet camp and the Warsaw Treaty Organization.

The actual proceedings of the negotiations had been carried on the radio and there could be no doubt as to the impression created on the nation and in the world: it was in fact the government that had become the supplicant. If the workers did concede on the points mentioned above, then everybody understood that it was because there had been, though not physically present, a third party to the business, looking over the negotiators' shoulders—reminding them of the facts of Poland's geographic location and the realities of international life.

One did not have to wait long for the consequences of the regime's apparent capitulation. On September 5 the party had a new leader. Gierek's departure was strikingly similar to that of the man he had ousted ten years before: having allegedly suffered a heart attack, he submitted his resignation within days of the Gdańsk agreement. The supposed mediator between East and West departed unlamented. In Moscow a state publishing house had been preparing a Russian edition of Gierek's speeches and articles; it would never be published. In Warsaw it was being intimated that the fallen leader might have to face criminal indictment. The new first secretary was Stanisław Kania, a colorless bureaucrat. From now until the proclamation of martial law there would be a constant flux within the upper ranks of the party and government hierarchies. The announcement of Gierek's dismissal was accompanied by a Central Committee statement that under other circumstances (i.e., without the USSR watching and the economic distress) would have been highly humorous: "The protest [of society] was not directed against the leading role of our party, the role dictated by history; it was caused by the mistakes the party has made."[24]

Following the Revolution of February 1917, what had been the Russian Empire found itself under what has often been described as "dual power": there was the Provisional Government, its legitimacy and authority constantly challenged, and the Petrograd Soviet of Workers and Soldiers, which claimed, and on many an occasion exercised, veto power over decisions of the tottering Kerensky regime— as the government came to be known, after its most conspicuous member. Poland's situation between August 31, 1980, and December 1981 was quite reminiscent of Russia's between February and October of 1917. Within a few weeks the entire pre-August fabric of the Communist political structure had come unraveled. The Gdańsk compact served as a model for similar agreements with rebellious workers elsewhere, in some cases the strikers' demands being even more far-reaching. At its height the strike movement embraced 1.5 million workers from some 2,000 factories. By the end of September this already vast industrial army coalesced into a federation of free labor unions—Solidarity. This then became the other half of the "dual power," which would rule Poland for little more than a year. And even when officially suppressed, Solidarity had not been vanquished. Once the umbilical cord linking the Communist Party to Moscow became severed in the late 1980s, Solidarity revived, and this time it could and did trounce the Communist regime.

Except for the factors, or rather *the* factor, mentioned above, Solidarity could have swept the party aside practically from the beginning of their tortuous coexistence. It very soon ceased to be just a workers' union, with the peasants, professionals, and students clamoring to join its ranks. It grew prodigiously until it had more than nine million members. The "government unions," as they were known, dwindled into insignificance.

If under Gierek, Polish society had already been the freest of all in the Communist states, then with Solidarity it assumed the appearance of what in the Kremlin's view must have seemed a veritable madhouse. The government lacked the courage and strength to maintain the usual practices of the police state. The regime was capable only of fighting a rearguard action, negotiating and pleading, no longer daring to threaten.

But what was happening in the meantime to "the vanguard of the proletariat"? Well, the new first secretary, whose entire background had been that of a conformist bureaucrat, struck the pose of a reformer. The game of musical chairs going on within the regime's high command was dubbed "renewal." Simultaneously, the authorities bared the depressing picture of corruption, bureaucratic abuses, and inefficiency that helped bring the country to its present straits, blaming it all, needless to say, not on the regime as such, but on Gierek and those officials who bit the dust along with him.

More than any previous crisis, this one showed the artificial nature of Communism in Poland. There were, to be sure, genuine reformers within the party, people who believed in the possibility of reconciling Marxism-Leninism with a measure of social pluralism and freedom. But it was now more obvious than before that most of those who were in the party had joined for careerist reasons. Among those who stayed in its ranks (and there had been a mass exodus since August), there was considerable support for a "renewal" of Polish socialism. Many Communists found nothing incompatible in their joining one of the Solidarity unions. In the upper echelons, some, whether out of opportunism or out of a genuine conviction, went along with the current mood of the nation. But others were hardened authoritarians and diehard conservatives who for all their liberal posturings were determined to fight tooth and nail to keep their jobs and official privileges.

Poland in 1980–81 offered a preview of what was to afflict Communism at large only a few years later: not only the failure to create a viable economy and a social consensus, but also the inability to preserve the full panoply of its powers in the face of mounting popular pressures.

For the moment, what had to preoccupy Moscow and other fraternal capitals was a related problem: whether and how the Communist Party of Poland could get back into the saddle. The threat seemed, and was, greater than in the case of Czechoslovakia in 1968. Then it had been the Communist leadership that had departed from the straight and narrow path and became mired in the quicksands of reform. Now it was the masses that made the party eat crow and were in a position to run it out of business. Solidarity's pledges not to interfere with the current pattern of Soviet-Polish relations were being taken by the Kremlin, and perhaps correctly, with more than a grain of salt. But the events in Poland had to be disturbing even to the "liberal" and anti-Soviet Communist rulers. The notion of genuinely free labor unions, emancipated from party control, was incompatible with every existing Marxist-Leninist system: leaders of East European regimes hastened to Moscow to plead with their hosts that something must be done to put an end to the scandalous situation lest the contagion spread. And this time Rumania's Ceauşescu also sought counsel and reassurances from Brezhnev. Delighted as they usually were whenever the Russians experienced troubles with their empire, the Chinese expressed their disapproval of the antiparty motif in the Polish revolution.

As we now know, Soviet contingency plans for an invasion of Poland were formulated within weeks of the August crisis. At the same time, a number of Polish party and military leaders were readying a scenario for the imposition of martial law and a crackdown on Solidarity by the Polish armed forces, whether in conjunction with, or in order to avoid, the Soviets' armed intervention.[25]

There were at the same time cogent reasons for the Kremlin to hesitate before using force directly or indirectly (i.e., through the Polish army) to suppress what it regarded as a counterrevolution immediately in the wake of the events of August. The mood of the Polish people was such that invading troops were likely to meet with armed resistance, and, whatever its high command might ordain, at least part of the Polish army would have joined in fighting the invaders. Poland appeared a much harder nut to crack than Czechoslovakia had been. It was much bigger than the latter, and anti-Soviet sentiments among the people were much stronger. Its occupation could not be merely symbolic in nature: sizable Soviet garrisons would have to be deployed throughout this country of 35 million people. Occupation would saddle the USSR, whose own economy was beginning to stagger, with the direct responsibility of running a bankrupt country where workers and farmers were bound to make the invader's task harder. With the economies of the socialist bloc heavily dependent on the flow of credits from the capitalist world, an invasion would spell the end of such bounty. There were bound to be heavy political costs as well: Moscow's attempts to loosen the ties between Western Europe and the United States were not going to be helped by the pictures of Soviet tanks in Warsaw. Several Communist parties, notably the Italian and Spanish, announced that an invasion would mean their definite and final break with the Fatherland of Socialism.

Such dilemmas were to be temporarily deflected by the events of December 13, 1981. But the events in Poland in 1980 must have been a vivid demonstration to the Kremlin of the costs and dangers of hanging on to its external empire, and thus prepared the ground for Gorbachev's willingness a few years later to preside over the liquidation of that empire.

While preparing for a possible military solution, the Soviets were hoping for a political one. The best eventuality from Moscow's point of view would have been to let the wave of unrest and popular enthusiasm in Poland subside, allowing the Communists to recover from the shock and to begin to close ranks. Once the regime gained some breathing space and economic realities curbed the insolence of Solidarity, the government could, ran the scenario, proceed gradually to undo the most scandalous reforms, bring the labor unions back into subjection, reestablish strict censorship, and deal out exemplary punishment to the troublemakers. In the meantime, the USSR proposed to keep up relentless psychological and political pressure that would discourage the hotheads among the workers and restore the courage and morale of the diehard Polish party members. Throughout late 1980 and most of 1981 there would be Soviet troop concentrations on the Polish border and suggestions leaked to the Western press about the imminence of invasion. A rather typical Soviet news story would hint at the presence in Warsaw of some dark forces that "were trying to overthrow the socialist system of Poland and to move the country out of the socialist alliance of the Warsaw Treaty Organization. . . . Under the mask of 'renewal' counterrevolutionary forces are striving toward the ultimate goal of the destruction of socialism in the country."[26]

Leaders and advisers of Solidarity were well aware of the danger and of the need to avoid unnecessary provocation of the country's powerful neighbor. At the time, the question of Soviet intervention quite apart, few Poles would have considered tampering with the socialist economic system as such. Wałęsa and his closest associates were carefully eschewing anti-Russian rhetoric and any criticism of Poland's membership in the Communist bloc. But there were influential members of Solidarity who questioned Wałęsa's moderation and caution. Looking back, it is difficult to see how the tortuous coexistence of Solidarity and the Communist regime could have continued indefinitely, but it is fair to say that at the time most Poles, if allowed to preserve internal freedom, would have tolerated the continuation of the Communist regime and agreed to the country remaining within the Soviet bloc.

But could the regime have endured such coexistence? Would the

Communist Party, repudiated by the working class, emasculated insofar as its authority was concerned, still be able to wield any power within the system? The Soviets evidently had some doubts on that count, for they now increasingly courted and communicated with the military figures of the Communist establishment rather than with the apparatchiks (those people of the party apparatus), epitomized by Kania. The civilian bosses were for once self-effacing and not averse to having generals advance to the forefront of their ranks. A soldier's uniform was still supposed to, and in fact did, have some sentimental associations for the nation; the party card by itself definitely did not. And so perhaps Communists in military uniform could help.

In February 1981, General Wojciech Jaruzelski, longtime minister of defense, was appointed prime minister. The general had a rather favorable reputation among the public because of rumors (unverified) that both in 1970 and in August he had opposed the use of army troops against the strikers. But as had been the case with every high-ranking officer of the Warsaw Pact countries, his military advancement would not have been possible without Moscow's express approval. His appointment, however, was not made solely for the sake of placating Polish public opinion. Kania was allowed to linger as the party chief for a bit longer, but the helm of the currently foundering Communist ship of state passed to the general. And he immediately embarked upon a rescue operation: according to the subsequent revelations, within days of this appointment Jaruzelski, who kept command of the army, began secretly planning for a crackdown on Solidarity.[27] He then, with Kania, traveled to Moscow to report to the Soviet comrades, currently holding their Party Congress. Brezhnev's view of the Polish events, as expressed in the general secretary's report, was unambiguous: "In fraternal Poland, enemies of socialism, helped by foreign forces, have been instigating anarchy, thus hoping to turn the course of events in a counterrevolutionary direction. . . . [But] the Polish Communists and working class can fully rely on their friends and allies; we shall not abandon fraternal Poland in its plight. . . . Communists have never faltered before the enemy, and they have always prevailed. Let no one doubt our firm resolve to protect our interests and safeguard the socialist achievements of our nations."[28]

There were elements of unconscious humor in Brezhnev's part-lamentation, part-threat: the image of the Polish working class eagerly awaiting Soviet help to free it from the yoke of Solidarity; those wicked foreign capitalists, abetting counterrevolution by pouring billions into the Polish economy. Brezhnev and his fellow Politburo members were more realistic in their private talks with Jaruzelski and his entourage. The discussion that ensued could not have been pleasant to the Polish side. It centered on the Soviet query "When and how?" According to one source, the general assured the Soviet comrades that he was working on contingency plans for the introduction of martial law, but the time for it was not quite ripe. When the moment was ripe, the Polish leadership, "conscious of its allies' backing, is determined to use all means for the protection of the country from the counterrevolution."[29]

The great euphoria with which society had greeted the founding and the victory of Solidarity was bound to be succeeded by a more sober mood. Predictably, the economic picture worsened, not only because of continuing mismanagement by the reigning bureaucracy, but also because of the very concessions granted to the workers. Sporadic strikes, in many cases disapproved of by Solidarity's leadership, both illustrated and compounded the crisis. The government, still not feeling itself strong enough to confront Solidarity in an all-out struggle, engaged in constant harassment: arrests of the more radical activists, and refusal or delay in registering new free unions. Some voices within the workers' movement urged the use of a general strike to compel the regime to abandon its double game. Considerations of what such a strike would do to the already tottering economy kept Wałęsa and the more cautious of Solidarity's leaders from authorizing the action. Another party strenuously opposed to a confrontation between the two components of the "dual power" was the Church. The majority of the rank-and-file clergy strongly supported Solidarity, but the hierarchy, especially after the death of Wyszyński and his replacement by a much less commanding figure, Józef Głemp, threw its weight on the side of moderation and against any action that might lead to violence and the risk of Soviet intervention.

Throughout the spring and summer of 1981 the situation grew more heated. There was a steady pressure on the authorities to dismiss those provincial officials and industrial managers who resisted the reforms or who retained attitudes that in the eyes of the workers were incompatible with the spirit of the time. There were signs that the government might be readying its forces for a counteroffensive. Unobtrusively, General Jaruzelski began to place military personnel in key posts within the civil administration. Not always so unobtrusively—for obvious reasons their visits were often made public. Soviet military and civil notables were traveling to Poland much more than before. The commander-in-chief of the Warsaw Pact forces was a frequent visitor. And few could read the news of Marshal Fyodor Kulikov's arrival "for professional talks" without reflecting nervously on what had happened in a "fraternal socialist" country in 1968.

Even though its patience was being sorely tried, the Kremlin had no cause for undue haste. After the initial alarm, it was soon realized that for the moment and the immediate future there was little danger of the Polish disease spreading to the other countries of the bloc. Much as the Hungarian or Czech worker envied the rights and freedoms won by his Polish counterpart, he would hardly try to emulate his example while Poland's economic situation was going from bad to worse. By the same token, the USSR and its allies could not view with equanimity the country's industrial production grinding to a halt and the standard of living declining to a point where the people's exasperation would lead to another, violent explosion. Here was another lesson to the USSR of how heavy the burden of empire had grown: between September 1980 and May 1981 the USSR, according to a Communist source, provided Poland with over $4 billion in goods and hard currency.

Whatever the resolution of the crisis, it was obvious both to the Kremlin and to the Polish leaders that any reintroduction of the Communist version of law and order had as its prerequisite a resuscitation of the Polish Communist Party. Post-Solidarity Poland could not be run just by a bunch of generals, and even if there was to be a Soviet occupation, there would have to be a native facade for the alien rule.

It appeared for a while that the Polish United Workers' Party would not be able to provide such support either for its own or for Soviet military rule. Buffeted by the forces of nationalism and democratization, the party stood in imminent danger of being transformed into something quite different from the traditional hierarchical Marxist-Leninist model. In view of the happenings, it was obviously necessary to call a special party congress. But in accordance with the now-reigning glasnost (to anticipate the future Soviet term), the manner of electing delegates to it was to depart radically from the usual Communist practice. Instead of lists of delegates having been prepared by the central authorities and then being "elected" unanimously by the local membership, there were to be real, free elections. Throughout the spring of 1981 the Communist oligarchs in the USSR and the fraternal countries watched with horror, the rest of the world with amazement, as the electoral meetings turned into tempestuous debates. The party notables were being berated by the rank and file, and many of them were being denied a seat at the congress. If the process went on unchanged, the congress might turn into a Western-type party convention, with the new leadership (i.e., the Central Committee and the Politburo) composed overwhelmingly of reformers. Some speakers at the electoral meetings did not hesitate to criticize the USSR for exploiting Poland economically and for its interference in Polish domestic politics. There was an open season on the party's past and, to a somewhat lesser extent, present, leadership. Unless the party healed itself, thundered one speaker, it would be reduced to "a body of a few hundred thousand, most of them administrative, security, and military officials—that is, the people who feel revulsion against physical labor."[30] If this orgy of glasnost continued, the party would become incapacitated to serve as a counterforce to Solidarity, in fact might be transformed into an ancillary organization of the latter.

And so Moscow spoke severely, ordering the Communist high command to put a stop to the party's self-destruction. The Soviet Central Committee's letter to the Polish leaders, sent on June 5 and made public six days later, spoke for itself. Decisive steps had to be taken to curb "enemies of socialist Poland. . . . A wave of anti-Communism and anti-Sovietism is gaining force. . . . We would like to believe that the Central Committee of the Communists of fraternal Poland will be equal to the task. . . . The party can and ought to change the course of events even before the Ninth Congress."[31] This menacing directive had its effect; the regime exerted whatever influence and pressure it could summon to assure that the electoral process be cleansed of its excessively democratic characteristics. Those efforts were largely successful, for the majority of the delegates to the congress turned out to be of the conformist variety.

The congress followed the traditional Communist practice of heaping abuse on those who had failed and fallen: Gierek and his discredited henchmen were ceremoniously read out of the party. Kania and Jaruzelski, both pillars of the regime for more than two decades, were confirmed in their posts. The majority of the Politburo was still cast in the pre-August 1980 model. For the moment the Soviet Union's bridgehead in Poland had been saved.

One year after the revolution the impasse between the regime and society still continued. The leaders evoked more and more the specter of "national catastrophe"—i.e., Soviet tanks—should Solidarity persist in its demands. The people in turn kept pressing the government to fulfill its promises, such as "social control of mass media," which of course would have meant the regime surrendering its last line of defense. Strikes were now almost daily occurrences; it was difficult for Wałęsa and other moderate leaders to control their more impatient followers.

September brought another congress, that of Solidarity. As might have been expected, aspirations of many in the movement now escalated: Solidarity no longer defined itself just as a federation of labor unions, but also as a "social movement," a sort of euphemism for a political party. But what must especially have drawn the attention of the Kremlin (and very likely raised the blood pressure of its aged inhabitants) was the message issued by the congress "to the workers of Eastern Europe." The message was addressed not only to the Czechs, Hungarians, etc., but also to "all the nations of the Soviet Union." And if that were not bad enough, the Polish workers proceeded to scandalize the Communist bosses everywhere by declaring Solidarity to be the first independent and self-governing labor union in postwar Poland. Sounding the traditional Polish refrain "for our freedom and yours," Solidarity expressed its support for those who in the countries it addressed had chosen to emulate its example and "enter the difficult path of struggle for free unions." It would not be long, the manifesto proclaimed, before the representatives of free unions from all those countries would meet with their Polish comrades.[32] Trade unions of all Eastern Europe were to unite, and it was not necessary to spell out what chains they would have to cast off.

One can well imagine the seething fury that prompted the subsequent communication from the Central Committee of the Communist Party of the Soviet Union *and* the Soviet government (it was quite unusual for both bodies to join in addressing a foreign party) to their Polish equivalents: "We expect that the leadership of the Polish United Workers' Party and the government of the Polish Republic will *immediately* take decisive and *drastic* measures to stop the slanderous anti-Soviet propaganda and to put an end to hostile acts directed against the Soviet Union."[33] (My italics.)

Under the circumstances, Solidarity's manifesto was obviously imprudent. Many in the movement's ranks were on the one hand intoxicated by the experience of a year of (near) freedom and, on the other, infuriated by Moscow's implied and open threats. And it was

argued, possibly correctly, that such ruffling of the Soviets' feelings
would not affect their eventual decisions—look how deferential
Dubček and Company had been toward Moscow, and where it got
them!

The regime and Solidarity now found themselves on a collision
course. On October 16, Jaruzelski took over from Kania as first secretary, still retaining his other posts. He immediately launched a series
of meetings that in times of crisis had become obligatory for the leaders
of Communist Poland: seeing the primate and representatives of society as well as receiving Soviet marshals and generals. Had the leaders of Solidarity been more vigilant, they could not have missed the
implication of a resolution the government presented to and had carried through the legislature: "If the nation's existence were threatened, the legislature would consider endowing the government with
appropriate powers."

Even today it is difficult to sort out the various explanations and
versions of the coup of December 13, 1981. Was the regime's action
the result of an ultimatum addressed by Brezhnev to Jaruzelski that
unless the Poles put their house in order the Soviets would march in?
Had the whole enterprise, on the contrary, been planned all along by
Moscow and its Warsaw friends, as asserted in the version to which
we have already alluded? Were Jaruzelski and his fellow conspirators
motivated by patriotism and a genuine desire to spare Poland from
what might have been the terrible cost of Soviet occupation? Or were
they, on the contrary, acting in accordance with the Kremlin's instructions? In any case, there can be no question that the USSR had
foreknowledge of the coup and that Marshal Kulikov had not been
visiting Warsaw just to exchange soldiers' reminiscences with Jaruzelski. Would the Soviets have moved with their own and fraternal
countries' forces if the regime's hand had faltered? Again this is something that we cannot be sure about, but hazardous as the application
of the Brezhnev Doctrine would have been in this case, it is difficult
to see how in 1981 the USSR could have tolerated a non-Communist
Poland.

On December 11 the members of the central directorate of Solidarity
assembled in Gdańsk, unmindful of the rumors that the government
was about to spring a surprise. Few in the leadership were ready to
credit the decrepit government with the strength and resolution to
carry out an *effective* coup. There had been recent negotiations about
the government and Solidarity joining forces in a front of national

unity that would cope with the worsening economic situation. On the regime's side this was apparently a ruse to mask its real intentions. As for Solidarity, its conditions for such cooperation included the unions' assuming a major role in directing the economic life of the country and further measures of liberalization. On December 12, Solidarity decided to respond by a general strike to any emergency measures by the government, and to hold in three months' time a national referendum on the question of whether the country should exchange its present system for a democratic one.

The government's coup took place during the night of December 12–13. It was carried out in the classical style of such enterprises: the Polish authorities placed troops and tanks everywhere. Telephones and other means of communication were cut off. A general curfew was imposed. Solidarity leaders grouped conveniently in Gdańsk were scooped up by security forces. Arrests followed all over the country, thousands being carried off to internment camps. At six o'clock in the morning General Jaruzelski spoke on the radio, announcing the creation of the new supreme state organ, the Military Council for National Salvation, over which he would preside and which assumed the plenitude of powers. Along with the proclamation of martial law came decrees dissolving Solidarity and kindred organizations, banning strikes, and even suspending temporarily most of the newspapers and magazines.

Officially, Poland was under a military dictatorship. All the members of the awkwardly named supreme council (in Polish it sounded even worse, since the initials spelled "crow") were military officers, ranging from the highest-ranking generals to a mere colonel, whose claim to fame was his participation in a Soviet space shot. In fact, it was the party in uniform that had taken over, the purely military veneer believed to be more acceptable to most Poles than an overt reassertion of the authority of the despised party bosses. The word "Communism" was not mentioned in Jaruzelski's speech, its stress placed on a patriotic appeal. "The Fatherland has found itself on the edge of an abyss. . . . Let us strive together to avoid the specter of civil war." And a rather extravagant and almost humorous pledge: "[The taking of power by] the military will not replace the usual processes of socialist democracy."[34]

Before the fateful night it had been widely believed both within Solidarity and by its foreign sympathizers that (1) the army would not allow itself to be used to suppress its fellow countrymen and that (2) any government blow at the movement would be answered and de-feated by a general strike. Both beliefs proved to be greatly overoptim-istic. But it is important to note that neither of those assumptions was fully tested. The actual mechanics of repression were handled by the special security troops, with the army serving as a backup. It was still not clear how the soldiers would behave in the event of a civil war. There were plenty of strikes and riots following the proclamation of martial law, and some of them had to be put down by armed force. But as the events of 1970 and 1980 had demonstrated, though in different ways, effective strike action requires leadership, and those would-be leaders were among the thousands who had been interned. Even in the very beginning the regime was careful not to push its repressive measures too far; had it resorted to executions and other measures like those applied in Hungary after its revolution, there is little doubt that Poland would have had an explosion surpassing that of August 1980.

As it was, a year and a half of continuing and deepening economic distress (in the course of 1981 the Polish GNP fell 13 percent) was bound to weaken the workers' willingness to suffer further sacrifices, both materially and as a consequence of repression. The Church threw its weight on the side of moderation. And to be fair, the reckless talk by the more radical elements within Solidarity gave at least a shadow of plausibility to the patriotic rationale offered by Jaruzelski: the army had to take over because otherwise the Soviets would surely have marched in. The coup, it can confidently be asserted, would never have been attempted, or if attempted could not have been successful, without the knowledge that the Soviet Union stood behind Jaruzelski.

And the USSR hastened to express its approval. "Tass has been authorized to declare that the Soviet leadership and people are follow-ing attentively the Polish developments. . . . We greet with satisfaction the statement of W. Jaruzelski that the Polish-Soviet alliance has been and will remain the foundation of the Polish national interest and that Poland will remain an inseparable member of the Warsaw Pact and of the socialist commonwealth of nations."[35] There must have been some misgivings as well as sighs of relief in the Kremlin. The former because it was a bit embarrassing and perhaps bad precedent to have the Communist Party rescued by the military. But it was certainly better than having to mount an invasion, with all the risks that would portend. How long would the USSR have to stand armed guard over the 110 million people of Eastern Europe?

The latter question was especially poignant in view of the realization that what had taken place in Poland had been a rescue operation and not a victory. As in the case of Czechoslovakia in 1968, it is important to note what did *not* happen in the wake of the repression of the reform movement. The regime, and its Soviet sponsors, did not feel strong enough to stamp out the opposition; it stopped at containing it, using chicanery rather than outright terror. That chicanery to be sure was on a large scale. "By December 1982 about 3,616 sentences for politically motivated offenses had been handed out."[36] But even when interned, Lech Wałęsa continued his political activity and intermittently negotiated with those who ordered his arrest. It was perhaps symptomatic that Wałęsa and a large number of Solidarity activists were released from internment within a few days of Brezhnev's death in November 1982. And by the end of the year the regime terminated the state of martial law. The USSR had entered an interregnum. As they watched Andropov and Chernenko—both already aged and infirm at the time of their elevation—preside in turn over the Soviet regime, leaders of other countries of the socialist bloc must have sensed portents of turmoil in the Fatherland of Socialism. And that in turn dictated caution and restraint in their own domestic policies. Solidarity, officially banned, went underground, and its presence there would be felt until its formal resurrection in 1989. During the intervening years, for example, "the four-page weekly of Warsaw's underground Solidarity had not missed a single issue. It was being printed in six different underground shops with a press run of about fifty thousand copies."[37] The government chose to turn a blind eye to much of the underground, though the security forces did engage in the harassment of the dissidents: arrests, beatings, and (in rare cases) murder. But the word "dissident" is inappropriate: most of the people *conformed* to a strongly antiregime feeling. Communism in Poland was no longer merely bankrupt; it became irrelevant to the nation, and if the latter was still dressed in Communist clothes, there could be no question that they would be discarded at the first occasion when this could be done without the fear of foreign intervention. But even with the shadow of the preperestroika USSR still present, the government's position would have been more than shaky except for the measure of qualified support extended to it by the Church. John Paul II's repeat visit to Poland signaled the Vatican's opting for the resolution of the regime-society clash through dialogue rather than violent means. After the disbanding of the military governing council, Polish politics returned to the usual party-bureaucracy pattern. Some in society would still see General Jaruzelski as acting largely out of concern for the nation's interests. Others, as a prominent member of what might be called the opposition establishment said to an American reporter, felt that "he has not been more repressive because society would not let him."[38]

And so even after a military coup this strange Communist regime was still inhibited in dealing with its enemies and critics, largely dependent on the Church for whatever toleration society extended to it, ultimately dependent on the shadow of Soviet tanks and troops. "I have seen the future and it works," wrote an American publicist after a visit to the USSR in the 1930s. By the 1980s so many premises of that exultant assertion had been shattered: as demonstrated by the Sino-Soviet dispute, Communism offered no easy path to a peaceful world; it had failed to match the economic progress of the capitalist West. And now in Poland, Marxism-Leninism and the party professing it had been repeatedly rejected by the very class whose viewpoint and interest they purported to represent.

12

THE RAVAGES OF GLASNOST

SOME YEARS AGO, well before the onset of perestroika, this writer was visited by a Polish economist. He immediately informed me that though long a member of the Polish United Workers' Party, he was a staunch enemy of everything connected with Communism and was far, indeed, from being an admirer of the Soviet Union. Our conversation soon turned out to be a monologue, with my visitor vehemently denouncing Marxism-Leninism and recounting the real and alleged crimes committed by the Russians (as, in common with many Europeans and Americans, he would habitually refer to the inhabitants of the USSR, no matter what their nationality) and their protégés and puppets ruling Eastern Europe. Having finished his harangue and on the point of leaving, he brightened up, patted me in the Polish fashion on the shoulder, and added, "Thank God the Soviet Union is a Communist country." Seeing my incomprehension, he, in turn, was amazed: "But it is obvious: if the Russians had any decent system of government, they would have ruled the world a long time ago."

My visitor's logic was somewhat flawed. But his statement was not just mischievously paradoxical and, if unwittingly, humorous. It hinted at an important truth: it had been the Soviet Union's role as a superpower and the directing force of the international Communist movement that obscured the internal weaknesses of the Soviet system. And conversely, the appeal and influence of Communism reflected not so much the inherent attractiveness of the doctrine but, certainly since World War II, the power of the USSR and its ability to inflict repeated discomfitures upon the democratic-capitalist camp headed by the United States. It would have been almost inconceivable to imagine Communism remaining an important factor in world politics without the presence and power of the Soviet Union.

What was less obvious was the extent to which the stability of the Soviet system was dependent on the image of the USSR as the leader of the "socialist camp," leading it in a continuous and successful struggle against the forces of capitalism. The Soviet rulers had lost their enthusiasm for spreading Marxism-Leninism long before they gave it up explicitly in the late 1980s. But if they kept it up for so long after they had lost their missionary zeal, it was because of the suspicion, whether conscious or not, that an ideological veneer was a necessary condition of the political security of the Soviet regime. In this sense Soviet foreign policy until perestroika was a gigantic advertising campaign for the Soviet system, the means of preserving its legitimacy in the eyes of the people and of the rulers themselves. For the former, Russia's power in world affairs and the ideological mission were supposed to be compensation for the domestic failures and shortcomings of the Soviet state. For the ruling elite, its exertions, allegedly on behalf of world Communism, provided a psychological reassurance that for all of its autocratic and repressive ways, it served not its own interests but those of the nation and humanity. Keep, if you will, your autocratic powers, but give up the ideology was the message addressed by Alexander Solzhenitsyn to the men in the Kremlin in his *Letter to the Soviet Leaders*, published in 1970. Well, no sooner did Gorbachev and Company start to follow that advice than power began to slip out of their hands. It is perhaps pertinent for the author to repeat what he wrote in 1982. "It is easy to imagine a Politburo member arguing that the USSR could not afford to become less feared abroad and more liberal internally. It would then be exposed to much greater pressures both from the outside and at home: growth of political dissidence; claims for real autonomy, if not independence, for the non-Russian ethnic groups; in fact, demands for reforms incompatible with the survival of the Soviet state and system."[1]

Why would the jettisoning of the ideology make the USSR "less feared abroad"? The outside world's dread of the USSR had not been caused entirely, or even mainly, by the awareness of its vast power, first in conventional arms, and then in nuclear weapons. It was also due to the Kremlin's posture as the champion of militant Marxism, bent, it was believed, upon conquering the world even at the price, if need be, of an all-out war. The period when the West stood most in fear of the Soviet Union was, as we have seen, when in fact it was in the weakest position vis-à-vis the United States. Between 1946 and 1953 the Kremlin's main concerns had to be the rebuilding of its war-shattered economy. Until 1949 it had no nuclear weapons, and then but a few and with no means of delivering them against the United States. But it was the ominous self-imposed isolation of the USSR and the awesome figure of Stalin that more than compensated for the Soviets' weakness and mesmerized the West with fear. Illogically, Khrushchev's Russia frightened the West less than Stalin's, though it now was an industrial as well as a military superpower and possessed a sizable stock of nuclear weapons and intercontinental bombers and missiles. The Kremlin spoke soothingly about peaceful coexistence and promoted summitry. To be sure, there was also Khrushchev's missile-rattling, but even his intermittent bluff and bluster was not as unnerving as Stalin's ominous silence had been. Still, the new leader exuded Communist fervor and, as he explained to Andrei Sakharov, believed it necessary to keep the capitalists in a state of constant nervous apprehension as to what the Soviet Union might do next. Khrushchev was considered a committed Communist and proponent of wars of "national liberation"—in plain English, of civil strife—often helped by the Soviets, against the pro-Western regimes. And so at times the great advocate of peaceful coexistence would be transformed into a zealot, unmindful of the risk of nuclear confrontation.

Nor could the West be too reassured about Khrushchev's successors, even though Brezhnev and Kosygin were certainly less flamboyant in their rhetoric and more circumspect in their actions. They were still seen as doctrinaire Marxists.

But it was during Brezhnev's reign that détente may have encouraged American statesmen to do something they would not have dreamed of in Stalin's time and hardly dared under Khrushchev: to try to pressure the Soviets about some aspects of their domestic policies. Yet for all the American initiatives on issues such as Jewish emigration and human rights under the Helsinki Accords, the USSR was still seen as a dangerous rival and potential enemy. It was a Communist state, hence its leaders were assumed to be free from the Western statesman's cautions and inhibitions.

The posture of what might be called controlled hostility toward the capitalists and hence the game of scaring the West thus had to be essential elements of Soviet foreign policy. Without them, that policy would have lost its ideological ingredient, with all the consequences to which we have previously alluded.

Yet as we have already seen, as the years went by, this posture became harder and harder to maintain for the Soviet Union. For one thing, it required the state to spend an enormous amount, estimated to constitute in Brezhnev's time up to 20 percent of its GNP, for military purposes, thus warping still further the structure of the Soviet economy. But the main dilemma of this ideologically contrived posture of defiance of the West, and of taking a position opposite to that of the United States on almost every issue of international life, lay in the possibility that, even if unwittingly, it might one day lead to a nuclear clash between the superpowers. Common sense urged that the Soviet leaders acknowledge that danger and as a major step toward eliminating it proclaim openly what they had known all along—that a nuclear war was unwinnable. And a necessary sequel to such an acknowledgment would be the recognition that the nuclear age required an entirely new approach to international relations, one that superseded all ideological and class criteria. We have seen how difficult it had been for the Soviet leadership to acknowledge that simple truth. And when it did come, in a 1978 speech by Brezhnev, it was still equivocal. An all-out nuclear war, declared the general secretary, would lead to a universal catastrophe. But he refused to go into any implications of that grudging admission. The general tone of Soviet foreign policy remained one of apparent unconcern about the United States and the USSR finding themselves repeatedly on a collision course, or about the possibility that one situation resulting from that course might escalate into a catastrophic clash. During the four years that remained to him, Brezhnev continued to discuss the possibility of a nuclear clash with the United States and on occasion, in private, between the USSR and China. At the Twenty-sixth Party Congress in 1981, he talked about the possible implications of NATO's deploying intermediate nuclear missiles in Europe (so as to offset the Soviet SS-22s). The general secretary denied that the USSR was seeking or had achieved a strategic superiority over the United States. He admitted that it would be sheer madness for either party "to count on achieving a victory in a nuclear war."[2] But there were enough nuances in his speech to make the West skeptical that the Soviet Union had given up, if not nuclear war, then nuclear blackmail as an instrument of its policy.

But quite apart from the dangers of a holocaust, there were other ominous consequences of the ideological components of Soviet foreign policy. Even during the brief period of the flowering of the Nixon-Brezhnev détente, the Kremlin felt it ideologically imperative to support anti-Western regimes and movements. Without alleging that the fault was exclusively the Soviet Union's, it is still a melancholy fact that the recent Iraqi war and the entire Middle East imbroglio were very largely a legacy of the cold war.

And so it was the growing evidence both of the futility and the danger of the ideologically defined rivalry with the West that was to a new generation of Soviet oligarchs an important stimulus to perestroika. For all of Brezhnev's belated and not quite convincing incantations about the danger of nuclear war, Gorbachev was the first Soviet leader whose repudiation of nuclear diplomacy had a ring of truth. It was also he who acknowledged that it was not enough to confront forthrightly the nuclear danger, but that the whole basis of Soviet foreign policy had to be rethought and freed of its Marxist-Leninist ballast.

Here, as we shall see, the cerebral conviction of the necessity of a new approach had to be reinforced by an emotional trauma. On April 26, 1986, there was a meltdown and an explosion at the Soviet nuclear plant at Chernobyl. It is still not clear how extensive and catastrophic the consequences of the disaster have been; one version would have much of Byelorussia's soil and rivers polluted for generations and much of its population condemned to suffer the aftereffects of radiation. But whatever the long-range implications, the immediate reaction, once the clumsy efforts of the Soviet authorities to prevent the spread of the news failed, was one of worldwide shock. The effects of the explosion were felt far beyond the boundaries of Byelorussia and the Ukraine. It did not take much reflection to realize that, catastrophic as the consequences of Chernobyl were, their total effect was only a pinprick compared to the devastation that even a "limited" nuclear war—if such a thing were possible—would bring, and not only to the belligerents. And this must have been on the mind of Mikhail Gorbachev when on May 14 he addressed the Soviet people on television.

In several ways the general secretary's address was a watershed between the old and the new, between Brezhnev's neo-Stalinist style of governance and what would be called perestroika. The old could be seen in the embarrassing delay before the regime's highest official decided to speak to the nation on a disaster of this magnitude. Obviously, the old guard in the Politburo had hoped the whole affair could be somehow minimized, and that this case of shocking mismanagement by a government agency would be presented as of minor significance. The new was evident in the relative candor with which Gorbachev discussed the whole business, his clearly genuine grief and solicitude for the victims.

It was not easy for the Soviet leader to change *entirely* the Soviet style of oratory on such occasions. Hence the lingering tendency to blame the West for its alleged attitude toward the disaster, and invidious references to a mishap at an American nuclear plant in 1979. Obviously troubled by the fact that eighteen days had been allowed to pass before he reported to his people on Chernobyl, the general secretary, with scant regard for the truth, informed his listeners that the American authorities took ten days to tell the Congress and one month to inform the world about the accident at the Three Mile Island nuclear reactor. The awkwardness of the Soviet leader's verbal calisthenics was of course compounded by the fact that there could be no comparison between the two incidents from the point of view of their consequences. The American one represented a *potential* disaster, Chernobyl an actual one. The speaker could not let the occasion pass without chastising "the ruling circles of the USA and their close allies" for supposedly gloating over Chernobyl. The same "circles" were also described as using the catastrophe as an argument against negotiating with the Soviet Union on nuclear arms control, an argument as specious as it was illogical.

For all such insinuations, which one might have expected in pre-perestroika Soviet propaganda, there was a fresh note in Gorbachev's speech. Not because the actual text of the speech contained conciliatory words, as well as the lashing of the West. But what would happen in the next few years proved that, overall, Gorbachev's speech really did signal a new era in Soviet foreign policy, and consequently domestic politics as well. "We look at the tragedy quite differently. We understand it as yet another tolling of the bell, another grave warning that the nuclear era calls for new political thinking, for new policies. . . . The nuclear age demands as imperative a new approach to international relations, the unification of efforts of states, no matter what their social systems, in order to put a stop to the ruinous arms race, and in order to radically improve the climate of world politics."[3]

What Gorbachev said on this occasion was really not much different from what he had said on the same subject three months before at the Party Congress. But this time he spoke against the background of a vivid demonstration of what might happen were the USSR to continue its foreign policies on the basis of the "old thinking": along the ideological lines and pursuing the path of "proletarian internationalism." Now, implied the Soviet leader, the USSR proposed to pursue the path to international stability, conciliation and accommodation with the West, free of the old ideological imperatives and inhibitions. Even when seeking détente in the early 1970s, the Kremlin had qualified it by stipulating that the ideological rivalry with the West must continue. Now even that caveat was abandoned. The phrase "ideological struggle" had been a euphemism for the Soviets' intention to pursue expansionist policies, to preserve and to add to their empire while avoiding a nuclear clash with the United States. Now, against the background of the exploded nuclear reactor spewing out radioactivity, came the realization that one had to make a choice: expansion, with its recurrent danger of a clash escalating into a catastrophic explosion, or a *real* peaceful coexistence.

"To be done with the export of revolution—that is the imperative of the nuclear age," Yevgeni Primakov, then one of Gorbachev's principal advisers on international relations, would soon write. Primakov's article was entitled "The New Philosophy of Foreign Policy."[4] While the author still paid lip service to the old Soviet propaganda motif that beginning with Lenin, Moscow's policies had always eschewed propagation of Communism by forcible means, he admitted that in the past the USSR had hardly practiced what it preached. "The crux of the matter is in the entirely new situation: in view of the accumulation of the means of mass destruction, there can be no victors in a thermonuclear war." Peaceful coexistence thus must not be a mere phrase. "It has become an absolute necessity for the survival of mankind. And isn't it essential that this situation demands urgently not only new methods in foreign policy on the part especially of the superpowers, but a completely new approach to problems of international life?" Why, he asks rhetorically, has that obvious, irrefutable truth been acknowledged by the rulers of his country only with the onset of perestroika? And here the reader can provide an answer: it had taken repeated setbacks of world Communism—Titoism, Hungary in 1956, Czechoslovakia in 1968, China's defection, the uprising of the Polish working class, to name only the most important ones—to demonstrate that the "export of revolution" was not only futile, but counterproductive as far as the interests of the Soviet state and people were concerned.

Our author goes on to argue that the pursuit of the ideological chimera has also been harmful to the internal condition of the USSR. His article was written at a time when it was not as evident as it is today how much damage the decades of Communism had done to the economy of the country. Primakov clearly implies, however, that the expansionist policies and the consequently enormous cost of the defense establishment crippled the Soviet economy: ". . . the organic connection between internal and foreign policies has never been as evident as today." Between 1976 and 1985 the rate of growth of the Soviet GNP had steadily decreased. And so "the gap in the GNP between the USSR and the United States has not only fallen, but has grown bigger."

Well, others within the Soviet establishment would soon chime in with arguments that it was not only the exorbitant military expenditures but the confining straitjacket of the anachronistic Marxist dogmas that had reduced the Soviet economy and society to such straits.

The Soviet scene, beginning in 1986–87, began to resound to the criticisms of orthodoxy on all counts. The stream of revelations about the horrors of Stalin's time, reduced to a trickle after the removal of Khrushchev, grew with glasnost into a veritable flood. The economic tenets of Marxism now became fair game for the critics, and the highest dignitaries of the regime would assail the "administrative command" system, i.e., the state monopoly of the means of production, as the source of all that was wrong with Soviet industry and agriculture. Public criticism of the Soviet past soon extended beyond Stalin. The new leaders somewhat uncharitably (and in view of their own performance, notably in the economic sphere, incautiously) took to referring to the lengthy reign of Brezhnev and the brief ones of Andropov and Chernenko as the period of stagnation. Criticism of the basic verities of Marxism-Leninism, of Soviet political culture, such as before 1985 would have come only from a dissident, now became commonplace, heard at party gatherings and seen in the columns of the newspapers and magazines. The notion of dissent became obsolete, the functions of samizdat virtually superfluous.

For all the breaches made in the Soviet system's outer defenses by the collapse of its ideological mission, one must ask, how could it, how did it, happen? Here was a regime that survived the kind of cataclysms that would have overturned any other government in modern times: the frightful ordeal of collectivization in the early 1930s, the virtual war waged by the Communist Party against the peasant majority of the nation, accompanied by a catastrophic drop in the standard of living and a famine that had held the country in an iron grip. Then came the Great Terror—the army and the security forces were all decimated. The country had still not recovered from that bloodbath and its economic and social consequences when it was struck by a military disaster, again unparalleled in modern history: in the first six months of the German war, the Red Army suffered a series of defeats that in any other conflict would have led to a belligerent's capitulation and a total collapse of its government and society. By December 1941 the extent of the defeat dwarfed that suffered by the tsarist regime in 1916–17, areas inhabited by 60 million people having been lost to the enemy.

With Stalin's death internal divisions and factional struggle shook the ruling oligarchy, and yet the authoritarian framework of the system remained unaltered. The Soviet regime had demonstrated a resilience unmatched in history. How trivial in comparison with its past disorders were the ailments that afflicted it in the beginning of the 1980s as far as the domestic scene was concerned: a lowered rate of growth of the GNP for the past decade, still at 1.5 to 2 percent per year, which does not compare so badly with that of the United States; an elderly and somnolent ruling oligarchy; active dissent by just a tiny segment of the intelligentsia, which the regime semitolerated as a sort of safety valve. How could one add up such flaws and deficiencies, no more serious than those afflicting many other contemporary societies, and come up with the picture of 1989–91, which included a catastrophic loss of power and prestige by the Communist Party, paralysis of the economy, the entire edifice of the Union rent by national strife with a high probability of civil wars erupting in various areas of the Soviet state. Attempts at reform had seemingly accomplished what famines, terror, and military defeat had failed to effect—the destruction of the Communist state.

One cannot dismiss the question with the old saw that an authoritarian system is never as weak as when it embarks upon reform and liberalization. For by 1990 the old system had in effect collapsed, leaving behind it incongruous fragments: the hobbled Communist Party, a largely emasculated security apparatus—the KGB—and a demoralized officers' corps. The problem then became not how one could preserve a liberalized Soviet system but whether in view of its collapse there was an alternative system that would be able to maintain social cohesion, such as it remains, and the very existence of the Soviet state. The questions asked by this writer in the beginning of the decade are still pertinent. "Is the [Communist] state now so firmly engrafted upon society that it cannot be removed or seriously altered without destroying the latter? Can anything but a centralized authoritarian government hold all the nations of the USSR together, or must any democratization or real liberalization lead to full independence for some of them? If all the above were by some miracle resolved, what could be a feasible form of government for a people who for sixty years were systematically taught to forget all the lessons in freedom and self-government they had learned before?"[5] By the summer of 1991, Mr. Gorbachev was valiantly striving to accomplish that miracle. Barring that, he or some successor of his may try to put all the disjointed pieces of the old discredited order together and inaugurate a new dictatorship (even though they would be unlikely to succeed).

Not that that feat would be unprecedented in Soviet history. Lenin and his Bolsheviks took over a society plunged into almost complete anarchy (to which they had very largely contributed by their activities between March and November 1917) and then within a few years re-created a centralized, authoritarian state. But there are clear differences between Lenin and Gorbachev, not to mention the vastly different circumstances under which they had to operate. Lenin was a revolutionary, dedicated to the smashing of the bourgeois world; Gorbachev is an enlightened bureaucrat who has tried to reform rather than destroy the system in which he had grown up and made a career. Lenin was driven by the vision of a world revolution; Gorbachev, far from an ideologue though by his lights a socialist, has sought to make his country a partner of the capitalist world. The father of the Revolution headed an army of zealots—the Bolsheviks. Gorbachev by 1991 had only a reduced and not very dependable power base within the bureaucracy and the army.

It is all the more astounding how this man, certainly not endowed with a charismatic gift, was able to change the course of Soviet and world history. Between 1985 and 1990 the orientation of Soviet domestic and foreign policies underwent a basic change. Whatever transformation he and his policies may undergo from now on, even if he tried to set the clock back, it is impossible to deny to Mikhail

Gorbachev the credit for making the terms "freedom" and "openness" relevant to the actual Soviet political scene. Why and how did a middle-aged apparatchik, whose entire past career presented a record of conformity to Communist orthodoxy, embark on such a hazardous course?

The answer is to be found largely in the circumstances attending the leadership and morale of the Communist Party during the last decade (1976–85) of the Brezhnev era. The ruling group, the Politburo circle, was aging, and not merely chronologically. Of Brezhnev it could have been said, as of a British prime minister, that he liked men who were boys when he had been a boy. He kept advancing people whose age in the United States would have entitled them, whether in business or academia, to retirement. In 1979 the general secretary, at the time seventy-three years old, promoted as prime minister in the place of the ailing Aleksei Kosygin, Nikolai Tikhonov, then one year older than himself. It was not only within the top elite that one found a predominance of old-timers. At the time of Gorbachev's ascension, the ministry supervising nuclear energy and nuclear weapons production was headed by an eighty-seven-year-old who had led it for thirty-eight years. Brezhnev's chief deputy as head of state, eighty-one years old, was a veteran of Stalin's last Politburo. The gerontocratic pattern was also characteristic of Communist regimes elsewhere, the incumbents of the highest party and government positions in East Germany, Hungary, Czechoslovakia, Bulgaria, and Romania having held them for decades.

Now this prevalence of the elderly in the highest councils of Communism did not necessarily have to be a bar to change. China, where the dominant influence since 1978 had been that of Deng—born in 1904—had launched on a course of basic economic reforms. But in the Soviet Union, as in most of Eastern Europe, the rule of old men (with practically no women in the highest political organs) was symptomatic both of the atrophy of the system and hence its vulnerability. What Milovan Djilas had pointed out many years before had by the 1980s become all too evident: the ruling Communist elites had congealed into a class. There was bound to be a shock when biological laws made the change of the guard inevitable.

The original impetus to perestroika, then, came from a generational change. At the time of Gorbachev's elevation to the inner circle as a secretary of the Central Committee in 1978, he became the only member of that select group who had been barely an adult at the time of

Stalin's death, and had neither served in the army nor held an important party or administrative position during World War II. He succeeded Fyodor Kulikov, who in his capacity as both party secretary and Politburo member had been touted as a probable successor to Brezhnev. Kulakov's sudden death at sixty had prompted rumors that, thwarted in his efforts to hasten the succession and about to be disgraced, he had committed suicide or had met his end in an even more dramatic manner. But the only, flimsy argument brought in support of the rumor was the fact that, contrary to custom, Brezhnev and some other oligarchs absented themselves from Kulakov's funeral. Gorbachev, by training a lawyer, but who had spent all of his official career in the rich agricultural region of Stavropol where he eventually became the party boss, was a fairly logical successor to Kulakov's portfolio as the Central Committee's secretary in charge of agriculture. What is less explicable was his subsequent rapid ascent: candidate member of the Politburo in 1979, full member one year later. Born in 1931, he was eight years the junior of the next-youngest member of the supreme council. Some writers[6] have speculated that his rise was quite fortuitous: Brezhnev and some other oligarchs would often vacation in the summer resorts in the Stavropol area and of course the local boss would greet them on those occasions, somewhat in the manner of a lord lieutenant of a British county receiving the Queen on her visit to his territory. The "youngster" made a favorable impression on them; hence his preferments. Even if such speculation falls short of the mark, it gives a good impression of the flavor of politics in the late Brezhnev era.

There are other stories tracing Gorbachev's reforming penchant to his student days. But there is nothing to support such tales. If he had been a closet liberal, he would have had to take great care to conceal such sentiments. One did not advance up the party ladder if one betrayed the slightest sign of differing from the official line. An essential ingredient of success was the ability to camouflage one's political personality so that it in no way stood out in the landscape of bureaucratic conformity and complacency. It was perhaps not accidental that although he had been boss of an important area and a member of the Central Committee since 1971, Gorbachev did not speak at any of the three party congresses held between that year and the year of Brezhnev's death, 1982.

But putting the aspiring politician aside, what could a man of his generation and background really feel about the past and present of the Soviet system? On this we have valuable testimony from Gorbachev himself, when already as president as well as general secretary he found himself under attack from both the left and the right. In a 1990 speech to "cultural workers" he pleaded for his concept of perestroika by recalling what had preceded it. "Take my two grandfathers. One was convicted for failing to fulfill the sowing plan in 1933, even though half of his family died of hunger. . . . And my other grandfather, a collective farm organizer and representative of the Ministry of Procurement—that was an important position in those days—he was a 'middle' peasant [i.e., neither poor, with almost no land, nor a kulak—a village exploiter]. He was also put in jail, questioned for fourteen months until he confessed to things he had not done. . . . Thank God he survived. But I had to live in that accursed house of an 'enemy of the people' that [my] relatives and friends dared not enter for fear they might share Grandfather's fate."[7]

As dramatic and undoubtedly sincere as this revelation is, one must bear in mind that many of the Soviet dignitaries of the 1970s and 1980s could have told a similar tale. But for them, unlike for Gorbachev, it was Stalin's time when they began, at a very young age (because their seniors were being liquidated right and left), their brilliant careers, a time when opportunity raced danger, just as in a war where you have frightfulness but also exhilaration. His older colleagues' retrospective revulsion against Stalinism could not have been as unambiguous and categorical as Gorbachev's.

The ascent to the Soviet Olympus involved Gorbachev in policy making. In the first years he still eschewed public notice and confined himself largely to his department in the Secretariat charged with supervision of agricultural and related policies. His record there was hardly brilliant if we judge it by the performance of Soviet agriculture during the years 1979 to 1984. Those were years of bad harvests, the 1981 crop being so low that the government did not announce how much grain had actually been produced.[8] Quite apart from the climatic factors, the reasons for the poor performance of Soviet agriculture could not have been remedied by even a much more innovative and enterprising boss than the Gorbachev of those years. Ever since the catastrophic Stalin reforms of the early 1930s, it had been evident that the collective-state farm system had been a bar to efficient food production and a curse on rural life. The government's ways of trying to grapple with the problem resembled the proverbial Procrustean bed; agrarian policies were continually alternating between efforts to appease the farmer, by giving him material incentives to produce more and loosening the framework of the collective's structure on the one hand, and limiting what the peasant could produce on his private plot and tightening up the work norms on the other. By the time Gorbachev took over the hopeless job, China was dismantling its collective system and restoring family farming. Beijing was rewarded for this unabashed jettisoning of one of the principal tenets of Communism by a great increase in food production and a new morale and spirit of enterprise in the countryside. But such a breach with orthodoxy was as yet unimaginable to the sclerotic mind of the Soviet leadership; anything which even remotely suggested restoration of private ownership in land was strictly taboo. And Gorbachev was enough of a child of the system to share that prejudice of his elders. Even under perestroika he would still, for all his grim memories, extol collectivization and be but slowly and incompletely converted to the idea of allowing families and individuals to rent (not own!) land.

If as yet not a shining administrator or policy maker, Gorbachev displayed considerable political skill in the Politburo circle's infighting. By 1978 it was evident to his colleagues that Brezhnev's mental and physical powers were slackening, and attention was focused on potential successors. Andrei Kirilenko, long the general secretary's deputy for party matters, was actually a bit older than Leonid Ilich and hardly in better shape. Brezhnev's own favorite was his longtime confidant and pal, Konstantin Chernenko, then in his late sixties.

The circumstances surrounding the struggles and intrigues of the last four years of Brezhnev's reign have still not been fully clarified. But it is evident that the general secretary's grip on power within the party was visibly weakening. The security service, run by Yuri Andropov, uncovered scandals and corruption reaching into Brezhnev's closest family, which of course weakened his prestige and his ability to assure Chernenko's succession by packing the Politburo. As already noted here, this could be only the tip of the iceberg. Corruption and nepotism were rampant throughout the upper ranks of the establishment. In the same speech we have quoted, Gorbachev told how insight into the party's inner sanctum filled him with disgust. He had shared his impressions, he recounted, with his friend Eduard Shevardnadze, then the party boss of Georgia, who in turn told about the mess he had found there. "We compared our experience, and he said that it had all gone rotten."[9]

Well, that part of the story may perhaps be overdramatized. By the time the two friends had exchanged melancholy reflections on the Soviet system, they had worked in local and central regime positions for quite a while (Shevardnadze at the time was a candidate member of the Politburo) and could hardly have been surprised and shocked by something they had not known before. Shevardnadze had been one of the most assiduous eulogists of Brezhnev and had repeatedly gone beyond the call of duty in extolling Georgia's debt and gratitude to the great Russian nation.

In any case, Gorbachev evidently lined up behind Andropov, his friend of many years' standing, in the latter's fight against corruption in high places. And that proved to be a correct political calculation. In January 1982, Mikhail Suslov, the embodiment and watchdog of Communist orthodoxy, died. A senior Politburo member (elected 1955), he probably could have succeeded Khrushchev in 1964 but preferred to be a kingmaker. In May, after some more intraelite sparring, Andropov took over Suslov's job as the Central Committee secretary for ideological affairs, thus challenging Chernenko's position as Brezhnev's heir apparent.

On Brezhnev's death in November there were but three men holding the two offices that traditionally gave their incumbents a special claim to be considered for the top leadership: secretary of the Central Committee *and* full Politburo member. Of the three, Chernenko had the disadvantage of having been the dead chief's favorite. Gorbachev as yet was not in the running because of his relative youth. Andropov was not helped by his long tenure (1967-82) as head of the KGB. In Soviet history no chief of the secret service had ever ascended to the very top; several had been disgraced, three executed. Yet on this occasion, the majority of the Politburo voted for Andropov.

There remains a mystery attending this succession. Brezhnev had been not only the party boss but also, since 1977, head of state. Yet for seven months this position remained unfilled, and it was only in June 1983 that Andropov became president of the USSR, or to use the formal title, chairman of the Presidium of the Supreme Soviet. Was there at first some attempt to dilute the general secretary's power by placing someone else, say Chernenko, in the presidency, and endowing the largely ceremonial office with real political significance? But whatever the explanation, the incident itself is of more than just Kremlinological interest. It illustrates the presumption of the ruling elite and the utter absence of what in a few years would become known as glasnost. Not only was the choice of the supreme ruler over some 260 million people made in complete secrecy, with only eleven men being privy to it, but the oligarchs did not deign to inform the nation why the highest state office was being kept vacant. And so it was not surprising that the people's long-suppressed need to know how the decisions affecting their lives were being made would explode, with glasnost, and eventually turn into distrust of all governmental authority.

Andropov, sixty-eight years old at his elevation and soon critically ill, proposed to deal with the problems his predecessor had kept sweeping under the rug, but was hardly given the time. There was the intensified drive against corruption in high places. Andropov also advanced the drive to impart new dynamism to the sluggish Soviet economy. The notion would be summarized as one of the trinity of Gorbachev's initial slogans when he assumed power: *uskoryenye*—acceleration—but then for obvious reasons it was soon dropped.

Traditionally, as officially announced every year, the Soviet budget had been balanced down to the last ruble. In fact, for quite a number of years expenditures had been far outrunning what the government had been able to earn through taxes and other income. The gap was being plugged mainly by the government borrowing its citizens' savings, something it could do without their realizing it, and very cheaply, since the state was the only banker. Eventually, however, the deficits were bound to lead to great inflationary pressures, partly concealed by the state's being able to fix prices arbitrarily. As with all such artificially manipulated systems, there were highly deleterious side effects: a shortage of consumer goods, hence disincentives to work since there was so little to buy with additional cash. The state savings banks would pay only 3 percent on deposits. It goes without saying that most of the hidden deficit was due to the vast costs of the defense establishment and, almost equally, the exorbitant expenditures on subsidies to keep the price of food and housing artificially low (and yet, by the same token, perpetuating a shortage of both).

Clearly, this vicious circle could not be continued forever. But where could it be breached? The USSR's competitive posture vis-à-vis the United States argued against cuts in military spending, especially now that America under the Reagan administration was raising its own defense budget and embarking on such costly programs as the Strategic Defense Initiative (SDI). The lessons of Poland in 1970 and 1980 warned against attempts to save and offset the hidden inflation by raising prices on the necessities of life. As Gorbachev would ruefully recall: "Already then we realized that the country was living beyond its means. . . . And that we were moving toward the brink."[10]

As has already been suggested here, Gorbachev may have been exaggerating the extent of the country's economic plight prior to his assuming command. For one thing, his speeches had never demonstrated a coherent grasp of economics, the advocate of pragmatism inside him battling with someone who simply could not shake off the doctrines on which he had been brought up. For another, even the most virtuous politician cannot escape the temptation to attribute his troubles when in power to the derelictions of his predecessors. And for Gorbachev, with the steadily worsening mess of the Soviet economy, that temptation must have been irresistible.

In the same speech Gorbachev related something that sounds almost incredible. He, a full member of the Politburo and presiding at the sessions of the Central Committee's Secretariat (probably because the general secretary's health did not allow him to do so regularly), was still not allowed by Andropov to have access to all the details concerning the state budget. On second thought, the story *is* incredible! After all, one of the main items of business before the Politburo had to be questions bearing on the country's economy and the budget. It would then appear absurd that the data at the disposal of the minister of finance, much lower in the hierarchy, just a Central Committee member, would not be accessible to one of the ruling oligarchs. But then the incredible and the absurd have not been absent from Soviet history.

There are many unanswered questions about Andropov's short term at the helm. One of them touches on Gorbachev's position under the ailing leader. Andropov had been his friend for twenty years and allegedly contributed to his rise in the hierarchy. But as Gorbachev's remark suggests, once Andropov was the general secretary, all did not go well with this relationship. Gorbachev's chances of eventually attaining that position appeared considerably diminished when on June 15, 1983, Grigori Romanov was made a secretary of the Central Committee. Prior to that, the boss of the Leningrad party organization and a member of the Politburo since 1976, Romanov was rumored to be a hard-liner and anti-Semitic, neither of which were believed in 1983 to be a bar to further preferment. At sixty years of age he probably would have been more acceptable to the septuagenarian members of the Politburo than Gorbachev. And indeed all the Kremlinological signs (e.g., who stands where on the Lenin Mausoleum, who gives this or that speech) seemed for a while to favor Romanov.[11] When Andropov, who according to the official communiqués was having an unusually long cold, died in February 1984, it was expected that the choice was between the two Politburo "youngsters." It was therefore with considerable surprise that the world learned on February 13 that it was Konstantin Chernenko, bypassed in 1982 and seemingly put on the shelf, who at the age of seventy-one had been elected to be the general secretary.

Nothing could better epitomize the creaky condition of the Communist Party apparatus than this twice-in-a-row election to the supreme position of a man who his colleagues knew was not well. In the case of Andropov there could have been at least the excuse of his undoubted intelligence and his varied, if not always savory, experience in domestic and foreign affairs. Chernenko's almost entire career centered around Brezhnev, long as a sort of personal secretary, then in the central party organs. He had never headed a major party organization or headed a ministry. Even within the party he was a little-known figure. A Soviet poet once wrote of Stalin that in his late years, "though alive [he] was cut off from life by the Kremlin Wall." In a different sense this was true of the Politburo in the late Brezhnev period. Chernenko as the party boss was flanked by the head of the government, Tikhonov, aged seventy-nine, and Foreign Minister Gromyko, aged seventy-five. It was therefore appropriate that, seeking an ideological formula for his reign, Chernenko pronounced that the Soviet Union had achieved the state of "ripe," or "developed," socialism. Perhaps a more significant indication of the new leader's views was the restoration of the party card to Vyacheslav Molotov, thrown out of the party in 1961. Though the former chairman of the council of Commissars was ninety-four years old, this could hardly be presented as a humanitarian gesture. Molotov had been one of Stalin's main accomplices. His rehabilitation came at a time when many of the eminent victims of the Terror, entirely innocent of the crimes with which they had been charged, still had not had their good names restored. This was then a small but not insignificant sign of the elderly hierarchs' determination not to reopen an inquiry into the past and hence not to countenance any basic reforms.

It was also in line with the general tenor of "ripe" socialism that when Dmitri Ustinov, minister of defense, died in 1984, he was succeeded by a colorless, seventy-three-year-old undistinguished professional soldier. The logical successor to Ustinov should have been the man recognized as the country's outstanding military commander, Marshal Nikolai Ogarkov. But it was precisely that reputation and the marshal's outspokenness that had led to his dismissal as chief of staff and to his being bypassed for the ministry. As any political elite on the eve of its demise, the Communist establishment was afflicted with political hypochondria and excessive suspiciousness.

How then can one account for Gorbachev's rise first to second-in-command during Chernenko's last weeks, and then to the highest post? In retrospect, Gorbachev appears to have been the very embodiment of what must have been his elderly Politburo colleagues' worst nightmares. But in 1984–85 it would have taken clairvoyance to see in Gorbachev a potential gravedigger of Communism. His record was that of a pliable, unobtrusive administrator, and even his unspectacular performance as overseer of agriculture was in a sense reassuring; he was certainly not a man to rock the boat. There was the troublesome matter of his age, but then that could in a way be turned to advantage for the party: after having been led by three invalids, its image would improve with an able-bodied and vigorous general secretary. There was another and less subjective element in his colleagues' growing preference for Gorbachev. By 1984–85 it was clear that Soviet foreign policy would have to undergo some fundamental changes in respect to relations with both the West and China. Gorbachev had a modicum of knowledge about the West: having traveled officially to Canada and Great Britain. The latter visit had been a great success, as evidenced by Mrs. Thatcher's remark that the Atlantic world could do business with him.

As against such encouraging signs, the political physiognomy of Romanov (the only feasible rival) appeared more problematic. Right age, right record, effective supervision of the armaments industry on behalf of the party, he still displayed some disturbing characteristics. As the oligarchs saw it, the thing to be avoided at all costs was the election of a potential Stalin, or even a Khrushchev, of someone who like the former would tyrannize them or like the latter would shake up the party with his improvisations and whims. And Romanov did have the reputation of having an authoritarian bent and of being hard on his subordinates. One is drawn to an inescapable conclusion: those men holding in their hands the destiny of their country were motivated in their choice primarily by personal and what might be called class reasons. History was going to play a trick on them.

It is, of course, an unanswerable question—what would have happened had somebody else rather than Gorbachev taken over the reins after Chernenko's death? One conjecture was to be offered by a rebellious Lithuanian Communist in 1990. Yes, he told the Central Committee meeting, the Soviet Union could have gone on in the old (Brezhnevite) way for another ten or fifteen years, but then there would have been a violent explosion, a bloodbath like the one that brought down the Ceauşescu regime in 1989. "Yes, except for perestroika we could have gone on peacefully and, from the point of view of the bureaucrats, very comfortably. But all along, and inevitably, the country would have been sliding down into an abyss, the kind of situation that arose in Romania."[12] Yet there are other less apocalyptic scenarios. Another leader may have chosen a path similar to that taken by the Chinese Communists after Mao: very far-reaching economic reforms, and yet the party holding on to the monopoly of political power. One might object that what happened in the spring of 1989 in Beijing went far to prove that once it starts on the path of reforms, a Communist regime risks an explosion if it seeks to limit them just to the economic sphere. But it is arguable that the Chinese students' aspirations and protest were part of the chain reaction initiated by perestroika and the already-visible crumbling of the authoritarian regimes in Eastern Europe.

A question that is more answerable and pertinent touches on Gorbachev's intentions on assuming the post of general secretary, to which he was elected by the Politburo on March 10, 1985, and confirmed by the Central Committee on the eleventh. With Romanov scratched, so to speak, the only other name supposedly put in nomination was that of Viktor Grishin, seventy years old and the party boss of Moscow. But it could not have been much of a contest. "Technically," Grishin did not qualify, since he was not a secretary of the Central Committee; what was more important, his name was linked with corrupt practices. The party bigwigs evidently believed that they were electing a man who would be a moderate and cautious reformer and abide by collective leadership, rather than trying to lord it over them the way Khrushchev did and Romanov might. As Gromyko said in his nominating speech to the Central Committee, "Mikhail Sergeievich always knows how to find solutions that fit the general policy of the party."[13]

Nothing in the first months of the reign could have warranted the conclusion that the new chief would preside over the virtual dismantling of the Communist order, that within five years the Communist

Party would have been emasculated and the entire political structure
of the USSR thrown into disarray. Later it would be represented that
perestroika and all those momentous changes were discussed and
initiated at the Central Committee meeting on April 23, 1985, an
occasion that allegedly marked a watershed in Soviet history, as Gorbachev himself repeated again and again. Well, if so, there is little
evidence of it in the address the general secretary gave at the April
plenum. As one might expect from a leader's speech on such an
occasion and soon after his elevation, it abounded in eulogistic references to the Soviet past, present, and future. "The country has
achieved great successes in all spheres of social life. Benefiting from
the superiority of the new [socialist] system, it achieved in what by
historical standards is a very short time the heights of economic and
social progress. . . . For the first time in history man has become master of his country, maker of his destiny."[14] Beyond such clichés, perhaps obligatory in a *public* speech on such an occasion, Gorbachev
stressed the aforementioned theme of *uskoryenye*, or acceleration, a
term that would recur several times in his speech. "The main sense
of acceleration of the socioeconomic development of the country is
seen by the Communist Party in the continuous rise in the well-being
of the nation, in the constant improvement of all aspects of the lives
of the Soviet people, in the creation of favorable conditions for harmonious development of personality." As usual with Gorbachev—not
a very inspiring speaker—he would repeat that theme several times.
There is one reference to glasnost, but as yet the term is used in a
sense closer to "publicity" than to "openness." The party organs are
to take care that their activities are well publicized, that they maintain
close ties with the masses, that they pay special attention to public
opinion and to ordinary citizens' criticisms and grievances. This is
still condescending bureaucratese, nothing that could not have been
said by Brezhnev.

The same may be said of Gorbachev's observations concerning international affairs. There were the usual chestnuts about the evil
designs of the imperialists: "Certain circles in the United States still
aspire to dominate the world, especially in the military sphere. . . .
Washington . . . wants to carry the arms race into outer space [an
obvious reference to SDI] and refuses to discuss the problem of limiting and controlling nuclear weapons." America is also pursuing economic imperialism through means such as "the robber transnational
corporations, politically dictated limitations on trade, boycotts and

sanctions."[15] On the other hand, "It is an unusually important historical achievement of the fraternal socialist countries that they have reached military and strategic parity with the states comprising the *aggressive* NATO bloc."[16] (My italics.)

The only unusual feature of the performance was Gorbachev's avoiding any reference to his three predecessors and mentioning Lenin only once.

Naturally, one would not have expected a seasoned politician to lay his cards on the table so early in the game. He had to build up his political base, and indeed this meeting of the Central Committee elected three new members of the Politburo, two of them known as proponents of reform, the third the head of the KGB. One of the two presumed partisans of Gorbachev's was Yegor Ligachev, then an innovative secretary of the Central Committee, soon to become a conservative critic of the general secretary. We have not been vouchsafed the minutes of this supposedly earthshaking meeting. And looking at the list of others who spoke—mostly party satraps plus, as was compulsory for decorative purposes on such occasions, a *single* rank-and-file worker—one wonders if indeed anything out of the ordinary did transpire in the plenum.

Still, by analyzing Gorbachev's moves during the next six years, it is possible to reconstruct what were probably his general aims in the beginning of his reign. First, as anyone of his generation, even if conservative, must have felt, the party and state machinery had to be revitalized. He would continue and intensify Andropov's campaign against corruption in public life. There might be the need for some democratization *within* the party, making its procedures and decisions more open to the public. This was to grow into glasnost.

On the economy the 1985 Gorbachev was as far from any ideas of restoring private property in agriculture, privatizing industry, a market economy, etc., as would have been any of his predecessors. The key to "acceleration" was to implement better administrative procedures, to select better administrators, and to improve the productivity of the Soviet worker by vigorous measures such as attacking alcoholism. The Chinese example was not one to emulate. The People's Republic's economy had gotten into a complete mess with the Great Leap Forward and the Cultural Revolution, and its leaders therefore resorted to drastic measures. The Soviet economic system had stood the test of time. It just needed adjustments.

The necessity for basic changes, Gorbachev and his followers probably felt, was most pronounced in foreign affairs. Even before Chernobyl was to prove to be the catalyst of a very fundamental policy shift on that count, there were signs that, his April speech notwithstanding, Gorbachev was contemplating an improvement in relations with the West. And that of course would have to include nuclear arms control. We have already mentioned the importance in this regard of the generational factor. A man who had lived through the formative years of Communism would have been hard put to abandon giving lip service to the idea of world revolution. A veteran Soviet politician was used to viewing the West both with suspicion and some contempt: he would have found it difficult to push the notion of peaceful coexistence to the point of actually having friendly relations with the United States. But in people of Gorbachev's generation, such inhibitions were much weaker. For them it went against common sense, and not only on account of the danger of a nuclear war, to maintain a rigidly antagonistic posture toward the United States. It was expensive and rather pointless. Communism was not going to inherit the world. And by the same token the capitalists, who had not been able to summon enough resolve to prevail in Vietnam, were not likely to attack the Soviet Union. Gorbachev did not propose to preside over the liquidation of the Soviet empire but could not see much sense in enlarging it. True, Soviet military efforts in Afghanistan intensified throughout 1985, but one assumes that that policy was being pursued in the vain hope of being done also with the issues that sharply divided the United States and the USSR, such as the Arab-Israeli conflict or Soviet assistance to the Marxist regimes in the Caribbean. The onset of the Gorbachev regime marked added caution and retrenchment.

The actual details of the new policy, of the results of the "new thinking" on the subject of East-West relations, are too well known to require a discussion here. The 1985 Geneva summit between Reagan and Gorbachev worked a seemingly magical transformation in the atmosphere of Soviet-American coexistence. We say "seemingly," for as we have seen, a rapprochement, a *real* détente between the two superpowers, had been a goal of Moscow's since Khrushchev's days. But as we have also seen, for reasons having to do with Soviet internal as well as intra-Communist-bloc politics, such a transformation could not have been sought *explicitly* until the leadership of the USSR passed into the hands of someone of Gorbachev's age, someone much freer of the traditional compunctions and aspirations of Leninism. Khrushchev and Brezhnev sought a rapprochement only if it could be presented as a victory for Communism. Gorbachev was content to seek and represent it as a victory for common sense.

Alas, common sense and virtue are not always rewarded in politics. The logic of friendly relations with the West would clash with the rationale of preserving an authoritarian Communist system in the Soviet Union.

For someone with a sense of history, that problem must have lurked in the background even earlier, ever since the "new thinking" had been applied to actual policies. The world watched with amazement and gratification as the knottiest issues separating the two superpowers were dissolved by the warmth of the new friendship. Take the issue of Euromissiles. In 1984 the Soviet Union refused to continue negotiations on nuclear arms control. The Kremlin would not tolerate the deployment by NATO of nuclear rockets and guided missiles of medium and intermediate range that could reach most of the European USSR in a few minutes (as against half an hour for the long-range ICBMs, originating in the United States). It appeared unrealistic to hope that the Soviets would agree to Washington's proposal that in return for NATO's abstaining from deploying such weapons they should dismantle their own medium-range rockets situated in Europe and Asia (there targeted presumably against the People's Republic). Yet in less than four years Gorbachev would eagerly embrace this so-called zero option, and what might have been a prelude to a dangerous confrontation between the two superpowers would become of historical interest only.

The four summits that followed Geneva worked a veritable revolution in world affairs. Perhaps the most interesting from the angle of Soviet motivations was the apparently abortive one in Reykjavik in October 1986. Rather unexpectedly proposed by the USSR and hastily convened, it proved barren of results. Gorbachev even more unexpectedly proposed phasing out *all* nuclear weapons in the hands of the USSR and the United States if the latter stopped developing SDI, something to which Reagan after initial hesitation could not agree. Now it is clear that the Soviet leader could not have meant his offer seriously. It would have been irresponsible and potentially catastrophic for world peace if the two superpowers gave up their nuclear deterrents entirely, while several other states retained their own atomic and hydrogen weapons and/or the capacity to develop them. What then was the real reason Moscow sought the meeting? The most reasonable explanation is that just before October 1986 some rather minor but troublesome obstacles appeared on the path to a U.S.-USSR accommodation (such as the arrest of an American journalist) and Moscow was eager to maintain the dialogue and erase the impression of the recent discomfitures.

But how auspicious the circumstances and results of the next three meetings: Washington in December 1987, Moscow in June 1988, New York in December of the same year! Reagan's trip to Russia in 1988 had to rival Nixon's to China in 1972 as the most spectacular event in post–World War II diplomatic history. Here was the most conservative American president of that era making a state visit to the Fatherland of Socialism. And on the occasion he not only conferred with the leaders but had an opportunity to address the Soviet people and talk to an audience of students. This, then, could be taken not as merely a diplomatic breakthrough but as the beginning of a new era. One by one the issues that had long bedeviled U.S.-Soviet relations began to disappear or were reduced to tractable proportions. The Soviet Union promised to and eventually did pull out its troops from Afghanistan. Progress was being made in the control and reduction of both strategic and conventional arms.

In the West the process was being greeted gleefully and with few reservations. Some saw it as the conclusion of a historical contest between Marxism-Leninism and democracy, with the latter clearly the victor. By the same token, and in a lighter vein, certain Soviet analysts of U.S. affairs commiserated with America: what would this country do without a visible and powerful enemy! Behind the witticism was a serious thought still tinged by Marxism-Leninism: the cohesion of American society and its economy were supposedly dependent on the armaments industry, and the rationale for the arms expenditures was the alleged Communist threat.

Well, the Soviet commentators' concern for America (and, alas, it soon ceased to be humorous as this country found itself at war in the Gulf) might have been with a much better justification turned around. Could the Soviet system preserve its authoritarian framework and social cohesion without an external enemy as an essential rationale of its legitimacy? Ever since its inception the Communist regime has sought to impress upon its citizens the mentality of a state of siege, has rationalized their deprivations as citizens and consumers on the grounds of an external threat, be it from the American imperialists or the German "revanchists," and has portrayed the dissenters and nonconformists as real or unwitting agents of the foreign enemy.

And so by abandoning the myth of "the capitalist danger" and of the "class enemy abroad," the regime had lost the justification for retaining its authoritarian features, even those that it still proposed to cling to under perestroika. Changes in foreign policy would put additional pressures on Gorbachev to push *domestic* reforms far beyond what had been his original intentions.

How the "new thinking" had subverted the traditional ideological rhetoric can be well seen in an article on foreign policy written by an outstanding Soviet dramatist and public figure (a member of the Council of the People's Deputies and of the short-lived Presidential Council), Chingiz Aitmatov. In a few sentences he destroys the case for treating the Soviet defense establishment as a sacred cow. "Under the current historical conditions [huge] defense expenditures are anachronistic. I see absolutely no reason that any countries—and I have in mind the highly developed ones—would want to start a war against us. There are no economic reasons. Those countries have plenty of their own goods . . . some say they want to establish world domination. Who would want such a vast burden and why?" So much for the standard Soviet argument justifying any and all sacrifices for the defense of the Fatherland, always threatened by the capitalists. And how about "proletarian internationalism" requiring the Soviet Union to assist with its armed might, as it did in Hungary and Czechoslovakia, any fraternal socialist country endangered by counterrevolution? If one follows our writer, the Brezhnev Doctrine would appear as something out of the distant past. "At one time, and without the Supreme Soviet having anything to say about it, our troops were sent into Afghanistan. We ought to adopt a law categorically forbidding sending our armies outside our country no matter what the alleged reasons, no matter who would request their intervention and why."[17] As soon as this sentiment received tacit endorsement by the Soviet government, in about 1989, it would mean a death sentence for the Communist regimes of Eastern Europe. With the repudiation of the Soviet state's mission as the vanguard of the world Communist movement and with the fiction of the capitalist threat abandoned, what justification could there remain for the one-party state and other authoritarian features that would be retained after the restructuring of the Soviet system?

Let us stress again that those inherent contradictions of the Communist system in the USSR would become apparent only in 1987, and they would take even Gorbachev himself by surprise. In 1985–

86 he still adhered to the traditional Communist themes. At the Party Congress in February 1986 he still talked about the inherent contradictions of the *capitalist* world. "The recent years have offered fresh evidence of the worsening of the general crisis of capitalism. . . . The contradictions between the ever-expanding productive forces of the [capitalist] economy and the private-property system became all the more evident with the scientific and technological revolution. They lead to growing unemployment and the worsening of capitalism's social problems. Permeating everything [in the capitalist world] is militarism. It is the most convenient way of propping up the economy. . . . A particular symptom of the crisis of capitalism is anti-Communism and anti-Sovietism. They influence not only foreign policy but constitute a most important element of domestic policy, the means of repression of everything that is enlightened and progressive."[18]

Little more than one year later such language would have sounded anachronistic. And so would much of the ritual and atmosphere still surrounding this traditionally most solemn and festive gathering of Communists of the Soviet Union. As of old, the speeches exuded the self-congratulatory and confident attitude of the movement that had set out to conquer the world. All the votes and elections were unanimous. The congress was attended by the greatest number of foreign guests and well-wishers to date: 152 parties from 113 countries were represented. Altogether, a fitting swan song for the party that had ruled Russia since 1917. The next, quite possibly the last, Congress of the Communist Party of the Soviet Union, held in 1990, would be quite different. It witnessed angry debates and recriminations as to who was responsible for the parlous state of the party and the country. The entire apparatus of the once dominant force of Soviet life would be thrown into disarray. And to signal the passing of an era no foreign delegations had been invited. Presumably, Gorbachev and his entourage did not want them to witness this wakelike occasion and to add their own tales of woe. What Gorbachev said in 1986 would have certainly struck a false note four years later. "The Communist Party of the Soviet Union is an inseparable part of the international Communist movement."[19]

Yet as we have already seen, when it came to the question of war, peace, and nuclear weapons, Gorbachev's speech at the Twenty-seventh Congress did contain hints of the new thinking on international affairs. And those hints on foreign policy were paralleled by the intimations of changes, also as yet vague and cautious, in domestic affairs. Thus "expanding the sphere of glasnost is for us a principal political task. Without glasnost you cannot have . . . political creativity of the masses or their participation in the process of government."[20]

One must not, however, think that what Gorbachev meant by glasnost in 1986 was synonymous with what would be understood by it and demanded by Soviet society within a few months: complete openness in politics, and the elimination of any vestiges of censorship about what had gone on in the past and what was now going on in Soviet society. The term came into the Russian political vocabulary under tsarism, during the great reforms of the 1860s. Emperor Alexander II decided that the country must not be ruled any longer in the style of his despotic father, Nicholas I. The government would no longer be conducted in a conspiratorial way, with only a handful of the highest-ranking bureaucrats privy to how and why policies were being made. But more extensive information about the operations of his government was for Alexander far from being synonymous with the freedom of speech and of the press. Censorship and other paraphernalia of the police state were retained.

Gorbachev's *initial* concept of glasnost was not greatly different from Alexander's. Unnecessary secrecy would be avoided; the Soviet people would be able to see and understand more of the decision making process, whether in politics or the economy. But the Soviet leader would at that point have balked at the idea that under the new dispensation the Russian citizen had the right to know exactly what went on at a Politburo meeting or that one could publish some forbidden work by Solzhenitsyn. How limited his conception of glasnost was in 1986 is seen in another passage of his speech at the Twenty-seventh Congress. "We need glasnost at the center [of the party and the government], but if anything, even more in places where the people actually live and work. They want to and should know not only how the government operates, but also about decisions being reached by the local party and state organs, management of enterprises and labor unions."[21] This is hardly a formula for democracy. It is an affirmation of the people's right to know what their superiors are up to, but not of their right to do anything about it.

The original concept of perestroika was thus far from envisaging the revolutionary upheaval that would shake Soviet politics and all other spheres of Soviet society beginning in 1987. The very term "restructuring" implied the retention of the inherited foundations:

socialism, the Communist Party's monopoly of power, and considerable (though compared with the pre-1985 conditions, somewhat reduced) constraints on the individual's freedom. Pertinent to the last point is Gorbachev's response to a French journalist who in Paris in the fall of 1985 questioned him about Andrei Sakharov. The distinguished physicist and dissenter had for some years been in exile, confined to the city of Gorky (now again Nizhny Novgorod). Gorbachev's brusque reply was not reassuring: the academician had broken Soviet laws and must bear the consequences. He was equally curt about related queries: no, there were no political prisoners in the USSR; no, his country did not have a Jewish problem.

Such prickly sensitivity to what he considered a foreign reporter's provocative questions, not unnatural in his debut abroad as the leader, probably did not represent Gorbachev's views. Everything indicates that from the beginning the elimination of the police-state characteristics of the Soviet Union was an essential ingredient of his agenda. German jurists in the nineteenth century developed the concept of the *Rechtsstaat*, the state in which, though it is not a democracy, its rulers abide by legal norms and constraints. Gorbachev's notion of perestroika envisaged what he called a "state under the law," a kind of Communist *Rechtsstaat*. The last vestiges of Stalinism would be removed, there would be much greater (but not complete) freedom of speech and of the press, though the latter of course would continue to be run by the party. Rules on emigration would be relaxed, and Soviet citizens would be freer to travel abroad. The constitution would have to be revamped in a way that allowed for free elections and yet guarantee the party's continued predominance. (And this incongruous combination would prove the source of unending trouble and a blow to perestroika.)

In the economic sphere, Gorbachev's views were, and to a large extent would remain, confused. There was the realization that the economy needed a new deal and yet uncertainty as to what precisely that might involve. Private initiative was to be encouraged, yet the notion of privatization was as yet taboo. Individuals and cooperatives were also to be permitted to engage in economic activity (this in fact would legalize what had been tolerated for some time) and yet "speculation" was to be severely punished. In brief, the loosening of state controls over the economy was to be accomplished through *adding* to the already existing and hugely overgrown body of bureaucratic regulations of economic life.

No Soviet leader, beginning with Lenin, had failed to rail against bureaucracy or had failed to increase it greatly. Alas, this was also to be true of Gorbachev, both as the reformer and later as the embattled president struggling to preserve the Soviet Union. In the promised land of perestroika, the command administrative system of running industries was to be simplified. The veritable horde of ministries supervising (and complicating) the management of various branches of the economy was to be reduced in numbers, and the remaining ones were to abstain from interference with the management of individual enterprises. But needless to say, while abolishing some branches of central administration, perestroika introduced new ones. The quality of much of Soviet industrial production was notoriously shoddy, so it appeared reasonable (but would prove most meddlesome) to create a new layer of bureaucracy to check the quality of products.

And of course, as any new leader would (but the three invalids who preceded him couldn't), Gorbachev hoped to create a fresh moral and political atmosphere that by itself would have beneficial effects on the economy. There would be a renewed and expanded struggle against corruption, the arm of justice not sparing even the highest party and state figures. The regime would resume Khrushchev's crusade against the ghost of Stalin and thus reinforce the moral prestige of the party.

Much was expected from the campaign against alcoholism in the way of elevation of the moral tone of society and of increasing its economic efficiency. Just as with drug addiction in the United States, so in the Soviet Union had alcoholism afflicted almost all spheres of national life. Perestroika began to the accompaniment of far-reaching measures to curb the plague: production and sale of strong spirits (to a lesser degree, also of wines and beer) was sharply reduced, their prices increased, and severe penalties were prescribed for sales of alcohol to underage persons and at unauthorized hours. This call to virtue was signaled by Soviet state functions, once celebrated for their copious potations, now becoming liquorless. Unfortunately, like many similar efforts in the past, notably Prohibition in America, the campaign has not succeeded in perceptibly reducing the consumption of liquor. And like many early perestroika initiatives, the means employed to attain the desired goal proved counterproductive: illegal domestic stills took up the slack left by the drop in production by government distilleries, the state losing much of the needed revenue from the sale of spirits. By 1989 the whole campaign was seen to have been a failure.

The original scheme for the reform was then much less than a systematic blueprint. Rather it was a motley collection of some actual legislation, but mostly goals and slogans looking toward a moral, political, and economic reconstruction of Soviet society, yet reaffirming its socialist character.

As such, it was evidently supported even by party hierarchs such as Yegor Ligachev, who by 1988 would be identified as the leader of the conservative opposition to Gorbachev. At the same time the general secretary was naturally eager to acquire control of the policy making organs of the party apparatus insofar as it was in his power to do so. Removed fairly expeditiously from the Politburo were such figures of the Brezhnev establishment as Gorbachev's unsuccessful rival Romanov; the man who allegedly ran against him for the general secretaryship, Viktor Grishin; and the eighty-year-old prime minister, Nikolai Tikhonov. Still, some old-timers would linger on in the highest party posts and thus limit Gorbachev's freedom of action.

By the same token, the general secretary would seek to place his allies and protégés in sensitive positions. The portfolio of foreign affairs vacated by Gromyko (who was pushed upstairs to become head of state, a position Gorbachev was unwilling or unable to claim at the time) went to Shevardnadze. The latter, though a very conformist bureaucrat under Brezhnev, was Gorbachev's personal friend, and thus, and perhaps because he had no foreign experience, was the logical choice to implement the new leader's "new thinking" in foreign policy. Brought back from his virtual banishment (as ambassador) to Canada was Aleksandr Yakovlev, a one-time student at Columbia University, who until 1990 would be the most influential and progressive figure in the general secretary's entourage.

Perestroika, conceived in an irreproachably socialist spirit, would soon acquire a life of its own and would shatter the foundations of the Communist order. How could it happen?

To revert to our theme, the major part of the explanation lies in the collapse of "proletarian internationalism," in the detachment, at first psychological, then actual, of the fortunes of the Soviet Union from those of the world Communist movement. For all of Gorbachev's phrases about the CPSU being an "inseparable part" of that movement, that detachment could be already read between the lines of his report to the Twenty-seventh Party Congress. Paradoxically, it could even have been inferred from the new attitude toward the People's Republic: "One can note with satisfaction the considerable improvement in the relations between the Soviet Union and its great neighbor—socialist China."[22] The two Communist giants were mending their relations not because of an ideological rapprochement, but precisely because that ideology was becoming irrelevant to their relations and would soon also be so to their domestic policies. Who on either side would now worry about the other party or charge it with "revisionism" or "dogmatism and left-wing sectarianism"? Both countries turned to the cultivation of their own respective gardens.

And in the Soviet case, at least, the domestic scene began to alter rapidly. The Chernobyl catastrophe had a traumatic impact on internal as well as foreign policies. It was a powerful spur to glasnost. What had been moderate dissent under Brezhnev was with his ultimate successor becoming the new orthodoxy: demands for enlarging the sphere of intellectual and artistic freedom. In February 1986, Gorbachev had declared: "Our socialist democratism should be expanded and further developed through the entire complex of the *sociopolitical and individual rights and freedoms of the Soviet man.*"[23] That was a rather elusive statement—democra*tism* rather than democracy; are those freedoms and rights already existing or to come? For most of 1986 it could have been considered a rhetorical flourish. But in December the general secretary personally telephoned Academician Sakharov to tell him he was free and hoped that he would come back to Moscow and work for the country. The era of glasnost had really begun.

Within another year, the Soviet Union ceased being a closed society and became one in which *almost* anything could be published and said in public. How did that happen?

The answer lies partly in politics, partly in something else. Abandoning his previous caution, Gorbachev became a much more fervent proponent of glasnost. Evidently, he became convinced that without it his proposed reforms would continue to be sabotaged by the bureaucracy and he himself might soon share Khrushchev's fate. And so all the stops were pulled from the campaign both against Stalin and Stalinism and against Brezhnevism, the era of stagnation. The conservatives within the party had now been shaken out of their torpor and realized what was going on. But how could they dare to try to push the clock back in view of what the party, the Soviet public, and the entire world was now being told about the past?

But apart from the political calculations of the ruling group, glasnost was spontaneously exploding on its own. Sakharov returned to a triumphant reception in Moscow. While declaring his support for perestroika, he also demanded the release of all political prisoners and an end to the Soviet military intervention in Afghanistan. The so-called "thick" literary magazines, already in the nineteenth century and up to the Soviet era often vehicles of political protest and of progressive thought, boldly resumed that mission. Novels and essays describing the horrors of the Stalin era, the harsh facts about forcible collectivization as well as the more recent travails of Soviet society were now being published, some like Pasternak's *Doctor Zhivago* having been in the past specifically anathematized by the party. Similar stirrings were felt in all the media. Books and movies dealing with hitherto forbidden themes pressed their message upon the Soviet reader and filmgoer. Prior to this wondrous year, a foreign student of Soviet affairs had little need to read the Soviet press: mention a topic or a political occurrence and he would have been able to recite accurately what might be written on the subject in *Pravda* or *Izvestia*. Glasnost revived real journalism, newspapers became real dispensers of news, tribunes for their readers' opinions and grievances, authentic reflections of Soviet life.

We noted how following Stalin's death there occurred the celebrated "thaw" in Russian society and how Nikita Khrushchev described the reaction of the Kremlin to that; compared to the 1987 glasnost, it was quite a modest intrusion of openness on the Soviet scene: "We were afraid the thaw might unleash a flood which we would not be able to control and which could drown us. It could have overflowed the banks of the Soviet riverbed and formed a tidal wave which would have washed away all the barriers and retaining walls of our society."[24] By late 1987 glasnost became a flood, and it did threaten to overflow the retaining walls of the Communist state.

Now, was Gorbachev unmindful of the danger to which he contributed by opening the floodgates? In his speech on the seventieth anniversary of the October Revolution he tried valiantly, and futilely, to strike a balance between historical truth and the need to preserve the fundament of the system, the authority of the Communist Party. "It is imperative to evaluate the past with a feeling of historical responsibility, and on the basis of historical truth."[25] But how could the responsibility for preserving the authority and power of the party be reconciled with telling the *full* truth about its past when it allowed itself to become an instrument of tyranny?

It is only a slight oversimplification to assert that the first phase of glasnost was about Stalin and Stalinism. The regime was now ready to rehabilitate the victims of Stalin's terror. But could one rehabilitate its main victim, the Communist Party of the Soviet Union? It would have required a very ingenious explanation to argue that even when it prostrated itself before the tyrant, it still remained true to its historical mission and hence deserved to remain the ruler of the country.

To rescue the reputation of Communism one had to qualify the condemnation of Stalin and assert that for all his criminal impulses, his policies had led the country to socialism, and that is why the party felt constrained to follow him. This was the line taken by Gorbachev in his speech commemorating the seventieth anniversary of the Revolution. "Through mass repressions and lawlessness Stalin and his entourage have sinned before the party and the nation. Their guilt is enormous and unforgivable. Let it stand as a lesson for all generations." And yet, "From the viewpoint of historical truth, it is indisputable that Stalin has contributed to the struggle for socialism and to its defense in the ideological struggle. . . . The core of the party headed by Stalin had successfully defended Leninism."

Even more jarring was Gorbachev's praise of Stalin's role during the world war: "What was an important factor in achieving victory was the strong political will, resolution, perseverance and the ability to organize and discipline [*sic!*] people displayed during the war years by J. V. Stalin."

Similar ambivalence characterized the general secretary's references to what was already being recognized by society as the greatest error and crime of Communist rule: the forced collectivization of Russian agriculture from 1929 to 1933. Sure, there were huge abuses in carrying out the reforms: "gross violations of the principles of [voluntary] collectivization occurred everywhere." And yet collectivization played "a positive role in introducing and strengthening socialism in the countryside . . . it created the social base for the modernization of the agrarian sector and for turning it onto the path of cultured development; [it] led to a considerable increase in productivity." All that about the unprecedentedly brutal feat of social engineering that cost millions of Soviet lives and whose fatal consequences have haunted Soviet agriculture and the economy in general to this very day.

If those passages were to indicate the permissible limits of the public debate about the Soviet past, then it was a bit late in the game. By November 1987 the Soviet public was already becoming familiar with a more realistic appraisal of Stalin's role, one that condemned him without any qualifications. Far from praising him for his wartime services, military experts blamed him for leaving the country unprepared for Hitler's invasion, for massacring the Soviet officer corps in the purges and thus contributing to the Red Army's catastrophic defeats in the fall of 1941 and the spring of 1942. No one would deny him the talent for, as Gorbachev quaintly put it, disciplining people, but his conduct as commander-in-chief was now being characterized as amateurish, and his perseverance consisted mainly in the insistence that no one but he should get the credit for the eventual victories. Several economists had already hinted at the need to abolish or drastically modify the collective farm system if the economy was to be healed.

Ever since the Twentieth Party Congress there had been insistent voices among Soviet as well as foreign Communists calling for official rehabilitation of the old Bolsheviks, the most eminent of whom had figured in the grotesque spectacles known in history as the great Moscow trials of 1936–38, in which they were convicted and subsequently shot. For reasons of intraparty politics, Khrushchev couldn't (and his successors wouldn't) acknowledge those trials as a surrealist travesty of justice and thus restore the good name of Lenin's closest collaborators. It fell to Gorbachev in the speech just mentioned to make the first step in that direction.

He did so indirectly by his laudatory reference to Nikolai Bukharin, one of the main victims of the 1938 "trial." For Communists as well as outsiders Bukharin stands as the most attractive figure in Lenin's old guard. Bukharin, said the general secretary, had rendered valuable services in fighting (alongside Stalin) Trotsky and his partisans. Alas, he later stumbled ideologically and opposed collectivization. Gorbachev proceeded to quote Lenin's characterization of Bukharin: " 'He is not only the most valuable major theoretician of our Party, but is also, and quite correctly, considered as its favorite. But his theoretical views can hardly be considered fully Marxist, because there is something rather scholastic about him (he never learned nor fully understood dialectic).' "[26] Lenin's somewhat inconsistent statement is matched by Gorbachev's qualified praise of this most likable of Bolshevik leaders. In any case, the first shoe was dropped: Bukharin was not a people's enemy, and the trials were phony. A special Politburo commission had been established, announced the general secretary, that would study the whole subject of the so-called trials of repression of Stalin's times. It had been thirty-one years since Khrushchev's secret speech. Some in the audience must have felt revulsion: why wait? What was there to study—it was all false and terrible.

Inevitably, on this count too Gorbachev was being outpaced by public opinion. It had been widely known for decades, and now it was being openly said and written, that the Moscow trials were a cruel farce, that all the charges under which all the accused (and not only Bukharin) were convicted had not only been fabricated, but were preposterous. And in 1988 the regime dropped the other shoe; the special Politburo commission gravely exonerated all the victims, with one exception. The one exception was the former chief of the secret police, Genrikh Yagoda, indisputably a scoundrel, but as innocent of most of the charges preferred against him as were the others. (Not that their hands were entirely clean either. They all at one time or another had been Stalin's helpers or allies.) But before the other shoe was dropped, there had been plenty of articles and studies about the victimized greats, as well as many other party and government leaders who were liquidated outside the glare of publicity. Some of those treatments discussed the most repellent feature of Stalin's justice: forcing the accused to confess to entirely fictitious crimes. There now could be no doubt in the mind of any intelligent Soviet citizen that in the vast majority of cases, such confessions were secured through physical and/or psychological torture.

Also freed of opprobrious charges was the memory of Lev Trotsky, the archfiend of Stalinist mythology. The creator of the Red Army was not (and is not) being presented in a favorable light, but even the tone in which Gorbachev referred to him in the speech we quoted indicated the preposterousness of branding him, as was done in the 1930s, as an agent of the German General Staff and the mastermind of all wrecking and sabotage allegedly committed within the USSR. In due time the Soviet reader would have a detailed description how on Stalin's orders, Soviet secret agents arranged Trotsky's murder.[27]

By the summer of 1988 it appeared as if the Soviet Union had lost its history. This is not merely a turn of phrase. The teaching of history became chaotic in the school year 1988–89. In the spring of 1989 high school and university examinations in history and social science were canceled. During the next academic year the old history textbooks were withdrawn from the classrooms. New ones were not ready until the fall of 1990.

Well, much of what the flood of glasnost had brought was hardly news to thinking Russians. But the total effect had to be shattering. It was now officially confirmed that for thirty years the country had been ruled by a sadistic maniac. Add to it the twenty years of the Brezhnev era, officially proclaimed to have been the period of stagnation. What was left of the glorious past of Communism in its birthplace? It was becoming difficult to maintain the cult of Lenin. To be sure, for a while he would still remain the paragon of all virtues, and his leadership in the Revolution, the Civil War, and the early 1920s would continue to be praised. But his active career came to an end with his illness in late 1922, and there was the uncomfortable fact that it was he who had elevated Stalin to be general secretary. Ten years of Khrushchev's reign became in the rapidly shifting official historiography first a subject of dispute, than a sort of gray area: the first secretary certainly meant well and did not deserve the ignominious treatment he received at the hands of Brezhnev and Company, but he was too impulsive and arbitrary in his actions.

A joke current in the preperestroika Soviet Union mocked the regime's frequent reassessments of the past. It was only the future that was certain (and glorious!). But former historical revisionism paled in comparison with what, as against the previous reevaluations, was like the effect of a nuclear bomb set against ordinary explosives. History in the Soviet Union, as in all Communist systems, was intimately connected with politics. By 1988 most intelligent Soviet people would have had to conclude with the historian Yuri Afanasiev that "there is not, and there has never been, a country and a nation whose history has been as falsified as ours."[28]

There were voices, and they would grow in intensity, protesting that such candor could be fatal to the survival of Communism. Journals such as Krasnaya Zvezda (The Red Star), organ of the army, and Sovetskaya Rossia (Soviet Russia) lined up alongside those who believed that glasnost had gone too far about the past. But the neoconformists, as one might call them, could not in the nature of things prevail against the ever-growing tide of revelations. Gorbachev left the door ajar, historians helped to open it more widely, and what was now flooding the Soviet media were recollections and personal testimonies of the surviving victims of the Terror, of their children and grandchildren. More recent, but in a different way as destructive of the Communist ethos, were the stories of corruption and arbitrariness under Brezhnev. Heads of huge party organizations such as the late boss of Uzbekistan and the very recent one of Kazakhstan were exposed as having been simultaneously chiefs of Mafia-like gangs, indulging in every kind of corruption.

The focal point of the contest between glasnost and Communist orthodoxy remained, at least through 1988, Stalin and Stalinism. All Soviet men and women under fifty at the beginning of perestroika had through their childhood and adolescence been brought up in the cult of the "genius leader of all progressive mankind." For them it was not only a question of whether they could retain vestiges of faith in the system that had produced him, but also a source of personal trauma. Was the cataclysm of Stalinism just the fault of the man and his close entourage, as Gorbachev would have it, or did part of the blame rest with society, themselves, their parents and relatives who allowed themselves to be mesmerized by the tyrant?

How deeply frightening that Soviet version of muckraking was to the dwindling band of believers in Communism is well illustrated in a letter that appeared in *Soviet Russia* on March 13, 1988, and created an instant, nationwide sensation. Its writer was Nina Andreyeva, a chemistry instructor at the Leningrad Technological Institute. Covering an entire page of the newspaper, the articlelike letter was a lengthy *cri de coeur* against the surfeit of glasnost and its dangerous consequences for the ideology, for the Soviet state. "Quite recently one of my students perplexed me by avowing that the concept of the class war was simply out of date and so was the notion about the leading role of the proletariat. It would not be so bad if it was only she who held such views. Not so long ago a respected academician provoked a sharp debate by maintaining that current relations between states belonging to two different socioeconomic systems have nothing to do with their class character. I shall grant that the academician has failed to explain why in the course of several decades he had argued exactly the opposite—that peaceful coexistence is [merely] the class war in the international arena. . . . What can you do, people change their views." As for herself, "I cannot give up my principles" [the heading of her piece]. Behind her irony there was a bitter resentment against those who traduced Soviet history and capitulated before the now fashionable ideological agnosticism masquerading as perestroika and glasnost. Her special target was the playwright Mikhail Shatrov, whose historical dramas offered a critical reevaluation of the beginnings of the Soviet state, damning Stalin and hinting even at a criticism of Lenin. Shatrov, notes Ms. Andreyeva indignantly, "departs fundamentally from the accepted principles of socialist realism." The term, of course, startlingly anachronistic under perestroika, evoked the memory of the stringent controls over Soviet arts and literature in the thirties and forties. And indeed it was the iconoclasm concerning Stalin and his era that provoked the writer's worst apprehensions. Not that Stalin could not be cruel or unjust. But so was Peter the Great. By trying to denigrate Stalin one discredited much of the achievements of Communism. "Take the question of J. V. Stalin in the history of our country. . . . [His] era is one of an unexampled rise of a whole generation of Soviet people who only now are gradually leaving the social and political arena. The formula of the period, 'a cult of personality,' is supposed to describe [those achievements] of industrialization, collectivization, and cultural revolution that brought our country the status of a superpower. All that is being questioned." Mass repressions of the thirties and forties were indeed reprehensible and regrettable, "but common sense argues against painting all those complex times and problems with the same brush as is being done in some of our journals." Ms. Andreyeva professed to be for perestroika and Gorbachev, but there was a thinly veiled reprimand of the latter when she condemned the tendency, presumably on the part of the new leadership, to find faults with and to discredit its predecessors. "From where and why has come to us that passion to undermine the authority and dignity of the leaders of the first country in the world to embrace socialism?"

Andreyeva's letter aroused considerable apprehension among the proglasnost elements, especially within the intelligentsia. It was reliably rumored to have been inspired by Ligachev, now clearly the leader of the conservative forces within the party elite. Not that Stalin did not find occasional defenders among wider circles. A letter to the press, criticizing a scholar's venture into the past, speaks for itself. "As that doctor of social sciences should know, the Trotskyites, Zinovievites, etc., became a counterrevolutionary opposition . . . that indulged in antiparty and anti-Soviet activities. . . . Not all the enemies of the party and of the people were crushed. Many survived, and afterward they revenged themselves on those who supposedly slandered them. . . . Now the consequences are blamed on Stalin. Yes, he *was* guilty: he failed to finish off all the enemies of the people."[29]

But such voices did not speak for the great majority. The problem lay elsewhere, as demonstrated in the long delay before Andreyeva's outburst was officially answered by the party, namely whether to keep criticisms of Stalinism within the bounds observed in Gorbachev's speech on the seventieth anniversary of the Revolution, or to endorse the truer and more devastating appraisals.

The dilemma was well portrayed by the main target of Andreyeva's attack, Mikhail Shatrov. In his latest play, he resurrected the great figures of the Revolution and has them discuss and reflect on the strange turn history has taken following it. His Stalin is unqualifiedly evil, and yet unwittingly the author sees him as having been made by the party and because of the party. One of the dictator's victims avows that there was something perversely imposing in the very scale of Stalin's crimes: "One who kills a single person becomes a murderer. He who kills hundreds of thousands [is glorified as] the leader."[30]

In the play Stalin is made to address his successors: "I'll give you some friendly advice. If you don't want a lot of malcontents getting after you and all sorts of other unpleasantness, leave me in peace. The edifice [of socialism and the Soviet state] has been built, one can live there somehow. . . . But if you really have to, make only cosmetic alterations. Change the decorations, the general setting, but concentrate on your current problems; certainly that should keep you busy."[31]

Perhaps without realizing it, the playwright got at the original formula for perestroika as conceived by Gorbachev's Politburo colleagues (if not the general secretary himself) who wanted *some* changes but nothing fundamental—above all, not too much fuss about what had happened during those unfortunate years. But as the party conservatives have found out, one simply could not ignore or minimize the importance of the past because so much of it was still sticking to the Soviet system. Shatrov concluded his play with Lenin and Stalin remaining on the stage, all the other historical figures having disappeared. "Lenin, very thoughtful, looks at the audience, obviously wants to say something important and from the heart, but he is waiting until he is alone. . . . Stalin does not leave. Lenin is waiting. . . . One would like very much that Stalin should leave. But he stays on. . . . Curtain."[32]

Here art captured very well the sense of Soviet history as conceived by the *reform-minded* party member. For him it was the lingering presence of Stalinism in the system that prevented Communism from blossoming into a new way of life as intended by the Father of the Revolution. For a diehard conservative, on the other hand, glasnost had already by 1988 removed some vital linchpins from the Soviet edifice and to go any further along that path would have been criminal.

Official silence in the wake of Andreyeva's salvo led to fears that once again, as in 1964–65, the demythologizing of the Soviet past would be brought to a halt and the regime would revert to its pre–1985 practices. Such fears were greatly exaggerated. It was much too late, short of initiating new terror, to turn the clock that far back. Rather, during those three weeks the Politburo must have discussed what kind of a rebuttal was needed to this manifestation of neo-Stalinism. The answer came on April 5 when an unsigned (and hence authoritative) article in *Pravda* chided *Soviet Russia* for the prominence it gave to one reader's distorted view of history. The author of *Pravda*'s article (quite possibly A. Yakovlev himself) granted that under the new dispensation Ms. Andreyeva had the right to disagree with the party line and the paper had the right to print her letter. But one did not help the party by suppressing the truth. "One still hears it said that Stalin did not know about the acts of lawlessness. Not only did he know, but he organized and directed them."[33] The latter sentence went beyond what Gorbachev had said about Stalin's criminality the preceding November.

There would be no further *official* attempts to defend Stalin's reputation or to minimize his crimes.

But as the dramatist put it, Stalin stayed on. Historians would continue to probe the crimes of his era. But what appeared the most urgent and onerous task for the regime was to prove that for all of his having been for thirty years the leader of Soviet and world Communism, worshiped as an infallible oracle of Marxism-Leninism, Stalin was really a historical accident, really outside the mainstream of Soviet history and of Communism.

The attempt to rehabilitate the party and Communism was foundering on the ever-growing mass of data about unpleasant and compromising incidents in the past. Never mind just Stalin. The tone of some of the *milder* reappraisals of the Communist past can be seen from the following: "The Stalin generation believed that the victory of Communism was at hand. . . . That is why [it was thought that] the liquidation of some 10 to 20 million people was unavoidable and justified. The Khrushchev generation still cultivated a belief in the coming of Communism. . . . And that is why the reviling of some 'insignificant' intellectuals [by the party] was felt to be like sweeping rubbish dirtying our grandiose path. The Brezhnev generation justified the suppression of dissidents as well as the toleration of [the regime's] corruption as quite appropriate to the greatness of a super-power endowed with nuclear weapons."[34] Were the flaws of the Khrushchev and Brezhnev reigns also accidental?

In attempting to erect the new retaining walls that would contain the flood of glasnost and prevent it from washing away what remained of the party's reputation, the regime resorted to a familiar motif: Leninism as the only true path to socialism, everything negative in Soviet life having resulted from the departure from Vladimir Ilich's wise counsels. But by the 1980s the whole complex of ideas and events associated with Lenin was for the average Soviet citizen, even for party members, ancient history, irrelevant to his and the country's life. One certainly could not explain or excuse the crimes and abuses of the past by a recourse to pseudosophisticated, in fact meaningless, phraseology! "In the most complex, dramatic, and decisive moments of history, Lenin turned again and again to dialectic as the living soul of Marxism, not only in order to understand those historical events, but also to arm the party and the masses with such understanding. Perestroika has the same idea behind it."[35] Such language made only too evident the anachronism of the Lenin cult and its doubtful value in defending the Communist Party's record and legitimacy.

It is interesting to note yet another line of defense designed to rescue something from the party's past and thus to justify its authority. Even before his rehabilitation Nikolai Bukharin was being presented by some Communist publicists as a sort of St. John the Baptist of perestroika. Had he, rather than Stalin, taken over the leadership of the party in the mid-twenties, as many Communists at the time allegedly wanted, the whole history of the Soviet Union would have been quite different and incomparably happier. And so it was not because there is some basic flaw in Communism that Stalin was able to seize power. It was simply through chicanery and deceit that he managed to occupy the place that rightfully should have been Bukharin's.

Needless to say, this budding cult of Bukharinism was based on very dubious historical foundations. Even granting that Bukharin by comparison with most other Communist leaders of the time stands out as an attractive and humane person, the fact remains that as a writer and theoretician who never held an administrative position, he was likewise never in the running for the top position. And for all his reputation for humanity, he was long an ally of Stalin's, seldom objecting to the latter's already brutal methods until the two men disagreed about collectivization. His story offers a different moral than that intended by those who wanted to save the party's honor. It shows how even decent men could be corrupted or terrorized into becoming accomplices of the tyrant.

With Lenin's legend punctured and Bukharin's a nonstarter, the makers of perestroika had to confront the melancholy fact that glasnost was making it almost impossible to retain the unreconstructed Communist Party as an integral part of the projected edifice of the Soviet state and society. "For some, perestroika would mean just the usual cosmetic repairs. Others have seen it as an opportunity to demolish the entire socialist system, and if so, the entire path traversed since the October [Revolution] has been false, and the values and principles of socialism are unreal. Others, still, are carried away by radical phraseology, jollying themselves and others with the illusion that one can bypass the unavoidable stages [toward perestroika],"[36] complained Yakovlev.

What then was to be done with those who wanted to retain socialism and proceed with reasonable reforms at a reasonable pace? The first priority in the mind of the general secretary and his partisans was clearly the restructuring of the Communist Party itself. This was presumably the task to be addressed by the special conference of the Communist Party summoned for the early summer of 1988.

13

THE UNRAVELING

I

WERE GLASNOST AND PERESTROIKA merely the means through
which Gorbachev sought and hoped eventually to achieve personal
dictatorship? Or, on the contrary, was he from the beginning a thoroughgoing liberal, intent on replacing Communist Party rule with
democracy, one whose earlier cautions and reservations were designed
to reassure the more conservative of his followers? Or did he try to
change his course only when he realized that the price of democracy
might be the dissolution of the Soviet state?

The most reasonable hypothesis is to place his original intentions
between those two extremes. Glasnost was not to be an end in itself
but the means to clear the path to a thorough reform of the state and
society. Socialism would remain the foundation of the system. In
politics the Communist Party would remain supreme, but it would be
internally democratized and would rule through persuasion rather
than coercion. In the economy overcentralization and the "command
administrative" system would give way to "market socialism," the
exact meaning of which was probably not clear to Gorbachev himself
but stood for something that would allow for private initiative and
foreign investments.

As of the spring of 1988, Gorbachev may well have felt that the
debate about the party's sinful past had gone too far. But at the same
time he undoubtedly must have expected that society's attention
would now be turned to the ambitious plan of constitutional and political reconstruction that he was about to propose. Glasnost had enabled him to discredit or immobilize the opponents of perestroika

within the party councils. Now it was time to turn to the tasks at hand. It was only later, after the elections of 1989, that the proponents of reform realized how much damage historical debate had done to the spell—if that's the word—that the party had exercised over society. And after another year, and with the territorial integrity of the Soviet Union threatened, the general secretary would have appreciated what a famous American baseball player and homespun philosopher once said: "Don't look back. Something may be gaining on you."

By the middle of 1988 Gorbachev stood at the height of his popularity at home and abroad. To the world he was the man who by creating an entirely new atmosphere in East-West relations had exorcised the specter of nuclear war. No one but the extreme doctrinaires begrudged him as yet the promise of perestroika and the new spirit of openness that pervaded the Soviet Union. The general secretary's assimilation of certain traits of Western political style, such as his taking his wife along on his state visits abroad, must have created some head shaking among the party stalwarts, but by the same token it enhanced his popularity among the progressive elements of society. The same was true about his gradual dismantling of the apparatus and phraseology of proletarian internationalism. The people at large, if not the remaining ideologues and some generals, welcomed the government's pledge to withdraw Soviet troops from Afghanistan by February 1989 and thus conclude what had been an endless and unpopular war.

As against this generally pleasing picture, there were portents of the trouble to come. One touched on the possibility of remaking the party so that it would fit into the scheme of things to come. The other was a preview of what would be the Achilles' heel of perestroika in the USSR, the nationalities question.

The Yeltsin affair ostensibly pitted a hotheaded party leader against his superiors and colleagues. But it was also the first major clash between Gorbachev the party boss and Gorbachev the reformer.

Boris Yeltsin was an early and enthusiastic follower of Gorbachev and of his drive for reforms. His speech at the Twenty-seventh Party Congress was a euphoric salute to the new and democratic tendency within the party. It must have embarrassed some of those present when he lapsed into what is often assumed to be the Russian itch for public confessions: "The delegates might ask me: why didn't you talk like that at the Twenty-sixth Party Congress? Well, let me tell you frankly: then I lacked the courage and political maturity to say those things."[1] Gorbachev elevated his enthusiastic follower to the Politburo and made him the Moscow party boss in the place of the discredited Grishin.

From the beginning Yeltsin's populistic style of administering the Moscow party organization irritated the old-timers. He would travel by subway rather than, as the custom ordained, in a limousine, and he demanded a similarly modest lifestyle and the forgoing of official perquisites from his subordinates. He publicly excoriated several notables of the Brezhnev period, implying, for example, that Grishin should face criminal charges rather than be holding a sinecure in the Presidium of the Supreme Soviet, where he was being sheltered by his old pal Gromyko, himself still on the Politburo, still the head of state. Yeltsin clashed repeatedly with Ligachev, who as the secretary of the Central Committee for personnel was his superior. Gorbachev, who as yet felt he could not ruffle unduly the conservative wing of the Politburo, stayed on the sidelines. At the October 1987 meeting of the Central Committee, Yeltsin erupted in an angry outburst against Ligachev, at the same time clearly displaying his bitterness against the general secretary, who had let him down. Gorbachev now decided he must sacrifice his protégé.

The ceremony of Yeltsin's dismissal took place at the November 12 session of the Moscow Committee of the party. Those who read the account of the meeting the next day in *Pravda* probably could not believe their eyes: the procedure and the style of the speeches sounded as if they were from Stalin's time. One by one the speakers, most of them Moscow officials, blasted their unfortunate boss. Yeltsin was brutally criticized, in some cases by the very people whom he brought to and elevated in the political and economic apparatus of the capital. Not a single speaker defended Yeltsin. Gorbachev, who attended the proceedings, accused his erstwhile protégé and friend of demagoguery and of trying to build up his personal following at the expense of the party's interest. Yeltsin's own speech could have been that of an official being purged in 1937. To use the terminology of that period, he recanted and admitted his guilt. He was obviously a broken man. Following his ouster from the Moscow post, he was dismissed from the Politburo. Even his subsequent appointment as deputy chairman of the State Committee on Construction was still in the Stalinist style. Notables of that period were usually given some inferior posts to keep them busy during the interval between their political and physical liquidation.

The latter, of course, was now out of the question, and perhaps in subsequent years Gorbachev would inwardly regret that it was so. The public degradation and humiliation of his overzealous lieutenant was to turn out, to paraphrase Talleyrand, worse than a display of moral insensitivity on the part of the general secretary; it was a political blunder of major proportions that would haunt Gorbachev for years to come. Perestroika now had its first major martyr, furthermore a martyr who against all Soviet precedents on that score would almost immediately bounce back into the political arena. Yeltsin had been very popular with Muscovites; he was a man with wit and the common touch, quite different from the grim, colorless satraps who had preceded him. For all of Gorbachev's considerable popularity, there was already a growing antiestablishment sentiment—and never mind how liberal the establishment. And here was the man who would epitomize that sentiment in a way that an intellectual like the academician Sakharov never quite could.

The Yeltsin affair, or rather what followed it, signaled the coming breakdown of intraparty discipline: what happened in the Caucasus in February 1988 portended an even greater danger to the future of perestroika, the unraveling of that pattern of authority that for seven decades had held the multinational state together.

The ethnic mosaic that is the Caucasus had been the scene of national and religious hostilities since time immemorial. That "prison house of nationalities," as Lenin called tsarist Russia, could not for all of its authoritarian character eradicate the most recurrent of these conflicts between the Moslem Tatars, or as they would be classified in Soviet times, Azerbaijanis, and the Christian Armenians. Racial, religious, and socioeconomic factors had all fueled the tension between the nationalities, which periodically would erupt into bloody clashes. The coming of Soviet power brought with it the eventual creation in the Caucasus of three Union republics, Georgia, Armenia, and Azerbaijan, but the old ethnic mix and the resultant tension persisted. According to the canon of Marxism-Leninism, with those major nationalities being given their own states, national animosities should have subsided, since the real cause for all the ostensible manifestations lay really in the economic and political enslavement of all the nationalities under the tsars' reign. Against such prognoses ethnic troubles continued, even though Communist rule proved much more effective in preserving its own version of law and order than the tsar did. Still, if ethnic enmities were an unwitting reaction to the frustrations of life under a despotic rule, that was truer of much of the Soviet period than before the Revolution. And with Stalin's death, the repressed national aspirations of the peoples of the Caucasus (as elsewhere) began to be aired in public, at first timidly, but with the onset of perestroika, quite boldly.

Officially, Nagorno-Karabakh had the status of an autonomous region within the Azerbaijan Republic. Ethnically, it was a predominantly Armenian enclave (some 80 percent of the population of 180,000), separated from the Armenian Republic by territory inhabited by the Azerbaijanis. For years, representatives of the district's majority, as well as those of Armenia itself, had been petitioning Moscow for the transfer of the district to the latter. All such pleas were met with bureaucratic indifference. As the Armenian party head was to complain at the Nineteenth Party Conference in June 1988: "The sources of the existing situation are found in the complex . . . problems arising from the distortion of the nationality policy during the periods of the cult of personality, and of stagnation."[2] In other words, under Stalin nobody would have dared to complain, under Brezhnev nobody would listen.

The "existing situation" to which the Armenian chief referred was that of virtual warfare between the two "fraternal" republics of the USSR over possession of the tiny enclave. As perestroika proceeded, so did the Armenians' insistence that the district be joined to their republic, a demand that ran into obdurate resistance by Azerbaijan officials. Riots erupted in the area in February. That in turn led to huge manifestations in Yerevan, the capital of Armenia, in which crowds estimated at nearly a million participated (the total population of the republic being around 3 million). Quite apart from the disputed district, there were a lot of Armenians living in Azerbaijan towns. And on February 27, in one of them, a clash between the two nationalities claimed at least 32 dead, the great majority of them Armenians. Their fellow nationals now began to flee from Azerbaijan, while in Armenia mass protests and manifestations escalated. Confronted by the crisis, Gorbachev appealed to both nations for calm, but privately complained that the Armenians "were stabbing perestroika in the back."[3] Troops were sent to Armenia to enforce order. To its people this signified that Moscow, as before, favored the cause of their hereditary antagonists.

The subsequent course of the Azerbaijan-Armenian conflict lies outside this study. Suffice it to say that all the Kremlin's efforts to resolve it—use of force, persuasion, the temporary imposition of direct rule from Moscow—proved unavailing. It has festered to this day. What is pertinent to our theme is that the initial phase of the crisis illuminated the vulnerability of the Communist system, especially during the attempts to liberalize it, to the enmities of the ethnic groups within the Soviet state. In the speech to which we've already referred, Armenia's party boss tried dutifully to deny that the trouble may have been intensified by the regime being no longer as tough and ruthless as it once was: "It would be blasphemous to maintain that the reasons for all those events are to be found in perestroika, democratization, and glasnost."[4] Yet, much as one does not like to agree with the party conservatives, the fact remains that by allowing the regime to be less feared, Gorbachev and his lieutenants helped make the nationalities issue more overt and explosive.

This is not to argue that democratization ought not to have been tried, or that the old ways could have been continued for long without bringing an even more violent explosion of national enmities and secessionist demands than that which would rack the USSR from 1989 on. But Gorbachev and his aides underestimated the gravity and urgency of the nationalities problem. He had demonstrated a certain insensitivity already in 1986 when he appointed a Russian to replace Dinmukhamed Kunayev, a Kazakh, as head of the party in Kazakhstan, an appointment which led to violent riots by Kazakh youth in the republic.

In itself, at least to an outsider, the issue in contention in the Caucasian dispute could appear preposterously small to have triggered such serious and mournful consequences. In the past a peremptory order from Moscow had led on occasion to the resettlement of a population several times the size of that of the unfortunate district. But in this situation, as on other issues, the post–1953 Soviet regime was not able to sustain such a level of repression. By 1988 the celebrated paradox from *Through the Looking-Glass* was applicable to the situation in the USSR: the regime would have to run very fast to keep in the same place. Freely translated, it carried a lesson that Gorbachev should avoid half-measures. Perestroika could not be accomplished through democratization. It could either set a course toward real democracy or it would run into trouble. The nationalities issue is a good case in point. If in 1987–88 the Kremlin had offered an imaginative plan to restructure the USSR by granting real and substantial autonomy to the fifteen republics, it would have, in all likelihood, been spared the subsequent demands for full independence. Events and the people's reaction to them showed that the Balts, the Georgians, and others who would have been content in 1988 if the Soviet Union had become a real rather than a fictitious federal commonwealth, would two years later be satisfied with nothing short of independence.

But the crucial consideration on this issue, just as on practically every other in Soviet life, was to be the role of the party. *Legally*, the republics and hence the major nationalities, did not need any new powers. Under the existing constitution (proclaimed by Stalin in 1936, amended slightly under Brezhnev in 1977) they enjoyed powers far surpassing those of the American states, including the right to secede from the Union. But up until now the constitution was a part of the mythology of Soviet life, rather than anything having really to do with the rights of the Union republics, or for that matter, with those of the individual citizens. The country was ruled by the party, and that again did not mean rule by its 19 million members, for the Party Statute was also a part of the mythology. Real power resided with the twenty to twenty-five men at the top of the party hierarchy, and as of 1988 they were chosen, just as under Brezhnev in the era of stagnation, by co-optation.

If perestroika was not to turn out to be just a show, all that had to be changed. Hence Gorbachev's first words to the five thousand delegates to the Nineteenth Party Conference that opened June 28, 1988: "The basic task [which faces us] is how to deepen and make irreversible the revolutionary perestroika that has been initiated and has been developing under the leadership of the party."[5]

The very atmosphere of this party gathering was to be a testimony both of how much had already been achieved and how much more had to be done in transforming the Soviet state and society. There would be and there were real political speeches and at times sharp debates, rather than those heavy ritualistic recitations and the automatic applause that had been the rule in the past, and was still prevalent at the Twenty-seventh Congress in 1986. Gorbachev actually welcomed being challenged and interrupted from the floor. The delegates' attitude toward their leader was one of what might be called reserved cordiality. Personally, he was obviously very popular and no one as yet would question his leadership. But for the traditionalist, perestroika had already gone too far, and the more impatient among the reformers were also developing doubts about the Gorbachev who had heartlessly demoted Yeltsin. The strain was evident to the general secretary, though he chose to joke about the tension. "We have not gathered here to deceive each other. Why do some of you believe that the leadership will always trick you, try to wrap you around its finger?"[6]

The problem underlying all others—what to do about the Communist Party—led to the most dramatic incident of the conference, the Yeltsin-Ligachev confrontation, though in the immediate context the real significance of the clash was obscured by the personal vendetta on both sides.

Instead of being quiet, as behooved one politically dead, Boris Yeltsin burst into the news with an interview he gave to foreign TV in which he explicitly named Ligachev as the one who was obstructing perestroika. There had been discreet efforts to keep him from speaking at the conference, but the incorrigible man, to the obvious discomfort of the leaders, insisted on having his say. The thrust of his remarks went beyond personalities. "Perestroika should have begun with the party. . . . But the party has lagged behind."[7] He criticized the party apparatus, which had not entirely lost its bad habits: it tried during the election of delegates to make sure most of them would be "safe." They must have *real* elections at every level. He exposed the hypocrisy of blaming all of the sins of stagnation on Brezhnev. How about those who sat on the Politburo with him? "Why did they keep silent when he, as instructed by the apparatus, decided by himself the fortunes of the party, the country, of socialism. . . . Why did they elect the incapacitated Chernenko. . . . They ought to explain how the party and the country have been brought to their present plight. And afterward . . . throw them out of the Politburo."[8] Not a single one of the five thousand delegates present could have ignored the fact that M.S. Gorbachev had, beginning with 1979, been a member of the Politburo.

Yeltsin was undergoing that political and psychological evolution that in some two years would make him give up his party card. They were all proud of socialism, yet "in seventy years we have not solved the main problems: how to feed and clothe the nation . . . how to solve social problems." The once contrite and humbled official now defiantly demanded to be rehabilitated, because "that would be in the spirit of perestroika and democracy and would help perestroika by making people believe [that it was real]."[9]

The unrepentant sinner was answered by his bête noire. Though Ligachev's intervention in the debate was loudly cheered, it could hardly have gained him much sympathy, certainly not outside the conference hall. It was an old-style denunciation of his tormentor for his undisciplined behavior. He, Ligachev, the number-two man in the party (as he stressed) fully supported perestroika and the general secretary. Hadn't he and other old-timers like Gromyko been instrumental in electing Gorbachev? Compare his record as a regional secretary with that of Yeltsin. *He* would not dream of discussing party affairs with bourgeois journalists. "Comrade Yeltsin evidently likes to make fun of himself and seek sympathy."[10] On perestroika, this exemplar of the party bureaucrat counseled patience. "You don't rush in politics. It is not like slurping cabbage soup."

The debate illustrated vividly how the winds of change were transforming the party without necessarily making it more democratic. Another delegate took up Yeltsin's call for throwing the rascals out, and again Gorbachev tried to joke about it: "You have some concrete proposals? We sit here and wonder, is it me or him that he has in mind?"[11] Unabashed, the delegate mentioned two members of the Politburo and some other notables whom he would put out to pasture. Who in the old and not so old days could have imagined that a rank-and-file delegate would dare to go that far! And how little some of those people reflected on what they were doing would be demonstrated within two years when our supercritical delegate turned into a thoroughgoing conservative who believed that perestroika had gone too far.

So far, that motif—open hostility to the idea of reform—was heard infrequently in the delegates' speeches. The closest to an explicit attack on glasnost and perestroika came not from a party official but from a writer. Yuri Bondarev compared perestroika to a plane that had taken off without the pilot knowing whether there was a landing strip at his destination. "It is not through demolishing our past that we should secure [a better] future."[12] Much of the trouble, charged this literary epigone of Stalinism, came from the media having been seized by intellectuals for whom Russian culture was alien. "Some of my fellow writers, who at meetings in the publishers' drawing rooms and in the lectures they give abroad about Russian culture pour ill-smelling filth on its past and present, mix with dirt our classical and contemporary writers, lie and slander." His was the voice of the new brand of reactionaries, for glasnost was undermining not only Communism but also the position of the Russian nation as the dominant one in the Soviet Union. Listening to him, one could almost imagine hearing Andrei Zhdanov, Stalin's satrap for cultural affairs after World War II, who had presided over the notorious campaign to cleanse

Soviet literature and the arts from the noxious influence of the Jews and other "cosmopolites."

Bondarev's insinuations represented, in a sophisticated version, much of the sentiment behind such movements as Pamyat (Memory), with its mixture of nostalgia à la Ms. Andreyeva for the old times and pronounced Russian chauvinism. What might be called an illegitimate child of glasnost, Pamyat, with its anti-Semitic and anti-intellectual tendencies, appeared in turn to be a throwback to a tsarist-era protofascist movement, the Black Hundreds, which had as its battle cry, "Beat the Jews and the intellectuals. Save our Russia." The party denounced the newfangled fascists, but some among its right wing could not conceal their glee that the liberals' precious glasnost had given birth to such misshapen progeny.

For the moment the danger from the right did not appear very serious. Gorbachev was still in command, and by and large the Party Conference acceded to his demands. Politically, perestroika was to be institutionalized. Though the resolutions and some speeches still carried some ritualistic phrases about solidarity with the international Communist movement, almost everyone present understood and approved the fact that "proletarian internationalism" was being quietly buried. With its foreign burden greatly reduced and with the political system restructured, the party could turn to the most basic and urgent task—getting the Soviet economy out of the doldrums.

Alas, the political side of perestroika was to prove much more difficult than Gorbachev and other liberal-minded members of the elite expected and hoped. Our reactionary author's simile was not far off the mark: perestroika had taken off, but Gorbachev at the controls could not be sure that he would be able to land at the desired destination.

For that destination was to prove to exist only in the pilot's imagination. The goal Gorbachev and his advisers set before themselves was unreachable. As of June 1988 the general secretary proposed and the conference agreed to establish a new political system in the Soviet Union, one that would combine democracy *and* one-party rule. How could a seasoned politician and a man endowed with his intelligence entertain such a fantastic notion? There were speakers at the conference, people then close to him, who tried delicately and indirectly to point out that the idea was as hard to realize as squaring the circle. But Mikhail Sergeievich was a party man not only by profession but also emotionally.

"How shall we be able, while preserving the Soviet form of society and the one-party system, to secure the democratic character of social life?"[13] It was Leonid Abalkin, soon to become deputy prime minister and already one of the principal economic advisers to the regime, who posed that question. The distinguished economist did not answer his own question directly; this was hardly the occasion and the forum from which to damn the party's monopoly of power. But for all his circumlocutions, what emerged from his speech was a strong conviction that if the country did not embrace political pluralism, it was bound to stagnate economically and socially.

Those seemingly incongruous bedfellows, democracy and one-party rule, were to be united under the auspices of the new Soviet constitution, whose general outline was presented at the conference. It was too much to expect that any constitution, no matter how finely crafted, could by itself smooth the path of perestroika. But quite apart from the glaring incongruity of its two main motifs, the new constitution would turn out to be a most unwieldy political instrument, with several of its provisions impractical or obsolete already by the time it came into force.

The central and most awkward feature of this Rube Goldberg–like contraption was to be the Congress of People's Deputies. Two-thirds of this assembly of 2,250 representatives was to be elected by popular suffrage and one-third by "social organizations," a description encompassing such diverse organizations as the Communist Party (one hundred delegates), the Academy of Sciences (twenty), and the Society of Philatelists (one). The Congress would meet annually and select one-fifth of its membership to constitute the Supreme Soviet; the two-tiered standing legislature would be expected to function like a Western-style parliament.

What was behind the cumbersome scheme was obvious. The Soviet state was to have real elections for the first time since 1918. Those 1,500 popular seats could—most of them would—be contested, rather than, as before, having just one candidate sponsored by the party. Thus quite a few, perhaps a sizable number, of the people elected by universal suffrage might turn out to be independents, critical of this or that aspect of the regime. But a great majority of those 750 deputies sent to the Congress by "social organizations" were bound to be individuals toeing the party line, and hence Gorbachev loyalists. There was to be the best of all possible worlds: democracy secured, one-party rule safeguarded, and an (almost) freely elected legislature with a firm proregime majority.

In any event, it did not turn out that way. Even on the procedural side there would be great confusion as to the powers of the Congress vis-à-vis those of the Supreme Soviet. The story of prerevolutionary Russia's brief experience with parliamentarism (1906–17) should have taught Gorbachev that you really cannot combine genuine parliamentarism with what might be called semiautocracy.

The tie-in between democracy and the party's leading role was to be secured by yet another political device, one which, unlike the unfortunate blueprint of the legislature, was widely discussed at the conference. The Gorbachev team proposed to expand the powers of the local legislative bodies—soviets—ranging from those at the district level to those of the Union republics. On its face, this was a return to Lenin's celebrated slogan, "All power to the soviets," which between the two 1917 revolutions garnered the Bolsheviks so much support among the workers and soldiers. But again there appeared a dilemma: wouldn't the soviets—well, some of them—be able to emancipate themselves from the party's guidance and thus increase the already evident centrifugal tendencies? One cannot do better than to quote Gorbachev: "I shall say once more, and I wish that my confidence would be shared by you. I think that political reforms should be carried out in a way that would lead to a tie-in: the role of the party as the vanguard of society should grow and, at the same time, so should the role and authority of the soviets; the two should be closely connected."[14] How was that to be secured? One way that was adopted by the conference on Gorbachev's insistence envisaged the first secretary of the party organization serving simultaneously as chairman of the corresponding soviet; the first secretary of, say, the Kiev Communist Party would also be chairman of the presidium of the Kiev regional soviet. Here several delegates, especially those democratically inclined, came up with obvious objections. If the soviet is to be an independent body, how can you guarantee that it would choose as its chairman the local secretary, or even that the latter would have been elected by the people of the given district or republic to its council? Where is your democracy? Gorbachev's rebuttal was hardly convincing. "Why are you comrades disturbed by it? I realize that there exist critical attitudes and distrust of certain party secretaries. And people are afraid. Won't it be worse if that man also becomes head of the soviet? . . . But the main thing is: he would be under popular control. More than that, if the local soviet refuses to elect him, then he is finished as the party secretary. If the deputies of the working people don't trust him enough to elect him as chairman of the soviet, he could hardly stay on as secretary."[15]

Here Gorbachev was either very naive or very Machiavellian. The latter interpretation would credit him with knowing in advance that the people were growing exasperated with the party bureaucrats, and hence quite a few of them would lose their bid to be elected to the given soviets. Those satraps, presumably the most reactionary, would then be fired as party officials and hence the scheme to strengthen Gorbachev's hand. And this version would have the general secretary quite willing to have the party suffer considerable setbacks if it enhanced his personal power.

But that interpretation is much too oversubtle and clashes with the general secretary's subsequent behavior. No, he was enough of a party man to believe that the electorate would indeed allow most of the local party bosses to get on the local legislatures and councils, and once there, they would earn the confidence of their fellow members. The few unworthy ones would be, and quite properly, chastised, but overall the party would continue as the "vanguard of society."

At the same time, there is little doubt that the conservative wing of the Politburo viewed the proposed reform as the means through which Gorbachev sought to destroy the collective, i.e., oligarchical, character of the leadership, so as to exalt his own role. Already by the summer of 1988 there was a growing suspicion both on the party's right and left that this man really aimed to become a dictator, and that was why he was systematically debasing the power and prestige of the party (as was believed on the right), or contrariwise, why he was being halfhearted and tentative in his proposals for democratization and economic reforms (from the left).

But in general the Nineteenth Party Conference resulted in considerable success for Gorbachev. The Party Conference followed the counsel of neither the right nor the left. It voted for the middle course, which was, for all his language about its revolutionary character, exactly what the general secretary expected from perestroika.

Within a few months the conservatives would suffer another resounding defeat. The meeting of the Central Committee on September 30 (called hurriedly and amid rumors of a possible coup) removed several old-timers, including the veteran Gromyko, from the Politburo.

Remaining, but with their responsibilities downgraded, were two other neo-Stalinists, Yegor Ligachev and Viktor Chebrikov, the former stripped of his functions as the secretary in charge of personnel, the latter no longer head of the KGB. They were made chairmen of rather meaningless commissions of the Central Committee. Gromyko had to resign simultaneously from what was known as the presidency of the USSR—officially, the chairmanship of the Presidium of the Supreme Soviet. He was succeeded by Gorbachev, whose title under the new constitution would be a bit different—chairman of the Supreme Soviet—and somewhat later he would be called, for all of its alien sound to the Russian ear, president. And under the new dispensation the office would be endowed with very considerable powers. Offices and honors apart, Mikhail Sergeievich stood at the apogee of his career by the end of 1988. For all the ominous portents we've listed, it still would have required special prophetic powers to predict that within one year his leadership would be challenged, that party authority would have suffered a catastrophic blow, and that the Soviet Union would be in the process of losing its East European empire, with its own unity endangered by separatist and nationalist forces.

One event accelerated all those developments and made them erupt simultaneously on the Soviet scene: the elections to the Congress of People's Deputies, which took place in March 1989 and which marked a watershed in Soviet history, perhaps even more significant than the events of March 1985.

We spoke before about the damage done to the reputation of the Communist Party because of what glasnost had revealed about its past and also because of the loss of a sense of mission. What happened as the result of the elections went, however, much further. It was a veritable body blow to the role of the party, one from which it would not recover.

If one pays attention merely to numbers, the election may well have appeared as justifying Gorbachev's expectations. The great majority of the successful candidates were in principle supporters of perestroika. The diehard party conservatives were for the most part defeated. Superficially, the results justified the prediction Gorbachev made while casting his own ballot on March 26—"Elections will carry us and perestroika far forward"[16]—and *Pravda*'s headline the morning after—"Millions Vote for Perestroika—A Vote of Confidence for the Policy of Regenerating Soviet Society." But the numbers don't begin to tell the whole story.

Properly understood, the vote was one of nonconfidence in the Communist establishment. That the party was able to secure a majority of sorts was due first of all to the complex electoral procedure, to the undoubted tampering with the ballots in several places in the provinces, and of course to those seats reserved to the "social organizations" where the *nomenklatura* could be expected to score heavily—and by and large it did, though there were also some surprises for the regime. (Thus, despite considerable pressure on the Academy of Sciences *not* to elect Andrei Sakharov, he was eventually voted in.) But the overall impression had to be one of spectacular setbacks dealt to the party, with humiliating defeats of several of its notables. This was most obvious in the big cities, where it would have been difficult to tamper with the ballots or to indulge in other chicaneries. The unofficial (there was no longer an official) party slate in Moscow and Leningrad was trounced. Many party bosses were repudiated by the voters in what had been their little kingdoms. There was, for example, the glaring defeat of the Leningrad first secretary and candidate member of the Politburo, Yuri Solovyov, who, though he ran unopposed, failed to get elected because he did not obtain the minimum prescribed quota of votes (50 percent). Gorbachev's ingenious scheme of linkage between the party organization and corresponding top organs of local government was demolished. The scheme was given up and even those party bigwigs who survived the electoral test (very often by opting for safe districts and/or discouraging would-be competitors) would not offer their candidacy to head the local legislatures and councils. There was no other party competing with the Communist one, so all the more eloquent was the people's repudiation of the way they had been ruled for decades.

But even the spectacular defeats of the Communist establishment figures were overshadowed by the spectacular victories of those who were identified with the antiestablishment. Outstanding among them was Boris Yeltsin, who in a district coterminous with Moscow received 6 million votes, crushing the party hack put up against him. In the Baltic republics, reformers grouped in "popular fronts"—regional organizations based (though not explicitly) on the ethnic principle—secured the majority of the seats, the Lithuanian one, Sajudis, winning in thirty-one out of thirty-nine districts. Communist leaders in those areas had to go along with the local nationalist aspirations in order to be elected. Those aspirations, demands for much wider autonomy or full independence, surfaced in other areas of the vast land.

The sum total of the developments centered around the elections to the Congress of People's Deputies spelled the end of the Communist Party's domination of Soviet politics and of the entire one-party political culture. The party would remain an important element in Soviet politics, but it definitely ceased to be the decisive one. If an outright dictatorship is one day restored in the USSR, it will have to rely mainly on another instrument of power, with what used to be "the vanguard of society" or "of the proletariat" playing but a subsidiary role.

The results of the elections had thus to be a blow to Gorbachev. He had hoped to nurse Soviet democracy through its infancy. He was suddenly confronted by an unruly adolescent. What he had hoped for was probably what happened when the Central Committee of the party gathered to elect those one hundred delegates it was empowered to send to the Congress. Some 10 percent of its members refused to cast their votes for Ligachev, and an almost equal number expressed its disapproval of the man identified with and blamed for the radical version of perestroika, Aleksandr Yakovlev—the right balance between two permissible extremes. The general secretary himself was denied only twelve votes out of four hundred, which led him to joke that not enough people voted against him. "I would have been disappointed if there had not been some opposition. Because then I would have felt that things were not going the way they should, not fast enough."[17] But then, growing serious, he maintained that they must not try to leap too far. After the popular elections it became clear that the measured pace of perestroika, as conceived by the general secretary, was not meeting with society's approval. The people were growing impatient, and Yeltsin's dazzling victory was but one symptom of that impatience.

How much the results of the elections unnerved the leadership was demonstrated before the Congress of People's Deputies assembled. A peaceful demonstration in Tbilisi, with the marchers carrying banners with nationalist slogans, was brutally dispersed by the troops of the local military districts. For reasons still not fully explained, soldiers resorted to the use of toxic gas and physically assailed the demonstrators. At least twenty demonstrators were killed, with many more injured. Orders for repression on that scale had to come from the center, and it is still not clear who issued the order to send in troops, and why, and whether Gorbachev himself was involved. The Georgian tragedy was only the most publicized of the many incidents of violence caused by ethnic tensions that were becoming endemic over large areas of the Soviet Union. As it was, the Tbilisi affair gave a powerful stimulus to the independence movement in Georgia.

When the Congress of People's Deputies assembled in May, it became immediately evident that insofar as its very mechanics were concerned, the course of reform would not be served well by the new constitutional setup. The cause of orderly government is best served by clarity in its structure and by clearly delineated lines of authority. From the beginning there was confusion between the functions of the Congress and those of its offspring, the Supreme Soviet. More fundamentally, Gorbachev's entire scheme of bringing up Soviet society *gradually* toward the goal of political pluralism, while preserving for a time what might be called a semiautocracy, clashed immediately with the new political realities. He had behind him a majority in the Congress and hence the Supreme Soviet, but in a revolutionary situation formal majorities in a legislature have seldom proved to be the decisive factor. What was increasingly destructive of the whole ethos and discipline of Communist society was the fact that for all the serried ranks of party functionaries on the Congress's benches, there was a sizable group of deputies unsparing in their criticisms of the regime because of its failure to proceed with reforms faster and more effectively. This opposition centered in the so-called Interregional Group, which counted some 250 members. Its leaders (or rather the leading figures among them, since it was in no sense an organized party) were people as eminent as academician Sakharov, Yeltsin, and the historian Yuri Afanasiev. Its attitude toward Gorbachev was growing more critical with every day: he was remiss on the economic reforms, slow with democratization, and quite unwilling to recognize the seriousness of the nationalities problem and to draw the appropriate conclusions. Such criticisms were seldom accompanied by concrete proposals. One could simply summarize the attitude of the Soviet left since the middle of 1989 by two words: "more" and "faster." Andrei Sakharov, who before his premature death came close to becoming the moral leader of the prodemocracy forces, chastised the Gorbachev team's reluctance to grant the most far-reaching freedom to the Union republics, and for its failure to base the future Soviet Union on an entirely free compact between the constituent units rather than trying to retain them through any other means. But such specific postulates were rare.

If the left was vague in its proposals, then the right—those nostalgic for the pre-1985 ways—was incoherent. Its partisans appeared thunderstruck by what had been happening around them, and they were unable to react in any organized fashion to the growing disintegration of the Communist order. The most choleric complaints came from the officer corps, some of whose members were understandably bitter because of the Afghan fiasco, of the Soviet Union's acquiescing in the loss of what the Red Army had won in Eastern Europe, and even on account of the new relationship with the West, which was bound to decrease the importance (and the financial pampering) of the Soviet military. To many in the predominantly Russian officer corps, it was outrageous how under glasnost the famous achievements of the Russian soldier were being traduced, and how in some non-Russian republics the Soviet soldiers were accused of being an army of occupation. One such worthy exclaimed: "We must have our own press to defend the army, which currently is under fire by practically all the media."[18] Another, incensed by the separatist movements, would let the discontented nationalities leave the Soviet family of nations, but not before they paid sizable reparations to the Russian Republic!

Indeed, Russian chauvinism combined with neo-Stalinism in the as yet impotent rage at the general tendency of perestroika. It is fair to add that a number of officers declared themselves on the side of the democratic reforms. "Liberals" were now to be found even in the ranks of officials of the KGB, which in accordance with the new fashion was attempting to erase its former sinister image and to replace it by a new one as the guardian of Soviet legality.

Where in all that increasingly chaotic situation was perestroika? Well, by the end of 1989 it had definitely ceased to be, if it ever was, a systematic program of reforms and had become a synonym for changes, some of them intended by the government, others to which it had been pushed by extraneous factors. What was also going on was what might be called rebellion perestroika, such as was inherent in the various units of the federal system adopting reforms on their own and pressing for independence.

Gorbachev's position had undergone a considerable alteration. He was still enormously popular in the West, where he was credited, and on good grounds, with bringing an end to the cold war and, somewhat less justifiably, with consciously helping East European countries to get rid of their Communist regimes. But at home his popularity began to decline. This was largely, though not completely, because of the worsening economic situation.

The task of bringing the Soviet economy out of the doldrums and setting it on a steady course that would lead to immediately recognizable benefits in raising the standard of living and of the amelioration of the environment would have overtaxed the resources of the most resolute leader, even one with absolute power. Gorbachev's position from 1989 on fitted neither of those criteria. He had accepted, though reluctantly, that the old dogmas of Marxism-Leninism had to be jettisoned. Soviet economists now virtually unanimously proclaimed that ideological superstitions were doing immeasurable harm to the well-being of the Soviet people and the vitality of the economy. The remedies were to be found in the free market, the open path to private initiative, and the dismantling of the entire collective-state farm system that had been the curse of Soviet agriculture for more than five decades. Most of the measures to implement those goals, while salutary in the end, were bound in the "short run" (conceivably taking years) to cause considerable hardships and unrest among the population. All of them involved tremendous administrative problems, as well as the overcoming of long-standing practices and prejudices.

The free market implied giving up government subsidies for food and other necessities, such as rent, which kept their prices artificially low. You could not compensate for this blow to the consumer by raising wages and pensions without magnifying the already considerable inflationary pressures. Encouragement of private entrepreneurship meant defying what through years of official indoctrination had become an article of faith for most Soviet citizens: that profit seeking meant "exploitation of man by man," and hence was antisocial. The peasant would find it hard to believe that this time the regime really wanted him to be a proprietor and leave the collective farm: he had grown wary of Moscow, now encouraging, now backtracking on allowing farmers to work independently of the collective. After what seemed like an eternity of the "command administrative" system, would your average peasant, or for that matter, factory manager, have enough self-reliance and business skill to be left on his own?

Many of the difficulties could have been avoided if Gorbachev, like Stalin or even Brezhnev, could just crack the whip and be obeyed, if for example, prices on the necessities of life could be doubled over night, and yet the people could be expected to suffer in silence rather than strike and riot. Now, with political power diffused and the regime no longer awesome, the Soviet consumer was unlikely to acquiesce in having his already unsatisfactory standard of living lowered still further and to suffer it in silence. Even without the government's resorting to measures of the kind described above, the worsening economic situation brought strikes, such as that of the Donbas miners in the summer of 1990, on a scale unimaginable only a few years before.

With the fervor of neophytes, growing numbers of Soviet economists were embracing the gospel of free enterprise. For them all the dangers and difficulties of the transition to the free market paled as against the urgency of changing the old economic ways that had brought the country to the brink of disaster. The people, went their argument, would put up with an interlude of hardships if at the end of the road there was a clearly discernible goal of a free and dynamic economy, no more shortages of basic commodities, no more shoddy goods, and the overall appearance of a Soviet society no longer reminiscent of that of a Third World country. As one of them wrote: "We must, we absolutely must, bring to our society the understanding that what is economically ineffective is by the same token immoral, what is effective is also morally right. . . . The economically deficient mechanism of planning led to the mindless waste of our national resources, indifference about what was happening to our national treasure; the fact that land and water have seemingly been free of charge led to such shocking consequences as the devastation of whole areas of the country [e.g., the drying up of the Aral Sea]. . . . We are facing a revolutionary situation in our country. The rulers can no longer cope, and the masses no longer want to live in the old way."[19]

Nikolai Shmelyov, the economist in question, was at one time quite close to Gorbachev, who through 1990 was quite prone to seek advice from progressive social scientists. Yet for all such contacts, Mikhail Sergeievich's attitude toward a free-market economy remained similar to his view about the possibility of introducing democracy in the Soviet Union: yes, up to a point; certainly not right away. And so progress toward economic perestroika has been episodic and inconsistent. Joint ventures with foreign entrepreneurs were authorized but have intermittently been overregulated. The same goes for cooperative enterprises. Privatization of Soviet industry was proclaimed to be a legitimate goal, but again bureaucratic hurdles have been erected in the path of its realization.

All along, the search for that elusive goal—market socialism—has been hampered and complicated by the authorities pondering that question worthy of Marxist scholasticism: when does legitimate, i.e., socially useful, profit seeking become sinful speculation? Since that question, like most scholastic conundrums, is difficult to resolve, the government's legislation on liberalizing the economic system has often been rendered ineffective by laws and decrees that could only scare off any prospective entrepreneurs and investors, foreign or domestic. Certainly, individuals in those categories would not be encouraged by a recent and not atypical government decree (signed by President Gorbachev) that gives the agents of the KGB and the Ministry of the Interior the right to raid all private and cooperative business offices and premises at their discretion. These agencies are empowered to check all the business transactions, examine financial records, and, in the case of enterprises producing articles of common use, to pass judgment on the quality of the product and on whether those enterprises do right by the Soviet consumer.[20] All such interventions can take place suddenly and without a judicial warrant. Granted the widespread abuses of the new economic freedoms (often resulting from the poorly drafted and contradictory legislation), this kind of remedy can only have a dampening effect on the entire economic side of perestroika.

The regime's indecisiveness on the economic front reflected not only concrete difficulties attending the proposed reforms, but also a very real psychological problem confronting the reformers, and especially their leader. As late as November 1987, Gorbachev hailed collectivization of agriculture as a great achievement of socialism. It took considerable and virtually unanimous pressure by the economic community to persuade the regime that individual peasants should be allowed to leave the kolkhozes, and that the kolkhozes (collective farms) could be legally dissolved, with the peasants being able to rent land for individual family farming. The peasant's response to that initiative, which would lead to their economic liberation, was hardly enthusiastic. As of this writing, relatively few peasants have sought to avail themselves of the opportunity to become individual farmers. As suggested before, part of the reason may lie in the attrition of the skills of economic self-reliance caused by the long years of socialized agriculture. But Soviet experts have laid the major portion of the blame on the regime's unwillingness to proclaim and establish firmly the principle of private property in agriculture, as well as elsewhere.

The difficulty has been epitomized by Gorbachev's own stand on the issue. In a somewhat emotional performance before a number of figures from the intellectual and cultural community, Mikhail Sergeievich avowed that there are some principles he could not give up, even for the sake of perestroika. He had been implored, he informed his listeners, to give up repeating and pledging that he was true to socialism. "But why should I renounce what I firmly believe in? I will not stop, as long as I am able, to say and do everything to affirm that [faith in socialism]."[21]

What did that devotion mean in practice? First, as we have already seen, Gorbachev's inability to condemn unreservedly the Soviet past. "We shall never, I hope, agree with those who throw mud at everything that has been done for decades, by ourselves, by our fathers and grandfathers."[22] How could he, Gorbachev, forget that his grandfather had been chairman of his collective farm for seventeen years and firmly believed in what he was doing? If one denounces Stalinism, does that mean that one must repudiate and slander the work of previous generations? And so the reawakened Marxist-Leninist in Gorbachev could not accept the notion of private property in land.

A statement followed, startling for its apparent illogic: "I have always been for and supported the free market . . . but do what you will to me, I shall not accept private property in land. I will not. I am for renting land [to individual farmers], be it for 100 years and with the right to sell and bequeath the renting right. But private property in land, with the right to buy and sell it, that is unacceptable."[23]

Was it only in regard to land that Gorbachev's socialist scruples did not permit him to accept economic freedom? Not quite. In another speech delivered about the same time, he expressed considerable doubts as to the possibility of completely abandoning controls over prices and wages. To buttress his argument, he resorted to some rather strange (and incorrect) statistics. "In Germany 50 percent of prices are controlled. Or another example: 56 to 57 percent of the financing of scientific research in Japan is done by the government."[24] One wonders where he got his figures, though the moral he attempted to draw—that in no state was the market absolutely free—was in itself plausible enough.

One might object that the speeches from which we have just quoted were delivered late in 1990 with the reforms already blocked on several fronts, and hence may not represent his real views during the middle of 1989 (the point from which dates the decline of Gorbachev's effective power and of perestroika). But his doubts about the principles that should govern economic reconstruction were already then amply evident. Economic perestroika stalled, and the whole political scene in the Soviet Union was thrown into disarray. To an outsider Gorbachev's scruples may appear pedantic to the point of silliness: how much difference is there between renting a plot of farmland for a hundred years and actually owning it? For Gorbachev, as for anyone even slightly influenced by Marxism-Leninism, the difference was real and important: if you tolerate private ownership of the means of production, you reintroduce capitalism; if you stop short of the taboo term, you have something you can call market socialism.

Mid-1989 concluded the first, and in retrospect, hopeful, phase of perestroika. With the meeting of the Congress of People's Deputies, the focus of political activity shifted not necessarily to the legislative bodies but certainly away from the Communist Party. What had been the struggle to remake the state and society would soon be preempted by another and desperate effort by Gorbachev to preserve as much as possible the existing structure of Soviet power and to cling to the vestiges of the Communist creed. The great reformer became simultaneously and incongruously a defender of the status quo on issues such as the rights of the republics versus those of the center.

Another incongruity and paradox that would plague Gorbachev from mid-1989 on was that the very rapidity of political change until then had made further advances of perestroika increasingly difficult. If he had intended to reduce the authority and power of the party (which as we have seen he did, but not to the extent to which it had actually taken place), then at one point he must have realized that he had been sawing off the very limb on which he had been sitting. With the party discredited and demoralized, what could now serve as an effective lever of power, and hence be a dependable instrument of reform? The party, even if Gorbachev did not control it completely, had been the glue that held the Soviet Union together and kept the lid on many other potentially explosive problems. It thus freed Gorbachev's hands to proceed with reforms, a role that after the Nineteenth Party Conference he would no longer be able to perform. Gone along with the party's monopoly of power was also its once-iron internal discipline. Prominent Communists would take political positions and express their views publicly with little concern as to what the official party line was on this or that issue. Some of them, like Yeltsin, would before too long turn in their party cards, their example followed by quite a number of rank-and-file members. The once eagerly sought membership—a key that opened doors to advancement in every sphere of Soviet life—had become greatly depreciated. By the same token, those

who stayed in now appeared to have shed almost all of the characteristics of an ideological order and had become explicitly what they
had really been for a long time, a kind of association of officeholders.
As such, the prevailing trend among the members was to grow more
critical of the alleged excesses of perestroika, which had made the
once-proud name "Communist" no longer a sign of distinction. And
apart from individual defections, several national subdivisions would
very soon seek autonomy, or even secede from the CPSU. The Lithuanian Communist Party had always been just a detachment of the
Soviet Communists in Lithuania. In 1989 the great majority of its
members opted for it to become truly Lithuanian and to side with
their people rather than with the bosses in Moscow.

With the party an uncertain and increasingly more vulnerable ally,
Gorbachev's political base was obviously shrinking. The new constitution endowed him in his capacity as head of state with an extensive
panoply of powers and they would be expanded in 1990. Critics at
home would accuse him of setting the stage for a dictatorhip, and
even his friends and allies would come to see Gorbachev being pushed
toward the goal. But they, as well as the Western analysts who by
1990 also began to credit the now-President Gorbachev with dictatorial
ambitions, overlooked the fact that formal powers, no matter how
extensive, could hardly prove to be the decisive factor when set against
the increasing disarray of the Soviet political scene.

Perhaps the best commentary on the charges of his seeking dictatorship was offered by Mikhail Sergeievich himself: "I recently saw
in some paper a caricature: Gorbachev is sitting and is trying an
imperial crown on for size. I hope, dear comrades, that I don't have
to tell you how absurd it is: that if Gorbachev was a man who lusts
after absolute power, then why did he give it up when he had it? I
did have it—the general secretary in those days was a dictator, with
powers unparalleled elsewhere in the world. Nobody had more power.
Do you understand? Nobody."[25] Well, in his exasperation Gorbachev
had exaggerated. One did not automatically become a Stalin upon
election as general secretary. Yet, without any doubt, when chosen
to that post in March 1985, he wielded more real power and was in
a much better position to seek personal dictatorship than President
Gorbachev would have in 1990. Circumstances may yet compel Gorbachev to seek absolute power, but had that been his original goal,
he would never have embarked upon perestroika, or licensed glasnost.

In a sense, the strength of Gorbachev's position after the first and bitter failures of perestroika reflected the vulnerability of the system. Things were not going fast enough for the reform camp, and were going too fast for the conservatives, but both sides would agree, at least until the end of 1990, that without Gorbachev it would have been worse.

With the decline of the Communist Party one would have expected the rise of another movement that would aspire to guide Soviet society. Once Gorbachev's popularity began to wane, there should have been some rivals aspiring to the top post. Yet it has been a peculiarity of Soviet politics under perestroika that it produced no party seeking power at the all-Union level. There has been a profusion of fronts, blocs, and even parties, but practically all of them have regional constituencies and goals. It is characteristic that even democratically inclined members of the first Congress of People's Deputies who banded together called their association the interregional *group*. Somehow the term "party" has taken on a pejorative meaning. In June 1917 at the All-Russian Congress of the Soviets, one speaker declared that there was no single party ready to assume the staggering burden of governing what had been the Russian Empire. Lenin aroused universal merriment and disbelief when he shouted from the Bolshevik benches that yes! there was such a party—his own. What was said in 1917 has up to now been true also of the perestroika period.

Equally repelling to society has become the notion of an individual being endowed with dictatorial powers. Never mind the Stalinist model, but even leadership à la Khrushchev or Brezhnev has become definitely out of fashion. So Gorbachev has been harassed by a multitude of critics, but none of them so far has displayed the ambition to replace him and to inherit his intractable problems. Boris Yeltsin has preferred to establish his political base by becoming head of the Russian Soviet Federated Socialist Republic, an ideal position from which to harass and block the initiatives of the central government, but not a post with commensurate responsibilities.

On the conservative side Yegor Ligachev kept up a constant stream of complaint, but avoided a pitched battle with Gorbachev. After the September 1989 Plenum of the Central Committee, Ligachev was shorn of his real power as the secretary for personnel of the Central Committee. He still failed to challenge Gorbachev openly, certainly not in the sense of demanding his dismissal. One suspects he was being retained on the Politburo more as a scarecrow for the liberals so that they would not criticize Gorbachev too much, rather than because of his political strength.

Seven decades of Communism in the Soviet Union has not only grievously damaged the country's economy and done incalculable harm to the environment in large areas of the land, but has also gone far to render the normal process of politics virtually impossible. During the 1980s the ever-deepening political and economic crisis was eroding the foundations of the regime. For all the frantic constitution- and lawmaking, those foundations were not being replaced by new and reliable ones. By the end of 1989 the crisis of the Soviet system had clearly merged with that of the worldwide Communist movement of which perestroika had been one of the catalysts. The problem before the Kremlin has become not so much that of restructuring and rehabilitating the system as of preserving the Soviet Union.

II

While the public in democratic countries cheered, the Communist world has watched the progress of reforms in the USSR with growing apprehension. As for many in the West, so for the leaders of the "fraternal parties" in both the East and West the original thrust for perestroika was puzzling and bewildering. What for the democratically minded was hopeful had to be for the Communists disturbing and attended with ominous possibilities.

The fact that Moscow abandoned a confrontational stance toward the West was bound to create uneasiness even among parties such as the Italian one, which has for a long time, if not consistently, criticized the Soviets for their rigid foreign policy and their autocratic ways at home. If Moscow had now explicitly rejected the class approach to international affairs and gone to such lengths to humor (many of the unreconstructed militants would say to appease) Washington, what would remain of the whole paraphernalia of Communist international philosophy? For many years the Italian Communists emphasized their differences from Moscow, condemned actions such as the invasion of Czechoslovakia, and repudiated the notion of the dictatorship of the proletariat and its corollary, the one-party state. By the 1980s Western Communism, certainly in Italy, had thrown off its subservience to the Soviet Union. But now the Kremlin leadership, engrossed in its own problems, had to all appearances lost its interest in the "fraternal parties" of the West. Official declarations such as the resolution at the Nineteenth Party Conference in 1988 still repeated the sacramental formulas about Soviet support for the progressive and national liberation forces throughout the world, but such stale rhetoric could no longer alarm or excite many outside of the USSR.

Many years earlier a French socialist quipped about the Communists in his country and in general that they were neither on the left nor on the right, but in the East—i.e., subservient to the USSR. Now that this subservience was almost totally gone, the Western Communist parties discovered that they were not becoming more popular with their people, but quite the contrary. "Being in the East," i.e., allegiance to the Fatherland of Socialism, had until the 1980s still carried with it an aura of militancy and hence a certain romanticism. Now that the USSR, absorbed in its internal problems, was exuding complete indifference toward the "fraternal parties," proletarian internationalism was clearly a thing of the past, the canons of Marxism-Leninism as anachronistic as medieval scholasticism. The outburst of glasnost in the USSR has discredited not only homegrown Communism, but the worldwide movement, so long devoutly servile to the tyrant in the Kremlin, and even after his death so deferential to his successors. The revelations of the parlous state of the Soviet economy and society threw somber light on the ability of "scientific socialism" to show the path to a better life. "There is no future for capitalist society," declared Leonid Brezhnev at theTwenty-fifth Party Congress in 1976. Ten years later Brezhnev's successor was engaged in vigorous courtship of such potentates of capitalist society as Reagan, Thatcher, and Kohl. And if not explicitly, then through their economic policies and plans, the leaders of the Soviet and Chinese Communist regimes were plainly indicating that in their view there was no future for socialist society as the term would have been understood by Leonid Brezhnev.

He would not renounce his faith in socialism, Gorbachev kept repeating, and his ideological scruples, as we have seen, played an important role in stymieing the progress of economic reforms. But how could an Italian or Spanish Communist argue the superiority of state control of the economy and its superiority to private ownership when the unanimous chorus of Soviet economists had roundly condemned the "command administrative" system for ruining the country's production and had pleaded for privatization of state enterprises? What then remained about the Communist parties in the democratic countries that distinguished them from other movements on the left, except for the now less than felicitous recollections and reflections associated with their name? Not surprisingly, many would rush to continue business under a different name, such as "the Democratic Socialist Party of the Left." The convoluted nature of the new name would in itself indicate the eagerness to get as far as possible from the old one and what it currently stood for: painful memories of submission to a tyrant, and now ideological vacuum and economic failure.

Marxism-Leninism remained important in certain areas of the Third World where the general socioeconomic situation made the militant part of its message still meaningful. But even there the Soviet Union's decline as a superpower, its and the People's Republic's nonconfrontational relations with the West, had deeply negative effects on the strength and élan of the local Communist and national liberation movements. Rapprochement with the United States put an effective end to Moscow's military aid to the Sandinista regime in Nicaragua and that in turn contributed to its defeat at the polls. With the Soviet economy in ever-deeper trouble, with even the pretense of ideological zeal disappearing from its foreign policy, the Kremlin could not afford to persist in its role as an avowed protector of radical and revolutionary movements all over the world. Considerations of prestige required that such longtime clients as Castro's Cuba and the Soviet-installed regime in Afghanistan should not have their material aid from the USSR cut off precipitously. But with Gorbachev at the helm and with Shevardnadze as foreign minister, the regime was firmly determined to avoid anything that might bring back the winds of the cold war. Instead of expanding its resources on the revolutionary and anti-Western goals, the Soviet Union was now counting on, and beginning to receive, material help from the West. By 1989 the international dimension of what remained of Communism appeared to have disappeared from the perspective of the leaders of the USSR. They were engrossed in the task of cultivating their own garden.

A moralist would not be edified by the reflection that this virtuous foreign policy did not bring the regime any readily perceptible dividends in terms of increased popularity or improved conditions at home. There was undeniably one huge benefit: the lessening of international tensions and the greater remoteness of the specter of nuclear war. But as mentioned before, aggressive foreign policy served the regime as a kind of public relations campaign extolling the Soviet system. The new thinking about international affairs made the Soviet Union

appear much less awesome and by the same token made both foreigners and its own citizens see more clearly the vulnerabilities and
weaknesses of the Soviet state and society. Due both to the circumstances and to its conscious policy, the Soviet Union would no longer
appear as the guardian and leader of world communism. But the
abdication of that role would in turn threaten not only the power, but
the very existence, of the Communist state.

It would not have taken much foresight to realize that any weakening of the Soviet image as a superpower could have speedy and
most drastic repercussions on Eastern Europe. The Communist governments there—Communism as a way of life—were maintained
above all by one factor: the physical presence or the shadow of Soviet
soldiers and tanks. This was most vividly demonstrated in Hungary
in 1956 and Czechoslovakia in 1968. But it was also inherent in the
Polish drama of 1980–81. Practically no one in Eastern Europe believed that the Jaruzelski regime would have dared to tame Solidarity,
and they certainly couldn't have succeeded in it, without the support
or an implicit threat of intervention by the Kremlin. Paradoxically, the
awe of Soviet power was largely responsible for the survival of the
Communist regime in Yugoslavia, though it was outside the Soviet
bloc, and in Romania, whose situation under Ceauşescu could be
described as partly inside the bloc and partly outside of it. In both,
popular acquiescence in the oppressive regimes was also due to the
conviction that the only practical alternative was not anything resembling a democracy, but another Communist government like that in
Prague or Sofia. Tito's discordant heirs (the marshal arranged the
politics of his country so that after his death no single person would
inherit his powers) and the increasingly oppressive and eccentric Romanian dictator were thought to be lesser evils, though by the late
1980s this view was quite questionable in regard to the latter.

Eastern Europe then posed perplexing problems for the new thinking on foreign policy, and even a more difficult one for overall Soviet
policies. If the Kremlin was to repudiate what had been (mis)called
the Brezhnev Doctrine, Eastern Europe might—almost certainly
would—explode. On the other hand, for the USSR to cling to its
protectorate over the area would have been inconsistent with the new
type of relationship Gorbachev and Shevardnadze were trying to develop with the West. It would also have run into considerable popular
opposition at home. Perestroika has created what might be legitimately
called public opinion in the USSR. The people applauded the with-

drawal from Afghanistan and judging by its manifestations, such as
the article by Chingiz Aitmatov that we've cited, they were definitely
opposed to fresh military ventures abroad.

However, the dilemma of what to do or not do about the Soviet
Union's clients in Eastern Europe transcended considerations of foreign policy and even those of putative popular reactions to another
coup like those in 1956 or 1968. Liquidation of the Communist regimes in Poland or Czechoslovakia—or even a rising against them—
was bound to have reverberations within the USSR. It did not take
much imagination to foresee what effect such an event might have
on the already aroused nationalist aspirations of various ethnic communities, and what further incentives it would provide for their efforts
to secure greater autonomy or even independence from Moscow.

Gorbachev's behavior through 1987–88 suggests strongly, even
though it would seem hardly credible, that he underestimated the
danger. Or, rather as with many domestic reforms he had initiated,
he had not realized that, once started, the momentum of liberalization
of East European Communism could not be arrested at a safe point.
In April 1987 he visited Czechoslovakia, which the Husák regime had
held under a tight rein ever since 1969, stamping down any attempts
to revive the spirit of the Prague Spring. To his hosts' obvious discomfiture, Gorbachev chose to expatiate on perestroika, implying that
its liberalizing tenets should be adopted by other Communist states
as well as the USSR. A member of his entourage was asked what the
difference was between the current reforms in the Soviet Union and
what Dubček had attempted in 1968. "Twenty years," was the evasive
answer. In July 1988 Mikhail Sergeievich paid a state visit to another,
even more imperiled forepost of Communism: Poland. Again, he be-
haved like a statesman visiting a friendly power rather than the supreme leader of Communism inspecting a vassal state. Again, during
his public appearances there were attempts to draw him out on the
kind of relations he envisaged between the USSR and the "fraternal
countries" and what the USSR might do if events like those of 1980
were to recur in Poland. He planned to write a book on the subject,
replied the visitor, undoubtedly raising the level of anxiety among his
official hosts and that of hope among the people at large. As in his
domestic policies, the general secretary was clearly underestimating
the explosive potential of nationalism and exhibiting unwarranted
confidence that democratization would strengthen rather than lead
to the end of one-party rule.

It is not clear whether Gorbachev really believed in what he said when questioned by American reporters on the subject of Eastern Europe. It was in May 1988 that some of them asked him pointedly whether he would tolerate Poland's adoption of "a pluralistic system in which the Communist Party might not play the leading role." In his reply Gorbachev expressed confidence that the great majority of people in Poland would want to continue on the path the country had followed since World War II.[26] No intelligent Russian, still less a man in his position, could have been that confident. But it may have been a case of wishful thinking: even the Poles, with their anti-Russian tradition, were bound to see that their national security must rest on an alliance with the Soviet Union. And that alliance in turn required the continuation of the Warsaw Treaty Organization and of the Communist Party's leading (but not necessarily exclusive) role in Poland's political life.

In other words, the 1988 Gorbachev would have been quite willing to go beyond Dubček's planned reforms in 1968 and to tolerate a considerable degree of pluralism in Eastern Europe. It may seem incredible now that he could have believed that the Poles, Hungarians, and other East Europeans would have been satisfied with such partial freedom. At the time, however, there were cogent reasons for a modicum of confidence on the subject. The USSR still loomed as a military colossus, not to be provoked lightly. At least two nations in the area— Poland and Czechoslovakia—were assumed to be apprehensive of the growing power of West Germany, and hence would, also out of self-interest, cling to Moscow for protection, with all that it implies.

At the same time, it must have been clear to Gorbachev as well as to others in the Kremlin that the old vassal status of Eastern Europe could not endure. As suggested above, the Soviet leader would until quite late cling to the belief that even under a new order the local Communist parties would continue to dominate the political scene. But for many official and unofficial Soviet analysts of international affairs, it was obvious early in perestroika that the last chance for Communism in those countries to be reconciled with popular aspirations had passed in 1968 with the invasion of Czechoslovakia. The nations of the area would not be appeased by promises or even by the liberalization of the existing regime. They wanted to get rid of them, and they would do so, once reasonably sure Soviet tanks and troops would not intervene. How then could the USSR retain influence over Eastern Europe and preserve such tangible elements of its presence as the Warsaw Pact if the Communist parties of the area were gone or reduced to impotence?

Searching for an answer, some Soviet scholars thought of the idea of the Finlandization of Eastern Europe. Their notions on the subject deserve our attention, not because by the time they were enunciated there still existed a chance of putting the idea into practice, but because the very formulation of it was a testimony of the utter collapse of Communism both as an ideology and as an international movement. ". . . a 'Finlandized' country is a country that has a western-type social system and links with the Western world's economy, but which conducts its foreign policy in accordance with the defense and political interests of the USSR," wrote a Soviet analyst in 1989.[27] Why should the USSR tolerate such a transformation of its erstwhile satellites and acquiesce in their throwing off Communism? Because "having stopped considering our system as an alternative model of social development for the whole world, and having recognized the organic weaknesses of our own economic and political system, we are consciously trying to change our attitude toward the already-existing ties with the West, and as far as possible to integrate ourselves with its [the West's] system." There could be no more explicit acknowledgment of the bankruptcy of the Communist system and not only in Eastern Europe. The author calls for the USSR to give up any effort to maintain in power the existing Communist regimes or to create new ones. "The principal [Soviet] political line in those regions [i.e., in the Third World], consequent upon the global strategy of the USSR . . . rejects the notion of creating new *left-wing totalitarian regimes*."[28] (My italics.) And if so, why try to perpetuate such regimes in Eastern Europe? "Changing the character of the relations between the USSR and [other] countries belonging to the Warsaw Treaty Organization . . . would create a more favorable image of the USSR both among societies of those countries and in the entire world." But wouldn't the erstwhile Communist and now Finlandized countries seek to sever their ties with the USSR even as far as their foreign and defense policies are concerned? Once emancipated, would they not gravitate toward the West? The author's answer is not very convincing. "It seems to me such apprehensions proceed from the old imperialist logic, according to which one must preserve the conflict and confrontation between the countries belonging to NATO and those of the Warsaw Pact."

By the time the article was published, both its tone and its recommendations appeared anachronistic. By August 20, 1989, it was no longer a question of the Soviet Union permitting the removal of the Polish, Hungarian, and other Communist parties from power, but of acquiescing in what was almost a fait accompli. *All* of the Soviet-sponsored East European regimes were already tottering, and would collapse within a few months, and except in the case of Romania with no bang and barely a whimper. The only alternatives before Moscow at that time were either to let events take their course or to authorize a massive military intervention, in the first place, in Poland, where the Polish United Workers' Party was in its death throes. In fact, there was no choice: by the middle of 1989 the situation inside the Soviet Union made it virtually impossible for the Kremlin to embark on a major military operation abroad.

Finlandization implied continued membership of the erstwhile satellites in the Warsaw Treaty Organization. As late as the end of 1988, not even the most fervent Polish or Hungarian patriot and anti-Communist could have imagined that even if it permitted the fall of their respective regimes, the USSR would let Eastern Europe slip entirely out of its sphere of domination and scrap the Warsaw Treaty Organization. But what could be the point and the possibility of pre-serving the pact once those regimes were gone? The main purpose of the Warsaw Treaty Organization was to protect Communism in Eastern Europe and to lend a veneer of legitimacy to actions such as the invasion of Czechoslovakia.[29] With Communism in the area stripped of power, the Warsaw Treaty Organization would become superfluous, reminiscent in its fatuity of the Holy Alliance of the nineteenth century. And Finlandization would become a mirage, van-ishing precisely when the Kremlin was belatedly ready to grasp it. There would have been a chance for it had Moscow been ready in 1968 to embrace Dubček, in 1980–81 to tolerate Solidarity. By August 1989 it was much too late.

Apart from the special case of Romania, the manner of the demise of the Communist regimes under Soviet tutelage[30] was pretty much the same. Already the first phase of perestroika (1985–87) had raised the peoples' hopes and their rulers' apprehensions. The latter re-sponded with attempts at liberalization, but for the most part drew back from trying to carry out their own version of perestroika. For the USSR the restructuring of the system and especially glasnost meant a leap into the unknown. But their colleagues in Warsaw, Prague, and the other East European capitals realized only too well where

such a leap would carry them: political turbulence, and insistent demands for further concessions and finally for freedom.

On February 8, 1988, the clock really started running out on Communism in Eastern Europe; that was the day Gorbachev made public
a tentative timetable for the withdrawal of Soviet troops from Afghanistan. In May the armed forces of the USSR began their withdrawal. In the same month, János Kádár was replaced as the head of
the Hungarian Communist Party. His name epitomized the Soviet-
controlled past, even though Hungary during the last two decades of
his leadership had liberalized its economic policies and had proclaimed
its own limited version of glasnost. Almost simultaneously there broke
out a wave of strikes in Poland, with the still officially banned Solidarity
acting as their catalyst. Political and industrial turbulence in Poland
and Hungary would continue throughout the rest of the year, with
the ruling (the term growing increasingly incongruous) parties fighting a rearguard action, promising reforms and putting out feelers to
the dissenters.

What the Hungarian and Polish bosses shared with their opposite
numbers in the other bloc countries was their growing appehension
and demoralization in view of what was happening in the Soviet
Union. In Budapest and Warsaw there was talk of concessions, in the
hope of buying time until their Soviet friends would return to their
senses and restore the healthy fear of the USSR among the nations
of the socialist bloc. Elsewhere, the same considerations and hopes
led to the opposite tactics. Husák stepped down as the leader of the
Czechoslovak regime (remaining as president), but instead of replacing him, as was done in Hungary, with someone who could conceivably tantalize the people as a Gorbachev-like reformer, the party's
choice fell upon an old-timer, a man with a consistent record as a
diehard conservative since 1968. In East Germany, Honecker still
held sway; the government banned the most glasnost-prone Soviet
newspapers and journals. Similar practices were adopted in Bulgaria
and Romania. The latter followed its own course under what had been
for some time a family dictatorship. There were other eccentric features about the Romanian situation. Far from tempering its economic
and social policies with a dose of pragmatism and tolerance, as was
attempted by other Communist states since the onset of the Brezhnev
era, Ceauşescu's rule had grown increasingly doctrinaire, the level of
the people's distress and restiveness surpassing that of other countries
in the bloc. But what was true everywhere on the eve of momentous

changes was that those regimes, after forty years in power, remained without any popular roots. Nowhere except perhaps in Bulgaria could an unreconstructed Communist Party have hoped for a sizable vote in a really free election.

Equally striking as the lack of genuine popular support was the ruling elites' all too obvious abdication of any sense of ideological mission. Little remained of that enthusiasm and conviction that they were building socialism which at least some in the Communist ranks felt when they first had come to power. What you had now at the top were mostly aged oligarchs, and below them the serried ranks of bureaucrats, whose chief preoccupation was how to hold on to their jobs and the perquisites that came with them. If in most cases they clung to the traditional dogmas of Marxism-Leninism, it was largely out of inherent conservatism and a sense of self-preservation—any comprehensive program of reforms, as demonstrated vividly in 1968 and 1980–81, was bound to increase popular aspirations and pressures for political pluralism and democracy. And so if the East European leaders felt constrained to initiate some features of perestroika, they were undoubtedly doing it reluctantly, and probably at Moscow's prompting.

But why didn't Gorbachev understand that under the circumstances no amount of reform was likely to make those regimes acceptable to their people, but only less feared and hence more vulnerable? What may have been obvious to an outside observer and the average Pole or Hungarian was not so to the Soviet statesman; for all of his iconoclastic ideas, he remained a believer.

But as we have already seen, Gorbachev's ideological bent yielded precedence to political realism and his commitment to the cause of reform at home. Both that cause and Communist power within the Soviet Union must not be imperiled by whatever happens within the Communist bloc. His predecessors acted out of the conviction that the fall of the government in a fraternal country would have a domino effect that might not stop at the frontiers of the USSR. Gorbachev's actions clearly bespoke his conviction that if one of those regimes was not strong and nimble enough to hold on to power by itself, then he was not going to endanger the cause of reforms at home, the newly forged ties with the West, and the whole edifice of perestroika by coming to its aid. In 1968 the invasion of Czechoslovakia led to a demonstration by *eight* people in Red Square. More expressed their disapproval in different ways, but still public protest on a large scale had been absent, and in the nature of things virtually impossible. A military intervention in the bloc in 1988 would have been followed by crowds demonstrating in Moscow and in other major cities in the USSR and by the Western powers not only returning to cold-war attitudes but also imposing economic and diplomatic sanctions. It would have meant a political suicide for Gorbachev, for in addition to the repudiation of all that he had been trying to achieve since 1985, he would now be at the mercy of the party and army conservatives. All in all, by the time the Nineteenth Party Conference assembled, a military intervention ceased to be a real option of practical politics. The best-case scenario envisaged people in those countries appeased by reforms and agreeable to the continuance of Communist rule, perhaps even in a coalition with another party (in Poland the regime had for some time been sympathetic to the creation of a Church-sponsored party, one that would be its junior partner and that would weaken the popular support for the still-illegal Solidarity). The worst-case scenario envisaged an actual uprising against a Communist regime, which might involve the Soviet troops stationed in the country, or in any case pose most difficult dilemmas for the Warsaw Pact allies: could they leave one of its members mired in a civil war; what if the rebels got aid from the West? etc. So if things reached a boiling point, it was not even safe to leave the Polish and other East European comrades to their own devices. One would have to give them a gentle push to be reasonable and to make the best deal they could, and if there was no other way, to avoid violence at all cost and to negotiate a surrender. By the end of 1988, at the latest, Gorbachev must have realized and those concerned in Eastern Europe must have at least suspected that this time the bid for freedom would not be followed by the appearance of Soviet tanks.

Still, we would give a great deal to know the gist of communications that passed at that time between the East European capitals and the Kremlin. The same goes for the consultations within the Kremlin. There must have been remonstrations, certainly from the Soviet military leaders, that the prospective abandonment of Eastern Europe, coming in the wake of the withdrawal from Afghanistan, would be a devastating blow to the morale of the army and to the cohesion of the Soviet system itself.

The most excruciating dilemma centered on East Germany. Preservation of Communist rule there transcended the now-obsolete considerations of "proletarian internationalism." It has been a cardinal point of Soviet foreign policy ever since the end of World War II. More than 300,000 Soviet soldiers were stationed on East German territory to defend it from external and internal enemies. For two generations the people of the USSR, indeed the entire world, had been told that the preservation of that outpost of Moscow's power, of the East German Communist regime, was vital to the national security of the Fatherland of Socialism. The Berlin Wall had long stood not merely as an expression of the division of Germany, and that of Europe between East and West; it stood also, and mainly, as a tangible symbol of the Soviet Union's status as a superpower. For almost thirty years no Western statesman, even in his most sanguine moments, could have believed that the Wall could be breached, let alone come down, without incurring an almost certain prospect of a nuclear war. And no one imagined that when it came the breach would be initiated from the East.

Moscow's acquiescence in the demise of what was misnamed the German Democratic Republic still remains the most astounding and the least-explained incident of the East European revolution of 1989–90. Again everything points to the probability that Gorbachev's earlier calculations and caution were outrun by the rush of events. By the beginning of 1989 he may well have reconciled himself to the fact that the old political structure in Eastern Europe was doomed. No matter how much and how fast the local Communist regimes might try to atone for their old sins and pursue their own version of perestroika, most of their Communist parties would not be able to maintain a monopoly on power, perhaps not even retain a share of it in some sort of coalition arrangement. But certainly East Germany had to be a special case. Its economy, as acknowledged even in the West, was much more efficient and advanced than those of the other countries of the socialist bloc. And though by now the Brezhnev Doctrine was clearly a thing of the past, still the mere presence of upward of 300,000 Soviet soldiers was bound to be a psychological deterrent to any precipitous challenge to Communist rule. Most of all, he could not afford to believe otherwise. No Soviet ruler since Stalin could have survived in power had he indicated that the Soviet Union was ready to give up its most significant conquest of World War II.

The persistence of that illusion of Gorbachev's is well illustrated by what he had to say about East Germany as late as December 9, 1989. The Wall was being razed, the East German Socialist Unity (Communist) Party was in its death throes. But Mikhail Sergeievich's language in reference to German affairs could have come from a speech by Brezhnev or Khrushchev. "As for our part, we must declare solemnly that we shall not let down the German Democratic Republic. It has been our strategic ally and member of the Warsaw Pact. One must accept the realities of the post–World War II situation—the existence of two sovereign states, both members of the U.N. To depart from that would threaten the stability of Europe."[31] In a few months the German Democratic Republic would be only a historical memory.

Could the general secretary, speaking as he was before the Central Committee, have been consciously deceiving his comrades, and trying to contain their indignation until such time as a united Germany became a fait accompli? It is difficult to perceive such Machiavellian motivations in Gorbachev's address. Rather, it was another case of his quite frequent lack of realism when dealing with the phenomenon of nationalism. In the same speech he admitted that "to a significant extent the position of our friends in the GDR and Czechoslovakia has become weaker." (A masterpiece of understatement!) But "the new situation requires from our friends decisive and thought-out steps to restore their influence and power within their society—a new strategy and tactics. First of all, there is the task of consolidating all the forces that stand for socialism, democracy, and progress." No, he was not being insincere. Socialism remained for Gorbachev a viable and powerful idea, and once purified of its abuses and excrescences it was bound to appeal to the majority of the people, whether in East Germany or Lithuania.

What is more difficult to understand is the apparent equanimity of other Soviet leaders, political and military, in the face of this rapid disintegration of Moscow's outer empire. Here a major role was undoubtedly played by the growing complexity and contentiousness of domestic problems. By 1989 it was only too obvious that the economic reform had been ineffective. Or rather, though there had been a profusion of legal enactments on the economy, its "command administrative" character had not been basically modified nor had the long-suffering Soviet consumer gotten a new and better deal. Of the three key terms that were to herald the new Soviet era, "acceleration" (of economic growth) has disappeared from the official rhetoric. With the economic side of perestroika stymied, its political meaning and goals were being increasingly, and at times acrimoniously, debated. Glasnost has taught the Soviet citizen that his economic deprivations had been due in the past to a flawed and repressive political system. And so if four years of Gorbachev failed to bring economic improvement, this could only mean that his concept of perestroika was itself flawed. The Soviet system had to be drastically changed, and not merely restructured. The issues that agitated the leadership and the public only a few months before, such as Stalinism, democratization of the party, and the permissible limits of glasnost, were no longer of prime importance. Their place was preempted by more fundamental questions: the very existence of the Communist Party as the source of authority in society, and the rights of the Union republics to fuller autonomy or even independence. With the nature and the territorial integrity of the Soviet state put in question, and with the growing economic distress, what was happening in Germany, and the fortunes of the Warsaw Pact, were increasingly irrelevant.

Yet domestic and intra-Communist-bloc troubles were but two sides of the same coin. The tangible effect of perestroika—decline in the authority and reputation of the CPSU—acted as a stimulant to the disintegration of Communism in the bloc, and vice versa. By losing its international mission and aspirations, Communism has become devoid of any concrete meaning. We have followed the successive steps of that decline ever since 1948, and have seen that even before perestroika Marxism-Leninism had been reduced to one principal proposition: autocratic rule by a self-sustaining oligarchy and bureaucracy. In the Soviet bloc that rule was not only oppressive but ran against the national feelings of the subjugated nations (unlike in China or Yugoslavia, where it took on a nationalist coloration). So it could maintain itself there only if it had the support of Moscow's military power. Once that support was no longer forthcoming, nothing could save the local Communist parties from collapsing in rapid succession like so many bowling pins. And that collapse was bound in turn to undermine the position of *the* Communist Party. By discarding, even if for the time being, its imperial role, the Soviet regime was abandoning its last line of ideological defense. If Communism was not going to inherit the world, then the party's right to rule over the multinational state could be justified only in terms of its domestic record. And that record spoke for itself.

The ideological bankruptcy of Communism and the practical consequences of that bankruptcy were amply illustrated by Gorbachev's state visit to China in May 1989. It was the first summit meeting between the top leaders of the two giant Communist states since 1959 and should have been a momentous event. Only a few years before it would have been seen as such, riveting the attention and hopes of what used to be called the Communist world, arousing vivid apprehensions in its democratic counterpart. To the faithful it would have held the promise that with the termination of the historic dispute and schism Communism would once again resume its advance on the international scene. In the Western capitals it would have been taken as a portent of future crises and confrontations. In 1989 the trip aroused no worldwide fears or hopes. While the clash between the USSR and the People's Republic changed the course of world history, the consummation of their reconciliation was only a diplomatic event.

What gave an unexpected (at first merely embarrassing, later on lurid) background to the summit was a course of events not directly connected with Sino-Soviet relations but illustrative of the plight of Communism in both countries. Hu Yaobang, former general secretary of the Chinese party, discharged in 1986 for his overly liberal tendencies, died one month before Gorbachev's scheduled arrival. His demise triggered student unrest and mass demonstrations in Beijing directed against corruption in high places and the unrelenting authoritarian ways of the regime headed by the eighty-four-year-old Deng Xiaoping. The question of how to deal with the unruly youth split the leadership, with General Secretary Zhao Ziyang inclined to conciliate the Democracy Movement (as it became known) and Deng, who though not holding any party office still exercised supreme power, urging repression.

The once-genial leader, who had sponsored the virtual restoration of capitalism to China's economy, balked at political reforms. Even to have a dialogue with the Democracy Movement, he argued, would place Chinese Communism on the same slippery path that had led to the current situation in Eastern Europe.

To the young rebels Gorbachev was not the embattled leader already facing some of Deng's dilemmas, but still the embodiment of a new spirit in Communism. Above all, his visit was an opportunity not to be missed to make the oppressive regime lose face. The crowds that had been demonstrating in Beijing's Tienanmen Square now began to camp there and grew in size until the whole vast area, the heart of the capital, became filled with a sea of humanity. The official reception of the Soviet guest scheduled for the square had to be hastily transferred elsewhere, and the rest of the visit took place under equally embarrassing circumstances.

With the domestic situation in their respective countries uppermost on their minds, and their meeting taking place in an atmosphere of an incipient revolution, the Soviet and Chinese leaders did not come to any real understanding. Had there been any substance left to proletarian internationalism, one would have expected Gorbachev and Deng to join in a ringing reaffirmation of the ideology. But apart from the ritualistic formulas of the official communiqués, the two sides could find no common language. The strong emotional undercurrent that characterized Sino-Soviet relations both when friendly and when hostile had by now vanished. For the moment neither side had much to fear or to expect from the other.

Gorbachev found it politic when talking with Zhao Ziyang, to whom he felt closer than to other Chinese leaders, to sympathize with his host's predicament. "We too have our hotheads who want to renovate socialism overnight, but that is impossible. It does not happen in real life, only in fairy tales."[32] Having met Deng, he was probably less sincere when he added, "I am sure you will sort out this problem to the benefit of your people." Less than three weeks after his departure the Chinese government did try to resolve the problem. Overruled by Deng and his fellow octogenarians in the leadership, Zhao Ziyang was dismissed and placed under arrest. Troops and tanks were used to clear Tienanmen Square, the resulting massacre claiming several hundred dead. Soviet media joined those of the rest of the world in condemning the slaughter. Moscow's official reaction was restrained.

Tienanmen, the subsequent trials of dissidents, and the general crackdown on opposition stamped the Beijing regime as one that would not be inhibited in using force to preserve one-party rule. This, however, was not a reassertion of orthodoxy but a clear case of clinging to power for power's sake. Beijing was not aspiring to the leadership of the world movement that was clearly slipping out of Moscow's hands, or more precisely was in fact being given up by the Gorbachev regime. Once, not so many years before, Beijing would have easily grasped the chance to displace the "revisionists" as the guide of international Communism. But gone were the days when the People's Republic defied both superpowers and put itself forth as the leader of the Third World and proclaimed its brand of Marxism-Leninism to be the only correct one. Now the missionary zeal was as absent in China as it was in the USSR. In its foreign policy, instead of striking a note of defiance in the face of worldwide reprobations over Tienanmen and what followed, Beijing sought patiently to mend its ties with the West. For all their avowed determination to preserve the socialist system in China, the aged rulers displayed little zeal on behalf of the ideology and the movement they embraced in their early youth and had followed through the vicissitudes of persecutions, wars, and revolutions. It was the Communist Party and their own power to which they were desperately clinging, and not Communism.

On the same day that the old men of Beijing unleashed armed force against its youth, an equally dramatic but nonviolent event took place in Poland. Polish Communism took the decisive step toward its exit from the political scene. Elections, even if only partially free, have almost never and nowhere favored the cause of Marxism-Leninism. Those to the Congress of People's Deputies in March crippled the Communist Party of the Soviet Union, and it would never be quite the same. But what happened to the Polish United Workers' Party as the result of the June 4, 1989 elections was much more disastrous. It was a death blow. For a few more weeks Polish Communism would writhe in convulsions, but then for all practical purposes it would be gone.

As with many important events in history, this one happened not through the conscious design of any of the parties involved, but resembled rather a comedy of errors with the final outcome astounding to all concerned.

Here is what preceded the elections. The 1988 strikes subsided only after the government promised that it was ready for a dialogue with society, in the first instance with Solidarity. In view of the regime's record on such promises, many within Solidarity criticized Wałęsa, who threw his personal prestige behind efforts to terminate the strikes. The regime, believed the hotheads in the movement, was on the run. Now was the time to pressure it until it would give up completely. Negotiations, believed the more impatient among Solidarity, were yet another ruse by the Jaruzelski government to gain time, quite possibly to wait for the Kremlin's position on Eastern Europe to harden again.

If there had been such hopes within the Polish Communist establishment, they must have collapsed after the March 26 elections to the Congress of People's Deputies in the USSR. With Soviet Communism in deep trouble Moscow was hardly in a position to exert itself on behalf of its friends abroad.

So it was a roundtable, rather than a violent coup, that brought Polish Communism down, something that few who had lived through the tumultuous dramas of 1980–81 could have believed possible only a few months earlier. It was a general and odd characteristic of the

East European revolution that when the moment of decision came, the Communist elites' willingness to give up power was much greater than their opponents' readiness to seize it. Both aspects of the paradox are easily explicable. The Communist bosses had been orphaned by Moscow and except in Romania were unable to conceive how they could stand up to their people unassisted. On the other side there was the fact of the utter weariness of East European societies. There was little that was romantic or picturesque about the fall of Communism. Political freedom came in the wake of the ideological bankruptcy of the rulers, and of the moral and economic disarray of the societies over which they had ruled for almost two generations.

The agreement the representatives of the Polish United Workers' Party reached with Solidarity did not on its face spell the doom of the regime. Solidarity was to be legalized. In the forthcoming elections to the Diet, it would be allowed to compete for one-third of the seats. The rest would be reserved for the Communists and their allies. The semifree elections for the Diet were to be balanced by completely free elections for the new legislative body, the Senate, in which Solidarity could offer candidates for all one hundred seats. It seemed like a sensible compromise: the moribund regime gained a lease on life, and Solidarity would function *openly* as the opposition. The Kremlin would surely be pleased by this exemplary Polish perestroika, while the West, impressed by this tangible if partial move toward democracy, would surely loosen its purse strings.

An émigré Russian publicist writing about the events of 1917 pointed out their bizarre setting: the revolutionaries were not ready; indeed Lenin, as late as January 1917, expressed his feeling that his generation might not see the overthrow of tsardom. But the Revolution—*it* was ready. And so with Poland in 1989. The first round of elections held on June 4 confounded the government's hopes and Solidarity's cautions: the Communists and their allies were smashed. Solidarity was triumphant, winning all the seats for which it had been licensed to compete in the elections to the Diet, and ninety-nine out of a hundred seats in the Senate. In many of the Diet constituencies where the Communists' and their allies' candidates were not contested by Solidarity, they still failed to obtain 50 percent of the votes and had to undergo the humiliation of going through a second round of voting. But the Diet elections were completely overshadowed by those for the Senate. There the voice of the people was fully free and its meaning unmistakable: ninety-nine to one against Communism. The turnout for the elections was not unduly high, just over 60 percent of those eligible casting votes. But what could be of no comfort to the regime was that most of those abstaining did so in response to the appeal of the radical wing of Solidarity which argued that the elections, coming as they did as part of a deal with the Jaruzelski government, had to prove meaningless.

Astounded in the first instance, embarrassed by the extent of its victory, Solidarity was still ready to live up to its April bargain with the regime. It was agreeable to a coalition with the Communists, with the latter retaining the key government posts, including that of premiership. But what followed the election was the defection of the Communists' allies, the two "quasi-parties" that had for forty years preserved exemplary obedience to the regime, surpassing in their docility even some of the Communists.[33] Now those hitherto decorative features of the political scene came alive, their members scurrying to leave the sinking Communist ship. The Polish United Workers' Party found itself in a minority also in the Diet, and its candidate for prime minister was unacceptable to the majority. A strong *political*—now the only one possible—intervention by the Kremlin might have still saved, for a while, an appearance of power for the Communists. But Gorbachev felt it unadvisable, and risky for the USSR, to prolong the agony of a discredited and impotent regime. On August 19, Tadeusz Mazowiecki, a veteran Solidarity partisan imprisoned in 1981 and the personal nominee of Wałęsa, was called upon to form the government. A Soviet correspondent in Warsaw felt constrained to pen a wistful obituary: "The [Communist] Party having ceased to be the ruler, and finding itself, to speak frankly, in a kind of opposition, intends to restructure itself and to work out a new program that would attract millions."[34]

Variants of the Polish drama were simultaneously being enacted all over Eastern Europe. There had been similar moves by the Communists in the other satellite countries to refurbish their image by choosing new leaders, and by attempting to negotiate with and appease the representatives of society, and there were last-minute vain appeals to secure some assistance or at least verbal encouragement from the Kremlin—and then came the crash. Much of the true sense of what was happening in that part of Europe was epitomized by what took place when, in September, Hungary opened its border with Austria. Thousands of East German "tourists" started escaping across it to the West. Others would camp on the grounds of West German embassies in Prague and Warsaw, seeking exit permits. This vividly confirmed that it was much too late for Communism to try to reform itself. People were fleeing not only, or even mainly, from the oppressiveness of an authoritarian system, but from the entire way of life produced by Communism. Nor was this flight to be understood merely in terms of the economic disparities between East and West and of the refugees' excessive hopes on that count. People were also fleeing from the tyranny of meaningless slogans, from the constant harassment of countless and needless regulations and of other affronts to what has become recognized as a civilized way of life for the modern individual.

Gorbachev's visit in October to the German Democratic Republic on the occasion of the fortieth anniversary of its foundation turned out to be a harbinger of its fall. The Wall was breached on November 9, and within one month, with something like 400,000 Soviet troops standing by, the East German Communist regime collapsed. A few days later a non-Communist government was installed in Prague. There would still be several weeks, maybe months, of formalities to achieve the definitive termination of Communist usurpation. The process was decorous. The very ease with which the once-formidable edifice of power and repression gave way argued against violence and the thirst for retribution. General Jaruzelski, the main architect of the repression of Solidarity in 1981, was allowed to remain for another year and a half as the president of the Polish (no longer People's) Republic. Other Communist chiefs and dignitaries were also, for the most part, allowed to retire in peace. It was not only humanity that dictated such tolerance to the forces of reform. It was also the recognition that once stripped of its foreign mainstay, local Communism had become not only powerless but almost unimportant. Only in Romania was the scenario different and marred by violence. Elsewhere, the regimes had peacefully disintegrated. Here the dictator, who had utterly lost the sense of political reality, held on tenaciously to power, unmindful of what was going on in the USSR or anywhere else. Hence the bloody end of Ceauşescu and his associates during the last days of 1989.

The balance sheet of the year marked a rout of Communism not only in Eastern Europe. What the events between 1945 and 1985 had clearly established was that the Soviet Union was not merely the most powerful of the Communist states and thereby had assured the survival of the client regimes in its spheres of domination. Even with the ideology having largely evaporated from the Soviet system during the era of stagnation, Communism elsewhere, even under regimes independent of Moscow, derived its meaning and vitality from the fact that it remained the ruling creed of the Fatherland of Socialism and that the latter was a superpower. Now that perestroika put in question both those propositions, other fraternal countries and parties found themselves under pressure to give up or to alter fundamentally their own ideologicopolitical structures. Yugoslavia and Albania, though each in its own way independent of the Soviet Union, still found themselves, largely as the result of what was happening to Communism elsewhere, politically adrift, their steering mechanisms no longer functioning. It was only a question of time (most likely short) before their ideological facade would also crumble. Beijing had defied the Soviet Union for two decades, but eventually it was not its armies but the reverberations of perestroika that had penetrated the borders of the People's Republic and led to the Democracy Movement and the Tienanmen confrontation. With the ideology for all practical purposes discarded or reduced to a meaningless ritual, the survival of the existing power structure in China and the remaining Communist states was now dependent solely on the efficacy of their political and police controls.

Communism was perceptibly losing its character as a world movement. By the end of 1989 several of its bastions had fallen, the remaining ones becoming isolated and beleaguered redoubts. The term "Communist" was now unfashionable, with most "fraternal parties" scurrying to change their names. Even those that like the Polish United Workers' Party did not have the embarrassing adjective in their title opted for a new name in the hope of making people forget the unfortunate associations clinging to the old one. Could Soviet Communism survive, in any meaningful way, its abdication as the leader of a worldwide movement? Could the Soviet state?

III

The foreign Communists' identity problems were paralleled by the Soviets' somewhat similar gyrations. Much of the political debate in the USSR centered in 1989–91 on the meaning of the two terms "socialism" and "sovereignty."

Communism, at least in the public mind, has come to have a straightforward meaning: the party's monopoly of power and all that it implied as illustrated by the decades of Soviet history. Socialism is a much more nuanced concept. Though Gorbachev, as we shall see, would balk at the party's abdicating its role, the general thrust of perestroika has meant the abandonment of Communism as defined above. But was the Soviet Union also to cease to be a *socialist* society? The mere posing of the question would bring a very emotional response from the architect of perestroika. He was a convinced socialist, Gorbachev declared in a speech previously cited. This is not only a matter of belief with him, it is a part of his personality. "We have agreed that we want real socialism; for us the idea of socialism is not a threat."[35]

By the time this resounding profession of faith was made, it was clear that the drift of perestroika, as far as the economic issues were concerned, was away from socialism. The usual definition of a socialist economy includes state ownership of the means of production, government control of prices and wages, and public policies designed to prevent great disparities in income. Now, some of those conditions, certainly not the last one, had never been fully implemented in the preperestroika USSR, yet they were the official policy of the state.

Gorbachev's initial notions of how to stimulate the Soviet economy did not go much beyond fresh administrative contrivances and the traditional rousing appeals for better performance by management and workers. When such panaceas once more proved ineffective, the regime at first reluctantly acknowledged the need for organic changes. By 1989 the command administrative system, i.e., centralized planning and management, was being roundly condemned. By then it had been recognized that the collective-state farm system, having failed, had to be replaced by a new approach to agriculture. Also urgent, it was argued, was the need for industry and commerce to receive an injection of private initiative. And, yes, the Soviet Union should be open not only to Western ideas of how to run the economy; it should also welcome investments by foreign capitalists. Now that glasnost enabled them to speak freely, Soviet economists virtually unanimously opted for giving up the old Marxist shibboleths and adopting measures that would enable this vast country, with its fabulous resources, to loosen the ideological straitjacket that kept its standard of living at the level of a Third World society. The boldest proponents of reforms would scorn the cautions and delays of a transition. They pleaded for the government to take the path that would be actually adopted by Poland in 1990: a direct plunge into a free-market economy through a deregulation of prices, aggressive pursuit of privatization of industry and agriculture, and an end to the state subsidization of food and other necessities.

As Poland's experience was to confirm, such a drastic change of course involved considerable hardships and hence posed political dangers. It would inevitably bring unemployment and, in the first instance, a massive increase of inflationary pressures. For all of the Soviet citizen's numerous economic grievances, he could at least take it for granted that the state protected him from being unemployed and from the fluctuation of prices for the necessities of life. In Poland the shock was cushioned by the popular acceptance of the hardships as a price for getting rid of an alien and repressive political system. No such rationale could be invoked in inflicting similar, even if temporary, sufferings upon the Soviet consumer. Political perestroika has made the task of economic perestroika much harder. The Kremlin's measures that before would have been accepted by its subjects, even if sullenly, could and would now bring about strikes and demonstrations, perhaps even more drastic reactions. Still far from being one, the Soviet Union became vulnerable to all the vicissitudes of a democracy.

It was not, however, such practical difficulties that were in the main responsible for the agonizingly slow progress of the economic reform. There was also the opposition to any new thinking on the subject by the vast administrative and managerial bureaucracy, which had a vested interest in preserving as much of the old system as possible. The complexity of the task offered its covert enemies within the government ample opportunties to sabotage reforms—for example, by attaching provisions to the liberalizing measures that in fact made them impracticable or hobbled their effectiveness. In 1987 the government authorized joint ventures with capitalist countries, but the law was accompanied by provisions that would make foreign investors chary of placing their money in a Soviet enterprise. The Soviet share of the business in question had to be at least 51 percent, its manager had to be a Soviet citizen, and there were a number of other vexatious regulations. To be sure, the law was subsequently amended, with some of the counterproductive provisions eliminated. But this has been far from an isolated example of the nervousness and indecision that has characterized the Gorbachev regime's efforts to shed the constraints of the administrative command system. The law authorizing private cooperatives in the service and industrial sectors was followed in short order by another subjecting their profits to exorbitant taxation. Nor, as we have already seen, would the government take the simplest and most logical route toward the eventual disbanding of the disastrous collective farm mechanism, by authorizing private ownership of land.

What flawed the reforms, apart from the political dangers inherent in a shock treatment for the Soviet economy, and bureaucratic resistance and inertia, was the trauma inherent in the repudiation of the basic canons of Marxism-Leninism. Granted, this repudiation was clothed in euphemisms—for example, describing the new economic order as "market socialism." Proponents of the new course tried to invoke Lenin's authority for their proposals. Abel Aganbegyan, an early Gorbachev adviser, stressed this motif. "Lenin fully understood that a socialist society could not be developed solely on enthusiasm and on the application of administrative measures." And like Gorbachev himself, he sought to classify this partial retreat into capitalism as the consummation of socialism: "The aim of socialist development in the final analysis lies in meeting the needs of all members of society more fully. Cooperatives and self-employment contribute to this end, and therefore reinforce our socialist principles. They completely correspond to Gorbachev's slogan for perestroika: 'Give us more socialism.' "[36]

But while it was easy for a professional economist grown impatient of the antiquated formulas and taboos to indulge in such self-deception or equivocation, a politician of the Gorbachev generation found the task much harder. One might well ask why the economic tenets of the creed have been more difficult to shed than those bearing, for example, on proletarian internationalism. This, however, can be better understood in psychological rather than ideological terms. To deny the validity of the Marxist-Leninist strictures on the economy meant a virtual repudiation of the entire Soviet experiment. One could rescue the reputation of the October Revolution by claiming that while it accidentally led to Stalin, its main meaning was to be found in such achievements as the modernization and industrialization of the USSR, in the collectivization of agriculture. What a radical change of the economic structure would imply was that the entire process had been wasteful. The country could have been much more efficiently modernized and industrialized under auspices other than the socialist one. Collectivization, especially, had been a horrendous mistake. Gorbachev's intermittent reaffirmation that he was and would remain a follower of socialism represented then a desperate attempt to cling to the Soviet past, a refusal to admit that those seventy years had been entirely in vain. And the same impulse made him and his subordinates superstitiously afraid of an adjective. "Private" would evoke those traditional bogies of common Marxist parlance: "exploitation" and "speculation."

Such quasi-ideological prejudices were not absent among the people at large. Three-quarters of a century of indoctrination failed to turn the mass of the people into believers, but it certainly conditioned them to feel that anything smacking of capitalism was suspicious, which in turn reinforced their inherent egalitarian instincts. Licensing of long-term leases failed to bring a mass exodus from the collective farms. Peasants by and large, especially in the Russian Republic, have preferred the low-level economic security provided by the old system to striking out on their own. Private cooperatives and budding entrepreneurs have had to grapple not only with a mass of superfluous regulations but also with a fairly widespread popular sentiment which holds that spectacular success in business is made possible only through something illicit.

It has been a combination of such diverse factors that held back economic perestroika. Or rather the picture was that of a Procrustean bed with the government here expanding the area of autonomous economic activity, there cutting it down in the name of restraining "speculation" and "exploitation." In retrospect, it is probable that the regime erred by not pushing reforms more energetically and decisively during the earlier period of perestroika, before the March 1989 elections to the Congress of People's Deputies. The imperfect democratization that then ensued weakened Gorbachev's powers without endowing his rule with a popular mandate. It was not only his socialist scruples but, for all his formal powers, the ever-growing constraints on his freedom of action that rendered economic perestroika so uncertain and chaotic. What could have been accomplished by a Kremlin decree in 1987 would two years later become a risky gamble.

The faltering pace of the economic reform was bound to become even more frustrating than the corresponding process in politics. In the fifth year of Gorbachev's tenure the average Soviet citizen could not note any perceptible improvement in his standard of living. There may have been stagnation under Brezhnev, went a standard complaint, but there were also goods on the shelves, while in this brave new world of perestroika basic commodities were often in short supply. Just as glasnost had demythologized the past, so it was casting a glaring light on the present. Television and newspapers kept the Soviet citizen informed of strikes, of shortages, of the rationing of basic commodities in numerous localities. It made him more aware than ever how primitive were the material conditions of his life, even when compared with those in other East European countries. Written in 1991, the following passage expresses the mood already prevalent at the end of 1989: "We would like here to raise a special question. Why has the direction of our economy become so impotent? Why is it in such a mess? What remains under the rubble of the command system? Should that system be restored or should we as fast as possible construct a market economy?"[37]

But wasn't there a middle road that might preserve for the Soviet economy some of the attributes and values of socialism while imparting to it the dynamism of a free market? There was the attractive model of Sweden, a country with a capitalist structure for its economy, balanced by highly egalitarian fiscal policies—and enjoying one of the highest standards of living in the world. But how distant the USSR was from Sweden when it came to its political and social culture! The crisis of authority, plainly visible already after the first meeting of the Congress of People's Deputies, both engendered and was itself a consequence of the sad state of the economy. "A power vacuum and lack of direction—those words are being heard more and more often both in the queues and from the speakers' platforms at meetings. It is being said by leaders who criticize the present executive branch of government, whether from the left or from the right. Yes, political authority in our country has never during the last seventy years been so unstable, weak, and lacking in solidity as it is now as we pass from 1990 to 1991," wrote a noted economist.[38]

The crisis of authority reflects above all the loss of a sense of direction by Gorbachev and Company. Having demolished several appurtenances of the old system, they paused in uncertainty as to what should replace them. An early economic adviser of Gorbachev and then his critic, Stanislav Shatalin, portrayed the dilemma when defining his political position. "I still consider myself a socialist, but socialism for me is real political democracy grounded in a multi-party system . . . an economic system based on a truly multi-faceted property basis, including of course private property and free enterprise."[39] Such a catholic (in the general sense) definition of socialism would, of course, permit us to classify the United States as a socialist country. Here again, one suspects, is a case of a modern economist exasperated

by obsolete formulas and trying to make economic and political pragmatism acceptable to politicians, more specifically, to Gorbachev.

Perhaps the latter's scruples could have been appeased if to the
confusion over the meaning of socialism had not been added the
turmoil and mischief associated with another term, "sovereignty."

Here we must return to the Achilles' heel of the Soviet system—
the nationalities question. The travails of the Soviet Union and Communism are reminiscent of those Russian dolls in which, after de-
taching the top segment of the figurine, one finds successively smaller
and smaller dolls. The breakdown of the unity and ideological mission
of the movement revealed and accentuated the tensions within the
smaller entity—the socialist bloc. And with that bloc disintegrating
and then reduced to the Soviet Union itself, its own unity and survival
became subject to increasing pressures.

Gorbachev had had his hands full fighting the battle of perestroika
on several fronts. Still, one must note his lack of foresight when it
came to the issue of nationalities and of preserving the unity of the
country. As a statesman setting out to remake his society, he should
have remembered how already in prerevolutionary Russia every attempt to liberalize the autocratic system and any advance toward
glasnost, no matter how modest, would bring the nationalities problem
to the surface and pose a quandary for the central government. Any
relaxation of the regime would prompt the inmates to try to break out
of their "prison house of nationalities." The Soviet period brought the
nationalities formal equality and the fiction of a federal state. The
primary and avowed purpose of perestroika had been to make those
rights—so impressive on paper, so irrelevant to the actual process of
Soviet politics—real.

The problem of nationalities is not *exactly* synonymous with that
of the rights of the various component units of the USSR to autonomy
or independence. The first reflected largely opposition in varying de-
grees of the non-Russian ethnic groups to the domination by the Elder
Brother, "the leading nation" in Communist parlance, which under
Soviet rule was as pronounced as under the tsars (and even more so
under the Georgian turned Russian chauvinist, Stalin). But there is
the other side of the coin. It comes out of the people's (including the
Russians') dislike of centralized authority, and the consequent feeling
that the government should not only be democratized, but also de-
centralized. Add to those two kindred issues the factor of interethnic
tensions, which in some areas pits cohabiting nationalities against

each other—for example, Azerbaijanis versus Armenians—and one gets the dangerous combination of aspirations and emotions which, once the iron grip of Moscow slackened, threatened not only peres-troika but the very existence of the Soviet Union.

It would be naive to think that even the wisest and most far-sighted policy on that count would have avoided trouble. Still, when the trouble came, it would not have had to be as far-reaching and seemingly intractable had Gorbachev and his associates shown themselves more sensitive to the problems of the multinational state emerging from autocracy and repression. He had tried to democratize the Soviet political scene while retaining the dominant role of the Communist Party; he now proposed to reform the economy and yet somehow preserve its socialist character. Likewise, Gorbachev planned to turn the USSR into a real federation while preserving undiminished the powers of the Union. He would find himself in the position of the sorcerer's apprentice: unable to stop the very forces he had evoked. And while in regard to political and economic reforms the architect of perestroika would let himself be pushed far beyond where he originally proposed to stop, he would prove much more recalcitrant when it came to preserving undiminished the Union of Soviet Socialist Republics.

That Union, he would declare with mounting passion, was the continuation of a community of nations going back almost one thousand years. That flamboyant rhetoric lacked one crucial word: it had never been a *voluntary* union. This fact was spectacularly underlined by a dramatic manifestation that opened the critical phase of what might be called the sovereignty crisis. On August 23, 1989, upward of 1 million citizens of Lithuania, Latvia, and Estonia had formed a human chain stretching through the territory of the three little Union republics. The demonstration commemorated the fiftieth anniversary of the Nazi-Soviet Pact, which surrendered the Baltic republics to Stalin and was a prelude to their annexation the next spring. The giant protest had been spurred by the Soviet Foreign Ministry's acknowledgment of the existence of the secret protocol to the agreement, which sealed Poland's fate as well as that of the three republics. Once again Stalin's sins were being visited on Gorbachev.

It was not only the tyrant's crimes but also his protestations of virtue that were to prove a heavy burden to his successor. Ironically, one of the most troublesome legacies from the era of the "cult of personality" was the 1936 constitution, most of which indeed added up to what had been advertised as—and on paper, with some exceptions, was—the most progressive and democratic document of that kind in the world. (The qualification touches largely on Article 6, about which more later.) And there it was—something no other federal constitution could boast of—Article 72: "Each Union republic shall retain the right freely to secede from the USSR." How inferior in that respect was the Constitution of the United States, that alleged champion of national self-determination, which in the language of a Supreme Court decision prescribed "an indestructible union of indestructible states."

It is unlikely that during the fifty-odd years since the Stalin constitution had been proclaimed Article 72 was given as much as a moment of thought by the average Soviet citizen of any nationality. To imagine that the Ukraine or Latvia might ever evoke that provision or that anyone in his right mind would raise the issue was simply out of the question. One might as well have believed that the time would come when there would be real elections for the Supreme Soviet, with several candidates contesting most seats, or when local authorities, and with impunity, could order statues of Lenin pulled down. Well, by 1989 all those impossible things were happening. Glasnost, and the examples of what was going on in Eastern Europe, transformed the dead letter of the law into a living reality that now stood threateningly before the Gorbachev regime.

Who in his wildest fantasy would have dared to predict that a moment would come when the foreign minister of *Czechoslovakia* would summon the *Soviet* ambassador and gravely ask him to explain why the Kremlin was cracking down on Lithuanian nationalism? Yet this was to happen in January 1991. Shades of 1968! And one also recalls how even a mild intervention by the United States on behalf of the dissidents in the USSR would be met by Gromyko with the glacial response that it was not the kind of language one could allow oneself when speaking to the Soviet Union.

That the virus of independence should manifest itself first and most violently among the population of Lithuania was both unexpected and logical. Unexpected because of the relatively tiny size of the Lithuanian nation, and because the economic and geographic situation of the republic would make its complete separation from the USSR fraught with great hardships for its inhabitants. One would have expected nationalist aspirations to explode more readily among the Ukrainians, the second-largest ethnic group in the Soviet Union, their country having ample resources and meeting other conditions for a

separate state existence. Stronger secessionist ambitions might have
been expected also in Georgia, with its long history of independent
statehood, or in Moldavia, where after its annexation in 1940 the
Kremlin had renamed the Romanian-speaking majority of the population Moldavians.

At the same time, once the atmosphere of fear that had pervaded
preperestroika Soviet politics abated, it was quite natural for Lithuania
to surge to the forefront of those Soviet political entities seeking sovereignty and for the spokesmen of its people to define this term as
implying secession from the Soviet state. Despite their previous in-
clusion in the Russian Empire and their forcible annexation in 1940,
the three Baltic countries had remained the least politically assimilated
area of the Soviet Union. Of the three, Lithuania has the highest
percentage of native inhabitants among the population, and its people
have shown themselves remarkably resistant to foreign domination,
be it cultural or political. Even so, Latvia and Estonia were not far
behind their fellow Baltic land in asserting, though more cautiously,
their right to seek independence. In May all three adopted legislation
proclaiming their sovereignty.

In the Soviet Union, 1990 might be called the year of sovereignty
and, by the same token, the testing time for the survival of the Union
itself. This is not the place to give a detailed account of the effort to
preserve some form of the Union, an ongoing struggle that will not
be resolved for some time. What is pertinent for us is the connection
between that process and the decline of Communism as a world movement, the abdication by its Soviet branch of its universal mission.
Here the causal relation is unmistakable. No sooner did the rulers of
the USSR explicitly abandon the mission to remake the world in a
Marxist-Leninist image than power began to slip out of their hands.
With Communism no longer able to sustain the fiction that it was the
wave of the future, the Communist Party could no longer act as the
glue which held the multinational state together.

The term "sovereignty," so loosely used on the Soviet contemporary
scene, recalls in a strange way the beginnings of the Soviet state and
of Communism. "Sovereignty" in common English use is a synonym
for "independence." Yet, as currently applied in the Soviet Union, its
meaning also embraces assertions of far-reaching autonomy or of the
right to claim independence. Thus sovereignty has been proclaimed
by a number of legislative bodies, including not only those of several
Union republics but also of autonomous republics or even smaller

units. Gorbachev's proposals for a new, "more perfect" Union envisaged at one time its being renamed the Union of *Sovereign* Socialist Republics. What's in a name? In Webster's dictionary, "soviet" comes after "sovereign." The current passion for sovereignty is the first cousin of the sentiment which in 1917 inspired "all power to the soviets," the slogan whose popularity was so cleverly exploited by Lenin. Both have appealed to the average citizen's resentment and distrust of big government, of the central bureaucracy. Both have reflected the desire to bring decision making on crucial issues closer to the people, to the local level. While he has tried to co-opt the term, Gorbachev has recognized its dangerous implications. Even when not used as the equivalent of "independence," "sovereign" has implied (in some cases it has been stated explicitly) that the laws of the given republic take precedence over those of the Union. In the same spirit some republican legislatures have passed laws purporting to establish their own armed forces, their own currency, invalidating some enactments of the Supreme Soviet of the USSR. And having asserted its sovereignty in May 1989, Lithuania on March 11, 1990, declared its full independence. The country where once some twelve or fifteen men in the Kremlin had the last word on every issue has become the stage for the "war of the laws," as the current saying goes.

Confronted by the most fundamental crisis of his political career, the harassed Gorbachev resorted again to constitutional and legal improvisations. On the dubious premise that Article 72 had not specified *how* a Union republic may opt out of the USSR, a new law spelled out a lengthy and cumbrous procedure for secession that would virtually make it impossible. More effective, in the short run, were economic sanctions against Lithuania that made its leaders suspend the operation of the independence law and open negotiations with Moscow.

The fashion for "sovereignty" (which as of the end of August 1991 has been proclaimed by fourteen out of fifteen Union republics and by several autonomous ones) and its more troublesome progeny—independence—has by now reached the stage where not only perestroika but the very existence of the Soviet state has been threatened. The March 17, 1991, referendum saw upward of 70 percent of those who voted agreeing that the USSR should continue as a federal union of "sovereign socialist states." But the validity of the vote as an effective barrier to centrifugal forces was severely limited by the fact that six Union republics—Lithuania, Latvia, Estonia, Georgia, Armenia, and

Moldavia—did not officially participate in the referendum, thereby dclaring their intention to seek full independence sooner or later.

The skill that Gorbachev had displayed in confounding his conservative rivals within the party during the first four years of his reign abandoned him in the most important political battle of his life. He who had retreated on so many issues has taken a stiff legalistic stand on a question that more than any other should have been approached in a spirit of conciliation and flexibility. The president has refused to countenance the right of the republics to claim independence, save through the tortuous procedure that would delay its consummation indefinitely. Had the law in question been passed in 1986 or 1987, it is possible it would have been effective. By 1989–90 it was too late for such palliatives. The same factor—poor timing—has flawed Gorbachev's proposed Treaty of the Union, i.e., the new federal compact, that would bestow considerable (though vaguely defined) new powers on the republics. Earlier, when still unscarred by political and economic setbacks, Gorbachev might well have shown himself more innovative in meeting the challenge. He might have acknowledged the fifteen republics' unconditional right to independence and then with the air cleared, asked them to subscribe to a meaningful federal arrangement. It would have been a gamble, but less so than has been the present course.

But how genuine and enduring is the present nationalities-constitutional crisis? Granted the enormous current frustrations—especially in the economic sphere—would the people of the secession-minded republics really seek a complete and permanent separation from the Union if their material conditions of life were better? Isn't it really the great failure of perestroika in the economic sphere that has made Lithuanians, Georgians, and some of the others so responsive to the call for separation?

The economic plight has undoubtedly aggravated the crisis. We've already located its basic source, however, in the political and ideological sphere. Before the sovereignty issue had heated up, Gorbachev had already lost another battle: over retaining the Communist Party, if no longer as the actual force assuring the country's unity, then at least its symbol.

As of the end of 1989, Article 6 of the Soviet constitution still proclaimed that "the Communist Party, armed with Marxism-Leninism, determines the general perspectives of the development of society and the course of the home and foreign policy of the USSR, directs the great constructive effort of the Soviet people, and imparts a planned, systematic, and theoretically substantiated character to their struggle for the victory of Communism."[40]

After its moral defeat in the elections for the Congress of People's Deputies, the party became a target of attack for the forces of reform, and the first major issue on which they *overtly* clashed with Gorbachev. He had already disenchanted his more progressive supporters by declaring—in the face of the palpable evidence to the contrary—that the elections had proved the Soviet Union did not need a multiparty system. Now confronted with the insistent demands that Article 6 be eliminated from the constitution, Gorbachev committed a major psychological error. He could have saved face, his and the party's, by saying in effect that it did not need a special constitutional entitlement to continue its leading role in the state and society. Instead, he pleaded, and that to the already converted (i.e., to the members of the Central Committee), that Article 6 be retained. "We consider the CPSU to be a consolidating, unifying force. We [see it] as the guarantor of the revolutionary revival of the Land of the Soviets, of the preservation and enhancement of its might and of its international authority and prestige. . . . The Central Committee will resolutely fight any attempts to denigrate the importance of the party and to undercut its authority among the masses. . . . [The demand to eliminate Article 6] is an attempt to demoralize Communists . . . to set the party apart from the workers."[41] Placed against the realities of the contemporary political scene in the Soviet Union, the speech must have sounded to some listeners as a throwback to preperestroika days. And within a few weeks the general secretary of the beleaguered party was compelled to give up his defense of Article 6. On February 27 the Congress of People's Deputies voted to eliminate the offending article from the constitution. It was little consolation that on the same day the parliament voted that additional powers be vested in the office of the president.

With the party debilitated, could "Soviet patriotism" take its place? Some years ago many would have argued that it was the Soviet citizen's attachment to and pride in his country, rather than the worn-out Communist formulas, that constituted the first line of defense of the Soviet system. It was, after all, by appealing to the basic patriotic urge, while ignoring slogans of Marxism-Leninism, that Stalin's regime had been able to survive the first and catastrophic period of World War II, and then to evoke from its sorely tried people the effort that assured victory.

The recent crisis has shown that the citizen's loyalty to his country when under attack cannot be readily translated into loyalty to a political system once it has palpably failed to respond to his needs and aspirations. "Soviet patriotism" has always been a nationalism with a difference: one might try to define it as Russian nationalism with a Communist ideological veneer. In 1943 the "Internationale," the symbol of the ideological origin and mission of the Soviet Union, was replaced as the state anthem by a frankly nationalist text. Its first two verses were much closer to capturing the essence of the nationalities question in the USSR than did Article 72: "An unbreakable union of free republics was forged forever by Great Rus'." *Rus'* was the emblem of the historical Russian state which, though multinational, had for centuries been clearly and oppressively dominated by its major ethnic group. Or rather, under the Soviets (certainly beginning with Stalin's ascendance) as under the tsars, Russian nationalism provided the psychological and cultural bulwark of autocratic rule. But like proletarian internationalism, Russian-Soviet nationalism has ceased to be a dependable ally and support of the Soviet regime. For many within the Soviet army's officer corps and the bureaucracy, and for a small segment of the intelligentsia of Russian origin, the Lithuanian or Georgian aspirations to independence are, of course, a blow to their national feelings. For them the greatness of Russia, whether under imperial or Communist auspices, has been synonymous with its expansion and domination over other nations. But as the recent political developments have demonstrated, the average Soviet citizen of Russian origin does not seem to feel that his national pride requires the preservation of the Soviet state in its present shape or size, especially if this cannot be done through other than forcible means. Being of "the leading nation of the Soviet Union," as Stalin phrased it, did not save the average Russian from feeling the effects of his tyranny, or of the present social and economic disarray, just as acutely as have members of other nationalities. Nationalism with an imperialist coloring has become increasingly unfashionable and unappealing during the last half-century.

The threat to the territorial integrity of the Soviet state has thus not led, at least up until now, to a great nationalist reaction among the ethnic Russians. In his predicament Gorbachev has appealed to Russian nationalism to save the Union, though to be fair to him, he has avoided a chauvinistic note. "History has decreed that a number of big and smaller nations became united around Russia. . . . This process was assisted by the openness of the Russian nation, its readiness to work as equals with people of other nationalities, and to accept with good will their traditions as well as to share their own."[42] Well, a Ukrainian or an Uzbek might question the Russians' (or rather their rulers') willingness to tolerate the other nations' traditions. But beyond such contentious points the fact remains that arguments based on history have seldom proved decisive in a heated political atmosphere such as has prevailed in the Soviet Union since the elections of March 1989.

Nor is the argument for the preservation of the Union strengthened when put in terms of the success of the Soviet experiment: "There has been a great deal of discussion about the union of nationalities produced as a consequence of the October Revolution. . . . But that was a tremendous achievement. . . . One can confidently say that our country has achieved a unique type of civilization, the result of joint endeavors of all our nationalities."[43] How far such arguments are out of tune with popular sentiments even in the Russian Republic has been shown by the great popularity there of Boris Yeltsin. Still seen as an antiestablishment figure, despite the fact that he is president of the Russian Republic, Yeltsin appeals to those who are not confident that the consequences of the October Revolution add up to a "tremendous achievement." He has expressed sympathy for the Baltic nations' struggle for fuller freedom, and while professing the desire to preserve the Union, he would have it based on the entirely voluntary adherence of the individual republics.

Whatever one thinks of the personalities of the two contenders, Gorbachev and Yeltsin, they stand for two opposing tendencies in the current Soviet political scene. The president of the Soviet Union and general secretary of the party has clung to the symbolism, if not the essence, of Marxism-Leninism, and to the preservation of the USSR basically in its present form. The chairman of the Presidium of the Supreme Soviet of the Russian Republic rejects, as does the majority of Soviet citizens (as of June 12, 1991), not only the substance but also the form of the old system and its creed. For him, as for them, Communism is an experiment that has demonstrably failed and socialism has become synonymous with scarcity of goods and the queue. The leader of the Soviet Union would keep its structure intact; the president of the biggest Soviet Republic wants to build the whole edifice anew rather than merely restructure it. Gorbachev, the one-time iconoclastic reformer, had throughout the spring of 1991 increasingly allied himself with the conservative forces in the party, the army, and the bureaucracy. On resigning as foreign minister, Shevardnadze, once Gorbachev's closest adviser, charged that the conservatives are pushing toward the restoration of authoritarian government and implied that the president had become their willing accomplice. For his part, Yeltsin, increasingly uninhibited in his attacks on Gorbachev, found himself accused in the Supreme Soviet of the USSR of "excessive ambition, seeking to split up the USSR, to provoke a civil war, and to replace the leader of our state."[44]

Apart from being a testimony to the current style of political polemic in the Soviet Union, the interchange was a good illustration of the waning of ideology. Gone are terms like "revisionism," "bourgeois nationalism," "leftist deviation," which were once the common currency of such debates.

Looking at the unraveling of the system, one cannot, indeed, exclude the possibilty of a push toward a dictatorship, or that of a civil war.

As to the first danger, proponents of a dictatorial solution must realize that it would require a vast application of force. An *occasional* resort to force, such as perpetrated by Soviet troops in seizing a Vilnius television station on January 13, 1991, when thirteen people were killed, can only aggravate passions; it has not deflected the majority of Lithuanians from their proindependence stand. A similar display of brutality in Tbilisi on April 9, 1989, when nineteen demonstrators were killed by soldiers spraying them with gas, merely solidified Georgian public opinion in its stand against Moscow. Could the multinational Soviet army, already plagued by indiscipline, desertion, and the widespread refusal of draftees to answer the call to colors, become an effective instrument of mass repression? Could Gorbachev, who after the first stage of perestroika (before the middle of 1989) has shown himself, whether prescribing reforms or repressions, halfhearted and indecisive, summon enough resolution and adequate support to be an effective dictator? Merely to ask such questions is to realize that to impose dictatorship upon Soviet society would be an even more difficult task than to endow it with democracy and an orderly economy.

Economic distress and challenges to the unity of the state, coming as they do from so many directions, constitute the main givens of the grim situation of the Soviet Union. It is difficult to see how even the most ingeniously devised plan of economic recovery could succeed without first resolving whether, how and within what territorial-national limits, what is still called the Union of Soviet Socialist Republics can survive.

At this point one should perhaps talk about the chances of effectively reconstituting the USSR, rather than of survival. With political authority being challenged at several levels, with the Union republics challenging Moscow on such basic issues as turning over to the central government its share of taxation, the issue is really the feasibility of building a new federal structure, rather than, as Gorbachev has attempted up to now, hanging on to the old while tinkering with the constitutional machinery. Perhaps the only nonviolent resolution of the dilemma at this time would be an immediate and unconditional recognition of the federal units' independence. Once this was done and the old suspicions and grievances appeased, the now really "free republics" would be invited to subscribe to really meaningful federal arrangements. The logic of economic interdependence and of the necessity of arresting the drift toward anarchy could be a strong argument in favor of the reconstitution of the Union upon new foundations. Those republics which, like the Baltic ones, would still prefer to stay outside the federation could be accommodated through treaty arrangements similar to those of the European Economic Community and NATO.

Whatever the political and constitutional arrangements of the territories now constituting the USSR, it will surely cease to be, in any meaningful sense of the term, a Communist state. The party itself, its membership hemorrhaging, its monolithic facade exposed, might have remained for a while an influential element in the situation. But it did so as a body comprising the mass of officeholders, a kind of pressure group, rather than, as of old, a disciplined order, the foundation of first personal, then collective, dictatorship.

Perestroika has not led to a redefinition of Communism; it has turned out to be its latest and probably most decisive defeat. To some extent this has been due to a peculiar configuration of personalities and circumstances. But there have been other and more fundamental reasons for the debacle. On the international plane the claims of partisans of Marxism-Leninism that it provided the only sure path to peace and the eventual world state had been discredited by the clash between the two giant Communist states. Domestically, the doctrine,

attuned to reactions to the Industrial Revolution and to the crisis of
Western liberalism as it had emerged from World War I, proved incapable of dealing with the economic and technological realities of
the second half of the twentieth century. The bankruptcy of the ideological premises of Communism was masked for a time by the growing military strength of the Soviet Union, its status as a superpower,
and its ability to expand its worldwide influence at the expense of the
democratic West. But that expansion could not be pursued without
creating situations that might have escalated into the frightful danger
of nuclear war. Khrushchev in his last year, the Brezhnev regime
throughout, had recognized the dreadful possibility. It was, however,
only Gorbachev who acknowledged the danger without any ambi-
guities and drew the logical conclusion—peaceful coexistence without any ifs or buts. This has been the historical merit of the Gorbachev
regime, one that will not be erased by its subsequent travails and
reversals. By the same token, this abdication of the universal claims
by Soviet Communism has stripped it of its last line of defense: the
foreign policy of the Soviet Union can no longer shield it from confronting its internal, largely intractable, problems.

Some would apply to Communism what has been said in defense
of Christianity: the trouble with it is that it has never been practiced.
Yet the historical record of the movement is replete with efforts at
reform, efforts to recoup what at different times and in various ways
has been claimed to be the genuine meaning of Marxism-Leninism.
All such efforts have foundered because of the reformers' inability to
cope with what has been the main, many would say the only, essential
characteristic of Communism: one party's monopoly of power. Mao's
attempt to curb his party's bureaucracy by unleashing fanatical youth
against it plunged China into chaos, from which it recovered not only
by jettisoning the Cultural Revolution (which in a bizarre way would
be reincarnated in the Democracy Movement of the late 1980s) but
also by reverting to the old oligarcho-bureaucratic pattern. At the other
end of the political spectrum, the Czechoslovak experiment with "socialism with a human face" threatened or promised, depending on
one's point of view, to lead to political pluralism with the Communist
Party, and eventually even socialism, fading away (as is happening
before our eyes in Eastern Europe). And has not perestroika set in
motion a similar process in what can no longer with any confidence
be described as the Fatherland of Socialism?

CONLUSION

THE MOMENT OF TRUTH

IN THE PRECEDING PAGES we set out the condition of the Soviet Union and of Communism as it stood at the end of the spring of 1991. What has happened since then has only confirmed the logic of the events set in motion by perestroika and glasnost, a logic which spelled the doom of Soviet Communism and the end of the Union of Soviet Socialist Republics. The abortive putsch merely speeded up the process. The Communist Party, rudderless and disintegrating ever since the March 26, 1989, elections to the Congress of the People's Deputies, now collapsed, rather than prolonging its agony for another year or two. Within days of the failure of the inept conspiracy, what had been the USSR took on the appearance of a ruined edifice, its skeleton barely standing, its interior gutted.

The Communist era in the country first known as Russia and later on as the Soviet Union began with the successful putsch of November 7, 1917, and concluded with an abjectly unsuccessful one of August 19, 1991. The first was a daring move by a handful of zealots leading a motley crowd of soldiers, workers, and sailors, not only to seize power but to ignite the fires of world revolution; the latter, a clumsy attempt by a junta of aging oligarchs to reimpose the Communist version of law and order, not in the name of any revolutionary ideas, but to preserve the power and privileges of a decrepit bureaucracy.

The failure of the putsch reaffirmed what had been said on a preceding page: an attempt to reimpose dictatorship in the USSR of 1991 would prove even more difficult than steering the state toward effective democracy and an orderly economy.

As of this writing the full story of what had led to the coup and what transpired during those crucial seventy hours has still not been told. Following the drama there have been muted hints that at one time or another during the preceding months Gorbachev himself had played with the idea of assuming dictatorial powers. In June, Prime Minister Valentin Pavlov urged the Supreme Soviet to endow the government with (undefined) emergency powers. The proposal encountered strong resistance from the deputies, with Gorbachev contributing to squelching it. But if the president of the USSR had been categorically opposed to such an unprecedented request by his subordinate, why didn't he dismiss him then and there?

The other shoe was dropped on August 19 when the Soviet citizens were informed of the creation of the State Committee for the Emergency Situation. The body, whose awkward name testified to the amateurish character of the enterprise (it was the plotters who created the emergency; one mindful of the revolutionary precedents would have baptized it Council for National Salvation or Unity) was headed by Vice-President Gennadi Yanayev, an obscure party hack whose election Gorbachev had literally to force upon the Parliament. The most important figures who joined him on that junta of eight men were Pavlov; Vladimir Kryuchkov, head of the KGB; Boris Pugo, minister of the interior; and Dmitri Yazov, minister of defense. In a transparent prevarication, Yanayev claimed that Gorbachev, vacationing in the Crimea, had fallen ill and he, Yanayev, assumed the presidency until such time that Mikhail Sergeievich could resume his duties. In fact, the reputed invalid was under house arrest, with his chief secretary and the agents responsible for his personal security being in on the plot.

"A wretched country; they don't even know how to hang properly," a nineteenth-century Russian revolutionary was reputed to have exclaimed when the hangman's rope broke under his weight. And now conspiratorial skill appeared to have been completely missing in such alleged experts of the craft as Kryuchkov and Pugo (himself with a long KGB background). They failed to move with dispatch, to secure such people bound to oppose the coup as Yeltsin and Shevardnadze; within hours Yeltsin was on the Moscow streets calling on the citizens to rise against the junta and for a general strike. In Leningrad another dauntless reformer, its mayor, Anatoli Sobchak, galvanized even bigger crowds to stand up for democracy. In seventy hours the foolish enterprise was over; seven of the junta arrested, one a suicide, and a shaken Gorbachev being flown back to Moscow.

Could a more professionally staged coup have succeeded? Those who would lean to that conclusion could point to the fact that most of the civilian government personnel (including virtually the entire council of ministers) and the higher military ranks initially supported the putsch. Most of the local party bosses did likewise, some of them being among the active plotters. And among the leaders of the non-Russian republics there were quite a few who for the first few hours adopted a wait-and-see attitude. But the essential condition for the success of such a venture—*firm* support by the officer corps, the KGB, and the party state machinery—was lacking. Ever since 1989, power in the Soviet Union had become too much diffused to be scooped up by one sudden blow, and then through the years of glasnost Soviet society had become, if not exactly democratic, too agitated to remain passive in the face of this blatant attempt to turn the clock back. On October 13, 1964, Nikita Khrushchev had been the generally venerated leader of the Soviet state and people. On October 14 it was announced that through a secretly arrived decision by some twelve to fifteen people (in the Politburo) he had become an emeritus, and the attitude of the mass of the people remained one of complete indifference. Now it was different. Soviet men and women, including those in uniform, now felt themselves to be citizens, and though most of them may have had scant sympathy for Gorbachev or concern for constitutional proprieties, they would not passively accept such presumption by a bunch of faceless bureaucrats. "We older folk used to express what we really thought by whispering in the kitchen. Now our children spoke out loudly in the city's streets and avenues," exultantly wrote a Soviet journalist.[1]

Well, one should not overromanticize what happened between August 19 and 22. Had the coup been carried out more efficiently, had not some army units taken Yeltsin's side, the plotters might have succeeded in seizing Moscow and Leningrad. But that would have meant bloodshed and a civil war, which the Yanayev-Kryuchkhov clique could not have won.

"Gorbachev Returns to Power," proclaimed Western press headlines on August 23. He did return, but the president's power, already severely constricted before the coup, was now at its nadir. Yeltsin, the hero of the hour, vetoed Gorbachev's appointments of new ministers and forced him to accept those he himself nominated. The triumphant president of the Russian republic could not resist the temptation of publicly humiliating the president of the USSR. At the session of the Russian parliament he kept interrupting his speech and bossing him

around. Gorbachev's first utterances upon his return showed his un-
awareness that the political situation and the public mood were now
greatly different than they had been on August 18. He still expressed
his belief that the Communist Party should not only continue to exist
but also act as a leading force in Soviet society, still thought that the
outdated Treaty of the Union should provide the basis for the future
USSR; yet at the very same time Yeltsin was decreeing the suspension
of all party activities on the territory of the Russian republic and
shutting down its press organs. Heads of the other republics, anxious
to compensate for their ambivalent reaction to the putsch, hastened
to follow in Yeltsin's footsteps. "Does Gorbachev understand that he
has returned to what is now a different country?" a newspaper headline perspicaciously asked.[2]

Rather belatedly, Mikhail Sergeievich did understand. Within a
week of his rescue he laid down the office of the general secretary
and called upon the Central Committee of the CPSU to dissolve itself.
By this time the appeal appeared superfluous: all over the USSR the
party offices were being raided and shut down, its archives and files,
as well as those of the KGB, seized by the local authorities. What for
seventy years had been hailed as "the pride and conscience of the
nation," "the vanguard of the world proletariat"—the celebrated and
mighty Communist Party of the Soviet Union—for all practical purposes ceased to exist; its formal dissolution would come merely as a
death certificate. All over the vast land crowds were dismantling statues of Lenin and other Communist notables. Along with those momentous developments there arose a very practical question: Who
would inherit the enormous wealth of the party, estimated at upward
of five billion rubles?

But that question seems trivial when compared with another problem of inheritance. It was the Communist Party that had, though in
the last three years increasingly shakily, held the Soviet Union together. Who or what could inherit that function? The trauma of August 19–21 made explicit what had been implicit ever since March
26, 1989: the Soviet Union was falling apart and it would take a quite
unexpected turn of events to arrest the trend. As it was, during those
post–August 21 days practically all the non-Russian republics, led by
the largest of them, the Ukraine, hurriedly proclaimed their independence. Again that term, like "sovereignty," could as yet be interpreted in various ways, expressing the desire of at least some of them
not necessarily to break off all the ties with Moscow but, rather, to

have the Soviet Union transformed into a loose form of confederation. But there could be no mistaking the resolve of the three Baltic republics to acquire the full paraphernalia of independent statehood. And even before Gorbachev and the Congress of the People's Deputies grudgingly acquiesced in their secession, foreign countries began to recognize formally the independence of Lithuania, Latvia, and Estonia.

The impetus to full independence among the non-Russians was undoubtedly strengthened not only by the putsch, but also by Yeltsin's incautious behavior following its failure. By bossing Gorbachev around, by giving a strong impression at least initially that Russia was intent on dominating what remained of the Soviet Union, the president of the Russian republic could not but intensify the long-standing fears and resentments among other nations of the USSR. Especially injudicious was Yeltsin's threat—to be sure, almost immediately withdrawn—that were some other republics to opt entirely out of the Union, Russia might demand border rectification, i.e., to claim those areas of sister republics where ethnic Russians constitute a high proportion of the populations. Said the head of Kazakhstan, Nursultan Nazarbayev, "Kazakhstan will never acquiesce in becoming an 'appendix' of another region, will never accept the role of being a 'younger brother' of another nation."[3]

As August gave way to September, the tumult and confusion have somewhat receded, Yeltsin and Gorbachev now joined in an attempt to find what was still salvageable from the USSR. Among the people the elation of the post-putsch days began to give way to a sober realization of the trials and dangers ahead. There could be no doubt now that perestroika had failed, that what had been conceived as restructuring had the effect of a demolition. As Anatoli Sobchak phrased it: "Our great mistake during those six years had been to try to reform what was unreformable."[4] There has been a hurried effort, through yet another constitutional improvisation, to patch up the foundering—can one really still call it Soviet?—ship of state, so that a completely new one might be launched in the future. The central feature of the provisional arrangement as voted by the Congress of the People's Deputies is the State Council, composed of Gorbachev and the presidents of those republics that have deigned to participate in the salvaging enterprise (as of the moment, ten: Georgia and Moldavia, and of course the Baltic states, not participating). There is little point in dwelling on this or another part of the constitutional apparatus, since undoubtedly before this sees print the entire scene could, in all likelihood, be greatly altered. What we have known as the Union of Soviet Socialist States is to be rebaptized into the Union of Sovereign States. If, indeed, there is to be a union of some kind, it would be, as currently envisaged, a most loose type of confederation with but defense and foreign affairs and some as yet unspecified economic and internal security functions reserved to the center, all the rest being within the competence of the republics.

The problems that we had already alluded to in talking about the pre-putsch draft of the Union Treaty now press even more insistently upon those who would cling to the idea of retaining a federation. Even those republics that have not expressed a wish to secede propose to acquire the appurtenances of full statehood: their own army, separate currency, diplomatic relations with the outside world. How could even the loosest type of federation be reconciled with such ambitions? Or will the grim economic realities moderate those nationalist impulses and prompt genuine integration?

Having approved the provisional and rather chaotic political arrangements, the Congress of the People's Deputies voted itself out of existence, a fitting end for an inept contrivance, which instead of creating a new order succeeded only in hastening the destruction of the old. Symbolic of this repudiation of the past, of the condemnation now not only of the eras of "stagnation" and of "the cult of personality" but also that of the Revolution itself, of Lenin, was the Congress's decision to restore its original name—St. Petersburg—to Leningrad. And it can be only a question of time before the Lenin Mausoleum is shut down and the earthly remains of the founder are relocated to a cemetary in the city that no longer bears his name.

The Soviet people's revulsion against their recent and not so recent past is understandable in view of their realization of how much that past still blocks the road to a better future. Seventy years of authoritarian rule have gone far in atrophying those skills and habits that are necessary for the proper functioning of both a democracy and an orderly economy. Excessive centralization has given way, once its instrument, the party, has weakened and then fallen, to excessive particularism, which threatens further fragmentation of what still remains of the Soviet Union. Economic skills and incentives inevitably decayed during those long years when it was the Kremlin that did the thinking and planning, whether for the individual farmer or a factory manager.

The lesson of the year of revolutions, 1917, teaches that overthrow of an autocracy does not by itself clear the path to democracy. The crowds that demonstrated their jubilation over the overthrow of tsarism were no less inspired by the passion for freedom than those that during the August days, answering the appeal of Yeltsin and Sobchak, poured onto the streets of Moscow and Leningrad. Enthusiasm alone, however, is not a sufficient foundation for a stable democratic society. The budding democracy of the 1917 Russia, which Lenin himself called the freest state in the world, failed to develop a network of institutional defenses, and hence succumbed rather easily to the Bolshevik coup in November.

Looking at today's political scene, one still does not see any forces that would guarantee the future Soviet state remaining both united *and* democratic. The democratic reform movement (again this instinctive recoiling from the term "party"), headed by people like Shevardnadze and A. Yakovlev, appears quite vigorous, but is mostly confined to the Russian republic. In fact, there is no party or movement that can count on a significant number of adherents, not only in Moscow but also in Kiev, Tbilisi, and other republican capitals. In the non-Russian regions it is a variety of nationalist movements that have preempted the political scene. And it is only political parties that can secure a normal functioning of democratic and federal systems. For the moment what used to be called Soviet patriotism appears to be as anachronistic and moribund as "proletarian internationalism." Arguments advanced for preserving what could be saved of the union are mostly negative in their character: one must not let those thousands of nuclear warheads and missiles slip away from Moscow's control; economic recovery and progress of any part of the USSR would be almost impossible if what is still a unified, even if flawed, economic organism were chopped up; the West would be unable to help, nor could its badly needed assistance be effective, if the vast country became completely balkanized.

To list such reservations is to realize the horrendous harm that Communism has done to societies over which it had ruled, and especially to the Soviet Union. If with Stalin dead and buried, Stalinism still had clung to Soviet policies, then with the Communist Party of the USSR in shambles its legacy—the disastrous condition to which it had brought society—still stands in the way of the Soviet nations' quest for democracy. And by the same token this legacy poses a threat to the world order: a fragmented USSR, its parts now independent states, some of them not inconceivably under a dictatorship, that might prove a no lesser danger to international stability than that which had been posed by the Soviet Union at the height of its power. For almost fifty years we had worried about what the "Communists" might do to us. Now the West is concerned, and justifiably so, about the consequences of what the Soviets have been doing to themselves.

Communism had drawn its strengths and appeal from the claim that it was the only ideology and movement that could rise above nationalism and establish a peaceful and stable state. Ever since 1948, that boast, as we have seen, was repeatedly refuted by events. And it is an irony of history that the claim of Communism being a force for peace among nations should finally be laid to rest in its birthplace.

NOTES

CHAPTER 1

1. McGeorge Bundy, *Danger and Survival: Choices About the Bomb in the First Fifty Years* (New York, 1988), p. 203.

2. Something that was to be amply demonstrated by Khrushchev's missile-rattling. The Soviets continued to play on the West's fear of nuclear confrontation even after the Cuban crisis, and their manipulation of the theme ceased only under Gorbachev.

3. *The Times*, March 6, 1946.

4. "The Sources of Soviet Conduct" (published originally in July 1947) in George Kennan, *American Diplomacy, 1900–1950* (New York, 1960), p. 121.

5. One still reads that it was at Yalta that a division of Europe took place, and that consequently postwar Eastern Europe had already in 1945 been conceded to Stalin by Roosevelt and Churchill. Though widely believed and found in history books, this is at best a huge oversimplification. The Crimean conference's decision on Poland virtually guaranteed the Soviets' preponderant influence there, and thus one might have suggested that the same would happen in the case of the countries occupied at the time or subsequently by the Soviet army. But if Eastern Europe had been conceded by the West before the end of the war against Germany, it was, at the most, to grant to the USSR a sphere of influence in the pre-1914 meaning of the term—i.e., the states in the region would have to accommodate themselves to Moscow's wishes insofar as their foreign and defense policies were concerned, but would preserve their internal autonomy. Thus Poland, Romania, etc., the Western statesmen believed, would be able to retain their political pluralism, the way Finland actually succeeded in doing.

6. Harry S. Truman, *Memoirs*, vol. II, *Years of Trial and Hope* (New York, 1955), p. 98.

7. Most likely because (1) it became superfluous, and (2) to reassure the United States and Britain at a turning point in the war that the USSR no longer pursued the goal of conquering the world for Communism.

8. *For a Lasting Peace, For a People's Democracy*, November 10, 1947. This unwieldy name for the Cominform's organ was allegedly decreed by Stalin himself.

9. With the partial exception of Czechoslovakia and, in a different way, also Yugoslavia.

10. Milovan Djilas, *Rise and Fall* (New York, 1985), pp. 83–84.

11. Kennan, *op. cit.*, p. 124.

12. Djilas, *op. cit.*, p. 106.

13. Boris Kidrich, *On the Construction of Socialist Economy in the Federal People's Republic of Yugoslavia* (Belgrade, 1948), p. 63.

14. Quoted in Mosha Pijade, *The Soviet Help in the Yugoslav Uprising* (Belgrade, 1950), pp. 11–12.

15. This censure was preposterously unfair because (1) France and Italy were liberated by the Anglo-American and not Soviet armies and hence their Communists were in quite a different situation from those in Eastern Europe, and (2) at the time (1944) it was Moscow itself that had ordered both parties to eschew anything that might have appeared as an armed bid for power.

16. Djilas, *op. cit.*, p. 90.

17. It is quite likely that in initially promoting the federation of the Balkan Communist states Stalin expected that under such an agreement the Kremlin would be able to play off the Bulgarian Communists against their Yugoslav brethren and thus dilute Tito's and his clique's domination. But on second thought the idea of a union may have struck Stalin as too risky; Tito might overawe the Bulgarians and become even harder to handle.

18. Djilas, *op. cit.*, p. 108.

19. In theory, to be sure, an autonomous grand duchy united to the Russian Empire by the person of the emperor.

20. Though the world outside was apprised of it only at the end of June.

21. The author may be forgiven a personal note. In 1987 I was at a conference where one of my fellow participants was Gennady Gerasimov, the spokesman for the Soviet foreign ministry. He subsequently described the proceedings in the *Moscow News*, where he took me to task for suggesting there that (1) the USSR should announce a timetable for the withdrawal of its troops from Afghanistan, and (2) it should acquiesce in the Finlandization of Eastern Europe. I met Mr. Gerasimov one year later and could not resist reminding him that Moscow appeared to have accepted my advice on point one. When would they follow on my second suggestion? All I received in answer was my interlocutor's typical diplomatic smile.

22. Thus Jewish party members became tarred with the brush of having Zionist connections and ties.

23. In open court Traicho Kostov took back his confession.

24. The incautious Pole was promptly stripped of his office and then placed under house arrest. There is little doubt that had Stalin not died while the

"case" against Gomułka was being prepared, he would have eventually shared the fate of Rajk and Slansky.

25. Djilas, *op. cit.*, p. 351.

26. *Ibid.*, pp. 3–4.

CHAPTER 2

1. Chiang agreed to them only after strong U.S. pressure, Stalin at Yalta having exacted Roosevelt's help as a price for the Soviets' entering the Pacific war.

2. Tang Tsou, *America's Failure in China* (Chicago, 1963), p. 304.

3. *Selected Works of Mao Zedong*, vol. 4 (Beijing, 1961; in English), p. 442. (Throughout these notes the language of a publication will be given only if it differs from that spoken in the city of publication. All titles are in English regardless of the original language.)

4. It was only after Stalin's death that Gao Gang was stripped of his office, arrested, and accused of trying to turn Manchuria into his private preserve. He died, allegedly by his own hand, in 1954.

5. Shi Zhe, "Accompanying Chairman Mao," in *Problems of the Far East* (Moscow, January 1989), p. 40. The author was Mao's interpreter in the 1949–50 talks. The account of the visit is based largely on his article and on that of the Soviet interpreter on the occasion, N. T. Fedorenko—"Stalin and Mao: Talks in Moscow"—in the same issue of the journal.

6. Chen Boda, *Stalin and the Chinese Revolution* (Beijing, 1953), p. 1.

7. Stuart R. Schram, *The Political Thought of Mao Tse Tung* (New York, 1963), p. 292.

8. Quoted in *U.S. Relations with China with Special Reference to the Period 1944–49* (Washington, 1949), p. 72.

9. *Ibid.*, p. xvi.

10. *Sino-Soviet Relations, 1917–1957* (Moscow, 1959), p. 216.

11. Mao Zedong, *People's Democratic Dictatorship* (London, 1950), p. 33.

12. *Sino-Soviet Relations, 1917–1957*, p. 221.

13. *Ibid.*, p. 227.

CHAPTER 3

1. Alexander Tvardovsky, "Horizon Beyond Horizon," *New World*, no. 5 (Moscow, 1960), p. 9.

2. Walter Bedell Smith, *My Three Years in Moscow* (New York, 1950), p. 50.

3. Harry Truman, *Memoirs*, vol. II, *Years of Trial and Hope* (New York, 1955), p. 215.

4. Actually, it was Genghis's son and successor whose death occurred at that point.

5. Well, not quite. Russia remained under Mongol domination for two centuries.

6. And some of whom obeyed when summoned from their countries to Moscow, though they knew what had already happened there to their countrymen. Especially hard hit were the Polish, Yugoslav, and German parties, and as in the case of the Soviet elite, the Terror claimed a disproportionate number of foreign Communists whose affiliation with the movement went back to Lenin's days.

7. I leave aside—since the term is employed in its realpolitik sense—how far it is in any nation's interest to pursue an aggressive, expansionist policy.

8. Quoted by John B. Dunlop in "Will the Soviet Union Survive Until the Year 2000?" *The National Interest*, no. 18 (Washington, D.C.), Winter 1989, p. 69.

9. A Soviet writer, artist, or critic was also not supposed to get overly enthusiastic over the achievements in those spheres of the *non-Russian* nationalities of his society.

10. The question of a separate party organization for the Russian Republic was revived in 1989–90 in reaction to the ethnic fissures that began to convulse the USSR under perestroika, and in the latter year such an organization was established.

11. Irwin M. Wall, *French Communism in the Era of Stalin* (Westport, Conn., 1983), p. 131.

12. The Soviets did not acquire a long-range bomber force until the mid-1950s.

13. *Documents on International Communism, 1952* (London, 1955), p. 88.

14. Both presidents have asserted in their memoirs that they resorted to hinting about America's possible use of the A-bomb, Truman to nudge the Soviet troops out of northern Iran, Eisenhower to pressure the Chinese to agree to the Korean truce, but there is no clear-cut evidence supporting either assertion.

15. Nikita Khrushchev, *Khrushchev Remembers: The Last Testament*, ed. and trans. Strobe Talbott (Boston, 1974), p. 243.

16. According to Khrushchev, Stalin rewarded Gao Gang for his services to the Russians by denouncing him to Mao. Like some other of Khrushchev's tales, this one must be taken with a grain of salt. Gao's special relationship with Moscow was obvious enough to condemn him in the eyes of the Chinese leadership without any special tricks on Stalin's part.

17. In 1956 the Chinese evidently did suggest to the Polish Communist leaders visiting them that they could be bolder in their attitude toward the Russians.

18. Allen S. Whiting, *China Crosses the Yalu* (Stanford, Calif., 1960), p. 42.

19. Acheson immediately qualified this exclusion by asserting that the responsibility for defending South Korea rested with the United Nations, but the Kremlin probably did not believe that the Americans would carry their pedantic legalism to the extent of fighting under U.N. auspices to protect the territory.

20. Thus on January 6, 1950, an editorial in the Cominform journal chided the Japanese Communists for not struggling vigorously enough against MacArthur's rule of their country. That criticism was then echoed by *Pravda.*

21. It appears rather irrational now, but the fact is that when one studies American public opinion during the first days of the Korean War, one discerns a real fear that the Soviets might react to the U.S. intervention in the conflict by attacking Western Europe or by other steps that might precipitate World War III.

22. Allen Whiting, *op. cit.*, p. 45.

23. The Chinese People's Institute of Foreign Affairs, *Oppose the US Occupation of Taiwan and 'Two Chinas' Plot* (Beijing, 1958), pp. 5–6.

24. Much later the Chinese Communists were to claim that their military experts had foreseen the vulnerability of the North Korean army to an American counterattack and had advised both Moscow and Pyongyang accordingly. Yufan Hao and Zhai Zhihai, "China's Decision to Enter the Korean War: History Revisited," *China Quarterly*, no. 121 (March 1990), pp. 97.

25. *Ibid.*, p. 96.

26. By analogy to the secretary of state, the Soviet recipient of the note should have been Foreign Minister Vyshinsky; by that to Stalin, head of the Soviet government as prime minister, Truman rather than Acheson.

27. Robert Leckie, *Conflict, The History of the Korean War, 1950–53* (New York, 1962), p. 157.

28. Rosemary Foot, *The Wrong War: American Policy and the Dimensions of the Korean Conflict, 1950–1953* (Ithaca and London, 1985), p. 74.

29. *Ibid.*, p. 75.

30. If the administration was so certain that the Korean affair was started and managed by the USSR, why, it might be asked, did the United States react to the invasion by also taking a step directed against the People's Republic? To repeat, in 1950 it was believed much safer to vent America's anti-Communist animus on China than on the USSR.

31. *Ibid.*, p. 75.

32. Yufan Hao and Zhai Zhihai, *op. cit.*, p. 101.

33. *Ibid.*, p. 105.

34. Foot, *op. cit.*, p. 29.

35. *Ibid.*, p. 117.

36. Such as the Philby-Maclean spy network.

37. Bundy, *op. cit.*, p. 232.

38. Partially correct: battleground nuclear weapons were just being developed.

39. His most startling performance on that count came at a conference of eighty-one Communist parties in Moscow on the occasion of the 40th anniversary of the October Revolution. There, surpassing even Khrushchev's bluster on the subject, the chairman declared that such a war, while it would undoubtedly destroy capitalism, would not stop the advance of Communism. What if such a war destroyed half of China's population? Some three hundred million would still survive and proceed with the building of a socialist society. But his own country would be totally destroyed, protested a delegate from one of the "fraternal parties." Unabashed, Mao allowed that some smaller nations might have to be sacrificed for the good of the cause!

40. McGeorge Bundy, *Danger and Survival* (New York, 1989), p. 203.

41. O. B. Borisov and B. T. Koloskov, *Sino-Soviet Relations, 1945–80* (Moscow, 1980), p. 54.

42. Yufan Hao and Zhai Zhihai, *op. cit.*, p. 113.

43. *Ibid.*

44. Xu Xionqin, *History Remembered* (Beijing, 1987), pp. 804–5.

45. Mikhail Yakovlev, *Seventeen Years in China* (Moscow, 1981), p. 10.

46. *Soviet News* (Moscow), September 27, 1952.

47. A. Lavrishchev and D. Tomashevsky, eds., *International Relations after the Second World War*, vol. II (Moscow, 1963), p. 357.

48. Borisov and Koloskov, *op. cit.*, p. 54.

49. *Pravda*, October 15, 1953.

50. *Pravda*, March 6, 1953.

51. Khrushchev, *op. cit.*, p. 79.

52. McGeorge Bundy, *op. cit.*, p. 240.

53. *Ibid.*, p. 241.

CHAPTER 4

1. Royal Institute of International Affairs (hereafter, RIIA), *Survey of International Affairs, 1953*, ed. Peter Calvocoressi (London, 1956), p. 29.

2. RIIA, *Documents on International Affairs, 1953* (London, 1956), p. 154.

This was, of course, before the construction of the Berlin Wall, when defection from East Germany to the West was both easy and widespread.

3. *Ibid.*, p. 156.

4. Nikita Khrushchev, *Khrushchev Remembers: The Last Testament*, ed. and trans. Strobe Talbott (Boston, 1974), p. 193. The heinous sins publicly ascribed to Beria have not usually included any initiatives in foreign policy, so this opaque reference by Khrushchev has a special significance.

5. *Documents on International Affairs, 1953*, p. 159.

6. Khrushchev, *loc. cit.*

7. The figures are from a speech by Khrushchev published in *Pravda*, January 15, 1960.

8. They had been broken off after the "discovery" of the "doctors' plot" in December 1952. The announcement included allegations that the culprits, most of them Jewish, had been recruited for subversive activities by Zionist organizations in conjunction with U.S. and British intelligence. The entire tissue of lies was repudiated by the Kremlin within days of Stalin's death.

9. Veljko Mićunović, *Moscow Diary* (New York, 1980), p. 435.

10. Which, despite Malenkov's initial primacy, can be dated from March 1953 to 1964.

11. No other group of foreign Communists who had the misfortune to reside in the USSR in the late thirties was purged as mercilessly and thoroughly as the Polish ones. And in 1938 the Comintern dissolved the Polish Communist Party for allegedly being shot through with Trotskyism. It was reborn during the war as the Polish Workers' Party, renamed in December 1948 the Polish United Workers' Party, which in September 1990 concluded its inglorious life.

12. Mikoyan's trips during the civil war were kept secret.

13. *Pravda*, September 2, 1964.

14. *Ibid.*, May 27, 1955.

15. RIIA, *Documents on International Affairs, 1955* (London, 1956), p. 267.

16. Quoted in Basil Dmytryshyn, *USSR: A Concise History*, 2d ed. (New York, 1971), p. 430.

17. *Ibid.*, p. 425.

18. *Ibid.*, p. 440.

19. Fyodor Burlatski, "Khrushchev," *Literary Gazette* (Moscow), February 24, 1988.

20. Quoted by Burlatski, *loc. cit.*

21. Khrushchev in Dmytryshyn, *op. cit.*, p. 443.

22. Burlatsky, *loc. cit.*

CHAPTER 5

1. The date was June 16, 1956; the newspaper was *Unità* (Rome).

2. Quoted in *The Anti-Stalin Campaign and International Communist: A Selection of Documents*, ed. Russian Institute, Columbia University (New York, 1956), pp. 105–9.

3. *Ibid.*, p. 129.

4. *Ibid.*, p. 137.

5. *Ibid.*, p. 135.

6. Cited in Paul E. Zinner, ed., *National Communism and Popular Revolt in Eastern Europe* (New York, 1956), p. 519.

7. *Ibid.*, p. 521.

8. Cited in Roderick MacFarquhar, Timothy Cheek, and Eugene Wu, eds., *The Secret Speeches of Chairman Mao* (Cambridge, Mass., 1989), p. 178.

9. *Ibid.*, p. 141.

10. *Ibid.*, p. 279.

11. *Ibid.*, p. 167.

12. As to the projected Hungarian role in the invasion, see Béla Király and Paul Jonas, eds., *The Hungarian Revolution of 1956 in Retrospect* (New York, 1978), p. 61.

13. The Polish Communists' reluctance to call their party by the proper name was in itself an eloquent testimony of how unpopular the term "Communist" was among the population.

14. The struggle against Catholicism went through several stages. At first the regime, conscious of its unpopularity, refrained from an explicit antireligious campaign against the institution which, after the forcible elimination of other forms of opposition, became the custodian of not only the religious but also the national sentiments of the overwhelming majority of the people. After 1948 the government increasingly subjected the Church to chicaneries but still avoided a frontal attack on its pastoral, as distinguished from other, activities. There was a concerted effort to undercut the authority of the Church hierarchy over the clergy, to promote associations of "progressive priests," and to take other steps designed to undermine the Church's cohesion and its prestige in society. Stalin's death did not at first arrest the momentum of the anti-Church campaign. The indomitable primate of Poland, Cardinal Wyszyński, was placed under arrest in 1953, as had been several other bishops. Catholic publishing houses and charitable institutions were being closed down. What appeared to be the government's long-term goal was a Church stripped of its ties with the papacy and constrained to become submissive to the state and nonhostile to Marxism-Leninism.

15. Antoni Czubiński, *June 1956 in Poznań* (Poznań, 1956), p. 18.

16. *Ibid.*, p. 200.

17. *Ibid.*, p. 25.

18. *Ibid.*, p. 34.

19. Teresa Torańska, *They* (London, 1956; in Polish), p. 51.

20. Czubiński, *op. cit.*, p. 48.

21. Torańska, *op. cit.*, p. 52.

22. From a speech by Gomułka quoted in *New Paths* (the journal of the Central Committee, Warsaw, October 1956), p. 23.

23. Quoted in Torańska, *op. cit.*, p. 146.

24. *Ibid.*, p. 56.

25. *Ibid.*, p. 58.

26. *Ibid.*, p. 63.

27. *Ibid.*, p. 64.

28. *New Paths*, October 1956, p. 17.

29. *Ibid.*, p. 20.

30. *Ibid.*, p. 21.

31. *Ibid.*, pp. 39–41.

32. *Trybuna Ludu* (*The People's Tribune*) (Warsaw), October 25, 1956.

33. Torańska, *op. cit.*, p. 151.

34. Quoted in Konrad Syrop, *Spring in October: The Polish Revolution in 1956* (London, 1957), p. 157.

35. Veljko Mićunović, *Moscow Diary* (New York, 1980), p. 126.

36. Paul Zinner, ed., *National Communism and Popular Revolt in Eastern Europe* (New York, 1956), p. 398.

37. Quoted *ibid.*, p. 403.

38. *Ibid.*, p. 403.

39. Miklós Molnár, *Victory in Defeat: Budapest 1956* (Paris, 1968).

40. Mićunović, *op. cit.*, p. 132.

41. *Ibid.*, p. 134.

42. *Ibid.*, p. 135.

43. Molnár, *op. cit.*, p. 186. If accurate, the number is still only a fraction of the number killed during the Soviet repression of the uprising and of those subsequently tried and sentenced to death.

44. Király and Jonas, eds., *op. cit.*, p. 74.

45. Mićunović, *op. cit.*, p. 149.

46. Quoted in Zinner, *op. cit.*, p. 59.

47. Mićunović, *op. cit.*, p. 188.

48. *Ibid.*, p. 187.

CHAPTER 6

1. John Wilson Lewis and Xue Litai, *China Builds the Bomb* (Stanford, Calif., 1988), p. 62.

2. *Ibid.*, p. 63.

3. Khrushchev would later talk quaintly about the "arithmetical majority" which had tried to unseat him. Marshal Zhukov's reward for the vital help he had rendered was his promotion to full presidum membership in June, and sudden dismissal from all his party and government posts in October. He had become too powerful for a professional soldier.

4. Veljko Mićunović, *Moscow Diary* (New York, 1980), p. 319.

5. Quoted in John Gittings, *Survey of the Sino-Soviet Dispute* (London, 1968), p. 82.

6. *Ibid.*, p. 82.

7. Mićunović, *op. cit.*, p. 323.

8. Roderick MacFarquhar, Timothy Cheek, and Eugene Wu, eds., *The Secret Speeches of Chairman Mao* (Cambridge, Mass., 1989), p. 123.

9. Mao's speech on August 17 to an enlarged Politburo conference. MacFarquhar, Cheek, and Wu, *op. cit.*, p. 408.

10. Roderick MacFarquhar, *The Origins of the Cultural Revolution*, vol. 2 (New York, 1983), p. 90.

11. E.g., the possibility of a West German nuclear bomb or missile being launched against a Soviet installation. The USSR would have to assume that the attack came from NATO as a whole, and respond with appropriate reprisals that, even if limited in scope, might lead the United States to launch a massive strike against the Soviet homeland.

12. Mićunović, *op. cit.*, p. 378.

13. RIIA, *Documents on International Affairs, 1957* (London, 1958), p. 238.

14. RIIA, *Documents on International Affairs, 1958* (London, 1961), p. 302.

15. *Ibid.*, p. 318.

16. Nikita Khrushchev, *Khrushchev Remembers: The Last Testament*, ed. and trans. Strobe Talbott (Boston, 1974), pp. 258–62. It is of course quite pos-

sible that, being old and ill at the time, Khrushchev's memory faltered when he recorded his recollections.

17. O. B. Borisov, *The History of Soviet-Chinese Relations* (Moscow, 1981), p. 46.

18. O. B. Borisov and B. T. Koloskov, *Sino-Soviet Relations, 1945–80* (Moscow, 1980), p. 167.

19. RIIA, *Documents of International Affairs, 1958* (London, 1961), p. 179.

20. *Ibid.*, p. 187.

21. *Ibid.*, p. 202.

22. Borisov and Koloskov, *op. cit.*, p. 167.

23. William Griffith, ed., *The Sino-Soviet Rift* (Cambridge, Mass., 1964), p. 399.

24. Quoted *ibid.*, p. 365.

25. *Ibid.*, p. 382.

26. *Documents of International Affairs, 1958*, p. 165.

27. *Twenty-first Congress of the Communist Party of the Soviet Union* (stenographic report) (Moscow, 1959), vol. I, p. 78.

28. Quoted in MacFarquhar, *op. cit.*, p. 221.

29. *Ibid.*, p. 237.

30. Khrushchev, *op. cit.*, p. 473.

CHAPTER 7

1. John Wilson Lewis and Xue Litai, *China Builds the Bomb* (Stanford, Calif., 1988), p. 140.

2. William Griffith, ed., *The Sino-Soviet Rift* (Cambridge, Mass., 1964), p. 374.

3. Dwight D. Eisenhower, *Waging Peace, 1956–61* (New York, 1965), p. 455.

4. Quoted in Griffith, *op. cit.*, p. 400.

5. Nikita Khrushchev, *Khrushchev Remembers: The Last Testament* (Boston, 1974), p. 308. In an earlier book of recollections, published in 1970, Khrushchev remembers Mao on that occasion as having been quite brusque and rude to him (*Khrushchev Remembers* [Boston, 1970], pp. 469–72).

6. *Ibid.*, p. 308.

7. RIIA, *Documents on International Affairs, 1960* (London, 1964), p. 185.

8. *Ibid.*, p. 189.

9. *Ibid.*, p. 195.

10. *Ibid.*, p. 184.

11. *Ibid.*, p. 183.

12. *Ibid.*, p. 187.

13. English version in *Peking Review*, April 26, 1960.

14. Dillon on April 20, *Documents on International Affairs, 1960*.

15. Quoted in Griffith, *op. cit.*, p. 401.

16. John Gittings, *Survey of the Sino-Soviet Dispute* (London, 1968), pp. 139–40.

17. Lewis and Xue Litai, *op. cit.*, p. 122.

18. *Ibid.*, p. 123.

19. Quoted in Griffith, *op. cit.*, p. 404.

20. *Documents on International Affairs, 1960*, p. 228.

21. Quoted in Gittings, *op. cit.*, p. 161.

22. RIIA, *Documents on International Affairs, 1961* (London, 1965), p. 33.

23. Long negotiations in Geneva finally concluded with the restoration of a coalition government in Laos.

24. *Twenty-second Congress of the Communist Party of the Soviet Union* (stenographic report) (Moscow, 1962), vol. II, p. 326.

25. *Ibid.*, p. 343.

26. Cited in Gittings, *op. cit.*, p. 156.

27. *Ibid.*, p. 157.

28. *Twenty-second Congress*, vol. I, p. 45.

29. *Peking Review*, August 16, 1963, p. 14.

30. Lewis and Xue Litai, *op. cit.*, p. 107.

31. *Pravda*, September 11, 1962.

32. For an extensive treatment of the crisis, see my *Expansion and Coexistence*, 2nd ed. (New York, 1974), pp. 666–77.

33. Alexander Alekseyev (then Soviet ambassador to Cuba), "The Caribbean Crisis—At the Edge of an Abyss," *Echo of the Planet* (Moscow), November 1988, no. 33.

34. Cited in Griffith, *op. cit.*, p. 383.

35. From Radio Liberty, *Digest of the 27th Congress of the Communist Party of the Soviet Union*, sec. 94, p. 11.

36. Cited in Griffith, *op. cit.*, p. 300.

37. *Ibid.*, p. 327.

38. *Ibid.*, p. 413.

39. *Ibid.*, p. 473.

40. *Ibid.*, p. 349.

CHAPTER 8

1. Mikhail Suslov, in *Plenum of the Central Committee of the CPSU, February 10–15, 1964* (Moscow, 1964), p. 495.

2. Suslov, *loc. cit.*, p. 546.

3. *Ibid.*, p. 551.

4. *Peking Review*, November 12, 1965.

5. *Ibid.*

6. *Ibid.*

7. *Ibid.*

8. *Twenty-third Congress of the Communist Party of the Soviet Union* (Moscow, 1966), vol. I, p. 322.

9. From the same speech, *loc. cit.*, p. 323.

10. *Twenty-third Congress*, vol. II, p. 295.

11. *Peking Review*, May 13, 1966.

12. *Pravda*, June 8, 1969. Clearly a slip on the part of the general secretary or his speechwriter, since the ritualistic phrase is "scientific *socialism.*"

13. Stuart Schram, ed., *Mao Tse-tung Unrehearsed: Talks and Letters, 1956–1971* (London, 1974), p. 154.

14. Yen Chio-chi and Kao Kao, *The Ten-Year History of the Chinese Cultural Revolution* (Beijing, 1987), p. 14.

15. *Ibid.*, p. 82.

16. *Ibid.*, p. 167.

17. Schram, *op. cit.*, p. 294.

18. Yen Chio-chi and Kao Kao, *op. cit.*, p. 56.

19. Unlike what at the time was widely believed in the West, terror and repression during the Cultural Revolution struck not only at the upper echelons of the party and government officialdom; a great number of ordinary citizens were affected, with thousands killed.

20. Yen Chio-chi and Kao Kao, *op. cit.*, p. 254.

21. Edgar Snow, *The Long Revolution* (New York, 1972), p. 19.

22. Quoted in Fyodor Burlatski, *Mao Zedong and His Successors* (Moscow, 1979), p. 124.

23. O. B. Borisov and B. T. Koloskov, *Sino-Soviet Relations, 1945–1980* (Moscow, 1980), p. 394.

24. Henry Kissinger, *The White House Years* (New York, 1979), p. 183.

25. Yen Chio-chi and Kao Kao, *op. cit.*, p. 222.

26. Contrariwise, a similar program started about the same time by the Soviets was more defensible. While equally useless in an all-out war with the United States, it could have served a purpose as a shield against the as yet and for the immediate future modest nuclear potential of China.

27. Burlatski, *op. cit.*, p. 147.

28. The breakdown of social controls had to have an adverse effect on agricultural and industrial production. As of the end of 1969 most of the commodities in common use were rationed.

29. Certainly a misnomer. The threat of military intervention against a Communist regime that defied the Kremlin had been inherent in Soviet policies under Stalin and Khrushchev, at least as much as with Brezhnev. In fact, it was a testimony of the loosening of the bonds of the Communist bloc that the Soviet Union's prescriptive right to chastise those bloc members that strayed away from the party of socialist righteousness had to be spelled out in 1968. In Stalin's time it would have been superfluous to stress the point. One might rebut that the Soviets did not invade Yugoslavia after Tito's challenge. But then Brezhnev's Russia also found it prudent to put up with Albania's defiance and Romania's independent ways.

30. Henry Kissinger, *Years of Upheaval* (Boston, 1982), p. 233.

CHAPTER 9

1. Richard P. Stebbins and Elaine R. Adams, eds., *American Foreign Relations 1972: A Documentary Record* (Washington, D.C., 1976), p. 76.

2. *Kontinent: An Anthology* (New York, 1976), p. 6.

3. Georgi Arbatov on Soviet-American Relations in *The Communist*, no. 3 (Moscow, February 1973), p. 111.

4. Václav Havel on the subject of opposition in Robin Remington, ed., *Winter in Prague: Documents on Czechoslovak Communism in Crisis* (Cambridge, Mass., 1969), p. 64.

5. *Ibid.*, p. 65.

6. Quoted *ibid.*, p. 105.

7. *Ibid.*, p. 105.

8. *Ibid.*, p. 148.

9. *Ibid.*, p. 148.

10. Ota Šik, *Czechoslovakia: The Bureaucratic Economy* (White Plains, N.Y., 1972), p. 46.

11. Remington, ed., *op. cit.*, p. 117.

12. *Ibid.*, p. 122.

13. *Ibid.*, p. 133.

14. Ever since the Communist coup of February 1948, which put an end to what had remained of parliamentary democracy in Czechoslovakia.

15. Ivan Sviták, *The Czechoslovak Experiment, 1968–69* (New York, 1971), p. 117.

16. *Ibid.*, p. 117.

17. *Ibid.*, p. 118.

18. Remington, ed., *op. cit.*, pp. 196–97.

19. *Ibid.*, p. 201.

20. I. Alexander, "Attack on the Socialist Foundations of Czechoslovakia," in *Pravda*, June 11, 1968.

21. Zdeněk Mlynář, *Night Frost in Prague* (New York, 1978), p. 136.

22. Remington, ed., *op. cit.*, p. 226.

23. *Ibid.*

24. *Ibid.*

25. Zdeněk Mlynář, in an interview in G. R. Urban, ed., *Communist Reformation. Nationalism, Internationalism, and Change in the World Communist Movement* (New York, 1979), p. 142.

26. Much of that pressure came from President Svoboda, who despite his previous stance now insisted on yielding to the Kremlin's demands.

27. Remington, ed., *op. cit.*, p. 378.

28. Mlynář, *Night Frost in Prague*, p. 239.

29. *Ibid.*, p. 241.

30. *Ibid.*, p. 384.

31. *Ibid.*, p. 386.

32. Urban, ed., *op. cit.*, p. 146.

33. Quoted from the *Peking Review* of August 23, 1968, *ibid*, p. 327.

34. From a lecture delivered before an American audience in 1969. Sviták, *op. cit.*, p. 218.

CHAPTER 10

1. *Twenty-fifth Congress of the Communist Party of the Soviet Union* (stenographic report) (Moscow, 1976), vol. II, p. 193.

2. *Ibid.*, vol. I, p. 53.

3. *Ibid.*, p. 55.

4. Mikhail Gorbachev at the Twenty-seventh Congress of the CPSU, *Radio Liberty Report* (1986), p. 41.

5. Quoted in *New York Times*, April 26, 1976.

6. *Pravda*, September 2, 1964.

7. *Peking Review*, November 4, 1977, p. 35.

8. *Pravda*, January 24, 1979.

9. V. Demchenko, "The Horizons of Cooperation," *Pravda*, April 6, 1979.

10. *Twenty-sixth Congress of the CPSU* (stenographic report) (Moscow, 1981), vol. I, p. 198.

11. *Ibid.*, p. 317.

12. Quoted in Bohdan Nahaylo and Victor Swoboda, *Soviet Disunion* (New York, 1990), p. 200.

13. *Ibid.*, p. 188.

14. *U.S. State Department Bulletin*, September 1, 1975, p. 325.

15. *Pravda*, December 30, 1979.

CHAPTER 11

1. It is a gross oversimplification to maintain, as many politicians and scholars have, that Yalta sanctioned the division of Europe, and that the Western Powers acquiesced in its eastern part coming under Communist rule. For both Churchill and Roosevelt the most that the Soviet Union could claim under the Yalta agreements and understandings was a sphere of influence in the old sense of the term, i.e., something not much different from the influence the United States exercised *then* in Latin America. Neither statesman believed that he was licensing Stalin to foist, as he would between the war's end and 1948, one-party Communist governments on most states of the area.

2. *December 1970* (Paris, 1986; in Polish), p. 32. This is a collective work put together by a Solidarity research team in 1981.

3. *Ibid.*, p. 48.

4. Zbysław Rykowski and Wiesław Władyka, *The Polish Calendar, 1944–1984* (Warsaw, 1987), p. 86.

5. Małgorzata Szejnert and Tomasz Zalewski, *Stettin* (London, 1986; in Polish), p. 71.

6. *Ibid.*, p. 74.

7. *December 1970*, pp. 104–6.

8. *Ibid.*, p. 108.

9. *Ibid.*, p. 145.

10. "Warsaw Surrenders," in *New York Times*, June 27, 1976.

11. Timothy Garton Ash, *The Polish Revolution: Solidarity, 1980–1982* (London, 1983), p. 18.

12. Thomasz Strzyżewski, *The Black Book of Censorship in the Polish People's Republic* (London, 1977; in Polish), p. 36.

13. *Ibid.*, pp. 48–49.

14. *Ibid.*, p. 47.

15. *Ibid.*, p. 71.

16. *Reporting to Edward Gierek* (Warsaw, 1988), p. 14.

17. *Ibid.*, p. 15.

18. J. F. Brown, "The Significance of Poland," in Lawrence L. Whetten, ed., *The Present State of Communist Internationalism* (Toronto, 1983), p. 131.

19. J. Kuroń in *The Information Bulletin of KOR*, no. 3/29, 1979.

20. Quoted in Władysław Ważniewski, *A Short History of People's Poland* (Warsaw, 1975), p. 176.

21. Rykowski and Władyka, *op. cit.*, p. 118.

22. *Pravda*, August 20, 1980.

23. Neal Ascherson, *The Polish August* (New York, 1982), p. 291.

24. Rykowski and Władyka, *op. cit.*, p. 120.

25. "The War Against the Nation as Seen from the Inside," *Kultura*, no. 4/475 (Paris, April 1987; in Polish). This account is based on an interview with a Polish staff officer who was engaged in preparing such blueprints and who defected before the proclamation of martial law.

26. *Pravda*, January 30, 1981.

27. "The War Against the Nation," *loc. cit.*, p. 28.

28. *Twenty-sixth Congress of the Communist Party of the Soviet Union* (stenographic report) (Moscow, 1981), vol. I, p. 26.

29. "The War Against the Nation," *loc. cit.*, p. 30.

30. *Quoted* in *Kultura*, no. 11/359 (Paris, November 1981), p. 158.

31. Rykowski and Władyka, *op. cit.*, p. 128.

32. *Ibid.*, p. 130.

33. *Ibid.*, p. 131.

34. *Ibid.*, p. 132.

35. *Pravda*, December 15, 1981.

36. George Sanford, *Military Rule in Poland* (London, 1986), p. 129.

37. Michael T. Kaufman, *Mad Dreams, Saving Graces: Poland—A Nation in Conspiracy* (New York, 1989), p. 80.

38. *Ibid.*, p. 129.

CHAPTER 12

1. Adam Ulam, *Dangerous Relations: The Soviet Union in World Politics, 1970–1982* (New York, 1983), p. 314.

2. *Twenty-sixth Congress of the Communist Party of the Soviet Union* (stenographic report) (Moscow, 1981), vol. I, p. 26.

3. *Pravda*, May 15, 1986.

4. *Pravda*, July 10, 1987.

5. Adam B. Ulam, *Russia's Failed Revolutions* (New York, 1981), p. 425.

6. E.g., Zhores Medvedev, *Gorbachev* (London, 1986), pp. 90–91.

7. *Pravda*, December 1, 1990.

8. Michel Tatu, *Gorbachev: Will the USSR Change?* (Paris, 1987), p. 96.

9. *Pravda*, December 10, 1990.

10. Gorbachev's speech on December 7, 1990, to industrial managers. *Pravda*, December 10, 1990.

11. See Tatu, *op. cit.*, pp. 104–5.

12. Y. Y. Paletskis, quoted in *Pravda*, February 9, 1990.

13. *Pravda*, March 12, 1985.

14. *Pravda*, April 24, 1985.

15. *Ibid.*

16. *Ibid.*

17. *Pravda*, April 2, 1989. The military intervention in Afghanistan was allegedly at the request of its government. Similar and false reasons were adduced in the case of Hungary and Czechoslovakia.

18. *Twenty-seventh Congress of the Communist Party of the Soviet Union, February 25–March 6, 1986* (Moscow, 1986), vol. I, p. 33.

19. *Ibid.*, p. 96.

20. *Ibid.*, p. 83.

21. *Ibid.*, p. 83.

22. *Ibid.*, p. 95.

23. *Ibid.*, p. 83.

24. Nikita Khrushchev, *Khrushchev Remembers: The Last Testament* (Boston, 1974), p. 78.

25. *Pravda*, November 3, 1987.

26. Quoted in Gorbachev's speech, *ibid.*

27. Nikolai Vasetski, "The Death of Trotsky," *Literary Gazette* (Moscow), January 4, 1989.

28. "Conference on History and Literature," *Problems of History* (Moscow), June 1988, p. 72.

29. Letter to the editor in *Soviet Culture* (Moscow), August 30, 1988.

30. Mikhail Shatrov, "On . . . and On . . . and On . . . ," in *The Banner* (Moscow), January 1988, p. 47.

31. *Ibid.*, p. 51.

32. *Ibid.*, p. 53.

33. *Pravda*, April 5, 1988.

34. Fyodor Burlatski, *Literary Gazette*, July 19, 1989.

35. "Principles of Perestroika" [an answer to Andreyeva's piece], *Pravda*, April 5, 1988.

36. *Ibid.*

CHAPTER 13

1. *Twenty-seventh Congress of the Communist Party of the Soviet Union* (Moscow, 1986), vol. I, p. 143.

2. *Nineteenth All-Union Party Conference of the CPSU* (Moscow, 1988), vol. I, p. 217.

3. Quoted in Bohdan Nahaylo and Victor Swoboda, *Soviet Disunion* (New York, 1990), p. 286.

4. *Nineteenth Party Conference*, vol. I, p. 216.

5. *Ibid.*, p. 19.

6. *Ibid.*, p. 250.

7. *Ibid.*, vol. II, p. 56.

8. *Ibid.*, p. 58.

9. *Ibid.*, p. 62.

10. *Ibid.*, p. 88.

11. *Ibid.*, vol. I, p. 270.

12. *Ibid.*, p. 233.

13. *Ibid.*, p. 119.

14. *Ibid.*, vol. II, p. 123.

15. *Ibid.*, p. 124.

16. *Pravda*, March 27, 1989.

17. *Ibid.*

18. *Red Star* (Moscow), December 9, 1989.

19. Nicholas Shmelev, "The New Troubles," *New World* (Moscow), April 1989, p. 175.

20. "The Presidential Decree on Measures to Fight Economic Sabotage and Other Crimes in the Economic Sphere," *Pravda*, January 28, 1991.

21. *Pravda*, December 1, 1990.

22. *Ibid.*

23. *Ibid.*

24. M. S. Gorbachev, "Strengthen the Key Links of the Economy," *Pravda*, December 10, 1990.

25. *Pravda*, December 1, 1990.

26. The scene is described in Robert G. Kaiser, *Why Gorbachev Happened: Making Sense of the Man and His Revolution* (New York, 1991), p. 200.

27. Andranik Migranian, "An Epitaph for the 'Brezhnev' Doctrine," *Moscow News*, August 20, 1989.

28. *Ibid.*

29. The usual assertion that the Warsaw Pact was created to counter NATO is easily disproved by the respective dates of their founding: 1949 for the latter, 1955 the former. From the purely military point of view, the USSR hardly needed the Pact. Even before, Moscow had tightly controlled its junior partners' military establishments, and the elaborate machinery of joint command set up in 1955 just ratified the status quo. But politically the Pact would serve several purposes. At first it was intended as a bargain chip to be traded against West Germany's giving up its rearmament and membership in NATO. After it failed on that count, it continued to provide

a convenient pretext for the stationing of Soviet troops in the fraternal countries and for enforcing the Brezhnev Doctrine.

30. Which excludes Yugoslavia and Albania.

31. From the speech before the Central Committee, *Pravda*, December 9, 1989.

32. Michael Fathers and Andrew Higgins, *Tienanmen: The Rape of Peking* (London, 1989), p. 64.

33. Those "parties" were but creatures of the regime, created and tolerated to give it a democratic gloss.

34. *Izvestia*, August 20, 1989.

35. *Pravda*, December 1, 1990.

36. Abel Aganbegyan, *The Economic Challenge of Perestroika* (Bloomington, Ind., 1988), p. 30.

37. D. Levchuk in *Izvestia*, February 7, 1991.

38. *Ibid.*

39. S. Shatalin in *El País* (Madrid) translated in *FBIS* (Foreign Broadcasts Information Service), March 20, 1991.

40. Quoted from John N. Hazard, *The Soviet System of Government* (Chicago, 1980), p. 250.

41. Quoted in *Pravda*, December 10, 1989.

42. Television speech reported in *Izvestia*, February 7, 1991.

43. *Ibid.*

44. "A Senseless Confrontation," *Izvestia*, February 20, 1991.

CONCLUSION

1. *Izvestia*, August 23, 1991.

2. *Ibid.*

3. *Izvestia*, August 27, 1991.

4. *Ibid.*

INDEX

Abalkin, Leonid, 434
Academy of Sciences, Soviet, 434, 438
Acheson, Dean, 44, 81, 86, 96
Action Program, 299
Adenauer, Konrad, 186, 210, 228
Afanasiev, Viktor, 65
Afanasiev, Yuri, 440
Afghanistan, 173, 288, 321, 328, 341
    Soviet intervention in, 290, 340–41,
        405, 406, 413, 425, 441, 453, 457
Aganbegyan, Abel, 472
Aitmatov, Chingiz, 406, 453
Albania, 20, 21, 134, 224, 306, 317, 469
    China and, 188, 215, 219–20, 223,
        227, 259, 282, 300
    defiance of Soviet Union by, 189
    in World War II, 14
Alexander II, Emperor of Russia, 408
Algerian War, 174
All-Russian Congress of the Soviets,
    448
Anderson, General Robert, 89
Andreyeva, Nina, 418–21, 433
Andropov, Yuri, 379, 388, 394–98
Angola, 288, 290, 321–24
Antifascist Council of National Libera-
    tion, 14
Anti-Semitism, 26, 67, 146, 302, 337,
    346, 397, 433
Arab League, 324
Argentina, 71
Armenia, 68, 331, 427–29, 476, 479
Atlantic Alliance, 88
Attlee, Clement, 95
Austria, 16, 119, 120, 164, 467
Azerbaijan, 328, 427–28, 476

Bandung Conference, 201
Bangladesh, 283
Bao Dai, 53
Baruch Plan, 74
*Basic Principles of Mutual Relations
    Between the United States and the
    Union of Soviet Socialist Republics,*
    288
Batista, Fulgencio, 220
Bay of Pigs invasion, 220, 222
Belgium, 212, 350
Beria, Lavrenti, 106, 109, 110, 123
Berlin, 197–200, 204–5, 208, 209, 214,
    222, 223, 225, 227–28, 232, 235
    blockade of, 3, 6, 10, 23, 48, 60, 69,
        70, 109
Berlin Wall, 222, 228, 460, 468
Bierut, Bolesaw, 139
Black Hundreds, 433
Bolsheviks, 26, 35, 113, 343, 390, 415,
    435, 448, 493
Bondarev, Yuri, 432–33
Bradley, General Omar, 88, 94–95
Brandt, Willy, 250
Brezhnev, Leonid, 59, 64, 225, 245–48,
    329–34, 342, 383–84, 388, 391,
    401, 426, 428, 442, 448, 450, 461,
    473
    and Afghanistan invasion, 340
    Chernenko and, 398
    corruption under, 417, 422
    Czechoslovakia and, 292, 294, 309,
        311, 313, 316, 331, 335
    death of, 379
    and détente with United States, 286,
        288, 319, 320, 385, 403

Brezhnev, Leonid (*cont.*)
  dissent under, 412, 423
  and emigration, 67
  Helsinki accords signed by, 336
  Indonesia and, 260
  Iran and, 327
  Mao and, 268
  on nuclear weapons, 111
  Poland and, 301, 361, 363, 364, 369,
    371, 372, 376
  Shevardnadze and, 395, 411
  in Stalinist bureaucracy, 245
  successor to, 394
  during Vietnam War, 250, 251, 261,
    263
  Yeltsin on, 431
Brezhnev Doctrine, 76, 134, 285, 316,
  376, 406, 452, 457, 460
Brinksmanship, 69, 70, 196
Bukharin, Nikolai, 415, 416, 422–23
Bukharinism, 422
Bulganin, Nikolai, 49, 109, 122, 136,
  144, 165, 173
Bulgaria, 7, 20–22, 26, 76, 88, 112,
  156, 391
  collapse of Communism in, 457, 458
  Czechoslovakia and, 309, 312
  Hungary and, 161
  purge trials in, 117, 138
  in World War II, 13, 14
Bundy, McGeorge, 107
Byelorussia, 332, 385

Cambodia, 252, 269, 339
Canada, 399
Carrillo, Santiago, 335
Carter, Jimmy, 326, 356
Castro, Fidel, 213, 214, 220, 221, 232,
  234, 261, 314–15, 317, 323, 451
Catholic Church, 8, 27, 29, 78, 116,
  139, 154, 344, 356, 358, 361, 362,
  372, 378–80, 459
Ceauşescu, Nicolae, 19, 282, 300, 306,
  310, 312, 315, 345, 369, 400, 452,
  457, 468
Central Intelligence Agency (CIA), 27,
  220, 252, 322
Chase Manhattan Bank, 363
Chebrikov, Viktor, 437
Chen Yi, Marshal, 206, 264
Chernenko, Konstantin, 379, 388, 394,
  395, 398–400, 431
Chernobyl nuclear accident, 357, 385–
  86, 403, 412

Chiang Kai-shek, 5, 37–41, 43, 46, 52, 80,
  87, 106, 121, 172, 192–93, 199, 213
China, 6, 22, 290, 298, 299, 333, 387, 399
  Berlin and, 198–99
  civil war in, 2, 5, 30, 36–43, 46, 48,
    52, 80
  Communist Party of, 41, 131, 147,
    206, 215, 243, 276, 281
  Cultural Revolution in, *see* Cultural
    Revolution
  Czechoslovakia and, 315
  Democracy Movement in, 400, 463–
    65, 469, 486
  de-Stalinization and, 132–33
  détente with United States, 241, 242,
    248, 277, 284–87, 289, 300, 405
  economic reforms in, 297, 338–39,
    391, 394, 400, 402, 450
  Great Leap Forward in, *see* Great
    Leap Forward
  Hungary and, 166, 167
  India and, 201–2, 206, 216, 234, 260,
    282–83
  Japanese invasion of, 37–38
  in Korean War, 69, 80–107, 202, 248,
    253–55
  and Mao's death, 65, 70, 337–38
  and Middle East, 189–91
  Poland and, 147–48, 369
  and Quemoy-Matsu crisis, 192–96
  Soviet Union and, 36–56, 60, 75–80,
    119–22, 125, 169–173, 175–89,
    199–209, 211–30, 233–44, 248–
    50, 307–8, 317, 329, 335, 337–40,
    380, 384, 411–12, 462–64
  and Third World, 322, 325, 451, 464
  and Vietnam War, 100, 241, 252–64,
    266–69
Chinese People's Volunteers (CPV), 92,
  93, 97–99, 102
Churchill, Winston, 4, 27, 60–62, 69
Cold war, 5, 6, 24, 52, 61, 65, 69, 70,
  190, 196, 208, 255, 385, 451
Columbia University, 411
Comecon, 227
Cominform, 7–9, 19, 24, 27, 118, 136,
  175, 177
Comintern, 7, 10, 17, 62, 130, 136, 138,
  365
Committee to Defend Workers (KOR),
  355–57, 360, 365
  Information Bulletin of, 362–63
Communist Manifesto (Marx and En-
  gels), 1

Conference on Security and Coopera-
tion in Europe, 335
Confucius, 281
Congo, 212
Containment, 5, 52, 74, 212, 248
Council of Experts, 358–60
Council of the People's Deputies, 406
Cuba, 212, 214, 248, 324, 451
    Angola and, 290, 322–23
    Bay of Pigs invasion of, 220, 222
    Communist Party of, 261
    Czechoslovakia and, 315
    missile crisis, 75, 228, 230–36, 244,
    250, 265
Cultural Revolution, 41, 181, 202, 240,
    250, 251, 253, 264, 267, 268, 270–
    86, 308, 338, 402, 486
Cyrankiewicz, Józef, 143, 350
Czechoslovakia, 7, 26, 28, 29, 72, 156,
    329, 332, 342, 344, 345, 391, 406,
    477, 486
    collapse of Communism in, 453, 454,
    457, 461, 468
    Communist Party of, 292–95, 304–5,
    307
    Communist seizure of power in, 5, 6,
    21, 23
    East Germany and, 186
    Hungary and, 161
    1968 invasion of, 24, 240, 248, 251,
    265, 282, 285, 290–301, 303–17,
    335, 345, 346, 361, 368, 369, 379,
    387, 449, 452, 454, 458
    Poland and, 373, 375
    purge trials in, 76, 117, 138
    in World War II, 116

Darwin, Charles, 66
De Gaulle, Charles, 7, 181, 228, 250
Deng Xiaoping, 70, 213, 217, 237, 273,
    274, 338, 391, 463, 464
De-Stalinization, 113, 122, 131, 134,
    138, 158, 251, 291, 294
Détente, 24, 169, 171, 203, 215–17,
    219, 223, 225, 236, 241, 255, 265,
    284, 319–20, 323, 330, 335–37,
    340, 387, 403
Dillon, Douglas, 209, 210
Djilas, Milovan, 11, 15, 18, 29, 31, 32,
    124, 132, 391
Doctor Zhivago (Pasternak), 413
Dubček, Alexander, 285, 291–93, 295,
    296, 298–301, 304, 306, 308, 310–
    14, 366, 376, 453, 454, 456

Dulles, John Foster, 69, 72, 110, 122,
    192–94, 255
Dziady ("Forefathers' Eve"; play)
    (Mickiewicz), 301

East German Socialist Unity Party, 460
East Germany, 72, 209–11, 232, 297,
    322, 391
    closing of borders of, 222
    collapse of Communism in, 164, 457,
    459–62, 467, 468
    creation of, 73
    Czechoslovakia and, 308, 309, 312
    1953 uprising in, 108–11, 134, 343
    recognition of, 186, 198, 233, 249,
    319, 336
Egypt, 189, 212, 251, 288, 325, 326
Ehrenburg, Ilya, 56
Eisenhower, Dwight D., 75, 88, 106,
    110, 190, 194, 204–8, 210, 214,
    220, 222
Eisenhower Doctrine, 189
Einstein, Albert, 66
Eliot, T. S., 209
Engels, Friedrich, 1, 42, 63, 183, 273,
    331
Estonia, 68, 476–78, 491
Ethiopia, 173, 288, 321, 323–25
Euro-Communism, 334–35
European Common Market, 249, 335
European Economic Community, 335,
    485

February Revolution, 343, 367
Federenko, Nikolai, 47
Finland, 5, 22–23, 70, 120, 310
Finlandization, 455, 456
Five-Year Plans, 28
Ford, Gerald, 356–57
France, 73, 96
    in Algerian War, 174
    China and, 243
    Communist Party of, 2, 4, 6, 7, 30,
    62, 63, 71, 73, 104, 130, 131, 135,
    180, 216, 310, 315, 334, 350, 450
    Germany and, 109, 197, 228, 249
    and Middle East, 190
    Poland and, 356, 363
    student upheaval in, 265, 308
    Vietnam and, 53, 121, 252
    in World War II, 4

Gang of Four, 280, 338
Gao Gang, 40, 77

Gdańsk Polytechnic Institute, 348
Geneva Conference (1954), 119, 251,
    267
Geneva Summit (1985), 403
Genghis Khan, 62
Georgia, 427, 439–40, 478–80, 482,
    491
German General Staff, 416
Germany, 52, 113, 215, 220, 227–28,
    242, 256, 286, 409
  Democratic Republic of, see East Ger-
    many
  Federal Republic of, see West Ger-
    many
  Hitler's rise to power in, 37
  occupation of, 71–73
  reunification of, 170
  in World War II, 12–14, 56, 126, 389
Gerö, Ernö, 158, 160, 162, 163
Ghana, 212
Gierek, Edward, 302, 350–54, 356–58,
    360, 361, 363–64, 366–68, 374
Giscard d'Estaing, Valéry, 356, 363
Glasnost, 65, 97, 109, 128, 330, 336,
    408, 411–13, 416, 418, 420, 424,
    429, 433, 437, 456, 457, 470, 473,
    477, 487
Głemp, Józef, 371
Gomułka, Władysław, 27, 118, 138–40,
    145–55, 157, 161, 164, 177, 294,
    296, 300–303, 308–9, 345–50
Gorbachev, Mikhail, 19, 114, 155, 245,
    298, 340, 361, 370, 390–91, 399–
    404, 424–54, 471–77
  and breakaway republics, 477, 479–
    84, 491
  and Chernobyl disaster, 385–86
  in China, 205, 462–64
  and collapse of communism in East-
    ern Europe, 457–62, 467, 468
  and Congress of People's Deputies,
    434–35, 437–40, 473, 481, 491
  constitution under, 333, 447, 479,
    480, 485
  coup attempt against, 488–90
  cultural and scientific exchanges with
    West under, 67
  foreign policy of, 386–87, 403–4,
    406–7, 451–52
  and free market economy, 442–46
  glasnost of, 412–13, 418, 424
  and nationalities issue, 428–30
  at Nineteenth Party Conference, 430–
    36

  on nuclear weapons, 111, 236, 284,
    385, 486
  perestroika of, 19, 225, 292, 408–11,
    424, 428, 429, 446, 448, 470, 475
  popularity in West of, 357, 441
  rise of, 391–97, 399–400
  Stalinism condemned by, 64, 65, 290,
    409, 413–21
  Yeltsin and, 425–27, 430–32, 483–84
Great Britain, 3, 16, 60–61, 73, 96, 184,
    196
  China and, 242
  Germany and, 109, 197
  Gorbachev in, 399
  and Korean War, 95
  and Middle East, 190
  and Suez Crisis, 174
  in World War II, 343
Great Depression, 4, 320
Great Leap Forward, 182–85, 201, 202,
    204, 212–13, 230, 242, 271, 338,
    401
Great Patriotic War, 62, 64
  See also World War II
Great Terror, 138, 245, 334, 389, 398
Greece, 2, 111
  civil war in, 44
  in World War II, 14
Grishin, Viktor, 400, 411
Gromyko, Andrei, 101, 226, 230, 323,
    398, 401, 411, 426, 432, 436, 437,
    477

Havel, Václav, 293–94
Helsinki Accords, 335–37, 383
Herter, Christian, 209
Hitler, Adolf, 15, 27, 37, 56, 70
Ho Chi Minh, 53, 55, 119, 257, 278
Holocaust, the, 302
Holy Alliance, 45
Honecker, Erich, 457
Hong Kong, 235
Hoxha, Enver, 215, 219, 300, 306
Hua Guofeng, 338
Hungary, 7, 20, 22, 26, 88, 116, 135,
    299, 329, 344, 391, 406
  collapse of Communism in, 189, 454,
    456–58, 467
  Czechoslovakia and, 309, 310, 312
  economic reform in, 354
  Mongol invasion of, 62
  1956 uprising in, 24, 131, 133, 139,
    149, 153–55, 157–68, 170, 173,
    174, 187–89, 265, 291, 294, 306,

308, 310, 311, 314, 335, 345, 378,
387, 452
and peaceful coexistence, 216
Poland and, 373, 375
purge trials in, 76, 117, 138, 157
in World War II, 13
Husák, Gustáv, 314, 453, 457
Hu Yaobang, 463

India, 33, 190
China and, 86, 106, 201–2, 206, 216,
234, 260, 282–83
Indonesia, 53, 216, 259–60, 284
Industrial Revolution, 298, 486
Interfactory Strike Committee, 364
International Institute for Human
Rights, 364
Interregional Group, 440
Iran, 327–28, 341
Iraq, 189, 326
Islam, 327, 328
Israel, 67, 111, 251, 301, 325–26, 403
Italy, 16, 119, 242
Communist Party of, 2, 4, 6, 7, 30,
62, 63, 73, 104, 129–31, 135, 180,
216, 310, 315, 334–35, 369, 449,
450
in World War II, 13
Izvestia, 413

Japan, 50, 51, 79, 80, 199
China and, 242, 243, 259
Communist Party of, 53
economy of, 445
and Korean War, 81–82
peace treaty with, 101
in World War II, 37–38, 56
Jaruzelski, Wojciech, 351, 371, 372,
374, 376–78, 380, 452, 465, 467,
468
Jews
emigration of, 337, 383
persecution of, see Anti-Semitism
Jiang Qing (Mao's wife), 272, 279, 338
John Paul II, Pope, 362, 379
Johnson, Lyndon B., 253–55, 265, 266,
313
Jordan, 189–90

Kádár, János, 160, 162–65, 167, 189,
309, 310, 312, 457
Kaganovich, Lazar, 114, 149, 150, 173
Kania, Stanisław, 366, 371, 374, 376
Kazakhstan, 429, 491

Kennan, George, 5, 6, 12, 60
Kennedy, John F., 214, 221, 222, 226,
229–31, 235
KGB, 19, 62, 76, 389, 402, 437, 441,
444, 488–90
Khmer Rouge, 339
Khomeini, Ayatollah, 327–28
Khrushchev, Nikita, 54, 59, 64, 70, 77,
114–15, 125–34, 139, 148–50,
153, 155–56, 160, 165–67, 169,
173–74, 193–211, 216–28, 258,
286, 293, 299, 303, 316, 383, 400,
403, 415–17, 421–22, 448
and Albania, 291–20, 223
and Cuba, 220–22, 231–30
de-Stalinization under, 65, 104, 110,
112–14, 122, 238, 292, 306, 345,
410, 413
fall of, 240, 244–49, 256, 294, 412,
489
foreign policy of, 109, 284
and Germany 185–86, 190, 197–98,
209–11, 227–28, 461
and India, 260
Mao and, 100, 120–21, 128, 131,
133, 171–72, 175–81, 184, 185,
191, 195, 200, 201, 203–4, 206,
213, 242–44
and nuclear weapons, 75, 199, 206–
7, 218–19, 486
and Poland, 301
and Quemoy-Matsu crisis, 193–96
Tito and, 123–25, 131, 136, 137, 145,
156, 161–63, 165, 235
on Tonkin Gulf incident, 253
at Twenty-second Party Congress,
224–27
in United States, 204–6, 214
and Yugoslavia, 187–88
Kirilenko, Andrei, 394
Kissinger, Henry, 270, 286, 290, 323
Kohl, Helmut, 450
Konev, Marshal Ivan, 151
Korean War, 30, 57, 69, 70, 75, 80–
107, 110, 119, 132, 178, 202, 248,
253–55, 267
Kostov, Traicho, 26, 117, 118
Kosygin, Alexei, 246–48, 251, 254, 257,
260, 277–79, 329, 340, 383, 391
Kovalev, S., 316
Krasnaya Zvezda (The Red Star) (jour-
nal), 417
Kriegel, Francis, 311
Kryuchkov, Vladimir, 488, 489

Kulikov, Marshal Fyodor, 373, 376, 392
Kunayev, Dinmukhamed, 429
Kuomintang, 2, 36–43, 46–48, 50–52,
    55, 79, 80, 83–85, 87, 95, 120, 267,
    273
Kuznetsov, Alexis, 68
Kuznetsov, V. V., 106

Laos, 220, 221, 252, 254, 269
Latvia, 476–78, 491
League of Yugoslav Communists, 31,
    124, 187
Lebanon, 189–90
Leningrad Technological Institute,
    418
Lenin, V. I., 12, 63, 79, 104, 117, 206,
    283, 332, 350, 390, 415, 422, 423,
    471
    bureaucracy denounced by, 410
    Communist International organized
        by, 365
    cult of, 417, 492
    death of, 70
    Gorbachev on, 402
    Khrushchev on, 65, 110, 127, 245
    Mao on, 45, 273
    on nationalities issue, 427
    during revolution, 435, 448, 466, 479,
        493
    Shatrov's play about, 420
    statues of, dismantled, 477, 490
    tomb of, 56, 57, 333
    and world revolution, 113, 215, 387
Leninism, 115, 208, 244, 403, 422
    See also Marxism-Leninism
Letter to the Soviet Leaders (Solzheni-
    tsyn), 382
Ligachev, Yegor, 402, 411, 419, 426,
    431, 432, 437, 439, 448
Lin Biao, 273, 275, 276, 279–81
Lithuania, 438, 447, 461, 476–80, 482,
    491
Liu Shaoqi, 41, 53, 75, 161, 202, 213,
    272, 273, 277
London Times, 4
Lysenko, Trofim, 66

Macao, 235
MacArthur, General Douglas, 53, 79,
    87, 91, 94, 95, 98, 103
Macmillan, Harold, 190
Malaya, 53
Malaysia, 259
Malenkov, Georgi, 49, 64, 70, 105, 106,

    109, 111, 112, 116, 122, 134, 145,
    161, 165, 166, 172, 173
Malik, Jacob, 89
Malinovsky, Marshal Rodion, 191, 224,
    225
Manchu empire, 37, 55, 120, 201, 242
Manchurian Railway, 38, 50, 54, 77,
    101
Mandelstam, Osip, 114
Maoism, 267, 268, 274, 280
Mao Zedong, 19, 77, 110, 126, 167,
    189, 224, 241, 325, 400
    during Chinese civil war, 30
    during Cultural Revolution, 268,
        270–82, 486
    death of, 65, 242, 280, 297, 337–38
    Great Leap Forward of, 182–85, 202,
        204, 213, 242
    Khrushchev and, 120–21, 128, 131,
        133, 171–72, 175–81, 191, 195,
        200, 201, 203–4, 206
    during Korean War, 82, 83, 85, 87,
        91–94, 99, 100, 132, 253
    liquidation of heirs apparent of, 70
    and nuclear weapons, 96–97, 207,
        225, 229–30, 233, 239
    and Sino-Soviet defense agreement,
        170
    and Sino-Soviet dispute, 208–9, 213,
        238, 243–44
    Stalin and, 36–51, 54–56, 69, 75, 78,
        85, 104–6, 132–33, 179, 192, 273
    United States and, 60, 196, 199, 284–
        85
    during Vietnam War, 253, 256, 264
Marshall, George C., 61
Marshall Plan, 2, 60, 63, 72, 73
Marx, Karl, 1, 42, 63, 183, 184, 273,
    283, 331
Marxism, 269, 302, 383, 443
    of Bukharin, 415
    in Caribbean, 403
    Catholic Church's opposition to, 154
    in China, 42, 183, 201, 208, 243, 289
    class consciousness in, 352
    in Czechoslovakia, 304
    dialectic in, 422
    economic and social consequences of,
        388, 470, 473
    in Poland, 353
    on spontaneous workers' uprisings,
        140, 343
Marxism-Leninism, 9, 12, 28, 35, 60,
    64, 78, 79, 116, 128, 235, 237–39,

290, 307, 318, 339, 382, 405, 421,
    442, 450, 458, 472, 478, 486
in Albania, 300
Brezhnev Doctrine and, 134–35
bureaucracy and, 462
criticism of, 388
and Czechoslovakia, 292, 296, 297,
    309, 314–16
in East Germany, 110
ethnic minorities and, 427
foreign policy and, 385
free elections and, 465
fundamentalist, 338
of Gorbachev, 445–46, 483
humanitarian claims of, 329
internationalism and, 11, 14, 15, 112,
    123
and Iranian revolution, 327
of Khrushchev, 112, 115, 125, 132,
    172, 200
of Mao, 49, 56, 65, 132, 172, 179,
    241–43, 284
in Poland, 344–45, 351, 353, 362,
    368–69, 373, 380, 381
postwar support in Western Europe
    for, 4
and Sino-Soviet dispute, 180–82, 185,
    216, 217, 224, 227, 235, 237–39,
    241, 268, 283, 485
Sputnik and reputation of, 174, 180
in Third World, 220, 252–53, 321–
    34, 451
and Vietnam War, 262, 268
during World War II, 481–82
in Yugoslavia, 25, 29–30, 65
Massachusetts Institute of Technology
    (MIT), 61
Matsu, see Quemoy-Matsu crisis
Matthews, Francis, 89
Mazowiecki, Tadeusz, 365, 467
Mengistu Haile Mariam, Colonel, 323,
    325
MGB, 62
Mikoyan, Anastas, 41, 122, 149, 158,
    160, 234
Military Council for National Salvation,
    377
Moczar, Mieczysław, 302
Moldavia, 478, 480, 491
Molotov, Vyacheslav, 43, 45, 49, 106,
    109, 113, 120, 122, 123, 134, 136,
    145, 148–50, 155, 161, 165, 166,
    172, 173, 389
Mongolia, 38, 51, 54, 62, 121, 242

Monroe Doctrine, 220
Moslems, 327–28, 427
Movement for the Protection of Human
    Rights, 363
Mujahedin, 341
Münnich, Ferenc, 163
Mussolini, Benito, 15

Nagy, Imre, 157–65, 167, 188, 189,
    291, 303
Nasser, Gamal Abdel, 189
National Front for the Liberation of An-
    gola (FNLA), 322
National Liberation Front (NLF), 252,
    261, 263, 268
National Socialism, 328
National Union for the Total Indepen-
    dence of Angola (UNITA), 322
NATO, 33, 69, 72, 73, 88, 95, 98, 119,
    155, 164, 186, 198, 315, 322, 335,
    384, 402, 404, 455, 485
Natolin group, 145–46, 148, 150, 152,
    154
Nazarbayev, Nursultan, 491
Nazis, 118, 316
Nazi-Soviet Pact (1939), 13, 49–50, 78,
    477
Nehru, Jawaharlal, 86, 206
Nenni, Pietro, 135
New Left, 265
New York Times, 58, 59
Nicaragua, 451
Nicholas I, Emperor of Russia, 408
Nixon, Richard M., 269, 270, 276, 278,
    286, 288, 289, 319, 320, 385, 405
Nomenklatura, 438
    Polish, 303, 345
North Atlantic Treaty (1949), 43
North Korea, 209, 216, 282
    See also Korean War
Norway, 71
Novotný, Antonin, 294
Nuclear Test Ban Treaty, 254
Nuclear weapons, 52, 72, 111, 121,
    171, 186, 218, 225, 247, 284, 286,
    315, 318, 383–85, 425
    ban on testing of, 214, 222, 223, 228,
        229, 236–37, 253–54
    China and, 170, 178–79, 197, 199,
        204, 207, 219, 233, 236, 239, 277
    and Cuban missile crisis, 230–33
    and Korean War, 89, 95–97, 106
    NATO deployment of, 404
    peace campaign against, 74–75

Nuclear weapons (*cont.*)
  in postwar years, 2–4, 33
  and Quemoy-Matsu crisis, 192–94, 196

Ochab, Edward, 139–40, 142–50, 161
October Revolution, 26, 35, 63, 112,
    113, 175, 215, 281, 343, 390, 413,
    414, 417, 420, 423, 471, 482
Ogarkov, Marshal Nikolai, 399
One Day in the Life of Ivan Denisovich
    (Solzhenitsyn), 115, 245
One Hundred Flowers campaign, 181,
    184
On Stalin's Watch (journal), 141
OPEC, 283, 310, 327
Organization of African Unity, 322
Ostpolitik, 319, 336

Pahlavi, Mohammed Reza, 327
Pakistan, 260, 282, 341
Palestinians, 325
Pamyat, 433
Pannikar, Kavalam, 91
Pasternak, Boris, 413
Path, The (journal), 363
Pavlov, Valentin, 488
Peaceful coexistence, 216, 284, 288,
    387
Peng Dehuai, 92, 202, 271, 273
Peng Zhen, 211, 273
People's Congress, Chinese, Military Af-
    fairs Committee of, 271
People's Liberation Army, 40, 41, 48,
    80, 85, 87, 98, 193
Perestroika, 65, 167, 216, 289, 296,
    304, 328, 329, 331, 336, 381, 394,
    406, 408–13, 417, 419, 422–25,
    427, 429–33, 436, 437, 439, 441,
    443, 445–49, 452, 454, 456, 458,
    466, 469–73, 484, 485, 487
  of Khrushchev, 112, 115, 128, 169
Persian Gulf War, 405
Peter the Great, 419
Petrograd Soviet of Workers and Sol-
    diers, 367
Philippines, 53
Poland, 7, 20, 27, 28, 77, 112, 116, 131,
    240, 242, 249, 294, 296, 300–303,
    307, 341, 476
  China and, 177
  collapse of Communism in, 453, 454,
    456–59, 465–69
  Czechoslovakia and, 308, 309, 312

de-Stalinization and, 138–39
East Germany and, 186
economic reforms in, 470–71
Hungary and, 164–65
Mongol invasion of, 62
and peaceful coexistence, 216
Soviet military presence in, 76
and Stalin's death, 117–18
unrest in, 140–57, 159–61, 170,
    343–80, 398, 452
western borders of, 319, 336
Polish United Workers' Party, 159, 373,
    375, 381, 456, 465–67, 469
Polish Workers' Party, 138, 159
Popular Liberation Movement of Angola
    (MPLA), 322
Port Arthur, 38, 50, 54, 56, 101, 120
Portugal, 322
Potsdam Conference (1945), 103, 336,
    343
Powers, Gary, 210
Prague Spring, 290–301, 303–17, 453
Pravda, 163–64, 243, 316, 413, 421,
    426, 437
Presidential Council, 406
Primakov, Yevgeni, 387–88
Pugo, Boris, 488

Quemoy-Matsu crisis, 192–96, 221

Rajk, László, 26, 117, 157, 158
Rákosi, Mátyás, 157, 158, 162, 163
Rapacki Plan, 197
Reagan, Ronald, 396, 403–5, 450
Red Army, 1, 14, 38, 64, 116, 134, 138,
    156, 389, 416, 441
Red Flag (journal), 208
Red Guards, 272, 274–77, 279
Rhee, Syngman, 91
Rockefeller, David, 363
Rokossovski, Konstantin, 76, 148, 150–
    52, 154
Romania, 7, 28, 76, 134, 188, 242, 282,
    299, 300, 317, 345, 346, 391, 452,
    466
  collapse of Communism in, 400, 456,
    457, 468
  Czechoslovakia and, 309, 310, 312,
    315
  Hungary and, 161
  Poland and, 369
Romanov, Grigori, 397–99, 401, 411
Roosevelt, Franklin D., 27, 43, 45, 60

Rusk, Dean, 226, 229
Russia, 68–69, 491, 493
  Mongol conquest of, 62
  tsarist, 45, 54, 331, 389, 408, 427
Russian Civil War, 112, 417
Russian Revolution, *see* February Revolution; October Revolution
Russification, 332
Russo-Japanese War, 38

Sadat, Anwar, 326
Sakharov, Andrei, 289, 316, 383, 409, 412, 427, 438, 440
SALT I, 289, 318
SALT II, 340
Samizdat, 330, 332, 334
Sandinistas, 451
Schmidt, Helmut, 356
Shanghai massacre, 37
Shatalin, Stanislav, 474
Shatrov, Mikhail, 418, 420
Shcherbitsky, Vladimir, 332
Shelest, Peter, 332
Shepilov, Dmitri, 161
Shevardnadze, Eduard, 331, 394–95, 411, 451, 452, 484, 488, 492
Shiites, 327
Shmelyov, Nikolai, 443
Šik, Ota, 298
Sino-Soviet New Defense Technical Agreement (1957), 170
Sino-Soviet Pact of Friendship and Mutual Aid (1950), 195, 281
Sino-Soviet Treaty of Friendship and Alliance (1945), 38, 49, 101
Six-Day War, 251, 301
Slansky, Rudolf, 26, 117, 118
Smith, General Walter Bedell, 61
Snow, Edgar, 275
Sobchak, Anatoli, 488, 493
Society of Philatelists, Soviet, 434
Solidarity, 344, 345, 350, 356, 367, 368, 370–79, 452, 456, 457, 459, 465–68
Solovyov, Yuri, 438
Solzhenitsyn, Alexander, 115, 128, 155, 245, 262, 382, 408
Somalia, 323–24
South Korea, 322
  See also Korean War
South Yemen, 324
Sovetskaya Rossia (Soviet Russia) (journal), 417, 418, 421

Soviet Union
  Afghanistan intervention by, 290, 340–41, 405, 406, 413, 425, 441, 453, 457
  China and, 36–56, 60, 75–80, 119–22, 125, 169–73, 175–89, 199–209, 211–30, 233–44, 248–50, 307–8, 317, 329, 335, 337–40, 380, 384, 411–12, 462–64
  collapse of Communism in, 490–94
  and collapse of Communism in Eastern Europe, 452–62, 465–69
  Communist Party of, 63, 68, 115, 125, 141, 152, 171, 180, 215, 223, 220, 238, 258–60, 292, 330, 389, 401, 407, 411, 413, 423–27, 430–38, 446–48, 462, 470, 476, 478, 480–81, 487, 490, 493
  Congress of People's Deputies of, 434–35, 437–40, 446, 448, 465, 474, 481, 487, 491, 492
  constitution of, 332–34, 337, 430, 434, 437, 447, 476–77, 480–81
  coup against Gorbachev in, 487–90
  Cuba and, 220–21, 230–36, 348
  and Cultural Revolution, 270, 274, 277–84
  Czechoslovakian invasion by, 24, 248, 251, 265, 282, 285, 290–301, 303–17, 335
  de-Stalinization in, 112–15, 122–39
  détente with United States, 171, 203–8, 215–17, 223, 225, 226, 236, 255, 265, 284–90, 315, 319–20, 323, 337, 340, 383, 387, 403
  dissent in, 329–30, 334, 356
  economic crisis in, 441–45, 461–62, 470–74
  and Euro-Communism, 334–35
  Gorbachev's reforms in, 357, 390–91, 400–412, 424–25, 449–50
  Gorbachev's rise to power in, 391–400
  and Helsinki accords, 335–37
  and Hungarian uprising, 157–68, 174
  ideological collapse of, 381–90
  India and, 283
  Japan and, 50–51
  and Korean War, 30, 69, 80–107
  Khrushchev's fall from power in, 244–49
  and Middle East, 189–91, 325–28
  military power of, 318–19, 335

Soviet Union (cont.)
   nationalities question in, 330–32,
      334, 425, 427–30, 475–85
   Poland and, 140–57, 159–61, 300–
      303, 343–47, 350, 353–58, 361–
      63, 366–80
   in postwar years, 1–9, 57–75, 383
   and Quemoy-Matsu crisis, 192–96
   reassessment of history of, 412–23
   space program of, 174–75
   and Stalin's death, 57–59, 64, 70, 71,
      104, 106, 108–12, 116–18
   and Third World, 247–49, 321–25,
      335, 451
   and Vietnam War, 100, 241, 242,
      250–69, 290
   West Germany and, 197–99
   in World War II, 4, 13–15, 56, 60,
      116, 126, 343, 414–15
   Yugoslavia's defiance of, 10–12, 15–
      33, 35, 42–43, 54, 68–69
Spain, Communist Party of, 335, 369,
   450
Sputnik, 174, 175, 178, 180
Stalin, Josif, 3, 7–9, 12, 30–32, 101,
   110, 113, 121, 130, 136, 139, 155,
   162, 166, 174, 188, 253, 316, 331,
   335, 347, 383, 391, 398, 422, 442,
   460, 472, 481–82
   and Berlin, 198
   collectivization of agriculture by, 182,
      202
   constitution under, 332–33, 430, 477
   cult of personality of, 63–64, 151, 243
   death of, 39, 49, 57, 77–78, 104–5,
      109, 117, 118, 131, 157, 235, 329,
      389, 392, 428, 493
   and ethnic minorities, 33–34
   and Finland, 23
   funeral of, 106, 107
   during Korean War, 57, 69, 81–83,
      85, 88, 92, 93, 97, 101–2, 248
   last public speech of, 103–4
   Lenin and, 417
   Mao and, 36–51, 54–56, 69, 75, 78,
      85, 86, 104–6, 132–33, 179, 192,
      273
   nationalism of, 332, 475
   pact with Hitler, 13, 476
   and Poland, 148, 151, 152
   purges of, 117, 126, 389, 415–16
   rehabilitation of memory of, 245–46,
      292
   repudiation of, 114, 125–28, 133–35,

      141, 167, 181, 227, 238, 244, 265,
      410
   revelations of horrors perpetrated by,
      388–89, 412–16, 421
   Shatrov's play about, 418–20
   Tito and, 15, 18, 19, 22, 24, 25, 28,
      30–33, 35, 43, 52, 60, 64, 69, 78–
      79, 105, 123, 125, 163, 201, 296,
      303, 342
   and Turkey, 111
Stalinism, 12, 119, 134, 135, 268, 329,
   393, 426, 432, 448, 493
   of Brezhnev, 245
   collapse of, 64–65
   in Czechoslovakia, 292, 294, 300, 314
   in East Germany, 110
   Gorbachev's campaign against, 409,
      412, 413, 418–21, 445, 462
   and Hungarian crisis, 187, 345
   Khrushchev and, 104, 112, 131, 160,
      166, 167, 225, 240, 290, 306, 345
   Mao and, 172, 181, 280
   of Molotov, 113
   in Poland, 143, 152, 301–2, 307
   proletarian internationalism and, 107
   and satellite states, 155, 164
   Tito and, 25–26, 30, 123, 124, 132,
      181
Stockholm Appeal, 74, 75
Strategic Defense Initiative (SDI), 396,
   401
Suez Crisis, 160, 166, 168, 174, 189,
   221
Sukarno, 259
Suslov, Mikhail, 160, 242–44, 395
Sviták, Ivan, 304, 305
Sweden, 474
Syria, 316

Taiwan, 36, 40, 42, 78, 80–83, 85–87,
   106, 107, 121, 172, 192, 199, 204,
   206, 222, 322
Tass, 230, 260, 378
Tatars, 427
Thatcher, Margaret, 399, 450
Third World, 2, 33–34, 78, 196, 212,
   247–49, 252, 259, 262, 268, 282,
   288, 321–25, 335, 451, 455, 464
Thorez (French Communist), 71, 104
Three Mile Island nuclear accident, 386
Tibet, 87, 201
Tienanmen Square, 463–64, 469
Tikhonov, Nikolai, 391, 398, 411
Tito (Josip Broz), 10, 13–22, 24–33, 35,

43, 44, 54, 60, 63–64, 69, 78, 88,
105, 134, 175, 201, 300
Castro on, 315
China and, 175, 176, 181, 200, 208,
215, 235, 237, 282
death of, 65, 70, 342
Djilas and, 31, 32, 132
foreign policy of, 16–17
Gomułka and, 118, 296, 303, 306, 345
and Hungarian crisis, 158–59, 161–
63, 165
Khrushchev and, 123–25, 131, 136,
137, 145, 156, 161–63, 165, 235
personality cult of, 132
and Prague Spring, 310
repercussions of apostasy of, 116, 138
security service of, 19
Zionism charges against, 26, 27
during World War II, 13–16
Titoism, 11, 26, 28, 44, 52, 73, 117,
137, 138, 145, 157, 160, 387
Togliatti, Palmiro, 104, 129–32
Tonkin Gulf incident, 253
Trotsky, Lev, 27, 238, 415, 416
Trotskyism, 26, 63, 138, 238, 419
Truman, Harry S., 6, 60, 61, 75, 79–81,
83, 84, 86, 89, 90, 92, 95–97, 105
Truman Doctrine, 2, 6, 111
Turkey, 2, 111

Ukraine, 332, 385, 477, 490
Ulbricht, Walter, 308–10
Union of Soviet Socialist Republics, see
Soviet Union
United Nations, 30, 74, 222, 259, 461
China and, 172
and Hungarian crisis, 161
Khrushchev at, 214, 232–33, 235
and Korean War, 84–90, 93–95, 98,
106
Security Council of, 89, 190, 191
United States, 23, 53, 61, 227, 247,
318, 384, 386, 401
Afghanistan and, 340
arms control agreements with, 228–
29
China and, 38–44, 46, 51, 52, 78–80,
86, 121, 170, 172, 184, 200, 201,
218, 239, 241, 242, 248, 277, 278,
284–87, 289, 300, 405
constitution of, 430, 477
containment policy of, 5, 52, 74, 212,
248
Cuba and, 220–22, 230–36

Czechoslovakia and, 313
détente with Soviet Union, 171, 203–
8, 215–17, 223, 225, 226, 236, 255,
265, 284–90, 315, 319–20, 323,
337, 340, 383, 387, 403
Germany and, 109, 177, 197–99
GNP of, 388, 389
India and, 283
Japan and, 50–51
in Korean War, 30, 81–107, 255
and Middle East, 189–90, 325–28
Nicaragua and, 451
and nuclear free zone proposal, 199
nuclear testing and, 229, 236, 237
Poland and, 356–57
in postwar years, 2–7, 10, 16, 60, 63,
69, 72–75, 383
and Quemoy-Matsu crisis, 192–96
and Soviet emigration, 67, 337
and Stalin's death, 58–59, 110–11
State Department of, 44, 86, 90, 122,
210
summits with, 172, 210–11, 220–22,
403–4
Supreme Court of, 477
and Third World, 321, 322, 324
in Vietnam War, 100, 107, 242, 250–
69, 276, 279, 283–87, 308, 341
in World War II, 44–45, 60, 343
Yugoslavia and, 30, 137, 188
United States–Republic of China Mutual Defense Treaty (1954), 192
Ustinov, Dmitri, 398
U-2 incident, 210, 218, 220

Vaculík, Ludvík, 305
Vatican II, 362
Vietcong, 248, 262–65, 269, 286
Vietnam, 53, 216, 321, 339–40
French defeat in, 121, 178
Vietnam War, 100, 107, 241, 242, 248,
250–69, 276, 282–88, 290, 308,
320, 341, 403
Vinson, Frederick, 61
Voroshilov, Marshal Klimenti, 173, 192
Vyshinsky, Andrei, 49

Wałęsa, Lech, 353, 364, 365, 370, 372,
375, 379, 465, 467
Warsaw Treaty Organization, 76, 300,
455, 456, 461, 462
Albania expelled from, 227
China and, 207
creation of, 164

Warsaw Treaty Organization (*cont.*)
  and Cuban missile crisis, 231
  Czechoslovakia and, 285, 291, 305,
    307, 308, 312, 315
  Hungarian crisis and, 161, 164
  Poland and, 366, 370, 371, 373, 378,
    454, 459
Watergate scandal, 283, 320, 321
West Germany, 6, 186, 190, 200, 210,
    319, 454
  China and, 242
  creation of, 71
  economy of, 445
  in NATO, 164
  nuclear weapons in, 197–98, 207,
    208, 228, 233
  Poland and, 356
  rearmament of, 73, 75, 88, 103, 177,
    249
  student upheaval in, 265, 308
World Committee of Peace, 74
World War I, 389, 486
World War II, 13–17, 22, 116, 125,
    138, 226, 249, 343, 389, 392, 414–
    15, 460, 482
  See also Great Patriotic War
Wyszyński, Cardinal Stefan, 154, 362,
    372

Yagoda, Genrikh, 416
Yakovlev, Aleksandr, 411, 421, 423,
    439, 493
Yalta Conference 27, 103, 343
Yanayev, Gennadi, 488, 489
Yazov, Dmitri, 488
Yeltsin, Boris, 425–27, 430–32, 438–
    40, 446, 448, 483, 484, 488–91,
    493
Yosuke, Matsuoko, 56
Yugoslavia, 7, 53, 59, 71, 88, 131, 134,

    150, 175, 216, 235, 240, 296, 300,
    315, 317, 333, 345, 461, 469
  Albania and, 215
  China and, 43, 52, 78, 176, 177, 180,
    187–88, 200, 282
  Hungary and, 159, 161–65, 168
  Khrushchev and, 122–25, 131–32,
    136–37, 156, 187–88
  Leninism in, 181
  Soviet Union defied by, 10–12, 15–
    33, 35, 42–43, 54, 68–69
  and Stalin's death, 106, 111
  and Tito's death, 65, 70, 342, 452
  in World War II, 12–15

Zambrowski, Roman, 139
Zero option, 404
Zhao Ziyang, 463, 464
Zhdanov, Andrei, 7, 8, 66, 68, 432
Zhou Enlai, 44, 55, 167, 194, 200, 224,
    237, 242, 256, 285, 338
  at Bandung Conference, 201–2
  during Cultural Revolution, 274, 275,
    277–79
  death of, 337
  at Geneva Conference, 120
  Khrushchev and, 227
  during Korean War, 85, 91, 93, 107
  Lin Biao and, 281
  in negotiations with Soviet Union,
    46–49, 101
  on nuclear weapons, 96
  on Poland, 147
  at Stalin's funeral, 106, 107
  United States denounced by, 226
  during Vietnam War, 264
Zhukov, Marshal Georgi, 144, 161, 162,
    173
Zionism, 26, 27, 63, 118, 122, 150, 294,
    302, 332